Create Your Own Assignments or Use Ours, All [...]

An **Assignment** area allows you to create **student homework** and **quizzes** by using **Wiley-provided question banks,** or by writing your own. You may also assign readings, activities and other work you want your students to complete. One of the most powerful features of eGrade Plus is that student assignments will be automatically graded and recorded in your gradebook. This will not only save you time but will provide your students with immediate feedback on their work.

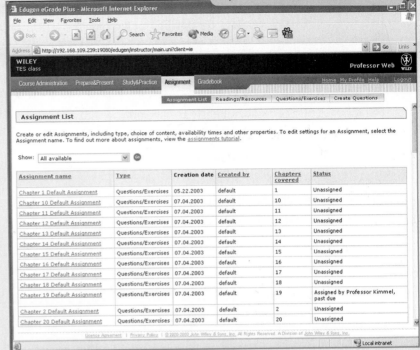

An **Instructor's Gradebook** will keep track of your students' progress and allow you to analyze individual and overall class results to determine their progress and level of understanding

Assess Student Understanding More Closely

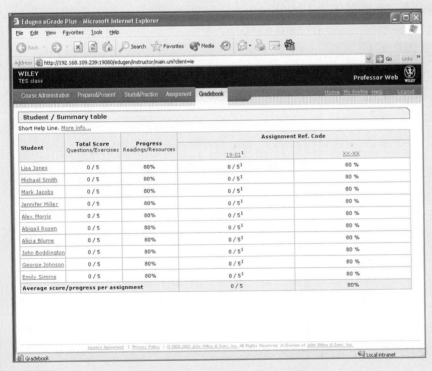

Students, eGrade Plus Allows You to:

Study More Effectively

Get Immediate Feedback When You Practice on Your Own

eGrade Plus problems link directly to relevant sections of the **electronic book content,** so that you can review the text while you study and complete homework online. Additional resources include **Powerpoint lecture slides, solutions manual material,** and other problem-solving resources.

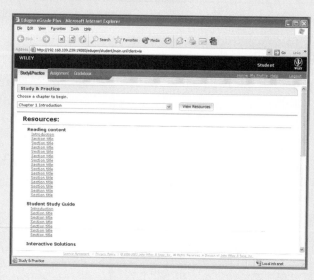

Complete Assignments / Get Help with Problem Solving

An **Assignment** area keeps all your assigned work in one location, making it easy for you to stay "on task." In addition, many homework problems contain a **link** to the relevant section of the **multimedia book,** providing you with a text explanation to help you conquer problem-solving obstacles as they arise. You will have access to a variety of **problem-solving tools,** as well as other resources for building your confidence and understanding.

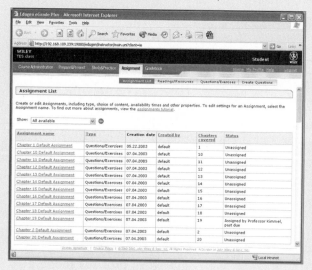

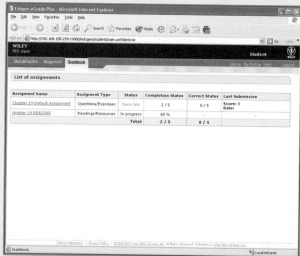

Keep Track of How You're Doing

A **Personal Gradebook** allows you to view your results from past assignments at any time.

OBJECTS, ABSTRACTION, DATA STRUCTURES AND DESIGN USING JAVA™

ELLIOT B. KOFFMAN
Temple University

PAUL A. T. WOLFGANG
Temple University

John Wiley & Sons, Inc.

81594

SENIOR ACQUISITIONS EDITOR	Paul Crockett
PROJECT MANAGER	Cindy Johnson, *Publishing Services*
SENIOR EDITORIAL ASSISTANT	Simon Durkin
SENIOR PRODUCTION EDITOR	Ken Santor
MARKET DEVELOPMENT MANAGER	Jennifer Powers
SENIOR DESIGNER	Kevin Murphy
COVER DESIGNER	Howard Grossman
TEXT DESIGN AND COMPOSITION	Greg Johnson, *Art Directions*
FRONT COVER PHOTO	© John Burcham/Image State
BACK COVER PHOTO	© Philip and Karen Smith/Image State

This book was set in 10 point Sabon, and printed and bound by R.R. Donnelley–Crawfordsville. The cover was printed by Phoenix Color Corporation.

This book is printed on acid free paper.

CREDITS: Figure 1.2, page 5, Booch, Jacobson, Rumbaugh, *Unified Modeling Language User Guide* (AW Object Tech Series), pg. 451, ©1999 by Addison Wesley Longman, Inc. Reprinted by permission of Pearson Education, Inc., publishing as Pearson Addison Wesley. Figure 6.1, page 296, ©AP/Wide World Photos.

To order books or for customer service please, call 1-800-CALL WILEY (225-5945).

ISBN 0-471-46756-1

WIE 0-471-66151-1

Printed in the United States of America

10 9 8 7 6 5 4 3 2 1

Preface

Our goal in writing this book was to combine a strong emphasis on problem solving and software design with the study of data structures. To this end, we discuss applications of each data structure to motivate its study. After providing the specification (interface) and the implementation (a Java class), we then cover case studies that use the data structure to solve a significant problem. Examples include a phone directory using an array and a list, postfix expression evaluation using a stack, simulation of an airline ticket counter using a queue, and Huffman coding using a binary tree and a priority queue. In the implementation of each data structure and in the solutions of the case studies, we reinforce the message "Think, then code" by performing a thorough analysis of the problem and then carefully designing a solution (using pseudocode and UML class diagrams) before the implementation. We also provide a performance analysis when appropriate. Readers gain an understanding of why different data structures are needed, the applications they are suited for, and the advantages and disadvantages of their possible implementations.

The text is designed for the second course in programming, especially those that apply object-oriented design (OOD) to the study of data structures and algorithms. The text could carry over to the third course in algorithms and data structures for schools with a three-course sequence. Besides coverage of the basic data structures and algorithms (lists, stacks, queues, trees, recursion, sorting), there are chapters on sets and maps, balanced binary search trees, graphs, and event-oriented programming. Although we expect that most readers will have completed a first programming course in Java, there is an extensive review chapter (included as an appendix) for those who may have taken a first programming course in a different object-oriented language, or for those who need a refresher in Java.

To help readers "Think, then code," we provide the appropriate software design tools and background in the first two chapters before they begin their formal study of data structures. The first chapter discusses two different models for the software life cycle and for object-oriented design (OOD), the use of the Uniform Modeling Language™ (UML) to document an OOD, the use of interfaces to specify abstract data types and to facilitate contract programming, and how to document classes using Javadoc-style comments. We develop the solution to an extensive case study to illustrate these principles. The second chapter focuses on program correctness and efficiency by discussing exceptions and exception handling, different kinds of testing and testing strategies, debugging with and without a debugger, reasoning about programs, and using big-O notation. As part of our emphasis on OOD, we introduce two design patterns in Chapter 3, the object factory and delegation. We make use of them where appropriate in the textbook.

As mentioned earlier, we apply these concepts to design and implement the new data structures and to solve approximately 20 case studies. Case studies follow a five-step process (problem specification, analysis, design, implementation, and testing). As is done in industry, we sometimes perform these steps in an iterative fashion rather than in strict sequence. Several case studies have extensive discussions of testing and include methods that automate the testing process. Some case studies are revisited in later chapters, and solutions involving different data structures are compared. We also provide additional case studies on the website (www.wiley.com/college/koffman) for the textbook, including one that illustrates a solution to the same problem using several different data structures.

Each data structure that we introduce faithfully follows the Java API for that data structure (if it exists) and readers are encouraged throughout the text to use the Java API as a resource for their programming. We begin the study of a new data structure by specifying an abstract data type as an interface, which we adapt from the Java API. Each class that implements the interface follows the approach taken by the Java designers where appropriate. However, when their industrial-strength solutions appear to be too complicated for beginners to understand, we have provided simpler implementations but have tried to be faithful to their approach. Therefore, our expectation is that readers who complete this book will be familiar with the data structures available in the Java Collections Framework and will be able to use them immediately and in their future programming. They will also know "what is under the hood" so they will have the ability to implement these data structures. The degree to which instructors cover the implementation of the data structures will vary, but we provide ample material for those who want to study it thoroughly.

Event-Oriented and GUI Programming

We provide a chapter-length appendix on graphical user interface programming which teaches the fundamentals of event-driven programming. Several applications throughout the text offer practice with GUI programming using Swing's JOptionPane class. There are some examples of applications with user-defined GUI classes; however, the GUI classes are kept separate from the classes that solve the problem and are discussed on the website for the textbook (www.wiley.com/college/koffman). This reinforces good program design and makes it possible for the instructor to keep the design of GUI classes optional. We also discuss the Java Locale feature in this appendix.

Intended Audience

This book was written for anyone with a curiosity or need to know about data structures, those essential elements of good programs and reliable software. We hope that the text will be useful to readers with either professional or educational interest. In developing the book, we paid careful attention to the ACM's *Computing Curricula 2001*, in particular, the curriculum for the second ($CS102_O$ – Objects and Data Abstraction) and third ($CS103_O$ – Algorithms and Data Structures) introductory programming courses in the three-course, "objects-first" sequence. The book is also suitable for $CS112_O$ – Object Oriented Design and Methodology, the second course in the two-course "objects-first" sequence. Further, although the book follows the object-oriented approach, it could be used after a first course that does not, because object-oriented programming principles are introduced and motivated in Chapters 1, 3, and the review chapter (Appendix A). Consequently it could be used for the following courses: $CS102_I$ (The Object-Oriented Paradigm), $CS103_I$ (Data Structures and Algorithms), and $CS112_I$ (Data Abstraction) in the "imperative-first" approach, or $CIS112_F$ (Objects and Algorithms) in the "functional-first" approach.

Prerequisites

Our expectation is that the reader will be familiar with the Java primitive data types including `int`, `boolean`, `char`, and `double`; control structures including `if`, `switch`, `while`, `for`, and `try-catch`; the `String` class; the one-dimensional array; input/output using either `JOptionPane` dialog windows or text streams (class `BufferedReader`) and console output. For those readers who lack some of the concepts or who need some review, we provide complete coverage of these topics in Appendix A. Although labeled an Appendix, the review chapter provides full coverage of the background topics and has all the pedagogical features (discussed below) of the other chapters. We expect most readers will have some experience with Java programming, but someone who knows another object-oriented language should be able to undertake the book after careful study of the review chapter. We do not require prior knowledge of inheritance, wrapper classes, or `ArrayLists` as we introduce them in Chapters 3 and 4.

Pedagogy

The book contains the following pedagogical features to assist inexperienced programmers in learning the material.

- Learning objectives at the beginning of each chapter tell readers what skills they should develop.
- Introductions for each chapter help set the stage for what the chapter will cover and tie the chapter contents to other material that they have learned.
- Problem solving is emphasized through numerous case studies that provide complete and detailed solutions to real-world problems using the data structures studied in the chapter.
- Chapter summaries review the contents of the chapter.
- Pitfall, Design Concept, and Program Style boxes help readers with common problems and provide tips for becoming better programmers.
- Syntax boxes are a quick reference for the Java structures they are learning.
- Quick-check and end-of-section exercises provide immediate feedback and practice for readers as they work through the chapter.
- Review exercises and longer programming projects in each chapter give readers a variety of skill-building activities.

Theoretical Rigor

Chapter 2 discusses algorithm correctness and algorithm efficiency. We use the concepts discussed in this chapter throughout the book. However, we have tried to strike a balance between pure "hand waving" and extreme rigor when determining the efficiency of algorithms. Rather than provide several paragraphs of formulas, we have provided simplified derivations of algorithm efficiency using big-O notation. We feel this will give readers an appreciation of the performance of various algorithms and methods and the process one follows to determine algorithm efficiency without bogging them down in unnecessary detail.

Java Language Versions

This version of the textbook is compatible with Java 1.4.2. However, a Java 1.5 version that illustrates how to use features such as generics, auto-boxing, and general **for** statements, will be available in Fall, 2004.

Overview of the Book

Object-oriented software design is introduced in the first chapter, as are UML class and sequence diagrams. We use UML sequence diagrams to describe several use cases of a simple problem: maintaining a phone number directory. We decompose the problem into two subproblems, the design of the user interface and the design of the phone directory itself. We emphasize the role of the Java interface as a contract between the developer and client and its contribution to good software design. We provide Java interfaces for each subproblem and present two implementations of the user interface, one with a JOptionPane GUI and one with streams. Javadoc-style documentation is also introduced in Chapter 1 and illustrated in the code segments throughout the text.

The next two chapters concentrate on software design topics. Following the introduction to software design in Chapter 1, the topics of algorithm efficiency and correctness are introduced in Chapter 2. Chapter 3 provides a thorough discussion of inheritance, class hierarchies, interfaces, abstract classes, and an introduction to object factories.

Next the Collections Framework is introduced as the foundation for the traditional data structures: lists (including ArrayList and LinkedList classes), stacks, and queues (Chapters 4 through 6). Each new data structure is introduced as an abstract data type (ADT) and its specification is written in the form of a Java interface. We carefully follow the Java API form of the interface (when available), so that readers will know how to use the standard data structures that are supplied by Java. Next, we show how to implement the data structure as a class that implements the interface. Finally, we study applications of the data structure by solving sample problems and case studies.

Chapter 7 covers recursion so that readers are prepared for the study of trees, a recursive data structure. As discussed below, this chapter could be studied earlier.

Chapter 8 discusses binary trees, including binary search trees, heaps, priority queues, and Huffman trees.

Chapter 9 covers the Set and Map interfaces. It also discusses hashing and hash tables and shows how a hash table can be used in an implementation of these interfaces. The Huffman tree case study is completed in this chapter.

Chapter 10 covers selection sort, bubble sort, insertion sort, Shell sort, merge sort, heapsort, and quicksort. We compare the performance of the various sorting algorithms and discuss their memory requirements.

Chapters 11 and 12 cover self-balancing search trees and graphs, focusing on algorithms for manipulating them. Included are AVL and Red-Black trees, 2-3 trees, 2-3-4 trees, and B-trees. We provide several well-known algorithms for graphs including Dijkstra's shortest path algorithm and Prim's minimum spanning tree algorithm. In most programs, the last few chapters would be covered in the second course of a two-course sequence.

Pathways Through the Book

Figure 1 shows the dependencies among chapters in the book. Most readers will start with Chapters 1, 2, and 3, which provide fundamental background on software design, exception classes, and class hierarchies and inheritance. In a course that emphasizes software design, these foundation chapters should be studied carefully.

FIGURE 1
Chapter Dependencies

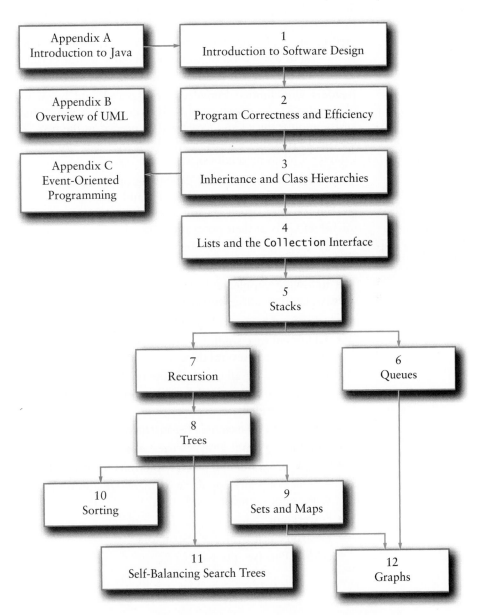

Readers with knowledge of this material from a prior course in Java programming may want to read these chapters quickly, focusing on material that is new to them. Similarly, those interested primarily in data structures should study Chapter 2 carefully, but they can read Chapters 1 and 3 quickly.

The basic data structures, lists (Chapter 4), stacks (Chapter 5), and queues (Chapter 6), should be covered by all. Recursion (Chapter 7) can be covered anytime after stacks. The chapter on trees (Chapter 8) follows recursion. Chapter 9 covers sets and maps and hash tables. Although this chapter follows the chapter on trees, it can be studied anytime after stacks if the case study on Huffman trees is omitted. Similarly, Chapter 10 on sorting can be studied anytime after recursion, provided the section on heapsort is omitted (heaps are introduced in Chapter 8). Chapter 11 (Self-Balancing Search Trees) and Chapter 12 (Graphs) would generally be covered at the end of the second programming course if time permits, or in the third course of a three-course sequence.

Readers with limited knowledge of Java should begin with the review chapter (Appendix A). An overview of UML is covered in Appendix B; however, features of UML are introduced and explained as needed in the text. The Appendix on Event-Oriented Programming (Appendix C) is optional and can be covered anytime after Chapter 3 (class hierarchies).

These paths can be modified depending on interests and abilities. Those who want to focus on programming techniques and event-oriented programming may spend less time on data structures and, instead, study Appendix C carefully and emphasize the use of GUIs in their programming.

Supplements

The following supplementary materials are available on the textbook website, www.wiley.com/college/koffman.

- Additional homework problems with solutions
- Additional case studies, including one that illustrates a solution to the same problem using several different data structures
- Source code for all classes in the book
- Solutions to end of section odd-numbered self-check and programming exercises (for students)
- Solutions to all exercises for instructors
- Solutions to chapter-review exercises for instructors
- Sample programming project solutions for instructors
- A choice of many popular compilers/IDEs (information available from your Wiley sales representative)
- PowerPoint slides
- Electronic test bank for instructors
- eGrade Plus (see pp. i–iv)

Acknowledgments

Many individuals helped us with the preparation of this book and improved it greatly. We are grateful to all of them. These include students at Temple University who have used notes that led to the preparation of this book in their coursework, and who have class-tested early drafts of the book. We would like to thank Anthony Hughes, James Korsh, and Rolf Lakaemper, colleagues at Temple University, who used preliminary drafts of this book in their classes. We would also like to thank a former Temple student, Michael Mayle, who provided preliminary solutions to many of the exercises.

We are especially grateful to our reviewers who provided invaluable comments that helped us correct errors in each version and helped us set our revision goals for the next version. The individuals who reviewed this book are listed below.

Sheikh Iqbal Ahamed, *Marquette University*
Justin Beck, *Oklahoma State University*
John Bowles, *University of South Carolina*
Tom Cortina, *SUNY Stony Brook*
Chris Dovolis, *University of Minnesota*
Vladimir Drobot, *San Jose State University*
Ralph Grayson, *Oklahoma State University*
Chris Ingram, *University of Waterloo*
Gregory Kesden, *Carnegie Mellon University*
Sarah Matzko, *Clemson University*
Ron Metoyer, *Oregon State University*
Rich Pattis, *Carnegie Mellon University*
Sally Peterson, *University of Wisconsin–Madison*
Mike Scott, *University of Texas–Austin*
Mark Stehlik, *Carnegie Mellon University*
Ralph Tomlinson, *Iowa State University*
Frank Tompa, *University of Waterloo*
Renee Turban, *Arizona State University*
Paul Tymann, *Rochester Institute of Technology*
Karen Ward, *University of Texas–El Paso*
Jim Weir, *Marist College*

Although all the reviewers provided invaluable suggestions, we do want to give special thanks to Chris Ingram who reviewed every version of the manuscript, including the preliminary pages for the book. His care, attention to detail, and dedication helped us improve this book in many ways, and we are very grateful for his efforts.

Besides the principal reviewers, there were a number of faculty members who reviewed sample pages online and made valuable comments and criticisms of their content. We would like to thank those individuals, listed below.

Razvan Andonie, *Central Washington University*
Ziya Arnavut, *SUNY Fredonia*
Antonia Boadi, *California State University–Dominguez Hills*
Christine Bouamalay, *Golden Gate University*

Amy Briggs, *Middlebury College*
Mikhail Brikman, *Salem State College*
Robert Burton, *Brigham Young University*
Debra Calliss, *Mesa Community College*
Tat Chan, *Methodist College*
Chakib Chraibi, *Barry University*
Teresa Cole, *Boise State University*
Jose Cordova, *University of Louisiana Monroe*
Joyce Crowell, *Belmont University*
Vladimir Drobot, *San Jose State University*
Francisco Fernandez, *University of Texas–El Paso*
Robert Franks, *Central College*
Barbara Gannod, *Arizona State University East*
Wayne Goddard, *Clemson University*
Simon Gray, *College of Wooster*
Bruce Hillam, *California State University–Pomona*
Wei Hu, *Houghton College*
Edward Kovach, *Franciscan University of Steubenville*
Sandeep Mitra, *SUNY Brockport*
Saeed Monemi, *California Polytechnic and State University*
Robert Noonan, *College of William and Mary*
Kathleen O'Brien, *Foothill College*
Michael Olan, *Stockton College*
Peter Patton, *University of St. Thomas*
Eugen Radian, *North Dakota State University*
Rathika Rajaravivarma, *Central Connecticut State University*
Sam Rhoads, *Honolulu Community College*
Rassul Saeedipour, *Johnson County Community College*
Vijayakumar Shanmugasundaram, *Concordia College Moorhead*
Gene Sheppard, *Georgia Perimeter College*
Meena Srinivasan, *Mary Washington College*
Stephen Weiss, *University of North Carolina–Chapel Hill*
Glenn Wiggins, *Mississippi College*

Finally, we want to acknowledge the participants in focus groups for the second programming course organized by John Wiley and Sons at the Annual Meeting of the SIGCSE Symposium in March, 2004. We thank those listed below who reviewed the preface, table of contents, and sample chapters and also provided valuable input on the book and future directions of the course:

Jay M. Anderson, *Franklin & Marshall University*
Claude Anderson, *Rose-Hulman Institute*
John Avitabile, *College of Saint Rose*
Cathy Bishop-Clark, *Miami University–Middletown*
Debra Burhans, *Canisius College*
Michael Clancy, *University of California–Berkeley*
Nina Cooper, *University of Nevada–Las Vegas*
Kossi Edoh, *Montclair State University*

Robert Franks, *Central College*
Evan Golub, *University of Maryland*
Graciela Gonzalez, *Sam Houston State University*
Scott Grissom, *Grand Valley State University*
Jim Huggins, *Kettering University*
Lester McCann, *University of Wisconsin–Parkside*
Briana Morrison, *Southern Polytechnic State University*
Judy Mullins, *University of Missouri–Kansas City*
Roy Pargas, *Clemson University*
J.P. Pretti, *University of Waterloo*
Reza Sanati, *Utah Valley State College*
Barbara Smith, *University of Dayton*
Suzanne Smith, *East Tennessee State University*
Michael Stiber, *University of Washington, Bothell*
Jorge Vasconcelos, *University of Mexico (UNAM)*
Lee Wittenberg, *Kean University*

We would also like to acknowledge the team at John Wiley and Sons who were responsible for the inception and production of this book. Our editor, Paul Crockett, was intimately involved in every detail of this book, from its origination to the final product. We are grateful to him for his confidence in us and for all the support and resources he provided to help us accomplish our goal and to keep us on track. Simon Durkin assisted Paul and provided us with additional help when needed. We would also like to thank Jenny Powers for her many contributions to marketing and sales of the book.

Cindy Johnson, the developmental editor and production coordinator, worked very closely with us during all stages of the manuscript development and production. We are very grateful to her for her tireless efforts on our behalf and for her excellent ideas and suggestions.

Greg Johnson was the text designer and compositor for the book, and he did an excellent job in preparing it for printing.

We would like to acknowledge the help and support of our colleague Frank Friedman, who read an early draft of this textbook and offered suggestions for improvement. Frank and Elliot began writing textbooks together almost thirty years ago and Frank's substantial influence on the format and content of these books is still present. Frank also encouraged Paul to begin his teaching career as an adjunct faculty member, then to teach full-time when he retired from industry. Paul is grateful for his continued support.

Finally, we would like to thank our wives who provided us with comfort and support throughout the creative process. We very much appreciate their understanding and sacrifices that enabled us to focus on this book, often during time we would normally be spending with them. In particular Elliot Koffman would like to thank

Caryn Koffman

and Paul Wolfgang would like to thank

Sharon Wolfgang.

Contents

Chapter 7   Recursion   337

Introduction to Software Design

In your first course in programming methods, you probably wrote a large number of small programs that solved particular programming problems but otherwise had little general use. Now that you have survived the first course in programming methods and are coming back for more, we can assume that you want to learn more about computer science and programming.

This chapter discusses software design and introduces tools and techniques used by professional programmers to facilitate the design and maintenance (upkeep) of large-scale programs.

The chapter shows how software designers use abstraction to create models of computer systems and how they use abstract data types to encapsulate data elements

1

and operators. You will learn how to specify the behavior of an abstract data type (ADT) using an interface and how to implement it using classes. You will see how interfaces, preconditions, and postconditions serve as contracts between system designers and programmers and between application programmers and implementors of classes in an API (Application Programming Interface). The use of interfaces enables programmers to develop systems with a high degree of flexibility and also enables a programmer to code program systems that have interchangeable parts.

Through examination of a large case study, you will learn how to follow a five-step software development process to design and implement new software applications. These steps include problem specification, analysis, design, implementation, and testing. You will see how to employ use cases to specify the interaction between the system and its users during problem specification and analysis. You will see how to use sequence diagrams and procedural abstraction to develop the algorithms for the class methods during the design phase. Carefully following the software development process will lead to more efficient implementations with fewer errors, making it easier to test and debug the completed system.

Introduction to Software Design

1.1 The Software Challenge

Programming in college is somewhat different from programming in the real world. In college an instructor generally gives you the problem specification. In many cases, the problem specification is ambiguous or incomplete, and interaction between the instructor and the class is necessary so that the students can pin down the details.

The goal of a college programming assignment is to give you some experience with a particular concept, thus reinforcing your mastery of it. The resulting program is used briefly to demonstrate to the instructor that you have mastered the assignment. The only users of the program are you (its author) and perhaps the instructor.

However, in industry, a software product is expected to be used for an extended period of time by someone who did not write the program and who is not intimately familiar with its internal design. The impetus for a software project comes from users of an existing software product or potential users of a new software product. The users see a need for improving the operation of an existing product or for computerizing an operation that is currently done "manually" (that is, without the use of computers). This need is communicated to the individual(s) responsible for providing software support in the organization (normally called *system analysts*).

Because the users are often naïve as to the capabilities of a computer, the initial specification for a software product may be incomplete. The specification is clarified through extensive interaction between the users of the software and the system analyst. Through this interaction, the system analyst determines precisely what the users want the proposed software to do, and the users learn what to expect from the software product. This way there are no surprises in the end.

Although it may seem like common sense to proceed in this way, very often a software product does not perform as its users expected. The reason is usually a communication gap between those responsible for the product's design and its eventual users; generally, both parties are at fault when the software fails to meet expectations. To avoid this possibility, it is imperative that a complete, written description of the requirements—a *requirements specification*—for a new software product be generated at the beginning of the project and that both users and designers review and approve the document.

1.2 The Software Life Cycle

A software product goes through several stages as it matures from an initial concept to a finished product in regular use. This series of stages could be compared to the stages that an insect goes through as is develops from egg, to larva, to pupa, to adult. This sequence of stages is known as the life cycle; thus, we speak of a *software life cycle*.

Software products can require years to develop and require the efforts of many individuals. A successful software product will be used for many years after it is first released. During the term of its use, new or updated versions may be released that contain changes to fit new situations or that fix errors that were previously undetected. For this reason, it is important to design and document software in an organized way so that it can be easily understood and maintained after its initial release. This is especially important because the person who maintains the software may not have been involved in its original design.

Software Life Cycle Models

Many different views of the software life cycle have been proposed over the years and are in use today. There are also many different ways of organizing the activities that transform the software from one stage to another. The simplest version is the *waterfall model*, in which the activities are performed in sequence and the result of

TABLE 1.1
Waterfall Model of the Software Life Cycle

1. Requirements	The requirements for the software system are determined.
2. Analysis	The requirements are studied and clarified, and the overall architecture of the solution is determined. Each major subsystem is analyzed, and its component classes are determined. Also, any interaction between components is determined.
3. Design	Methods and data fields are defined for classes. Detailed algorithms for the methods are defined.
4. Implementation	The individual classes and methods are coded in the target programming language.
5. Testing	The methods of each class are tested in isolation and as a class *(unit testing)*. The methods and classes are tested together *(integration testing)* to verify that they work together and meet the requirements.

one flows into the next (indicated by downward-pointing arrows in Figure 1.1), much like water flowing down a cascading waterfall.

Table 1.1 describes the activities that are performed in each of the five phases of the waterfall model. We will provide more details later in this section.

Although simple in concept, the waterfall model has proved to be unworkable in practice. The fundamental flaw in this model is the assumption that each stage can and must be completed before the next one starts. However, this is rarely the case in actual practice. For example, system designers may identify incomplete or inconsistent requirements during the design process, or programmers may find during the implementation phase that there are areas of the design that are incomplete or inconsistent. Sometimes it is not until the product is finished and the user first sees it that the user can fully express his requirements by stating, "That's not what I meant!"

Various alternatives have been proposed. The common theme is to develop a software product in stages or cycles. Each stage is a mini-version of the waterfall with varying amounts of emphasis for the particular cycles. At the end of each cycle there is a review with the users to obtain feedback to be used in the requirements specification for the next cycle.

One example of such a model is the *Unified Model,* shown in Figure 1.2. The cycles, called *phases* and *iterations,* are shown along the horizontal axis, and the activities, called *workflows,* are shown down the vertical axis. The four phases are inception, elaboration, construction, and *transition* (switching over to the new system). Time moves across the horizontal axis from iteration 1 to iteration *n* and each iteration is a mini-waterfall. The five activities are the same as in the simple waterfall model. The shaded areas under the curves next to each activity are intended to show the relative amount of effort spent on that activity during each iteration. For example, during the *inception phase* (iterations 1 and 2), most effort is spent on specifying requirements. In fact, requirements specification is the only activity performed during iteration 1. During iteration 2, some effort is also spent on analysis, with a *tiny*

FIGURE 1.1
The Waterfall Software
Life Cycle Model

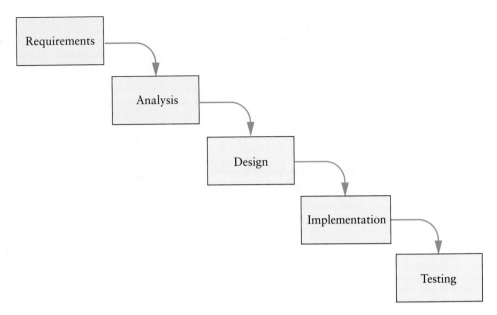

FIGURE 1.2
The Unified Software
Life Cycle Model

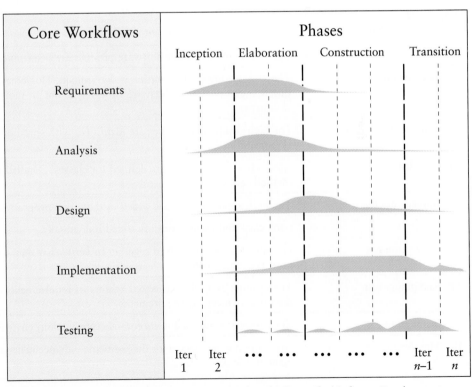

Source: Grady Booch, Ivar Jacobson, and James Rumbaugh, *The Unified Software Development Process* (Addison-Wesley, 1999)

amount on design and implementation. As the software developers move into the *elaboration phase,* they continue to work on requirements and analysis but also start to spend more time on design and implementation, particularly toward the end of the elaboration phase. In the *construction phase,* the requirements specification and analysis activities are completed, and most effort is spent on design and implementation. The diagram also shows that some time is spent on testing during all phases after inception, but more time is spent on testing during the *construction* and *transition phases.* We will discuss testing in more detail in Chapter 2.

Software Life Cycle Activities

Independently of how they are organized, there is general consensus that the activities shown in Table 1.2 are essential for the development of a software product. We will consider activities 1 through 5 in the rest of this chapter; activities 6 through 8 will be the subject of the next chapter.

Because our case studies are relatively small compared to a commercial software project, we generally follow the simple waterfall model. However, we do revisit some case study solutions in later chapters and iterate through the five activities, much as in the Unified Model.

TABLE 1.2
Software Life Cycle Activities

1. **Requirements specification**	The requirements for the software product are determined and documented.
2. **Architectural design**	The architecture of the solution is determined. This breaks the solution into different components, which are allocated to one or more processing resources.
3. **Component design**	For each component, classes are identified, with specified roles and responsibilities.
4. **Detailed design**	Methods and data fields are defined for classes. Detailed algorithms for the methods are defined.
5. **Implementation**	The individual methods are coded in the target programming language.
6. **Unit test**	Each class and its methods are tested individually.
7. **Integration test**	Groups of classes are tested together to verify that they work together and meet the requirements.
8. **Acceptance test**	The product as a whole is tested against its requirements to demonstrate that the product meets its requirements.
9. **Installation**	The product is installed in its end-use (production) environment.
10. **Maintenance**	Based upon experience with the software, enhancements and corrections are made to the product.

Requirements Specification

The system analyst works with the software users to clarify the detailed system requirements. Some of the questions that need to be answered deal with the format of the input data, the desired form of any output screens or printed forms, and the need for data validation. You often need to mimic this process by interrogating your instructor or teaching assistant to determine the precise details of a programming assignment.

For example, assume that your instructor has given you the following incomplete specification of a programming assignment.

> **Problem:** Write an interactive telephone directory program that will contain a collection of names and telephone numbers. You should be able to insert new entries in the directory, retrieve an entry in the directory, or change a directory entry.

Some of the questions that come to mind and might require clarification are the following:

- Is there an initial list of names and numbers to be stored in the directory beforehand, or are all entries inserted at the same time?
- If there is an initial list, is it stored in a file, or should it be entered interactively?
- If the initial directory is stored in a file, is the file a text file (file of characters) or a binary file (file of binary values)?
- If the file is a text file, are there any formatting conventions (for example, the name starts in column 1 and the phone number starts in column 20). Are the name and number on the same data line or on separate lines? How are the names stored (for example, *last, first* or *first last*)?
- Is it possible for there to be more than one telephone number associated with a particular name? If so, should the first number be retrieved, the last number, or all numbers?
- Is it possible to change a person's name as well as the person's phone number?
- When a number is retrieved, should both the person's name and number be displayed or just the number? What form should this display take?
- What action should be taken if a "new" entry has the same name as a person already in the directory? Should this be flagged as an error?

As you can see, there are plenty of questions left unanswered by the initial problem statement. To complete the requirements specification, you should answer these questions and more. Many of the questions deal with details of input data, handling of potential errors in input data, and formats of input data and output lists.

Analysis

Once the system requirements are specified, the analysis stage begins. Before you can embark on the design of a program solution, you should make sure that you completely understand the problem. If the requirements specification has been carefully done, this will be easy. If there are any questions remaining, they should be cleared up at this time.

The next step is to evaluate different approaches to the program design. In industry, the system analyst and users may consider whether there are commercial software packages that can be purchased to satisfy their requirements (as an alternative to developing the software in-house). They must also determine the impact of the new software product on existing computer systems and what new hardware or software will be needed to develop and run the new system. They determine the feasibility of each approach by estimating its cost and anticipated benefits. The analysis stage culminates with the selection of what appears to be the best design approach.

In your coursework, you do not have this flexibility. You must design and implement each program. During the analysis, your goal is to carefully determine the input/output requirements for the system and its interaction with the user. You will also find it helpful to break your system up into a set of small and manageable components, which you can then design and code separately. To do so, you need to identify the modules or components that will constitute the system and specify the interactions between them. You complete this process in the design phase, which we discuss next.

Design

Once you understand the problem and have selected the overall approach, it is time to develop a high-level design of the system. Professional software engineers make use of several design approaches in their work. The *top-down* approach, in which you break a system into a set of smaller subsystems, break each of those subsystems into smaller components, and so forth until components are small and simple enough to be coded easily, has been used successfully for many years. More recently, the *object-oriented* approach, in which you identify a set of objects and specify their interaction, has been increasingly used. In this text we will utilize both the top-down and object-oriented approaches to software design.

Top-Down Design

The top-down approach to software design (also called *stepwise refinement*) instructs us to start at the top level (the original problem) and divide it into subproblems. For each subproblem we identify a subsystem with the responsibility of solving that subproblem. You can use a *structure chart* to indicate the relationship between the subproblems (and subsystems). For example, a structure chart for the telephone directory problem is shown in Figure 1.3.

Figure 1.3 shows the two top levels of the structure chart, which include the original problem and its major subproblems. Each of these subproblems may be further refined and divided into still smaller subproblems. Figure 1.4 shows that to solve the subproblem "Read the initial directory" you must be able to "Read an entry from file" and "Store an entry in the directory". Figure 1.5 shows that to solve the subproblem "Retrieve and display an entry" you must be able to "read a name", "find a name in the directory", "get the entry information from the directory", and "display an entry".

Figure 1.3 indicates that you can solve the original problem (level 0) by providing solutions to four level 1 subproblems. Figures 1.4 and 1.5 represent the solutions to two level 1 subproblems in terms of six level 2 subproblems.

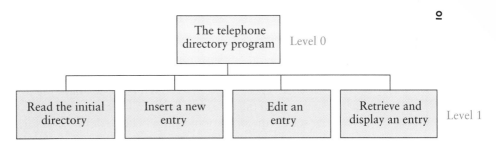

FIGURE 1.3
Structure Chart for
Telephone Directory
Problem

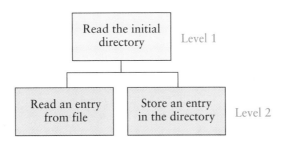

FIGURE 1.4
Refinement of "Read
the initial directory"

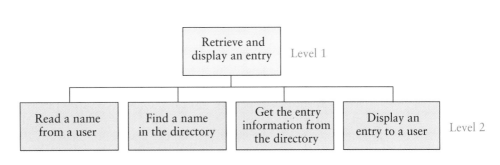

FIGURE 1.5
Refinement of
"Retrieve and display
an entry"

Object-Oriented Design

Top-down design is process-oriented in that it focuses on the actions that are needed rather than the data structures. In contrast, object-oriented design (OOD) focuses on the data elements that are needed and operations to be performed on those data elements. In OOD, you first identify the *objects* that participate in your problem, and then identify how they interact to form a solution. The common characteristics of an object define a *class,* and the interactions are identified as *messages* that one object sends to another. For an object to receive a message, its class must provide an *operator* to process that message. Looking at the nouns in the problem statement can help you identify objects, and looking at the verbs can point to the operators.

We assume that you have had a basic introduction to Java objects and classes in your first programming course. If you need to review the design of classes in Java, you should refer to Appendix A, which reviews several features of Java, including writing Java classes.

In looking at the phone directory problem statement, we have identified that there is a *directory* and that the directory contains *entries*. An entry consists of a *name* and a *number*. There is also a *user,* and there is a *data file* that contains entries. The user is external to the program and is called an *actor* in object-oriented terminology. The user selects the operations that will be performed on the directory and data file.

Object-oriented design incorporates some of the elements of top-down design. It also incorporates some of the elements of *bottom-up design,* which focuses on the design of individual system components. So OOD is a combination of both of these earlier techniques.

UML as a Design Tool

In this textbook we will use Unified Modeling Language (UML) diagrams as a design tool to illustrate the interaction between classes and between classes and external entities (users). We will introduce several features of UML in this textbook on an as-needed basis. Appendix B provides a summary of UML diagrams.

Figure 1.6 is a UML class diagram for the telephone directory program, showing the classes that are used and their interaction and relationships. The classes (Directory, Entry, and File) are identified by rectangles, whereas lines show the interaction and relationships. The lines ending with the diamond symbol at classes Directory and File indicate that class Entry is a component of both these classes. The lines ending with an arrow indicate an interaction between classes. For example, the class Directory has methods that read or write information from class File. External entities, called *actors,* are represented by a small figure. This seems to imply that the external entity is a person, but that is not necessarily the case. So far our class diagrams have no detail, because we have not yet identified their data elements and methods; we are focusing here on the interaction between classes.

UML diagrams are a standard means of documenting class relationships that are widely used in industry. We recommend that you use UML diagrams to describe the classes that you develop in solving your programming assignments.

FIGURE 1.6
Initial Class Diagram
for Phone Directory
Program

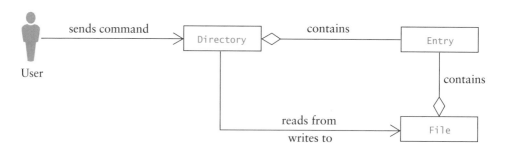

EXERCISES FOR SECTION 1.2

SELF-CHECK

1. What are the advantages of the Unified Model over the waterfall model of the software life cycle?
2. What are the five activities in the software development life cycle followed in this book?
3. Name the four phases of the Unified Model. Name the five activities in the Unified Model.
4. Draw a structure chart showing the refinement of the subproblem "Insert a new entry".
5. Draw a structure chart showing the refinement of the subproblem "Edit an entry".

1.3 Using Abstraction to Manage Complexity

Abstraction is a powerful technique that helps programmers (or problem solvers) deal with complex issues in a piecemeal fashion. An *abstraction* is a model of a physical entity or activity. In this book, we use abstraction to develop models of entities (objects and classes) and also of the operations performed on these objects. One example of the use of abstraction is the description of a program variable (for example, name or number) as a storage location in memory for a data value. We need not be concerned with the details of the physical structure of memory or the actual bits (binary digits) that are used to represent the value of a variable; we don't need to know this to use variables in programming. This is analogous to driving a car. You need to know how to use a key to start the engine, how to use the accelerator and brake pedals to control speed, and how to use the steering wheel to control direction. However, you don't need to know details of the car's electrical system, drive train, braking system, or steering mechanism.

Procedural Abstraction

Procedural abstraction is the philosophy that procedure development should separate the concern of *what* is to be achieved by a procedure (a Java method) from the details of *how* it is to be achieved. In other words, you can specify what you expect a method to do, then use that method in the design of a problem solution before you know how to implement the method. As an example of procedural abstraction, let's assume we have methods available to perform all the level 2 steps in Figure 1.5; we can write the following Java fragment to retrieve an entry from the directory using these methods.

```
name = readName();              // Reads a name
number = directory.get(name);   // Gets number associated with name
if (number != null)
    // Display name and number.
    System.out.println("Phone number for " + name
                            + " is " + number);
else
    // Display message that name is not in directory.
    System.out.println(name + " is not in directory");
```

Data Abstraction

In this course we will also use another type of abstraction: *data abstraction*. The idea of data abstraction is to specify the data objects for a problem and the operations to be performed on these data objects without being overly concerned with how they (the data objects) will be represented and stored in memory. We can describe *what* information is stored in the data object without being specific as to *how* the information is organized and represented. This is the *logical view* of the data object, as opposed to the *physical view*, its actual internal representation in memory. Once you understand the logical view, you can use the data object and its operators in your programs; however, you (or someone else) will eventually have to implement the data object and its operators before you can run any program that uses them. In Java, the operators are called methods, so we will use these terms interchangeably.

As an example, you have already practiced data abstraction in that you have used the String data type to represent sequences of characters without knowing how a character sequence is actually stored in memory. The Java String is an abstraction for a sequence of characters. You can use String objects and their operators (length, charAt, and so on) without knowing the details of their implementation.

Information Hiding

One advantage of procedural abstraction and data abstraction is that they enable the designer to make implementation decisions in a piecemeal fashion. The designer can postpone making decisions regarding the actual internal representation of the data objects and the implementation of its operators. At the top levels of the design the designer focuses on how to use a data object and its operators; at the lower levels of design the designer (or perhaps a different designer or programmer on the team) works out the implementation details. In this way, the designer can control or reduce the overall complexity of the problem.

If the details of a data object's implementation are not known when the higher-level module (a Java class) is designed, the higher-level class can access the data object only through its methods. From a software engineering viewpoint, this is an advantage rather than a limitation. It allows the designer of each class to make changes at a later date to accommodate new government regulations or to implement a method in a more efficient way. If the higher-level classes reference a data object only through its methods, the higher-level class will not have to be rewritten. The process of "hiding" the details of a class's implementation from users of the class is called *information hiding*.

As an example of how information hiding works, let's see how you might access the name part of a new entry (called myEntry) for the phone directory. If you assume that myEntry is an object with a field called name, you could use the qualified identifier

    myEntry.name

As implementation proceeds, you might change your mind and decide to use an array of two strings to hold each entry's name and telephone number. In this case, you would have to go back and change the preceding reference (and all similar references) to

    myEntry[0]

It is much cleaner to hide the structure of an entry and instead use a method to retrieve the name string. If getName is a method that extracts the name string from an Entry object, the statement

    aName = myEntry.getName();

will return the name string stored in myEntry and assign it to aName regardless of the internal representation chosen for an entry. If you decide to change the internal representation, you only have to change the body of method getName. You will not need to change any of the higher-level modules that call getName.

The rest of this chapter assumes that you are familiar with classes, array processing, and I/O fundamentals in Java. If you are not, you can learn about them in Appendix A.

EXERCISES FOR SECTION 1.3

SELF-CHECK

1. How is information hiding related to data abstraction?
2. How does information hiding relate to procedural abstraction?
3. How does the logical view of a data object differ from its physical view?
4. Explain why type int is an abstraction for integers in mathematics.

1.4 Abstract Data Types, Interfaces, and Pre- and Postconditions

One of the goals of software engineering is to write *reusable code,* which is code that can be reused in many different applications, preferably without having to be recompiled. One way to make code reusable is to *encapsulate* or combine data elements together with methods that operate on that data in a separate program module (a class). As we discussed in the previous section, a new program can use the methods to manipulate the data without being concerned about details of the data representation and the method implementation. In this way, the class can be used as a building block to construct new application programs. The combination of data together with its methods is called an *abstract data type* (ADT).

FIGURE 1.7

Diagram of an ADT

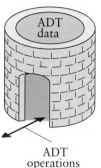

ADT
operations

Figure 1.7 shows a diagram of an abstract data type. The data values stored in the ADT are hidden inside the circular wall. The bricks around this wall are used to indicate that these data values cannot be accessed except by going through the ADT's methods.

A class provides one way to implement an ADT in Java. If the data fields are private, they can be accessed only through public methods. Therefore, the methods control access to the data and determine the manner in which the data is manipulated.

A primary goal of this text is to show you how to write and use ADTs in programming. As you progress through this book, you will create a large collection of ADT implementations (classes) in your own program library. Because each ADT implementation in your library will already have been coded, debugged, and tested, using them will make it much easier for you to design and implement new application programs. Also, the Java Application Programming Interface (API) provides a rich collection of ADT implementations. You will be introduced to many of these ADTs and their implementations as you progress through this book.

Interfaces

A Java *interface* is a way to specify (but not implement) an ADT. A Java interface specifies the names, parameters, and return values of the ADT methods without specifying how the methods perform their operations and without specifying how the data is internally represented. The method descriptions in an interface are called *method declarations*. An interface is even more abstract than a class, because it does not specify the data fields or define the method bodies. Unlike a class, an interface cannot be *instantiated*—that is, one cannot create objects, or *instances,* of it.

The classes that declare the data fields and code the method bodies are said to *implement* the interface. There may be more than one way to implement the methods; hence, there may be more than one class that implements the interface. Therefore, an interface describes a set of classes that code the interface methods.

Each class that implements an interface must provide the complete definition (implementation) of all methods declared in the interface. In addition, it may declare data fields and define other methods. For example, a class that implements an interface can define constructors, but an interface can't declare them, because an interface cannot be instantiated. Unlike an interface, a class that implements an interface is an actual class, so it can be instantiated and may have constructors. We provide further discussion of interfaces in Chapter 3.

EXAMPLE 1.1   For a phone directory program, you may want to provide user-interaction through the console or through a simple graphical user interface (GUI). Note that this use of the word interface refers to a control program that interacts with the user, not the Java construct interface that we have just discussed. Regardless of the kind of user-interaction, there must be a method that has the capability of responding to user commands (method processCommands). We can define a Java interface PDUserInterface that describes the form of method processCommands. Therefore, any class that implements this interface must provide this method. We define the Java interface next.

```
/** The interface for the phone directory user interface. */
public interface PDUserInterface {
    /** Abstract method that processes user's commands.
        @param thePhoneDirectory The PhoneDirectory object that
               contains the data to be displayed and/or changed
    */
    void processCommands(PhoneDirectory thePhoneDirectory);
}
```

This definition begins with the keywords **public interface** instead of **public class**. Like a class, an interface is saved in a file with the same name as the interface (in this case, the file PDUserInterface.java). The interface definition shows the heading for method processCommands. Because only the heading for method processCommands is shown and not its body, processCommands is considered an *abstract method*. The actual method with its body must be defined in a class that implements the interface. Therefore, a class that implements this interface must provide a **void** method called processCommands with an argument of type PhoneDirectory. The key words **public abstract** are implicit in the method heading.

We will provide two actual classes that implement interface PDUserInterface: PDConsoleUI and PDGUI. We can use UML to document the relationship between both these classes and the interface. Figure 1.8 shows the UML diagram. UML uses the notation "«interface» *PDUserInterface*" to indicate that PDUserInterface is an interface, not a class. The dashed lines and arrows indicate that both classes at the bottom of the diagram implement the interface.

SYNTAX   Interface Definition

FORM:
```
public interface interfaceName {
    abstract method headings
    constant declarations
}
```

EXAMPLE:
```
public interface Payable {
    public abstract double calcSalary();
    public abstract boolean salaried();
    public static final double DEDUCTIONS = 25.5;
}
```

MEANING:

Interface *interfaceName* is defined. The interface body provides headings for abstract methods and constant declarations. Each abstract method must be implemented in a class that realizes the interface. Constants defined in the interface (for example, DEDUCTIONS) are accessible in classes that realize the interface.

NOTES:

The keywords **public** and **abstract** are implicit in each abstract method definition, and the keywords **public static final** are implicit in each constant declaration. We show them in color in the example here, but we will omit them from now on.

FIGURE 1.8

Classes That Implement
`PDUserInterface`

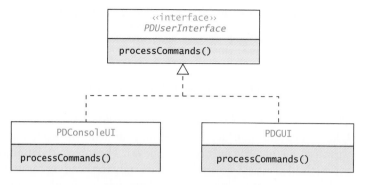

The `implements` Clause

The class headings for two classes that implement interface `PDUserInterface` are

```
public class PDConsoleUI implements PDUserInterface
public class PDGUI implements PDUserInterface
```

Each class heading ends with the clause `implements PDUserInterface`. When compiling these classes, the Java compiler will verify that they define the method `processCommands`. If a class implements more than one interface, list them all after `implements` with commas as separators.

 PITFALL

Not Properly Defining a Method to Be Implemented

If you neglect to define the method processCommands in class PDGUI or if you use a different signature, you will get the following syntax error:

```
class PDGUI should be declared abstract; it does not define method
processCommands(PhoneDirectory) in interface PDUserInterface.
```

The text after the semicolon indicates that the method processCommands was not properly defined. We will explain the meaning of the first part of this error message in Chapter 3. If you use a result type other than **void**, you will also get a syntax error.

 PITFALL

Instantiating an Interface

An interface is not a class, so you cannot instantiate an interface. The statement

```
PDUserInterface aPDGUI = new PDUserInterface();    // invalid statement
```

will cause the following syntax error:

```
interface PDUserInterface is abstract; cannot be instantiated.
```

Declaring a Variable of an Interface Type

In the previous programming pitfall, we mentioned that you cannot instantiate an interface. However, you may want to declare a variable that has an interface type and use it to reference an actual object. This is permitted if the variable references an object of a class type that implements the interface:

```
PDUserInterface aPDGUI = new PDGUI();    // valid statement
```

An Interface for a Telephone Directory Class

There are many different ways to represent a telephone directory. One of our goals in this course is to show you several ways to do this task and to compare their performance. Consequently, rather than provide a single class of type PhoneDirectory, we will define an interface that specifies the methods required of all implementors of this class. This will enable other programmers (including ourselves) to invoke the telephone directory methods without knowing exactly how the directory is represented or how its methods are implemented. We show this interface (Listing 1.1) with two abstract methods that perform the operations described in the structure charts shown earlier (Figure 1.4 and Figure 1.5). Other methods will be described later in the case study.

LISTING 1.1
Part of PhoneDirectory.java

```
/** The interface for the telephone directory.
 */
public interface PhoneDirectory {

    /** Load the data file containing the directory, or
        establish a connection with the data source.
        @param sourceName The name of the file (data source)
                          with the phone directory entries.
     */
    void loadData(String sourceName);

    /** Look up an entry.
        @param name The name of the person to look up
        @return The number or null if name is not in the directory
     */
    String lookupEntry(String name);
    . . .

}
```

Javadoc Comments

Java provides a standard form for writing comments and documenting classes, which we use in Listing 1.1 and throughout this book. If you use this form, you can run a program called Javadoc, which is included with the Java Software Development Kit (SDK), to generate a set of HTML pages describing each class and its data fields and methods. These pages will look just like the ones that document the Java API classes on the Sun Microsystems Java Web site (java.sun.com). For more information on how to use the Javadoc program, refer to Appendix A.

The Javadoc program focuses on text that is enclosed within the delimiters /**, */. The introductory comment that describes the class is displayed on the HTML page exactly as it is written, so you should write that carefully. The lines that begin with the symbol @ are Javadoc tags. They are described in Table 1.3. We use the @author tag in the initial comment for a class or interface, because the class author is also responsible for writing all the methods (but for the programs we show in this book, we will omit the @author tag because they are all written by the textbook authors.) We will use one @param tag for each method parameter. We will use the @return tag to describe the method result, so we will not use a @return tag for **void** methods.

Contracts and Interfaces

A Java interface is a *contract* between the interface designer and the programmer who codes a class that implements the interface. This programmer must code methods that perform the operations specified in the interface, and the Java compiler verifies that this is actually done. Therefore, any programmer who uses a class that implements the interface knows exactly what methods are available in that class and what operations they will perform. This allows that programmer to proceed to write application programs without needing to coordinate with the person who is coding classes that implement the interface. Similarly, the programmer who is coding a class that implements the interface can proceed independently of what the application programmers are doing.

There may be several classes that implement the interface, and each class can code the data and the methods in a different way. One class may be more efficient than another class at performing certain kinds of operations (for example, retrieving information from a directory), so that class will be used if retrieval operations are more likely in a particular application. In our example we will provide a GUI-like interface for those who have access to graphics terminals; others will want to use console-interaction. The important point is that either implementation can be used without affecting other classes that interact with it, because they both satisfy the contract.

TABLE 1.3
Javadoc Tags

Javadoc Tag and Example of Use	Purpose
@author *Koffman and Wolfgang*	Identifies the class author.
@param sourceName *The name of the file*	Identifies a method parameter, sourceName, and describes its use.
@return *The person's age*	Identifies a method return value.

Preconditions and Postconditions

At a lower level, we communicate the intent of a method through its precondition and postcondition comments, which are part of the multiline Javadoc comment that precedes a method definition (or declaration for an interface). A *precondition* is a statement of any assumptions or constraints on the method data (input parameters) before the method begins execution. A *postcondition* is a statement that describes the result of executing a method. A method's preconditions and postconditions serve as a contract between a method caller and the method programmer—if a caller satisfies the precondition, the method result will satisfy the postcondition. If the precondition is not satisfied, there is no guarantee that the method will do what is expected, and it may even fail. We discuss this further in Chapter 2. The preconditions and postconditions allow a method user and method implementor both to proceed without further coordination.

Although some programmers write preconditions and postconditions for every method that they write, we will use them only when they provide additional information that is not readily apparent. If a method has specific requirements for its arguments (for example, an argument must be positive), we will express these requirements through precondition comments. We will use postconditions to describe the change in object state caused by executing a mutator method. As a general rule, you should write a postcondition comment for all **void** methods. If a method returns a value, you do not usually need a postcondition comment because the @return comment describes the effect of executing the method.

EXAMPLE 1.2   A class BankAccount might define the following method processDeposit. The precondition (after *pre:*) shows that the deposit amount is positive. The postcondition (after *post:*) shows that data field balance is increased by the value of amount. The words *pre:* and *post:* are not Javadoc tags, so these comments are not processed by the Javadoc program.

```
/**
    Processes a deposit in a bank account.
    pre: amount is positive.
    post: Adds the specified amount to balance.
*/
public void processDeposit(double amount) {
    balance = balance + amount;
}
```

EXERCISES FOR SECTION 1.4

SELF-CHECK

1. What are the the two parts of an ADT? Which part is accessible to a user and which is not? Explain the relationships between an ADT and a class; between an ADT and an interface; and between an interface and classes that implement the interface.

2. Assume there is an interface named `Comparable` with the following definition:
```
public interface Comparable {
    int compareTo(Object obj);
}
```
Do you think class `String` implements interface `Comparable`? Provide a reason for your answer.

3. Correct each of the following statements that is incorrect, assuming that class `PDGUI` and class `PDConsoleUI` implement interface `PDUserInterface`.
   a. `PDGUI p1 = new PDConsoleUI();`
   b. `PDGUI p2 = new PDUserInterface();`
   c. `PDUserInterface p3 = new PDUserInterface();`
   d. `PDUserInterface p4 = new PDConsoleUI();`
   e. `PDGUI p5 = new PDUserInterface();`
   `PDUserInterface p6 = p5;`
   f. `PDUserInterface p7;`
   `p7 = new PDConsoleUI();`

4. Explain how interfaces and preconditions and postconditions serve as contracts.

5. What are two different uses of the term *interface* in programming?

PROGRAMMING

1. Define an interface named `Resizable` with just one abstract method, `resize`, that is a **void** method with no parameter.

2. Write a Javadoc comment for the following method of a class `Person`. Assume that class `Person` has two `String` data fields `lastName` and `firstName` with the obvious meanings. Provide preconditions and postconditions if needed.
```
public int compareTo(Person per) {
    if (lastName.equals(per.lastName))
        return firstName.compareTo(per.firstName);
    else
        return lastName.compareTo(per.lastName);
}
```

3. Write a Javadoc comment for the following method of class `Person`. Provide preconditions and postconditions if needed.
```
public void changeLastName(boolean justMarried, String newLast) {
    if (justMarried)
        lastName = newLast;
}
```

1.5 Requirements Analysis, Use Cases, and Sequence Diagrams

In this section, we will illustrate how to solve a programming problem similar to the telephone directory assignment introduced earlier. The solution will have multiple classes and interfaces. Our goal in this case study is to show you the process that would be followed in the software design and implementation. Don't be concerned at this point if you do not understand all the details of the final program. In this section, we show the requirements specification and analysis and introduce two new tools: the use case and sequence diagram.

CASE STUDY   Designing a Telephone Directory Program

Problem   You have a client who wants to store a simple telephone directory in her computer that she can use for storage and retrieval of names and numbers. She has a data file that contains the names and numbers of her friends. She wants to be able to insert new names and numbers, change the number for an entry, and retrieve selected telephone numbers. She also wants to save any changes in her data file.

Input/Output Requirements

Earlier we discussed some questions that would have to be answered in order to complete the specification of the requirements for the phone directory problem. Most of the questions dealt with input and output considerations. We will list some answers to these questions next.

INPUTS

Initial phone directory	Each name and number will be read from separate lines of a text file. The entries will be read in sequence until all entries are read.
Additional entries	Each entry is typed by the user at the keyboard when requested.

OUTPUTS

Name and phone numbers	The name and number of each person selected by the program user are displayed on separate output lines.
Updated phone directory	Each name and number will be written to separate lines of a text file. The entries will be written in sequence until all entries are written.

Analysis   The first step in the analysis is to study the problem input and output requirements carefully to make sure that they are understood and make sense. You can use a tool called a *use case* to help you refine the system requirements.

Use Cases

A use case is a list of the user actions and system responses for a particular sub-problem in the order that they are likely to occur.

The following four subproblems were identified for the telephone directory program:

- Read the initial directory from an existing file
- Insert a new entry
- Edit an existing entry
- Retrieve and display an entry

The use case (Table 1.4) for the first subproblem ("Read the initial directory") shows that the user issues a single command and the system responds by either reading a directory from a file or by creating an empty directory if there is no file. The second use case (Table 1.5) is for the subproblems "Insert a new entry" and "Edit an existing entry". Because the names in the directory must be unique, inserting a new entry and editing an existing entry require a search to determine whether the name is already present. Thus, from the user's point of view, the insert and edit processes are the same. The last use case (Table 1.6) shows the user interaction for the last subproblem ("Retrieve and display an entry").

The steps shown in each use case flesh out the user interaction with the program. The use cases should be reviewed by the client to make sure that your intentions are the same as hers. For most of the problems we study in this book, the user interaction is straightforward enough that use cases will not be required.

TABLE 1.4

Use Case for Reading the Initial Directory

Step	User's Action	System's Response
1.	User issues a command to the operating system to load and run the Phone Directory program, specifying the name of the file that contains the directory.	
2.		The Phone Directory program is started, and the directory contents initialized from the data file. If the data file does not exist, an initially empty directory is created.

TABLE 1.5
Use Case for Inserting a New Entry or Editing an Existing Entry

Step	User's Action	System's Response
1.	User issues the command to insert or change an entry.	
2.		System prompts for the name.
3.	User enters name.	If user cancels entry of name, process terminates.
4.		System prompts for the number.
5.	User enters number.	If user cancels entry of number, process terminates.
6.		The directory is updated to contain the new name and number. If the name was not already in the directory, the user is notified that a new name was entered. If the name already exists, the user is notified that the number was changed and is shown both the old and new numbers.

TABLE 1.6
Use Case for Retrieving and Displaying an Entry

Step	User's Action	System's Response
1.	User issues the command to retrieve and display an entry.	
2.		System prompts for the name.
3.	User enters name.	If user cancels entry of name, process terminates.
4.		The system retrieves the entry from the directory. If found, the name and number are displayed; otherwise, a message is displayed indicating that the name is not in the directory.

Refinement of Initial Class Diagram

Earlier we used the top-down design approach to identify the subproblems to be solved (see Figures 1.3 to Figure 1.5) and came up with the list of level 1 subproblems shown in the previous section. As discussed, you can combine the second and third subproblems ("Insert a new entry", "Edit an existing entry") and add a subproblem to save the directory. The modified list follows:

- Read the initial directory from an existing file
- Insert a new entry or edit an existing entry.
- Retrieve and display an entry.
- Save the modified directory back to the file.

FIGURE 1.9
Phone Directory Application Class Diagram: Revision 1

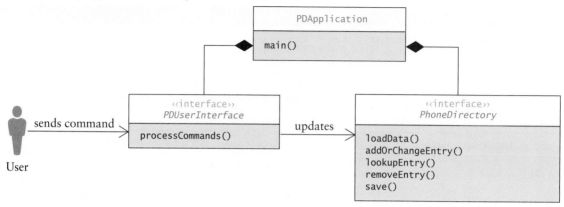

The directory should be saved whenever the program is exited. The phone directory has limited usefulness if updates to the directory cannot be saved from one run to the next.

There is another way to split this problem into subproblems. Overall, we want a phone directory application that combines a user interface as the front end and a persistent (permanent) storage of data as the back end. Thus, Figure 1.6 can be refined as shown in Figure 1.9. The black diamonds in Figure 1.9 indicate that a PDApplication object has objects of type PDUserInterface and PhoneDirectory as its components, and that they are created by the PDApplication object.

In Section 1.4, we identified two abstract data types: the PDUserInterface and the PhoneDirectory. They are shown in the class diagram as interfaces. In Section 1.6 classes that implement these interfaces will be designed. By splitting the design between the user interface and the directory, we can work on them independently. As long as the requirements defined by the interfaces are met, the front-end user interface does not care which back end it is dealing with, and the back-end directory does not care which front end it is dealing with.

Design   Overview of Classes and Their Interaction

Next, we identify all classes that will be part of the problem solution and describe their interaction. Besides the classes that implement the two interfaces shown in Figure 1.9, classes from the Java API will be used to perform input/output. We also need a class with a main method. Table 1.7 shows a summary of some of the classes and interfaces that will be used in our solution.

TABLE 1.7
Summary of Classes and Interfaces Used in Phone Directory Solution

Class/Interface	Description
PDApplication	Contains the main method. It instantiates classes that implement the PhoneDirectory and PDUserInterface interfaces.
DirectoryEntry	Contains a name-number pair.
PhoneDirectory	The interface that specifies methods to retrieve, insert, modify, load, and save the phone directory.
PDUserInterface	The interface that defines the user interface, which accepts commands from the user and calls the appropriate methods in the PhoneDirectory class to perform the desired action.
BufferedReader	A class in the Java API that breaks a stream of input characters into lines through a Reader object.
PrintWriter	A class in the Java API that provides output lines through a Writer object.

The first class in Table 1.7, PDApplication, contains a main method which starts program execution. From the use case in Table 1.4, we know that this method must create the PhoneDirectory object and read in the initial directory. Next, it must create a PDUserInterface object that interacts with the user to determine which operations should be performed. The list of steps for method main follows.

Algorithm for main Method

1. Create a new PhoneDirectory object.
2. Send it a message to read the initial directory data from a file.
3. Create a new PDUserInterface object.
4. Send it a message to perform all user operations on the PhoneDirectory object.

To perform Step 4, the PDUserInterface method processCommands will call its own internal methods that will, in turn, call PhoneDirectory methods that perform the specified operation on the PhoneDirectory object.

Next we show the UML *sequence diagram* for the main method. A sequence diagram (see Appendix B) is an OOD tool that documents the interaction between the objects in a program. Sequence diagrams are used to show the flow of information through the program and to identify the messages that are passed from one object to another.

FIGURE 1.10
Sequence Diagram for **main** Method

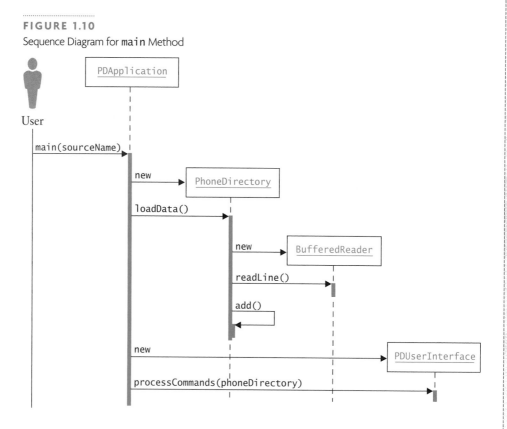

Sequence Diagram for **main** Method

The sequence diagram for the main method is shown in Figure 1.10. The first (and only) parameter for main will be the name of the file containing the directory data. We show this event in the sequence diagram as the user issuing the message main(sourceName) to the PDApplication class.

The sequence diagram shows all the objects involved in this use case across the horizontal axis, with each object's type underlined. Time is shown along the vertical axis. There is a dashed line coming down from each object that represents the object's *life line*. When a method of this object is called, the dashed line becomes a solid line indicating that the method is executing. All interaction with an object is indicated by a horizontal line that terminates at the object's life line.

The PDApplication object is created when the application begins execution. Tracing down its life line, you can see that its main method first sends the new message to a class that implements the PhoneDirectory interface, creating a new PhoneDirectory object. Next, main sends that object the loadData message. Method loadData is described in the `PhoneDirectory` interface. Looking at the life line for this `PhoneDirectory` object, you see that method `loadData` creates a new `BufferedReader` object and sends it a `readLine` message. Next, `loadData` sends the add message to the `PhoneDirectory` object. (Note that add is a new method that was not identified earlier.) This is the same object as the one that received the `loadData` message, so this add message is known as a *message to self*. Although the sequence diagram cannot show looping, the process of reading lines and adding entries continues until there are no remaining entries.

After all entries are read and saved, method `main` creates a new object (type `PDUserInterface`) and sends it the `processCommands` message, passing it the `PhoneDirectory` object as an argument. This provides the `PDUserInterface` object the necessary access to the `PhoneDirectory` object to process the commands. This completes the sequence diagram for reading the initial directory from a file. It shows all the steps performed by method `main`, including calling `processCommands` after the directory is loaded. Method `processCommands` will continue executing until the user issues the "Exit program" command.

The sequence diagram (Figure 1.10) shows that method `loadData` of the `PhoneDirectory` object performs most of the work for the "Read initial directory data" use case. Method `loadData` calls all the methods shown after it on the life line for the `PhoneDirectory` object.

EXERCISES FOR SECTION 1.5

SELF-CHECK

1. Provide a use case for saving the directory to a file.
2. Draw a sequence diagram for "Insert or change an entry".
3. Draw a sequence diagram for "Write the directory back to the file".

1.6 Design of an Array-Based Phone Directory

The case study continues with the design, implementation, and testing of class DirectoryEntry and classes that implement the interfaces PhoneDirectory and PDUserInterface. We will identify data fields for these classes and provide algorithms for their methods. As we design the methods of each class, we will identify new methods needed for that class. Because there are so many classes involved in this case study, their design, implementation, and testing are discussed in the remaining sections of this chapter.

CASE STUDY Designing a Telephone Directory Program (cont.)

Design Design of Data Structures for the Phone Directory

Next, we consider the actual data elements that will be involved in the telephone directory problem. We will define a class DirectoryEntry, which will contain the name-number pairs, and a class ArrayBasedPD, which implements the PhoneDirectory interface. This class will contain an array of DirectoryEntrys. In later chapters we will show alternative designs that use classes that are part of the Java API (for example, class ArrayList).

Our new class diagram is shown in Figure 1.10. The open diamond indicates that DirectoryEntry objects are components of ArrayBasedPD objects, but they can also be associated wth other objects (for example, the data file). For class DirectoryEntry, we show data fields (attributes) in the light-color screen and methods in the darker-color screen. Next, we discuss the two actual classes shown in this diagram: DirectoryEntry and ArrayBasedPD.

SYNTAX UML Syntax

In UML class diagrams, the + sign next to the method names indicate that these methods are public. The – sign next to the attributes name and number indicate that they are private. For the class DirectoryEntry we show the types of the attributes, and the parameter types and return types of the methods. Showing this information on the diagram is optional. We will generally show this information in separate tables such as Table 1.7. Appendix B provides a summary of UML.

FIGURE 1.11
Phone Directory Application Class Diagram: Revision 2

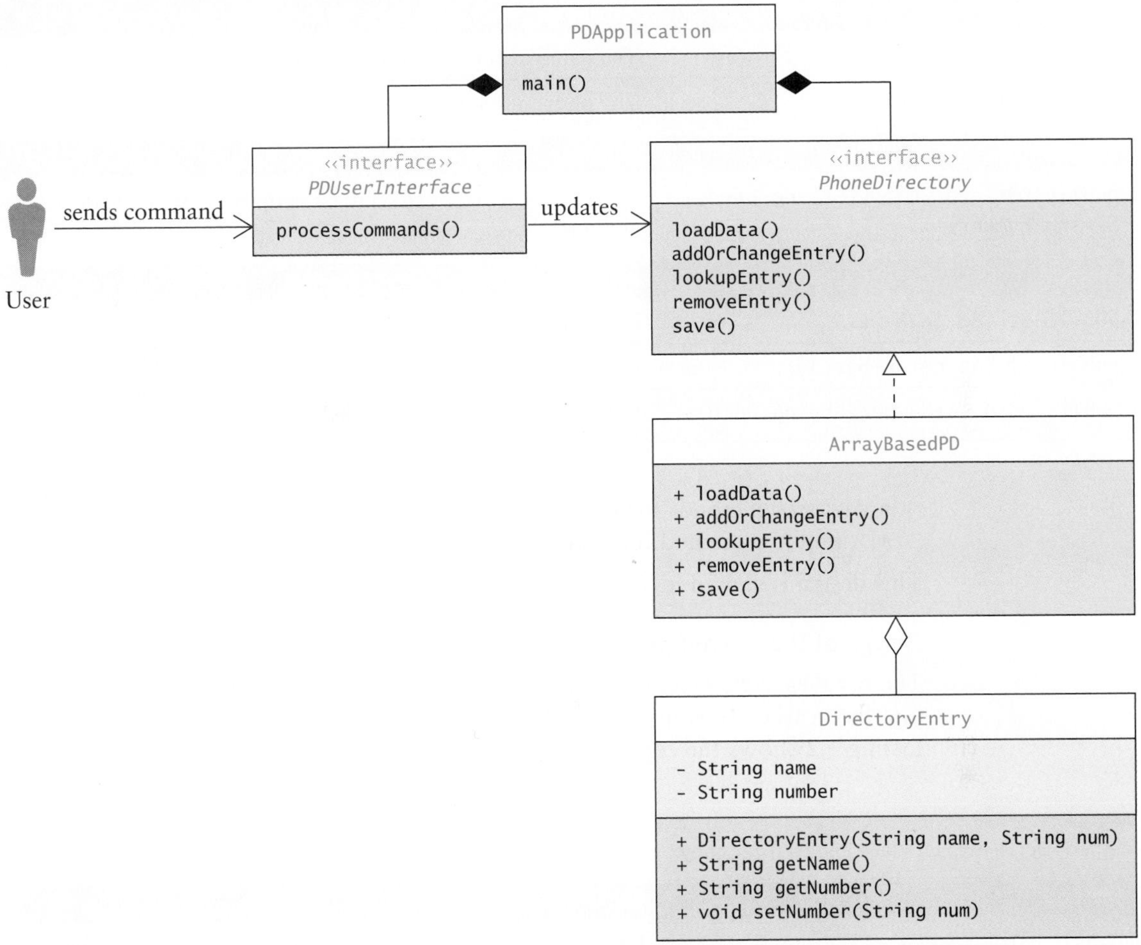

Design of the DirectoryEntry Class

The DirectoryEntry objects will contain the name-and-number pairs. The name is immutable; that is, it cannot be changed. For the purposes of your design, if you need to change the name of a person in your directory, you must remove the old entry and create a new one. The number, however, can be changed. Thus a straightforward design consists of

- Two data fields: name and number
- A constructor that sets both name and number

TABLE 1.8
Design of the `DirectoryEntry` Class

Data Field	Attribute
`private String name`	The name of the individual represented in the entry.
`private String number`	The phone number for this individual.
Constructor	**Behavior**
`public DirectoryEntry(String name, String number)`	Creates a new `DirectoryEntry` with the specified name and number.
Method	**Behavior**
`public String getName()`	Retrieves the name.
`public String getNumber()`	Retrieves the number.
`public void setNumber(String number)`	Sets the number to the specified value.

- Accessor methods for both `name` and `number`
- A mutator method for `number`

This design is shown in Table 1.8.

Design of the **ArrayBasedPD** Class

The `ArrayBasedPD` class implements `PhoneDirectory`. We showed a portion of this interface earlier (Listing 1.1); Table 1.9 shows the methods for the interface and Listing 1.2 shows the complete interface.

TABLE 1.9
Methods Declared in Interface `PhoneDirectory`

Method	Behavior
`public void loadData(String sourceName)`	Loads the data from the data file whose name is given by `sourceName`.
`public String addOrChangeEntry (String name, String number)`	Changes the number associated with the given name to the new value, or adds a new entry with this name and number.
`public String lookupEntry (String name)`	Searches the directory for the given name.
`public String removeEntry (String name)`	Removes the entry with the specified name from the directory and returns that person's number or **null** if not in the directory (left as an exercise).
`public void save()`	Writes the contents of the array of directory entries to the data file.

LISTING 1.2
PhoneDirectory.java

```java
/** The interface for the telephone directory.
*/
public interface PhoneDirectory {

    /** Load the data file containing the directory, or
        establish a connection with the data source.
        @param sourceName The name of the file (data source)
                           with the phone directory entries
    */
    void loadData(String sourceName);

    /** Look up an entry.
        @param name The name of the person to look up
        @return The number or null if name is not in the directory
    */
    String lookupEntry(String name);

    /** Add an entry or change an existing entry.
        @param name The name of the person being added or changed
        @param number The new number to be assigned
        @return The old number or, if a new entry, null
    */
    String addOrChangeEntry(String name, String number);

    /** Remove an entry from the directory.
        @param name The name of the person to be removed
        @return The current number. If not in directory, null is
                returned
    */
    String removeEntry(String name);

    /** Method to save the directory.
        pre:  The directory has been loaded with data.
        post: Contents of directory written back to the file in the
              form of name-number pairs on adjacent lines
              modified is reset to false.
    */
    void save();
}
```

Class `ArrayBasedPD` must implement these methods. It must also declare a data field for storage of the phone directory. Table 1.10 describes the data fields of class `ArrayBasedPD`. In addition to the array of directory entries, the class includes data fields to help keep track of the array `size` and `capacity` and whether it has been modified. The methods will be designed in the next section.

TABLE 1.10
Data Fields of Class ArrayBasedPD

Data Field	Attribute
private static final int INITIAL_CAPACITY	The initial capacity of the array to hold the directory entries.
private int capacity	The current capacity of the array to hold the directory entries.
private int size	The number of directory entries currently stored in the array.
private DirectoryEntry[] theDirectory	The array of directory entries.
private String sourceName	The name of the data file.
private boolean modified	A boolean variable to indicate whether the contents of the array have been modified since they were last loaded or saved.

Design of ArrayBasedPD Methods

In this section you will complete the design of the ArrayBasedPD class. At this stage you need to specify the method algorithms. We will develop *pseudocode* descriptions of the algorithms. Pseudocode is a combination of English and Java language constructs.

Method loadData

Method loadData is used to read the initial directory from a data file. The file name is passed as an argument to loadData when it is called.

Algorithm for Method loadData

1.   Create a BufferedReader for the input file.
2.   Read the name.
3.   **while** the name is not **null**
4.   Read the number.
5.   Add a new entry using method add.
6.   Read the name.

Note that we have identified a new method, add, for class ArrayBasedPD.

Method addOrChangeEntry

Method addOrChangeEntry is used to either add a new entry to the directory or change an existing entry if the name is already in the directory. The name and number are passed as arguments to addOrChangeEntry.

Algorithm for Method addOrChangeEntry

1.   Call method `find` to see whether the name is in the directory.
2.   `if` the name is in the directory
3.   Change the number using the `setNumber` method of the `DirectoryEntry`.
4.   Return the previous value of the number.

      `else`

5.   Add a new entry using method `add`.
6.   Return **null**.

Note that we have identified another new method, `find`, for class `ArrayBasedPD`.

Method `lookupEntry`

Method `lookupEntry` is passed a person's name as an argument. It retrieves the person's number or **null** if the name is not found.

Algorithm for `lookupEntry`

1.   The `PhoneDirectory` object uses its internal `find` method to locate the entry.
2.   `if` the entry is found
3.   `DirectoryEntry`'s `getNumber` method retrieves the number, which is returned to the caller.

      `else`

4.   **null** is returned.

Method **save**

Method `save` creates an output file and then writes all information stored in the array to this file. The file name is stored in data field `sourceName`. The algorithm for the save method follows.

Algorithm for save

1.   Create a `PrintWriter` object associated with the file.
2.   `for` each entry in the array
3.   Call `getName` to get the name from the entry.
4.   Write the name on a line.
5.   Call `getNumber` to get the number from the entry.
6.   Write the number on a line.
7.   Close the `PrintWriter` object.

Figure 1.12 shows the final class diagram with the additional methods.

FIGURE 1.12
Phone Directory Application Class Diagram: Revision 3

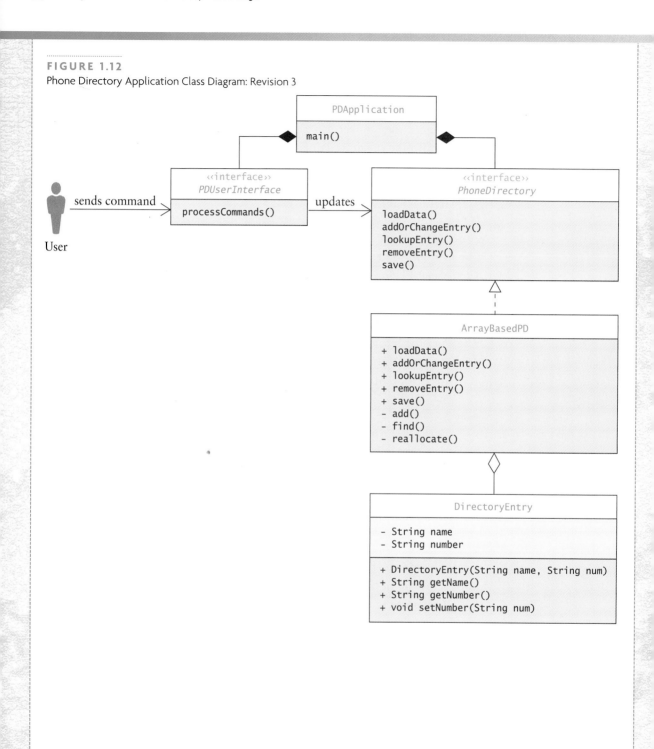

EXERCISES FOR SECTION 1.6

SELF-CHECK

1. Write the algorithm for the use case "Remove entry".

PROGRAMMING

1. Code class DirectoryEntry.

1.7 Implementing and Testing the Array-Based Phone Directory

In this section, the case study continues to illustrate implementation and testing of the array-based phone directory.

CASE STUDY Designing a Telephone Directory Program (cont.)

Implementation Next we write the code for class ArrayBasedPD. Listing 1.3 shows the data field declarations for the class. We use the Javadoc style for commenting the data fields.

LISTING 1.3
Data Field Declarations for ArrayBasedPD.java

```java
import java.io.*;

/** This is an implementation of the PhoneDirectory interface that uses
    an array to store the data.
*/
public class ArrayBasedPD implements PhoneDirectory {

    // Data Fields

    /** The initial capacity of the array */
    private static final int INITIAL_CAPACITY = 100;

    /** The current capacity of the array */
    private int capacity = INITIAL_CAPACITY;

    /** The current size of the array (number of directory entries) */
    private int size = 0;
```

```
/** The array to contain the directory data */
private DirectoryEntry[] theDirectory =
    new DirectoryEntry[capacity];

/** The data file that contains the directory data */
private String sourceName = null;

/** Boolean flag to indicate whether the directory was
    modified since it was either loaded or saved. */
private boolean modified = false;

...
}
```

Coding the Methods

Table 1.11 reviews the private methods of class ArrayBasedPD. They are private because they were not declared in the PhoneDirectory interface and should not be called by a client. Two of these, add and find, were discussed previously. Method reallocate will be discussed later in this section. Method removeEntry is left as an exercise.

The loadData Method

The loadData method (Listing 1.4) is called by the main method of class PDApplication to read the initial directory data from an input file (parameter sourceName). The data entry process takes place in the **while** loop inside the **try-catch** statement. (If you are unfamiliar with the use of **try-catch** statements for exception handling during file processing, you can review Appendix A. We also discuss these topics in the next chapter.) The **while** loop implements Steps 4 through 6 of the algorithm for loadData shown earlier. This method reads each name and number from two consecutive data lines and adds that entry to the array.

TABLE 1.11
Private Methods of **ArrayBasedPD** class

Private Method	Behavior
private int find(String name)	Searches the array of directory entries for the name.
private void add(String name, String number)	Adds a new entry with the given name and number to the array of directory entries.
private void removeEntry(int index)	Removes the entry at the given index from the directory array.
private void reallocate()	Creates a new array of directory entries with twice the capacity of the current one.

LISTING 1.4
Method `loadData` for `ArrayBasedPD.java`

```java
/** Method to load the data file.
    pre:  The directory storage has been created and it is empty.
          If the file exists, it consists of name-number pairs
          on adjacent lines.
    post: The data from the file is loaded into the directory.
    @param sourceName The name of the data file
*/
public void loadData(String sourceName) {
    // Remember the source name.
    this.sourceName = sourceName;
    try {
        // Create a BufferedReader for the file.
        BufferedReader in = new BufferedReader(
            new FileReader(sourceName));
        String name;
        String number;

        // Read each name and number and add the entry to the array.
        while ((name = in.readLine()) != null) {
            // Read name and number from successive lines.
            if ((number = in.readLine()) == null) {
                break;      // No number read, exit loop.
            }
            // Add an entry for this name and number.
            add(name, number);
        }

        // Close the file.
        in.close();
    } catch (FileNotFoundException ex) {
        // Do nothing - no data to load.
        return;
    } catch (IOException ex) {
        System.err.println("Load of directory failed.");
        ex.printStackTrace();
        System.exit(1);
    }
}
```

The `readLine` method of the `BufferedReader` class reads a line and returns it as a `String` object. If there is no more data to be read, **null** is returned, so we exit the **while** loop. Note that we combined the assignment statement and the test for **null** in the **while** statement condition

```java
while ((name = in.readLine()) != null) {...}
```

Similarly we combined the assignment and test when reading the number in the **if** condition

```java
if ((number = in.readLine()) == null) {
    break;      // No number read, exit loop.
}
```

Therefore, we also exit the loop (through execution of a **break** statement) if a name was read but a number was not. If both a name and number are read, then a new entry is added to the directory and we continue reading and adding entries.

If a file with name sourceName is not found, we immediately return (no data to read). (Later, we will write the new directory to file sourceName.) If an input/output error occurs, a stack trace is displayed and we exit the program with an exit code of 1, indicating an error.

PROGRAM STYLE

Use of Assignment in a Condition and Use of break

The **while** loop in this section uses two features of Java that simplify the code but are considered controversial. Some programmers prefer not to combine assignment with the evaluation of a condition. However, in this case, it simplifies the code to do it this way. Also, the requirement to exit the loop without storing an entry is met very naturally using the **break** statement. Some programmers prefer to provide only one way to exit a loop: when the **while** condition fails.

The addOrChangeEntry Method

This method calls the internal method find to locate the name in the array. Method find will either return the index of the entry, or return −1 (minus 1) to indicate that the entry is not in the array. If the entry is in the array, that entry's setNumber method is called to change the number; otherwise a new entry is added by calling the add method:

```
/** Add an entry or change an existing entry.
    @param name The name of the person being added or changed
    @param number The new number to be assigned
    @return The old number or, if a new entry, null
*/
public String addOrChangeEntry(String name, String number) {
    String oldNumber = null;
    int index = find(name);
    if (index > -1) {
        oldNumber = theDirectory[index].getNumber();
        theDirectory[index].setNumber(number);
    } else {
        add(name, number);
    }
    modified = true;
    return oldNumber;
}
```

The `lookupEntry` Method

This method also uses the internal `find` method to locate the entry in the array. If the entry is located, it is returned; otherwise **null** is returned.

```
/** Look up an entry.
    @param name The name of the person
    @return The number. If not in the directory, null is returned
*/
public String lookupEntry(String name) {
    int index = find(name);
    if (index > -1) {
        return theDirectory[index].getNumber();
    } else {
        return null;
    }
}
```

The **save** Method

If the directory has not been modified, method save (Listing 1.5) does nothing. Otherwise it creates a `PrintWriter` object and writes all phone directory entries to it. The output file name is the same as the input file name (sourceName), so an existing directory file will be overwritten. The **while** loop inside the **try-catch** statement writes the entries.

LISTING 1.5
Method save for `ArrayBasedPD.java`

```
/** Method to save the directory.
    pre:  The directory has been loaded with data.
    post: Contents of directory written back to the file in the
          form of name-number pairs on adjacent lines.
          modified is reset to false.
*/
public void save() {
    if (modified) { // If not modified, do nothing.
        try {
            // Create PrintWriter for the file.
            PrintWriter out = new PrintWriter(
                new FileWriter(sourceName));

            // Write each directory entry to the file.
            for (int i = 0; i < size; i++) {
                // Write the name.
                out.println(theDirectory[i].getName());
                // Write the number.
                out.println(theDirectory[i].getNumber());
            }
```

```
                    // Close the file.
                    out.close();
                    modified = false;
                } catch (Exception ex) {
                    System.err.println("Save of directory failed");
                    ex.printStackTrace();
                    System.exit(1);
                }
            }
        }
```

The **find** Method

The find method uses a **for** loop to search the array for the requested name. If
located, its index is returned; otherwise –1 (minus 1) is returned.

```
/** Find an entry in the directory.
    @param name The name to be found
    @return The index of the entry with the requested name.
            If the name is not in the directory, returns -1
*/
private int find(String name) {
    for (int i = 0; i < size; i++) {
        if (theDirectory[i].getName().equals(name)) {
            return i;
        }
    }
    return -1;      // Name not found.
}
```

 PITFALL

Returning –1 (Failure) Before Examining All Array Elements

A common logic error is to code the search loop for method find as follows:

```
for (int i = 0; i < size; i++) {
    if (theDirectory[i].getName().equals(name)) {
        return i;
    } else {
        return -1;  // Incorrect! - tests only one element.
    }
}
```

This loop incorrectly returns a result after testing just the first element.

The add Method

The add method checks to see whether there is room in the array by comparing the size to the capacity. If the size is less than the capacity, the new entry is stored at the end of the array and size is incremented by one after the entry is stored (size++). If the size is greater than or equal to the capacity, then the reallocate method is called to increase the size of the array before the new item is inserted.

```java
/** Add an entry to the directory.
    @param name The name of the new person
    @param number The number of the new person
*/
private void add(String name, String number) {
    if (size >= capacity) {
        reallocate();
    }
    theDirectory[size] = new DirectoryEntry(name, number);
    size++;
}
```

The reallocate Method

This method allocates a new array whose size is twice the current array. Method System.arraycopy (see Appendix A) copies the contents of the old array (theDirectory) to the new array (newDirectory):

```java
System.arraycopy(theDirectory, 0, newDirectory, 0, theDirectory.length);
```

and theDirectory is changed to refer to the new array. The storage allocated to the old array will be recycled by the Java Virtual Machine (JVM)'s garbage collector.

By doubling the size each time that a reallocation is necessary, we reduce the number of times we need to do this. Surprisingly, if we do this only fourteen times, we can store over 1 million entries.

```java
/** Allocate a new array to hold the directory. */
private void reallocate() {
    capacity *= 2;
    DirectoryEntry[] newDirectory = new DirectoryEntry[capacity];
    System.arraycopy(theDirectory, 0, newDirectory, 0,
                     theDirectory.length);
    theDirectory = newDirectory;
}
```

Using a Storage Structure Without Reallocation

In Chapter 4, you will study the ArrayList data structure, which will enable you to store a directory of increasing size without needing to reallocate storage. You will see that we can change to a different data structure for storing the directory with very little effort, because the problem solution has been so carefully designed. We will only need to code the methods declared in the PhoneDirectory interface so that they perform the same operations on an ArrayList.

Testing   Class **ArrayBasedPD**

To test this class, you should run it with data files that are empty or that contain a single name-and-number pair. You should also run it with data files that contain an odd number of lines (ending with a name but no number). You should see what happens when the array is completely filled and you try to add a new entry. Does method reallocate properly double the array's size? When you do a retrieval or an edit operation, make sure you try to retrieve names that are not in the directory as well as names that are in the directory. If an entry has been changed, verify that the new number is retrieved. Finally, check that all new and edited entries are written correctly to the output file. We will discuss testing further in the next chapter.

EXERCISES FOR SECTION 1.7

PROGRAMMING

1. Code the removeEntry method.
2. Rewrite method loadData so that the assignment is not part of the **while** condition. Also, rewrite the loop so that an entry with a **null** number is still not stored, but loop exit can occur only when the **while** condition is false.

1.8 Two Classes That Implement PDUserInterface

So far we have introduced the interface PDUserInterface, but we have not discussed any classes that implement the interface. In this section, the case study concludes with an illustration of two different classes that fulfill the requirements of the interface.

CASE STUDY   **Designing a Telephone Directory Program (cont.)**

Analysis   Through the description of the interface, we know that a class that implements PDUserInterface must contain a public method, processCommands, declared as follows in the interface:

```
void processCommands(PhoneDirectory theDirectory);
```

The interface enables clients to use method processCommands without knowing the details of its implementation (information hiding). We will introduce new private methods that are called by processCommands to perform its tasks, but are unavailable to a client.

The kind of user interaction that will take place will be determined by the input/output facilities used in a class that implements the interface. Three options would be console input, GUI input using a specially designed GUI for this problem, and GUI input using JOptionPane dialog windows. We will write classes that use the first and last options. (If you are unfamiliar with any of these Java input/output features, review Appendix A.)

For both classes, method processCommands should present a menu of choices to the user:

- Add or Change an Entry
- Look Up an Entry
- Remove an Entry
- Save the Directory Data
- Exit the Program

Design   For both classes, method processCommands will use a "menu-driven" loop to control the interaction with the user. In a true GUI, a loop would not be necessary. After each command is processed, the menu of choices is displayed again. This process continues until the user selects "Exit the program".

```
do {
    // Get the action to perform from the user.
    // The user's choice will be a number from 0 through 4.
    . . .
    switch (choice) {
        case 0: doAddChangeEntry(); break;
        case 1: doLookupEntry(); break;
        case 2: doRemoveEntry(); break;
        case 3: doSave(); break;
        case 4: doSave(); break;
    }
} while (choice < commands.length - 1);
```

The method processCommands calls a private method shown in the foregoing **switch** statement to perform the user's choice. Note that method doSave is called by the last two cases. We discuss the design and coding of these methods next.

Implementation   The PDGUI Class

Our first class will interact with the user through a GUI. It uses method showOptionDialog of the JOptionPane class, which is part of the Java Swing API, to present the menu to the user, request data from the user, and display the results to the user. The initial menu is as follows:

Method **doAddChangeEntry**

The doAddChangeEntry method uses the JOptionPane.showInputDialog method to request the name and new number. Here are examples of these dialogs:

 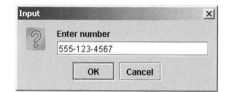

If the user selects Cancel, a null string is returned. In that case the method will return immediately without changing the directory.

The PhoneDirectory.addOrChangeEntry method is called if values are entered for the name and number. A return value of **null** indicates that this is a new entry, and a confirmation dialog is displayed by JOptionPane.showMessageDialog:

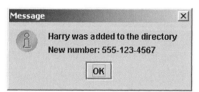

If the name was already in the directory, the previous value of the number is returned, and the confirmation shows both the old and the new number, as follows:

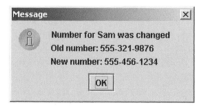

Algorithm for Method doAddChangeEntry

1. Read the name of the entry.
2. Read the number of the entry.
3. Send the addOrChangeEntry message to the PhoneDirectory object.
4. **if** the result of addOrChangeEntry was **null**
5.   The message "*name* was added to the directory" is displayed and the new number is displayed.

    else

6.   The message "number for *name* was changed", and the old and new number are displayed.

Method **doLookupEntry**

The doLookupEntry method uses the same dialog as doAddChangeEntry to request the name. If the user cancels the dialog, the method returns. Otherwise the number is looked up by calling the PhoneDirectory.lookupEntry method, and the result is displayed. If the name is not in the directory, a message is displayed. Examples of both are as follows:

Algorithm for doLookupEntry

1. Read the name.
2. Issue a lookupEntry message to the PhoneDirectory object.
3. **if** the result is not **null**
4.   The name and number are displayed.

    else

5.   A message indicating that the name is not in the directory is displayed.

Method **doSave**

The doSave method calls the save method of the PhoneDirectory object.

Listing 1.6 shows the code for the PDGUI class. It implements all the methods discussed above.

LISTING 1.6
PDGUI.java

```java
import javax.swing.*;

/** This class is an implementation of PDUserInterface
    that uses JOptionPane to display the menu of command choices.
*/
public class PDGUI implements PDUserInterface {

    /** A reference to the PhoneDirectory object to be processed.
        Globally available to the command-processing methods.
    */
    private PhoneDirectory theDirectory = null;

    // Methods
    /** Method to display the command choices and process user
        commands.
        pre:  The directory exists and has been loaded with data.
        post: The directory is updated based on user commands.
        @param thePhoneDirectory A reference to the PhoneDirectory
               to be processed.
    */
    public void processCommands(PhoneDirectory thePhoneDirectory) {

        String[] commands = {"Add/Change Entry",
                             "Look Up Entry",
                             "Remove Entry",
                             "Save Directory",
                             "Exit"};

        theDirectory = thePhoneDirectory;
        int choice;

        do {
            choice = JOptionPane.showOptionDialog(
                null,                               // No parent
                "Select a Command",                 // Prompt message
                "PhoneDirectory",                   // Window title
                JOptionPane.YES_NO_CANCEL_OPTION,   // Option type
                JOptionPane.QUESTION_MESSAGE,       // Message type
                null,                               // Icon
                commands,                           // List of commands
                commands[commands.length - 1]);     // Default choice
            switch (choice) {
                case 0: doAddChangeEntry(); break;
                case 1: doLookupEntry(); break;
                case 2: doRemoveEntry(); break;
                case 3: doSave(); break;
                case 4: doSave(); break;
            }
        } while (choice < commands.length - 1);
        System.exit(0);
    }
```

```java
/** Method to add or change an entry.
    pre:  The directory exists and has been loaded with data.
    post: A new name is added, or the value for the name is
          changed, modified is set to true.
*/
private void doAddChangeEntry() {
    // Request the name
    String newName = JOptionPane.showInputDialog("Enter name");
    if (newName == null) {
        return; // Dialog was cancelled.
    }
    // Request the number
    String newNumber = JOptionPane.showInputDialog("Enter number");
    if (newNumber == null) {
        return; // Dialog was cancelled.
    }
    // Insert/change name-number
    String oldNumber = theDirectory.addOrChangeEntry(newName,
                                              newNumber);

    String message = null;
    if (oldNumber == null) {    // New entry.
        message = newName + " was added to the directory"
                  + "\nNew number: " + newNumber;
    } else {    // Changed entry.
        message = "Number for " + newName + " was changed "
                  + "\nOld number: " + oldNumber
                  + "\nNew number: " + newNumber;
    }
    // Display confirmation message.
    JOptionPane.showMessageDialog(null, message);
}

/** Method to look up an entry.
    pre:  The directory has been loaded with data.
    post: No changes made to the directory.
*/
private void doLookupEntry() {
    // Request the name.
    String theName = JOptionPane.showInputDialog("Enter name");
    if (theName == null) {
        return; // Dialog was cancelled.
    }
    // Look up the name.
    String theNumber = theDirectory.lookupEntry(theName);
    String message = null;
    if (theNumber != null) {    // Name was found.
        message = "The number for " + theName + " is " + theNumber;
    } else {    // Name was not found.
        message = theName + " is not listed in the directory";
    }
    // Display the result.
    JOptionPane.showMessageDialog(null, message);
}
```

```
/** Method to remove an entry.
    pre:  The directory has been loaded with data.
    post: The requested name is removed, modified is set to true.
*/
private void doRemoveEntry() {
    // Programming Exercise
}

/** Method to save the directory to the data file.
    pre:  The directory has been loaded with data.
    post: The current contents of the directory have been saved
          to the data file.
*/
private void doSave() {
    theDirectory.save();
}
}
```

Testing   Testing Class PDGUI

To test this class you need a main method that creates an ArrayBasedPD object and a PDGUI object. Method main must invoke method loadData of class ArrayBasedPD to read the directory from a file, passing the file name as an argument; main must then invoke method processCommands of class PDGUI, passing the PhoneDirectory object as an argument.

```
/** Program to display and modify a simple phone directory. */
public class PDApplication {

    public static void main (String args[]) {
        // Check to see that there is a command line argument.
        if (args.length == 0) {
            System.err.println("You must provide the name of the file"
                                  + " that contains the phone directory.");
            System.exit(1);
        }

        // Create a PhoneDirectory object.
        PhoneDirectory phoneDirectory = new ArrayBasedPD();
        // Load the phone directory from the file.
        phoneDirectory.loadData(args[0]);

        // Create a PDUserInterface object.
        PDUserInterface phoneDirectoryInterface = new PDGUI();
        // Process user commands.
        phoneDirectoryInterface.processCommands(phoneDirectory);
    }
}
```

When this method runs, make sure you test all possible commands. Try exiting without first saving the directory and verify that the file is correctly updated and saved.

Implementation

The **PDConsoleUI** Class

Listing 1.7 shows the code for the PDConsoleUI class. This class uses System.out to display the menu of choices and results. It also uses System.in to read data from the user.

The constructor creates a BufferedReader object that is attached to System.in. This object has a readLine method, which reads a line of input and returns it as a String.

Method **processCommands**

The readLine method may throw an IOException, so the processCommands method uses a **try-catch** block to enclose the processing of user commands. Each of the individual methods that process the commands is declared to throw an IOException. Thus they do not need a **try-catch** block. (We provide thorough coverage of exceptions in Chapter 2.)

Should an IOException be thrown, an error message will be written to System.err and the program will exit with an exit code of 1 (error).

The initial menu is as follows:

Method **doAddChangeEntry**

The doAddChangeEntry method requests the name followed by the number. The PhoneDirectory.addOrChangeEntry method is called after values are entered for the name and number. A return value of **null** indicates that this is a new entry, and a confirmation dialog is displayed as follows:

```
Command Prompt - java PhoneDirectoryApplication3 Phone.dat
Select 0: Add/Change Entry
Select 1: Look Up Entry
Select 2: Remove Entry
Select 3: Save Directory
Select 4: Exit
0
Enter name
Quincy
Enter number
555-111-3333
Quincy was added to the directory
New number: 555-111-3333
Select 0: Add/Change Entry
Select 1: Look Up Entry
Select 2: Remove Entry
Select 3: Save Directory
Select 4: Exit
```

If the name was already in the directory, the previous value of the number is returned, and the confirmation shows both the old and new number as follows:

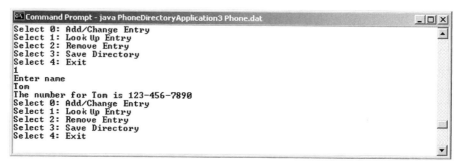

Method doLookupEntry

The doLookupEntry method uses the same prompt as doAddChangeEntry to request the name. If the user cancels the data entry, the method returns. Otherwise the number is looked up by calling the PhoneDirectory.lookupEntry method, and the result is displayed. If the name is not in the directory, a message is displayed. Examples of both cases follow:

```
Command Prompt - java PhoneDirectoryApplication3 Phone.dat
Select 0: Add/Change Entry
Select 1: Look Up Entry
Select 2: Remove Entry
Select 3: Save Directory
Select 4: Exit
1
Enter name
Tom
The number for Tom is 123-456-7890
Select 0: Add/Change Entry
Select 1: Look Up Entry
Select 2: Remove Entry
Select 3: Save Directory
Select 4: Exit
```

```
Command Prompt - java PhoneDirectoryApplication3 Phone.dat
The number for Tom is 123-456-7890
Select 0: Add/Change Entry
Select 1: Look Up Entry
Select 2: Remove Entry
Select 3: Save Directory
Select 4: Exit
1
Enter name
Dick
Dick is not listed in the directory
Select 0: Add/Change Entry
Select 1: Look Up Entry
Select 2: Remove Entry
Select 3: Save Directory
Select 4: Exit
```

Method **doSave**

The doSave method calls the save method of the PhoneDirectory.

LISTING 1.7
PDConsoleUI.java

```java
import java.io.*;

/** This class is an implementation of PDUserInterface
    that uses the console to display the menu of command choices.
*/
public class PDConsoleUI implements PDUserInterface {

    /** A reference to the PhoneDirectory object to be processed.
        Globally available to the command-processing methods.
    */
    private PhoneDirectory theDirectory = null;
    /** Buffered reader to read from the input console. */
    private BufferedReader in = null;

    // Constructor
    /** Default constructor. */
    public PDConsoleUI() {
        in = new BufferedReader(new InputStreamReader(System.in));
    }

    // Methods
    /** Method to display the command choices and process user
        commands.
        pre:  The directory exists and has been loaded with data.
        post: The directory is updated based on user commands.
        @param thePhoneDirectory A reference to the PhoneDirectory
               to be processed
    */
    public void processCommands(PhoneDirectory thePhoneDirectory) {
        String[] commands = {"Add/Change Entry",
                             "Look Up Entry",
                             "Remove Entry",
                             "Save Directory",
                             "Exit"};

        theDirectory = thePhoneDirectory;
        int choice;
        try {
            do {
                for (int i = 0; i < commands.length; i++) {
                    System.out.println("Select " + i + ": "
                                       + commands[i]);
                }
```

```
                    String line = in.readLine();
                    if (line != null)
                        choice = Integer.parseInt(line);
                    else
                        choice = commands.length - 1;
                    switch (choice) {
                        case 0: doAddChangeEntry(); break;
                        case 1: doLookupEntry(); break;
                        case 2: doRemoveEntry(); break;
                        case 3: doSave(); break;
                        case 4: doSave(); break;
                    }
                } while (choice < commands.length - 1);
                System.exit(0);
            } catch (IOException ex) {
                System.err.println
                    ("IO Exception while reading from System.in");
                System.exit(1);
            }
        }

        /** Method to add or change an entry.
            pre:  The directory exists and has been loaded with data.
            post: A new name is added, or the value for the name is
                  changed, modified is set to true.
            @throws IOException - if an IO error occurs
        */
        private void doAddChangeEntry() throws IOException {
            // Request the name.
            System.out.println("Enter name");
            String newName = null;
            newName = in.readLine();
            if (newName == null) {
                return;
            }
            // Request the number.
            System.out.println("Enter number");
            String newNumber = null;
            newNumber = in.readLine();
            if (newNumber == null) {
                return;
            }
            // Insert/change name-number.
            String oldNumber =
                    (theDirectory.addOrChangeEntry(newName, newNumber));
            String message = null;
            if (oldNumber == null) {   // New entry.
                message = newName + " was added to the directory"
                        + "\nNew number: " + newNumber;
```

```java
        } else {    // Changed entry.
            message = "Number for " + newName + " was changed"
                        + "\nOld number: " + oldNumber
                        + "\nNew number: " + newNumber;
        }
        // Display confirmation message.
        System.out.println(message);
    }

    /** Method to look up an entry.
        pre:  The directory has been loaded with data.
        post: No changes made to the directory.
        @throws IOException - If an IO error occurs
    */
    private void doLookupEntry() throws IOException {
        // Request the name.
        System.out.println("Enter name");
        String theName = null;
        theName = in.readLine();
        if (theName == null) {
            return;    // Dialog was cancelled.
        }
        // Look up the name.
        String theNumber = theDirectory.lookupEntry(theName);
        String message = null;
        if (theNumber != null) {    // Name was found.
            message = "The number for " + theName + " is " + theNumber;
        } else {    // Name was not found.
            message = theName + " is not listed in the directory";
        }
        // Display the result.
        System.out.println(message);
    }

    /** Method to remove an entry.
        pre:  The directory has been loaded with data.
        post: The requested name is removed, modifed is set to true.
        @throws IOException - If there is an IO Error
    */
    private void doRemoveEntry() throws IOException {
        // Programming Exercise
    }

    /** Method to save the directory to the data file.
        pre:  The directory has been loaded with data.
        post: The current contents of the directory have been saved
              to the data file.
    */
    private void doSave() {
        theDirectory.save();
    }
}
```

EXERCISES FOR SECTION 1.8

PROGRAMMING

1. Code the doRemoveEntry method for class PDConsoleUI.
2. Code the doRemoveEntry method for class PDGUI.

Chapter Review

- We discussed the software engineering process. We introduced two software life cycle models (waterfall and Unified) and discussed the activities performed in each stage of these models. In this text we will use a simplified five-step process for developing software:

  1. Requirements   4. Coding
  2. Analysis   5. Testing
  3. Design

  Although these steps are shown in sequence, in reality there is quite a bit of interaction between them. During the design phase, you may need to go back and redo the requirements and analysis steps. Of course, this is provided for in the full Unified Model.

- Procedural abstraction, data abstraction, and information hiding are tools for managing program complexity, so that progams can be designed as a collection of separate but interacting classes. Procedural abstraction focuses on the operations to be performed; data abstraction focuses on the data elements and their operations; information hiding means that users of a class or method need to know only how to use the class or method, not how it is implemented.

- A Java interface can be used to specify an abstract data type (ADT) and a Java class can be used to implement an ADT. An interface can have several classes that implement it (define its methods).

- Use cases summarize the interaction between the user and the system during requirements specification and analysis.

- UML class diagrams are used during the analysis and design phases to document the interaction of classes with each other and with the user.

- Sequence diagrams and pseudocode can be used to describe the sequence of actions performed by a program that is implemented as a collection of multiple interacting classes. Sequence diagrams are employed during the design phase of the software life cycle.

Java Constructs Introduced in This Chapter

```
interface
```

Java API Classes Introduced in This Chapter

```
javax.swing.JOptionPane
java.io.BufferedReader
java.io.FileReader
java.io.InputStreamReader
java.io.PrintWriter
java.lang.FileWriter
```

User-Defined Interfaces and Classes in This Chapter

```
class DirectoryEntry
interface PhoneDirectory
class ArrayBasedPD implements PhoneDirectory
interface PDUserInterface
class PDConsoleUI implements PDUserInterface
class PDGUI implements PDUserInterface
```

Quick-Check Exercises

1. The _____ of the _____ model is that it assumes that the software life cycle stages are performed in sequence and not revisited once completed. The _____ consists of _____, and _____ and the system designer can work on more than one _____ during each iteration.

2. Procedural abstraction enables a system designer to model _____; data abstraction focuses on the _____ and _____.

3. An _____ specifies the requirements of an ADT as a contract between the _____ and _____; a _____ implements the ADT.

4. An interface can be implemented by multiple classes (True/False).

5. A _____ is a statement that must be true before a _____ executes, and a _____ represents the _____ of executing a _____.

6. A _____ _____ specifies the interaction between an _____ _____ and a system.

7. _____ _____ means that a class _____ does not need to know its implementation details.

8. _____ _____ and _____ are used to design Java methods.

Answers to Quick-Check Exercises

1. The *disadvantage* of the *waterfall* model is that it assumes that the software life cycle stages are a sequence and not revisited once completed. The *Unified Model* consists of *activities/workflows* and *phases*, and the system designer can work on more than one *activity* during each iteration.

2. Procedural abstraction enables a system designer to model *processes/operations*; data abstraction focuses on the *data elements* and *operations on that data*.

3. An *interface* specifies the requirements of an ADT as a contract between the *developer* and *user*; a *class* implements the ADT.

4. True.
5. A *precondition* is a statement that must be true before a *method* executes, and a *postcondition* represents the *result* of executing a *method*.
6. A *use case* specifies the interaction between an *external entity* and a system.
7. *Information hiding* means that a class *user* does not need to know its implementation details.
8. *Sequence diagrams* and *pseudocode* are used to design Java methods.

Review Questions

1. Explain why the principle of information hiding is important to the software designer.
2. Discuss the differences between the waterfall model and Unified Model of the software life cycle.
3. Define the terms *procedural abstraction* and *data abstraction*.
4. Explain the role of method preconditions and postconditions.
5. What is the advantage of specifying an abstract data type as an interface instead of just going ahead and implementing it as a class?
6. Define an interface to specify an ADT Money that has methods for arithmetic operations (addition, subtraction, multiplication, and division) on real numbers having exactly two digits to the right of the decimal point, as well as methods for representing a Money object as a string and as a real number. Also include methods equals and compareTo for this ADT.
7. Answer Review Question 6 for an ADT Complex that has methods for arithmetic operations on a complex number (a number with a real and imaginary part). Assume that the same operations (+, -, *, /) are supported. Also provide methods toString, equals, and compareTo for the ADT Complex.

Programming Projects

1. Modify the telephone directory project in this chapter so that it could be used by a company. Each employee's information should contain a name, job description, telephone number, and room number. Assume that the information for each person is available on a single line of a data file in the form *last name, first name, job description, phone number, room number* with commas as separators between data items. Provide a submenu for the edit operation that allows the user to edit any of the person's data fields. After using the directory and updating it, save the data file in the same format as before.
2. Follow the software development model illustrated in this chapter to design and implement an array-based program application that manages a collection of DVDs. The data for each DVD will consist of a title, a category, running time, year of release, and price. Use a file to save the collection after it has been updated. The user should be able to add new DVDs to the collection, remove a DVD, edit the information stored for a DVD, list all DVDs in a specified category, and retrieve and display the information saved for a DVD given its title. Also, the user should be able to sort the collection of DVDs by year or by title.
3. Follow the software development model illustrated in this chapter to design and implement an array-based program application that manages your personal library. The data for each book will consist of a title, author, number of pages, year of publication, price, and the name of the person who has borrowed it (if any). Use a file to save the collec-

tion after it has been updated. The user should be able to add new books to the collection, remove a book, edit the information stored for a book, list all books by a specified author, list all books loaned to a particular person, and retrieve and display the information saved for a book given its title. Also, the user should be able to sort the collection of books by author or by title.

4. Assume that you have decided to loan DVDs in your DVD collection to friends (see Project 2) but just one DVD at a time to each friend. Assume that you also have a collection of friends. For each friend, you need to store the friend's name and phone number and the number of the DVD your friend has borrowed (–1 if none). Besides managing your DVD collection as in Project 2, you should also be able to manage your list of friends (add friend, edit friend, and so on). One of the edit operations should allow your friend to return a DVD or to exchange it for another. You should also be able to display each friend and the name of the DVD that the friend currently has (if any). Draw UML class diagrams before you start to code the program.

5. Develop a program that could be used to determine election results for a town. Assume that the town is divided into a number of precincts (an input item) and that the number of candidates is variable (an input item). The votes received for each candidate by precinct should be stored in a two-dimensional array that is part of class `VoteTabulation`. Your program should allow its user to issue any of the following instructions:

—Load the vote data from a file

—Load the vote data interactively

—Edit the vote data interactively to account for absentee ballots just received

—Request a table showing the raw vote results by precinct and candidate

—Request a table showing the percentage of votes by precinct and candidate

—Request a table showing the raw vote results by candidate and precinct

—Request a table showing the precentage of votes by candidate and precinct

—Display the top *n* vote getters for the township and their results in decreasing order, where *n* is a data item

6. Develop a program that could be used as a point-of-order inventory system. Read in a database from a file that represents the store inventory. Each item consists of an ID, a description, a price, a quantity on hand, and a reorder point. Assume that the database can be updated at a terminal by the operator when a customer purchases an item. The quantity purchased for an item is deducted from that item's quantity (if sufficient) and a register receipt is displayed after all purchases are entered. An operator can also process the return of an item by adding the quantity returned to the inventory. A register receipt should also be displayed for a return. Finally, the operator can process new items received from a supplier by adding the items to the database. It should also be possible for an operator to update the price of an item, provided the operator enters the correct security key. Also, the operator should be able to display a list of all items whose quantity on hand is less than the reorder point for that item.

7. Develop a sales-tracking program that enables a company to keep track of its sales force's performance by quarter. The program should read in each person's name and the past performance of that salesperson for the last *n* quarters, where *n* is a data item. The operator should be able to enter the results for each person for the current quarter interactively. The operator should be able to add a new salesperson to the system (past performances set to 0) and edit the information stored for a salesperson. The operator should be able to request any of the following tables:

—Total sales by quarter (for all quarters or for a specified quarter)

—Sales for each person by quarter (for all quarters or for a specified quarter)

—Rank of each person by quarter (for all quarters or for a specified quarter)

—A list of salespeople and amounts in decreasing order by quarter (for all quarters or for a specified quarter)

2

Program Correctness and Efficiency

Chapter Objectives

- ◆ To understand the differences between the three categories of program errors
- ◆ To understand the effect of an uncaught exception and why you should catch exceptions
- ◆ To become familiar with the Exception hierarchy and the difference between checked and unchecked exceptions
- ◆ To learn how to use the **try-catch-finally** sequence to catch and process exceptions
- ◆ To understand what it means to throw an exception and how to throw an exception in a method
- ◆ To understand different testing strategies and when and how they are performed
- ◆ To learn how to write special methods to test other methods and classes
- ◆ To become familiar with debugging techniques and debugger programs
- ◆ To be introduced to the process of program verification and the use of assertions and loop invariants
- ◆ To understand the meaning of big-**O** notation and how it is used to analyze an algorithm's efficiency

This chapter discusses program correctness and efficiency. You will learn about program defects and how to avoid them in your programs: through careful program design and by using other members of your programming team to help detect errors in logic before they become part of the code. As in all other situations in life, early detection leads to the best results.

You will study the different kinds of errors that can occur in programs: syntax errors, run-time errors or exceptions, and logic errors. You will learn about the different kinds of exceptions in Java, how to handle exceptions in programs, and the benefit of doing so.

The chapter discusses program testing in some detail. You will learn how to generate a proper test plan and the differences between unit and integration testing as they apply to an object-oriented design. You will also learn how to use drivers and stubs, special methods that are written to test other methods and classes.

You will learn how to detect errors during debugging and techniques for generating diagnostic information to help in debugging. You will also see what features are available in debugger programs to help with this process.

You will also see how formal verification can be used to help you reason about a program. We don't expect you to write a program like a mathematical proof, but you can use these ideas to help in the design and documentation of your programs and to increase your confidence that critical parts of programs operate as intended.

Finally, you will learn about algorithm efficiency and how to characterize the efficiency of an algorithm. You will learn about big-**O** notation, which you can use to compare the relative efficiency of different algorithms.

Program Correctness and Efficiency

2.1 Program Defects and "Bugs"

This chapter is about program errors or defects and how to avoid them. It does not matter much whether a program runs efficiently if it does not do what it is supposed to do. Very often, defects appear in a software product after it is delivered, with sometimes disastrous results. Some notable software defects have caused power brownouts, telephone network saturation, space flight delays, loss of spacecraft, and even loss of life.

One way to show that a program is correct is by thorough testing, but it is difficult to determine how much testing needs to be done. In fact, testing can never demonstrate the complete absence of defects. Furthermore, in some situations it is very difficult to test a software product completely in the environment in which it is used, such as software that controls a missile or prevents a meltdown in a nuclear power plant.

You may also hear the term "bug" used to refer to a software defect. "Debugging" is a commonly used term for removing defects, and a debugger is a commonly used testing tool that helps find defects, as we discuss in Section 2.6. Because of society's ever-increasing dependence on computer systems, however, many software professionals have come to believe that calling software defects "bugs" tends to trivialize their serious consequences.

Careful design and careful testing can reduce program defects. Obviously, it is much easier to eliminate defects by design rather than by removing them later through testing.

There are three kinds of defects or errors that you might encounter:

- Syntax errors
- Run-time errors or exceptions
- Logic errors

Syntax Errors

Syntax errors are mistakes in your use of the grammar (or syntax) of the Java language (for example, using = as the equality operator instead of ==). The Java compiler will detect most syntax errors during compilation and will require you to correct them before it can successfully compile your program. The following are some other common syntax errors:

- Omitting or misplacing braces that bracket compound statements
- Performing an incorrect type of operation on a primitive type value (for example, using + with **boolean** data or assigning a real number to a type **int** variable)
- Invoking an instance method that is not defined for the object it is applied to
- Not declaring a variable before using it
- Providing multiple declarations of a variable
- Not assigning a value to a local variable before referencing it
- Not returning a value from a method whose result type is not **void**

Some syntax errors are the result of typographical errors (for example, misspelling a variable name or typing { instead of } or [).

The compiler does not detect all typographical errors. For example, if you omit a } where you intended it but insert an extra } at a later point in the program, the syntax may still be valid but not what you intended. This will result in the computer performing a different operation from the one intended. Because a syntactically correct program can contain errors, careful review and testing are essential.

Run-time Errors or Exceptions

Run-time errors occur during program execution. A run-time error occurs when the Java Virtual Machine (JVM) detects an operation that it knows to be incorrect. Table 2.1 shows some examples of common run-time errors. A run-time error will cause the JVM to *throw an exception*—that is, to create an object of an exception type that identifies the kind of incorrect operation and to interrupt normal processing. This is

TABLE 2.1
Subclasses of java.lang.RuntimeException

Run-time Exception	Cause/Consequence
ArithmeticException	Integer division by zero.
ArrayIndexOutOfBoundsException	An attempt to access an element in an array with an index value (subscript) less than zero or greater than or equal to the array's length.
IllegalArgumentException	An attempt to call a method with an argument of incorrect type or inappropriate format.
NumberFormatException	An attempt to convert a string that is not numeric to a number (real or integer).
NullPointerException	An attempt to use a **null** reference value to access an object.
NoSuchElementException	An attempt to get a next token after all tokens were extracted from the string that was tokenized.

a "good news, bad news" situation. The good news is that the error has been detected. The bad news is that your program is no longer executing. We will discuss exceptions in more detail in Sections 2.2 and 2.3 and show how to prevent the bad-news situation from occurring. Following are brief discussions and examples of some of the errors listed in the table.

Division by Zero

If count represents the number of items being processed and it is possible for count to be zero, then the assignment statement

```
average = sum / count;
```

can cause a division-by-zero error. If sum and count are **int** variables, this error is indicated by the JVM throwing an ArithmeticException. You can easily guard such a division with an **if** statement so that the division operation will not be performed when count is zero:

```
if (count == 0)
    average = 0;
else
    average = sum / count;
```

Normally you would compute an average as a **double** value, so you could cast an **int** value in sum to type **double** before doing the division. In this case an exception is not thrown if count is zero. Instead average will have one of the special values Double.POSITIVE_INFINITY, Double.NEGATIVE_INFINITY, or Double.NaN depending on whether sum was positive, negative, or zero.

Array Index Out of Bounds

An `ArrayIndexOutOfBoundsException` is thrown by the JVM when an index value (subscript) used to access an element in an array is less than zero or greater than or equal to the array's length. For example, suppose we define the array `scores` as follows:

```
int[] scores = new int[500];
```

The subscripted variable `scores[i]` uses `i` (type **int**) as the array index. An `ArrayIndexOutOfBoundsException` will be thrown if `i` is less than zero or greater than 499.

Array-index-out-of-bounds errors can be prevented by carefully checking the boundary values for an index that is also a loop control variable. A common error is using the array size as the upper limit rather than the array size minus 1.

EXAMPLE 2.1   The following loop would cause an `ArrayIndexOutOfBoundsException` on the last pass, when `i` is equal to `x.length`.

```
for (int i = 0; i <= x.length; i++)
    x[i] = i * i;
```

The loop repetition test should be `i < x.length`.

If an array index is passed as a method argument, the method should validate the argument before using it as an array subscript. The next example shows one way to guard against this type of error; later in the chapter, you will learn another technique for handling illegal arguments.

EXAMPLE 2.2   Method `setElementOfX` stores its second argument (`val`) in the element of array `x` (a type `int[]` data field) selected by its first argument (`index`). The **if** statement validates that `index` is in bounds before the assignment. The method returns a **boolean** value indicating whether or not the array element was changed. If the method did not validate that `index` is in bounds, an out-of-bounds value would cause an `ArrayIndexOutOfBoundsException` to be thrown.

```
/** Stores val in the element of array x with subscript index.
    @param index The subscript of element to be changed
    @param val The value to be stored
    @return true if val is stored; otherwise, false
 */
public boolean setElementOfX(int index, int val) {
    if (index >= 0 && index < x.length) {
        x[index] = val;
        return true;
    } else {
        return false;
    }
}
```

PROGRAM STYLE

Using a Boolean Result to Indicate Success or Failure

What is gained by returning a **boolean** value when we execute method seElementOfX? The caller of the method can use this result to display an error message to the program user if desired. The following **if** statement applies method setElementOfX to object myXArray and writes an error message to stream System.err (the standard error stream) if the assignment did not take place.

```
if (!myXArray.setElementOfX(sub, data))
    System.err.println("***** Did not assign " + data
                        + " to element " + sub + " of array x");
```

The use of a **boolean** value to indicate success or failure is a technique that was used before exceptions were added to programming languages. Because exceptions are part of the Java language, using them is the preferred way to indicate an error.

EXAMPLE 2.3   A common technique for communicating the name of a data file to a program is to pass the file name as a parameter to method main. If you are using the Java Software Development Kit (SDK), you can do this by listing the file name on the command line that initiates program execution. If you are using an IDE, you can enter parameters in a special window. When the main method executes, any parameters are stored as strings in array args.

The following main method expects the first string to be the input file name, so it contains an **if** statement that validates that at least one string was passed to array args before the method attempts to store args[0] in inputFileName. If a parameter is not supplied, then we use the string "Phone.dat" as the default name of the input file. Without the **if** statement, Java would throw an ArrayIndexOutOfBoundsException when args[0] was referenced and no parameters were passed.

```
public static void main(String[] args) {
    String inputFileName;

    if (args.length > 0)
        inputFileName = args[0];
    else
        inputFileName = "Phone.dat";
}
```

Number Format Error

The NumberFormatException is thrown when a program attempts to convert a non-numeric string (usually a data value) to a numeric value. For example, if the user types in the string "2.6e", method parseDouble in the following code,

```
String speedStr =
    JOptionPane.showInputDialog("Enter speed");
double speed = Double.parseDouble(speedStr);
```

would throw a `NumberFormatException` because "2.6e" is not a valid numeric string (it has no exponent after the e). There is no general way to avoid this exception because it is impossible to guard against all possible data entry errors the user can make.

Null Pointer

The `NullPointerException` is thrown when there is an attempt to access an object that does not exist; that is, the reference variable being accessed contains a special value, known as **null**. You can guard against this by testing for **null** before invoking a method.

EXAMPLE 2.4   After the following loop has read all data lines, the value of name is **null** and the value of count gives the number of times the `String` referenced by `specialName` was read as data. The **while** condition stores the next data line in name and compares it to **null**. This ensures that the method invocation `name.equals(specialName)` executes only when name references an actual `String` object.

```
// Count occurrences of specialName.
int count = 0;
while ((name = in.readLine()) != null) {
    if (name.equals(specialName))
        count++;
}
System.out.println("The number of times " + specialName
                  + " was found is " + count);
```

Logic Errors

Logic errors are the final category of error. A logic error occurs when the programmer/analyst has made a mistake in the design of a class or a class method or has implemented an algorithm incorrectly. In either case, the Java code will not meet the specification for that method—that is, it will run but produce incorrect results. If the user is fortunate, a logic error may cause a run-time error in another method that relies on the results generated by the faulty method, but this may not happen. Most logic errors do not cause syntax or run-time errors and, consequently, are difficult to find. An example is the Pitfall on page 40.

Sometimes logic errors are found during testing by careful comparison of the actual program output with the expected results. This can happen only if the tester provides test cases that cause execution of the incorrect portion of the algorithm. Also, the tester must determine beforehand the output that should be generated, so that the expected output can be compared with the actual output.

A worse scenario is when logic errors are encountered during real-world operation of a program. There are many examples in which logic errors have made the popular news. The original Mars Lander spacecraft crashed due to type inconsistencies (feet versus meters). Billing programs have sent out bills for exorbitant amounts of money. Logic errors in automatic-teller-machine (ATM) programs or off-track betting programs have caused machine owners to lose significant amounts of money. Many popular operating systems have been released with logic errors that have enabled hackers to access computers easily. One popular word processor, when integrated with any document management system, frequently would "eat" the document off the server and leave an empty file in its place. In the 1980s several patients died after errors in the software that controlled therapeutic radiation machines gave them massive overdoses. To avoid these kinds of catastrophes, software professionals must be very diligent about detecting and correcting logic errors.

In Section 2.5 we show you how to reduce logic errors by carefully checking the program design. We also show how to detect logic errors through testing.

EXERCISES FOR SECTION 2.1

SELF CHECK

1. Explain and correct any syntax errors in the following `main` method.
```
public static void main(args[]) {
    int x = 3.45;
    float w = x / 2;
    char ch = 'a' + 'b';
    if (x = y) {
        int z = x++;
    else
        int z = y++;
    }
    System.out.println(z + "***" + sqrt(z));
}
```

2. Identify any of the following statements that would throw an exception. Identify the kind of exception.
```
int[] x = new int[10];
x[x.length] = 5;
x[x.length - 1] = -95;
x[0] = 7;
int n = 0;
x[n] = x.length / n;
String num = "334.e5";
n = Integer.parseInt(num);
double y = Double.parseDouble(num);
```

PROGRAMMING

1. Write an instance method that returns a type **int** value stored in an array data field x. The method argument is the subscript of the value to be retrieved. Validate the argument to prevent an `ArrayIndexOutOfBoundsException`. Return `MIN_VALUE` if the subscript is not valid.

2.2 The Exception Class Hierarchy

When an exception is thrown, one of the Java exception classes is instantiated. In this section we discuss the hierarchy of exception classes.

Exceptions are defined within a class hierarchy that has the class `Throwable` as its superclass (see the UML diagram in Figure 2.1). (We cover class hierarchies in detail in Chapter 3. Refer to the beginning of Section 3.1 if you are unfamiliar with the terms subclass and superclass.) The UML diagram shows that classes `Error` and `Exception` are subclasses of `Throwable`. Each of these classes has subclasses that are shown in the figure. We will focus on class `Exception` and its subclasses in this chapter. Because `RuntimeException` is a subclass of `Exception`, it is also a subclass of `Throwable` (the subclass relationship is transitive).

The Class `Throwable`

The class `Throwable` is the superclass of all exceptions. The methods that you will use from class `Throwable` are summarized in Table 2.2. Because all exception classes are subclasses of class `Throwable`, they inherit all of its methods. That is, any exception class can use a method defined in the `Throwable` class. If `ex` is an `Exception` object, the call

        ex.printStackTrace();

displays a *stack trace,* discussed in Section 2.3. The statement

        System.err.println(ex.getMessage());

displays a *detail message* (or error message) describing the exception. The statement

        System.err.println(ex.toString);

displays the name of the exception followed by the detail message.

FIGURE 2.1

Summary of Exception Class Hierarchy

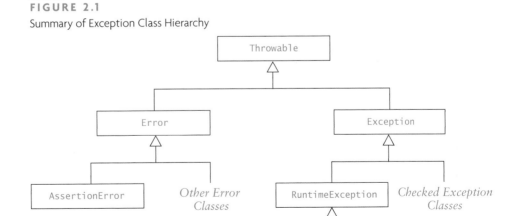

TABLE 2.2

TABLE 2.2
Summary of Commonly Used Methods from the `java.lang.Throwable` Class

Method	Behavior
`String getMessage()`	Returns the detail message.
`void printStackTrace()`	Prints the stack trace to `System.err`.
`String toString()`	Returns the name of the exception followed by the detail message.

Checked and Unchecked Exceptions

There are two categories of exceptions: *checked* and *unchecked*. A *checked exception* is an error that is normally not due to programmer error and is beyond the control of the programmer. All exceptions caused by input/output errors are considered checked exceptions. For example, if the programmer attempts to access a data file that is not available because of a user or system error, a `FileNotFoundException` is thrown. The class `IOException` and its subclasses (see Table 2.3) are checked exceptions. Even though checked exceptions are beyond the control of the programmer, the programmer must be aware of them and must handle them in some way. We show how to handle them in the next two sections. All checked exceptions are subclasses of `Exception`, but they are not subclasses of `RuntimeException`.

The *unchecked* exceptions represent error conditions that may occur as a result of programmer error or as a result of serious external conditions that are considered unrecoverable. For example, exceptions such as `NullPointerException` or `ArrayIndexOutOfBoundsException` are unchecked exceptions that are generally due to programmer error. These exceptions are all subclasses of `RuntimeException`. While you can sometimes prevent these exceptions via defensive programming, it is impractical to try to prevent them all or to provide exception handling for all of them. Therefore, you can handle these exceptions, but Java does not require you to.

The class `Error` and its subclasses represent errors that are due to serious external conditions. An example of such an error is `OutOfMemoryError`, which is thrown when there is no memory available. You can't foresee or guard against these kinds of errors. You can attempt to handle these exceptions, but you are strongly discour-

TABLE 2.3
Class `java.io.IOException` and Some Subclasses

Exception Class	Cause
`IOException`	Some sort of input/output error.
`EOFException`	An attempt to read beyond the end of the data in a file.
`FileNotFoundException`	A file that cannot be found.

aged from trying because your attempts will probably be unsuccessful. For example if an `OutOfMemoryError` is thrown, there is no memory available to process the exception-handling code, so the exception would be thrown again.

Figure 2.2 is a more complete diagram of the `Exception` hierarchy.

How do we know which exceptions are checked and which are unchecked? Exception classes that are subclasses of `RuntimeException` and `Error` are unchecked. All other exception classes are checked exceptions.

FIGURE 2.2
Exception Hierarchy Showing Selected Checked and Unchecked Exceptions

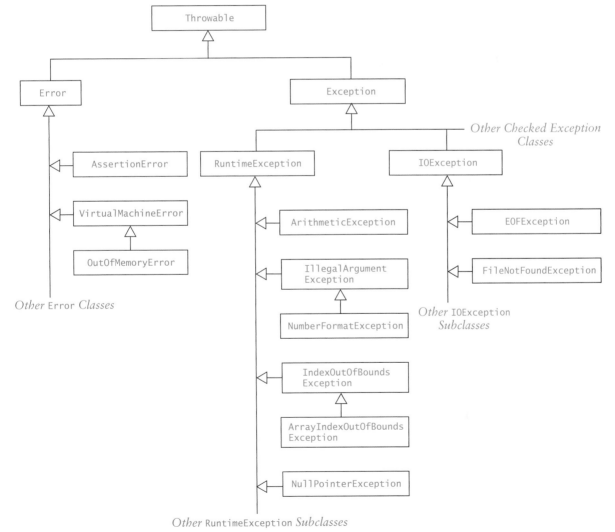

EXERCISES FOR SECTION 2.2

SELF-CHECK

1. Explain the key difference between checked and unchecked exceptions. Give an example of each kind of exception. What criterion does Java use to decide whether an exception is checked or unchecked?
2. What is the difference between the kind of unchecked exceptions in class `Error` and the kind in class `Exception`?
3. List four subclasses of `RuntimeException`.
4. List two subclasses of `IOException`.

2.3 Catching and Handling Exceptions

In the previous section we stated that when the Java Virtual Machine detects a run-time error, it throws an exception. When an exception is thrown, the normal sequence of execution is interrupted because the execution of subsequent statements would most likely be erroneous. The default behavior is for the program to stop and for the JVM to display an error message indicating which type of exception was thrown and where in the program it was thrown. The programmer can override this default behavior by enclosing the statements that might cause an exception in a **try** block and then processing the exception in a corresponding **catch** block.

Uncaught Exceptions

When an exception occurs that is not caught, the program stops and the JVM displays an error message and a stack trace. The *stack trace* shows the sequence of method calls, starting at the method that threw the exception, then showing the method that called that method, and so on, all the way back to the main method.

The stack trace in Figure 2.3 shows that an exception occurred during the execution of class `ExceptionDemo`. The uncaught exception was a `NullPointerException`. The exception was thrown in method `doSomethingElse` (at line 18 of class `ExceptionDemo`). Method `doSomethingElse` was called from method `doSomething` (at line 13). Method `doSomething` was called from method `main` (at line 7).

FIGURE 2.3

Example of a Stack Trace for an Uncaught Exception

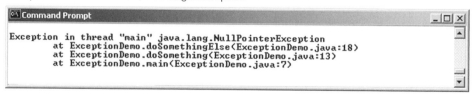

```
Exception in thread "main" java.lang.NullPointerException
        at ExceptionDemo.doSomethingElse(ExceptionDemo.java:18)
        at ExceptionDemo.doSomething(ExceptionDemo.java:13)
        at ExceptionDemo.main(ExceptionDemo.java:7)
```

In the next few subsections you will see how to avoid the default behavior when you write a method that may throw an exception. You will also see why it is advantageous to do this.

The `try-catch-finally` Sequence

One way to avoid uncaught exceptions is to write a **try-catch** sequence that actually "catches" an exception and "handles it" rather than relying on the JVM to do this.

```
try {
    // Statements that perform file-processing operations.
}
catch (IOException ex) {
    ex.printStackTrace();    // Display stack trace.
    System.exit(1);    // Exit with an error indication.
}
```

If all statements in the **try** block execute without error, the **catch** block is skipped. If an IOException occurs, the **try** block is exited and the **catch** block executes. This particular **catch** block simply displays the sequence of method calls that led to the error (starting with the most recent one and working backwards) in the console window (System.err – the standard error stream) and then exits with an error indication.

Although this handles the exception, it basically duplicates the default behavior for uncaught exceptions. Next, we show you how to use the **try-catch** sequence to recover from errors and continue execution of your program.

Handling Exceptions to Recover from Errors

In addition to reporting errors, exceptions provide us with the opportunity to recover from errors. One common source of exceptions is user input. For example, the method JOptionPane.showInputDialog displays a dialog window and allows the user to enter input. After the user enters input and presses the Enter key, the method will return a string containing the input characters. If we are expecting an integer value, we need to convert this string to an integer. The conversion is performed by method parseInt, which can cause a NumberFormatException to be thrown.

EXAMPLE 2.5   Method readInt (Listing 2.1) returns the integer value that was typed into a dialog window by the program user. The method argument is the dialog window prompt.

The **while** loop repetition condition (**true**) ensures that the **try-catch** sequence will execute "forever" or until the user enters a correct data item. The statements

```
String numStr = JOptionPane.showInputDialog(prompt);
return Integer.parseInt(numStr);
```

display the dialog window and return an integer value if numStr contains only digit characters. If not, a NumberFormatException is thrown, which is handled by the **catch** clause. The **catch** block displays an error message window by calling JOptionPane.showMessageDialog. The last argument, JOptionPane.ERROR_MESSAGE, causes a window with a stop sign to appear (see Figure 2.4). After closing this window, the user has another opportunity to enter a valid numeric string.

FIGURE 2.4
Bad-Numeric-String
Error

LISTING 2.1
Method `readInt` (part of class `MyInput.java`) with One Parameter

```
/** Method to return an integer data value.
    @param prompt Message
    @return The data value read as an int
*/
public static int readInt(String prompt) {
    while (true) {    // Loop until valid number is read.
        try {
            String numStr = JOptionPane.showInputDialog(prompt);
            return Integer.parseInt(numStr);
        }
        catch (NumberFormatException ex) {
            JOptionPane.showMessageDialog(
                null,
                "Bad numeric string – Try again",
                "Error", JOptionPane.ERROR_MESSAGE);
        }
    }
}
```

The **try** Block

The syntax for the **try** block is as follows:

```
try {
    Code that may throw an exception
}
```

The **catch** Clauses and Blocks

Exceptions are caught by what is appropriately called a catch clause. A catch clause resembles a method and has the following syntax.

```
catch (ExceptionClass exceptionArgument) {
    Code to handle the exception
}
```

The code within the brackets is called the **catch** *block*. The **catch** clause(s) must follow a **try** block. There may be multiple **catch** clauses, one for each exception class that you wish to handle.

An exception matches a **catch** clause if the type of the exception is the same as the argument of the **catch** clause or is a subclass of the argument type. When an exception is thrown from within a **try** block, the associated **catch** clause(s) is (are) examined to see whether there is a match in the exception class for any **catch** clause. If so, that **catch** block executes. If not, a search is made back through the chain of method calls to see whether any of them occurs in a **try** block with an appropriate **catch**. If so, that **catch** block executes. If none is found, the exception is uncaught.

EXAMPLE 2.6   The body of method readIntTwo below contains just the statements in the **try** block of method readInt (Listing 2.1).

```
public static int readIntTwo(String prompt) {
    String numStr = JOptionPane.showInputDialog(prompt);
    return Integer.parseInt(numStr);
}
```

In this case, if a NumberFormatException is thrown by method parseInt, method readIntTwo will not be able to handle it (no **catch** clause), so readIntTwo is exited and a search is made for an appropriate **catch** clause in the caller of method readIntTwo. If method readIntTwo is called to read a value into age by the following **try** block:

```
try {
    // Enter a value for age.
    age = readIntTwo("Enter your age");
} catch (Exception ex) {
    System.err.println("Error occurred in call to readInt");
    age = DEFAULT_AGE;
}
```

the **catch** clause will handle the NumberFormatException (because NumberFormatException is a subclass of Exception) and assign the value of DEFAULT_AGE to age. It will also display an error message on the console, and program execution will continue with the statement that follows this **try-catch** sequence.

Note that a **catch** clause is like a method, and the **catch** block is like a method body. The term **catch** *clause* refers to both the header and the body, whereas the term **catch** *block* refers to the body alone. This distinction is not generally that important, and you may see the terms used interchangeably in other texts and documentation.

 PITFALL

Unreachable catch Block

Note that only the **catch** block within the first **catch** clause having an appropriate exception class executes. All other **catch** blocks are skipped. If a **catch** clause exception type is a subclass of an exception type in an earlier **catch** clause, the **catch** block in the later **catch** clause cannot execute, so the Java compiler will display a catch is unreachable syntax error. To correct this error, switch the order of the **catch** clauses so that the **catch** clause whose exception class is the subclass comes first.

EXAMPLE 2.7 EOFException is a subclass of IOException. The two **catch** clauses in the following code must appear in the sequence shown to avoid a catch is unreachable syntax error. The first **catch** block handles an EOFException that occurs when all the data in the file was processed (not an error). This **catch** block tells the program user so and then exits the program. The second **catch** clause processes any other input/output exception (which does indicate an error) by calling method printStackTrace to display a stack trace like the one shown in Figure 2.3 It exits the program with an error indication (System.exit(1)). (*Note:* The method printStackTrace is defined in the Throwable class and is inherited by all exception objects.)

```
catch (EOFException ex) {
    System.out.print("End of file reached ")
    System.out.println(" - processing complete");
    System.exit(0);
}
catch (IOException ex) {
    System.err.println("Input/Output Error:");
    ex.printStackTrace();
    System.exit(1);
}
```

The finally Block

When an exception is thrown, the flow of execution is suspended and continues at the appropriate **catch** clause. There is no return to the **try** block. Instead, processing continues at the first statement after all of the **catch** clauses associated with the **try** from which the exception was thrown.

There are situations in which allowing the program to continue after an exception could cause problems. For example, if some calculations needed to be performed before returning from the method, these calculations would have to be duplicated in both the **try** block and every **catch** clause. To avoid such a duplication (which can be error-prone), the **finally** block can be used. The code in the **finally** block is executed either after the **try** block is exited or after a **catch** clause is exited (if one is executed). The **finally** block is optional. We show an example in the following syntax summary.

SYNTAX **try-catch-finally Sequence**

FORM:

```
try {
    Statements that may throw an exception
}
catch (ExceptionClass₁ exceptionArgument₁) {
    Statements to process ExceptionClass₁
}
```

```
catch (ExceptionClass₂ exceptionArgument₂) {
    Statements to process ExceptionClass₂
}
catch (ExceptionClassₙ exceptionArgumentₙ) {
    Statements to process ExceptionClassₙ
}
finally {
    Statements to be executed after the try block or the exception block exits
}
```

EXAMPLE:

```
try {
    String sizeStr =
            JOptionPane.showInputDialog("Enter new size");
    size = Integer.parseInt(sizeStr);
}
catch (NumberFormatException ex) {
    size = DEFAULT_SIZE;   // Use default value if input error.
}
finally {
    if (size > MAX_CAPACITY)
        size = MAX_CAPACITY;
}
```

MEANING:

The statements in the **try** block execute through to completion unless an exception is thrown. If there is a **catch** clause to handle the exception, its **catch** block executes to completion. After the **try** block or **catch** block executes, the **finally** block executes to completion.

If there is no **catch** clause to handle the exception thrown in the **try** block, the **finally** block is executed, and then the exception is passed up the call chain until either it is caught by some other method in the call chain or it is processed by the JVM as an uncaught exception.

Reporting the Error and Exiting

There are many cases in which an exception is thrown but there is no obvious way to recover. For example, reading from a file or the system console can result in an IOException being thrown. In this case the **catch** clause should print the stack trace and exit, as follows:

```
catch (IOException ex) {
    ex.printStackTrace();
    System.exit(1);
}
```

The method call System.exit(1) causes a return to the operating system with an error indication.

PITFALL

Ignoring Exceptions

Exceptions are designed to make the programmer aware of possible error conditions and to provide a way to handle them. Some programmers do not appreciate this feature and do the following:

```
catch (Exception e){}
```

Although this clause is syntactically correct and eliminates a lot of pesky error messages, it is almost always a bad idea. The program continues execution after the **try-catch** sequence with no indication that there was a problem. The statement that caused the exception to be thrown did not execute properly. The statements that follow it were not executed at all. The program will have hidden defects that will make its users very unhappy and could have even more serious consequences.

PROGRAM STYLE

Using Exceptions to Enable Straightforward Code

In computer languages that did not provide exceptions, programmers had to incorporate error-checking logic throughout their code to check for many possibilities, some of which were of low probability. The result was sometimes messy, as follows:

```
Step A
if (Step A successful) {
    Step B
    if (Step B successful) {
        Step C
    } else {
        Report error in Step B
        Cleanup after Step A
    }
} else {
    Report error in Step A
}
```

With exceptions this becomes much cleaner, as follows:

```
try {
    Step A
    Step B
    Step C
} catch (exception indicating Step B failed) {
    Report error in step B
    Cleanup after step A
} catch (exception indicating Step A failed) {
    Report error in step A
}
```

EXERCISES FOR SECTION 2.3

SELF-CHECK

1. Assume that method `main` calls method `first` at line 10 of class `MyApp`, method `first` calls method `second` at line 10 of class `Others`, and method `second` calls method `parseInt` at line 20 of class `Other`. These calls result in a `NumberFormatException` at line 430 of class `Integer`. Show the stack trace.

2. Assume that you have **catch** clauses for exception classes `Exception`, `NumberFormatException`, and `RuntimeException` following a **try** block. Show the required sequence of **catch** clauses.

PROGRAMMING

1. For the **try** block
```
try {
    numStr = in.readLine();
    num = Integer.parseInt(numStr);
    average = total / num;
}
```
write a **try-catch-finally** sequence with **catch** clauses for `ArithmeticException`, `NumberFormatException`, and `IOException`. For class `ArithmeticException`, set average to zero and display an error message indicating the kind of exception, display the stack trace, and exit with an error indication. After exiting the **try** block or the **catch** block for `ArithmeticException`, display the message "That's all folks" in the **finally** block.

2.4 Throwing Exceptions

In the last section we showed how to catch and handle exceptions using the **try-catch** sequence. As an alternative to catching an exception in a lower-level method, you can allow it to be caught and handled by a higher-level method. You can do this in one of two ways:

1. You declare that the lower-level method may throw a checked exception by adding a **throws** clause to the method header.
2. You throw the exception in the lower-level method, using a **throw** statement, when the exception is detected.

The throws Clause

The next example illustrates the use of the **throws** clause to declare that a method may throw a particular kind of checked exception. This is a useful approach if a higher-level module already contains a **catch** clause for this exception type. If you don't use the **throws** clause, you must duplicate the **catch** block in the lower-level method to avoid an `unreported exception` syntax error.

EXAMPLE 2.8   Method readData reads two strings from the BufferedReader object console associated with System.in (the system console) and stores them in data fields firstName and lastName. Each call to method readLine may throw a checked IOException, so method readData cannot compile without the **throws** clause. If you omit it, you will get the syntax error unreported exception: Java.io.IOException; must be caught or declared to be thrown.

```
public void readData() throws IOException {
    BufferedReader console = new BufferedReader(
        new InputStreamReader(System.in));
    System.out.print("Enter first name: ");
    firstName = console.readLine();
    System.out.print("Enter last name: ");
    lastName = console.readLine();
}
```

If method readData is called by method setNewPerson, method setNewPerson must have a **catch** block that handles exceptions of type IOException.

```
public void setNewPerson() {
    try {
        readData();
        // Process the data read.
        . . .
    }
    catch (IOException iOEx) {
        System.err.println("Call to readLine failed in readData");
        iOEx.printStackTrace();
        System.exit(1);
    }
}
```

If a method can throw more than one exception type, list them all after **throws** with comma delimiters. You will get an unreported exception syntax error if you omit any checked exception type. The compiler verifies that all class names listed are exception classes.

PROGRAM STYLE

Using Javadoc @throws for Unchecked Exceptions

Listing unchecked exceptions in the **throws** clause is legal syntax but is considered poor programming practice. Instead you should use the Javadoc **@throws** tag to document any unchecked exceptions that may reasonably be expected to occur but are not caught in the method.

The throw **Statement**

You can use a **throw** statement in a lower-level method to indicate that an error condition has been detected. When the **throw** statement executes, the lower-level method stops executing immediately, and the JVM begins the search for an exception handler as described earlier. This approach is usually taken if the exception is unchecked and is likely to be caught in a higher-level method. If the exception thrown is a checked exception, this exception must be declared in the **throws** clause of the method containing the **throw** statement.

EXAMPLE 2.9   The method addOrChangeEntry of the PhoneDirectory interface takes two String parameters: the name and the number. The number parameter is intended to represent a valid phone number. Therefore, we wish to validate its format to ensure that only validly formatted numbers are entered. Assuming that we have a method isPhoneNumberFormat that checks for a valid phone number, we could code the addOrChangeEntry method as follows:

```
public String addOrChangeEntry(String name, String number) {
    if (!isPhoneNumberFormat(number)) {
        throw new IllegalArgumentException
            ("Invalid phone number: " + number);
    }
    // Add/change the number.
    ...
}
```

The **throw** statement creates and throws a new IllegalArgumentException, which can be handled farther back in the call chain or by the JVM if it is uncaught. The constructor argument ("Invalid phone number: " + number) for the new exception object is a message that describes the cause of the error.

If we call this method using the following **try-catch** sequence:

```
try {
    addOrChangeEntry(myName, myNumber);
} catch (IllegalArgumentException ex) {
    System.err.println(ex.getMessage());
}
```

and myNumber references the string "1xx1", which is not a valid phone number, the console output would be:

```
Invalid phone number: 1xx1
```

SYNTAX   **throw Statement**

FORM:

throw new *ExceptionClass*();

throw new *ExceptionClass*(*detailMessage*);

EXAMPLE:

throw new FileNotFoundException("File " + fileSource
                                           + " not found");

MEANING:

A new exception of type *ExceptionClass* is created and thrown. The optional String parameter *detailMessage* is used to specify an error message associated with this exception. If the higher-level method that catches this exception has the **catch** clause

catch (*ExceptionClass* ex) {
    System.err.println(ex.getMessage());
    System.exit(1);
}

the *detailMessage* will be written to the system error stream before system exit occurs.

EXAMPLE 2.10   Listing 2.2 shows a second method readInt that has three arguments. As in method readInt in Example 2.5, the first argument is a prompt. The second and third arguments represent the end points for a range of integer numbers. The method returns the first integer value entered by the program user that is between the end points.

The **if** statement tests whether the end points define an empty range (minN > maxN). If so, the statement

throw new IllegalArgumentException(
    "In readInt, minN " + minN
    + " not <= maxN " + maxN);

throws an IllegalArgumentException, creating an instance of this class. The message passed to the constructor gives the cause of the exception. This message would be displayed by printStackTrace or returned by getMessage or toString.

If the range is not empty, the **while** loop executes. Its repetition condition (!inRange) is true as long as the user has not yet entered a value that is within the range defined by the end points. The **try** block displays a dialog window with a prompt that shows the valid range of values. The statement

inRange = (minN <= n && n <= maxN);

sets inRange to true when the value assigned to n is within this range. If so, the loop is exited and this value is returned. However, if the user enters a string that is not numeric, the **catch** block displays an error message. If the string is not numeric or its value is not in range, inRange remains false, so (!inRange) is true and the loop repeats, giving the user another opportunity to enter a valid number.

....
LISTING 2.2
Method `readInt` (part of `MyInput.java`) with Three Parameters

```
/** Method to return an integer data value between two
    specified end points.
    pre: minN <= maxN.
    @param prompt Message
    @param minN Smallest value in range
    @param maxN Largest value in range
    @throws IllegalArgumentException
    @return The first data value that is in range
*/
public static int readInt(String prompt, int minN, int maxN) {
    if (minN > maxN) {
        throw new IllegalArgumentException(
            "In readInt, minN " + minN
            + " not <= maxN " + maxN);
    }
    // Arguments are valid, read a number.
    boolean inRange = false; // Assume no valid number read.
    int n = 0;
    while (!inRange) {  // Repeat until valid number read.
        try {
            String line = JOptionPane.showInputDialog(
                    prompt + "\nEnter an integer between "
                    + minN + " and " + maxN);
            n = Integer.parseInt(line);
            inRange = (minN <= n && n <= maxN);
        } catch (NumberFormatException ex) {
            JOptionPane.showMessageDialog(
                null,
                "Bad numeric string - Try again",
                "Error", JOptionPane.ERROR_MESSAGE);
        }
    }   // End while
    return n;  // n is in range
}
```

PROGRAM STYLE

Reasons for Throwing Exceptions

You might wonder what is gained by intentionally throwing an exception. If it is not caught farther back in the call chain, it will go uncaught and will cause your program to terminate. However, in the examples in this section, it would not make any sense to continue with either an empty range (in `readInt`) or an invalid phone number (in `readData`). In fact, the loop in method `readInt` would execute forever if the range of acceptable values were empty. Because the boundary parameters `minN` and `maxN` are defined in a higher-level method, it would also make no sense to try to get new values in `readInt`. However, if the exception is passed back and caught at the point where the boundary points are defined, the programmer can get new boundary values and call method `readInt` again instead of terminating the program.

Catching Exceptions in the Phone Directory Application

The telephone directory case study in Section 1.5 illustrates handling of exceptions in the context of a large program. Methods `loadData` and save both have **try-catch** sequences for handling file processing errors. Listing 2.3 shows the **try-catch** sequence from `loadData`, which loads the phone directory array from a file. The **try** block contains several opportunities for an `IOException`. The statement

```
in = new BufferedReader(new FileReader(sourceName));
```

throws a `FileNotFoundException` if there is no file with the name stored in string `sourceName`. The first **catch** block handles this error by simply doing nothing, because there is no data to load if the file does not exist.

Each call to method `readLine` and the call to method `close` can throw an `IOException`, which is handled by the second **catch** block. The second **catch** block displays the stack trace and exits the program with an abnormal termination indication (`System.exit(1)`).

Note that the **catch** clause for `FileNotFoundException` must precede the one for `IOException`. This is because the former exception class is a subclass of the latter, so a `FileNotFoundException` could be caught by a **catch** clause whose exception class was `IOException`. If the **catch** clause for `FileNotFoundException` came second, we would get a `catch is unreachable` syntax error.

LISTING 2.3
Method `loadData` with Its **try-catch** Sequence (`ArrayBasedPD.java`)

```java
/** Method to load the data file.
    pre:  The directory has been created and it is empty.
          If the file exists, it consists of name-number pairs
          on adjacent lines.
    post: The data from the file is loaded into the directory.
    @param sourceName The name of the data file
*/
public void loadData(String sourceName) {
    // Remember the source name.
    this.sourceName = sourceName;
    try {
        // Create a BufferedReader for the file.
        BufferedReader in = new BufferedReader(
            new FileReader(sourceName));
        String name;
        String number;

        // Read each name, number and add entry to array.
        while ((name = in.readLine()) != null) {
            // Read name and number from successive lines.
            if ((number = in.readLine()) == null) {
                break;      // No number read, exit loop.
            }
            // Add an entry for this name and number.
            add(name, number);
        }
```

```
        // Close the file.
        in.close();
    } catch (FileNotFoundException e) {
        // Do nothing - no data to load.
        return;
    } catch (IOException ex) {
        System.err.println("Load of directory failed.");
        ex.printStackTrace();
        System.exit(1);
    }
}
```

The processCommands method in the user interface for the phone directory program in Chapter 1 also has a **try-catch** sequence (Listing 2.4) that handles an IOException. A possible source of such errors is the call to method readLine shown in Listing 2.4. Other possible sources are the calls to method readLine that occur in methods doAddChangeEntry, doLookupEntry, and doRemoveEntry. Each of these methods has a **throws** IOException clause in its heading, so any IOException thrown during the execution of one of these methods is caught by the **catch** block in its caller: method processCommands.

LISTING 2.4
The **try-catch** Sequence in Method processCommands (PDConsoleUI.java)

```
try {
    do {
        for (int i = 0; i < commands.length; i++) {
            System.out.println("Select " + i + ": "
                                + commands[i]);
        }
        String line = in.readLine();
        if (line != null) {
            choice = Integer.parseInt(line);
        }
        switch (choice) {
            case 0: doAddChangeEntry(); break;
            case 1: doLookupEntry(); break;
            case 2: doRemoveEntry(); break;
            case 3: doSave(); break;
            case 4: doSave(); break;
        }
    } while (choice < commands.length - 1);
    System.exit(0);
} catch (IOException ex) {
    System.err.println(
            "IO Exception while reading from System.in");
    System.exit(1);
}
```

PROGRAM STYLE

Catching versus Throwing Exceptions

You can always avoid handling exceptions where they occur by declaring that they are thrown, or throwing them and letting them be handled farther back in the call chain. In general, though, it is better to handle an exception where it occurs rather than to pass it back. This gives you the opportunity to recover from the error and to continue on with the execution of the current method. We did this, for example, for NumberFormatExceptions in both readInt methods (see Listings 2.1 and 2.2). If an error is a nonrecoverable error, however, and is also likely to occur farther back in the call chain, you might as well allow the exception to be handled at the farthest point back in the call chain rather than duplicate the error-handling code in several methods. That was the situation with method processCommands and the methods called by it to process individual commands. We recommend the following guidelines:

- If an exception is recoverable in the current method, handle the exception in the current method.
- If a checked exception is likely to be caught in a higher-level method, declare that it can occur using a **throws** clause, and use a **@throws** tag to document this in the Javadoc comment for this method.
- If an unchecked exception is likely to be caught in a higher-level method, use a **@throws** tag to document this fact in the Javadoc comment for the method. However, it is not necessary to use a **throws** clause with unchecked exceptions.

EXERCISES FOR SECTION 2.4

SELF-CHECK

1. Explain the difference between the **throws** clause and the **throw** statement.
2. When would it be better to declare an exception rather than catch it in a method?
3. When would it be better to throw an exception rather than catch it in a method?
4. What kind of exceptions should appear in a **throws** clause?
5. For the following situations, indicate whether it would be better to catch an exception, declare an exception, or throw an exception in the lower-level method. Explain your answer and show the code required for the lower-level method to do it.
   a. A lower-level method contains a call to method readLine; the higher-level method that calls it contains a **catch** clause for class IOException.
   b. A method contains a call to method readLine to enter a value that is passed as an argument to a lower-level method. The lower-level method's argument must be a positive number.
   c. A lower-level method contains a call to method readLine, but the higher-level method that calls it does not have a **catch** clause for class IOException.

d. A lower-level method reads a data string and converts it to type **int**. The higher-level method contains a **catch** clause for class NumberFormatException.

e. A lower-level method detects an unrecoverable error that is an unchecked exception.

PROGRAMMING

1. The syntax display for the **throw** statement had the following example:

```
throw new FileNotFoundException("File " + fileSource
                               + "not found");
```

Write a **catch** clause for a method farther back in the call chain that handles this exception.

2. A modified version of method setElementOfX from Example 2.2 is shown here. It validates that the parameters index and val are in bounds before accessing array x. Rewrite this method so that it throws an exception during array access if val is out of bounds. (The JVM will throw an exception if index is out of bounds, but the detail message will only contain the value of index). Pass an appropriate detail message to the new exception object. Your modified method should be type **void**, because there is no longer a reason to return a **boolean** error indicator. Show a **catch** block for a higher-level method that would handle this exception.

```
public boolean setElementOfX(int index, int val) {
    if (index >= 0 && index < x.length
        && val >= MIN_VAL && val <= MAX_VAL) {
        x[index] = val;
        return true;
    } else {
        return false;
    }
}
```

2.5 Testing Programs

After you have removed all syntax errors and run-time errors, a program will execute through to normal completion. That is no guarantee that the program does not contain logic errors, however. Because logic errors do not usually cause an error message to be displayed, they frequently go undetected.

Logic errors can be difficult to detect and isolate. If the logic error occurs in a part of the program that always executes, then each run of the program may generate incorrect results. Although this sounds bad, it is actually the best situation, because the error is more likely to be detected if it occurs frequently. If the value that is being computed incorrectly is always displayed, it will be easier to find the logic error. However, if this value is part of a computation and is not displayed, it will be very difficult to track down the error and the section of code that caused it.

The worst kind of logic error is one that occurs in a relatively obscure part of the code that is infrequently executed. If the test data set does not exercise this section of code, the error will not occur during normal program testing. Therefore, the software product will be delivered to its users with a hidden defect. Once that happens, it becomes much more difficult to detect and correct the problem.

Structured Walkthroughs

Most logic errors arise during the design phase and are the result of an incorrect algorithm. They can, however, also result from typographical errors during coding that do not cause syntax or run-time errors. One form of testing that does not involve execution of the program is checking the algorithm carefully before implementing it and checking that the program implements the algorithm. This can be done by hand-tracing the algorithm or program, carefully simulating the execution of each step and comparing its execution result to one that is calculated by hand.

Hand-tracing an algorithm or program is complicated by the fact that the designer often anticipates what a step should do. Because the designer knows the purpose of each step, it requires quite a bit of discipline to simulate each individual step carefully. For this reason, programmers often work in teams. The designer must explain the algorithm or program to the other team members and simulate its execution with the other team members looking on (called a *structured walkthrough*). Industrial experience has shown that the use of structured walkthroughs is effective in detecting errors and removing defects.

Levels and Types of Testing

Testing is the process of exercising a program (or part of a program) under controlled conditions and verifying that the results are as expected. The purpose of testing is to detect program defects after all syntax errrors have been removed and the program compiles successfully. The more thorough the testing, the greater the likelihood that the defects will be found. However, no amount of testing can guarantee the absence of defects in sufficiently complex programs. The number of test cases required to test all possible inputs and states that each method may execute in can quickly become prohibitively large. That is often why commercial software products have different versions or patches that the user must install. Version n usually corrects the errors that were still present in version $n - 1$.

Testing is generally done at the following levels:

- *Unit testing* refers to testing the smallest testable piece of the software. In object-oriented design (OOD), the unit will be either a method or a class. The complexity of a method determines whether it should be tested as a separate unit or whether is can be tested as part of its class.
- *Integration testing* involves testing the interactions among units. If the unit is the method, then integration testing includes testing interactions among methods within a class. However, generally it involves testing interactions among several classes.

- *System testing* is the testing of the whole program in the context in which it will be used. A program is generally part of a collection of other programs and hardware, called a system. Sometimes a program will work correctly until some other software is loaded onto the system, and then it will fail for no apparent reason.
- *Acceptance testing* is system testing designed to show that the program meets its functional requirements. It generally involves use of the system in the real environment or as close to the real environment as possible.

There are two types of testing:

- *Black-box testing* tests the item (method, class, or program) based on its interfaces and functional requirements. This is also called *closed-box testing* or *functional testing*. For testing a method, the input parameters are varied over their allowed range and the results compared against independently calculated results. In addition, values outside the allowed range are tested to ensure that the method responds as specified (for example, throws an exception or computes a nominal value). Also, the inputs to a method are not only the parameters of the method, but also the values of the data fields and global variables that the method accesses.
- *White-box testing* tests the software element (method, class, or program) with the knowledge of its internal structure. Other terms used for this type of testing are *glass-box testing, open-box testing,* and *coverage testing*. The goal is to exercise as many paths through the element as possible or practical. There are various degrees of coverage. The simplest is *statement coverage,* which ensures that each statement is executed at least once. *Branch coverage* ensures that each choice of each branch (**if** statements, **switch** statements, and loops) is taken. For example, if there are only **if** statements, and they are not nested, then each **if** statement is tried with its condition true and with its condition false. This could possibly be done with two test cases: one with all of the **if** conditions true and one with them all false. *Path coverage* tests each path through a method. If there are *n* **if** statements, path coverage could require 2^n test cases if the **if** statements are not nested (each condition has two possible values, so there could be 2^n possible paths).

EXAMPLE 2.11 Method testMethod has a nested **if** statement and displays one of four messages, path 1 through path 4, depending on which path is followed. The values passed to its arguments determine the path.

```
public void testMethod(char a, char b) {
    if (a < 'M') {
        if (b < 'X') {
            System.out.println("path 1");
        } else {
            System.out.println("path 2");
        }
    } else {
        if (b < 'C') {
            System.out.println("path 3");
```

```
        } else {
            System.out.println("path 4");
        }
    }
}
```

To test this method, we need to pass it values for its arguments that cause it to follow the different paths. Table 2.4 shows some possible values and the corresponding path:

TABLE 2.4
Testing All Paths of `testMethod`

a	b	Message
'A'	'A'	path 1
'A'	'Z'	path 2
'Z'	'A'	path 3
'Z'	'Z'	path 4

The values chosen for a and b in Table 2.4 are the smallest and largest uppercase letters. For a more thorough test, you should see what happens when a and b are passed values that are between A and Z. For example, what happens if the value of a changes from L to M? We pick those values because the condition (a < 'M') has different values for each of them.

Also, what happens when a and b are not uppercase letters? For example, if a and b are both digit characters (for example, '2'), the path 1 message should be displayed because the digit characters precede the uppercase letters (see Appendix A, Table A.2). If a and b are both lowercase letters, the path 4 message should be displayed (Why?). If a is a digit and b is a lowercase letter, the path 2 message should be displayed (Why?). As you can see, the number of test cases required to test even a simple method like `testMethod` thoroughly can become quite large.

Preparations for Testing

Although testing is usually done after each unit of the software is coded, a test plan should be developed early in the design stage. Some aspects of a test plan include deciding how the software will be tested, when the tests will occur, who will do the testing, and what test data will be used. If the test plan is developed early in the design stage, testing can take place concurrently with the design and coding. Again, the earlier an error is detected, the easier and less expensive it is to correct it.

Another advantage of deciding on the test plan early is that this will encourage programmers to prepare for testing as they write their code. A good programmer will practice *defensive programming* and include code that detects unexpected or invalid data values. For example, if a method has the precondition

pre: n greater than zero.

you can place the **if** statement

```
if (n <= 0)
    throw new IllegalArgumentException("n <= 0: " + n);
```

at the beginning of the method. This **if** statement will provide a diagnostic message in the event that the parameter passed to the method is invalid.

Similarly, if a data value being read from the keyboard is supposed to be between 0 and 40, a defensive programmer would use the three-parameter `readInt` method (see Listing 2.2):

```
hours = MyInput.readInt("Enter number of hours worked", 0, 40);
```

As discussed earlier, the second and third parameters of `readInt` define the range of acceptable values for its return value.

Testing Tips for Program Systems

Most of the time, you will be testing program systems that contain collections of classes, each with several methods. We provide a list of testing tips to follow in writing these methods next.

1. If the method implements an interface, the interface specification should document the input parameters and the expected results.
2. Carefully document each method parameter and class attribute using comments as you write the code. Also describe the method operation using comments, following the Javadoc conventions discussed in Section 1.4.
3. Leave a trace of execution by displaying the method name as you enter it.
4. Display the values of all input parameters upon entry to a method. Also display the values of any class attributes that are accessed by this method. Check that these values make sense.
5. Display the values of all method outputs after returning from a method. Also, display any class attributes that are modified by this method. Verify that these values are correct by hand computation.

You should plan for testing as you write each module rather than after the fact. Include the output statements required for Steps 2 through 4 in the original Java code for the method. When you are satisfied that the method works as desired, you can "remove" the testing statements. One efficient way to remove them is to enclose them in an **if** (TESTING) block as follows:

```
if (TESTING) {
    // Code that you wish to "remove"
    . . .
}
```

You would then define TESTING at the beginning of the class as **true** to enable testing,

```
private static final boolean TESTING = true;
```

or as **false** to disable testing,

```
private static final boolean TESTING = false;
```

If you need to, you can define different **boolean** flags for different kinds of tests.

Developing the Test Data

The test data should be specified during the analysis and design phases. This should be done for the different levels of testing: unit, integration, and system. In black-box testing, we are concerned with the relationship between the unit inputs and outputs. There should be test data to check for all expected inputs as well as unanticipated data. The test plan should also specify the expected unit behavior and outputs for each set of input data.

In white-box testing we are concerned with exercising alternative paths through the code. Thus the test data should be designed to ensure that all **if** statement conditions will evaluate to both **true** and **false**. For nested **if** statements, test different combinations of **true** and **false** values. For **switch** statements, make sure that the selector variable can take on all values listed as case labels and some that are not.

For loops, verify that the result is correct if an immediate exit occurs (zero repetitions). Also verify that the result is correct if only one iteraton is performed and if the maximum number of iterations is performed. Finally, verify that loop repetition can always terminate.

Testing Boundary Conditions

When hand-tracing through an algorithm or performing white-box testing, you must exercise all paths through the algorithm. It is also important to check special cases called *boundary conditions* to make sure that the algorithm works for these cases as well as the more common ones. For example, if you are testing a method that searches for a particular target element in an array, the code may contain a search loop such as

```
for (int i = 0; i < x.length; i++) {
    if (x[i] == target)
        return i;
}
```

Testing the boundary conditions means that you should make sure that the method works for all the cases in the following list. The first four test the boundary conditions for the loop and would be required in white-box testing. However, a program tester using black-box testing should also test these four cases. The next case (target in the middle) is not a boundary case, but it is a typical situation that should also be tested. The rest are boundary conditions for an array search that should be tested in either white-box or black-box testing.

- The target element is the first array element (x[0] == target is **true**).
- The target element is only in the last array element (x[x.length - 1] == target is **true**).
- The target element is not in the array (x[i] == target is always **false**).
- There are multiple occurrences of the target element (x[i] == target is **true** for more than one value of i).
- The target element is somewhere in the middle of the array.
- The array has only one element.
- The array has no elements.

To carry out the test, you can write a main method that creates an array to be searched. The easiest way to create such an array is to declare it using an initializer list. Listing 2.5 shows a main method that tests all the listed cases for an array search method. In method search, the array to be searched is the first parameter, and the target of the search is the second parameter.

The method verify is passed the array to be searched, the target value, and the expected return value. It calls the search method and then prints the actual and expected results.

```
int actual = search(x, target);
System.out.print("search(x, " + target + ") is "
                + actual + ", expected " + expected);
```

It then prints either ":   Pass" or ":   ***Fail" depending on whether or not the expected value is equal to the actual value.

```
if (actual == expected)
    System.out.println (":   Pass");
else
    System.out.println(":   ****Fail");
```

There are calls to verify for each one of the test cases in the list. For example, the first call,

```
verify(x, 5, 0);
```

searches array x for a target 5, which is at x[0]. The expected result (the third argument) is therefore 0. The line displayed should be:

```
search(x, 5) is 0, expected 0:   Pass
```

Figure 2.5 shows the result of a sample run. To verify that method search is correct, check for Pass at the end of each output line. For large-scale testing, you could write a program to do this.

LISTING 2.5
ArraySearch.java

```
/** Provides a static method search for searching an array. */
public class ArraySearch {

    /** Searches an array to find the first occurrence of a target.
        @param x Array to search
        @param target Target to search for
        @return The subscript of first occurrence if found;
                otherwise, return -1.
    */
    public static int search(int[] x, int target) {
        for (int i = 0; i < x.length; i++) {
            if (x[i] == target)
                return i;
        }

        // target not found
        return -1;
    }
}
```

```
/** Test method.
    @param args Command line arguments. Not used.
*/
public static void main(String[] args) {
    int[] x = {5, 12, 15, 4, 8, 12, 7};    // Array to search.

    // Test for target as first element.
    verify(x, 5, 0);
    // Test for target as last element.
    verify(x, 7, 6);
    // Test for target not in array.
    verify(x, -5, -1);
    // Test for multiple occurrences of target.
    verify(x, 12, 1);
    // Test for target somewhere in middle.
    verify(x, 4, 3);

    // Test for 1-element array
    x = new int[1];
    x[0] = 10;
    verify(x, 10, 0);
    verify(x, -10, -1);

    // Test for an empty array
    x = new int[0];
    verify(x, 10, -1);
}

/** Call the search method with the specified parameters and
    verify the expected result.
    @param x The array to be searched
    @param target The target to be found
    @param expected The expected result
*/
private static void verify(int[] x, int target, int expected) {
    int actual = search(x, target);
    System.out.print("search(x, " + target + ") is "
                        + actual + ", expected " + expected);
    if (actual == expected)
        System.out.println(":  Pass");
    else
        System.out.println(":  ****Fail");
}
}
```

....

FIGURE 2.5

Testing Method search

```
Command Prompt                                                     _|□|×|
search(x, 5) is 0, expected 0:  Pass
search(x, 7) is 6, expected 6:  Pass
search(x, -5) is -1, expected -1:  Pass
search(x, 12) is 1, expected 1:  Pass
search(x, 4) is 3, expected 3:  Pass
search(x, 10) is 0, expected 0:  Pass
search(x, -10) is -1, expected -1:  Pass
search(x, 10) is -1, expected -1:  Pass
```

Who Does the Testing?

Normally testing is done by the programmer, by other members of the software team who did not code the module being tested, and by the final users of the software product. It is extremely important not to rely only on the programmers who coded a module for testing it, because programmers are often blind to their own oversights. If they neglected to account for a possible error in the design, they are also likely to neglect to test for it. Some companies have special testing groups who are experts at finding defects in other programmers' code.

The reason for involving future users is to determine whether they have difficulty in interpreting prompts for data. Because they are not as knowledgeable about coding, users are more likely to make data entry errors than are members of the programming or testing teams.

Companies also have quality assurance (QA) organizations that verify that the testing process is performed correctly. Members of the QA organization typically do not do the testing themselves, but they independently review the test plans, witness the conduct of the tests, and independently verify the results.

Generally the programmer who wrote the unit does unit testing, while a separate test team does integration testing and system testing. However, many organizations are finding that having other members of the programming team do unit testing is very effective. There is one methodology (called *Extreme Programming*) in which programmers work in pairs; one writes the code and the other writes the tests. The tester also observes the coder while the code is being written. They take turns so that each team member is involved in both coding and testing. The units are kept small so that they can be coded and tested quickly.

Stubs

Although we want to do unit testing as soon as possible, it may be difficult to test a method or a class that interacts with other methods or classes. The problem is that not all methods and not all classes will be completed at the same time. So if a method in class A calls a method defined in class B (not yet written), the unit test for class A can't be performed without the help of a replacement method for the one in class B. The replacement for a method that has not yet been implemented or tested is called a *stub*. A stub has the same header as the method it replaces, but its body only displays a message indicating that the stub was called.

EXAMPLE 2.12   The following method is a stub for a **void** method save. The stub will enable a method that calls save to be tested even though the real method save has not been written.

```
/** Method to save the directory.
    pre:  The directory has been loaded with data.
    post: Writes the directory contents back to the
          file as name-number pairs on adjacent lines.
          modified is reset to false.
```

```
*/
public void save() {
    System.out.println("Stub for save has been called");
    modified = false;
}
```

Besides displaying an identification message, a stub can print out the values of the inputs and can assign predictable values (e.g., 0 or 1) to any outputs to prevent execution errors caused by undefined values. Also, if a method is supposed to change the state of a data field, the stub can do so (modified is set to false by the stub just shown). If a client program calls one or more stubs, the message printed by each stub when it is executed provides a trace of the call sequence and enables the programmer to determine whether the flow of control within the client program is correct.

Drivers

Another testing tool for a method is a driver program. A *driver* program declares any necessary object instances and variables, assigns values to any of the method's inputs (as specified in the method's preconditions), calls the method, and displays the values of any outputs returned by the method. Since each class can have a main method, you can put a main method in a class to serve as the test driver for that class's methods. When you run a Java program, execution begins at the main method in the class you designate as the one to execute; any other main methods are ignored. The main method shown in Listing 2.5 is a driver program to test method search.

Testing a Class

In Section 1.5, we specified the DirectoryEntry class. The coding of this class was left as an exercise. Below we show a test driver as a main method for this class. The test driver contains several test cases.

When main executes, two DirectoryEntry objects are created and then displayed on the console. Both the name and number attributes are displayed. We can use these test cases to verify that the constructor and methods getName and getNumber perform as expected.

```
public static void main(String[] args) {
    // Create some directory entries.
    DirectoryEntry tom =
        new DirectoryEntry("Tom", "123-555-4567");
    DirectoryEntry dick =
        new DirectoryEntry("Dick", "321-555-9876");

    // Display the entries
    System.out.println("tom - name:" + tom.getName()
                        + " number: " + tom.getNumber());
    System.out.println("dick - name:" + dick.getName()
                        + " number: " + dick.getNumber());
```

Next we test the equals method. Because the two objects have different name fields, we expect that they are not equal.

```
    // See whether they are equal.
    if (tom.equals(dick))
        System.out.println
            ("FAILURE -- Tom and Dick are equal");
    else
        System.out.println
            ("SUCCESS -- Tom and Dick are not equal");

    if (dick.equals(tom))
        System.out.println
            ("FAILURE -- Tom and Dick are equal");
    else
        System.out.println
            ("SUCCESS -- Tom and Dick are not equal");
```

Then we create a third DirectoryEntry object with the same name as one of the others. We expect this to be equal to the one with the same name.

```
    DirectoryEntry tom2 =
        new DirectoryEntry("Tom", "888-555-9999");
    System.out.println("tom2 -- name:" + tom2.getName()
                        + " number: " + tom2.getNumber());
    // See whether the two toms are equal.
    if (tom.equals(tom2))
        System.out.println
            ("SUCCESS -- tom and tom2 are equal");
    else
        System.out.println
            ("FAILURE -- tom and tom2 are not equal");

    if (tom2.equals(tom))
        System.out.println
            ("SUCCESS -- tom2 and tom are equal");
    else
        System.out.println
            ("FAILURE -- tom2 and tom are not equal");
```

Finally we test the setNumber method by changing the number of one of the objects and displaying it.

```
    dick.setNumber(tom.getNumber());
    // Dick and Tom should have the same number.
    System.out.println("dick -- name:" + dick.getName()
                        + " number: " + dick.getNumber());
    }
```

Figure 2.6 shows the results of testing the DirectoryEntry class.

....

FIGURE 2.6

Test of DirectoryEntry Class

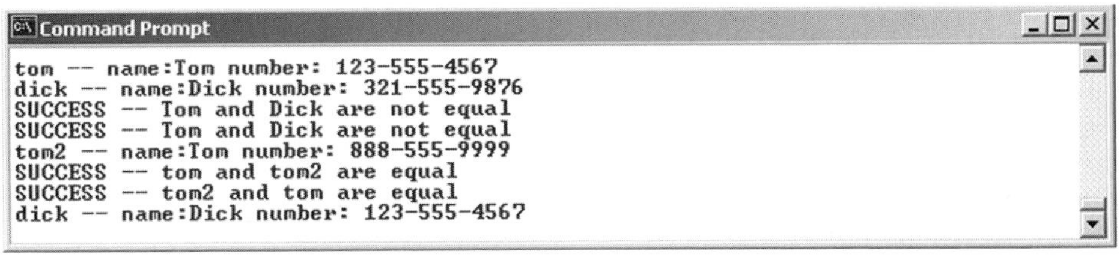

```
tom -- name:Tom number: 123-555-4567
dick -- name:Dick number: 321-555-9876
SUCCESS -- Tom and Dick are not equal
SUCCESS -- Tom and Dick are not equal
tom2 -- name:Tom number: 888-555-9999
SUCCESS -- tom and tom2 are equal
SUCCESS -- tom2 and tom are equal
dick -- name:Dick number: 123-555-4567
```

Using a Test Framework

The test driver for the DirectoryEntry class relied on visual verification of the output. In some instances the user needed to know the expected result, and in others we displayed a success/failure indication. We could have added code to verify the expected result for all of the tests, but that would have made our test code much longer.

This test driver contained several *test cases*. A test case is an individual test. A collection of test cases is known as a *test suite*. A program that executes a series of tests and reports the results is known as a *test harness*. Thus the test driver for the DirectoryEntry class was both a test harness and a test suite.

A *test framework* is a software product that facilitates writing test cases, organizing the test cases into test suites, running the test suites, and reporting the results. One test framework often used for Java projects is JUnit, an open-source product that can be used in a stand-alone mode and is available from junit.org. It is also bundled with at least two popular IDEs (NetBeans and JBuilder). Below we show a test suite for the DirectoryEntry class constructed using the JUnit framework. The class for the test suite must extend class TestCase (defined in JUnit). The setUp method is used to declare the test objects.

```
import junit.framework.*;

public class TestDirectoryEntry extends TestCase {

    private DirectoryEntry tom;
    private DirectoryEntry dick;
    private DirectoryEntry tom2;

    public void setUp() {
        tom = new DirectoryEntry("Tom", "123-456-7890");
        dick = new DirectoryEntry("Dick", "908-765-4321");
        tom2 = new DirectoryEntry("Tom", "111-222-3333");
    }
```

We then write a series of test cases by writing methods named test*Xxxxx*. For example to test that the object tom was created correctly, we write the method testTomCreate as follows:

```
public void testTomCreate() {
    assertEquals(tom.getName(), "Tom");
    assertEquals(tom.getNumber(), "123-456-7890");
}
```

The method assertEquals will report an error if its arguments are not equal, indicating that the results of getName or getNumber are not as expected. The various assert*Xxxxx* methods are specific to JUnit. This should not be confused with the Java assert statement, which we will discuss in Section 2.7.

We can test the DirectoryEntry.equals method as follows:

```
public void testTomEqualsDick() {
    assertFalse(tom.equals(dick));
    assertFalse(dick.equals(tom));
}
```

```
public void testTomEqualsTom2() {
    assertTrue(tom.equals(tom2));
    assertTrue(tom2.equals(tom));
}
```

We expect that `tom` is not equal to `dick`, so we use `assertFalse` in the first case, and we expect that `tom` and `tom2` are equal, so we use `assertTrue` in the second case.

Finally, we write a test case for the `setNumber` method.

```
public void testSetNumber() {
    dick.setNumber(tom.getNumber());
    assertEquals(tom.getNumber(), dick.getNumber());
}
```

Figure 2.7 shows the results of running this test suite under the control of the test harness. It shows that all of the test cases passed. If any of them had failed, there would have been an indication of which test failed and the line number of the assert*Xxxxx* method call that failed.

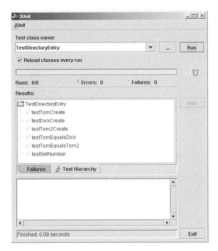

Regression Testing

The test plan, test suite (stubs and drivers), and test results should be saved. Whenever a change is made to a method, class, or program, the tests can and should be rerun to determine that the change did not cause an unintended consequence. This rerunning of tests and verifying that nothing changed is called *regression testing*.

Integration Testing

Another aspect of testing a system is called integration testing. In integration testing, the program tester must determine whether the individual components of the system, which have been separately tested, can be integrated with other components. (In this context the word *component* is used to represent a method, a class, or a collection of classes.)

Each phase of integration testing deals with larger components, progressing from individual units, such as methods or classes, and ending with the entire system. For example, after two units are completed, integration testing must determine whether the two units can work together. Once the entire system is completed, integration testing must determine whether that system is compatible with other systems in the computing environment in which it will be used.

Integration testing is generally use-case driven. Based on information in the UML sequence diagrams, the tester attempts to validate that the program is interacting correctly with the user and external devices.

EXERCISES FOR SECTION 2.5

SELF-CHECK

1. Why is it a good idea to use the structured walkthrough approach when hand-tracing an algorithm?
2. List two boundary conditions that should be checked when testing method readInt (see Listing 2.2).
3. Explain why a method that does not match its declaration in the interface would not be discovered during white-box testing.
4. Devise a set of data to test the method readInt with three parameters (Listing 2.2) using:
   a. white-box testing
   b. black-box testing
5. During which phase of testing would each of the following tests be performed?
   a. Testing whether a method worked properly at all its boundary conditions
   b. Testing whether class A can use class B as a component
   c. Testing whether a phone directory application and a word-processing application can run simultaneously on a PC
   d. Testing whether method search can search an array that was returned by method buildArray
   e. Testing whether a class with an array data field can use static method search in class ArraySearch

PROGRAMMING

1. Write a driver program to test method readInt using the test data derived for Self-Check Exercise 2.
2. Write a stub to use in place of method readInt.
3. Write a search method with four parameters: the search array, the target, the start subscript, and the finish subscript. The last two parameters indicate the part of the array that should be searched. Your method should catch or throw exceptions where warranted. Write a driver program to test this method.

2.6 Debugging a Program

In this section we will discuss the process of *debugging* (removing errors), both with and without the use of a debugger program. Debugging is the major activity performed by programmers during the testing phase. Testing determines whether you have an error; during debugging you determine the cause of run-time and logic errors and correct them, without introducing new ones. If you have followed the suggestions for testing described in the previous section, you will be well prepared to debug your program.

Debugging is like detective work. To debug a program, you must inspect carefully the information displayed by your program, starting at the beginning, to determine whether what you see is what you expect. For example, if the result returned by a method is incorrect but the arguments (if any) passed to the method had the correct values, then there is a problem inside the method. You can try to trace through the method to see whether you can find the source of the error and correct it. If you can't, you may need more information. One way to get that information is to insert additional diagnostic output statements in the method. For example, if the method contains a loop, you may want to display the values of loop control variables during loop execution.

EXAMPLE 2.13   The loop in Listing 2.6 does not seem to terminate when the user enters the sentinel string ("***"). The loop exits eventually after the user has entered 10 data items (or clicked Cancel), but the string returned contains the sentinel.

LISTING 2.6

The Method `getSentence`

```java
/** Return the individual words entered by the user.
    The user can enter the sentinel ***
    or click Cancel to terminate data entry.
    @return A string with a maximum of ten words
*/
public static String getSentence() {
    String sentence = "";
    int count = 0;
    String word =
        JOptionPane.showInputDialog("Enter a word or *** to quit");
    while (word != "***" && word != null && count < 10 ) {
        // Append word to sentence.
        sentence = sentence + word + " ";
        count++;
        word =
            JOptionPane.showInputDialog("Enter a word or *** to quit");
    }
    return sentence;
}
```

To determine the source of the problem, you should insert a diagnostic output statement that displays the values of word and count to make sure that word is receiving the sentinel string ("***"). You could insert the line

```
System.out.println("!!! Next word is " + word + ", count is " + count);
```

as the first statement in the loop body. If the third data item you enter is the sentinel string, you will get the output line:

```
!!! next word is ***, count is 2
```

This will show you that word does indeed receive the sentinel string, but the loop body continues to execute. Therefore, there must be something wrong with the loop repetition condition. In fact, the loop header must be changed to

```
while (word != null && !word.equals("***") && count < 10) {
```

because word != "***" compares the *address* of the string stored in word with the *address* of the literal string "***", not the *contents* of the two strings as intended. The strings' addresses will always be different, even when their contents are the same. To compare their contents, the equals method must be used.

Using a Debugger

If you are using an integrated development environment (IDE), you will most likely have a debugger program as part of the IDE. A debugger can execute your program incrementally rather than all at once. After each increment of the program executes, the debugger pauses, and you can view the contents of variables to determine whether the statement(s) executed as expected. You can inspect all the program variables without needing to insert diagnostic output statements. When you have finished examining the program variables, you direct the debugger to execute the next increment.

You can choose to execute in increments as small as one program statement (called *single-step execution*) to see the effect of each statement's execution. Another possibility is to set *breakpoints* in your program to divide it into sections. The debugger can execute all the statements from one breakpoint to the next as a group. For example, if you wanted to see the effects of a loop's execution but did not want to step through every iteration, you could set breakpoints at the statements just before and just after the loop.

When your program pauses, if the next statement contains a call to a method, you can select single-step execution in the method being called (that is, *step into* the method). Alternatively, you can execute all the method statements as a group and pause after the return from the method execution (that is, *step over* the method).

The actual mechanics of using a debugger depend on the IDE that you are using. However, the process that you follow is similar among IDEs, and if you understand the process for one, you should be able to use any debugger. In this section we demonstrate how to use the debugger in NetBeans, the IDE that is distributed by Sun along with the SDK.

Figure 2.8 is the display produced by this debugger at the beginning of debugging the GetSentence class. The source editor window displays the code to be debugged.

The Debug pull-down menu shows the options for executing the code. The selected item, Step Into, is a common technique for starting single-step execution, as we have just described. A window (such as window Local Variables in the center left) typically shows the values of data fields and local variables. In this case there is one local variable for method main: the String array args, which is empty. The arrow to the left of the highlighted line in the source editor window indicates the next step to execute (the call to method getSentence). Select Step Into again to execute the individual statements of method getSentence.

Figure 2.9 shows the editor and Local Variables windows after we have entered "Hello", "world", and "***". The contents of sentence is "Hello world", the value of count is 2, and the contents of word is "***". The next statement to execute is highlighted. It is the loop header, which tests the loop repetition condition. Although we expect the condition to be false, it is true (why?), so the loop continues to execute and "***" will be appended to sentence.

FIGURE 2.8

Using the Debugger for NetBeans

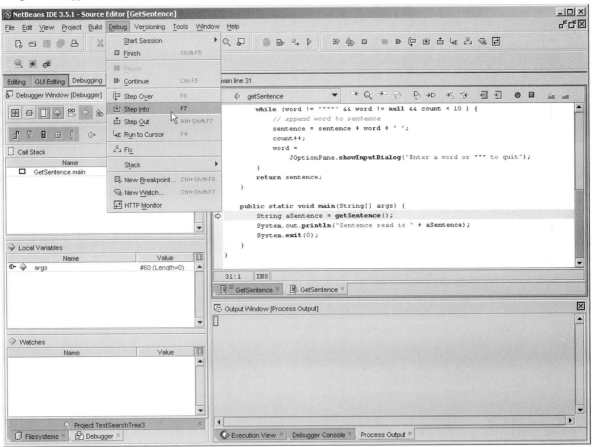

FIGURE 2.9

Editor and Debugging Windows

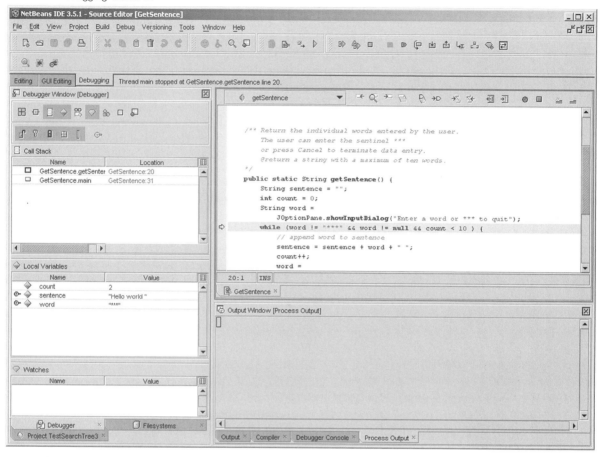

Next we illustrate the use of break points. Figure 2.10 shows the source editor window with two breakpoints set before we begin execution: one at the loop header and one after the loop. In NetBeans you set a breakpoint by clicking in the vertical bar just to the left of the statement that you want to select as a breakpoint. The small squares and highlighted bars indicate the breakpoints. You can click again on a small square to remove the breakpoint. We selected Step Into and then Continue, so the program displayed a dialog window (where we entered "Hello") and paused at the first breakpoint (Figure 2.11). If we select Continue again, the program will display another dialog window and then pause at the next breakpoint. In this case, it will pause again at the loop header. If we select Continue and click the Cancel button in the dialog window, the program will pause again at the loop header. If we select Continue again, the program will exit the loop and pause at the breakpoint following the loop.

FIGURE 2.10
Two Breakpoints Selected

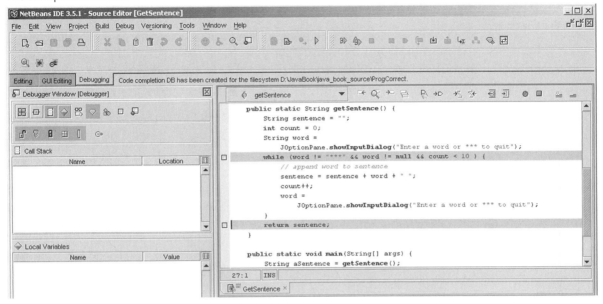

FIGURE 2.11
Stop at Breakpoint

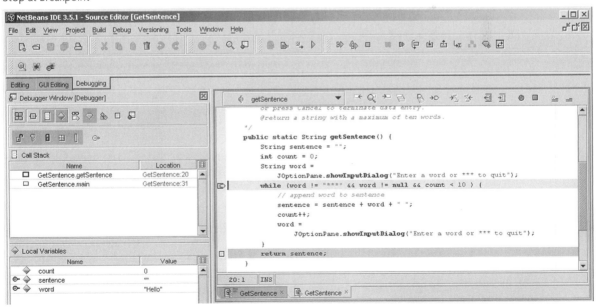

EXERCISES FOR SECTION 2.6

SELF-CHECK

1. The following method does not appear to be working properly. Explain where you would add diagnostic output statements to debug it, and give an example of each statement. Write a driver program and test the method.

```
/** Finds the target value in array elements x[start] through x[last].
    pre: first <= last.
    @param x Array whose largest value is found
    @param start First subscript in range
    @param last Last subscript in range
    @return The largest value of x[start] through x[last]
*/
public int findMax(int[] x, int start, int last) {
    if (start > last)
        throw new IllegalArgumentException("Empty range");
    int maxSoFar = 0;
    for (int i = start; i < last; i++) {
        if (x[i] > maxSoFar)
            maxSoFar = i;
    }
    return maxSoFar;
}
```

2. Explain the difference between selecting Step Into and Step Over during debugging.
3. Explain the rationale for the position of the breakpoints in method getSentence.
4. How would the execution of method getSentence change if the breakpoint were set at the statement just before the loop instead of at the loop heading?

PROGRAMMING

1. After debugging, provide a corrected version of the method in Self-Check Exercise 1. Leave the debugging statements in, but execute them only when the global constant TESTING is **true**.

2.7 Reasoning about Programs: Assertions and Loop Invariants

In Section 2.5 we discussed some aspects of program and system testing. In this section we describe some formal concepts that are intended to help a programmer prove that a program or method is correct. We will focus on using assertions and loop invariants to help you reason about an algorithm. Our goal is just to introduce the concepts and give you a feel for what can be done. Although it would be very desirable to be able to prove the correctness of a program, we usually cannot do this. In practice, formal verification is used more as a documentation tool and to enable a programmer to reason about a program than as a strict proof of correctness. Formal verification of programs is an active area of computer science research.

Assertions

An important part of formal verification is to document a program using *assertions:* logical statements about the program that are "asserted" to be true. An assertion is generally written as a comment, and it describes what is supposed to be true about the program variables at that point. Preconditions and postconditions are assertion statements. A precondition is an assertion about the state of the program (generally the input parameters) before a method is executed, and a postcondition is an assertion about the state when the method finishes.

EXAMPLE 2.14   We rewrite method search, shown earlier, with an assertion comment following loop exit.

```
public static int search(int[] x, int target) {
    for (int i = 0; i < x.length; i++) {
        if (x[i] == target)
            return i;
    }

    // assert: all elements were tested and target not found.
    return -1;
}
```

The assertion states what we know to be true at this point: All elements were tested and the target was not found, because, if it had been, we would have executed the **return** statement in the loop.

Loop Invariants

We stated earlier that loops are a very common source of program errors. It is often difficult to determine that a loop body executes exactly the right number of times or that loop execution causes the desired change in program variables. Programmers can use a special type of assertion, called a *loop invariant,* to help prove that a loop meets its specification. A loop invariant is a statement (a Boolean expression) that is true before loop execution begins, at the beginning of each repetition of the loop body, and just after loop exit. It is called an invariant because it is a relationship that remains true at all times as loop execution progresses; that is, the execution of the loop body *preserves the invariant*. If we can determine the loop invariant for the process that we want a loop to perform and then verify that the execution of a Java loop preserves the invariant, then we can be quite confident that the Java loop is correct.

A proposed invariant for a search loop that finds the first occurrence of a target value might be the following: If i is the subscript of the array element we are testing in the loop,

```
for all k, such that 0 <= k < i, x[k] != target
```

In English, this means "For all nonnegative integer values of k less than i, the kth element of x is not equal to the target. Let's verify that this is an invariant.

- *The invariant must be true before loop execution begins:* Before loop execution begins, i would be 0 and there is no nonnegative integer less than 0, so there are no possible values of k and thus no value of k such that x[k] is equal to target, so the invariant must be true.

- *The invariant must be true at the beginning of each repetition of the loop:* During loop repetition, we should compare x[i] to the target and exit the loop if the target is found. However, if x[k] was equal to target for a value of k < i, we would have already found the target, exited the loop, and would have not started the present repetition, so the invariant must be true.

- *The invariant must be true after loop exit:* We exit the loop after testing all array elements and finding that x[k] != target for all k < x.length, so the invariant must be true.

Now that we have the invariant, we must write a Java loop that preserves it. Of course, we already have one, but let's pretend that we don't.

```
int i = 0;
// invariant:  for all k, such that 0 <= k < i, x[k] != target
while (i < x.length) {
    if (x[i] == target)
        return i;   // target found at i
    i++;            // Test next element
}

// assert: for all k, such that 0 <= k < i, x[k] != target
//         and i >= x.length
return -1;          // target not found
```

Let's show that this loop preserves the invariant. Variable i is initially 0, so the invariant is certainly true before loop repetition begins. Prior to each loop repetition, the invariant must be true for the current value of i, or we would have executed the **return** statement with a value of k less than i. Loop exit occurs when the loop repetition condition fails (i is x.length), and because this occurs only if we did not find the target, x[k] != target must be true for all k < x.length (the current value of i), so the loop invariant is still true. When the loop ends, the invariant is still true, but the loop repetition condition is now false. We can therefore combine the loop invariant and the negation of the loop repetition condition to create the assertion that follows the loop.

This discussion used the loop invariant as a guide to writing a loop that preserved the invariant. A topic of computer science research is proving that a loop is correct by writing an assertion that is a loop precondition and an assertion that is a loop postcondition (an assertion that "ANDs" the loop invariant and the negation of the loop repetition condition), and then proving that the postcondition assertion follows from the precondition assertion. This would be a proof that the loop is correct.

DESIGN CONCEPT

Loop Invariants as a Design Tool

You can write the loop invariant as a specification for a loop and use that specification to help determine the loop initialization, the loop repetition condition, and the loop body. For example, we can write the following loop invariant to describe a summation loop that adds *n* data items:

```
// invariant: sum is the sum of all the data read so far, and the
// count of data items read is less than or equal to n.
```

From the loop invariant we can determine that

- The loop initialization is:
```
sum = 0.0;
count = 0;
```

- The loop repetition test is
```
count < n
```

- The loop body is
```
next = MyInput.readDouble("Enter next number");
sum = sum + next;
count = count + 1;
```

Given all this information, it becomes a simple task to write the summation loop (see Programming Exercise 2).

Enrichment Topic: The Java assert statement

Assertions may also be written using the Java **assert** statement. This statement was introduced in version 1.4 of the SDK. With this version of the SDK a special compiler switch is required to enable assertions. Assertions may be enabled on a method-by-method basis. The use of the assertion statement is beyond the scope of this text, but we describe its form next.

SYNTAX **Assertion Statement**

FORM:

assert *Boolean expression*;

EXAMPLE:

assert x == 5;

INTERPRETATION:

If the *Boolean expression* evaluates to **false**, then an AssertionError is thrown. AssertionError is a subclass of Error, which is a category of unchecked exceptions that the designers of Java strongly recommend not to be caught.

EXERCISES FOR SECTION 2.7

SELF-CHECK

1. Write the loop invariant and the assertion following the **while** loop in method readInt (Listing 2.2).

PROGRAMMING

1. Write a method that returns the number of digits in an arbitrary integer (number). Your solution should include a **while** loop for which the following is a valid loop invariant:

   ```
   // invariant:
   // count >= 0 and number has been
   // divided by 10 count times.
   ```

   and the following assertion would be valid after exit from the loop:

   ```
   // assert: count is the number of digits.
   ```

2. Write a program fragment that implements the loop whose invariant is described in the Design Concept discussion "Loop Invariants as a Design Tool."

2.8 Efficiency of Algorithms

You can't easily measure the amount of time it takes to run a program with modern computers. When you issue the command

    java *MyProgram*

(or click the Run button of your IDE), the operating system first loads the Java Virtual Machine. The JVM then loads the .class file for *MyProgram,* it then loads other .class files that *MyProgram* references, and finally your program executes. (If the .class files have not yet been created, the Java IDE will compile the source file before executing the program.) Most of the time it takes to run your program is occupied with the first two steps. If you run your program a second time immediately after the first, it may seem to take less time. This is because the operating system may have kept the files in a local memory area called a cache. However, if you have a large enough or complicated enough problem, then the actual running time of your program will dominate the time required to load the JVM and .class files.

Because it is very difficult to get a precise measure of the performance of an algorithm or program, we normally try to approximate the effect of a change in the number of data items, *n,* that an algorithm processes. In this way, we can see how an algorithm's execution time increases with respect to *n,* so we can compare two algorithms by examining their growth rates.

For many problems there are algorithms that are relatively obvious, but inefficient. Although computers are getting faster, with larger memories, every day, there are algorithms whose growth rate is so large that no computer, no matter how fast or with how much memory, can solve the problem above a certain size. Furthermore, if a problem that has been too large to be solved can now be solved with the latest, biggest, and fastest supercomputer, adding a few more inputs may make the problem impractical, if not impossible, again. Therefore, it is important to have some idea of the relative efficiency of different algorithms. Next, we see how we might obtain such an idea by examining three methods in the following examples.

EXAMPLE 2.15   Consider the following method, which searches an array for a value:

```
public static int search(int[] x, int target) {
    for (int i = 0; i < x.length; i++) {
        if (x[i] == target)
            return i;
    }

    // target not found
    return -1;
}
```

If the target is not present in the array, then the **for** loop body will be executed x.length times. If the target is present, it could be anywhere. If we consider the average over all cases where the target is present, then the loop body will execute x.length/2 times. Therefore the total execution time is directly proportional to x.length. If we doubled the size of the array, we would expect the time to double (not counting the overhead discussed earlier).

EXAMPLE 2.16   Now let us consider another problem. We want to find out whether two arrays have no common elements. We can use our search method to search one array for values that are in the other.

```
/** Determine whether two arrays have no common elements.
    @param x One array
    @param y The other array
    @return true if there are no common elements
*/
public static boolean areDifferent(int[] x, int[] y) {
    for (int i = 0; i < x.length; i++) {
        if (search(y, x[i]) != -1)
            return false;
    }
    return true;
}
```

The loop body will execute x.length times. But it will call search, whose loop body will execute y.length times for each of the x.length times it is called. Therefore, the total execution time would be proportional to the product of x.length and y.length.

EXAMPLE 2.17   Let us consider the problem of determining whether each item in an array is unique. We could write the following method.

```
/** Determine whether the contents of an array are all unique.
    @param x The array
    @return true if all elements of x are unique
*/
public static boolean areUnique(int[] x) {
    for (int i = 0; i < x.length; i++) {
        for (int j = 0; j < x.length; j++) {
            if (i != j && x[i] == x[j])
                return false;
        }
    }
    return true;
}
```

If all values are unique, the **for** loop with i as its index will execute x.length times. Inside this loop the **for** loop with j as its index will also execute x.length times. Thus the total number of times the loop body of the innermost loop will execute is $(\text{x.length})^2$.

EXAMPLE 2.18   The method we showed in Example 2.17 is very inefficient. We do twice as many tests as necessary. We can re-write it as follows:

```
/** Determine whether the contents of an array are all unique.
    @param x The array
    @return true if all elements of x are unique
*/
public static boolean areUnique(int[] x) {
    for (int i = 0; i < x.length; i++) {
        for (int j = i + 1; j < x.length; j++) {
            if (x[i] == x[j])
                return false;
        }
    }
    return true;
}
```

The first time the **for** loop with the j index will execute x.length-1 times. The second time it will execute x.length-2 times, and so on. The last time it will execute just once. The total number of times it will execute is:

    x.length-1 + x.length-2 + … + 2 + 1

The series $1 + 2 + 3 + \cdots + (n - 1)$ is a well known series that has a value of

$$n \times \frac{(n-1)}{2}$$

therefore, this sum is

    x.length × (x.length − 1)/2 or 0.5 × (x.length)² − 0.5 × x.length.

Big-O Notation

Today, the type of analysis just illustrated is more important to the development of efficient software than measuring the milliseconds in which a program runs on a particular computer. Understanding how the execution time (and memory requirements) of an algorithm grow as a function of increasing input size gives programmers a tool for comparing various algorithms and how they will perform. Computer scientists have developed a useful terminology and notation for investigating and describing the relationship between input size and execution time. For example, if the time is approximately doubled when the number of inputs, *n*, is doubled, then the algorithm grows at a linear rate. Thus we say that the growth rate has an order of *n*. On the other hand, if the time is approximately quadrupled when the number of inputs is doubled, then the algorithm grows at a quadratic rate. In this case we say that the growth rate has an order of n^2.

In the previous section we looked at four methods: one whose execution time was related to x.length, another whose execution time was related to x.length times y.length, one whose execution time was related to (x.length)^2, and one whose execution time was related to (x.length)^2 and x.length. Computer scientists use the notation O(*n*) to represent the first case, O(*n* × *m*) to represent the second, and O(n^2) to represent the third and fourth, where *n* is x.length and *m* is y.length. The symbol O (which you will see in a variety of type faces and styles in computer science literature) can be thought of as an abbreviation for "order of magnitude". This notation is called *big-O notation*.

A simple way to determine the big-O of an algorithm or program is to look at the loops and to see whether the loops are nested. Assuming that the loop body consists only of simple statements, a single loop is O(*n*), a nested loop is O(n^2), a nested loop in a nested loop is O(n^3), and so on. However, you also must examine the number of times the loop executes.

Consider the following:

```
for (i = 1; i < x.length; i *= 2) {
    Do something with x[i]
}
```

The loop body will execute *k* – 1 times with i having the following values: 1, 2, 4, 8, 16, 32, . . . , 2^k until 2^k is greater than x.length. Since 2^{k-1} ″ x.length < 2^k and $\log_2 2^k$ is *k*, we know that *k* – 1 ″ $\log_2$(x.length) < *k*. Thus we say that this loop is O(log *n*). The logarithm function grows slowly. The log to the base 2 of 1,000,000 is approximately 20. Typically, in analyzing the running time of algorithms, we use logarithms to the base 2.

Formal Definition of Big-O

Consider a program that is structured as follows:

```
for (int i = 0; i < n; i++) {
    for (int j = 0; j < n; j++) {
        Simple Statement
    }
}
```

```
for (int k = 0; i < n; k++) {
```
Simple Statement 1
Simple Statement 2
Simple Statement 3
Simple Statement 4
Simple Statement 5
```
}
```
Simple Statement 6
Simple Statement 7
. . .
Simple Statement 30

Let us assume that each *Simple Statement* takes one unit of time and that the **for** statements are free. The nested loop executes a *Simple Statement* n^2 times. Then 5 *Simple Statements* are executed n times. Finally, 25 *Simple Statements* are executed. We would then conclude that the expression

$$T(n) = n^2 + 5n + 25$$

expresses the relationship between processing time and n (the number of data items processed in the loop), where $T(n)$ represents the processing time as a function of n.

In terms of $T(n)$, formally, the big-**O** notation

$$T(n) = \mathbf{O}(f(n))$$

means that there exist two constants, n_0 and c greater than zero, and a function, $f(n)$, such that for all $n > n_0$, $cf(n) \geq T(n)$. In other words, as n gets sufficiently large (larger than n_0), there is some constant c for which the processing time will always be less than or equal to $cf(n)$, so $cf(n)$ is an upper bound on the performance. The performance will never be worse than $cf(n)$ and may be better.

If we can determine how the value of $f(n)$ increases with n, we know how the processing time will increase with n. Often the growth rate of $f(n)$ will be determined by the growth rate of the fastest-growing term (the one with the largest exponent), which in this case is the n^2 term. This means that the algorithm in this example is an $\mathbf{O}(n^2)$ algorithm rather than an $\mathbf{O}(n^2 + 5n + 25)$ algorithm. In general, it is safe to ignore all constants and drop the lower-order terms when determining the order of magnitude for an algorithm.

EXAMPLE 2.19   Given $T(n) = n^2 + 5n + 25$, we want to show that this is indeed $\mathbf{O}(n^2)$. Thus we want to show that there are constants n_0 and c such that for all $n > n_0$, $cn^2 > n^2 + 5n + 25$.

To solve this we need to find a point where

$$cn^2 = n^2 + 5n + 25$$

If we let n be n_0 and solve for c, we get

$$c = 1 + 5/n_0 + 25/n_0^2$$

For an n_0 of 5, this gives us a c of 3. So $3n^2 > n^2 + 5n + 25$ for all n greater than 5, as shown in Figure 2.12.

FIGURE 2.12
$3n^2$ vs. $n^2 + 5n + 25$

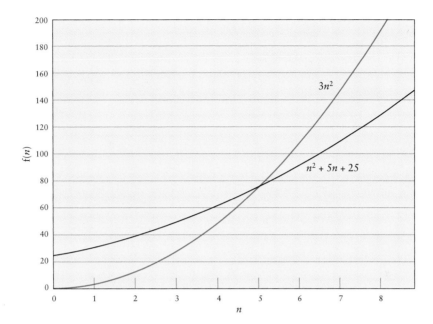

FIGURE 2.12
$3n^2$ vs. $n^2 + 5n + 25$

EXAMPLE 2.20   Consider the following program loop:

```
for (int i = 0; i < n - 1; i++) {
    for (int j = i + 1; j < n; j++) {
        3 simple statements
    }
}
```

The first time through the outer loop, the inner loop is executed $n - 1$ times; the next time $n - 2$, and the last time once. The outer loop is executed $n - 1$ times. So we get the following expression for $T(n)$:

$$3(n - 1) + 3(n - 2) + \cdots + 3$$

We can factor out the 3 to get

$$3(n - 1 + n - 2 + n + \cdots + 1)$$

The sum $1 + 2 + \cdots + n - 1$ (in parentheses above) is equal to

$$\frac{n \times (n - 1)}{2}$$

Thus our final $T(n)$ is

$$T(n) = 1.5n^2 - 1.5n$$

This polynomial is zero when n is 1. For values greater than 1, $1.5n^2$ is always greater than $1.5n^2 - 1.5n$. Therefore we can use 1 for n_0 and 1.5 for c to conclude that our $T(n)$ is $O(n^2)$ (see Figure 2.13).

FIGURE 2.13
$1.5n^2$ versus $1.5n^2 - 1.5n$

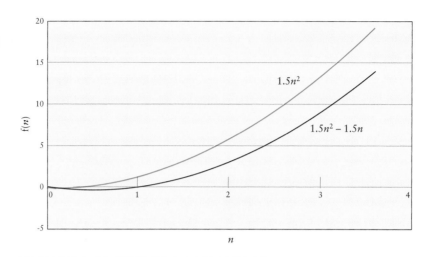

If T(n) is the form of a polynomial of degree d (the highest exponent), then it is O(n^d). A mathematically rigorous proof of this is beyond the scope of this text. An intuitive proof of this is demonstrated in the previous two examples. If the remaining terms have positive coefficients, find a value of n where the first term is equal to the remaining terms. As n gets bigger than this value, the n^d term will always be bigger.

We use the expression O(1) to represent a constant growth rate. This is a value that doesn't change with the number of inputs. The simple steps all represent O(1). Any finite number of O(1) steps is still considered O(1).

Summary of Notation

In this section we have used the symbols T(n), f(n), and O(f(n)). Their meaning is summarized in Table 2.5.

TABLE 2.5
Symbols Used in Quantifying Software Performance

T(n)	The time that a method or program takes as a function of the number of inputs, n. We may not be able to exactly measure or determine this.
f(n)	Any function of n. Generally f(n) will represent a simpler function than T(n), for example, n^2 rather than $1.5n^2 - 1.5n$.
O(f(n))	Order of magnitude. O(f(n)) is the set of functions that grow no faster than f(n). We say that T(n) = O(f(n)) to indicate that the growth of T(n) is bounded by the growth of f(n).

Comparing Performance

Throughout this text, as we discuss various algorithms, we will discuss how their execution time or storage requirements grow as a function of the problem size using this big-O notation. There are several common growth rates that will be encountered. These are summarized in Table 2.6.

TABLE 2.6
Common Growth Rates

Big-O	Name
$O(1)$	Constant
$O(\log n)$	Logarithmic
$O(n)$	Linear
$O(n \log n)$	Log-linear
$O(n^2)$	Quadratic
$O(n^3)$	Cubic
$O(2^n)$	Exponential
$O(n!)$	Factorial

Figure 2.14 shows the growth rate of a logarithmic, a linear, a log-linear, a quadratic, a cubic, and an exponential function by plotting $f(n)$ for each function. Notice that for small values of n the exponential function is smaller than all of the others. As shown, it is not until n reaches 20 that the linear function is smaller than the quadratic. This illustrates two points. For small values of n, the less efficient algorithm may be actually more efficient. If you know that you are going to process only a limited amount of data, the $O(n^2)$ algorithm may be much more appropriate than the $O(n \log n)$ algorithm that has a large constant factor. On the other hand, algorithms with exponential growth rates can start out small but very quickly grow to be quite large.

The raw numbers in Figure 2.14 can be deceiving. Part of the reason is that big-O notation ignores all constatnts. An algorithm with a logarithmic growth rate $O(\log n)$ may be more complicated to program, so it may actually take more time per data item than an algorithm with a linear growth rate $O(n)$. For example, at $n = 25$, Figure 2.14 shows that the processing time is approximately 1800 units for an algorithm with a logarithmic growth rate and 2500 units for an algorithm with a linear growth rate. Comparisons of this sort are pretty meaningless. The logarithmic algorithm may actually take more time to execute than the linear algorithm for this relatively small data set. Again, what is important is the growth rate of these two kinds of algorithms, which tells you how performance of each kind of algorithm changes with n.

FIGURE 2.14
Different Growth Rates

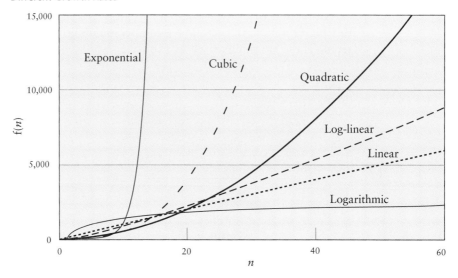

EXAMPLE 2.21   Let's look at how growth rates change as we double the value of n (say, from $n = 50$ to $n = 100$). The results are shown in Table 2.7. The third column gives the ratio of processing times for the two different data sizes. For example, it shows that it will take 2.35 times as long to process 100 numbers as it would to process 50 numbers with an $O(n \log n)$ algorithm.

TABLE 2.7
Effects of Different Growth Rates

O(f(n))	f(50)	f(100)	f(100)/f(50)
$O(1)$	1	1	1
$O(\log n)$	5.64	6.64	1.18
$O(n)$	50	100	2
$O(n \log n)$	282	664	2.35
$O(n^2)$	2500	10,000	4
$O(n^3)$	12,500	100,000	8
$O(2^n)$	1.126×10^{15}	1.27×10^{30}	1.126×10^{15}
$O(n!)$	3.0×10^{64}	9.3×10^{157}	3.1×10^{93}

Algorithms with Exponential and Factorial Growth Rates

Algorithms with exponential and factorial (even faster) growth rates have an effective practical upper limit on the size of problem they can be used for, even with faster and faster computers. For example, if we have an $O(2^n)$ algorithm that takes an hour for 100 inputs, adding the 101st input will take a second hour, adding 5 more inputs will take 32 hours (more than a day!), and adding 14 inputs will take 16,384 hours, which is almost two years!

This relation is the basis for cryptographic algorithms. Some cryptographic algorithms can be broken in $O(2^n)$ time, where n is the length of the key. A key length of 40 bits is considered breakable by a modern computer, but a key length of 100 (60 bits longer) is not, because the key with a length of 100 bits will take approximately a billion-billion (10^{18}) times as long as the 40-bit key to crack.

EXERCISES FOR SECTION 2.8

SELF-CHECK

1. Determine how many times the output statement is displayed in each of the following fragments. Indicate whether the algorithm is $O(n)$ or $O(n^2)$.

   a.
   ```
   for (int i = 0; i < n; i++)
       for (int j = 0; j < n; j++)
           System.out.println(i + "   " + j);
   ```

   b.
   ```
   for (int i = 0; i < n; i++)
       for (int j = 0; j < 2; j++)
           System.out.println(i + "   " + j);
   ```

   c.
   ```
   for (int i = 0; i < n; i++)
       for (int j = n - 1; j >= i; j--)
           System.out.println(i + "   " + j);
   ```

   d.
   ```
   for (int i = 1; i < n; i++)
       for (int j = 0; j < i; j++)
           if (j % i == 0)
               System.out.println(i + "   " + j);
   ```

2. For the following $T(n)$ find values of n_0 and c such that cn^3 is larger than $T(n)$ for all n larger than n_0.

   $$T(n) = n^3 - 5n^2 + 20n - 10$$

3. How does the performance grow as n goes from 2000 to 4000 for the following? Answer the same question as n goes from 4000 to 8000. Provide tables similar to Table 2.7.

   a. $O(\log n)$
   b. $O(n)$
   c. $O(n \log n)$
   d. $O(n^2)$
   e. $O(n^3)$

4. According to the plots in Figure 2.14, what are the processing times at $n = 20$ and at $n = 40$ for each of the growth rates shown?

PROGRAMMING

1. Write a program that compares the values of y1 and y2 in the following expressions for values of n up to 100 in increments of 10. Does the result surprise you?

```
y1 = 100 * n + 10
y2 = 5 * n * n + 2
```

Chapter Review

- There are three kinds of defects ("bugs") that can occur in programs. Syntax errors, which prevent your program from compiling, are generally the simplest to detect and fix. These are generally due to a typographical error or a misunderstanding of the language syntax. However, not all typographical errors result in syntax errors.

- Run-time errors are those errors that arise during the execution of your program and are generally indicated by exceptions. You can reduce the occurrence of run-time errors by using **if** statements to test the validity of variables before executing statements that can throw run-time exceptions.

- Logic errors occur when your program does not produce the correct result. Some logic errors are easy to find because the program always produces the wrong result. Other logic errors are difficult to find, because they occur only under special cases that are sometimes difficult to reproduce.

- All exceptions in the Exception class hierarchy are derived from a common superclass called Throwable. This class provides methods for collecting and reporting the state of the program when an exception is thrown. The commonly used methods are getMessage and toString, which return a detail message describing what caused the exception to be thrown, and printStackTrace, which prints the exception and then shows the line where the exception occurred and the sequence of method calls leading to the exception.

- The default behavior for exceptions is for the JVM to catch them by printing an error message and a call stack trace and then terminating the program. You can use the **try-catch-finally** sequence to catch and handle exceptions, possibly to recover from the error and continue, thereby avoiding the default behavior.

- There are two categories of exceptions: checked and unchecked. Checked exceptions are generally due to an error condition external to the program. The unchecked exceptions are generally due to a programmer error or a dire event.

◆ A method that can throw a checked exception must either catch it or declare that it is thrown using the **throws** declaration. If you throw it, you must catch it further back in the call sequence. Methods do not have to catch unchecked exceptions, and they should not be declared in the **throws** clause.

◆ Use the **throw** statement to throw an unchecked exception when you detect one in a method. You should catch this exception further back in the call sequence, or it will be processed by the JVM as an uncaught exceptions.

◆ Program testing is done at several levels starting with the smallest testable piece of the program, called a unit. A unit is either a method or a class, depending on the complexity.

◆ Once units are individually tested, they can then be tested together; this level is called integration testing.

◆ Once the whole program is put together, it is tested as a whole; this level is called system testing.

◆ Finally, the program is tested in an operational manner demonstrating its functionality; this level is called acceptance testing.

◆ Black-box (also called closed-box) testing tests the item (unit or system) based on its functional requirements without using any knowledge of the internal structure.

◆ White-box (also called glass-box or open-box) testing tests the item using knowledge of its internal structure. One of the goals of white-box testing is to achieve test coverage. This can range from testing every statement at least once, to testing each branch condition (**if** statements, **switch** statements, and loops) for each path, to testing each possible path through the program.

◆ Test drivers and stubs are tools used in testing. A test driver exercises a method or class and drives the testing. A stub stands in for a method that the unit being tested calls. This can be used to provide a test result, and it can be used to enable a caller of that method to be tested when the method being called is not yet coded.

◆ We described the debugging process and showed an example of how a debugger can be used to obtain information about a program's state.

◆ We discussed formal verification of programs and how assertions and loop invariants can help in the design and verification of our programs.

◆ Computer scientists are interested in comparing the efficiency of different algorithms. We introduced big-O notation and showed how to determine it by examining the loops in a program. We will use this notation through out the text to describe the relative efficiency of different data structures and algorithms that act on them.

Java Constructs Introduced in This Chapter

catch   throws
finally   try
throw

Java API Classes Introduced in This Chapter

Throwable   IllegalArgumentException
IOException   NumberFormatException
EOFException   NullPointerException
FileNotFoundException   NoSuchElementException
ArithmeticException   RuntimeException
ArrayIndexOutOfBoundsException

User-Defined Interfaces and Classes in This Chapter

class ArraySearch   class TestDirectoryEntry
class DirectoryEntry   interface PhoneDirectory
class MyInput

Quick-Check Exercises

1. What are the three broad categories of program defects discussed in this chapter?
2. What is the purpose of a structured walkthrough of an algorithm?
3. _____ testing requires the use of test data that exercise each statement in a module.
4. _____ testing focuses on testing the functional characteristics of a module.
5. _____ determines whether a program has an error; _____ determines the _____ of the error and helps you _____ it.
6. Assume you have the following exception classes in **catch** clauses following a **try** block. List the sequence in which they must occur:

   Exception
   IOException
   FileNotFoundException

7. Indicate which of the following may be false: loop invariant, **while** condition, assertion
8. Write a loop invariant for the following code segment:

   ```
   product = 1;
   counter = 2;
   while (counter < 5) {
       product *= counter;
       counter++;
   }
   ```

9. Determine the order of magnitude (big-O) for an algorithm whose running time is given by the equation $T(n) = 3n^4 - 2n^2 + 100n + 37$.
10. If a loop processes n items and n changes from 1024 to 2048, how does that affect the running time of a loop that is $O(n^2)$? How about a loop that is $O(\log n)$? How about a loop that is $O(n \log n)$?

Answers to Quick-Check Exercises

1. Syntax errors, run-time errors, logic errors.
2. To increase the likelihood of finding program logic errors.
3. *White-box* testing requires the use of test data that exercise each statement in a module.
4. *Black-box* testing focuses on testing the functional characteristics of a module.
5. *Testing* determines whether a program has an error; *debugging* determines the *cause* of the error and helps you *correct* it.
6. The exception clauses must be in the order `FileNotFoundException`, `IOException`, and finally `Exception`.
7. A `while` condition
8. invariant: product *contains product of all positive integers* < counter *and* counter *is between 2 and 5, inclusive.*
9. $O(n^4)$
10. The running time quadruples for the $O(n^2)$ loop; it increases by a factor of 1.1 for the $O(\log n)$ loop (11/10); it increases by a factor of 2.2 for the $O(n \log n)$ algorithm ($2048 \times 11 / 1024 \times 10$).

Review Questions

1. Describe a technique for preventing a run-time error caused by the user typing a bad character while entering a numeric value.
2. Describe the differences between stubs and drivers.
3. Discuss the differences between the **throws** clause and the **throw** statement. When would you use each one? What should you do if you decide to throw an exception rather than catch it in a method? Give two circumstances where it would be beneficial to throw an exception rather than handle it.
4. Indicate what kind of exception each of the following errors would cause. Indicate whether each error is a checked or unchecked exception.
   a. Attempting to create a `BufferedReader` for a file that does not exist
   b. Attempting to call a method on a variable that has not been initialized
   c. Using –1 as an array index
   d. Calling the `nextToken` method of a `StringTokenizer` without checking the results of `hasMoreTokens`
5. Briefly describe a test plan for the telephone directory program described in Chapter 1. Assume that integration testing is used.
6. Indicate in which stage of testing (unit, system, integration) each of the following kinds of errors should be detected:
   a. An array index is out of bounds.
   b. A `FileNotFound` exception is thrown.
   c. An incorrect value of withholding tax is being computed under some circumstances.
7. Which of the following statements is incorrect?
   a. Loop invariants are used in loop verification.
   b. Loop invariants are used in loop design.
   c. A loop invariant is always an assertion.
   d. An assertion is always a loop invariant.

8. Write a method that counts the number of adjacent data items out of place in an array (assume increasing order is desired). Include loop invariants and any other assertions necessary to verify that the procedure is correct.

9. Write a big-O expression for the following loops.

a.
```
for (int i = 1; i <= n; i++)
    for (int j = 1; j <= n; j++)
        for (int k = n; k >= 1; k--) {
            sum = i + j + k;
            System.out.println(sum);
        }
```

b.
```
for (int i = 0; i < n; i++)
    for (int j = 0; j < i * i; j++)
        System.out.println(j);
```

c.
```
for (int i = n; i >= 0; i -= 2)
    System.out.println(i);
```

d.
```
for (int i = 0; i < n; i++)
    for (int j = i; j > 0; j /= 2)
        System.out.println(j);
```

Programming Projects

1. Write a program that determines the average number of array locations that were examined in successful searches to locate an integer in an array of 100 unordered integers using sequential search. Your program should also compute the average number of array calculations that were examined for a failed search in the same array. Your average calculations should be based on trials involving searching for at least 50 different numbers.

2. Redo Project 1 using an array of integers sorted in ascending order. Modify the sequential search algorithm to halt a search as soon as the array values are larger than the target value being sought.

3. Write a program that allows you to examine the effects of array size and initial data order when your favorite sort operates on an array of integers. Test three different array sizes ($n = 100$, $n = 1,000$, and $n = 10,000$) and three different array orderings (ascending order, inverse order, and random order). This should produce nine test results. The Java method `Math.random()` may be helpful in building the randomly ordered arrays. If you don't have a favorite sort, use method `Arrays.sort` in the Java API `java.util`.

4. Write a set of stub methods for the `ArrayBasedPD` class (Section 1.5) that could be used to test the logic of either the `PDGUI` or the `PDConsoleUI` (Section 1.8) classes.

5. Design and program a white-box test for a class that computes the sine and cosine functions in a specialized manner. This class is going to be part of an embedded system running on a processor that does not support floating-point arithmetic or the Java `Math` class. The class to be tested is shown in Listing 2.9. Your job is to test the methods `sin` and `cos`; you are to assume that the methods `sin0to45` and `sin45to90` have already been tested.

You need to design a set of test data that will exercise each of the **if** statements. To do this, look at the boundary conditions and pick values that are

- Exactly on the boundary
- Close to the boundary
- Between boundaries

LISTING 2.9
SinCos.java (Except for the Test Driver)

```java
/** This class computes the sine and cosine of an angle
    expressed in degrees. The result will be
    an integer representing the sine or cosine as
    ten-thousandths. For example, a result of 7071 represents
    7071e-4 or 0.7071.
*/
public class SinCos {
    /** Compute the sine of an angle in degrees.
        @param x The angle in degrees
        @return The sine of x
    */
    public static int sin(int x) {
        if (x < 0) {
            x = -x;
        }
        x = x % 360;
        if (0 <= x && x <= 45) {
            return sin0to45(x);
        } else if (45 <= x && x <= 90) {
            return sin45to90(x);
        } else if (90 <= x && x <= 180) {
            return sin(180 - x);
        } else {
            return -sin(x - 180);
        }
    }

    /** Compute the cosine of an angle in degrees.
        @param x The angle in degrees
        @return The cosine of x
    */
    public static int cos(int x) {
        return sin(x + 90);
    }

    /** Compute the sine of an angle in degrees
        between 0 and 45.
        pre: 0 <= x < 45
        @param x The angle
        @return The sine of x
    */
    private static int sin0to45(int x) {
        // In a realistic program this method would
        // use a polynomial approximation that was
        // optimized for the input range.
        Code to compute sin(x) for x between 0 and 45 degrees
    }
```

```
/** Compute the sine of an angle in degrees
       between 45 and 90.
    pre: 45 <= x <= 90
    @param x The angle
    @return The sine of x
*/
private static int sin45to90(int x) {
    // In a realistic program this method would
    // use a polynomial approximation that was
    // optimized for the input range.
    Code to compute sin(x) for x between 45 and 90 degrees
}
}
```

6. Develop a test plan and test drivers/stubs as required to test Programming Project 2 in Chapter 1.

7. Update the test plan and test drivers/stubs to test the modified version of the DVD collection project described in Programming Project 4 in Chapter 1.

8. Develop a test plan and test drivers/stubs as required to test Programming Project 5 in Chapter 1.

9. Develop a test plan and test drivers/stubs as required to test Programming Project 6 in Chapter 1.

Inheritance and Class Hierarchies

This chapter describes important features of Java that can make your code more reusable. Object-oriented languages allow you to build and exploit hierarchies of classes, abstract classes, and interfaces to group common features and methods in your program designs. You will learn how to extend an existing Java class to define a new class that inherits all the attributes of the original, as well as having additional attributes of its own. At the top of the class hierarchy is the class Object, which all classes extend, so we describe this class and several of its methods that may be used in classes you create. Because there may be many versions of the same method in a class hierarchy, we show how polymorphism enables Java to determine which version to execute at any given time. Finally, we discuss multiple inheritance and show how desirable features of multiple inheritance can be exploited in Java.

You will also see how to use an object factory to creates instances of other classes. Finally you will learn how to create packages in Java, and about the different kinds of visibility for instance variables (data fields) and methods.

3.1 Introduction to Inheritance and Class Hierarchies

A major reason for the popularity of object-oriented programming (OOP) is that it enables programmers to reuse previously written code saved as classes, reducing the time required to code new applications. Because previously written code has already been tested and debugged, the new applications should also be more reliable and therefore easier to test and debug. The Java API gives the Java programmer a head-start in developing new applications. Java programmers can also build and reuse their own individual libraries of classes.

However, OOP provides additional capabilities beyond the reuse of existing classes. If an application needs a new class that is similar to an existing class, the programmer can create it by *extending* the existing class, rather than rewriting the original class. The new class (called the *subclass*) can have additional data fields and methods for increased functionality. Its objects also *inherit* the data fields and methods of the original class (called the *superclass*).

All Java classes are arranged in a hierarchy, starting with class Object, which is the superclass of all Java classes. Figure 3.1 shows the Exception class hierarchy discussed in the previous chapter. The entities farther down the hierarchy inherit data fields (attributes) and methods from those farther up, but not vice versa. Because all Exception classes are subclasses of Throwable, they can all use the methods getMessage and printStackTrace, which are defined in class Throwable. There is no need to redefine these methods in each exception class. Similarly, they can all use methods defined in class Object. All the unchecked exceptions (for example, ArithmeticException) are subclasses of RuntimeException, so they inherit data and methods defined in that class. Furthermore, the subclass/superclass relationship is

FIGURE 3.1

Summary of **Exception** Class Hierarchy

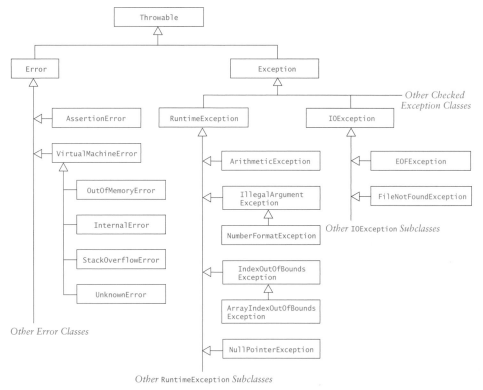

transitive, so all unchecked exceptions are subclasses of `Exception`, `Throwable`, and `Object` but not of `Error` or `IOException`.

Inheritance in OOP is analogous to inheritance in humans. We all inherit genetic traits from our parents. If we are fortunate, we may even have some earlier ancestors who have left us an inheritance of monetary value. As we grow up, we benefit from our ancestors' resources, knowledge, and experiences, but our experiences will not affect how our parents or ancestors developed. Although we have two parents to inherit from, Java classes can only have one parent. We will discuss the rationale for this in Section 3.5.

Inheritance and hierarchical organization allow you to capture the idea that one thing may be a refinement or extension of another. For example, an object that is a `RuntimeException` *is an* `Exception`. This means that an object of type `RuntimeException` has all the data fields and methods defined by class `Exception`, but it may also have more. Objects further down the hierarchy are more complex and less general than those further up. For this reason an object that is a `RuntimeException` is an `Exception`, but the converse is not true, because an `Exception` object does not necessarily have the additional properties defined by class `RuntimeException`.

Is-a Versus *Has-a* Relationships

One misuse of inheritance is confusing the *has-a* relationship with the *is-a* relationship. The *is-a* relationship between classes means that one class *is a* subclass of the other class. For example, to say that a jet plane is an airplane means that the jet plane class *is a* subclass of the airplane class. The *is-a* relationship is achieved by extending a class.

The *has-a* relationship between classes means that one class *has* the second class as an attribute. For example, a jet plane *has a* jet engine. The *has-a* relationship is achieved by declaring a data field whose type is one class in another class.

We can combine *is-a* and *has-a* relationships. For example, a jet plane *is an* airplane and it *has a* jet engine. A jet plane also *has a* tail because it *is an* airplane (a tail is an attribute of all airplane objects).

Java allows you to capture both the inheritance (*is-a*) relationship and the *has-a* relationship. For example, a class JetPlane might be declared as:

```
public class JetPlane extends Airplane {
    private JetEngine[] jets;        // Jet planes have multiple engines
    ...
}
```

The keyword **extends** specifies that JetPlane is a subclass of Airplane. The data field jets is of type JetEngine[] and indicates that a JetPlane *has* JetEngines.

A Superclass and a Subclass

FIGURE 3.2
Classes LapTop and Computer

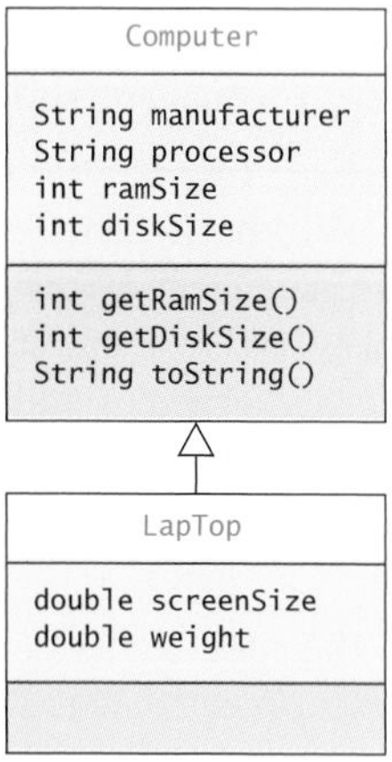

To illustrate the concepts of inheritance and class hierarchies, let's consider a simple case of two classes: Computer and LapTop. A Computer object has a manufacturer, processor, RAM, and disk. A laptop computer is a kind of computer, so it has all the properties of a computer plus some additional features (screen size and weight). Therefore, we can define class LapTop as a subclass of class Computer. Figure 3.2 shows the class hierarchy.

Class **Computer**

Listing 3.1 shows class Computer. It is defined like any other class.

LISTING 3.1
Class Computer.java

```
/** Class that represents a computer. */
public class Computer {
    // Data Fields
    private String manufacturer;
    private String processor;
    private int ramSize;
    private int diskSize;

    // Methods
    /** Initializes a Computer object with all properties specified.
        @param man The computer manufacturer
        @param processor The processor type
        @param ram The RAM size
        @param disk The disk size
```

```
    */
    public Computer(String man, String processor, int ram, int disk) {
        manufacturer = man;
        this.processor = processor;
        ramSize = ram;
        diskSize = disk;
    }

    public int getRamSize() { return ramSize; }

    public int getDiskSize() { return diskSize; }

    // Insert other accessor and modifier methods here.

    public String toString() {
        String result = "Manufacturer: " + manufacturer +
                        "\nCPU: " + processor +
                        "\nRAM: " + ramSize + " megabytes" +
                        "\nDisk: " + diskSize + " gigabytes";
        return result;
    }
}
```

Use of this.

In the constructor for the Computer class, the statement

```
    this.processor = processor;
```

sets data field processor in the object under construction to reference the same string as parameter processor. The prefix **this.** makes data field processor visible in the constructor. This is necessary because the declaration of processor as a parameter hides the data field declaration.

Class **LapTop**

In the LapTop class diagram in Figure 3.2, we show just the data fields declared in class LapTop; however, LapTop objects also have the data fields that are inherited from class Computer (processor, ramSize, and so forth). The first line in class LapTop (Listing 3.2),

```
    public class LapTop extends Computer {
```

 PITFALL

Not Using this. **to Access a Hidden Data Field**

If you write the preceding statement as

```
    processor = processor;   // Copy parameter processor to itself.
```

you will not get an error, but the data field processor in the Computer object under construction will not be initialized and will retain its default value (null). If you later attempt to use data field processor, you may get an error (for example, a NullPointerException) or just an unexpected result.

indicates that class LapTop extends class Computer and inherits its data and methods. Next, we define any additional data fields

```
// Data Fields
private double screenSize;
private double weight;
```

Initializing Data Fields in a Subclass

The constructor for class LapTop must begin by initializing the four data fields inherited from class Computer. Because those data fields are private to the superclass, Java requires that they be initialized by a superclass constructor. Therefore, a superclass constructor must be invoked as the first statement in the constructor body using a statement such as

```
super(man, proc, ram, disk);
```

This statement invokes the superclass constructor with the signature Computer(String, String, int, int), passing it the four arguments listed. (A method *signature* consists of the method's name followed by its parameter types.) The following constructor for LapTop also initializes the data fields that are not inherited. Listing 3.2 shows class LapTop.

```
public LapTop(String man, String proc, int ram, int disk,
              double screen, double wei) {
    super(man, proc, ram, disk);
    screenSize = screen;
    weight = wei;
}
```

SYNTAX **super(. . .);**

FORM:

```
super();
super(argumentList);
```

EXAMPLE:

```
super(man, proc, ram, disk);
```

MEANING:

The **super()** call in a class constructor invokes the superclass's constructor that has the corresponding *argumentList*. The superclass constructor initializes the inherited data fields as specified by its *argumentList*. The **super()** call must be the first statement in a constructor.

LISTING 3.2

Class LapTop

```
/** Class that represents a laptop computer. */
public class LapTop extends Computer {
    // Data Fields
    private double screenSize;
    private double weight;
```

```
     // Methods
     /** Initializes a LapTop object with all properties specified.
         @param man The computer manufacturer
         @param proc The processor type
         @param ram The RAM size
         @param disk The disk size
         @param screen The screen size
         @param wei The weight
     */
     public LapTop(String man, String proc, int ram, int disk,
                   double screen, double wei) {
         super(man, proc, ram, disk);
         screenSize = screen;
         weight = wei;
     }
}
```

The No-Parameter Constructor

If the execution of any constructor in a subclass does not invoke a superclass constructor, Java automatically invokes the no-parameter constructor for the superclass. Java does this to initialize that part of the object inherited from the superclass before the subclass starts to initialize its part of the object. Otherwise, the part of the object that is inherited would remain uninitialized.

Protected Visibility for Superclass Data Fields

The data fields inherited from class Computer have private visibility. Therefore, they can be accessed only within class Computer. Because it is fairly common for a subclass

 PITFALL

Not Defining the No-Parameter Constructor

If no constructors are defined for a class, the no-parameter constructor for that class will be provided by default. However, if any constructors are defined, the no-parameter constructor must also be defined explicitly if it needs to be invoked. Java does not provide it automatically, because it may make no sense to create a new object of that type without providing initial data field values. (It was not defined in class Laptop or Computer because we want the client to specify some information about a Computer object when that object is created.) If the no-parameter constructor is defined in a subclass but is not defined in the superclass, you will get a syntax error constructor not defined. You can also get this error if a subclass constructor does not explicitly call a superclass constructor. There will be an implicit call to the no-parameter superclass constructor, so it must be defined.

method to reference data fields declared in its superclass, Java provides a less-restrictive form of visibility called *protected visibility*. A data field (or method) with protected visibility can be accessed in either the class defining it, in any subclass of that class, or any class in the same package. Therefore, if we had used the declaration

```
protected String manufacturer;
```

in class Computer, the following assignment statement would be valid in class LapTop:

```
manufacturer = man;
```

We will use protected visibility on occasion when we are writing a class that we intend to extend. However, in general, it is better to use private visibility, because subclasses may be written by different programmers, and it is always a good practice to restrict and control access to the superclass data fields. We discuss visibility further in Section 3.6.

EXERCISES FOR SECTION 3.1

SELF-CHECK

1. Explain the effect of each valid statement in the following fragment. Indicate any invalid statements.
```
Computer c1 = new Computer();
Computer c2 = new Computer("Ace", "AMD Athlon 2000", 512, 60);
LapTop c3 = new LapTop("Ace", "AMD Athlon 2000", 512, 60);
LapTop c4 = new LapTop("Ace", "AMD Athlon 2000", 512, 60, 15.5, 7.5);
System.out.println(c2.manufacturer + ", " + c4.processor);
System.out.println(c2.getDiskSize() + ", " + c4.getRamSize());
System.out.println(c2.toString() + "\n" + c4.toString());
```

2. Indicate where in the hierarchy you might want to add data fields for the following and the kind of data field you would add.
   Cost
   The battery identification
   Time before battery discharges
   Number of expansion slots
   Wireless Internet available

3. Can you add the following constructor to class LapTop? If so, what would you need to do to class Computer?
```
public LapTop() {}
```

PROGRAMMING

1. Write accessor and modifier methods for class Computer.
2. Write accessor and modifier methods for class LapTop.

3.2 Method Overriding, Method Overloading, and Polymorphism

In the preceding section we discussed inherited data fields. We found that we could not access an inherited data field in a subclass object if its visibility was private. Next, we consider inherited methods. Methods generally have public visibility, so we should be able to access a method that is inherited. However, what if there are multiple methods with the same name in a class hierarchy? How does Java determine which one to invoke? We answer this question next.

Method Overriding

Let's use the following `main` method to test our class hierarchy.

```
/** Tests classes Computer and LapTop. Creates an object of each and
    displays them.
    @param args[] No control parameters
*/
public static void main(String[] args) {
    Computer myComputer =
        new Computer("Acme", "Intel P4 2.4", 512, 60);
    LapTop yourComputer =
        new LapTop("DellGate", "AMD Athlon 2000", 256, 40,
                    15.0, 7.5);
    System.out.println("My computer is :\n" + myComputer.toString());
    System.out.println("\nYour computer is :\n" +
                    yourComputer.toString());
}
```

In the second call to `println`, the method call

```
yourComputer.toString()
```

applies method `toString` to object `yourComputer` (type `LapTop`). Because class `LapTop` doesn't define its own `toString` method, class `LapTop` inherits the `toString` method defined in class `Computer`. Executing this method displays the following output lines:

```
My computer is:
Manufacturer: Acme
CPU: Intel P4 2.4
RAM: 512 megabytes
Disk: 60 gigabytes

Your computer is:
Manufacturer: DellGate
CPU: AMD Athlon 2000
RAM: 256 megabytes
Disk: 40 gigabytes
```

Unfortunately, this output doesn't show the complete state of object `yourComputer`. To show the complete state of a laptop computer, we need to define a `toString` method for class `LapTop`. If class `LapTop` has its own `toString` method, it will *override* the inherited method and will be invoked by the method call `yourComputer.toString()`. We define method `toString` for class `LapTop` next.

```
public String toString() {
    String result = super.toString()
                    + "\nScreen size: " + screenSize + " inches"
                    + "\nWeight: " + weight + " pounds";
    return result;
}
```

This method `LapTop.toString` returns a string representation of the state of a `LapTop` object. The first line,

```
String result = super.toString()
```

uses method call **super**.`toString()` to invoke the `toString` method of the superclass (method `Computer.toString`) to get the string representation of the four data fields that are inherited from the superclass. The next two lines append the data fields defined in class `LapTop` to this string.

SYNTAX   super.

FORM:

super.*methodName*()
super.*methodName*(*argumentList*)

EXAMPLE:

super.toString()

MEANING:

Using the prefix **super.** in a call to method *methodName* calls the method with that name defined in the superclass of the current class.

PROGRAM STYLE

Calling Method toString() Is Optional

In the `println` statement shown earlier,

```
System.out.println("My computer is :\n" + myComputer.toString());
```

the explicit call to method toString is not required. The statement could be written as

```
System.out.println("My computer is :\n" + myComputer);
```

Java automatically applies the toString method to an object referenced in a String expression.

PITFALL

Overridden Methods Must Have the Same Return Type

If you write a method in a subclass that has the same signature as one in the superclass but a different return type, you will get the error message: in *subclass-name* cannot override *method* in *superclass-name*; attempting to use incompatible return type. The subclass method must have the same return type as the superclass method.

Method Overloading

Let's assume we have decided to standardize and purchase our laptop computers from only one manufacturer. We could then introduce a new constructor with one less parameter for class LapTop.

```
public LapTop(String proc, int ram, int disk,
              double screen, double wei) {
    this(DEFAULT_LT_MAN, proc, ram, disk, screen, wei);
}
```

The method call

```
    this(DEFAULT_LT_MAN, proc, ram, disk, screen, wei);
```

invokes the six-parameter constructor (see Listing 3.2), passing on the five arguments it receives and the constant string DEFAULT_LT_MAN (defined in class LapTop). The six-parameter constructor begins by calling the superclass constructor, satisfying the requirement that it be called first. We now have two constructors with different signatures in class LapTop. Having multiple methods with the same name but different signatures in a class is called *method overloading.*

Now we have two ways to create new LapTop objects. Both of the following statements are valid:

```
    LapTop lTP1 = new LapTop("Intel P4 2.4", 256, 40, 14, 6.5);
    LapTop lTP2 = new LapTop("MicroSys", "AMD Athlon 2000", 256, 40, 15, 7.5);
```

The manufacturer of lTP1 is DEFAULT_LT_MAN.

SYNTAX **this(. . .);**

FORM:
this(*argumentList*);

EXAMPLE:
this(DEFAULT_LT_MAN, proc, ramSize, diskSize);

MEANING:

The call to **this()** invokes the constructor for the current class whose parameter list matches the argument list. The constructor initializes the new object as specified by its arguments. The invocation of another constructor (through either **this()** or **super()**) must be the first statement in a constructor.

FIGURE 3.3
Revised UML Diagram
for **Computer** Class
Hierarchy

Listing 3.3 shows the complete class LapTop. Figure 3.3 shows the UML diagram, revised to show that LapTop has a toString method and a constant data field.

LISTING 3.3
Complete Class LapTop with Method toString

```java
/** Class that represents a lap top computer. */
public class LapTop extends Computer {
    // Data Fields
    private static final String DEFAULT_LT_MAN = "MyBrand";
    private double screenSize;
    private double weight;

    /** Initializes a LapTop object with all properties specified.
        @param man The computer manufacturer
        @param proc The processor type
        @param ram The RAM size
        @param disk The disk size
        @param screen The screen size
        @param wei The weight
    */
    public LapTop(String man, String proc, int ram, int disk,
                  double screen, double wei) {
        super(man, proc, ram, disk);
        screenSize = screen;
        weight = wei;
    }

    /** Initializes a LapTop object with 5 properties specified. */
    public LapTop(String proc, int ram, int disk,
                  double screen, double wei) {
        this(DEFAULT_LT_MAN, proc, ram, disk, screen, wei);
    }

    public String toString() {
        String result = super.toString()
                        + "\nScreen size: " + screenSize + " inches"
                        + "\nWeight: " + weight + " pounds";
        return result;
    }
}
```

Polymorphism

Suppose you are not sure whether a computer referenced in a program will be a laptop or a regular computer. If you declare the reference variable

```java
Computer theComputer;
```

you can use it to reference an object of either type, because a type LapTop object can be referenced by a type Computer variable. In Java, a variable of a superclass type (general) can reference an object of a subclass type (specific). LapTop objects are Computer objects with more features. When the following statements are executed,

```
theComputer = new Computer("Acme", "Intel P4 2.4", 512, 60);
System.out.println(theComputer.toString());
```

you would see four output lines, representing the state of the object referenced by `theComputer`.

Now suppose you have purchased a laptop computer instead. What happens when the following statements are executed?

```
theComputer = new LapTop("Bravo", "Intel P4 2.4", 256, 40, 15.0, 7.5);
System.out.println(theComputer.toString());
```

Recall that `theComputer` is type `Computer`. Will the method call `theComputer.toString()` return a string with all six data fields or just the four data fields defined for a `Computer` object? The answer is a string with all six data fields. The reason is that the type of the object receiving the `toString` message determines which `toString` method is called. Even though variable `theComputer` is type `Computer`, it references a type `LapTop` object, and the `LapTop` object receives the `toString` message. Therefore, the method `toString` for class `LapTop` is the one called.

The fact that the `toString` method invoked depends on the type of the object referenced, and not the type of the reference variable (`theComputer` is type `Computer`), is a very important feature of object-oriented programming languages. This feature is called *polymorphism*, which means many forms or many shapes. Polymorphism enables the JVM to determine which method to invoke at run time. At compile time, the Java compiler can't determine what type of object `theComputer` will reference (type `Computer` or type `LapTop`), but at run time the JVM knows the type of the object that receives the `toString` message and can call the appropriate `toString` method.

EXAMPLE 3.1

In the preceding discussion, you could determine from each assignment statement whether variable `theComputer` was referencing a type `Computer` object or a type `LapTop` object. However, if we declare the array `labComputers` as follows,

```
Computer[] labComputers = new Computer[10];
```

the subscripted variable `labComputers[i]` can reference either a `Computer` object or a `LapTop` object. However, polymorphism works the same way for the method call `labComputers[i].toString()`. For each value of subscript i, the actual type of the object referenced by `labComputers[i]` determines which `toString` method will execute (`Computer.toString` or `LapTop.toString`).

EXERCISES FOR SECTION 3.2

SELF-CHECK

1. Explain the effect of each of the following statements. Which one(s) would you find in class `Computer`? Which one(s) would you find in class `LapTop`?
```
super(man, proc, ram, disk);
this(man, proc, ram, disk);
```

2. Indicate whether methods with each of the following signatures and return types (if any) would be allowed and in what classes they would be allowed. Explain your answers.

```
Computer()
LapTop()
int toString()
double getRamSize()
String getRamSize()
String getRamSize(String)
String getProcessor()
double getScreenSize()
```

3. For the loop body in the following fragment, indicate which method is invoked for each value of i. What is printed?

```
Computer comp[] = new Computer[3];
comp[0] = new Computer("Ace", "AMD Athlon 2500", 512, 60);
comp[1] = new LapTop("Intel P4 2.4", 256, 40, 15.5, 7.5);
comp[2] = comp[1];
for (int i = 0; i < comp.length; i++) {
    System.out.println(comp[i].getRamSize() +"\n" +
                       comp[i].toString());
}
```

4. When does Java determine which toString method to execute for each value of i in the for statement in the preceding question: at compile time or at run time? Explain your answer.

PROGRAMMING

1. Write constructors for both classes that allow you to specify only the processor, RAM size, and disk size.
2. Complete the accessor and modifier methods for class Computer.
3. Complete the accessor and modifier methods for class LapTop.

3.3 Abstract Classes, Assignment, and Casting in a Hierarchy

In this section we introduce another kind of class called an *abstract class*. Recall that an interface can declare methods but does not provide an implementation of those methods. The methods declared in an interface are therefore called *abstract methods*. Like an interface, an abstract class can have abstract methods, but it can also have data fields (instance variables) and can define concrete methods (that is, provide the implementation of those methods). It differs from an actual class (sometimes called a *concrete class*) in two respects:

- An abstract class cannot be instantiated.
- An abstract class can declare abstract methods, which must be implemented in its subclasses.

We introduce an abstract class in a class hierarchy when we need a base class for two or more actual classes that share some attributes. We may want to declare some of the attributes and define some of the methods that are common to these base classes. Consequently, we can't use an interface. However, we may also want to require that the actual subclasses implement certain methods. We can accomplish this by declaring these methods abstract, which would make the superclass abstract as well.

EXAMPLE 3.2   The Food Guide Pyramid provides a recommendation of what to eat each day based on established dietary guidelines. There are six categories of foods in the pyramid: fats, oils, and sweets; meats, poultry, fish, and nuts; milk, yogurt, and cheese; vegetables; fruits; and bread, cereal, and pasta. If we wanted to model the Food Guide Pyramid, we might have each of these as actual subclasses of an abstract class called Food:

```
/** Abstract class that models a kind of food. */
public abstract class Food {
    // Data Field
    private double calories;

    // Abstract Methods
    /** Calculates the percent of protein in a Food object. */
    public abstract double percentProtein();
    /** Calculates the percent of fat in a Food object. */
    public abstract double percentFat();
    /** Calculates the percent of carbohydrates in a Food object. */
    public abstract double percentCarbohydrates();

    // Methods
    public double getCalories() { return calories; }
    public void setCalories(double cal) {
        calories = cal;
    }
}
```

The three abstract method declarations

```
public abstract double percentProtein();
public abstract double percentFat();
public abstract double percentCarbohydrates();
```

impose the requirement that all actual subclasses implement these three methods. We would expect a different method definition for each kind of food. The keyword **abstract** must appear in all abstract method declarations in an abstract class, whereas **abstract** is optional (and usually omitted) in an interface because all methods declared in an interface are abstract by default.

SYNTAX **Abstract Class Definition**

FORM:

```
public abstract class className {
    data field declarations
    abstract method declarations
    actual method definitions
}
```

EXAMPLE:

```
public abstract class Food {
    // Data Field
    private double calories;

    // Abstract Methods
    public abstract double percentProtein();
    public abstract double percentFat();
    public abstract double percentCarbohydrates();

    // Methods
    public double getCalories() { return calories; }
    public void setCalories(double cal) {
        calories = cal;
    }
}
```

INTERPRETATION:

Abstract class *className* is defined. The class body may have declarations for data fields and abstract methods as well as actual method definitions. Each abstract method declaration consists of a method heading containing the keyword **abstract**. All of the declaration kinds shown above are optional.

 PITFALL

Omitting the Definition of an Abstract Method in a Subclass

If you write class Vegetable and forget to define method percentProtein, you will get the syntax error class Vegetable should be declared abstract, it does not define method percentProtein in class Food. Although this error message is misleading (you did not intend Vegetable to be abstract), any class with undefined methods is abstract by definition. The compiler's rationale is that the undefined method is intentional, so Vegetable must be an abstract class, with a subclass that defines percentProtein.

Referencing Actual Objects

Because class Food is abstract, you can't create type Food objects. However, you can use a type Food variable to reference an actual object that belongs to a subclass of type Food. For example, an object of type Vegetable can be referenced by a Vegetable or Food variable because Vegetable is a subclass of Food (that is, a Vegetable object is also a Food object).

EXAMPLE 3.3   The following statement creates a Vegetable object that is referenced by variable mySnack (type Food).

```
Food mySnack = new Vegetable("carrot sticks");
```

Abstract Classes and Interfaces

Like an interface, an abstract class can't be instantiated. However, unlike an interface, an abstract class can have constructors that initialize its data fields when a new subclass object is created. The subclass constructor will use **super(...)** to call such a constructor.

An abstract class may implement an interface just as an actual class does, but unlike an actual class it doesn't have to define all of the methods declared in the interface. It can leave the implementation of some of the abstract methods to its subclasses.

Abstract Class Number and the Java Wrapper Classes

The abstract class Number is predefined in the Java class hierarchy. It has as its subclasses all the wrapper classes for primitive numeric types (for example, Byte, Double, Integer, Short). A *wrapper class* is used to store a primitive-type value in an object type. Each wrapper class contains constructors to create an object that stores a particular primitive type value. For example, Integer(35) or Integer("35") creates a type Integer object that stores the int 35. A wrapper class also has methods for converting the value stored to a different numeric type.

Figure 3.4 shows a portion of the class hierarchy with base class Number. Italicizing the class name Number in its class box indicates that Number is an abstract class and, therefore, cannot be instantiated. Listing 3.4 shows part of the definition for class Number. Two abstract methods are declared (intValue and doubleValue), and one actual method (byteValue) is defined. In the actual implementation of Number, the body of byteValue would be provided, but we just indicate its presence in Listing 3.4.

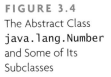

FIGURE 3.4
The Abstract Class
`java.lang.Number`
and Some of Its
Subclasses

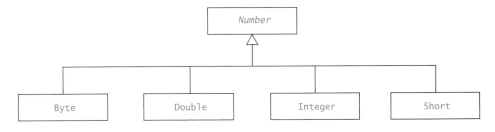

LISTING 3.4
Part of Abstract Class `java.lang.Number`

```
public abstract class Number {
    // Abstract Methods
    /** Returns the value of the specified number as an int.
        @return The numeric value represented by this object after
                conversion to type int
    */
    public abstract int intValue();

    /** Returns the value of the specified number as a double.
        @return The numeric value represented by this object
                after conversion to type double
    */
    public abstract double doubleValue();

    . . .

    // Methods
    /** Returns the value of the specified number as a byte.
        @return The numeric value represented by this object
                after conversion to type byte
    */
    public byte byteValue() {
        // Implementation not shown.
        . . .
    }
}
```

Summary of Features of Actual Classes, Abstract Classes, and Interfaces

Students often get confused between abstract classes, interfaces, and actual classes (concrete classes). Table 3.1 summarizes some important points about these constructs.

TABLE 3.1

Comparison of Actual Classes, Abstract Classes, and Interfaces

Property	Actual Class	Abstract Class	Interface
Instances (objects) of this can be created	Yes	No	No
This can define instance variables and methods	Yes	Yes	No
This can define constants	Yes	Yes	Yes
The number of these a class can extend	0 or 1	0 or 1	0
The number of these a class can implement	0	0	Any number
This can extend another class	Yes	Yes	No
This can declare abstract methods	No	Yes	Yes
Variables of this type can be declared	Yes	Yes	Yes

EXERCISES FOR SECTION 3.3

SELF-CHECK

1. What are two important differences between an abstract class and an actual class? What are the similarities?
2. What do abstract methods and interfaces have in common? How do they differ?
3. Explain the effect of each statement in the following fragment and trace the loop execution for each value of i, indicating which doubleValue method executes, if any. What is the final value of x?

```
Number[] nums = new Number[5];
nums[0] = new Integer(35);
nums[1] = new Double(3.45);
nums[4] = new Double("2.45e6");

double x = 0;
for (int i = 0; i < nums.length; i++) {
    if (nums[i] != null)
        x += nums[i].doubleValue();
}
```

4. What is the purpose of the **if** statement in the loop in Exercise 3? What would happen if it were omitted?

PROGRAMMING

1. Write class Vegetable. Assume that a vegetable has three **double** constants: VEG_PROTEIN_CAL, VEG_FAT_CAL, and VEG_CARBO_CAL. Compute the fat percentage as VEG_FAT_CAL divided by the sum of all the constants.
2. Earlier we discussed a Computer class with a LapTop class as its only subclass. However, there are many different kinds of computers. An organization may have servers, mainframes, desktop PCs, and laptops. There are also personal data assistants and game computers. So it may be more appropriate to declare class Computer as an abstract class that has an actual subclass for each category of computer. Write an abstract class Computer that defines all the methods shown earlier and declares an abstract method with the signature costBenefit(double) that returns the cost-benefit (type **double**) for each category of computer.

3.4 Class Object, Casting, and Cloning

The class Object is a special class in Java because it is the root of the class hierarchy, and every class has Object as a superclass. All classes inherit the methods defined in class Object; however, these methods may be overridden in the current class or in a superclass (if any). Table 3.2 shows a few of the methods of class Object. We discuss method toString next and the other Object methods shortly thereafter.

The Method `toString`

You should always override the `toString` method if you want to represent an object's state (information stored). If you don't override it, the `toString` method for class `Object` will execute and return a string, but not what you are expecting.

EXAMPLE 3.4   Because we don't have a `toString` method in class `ArrayBasedPD` (See Section 1.6) the method call `phoneDirectory.toString()` would call the `toString` method inherited from class `Object`. This method would return a string such as `"ArrayBasedPhoneDirectory@ef08879"`, which shows the object's class name and a special integer value that is its "hash code"—not its state. Method `hashCode` is discussed in Chapter 10.

Operations Determined by Type of Reference Variable

You have seen that a variable can reference an object whose type is a subclass of the variable type. Because `Object` is a superclass of class `Integer`, the statement

```
Object aThing = new Integer(25);
```

will compile without error, creating the object reference shown in Figure 3.5. However, even though aThing references a type `Integer` object, we can't process this object like other `Integer` objects. For example, the method call `aThing.intValue()` would cause the syntax error method `intValue()` not found in class `java.lang.Object`. The reason for this is that the type of the reference, not the type of the object referenced, determines what operations can be performed, and class `Object` doesn't have an `intValue` method. During compilation, Java can't determine what kind of object will be referenced by a type `Object` variable, so the only operations permitted are those defined for class `Object`. The type `Integer` instance methods not defined in class `Object` (for example, `intValue`, `doubleValue`) can't be invoked.

The method call `aThing.equals(new Integer("25"))` will compile, because class `Object` has an `equals` method, and a subclass object has everything that is defined in its superclass. During execution, the `equals` method for class `Integer` is invoked, not class `Object`. (Why?)

TABLE 3.2
Methods of Class `java.lang.Object`

Method	Behavior
`Object clone()`	Makes a copy of an object.
`boolean equals(Object obj)`	Compares this object to its argument.
`int hashCode()`	Returns an integer hash code value for this object.
`String toString()`	Returns a string that textually represents the object.

FIGURE 3.5

FIGURE 3.5
Type `Integer` Object
Referenced by `aThing`
(type `Object`)

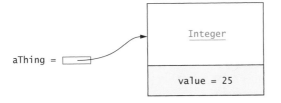

Another surprising result is that the assignment statement

```
Integer aNum = aThing;        // Incompatible types
```

won't compile even though aThing references a type Integer object. The syntax error: `incompatible types: found: Java.lang.Object, required: Java.lang.Integer` indicates that the expression type is incorrect (type Object, not type Integer). The reason Java won't compile this assignment is that Java is a *strongly typed language,* so the Java compiler always verifies that the type of the expression (aThing is type Object) being assigned is compatible with the variable type (aNum is type Integer). We show how to use casting to accomplish this in the next section.

Strong typing is also the reason that aThing.intValue() won't compile; the method invoked must be an instance method for class Object because aThing is type Object.

Casting in a Class Hierarchy

Java provides a familiar mechanism, *casting,* that enables us to process the object referenced by aThing through a reference variable of its actual type, instead of through a type Object reference. The expression

```
(Integer) aThing
```

casts the type of the object referenced by aThing (type Object) to type Integer. The casting operation will succeed only if the object referenced by aThing is, in fact, type Integer; if not, a ClassCastException will be thrown.

 DESIGN CONCEPT

The Importance of Strong Typing

Suppose Java did not check the expression type and simply performed the assignment

```
Integer aNum = aThing;        // Incompatible types
```

Further down the line, we might attempt to apply an Integer method to the object referenced by aNum. Because aNum is type Integer, the compiler would permit this. If aNum were referencing a type Integer object, then performing this operation would do no harm. But if aNum were referencing an object that was not type Integer, performing this operation would cause either a run-time error or an undetected logic error. It is much better to have the compiler tell us that the assignment is invalid.

What is the advantage of performing the cast? Casting gives us a type `Integer` reference to the object in Figure 3.5 that can be processed just like any other type `Integer` reference. The expression

```
((Integer) aThing).intValue()
```

will compile because now `intValue` is applied to a type `Integer` reference. Similarly, the assignment statement

```
Integer aNum = (Integer) aThing;
```

is valid because a type `Integer` reference is being assigned to `aNum` (type `Integer`).

Keep in mind that the casting operation does not change the object referenced by `aThing`; instead, it creates a type `Integer` reference to it. (This is called an *anonymous* or *unnamed reference*.) Using the type `Integer` reference, we can invoke any instance method of class `Integer` and process the object just like any other type `Integer` object.

The cast

```
(Integer) aThing
```

is called a *downcast* because we are casting from a higher type (`Object`) to a lower type (`Integer`). It is analogous to a narrowing cast when dealing with primitive types:

```
double x = . . . ;
int count = (int) x;    // Narrowing cast, double is wider type than int
```

You can downcast from a more general type (a superclass type) to a more specific type (a subclass type) in a class hierarchy, provided that the more specific type is the same type as the object being cast (for example, `(Integer) aThing`). You can also downcast from a more general type to a more specific type that is a superclass of the object being cast (for example, `(Number) aThing`). *Upcasts* (casting from a more specific type to a more general type) are always valid; however, they are unnecessary and are rarely done.

 PITFALL

Performing an Invalid Cast

Assume that `aThing` (type `Object`) references a type `Integer` object as before, and you want to get its string representation. The downcast

```
(String) aThing    // Invalid cast
```

is invalid and would cause a `ClassCastException` (a subclass of `RuntimeException`), because `aThing` references a type `Integer` object, and a type `Integer` object cannot be downcast to type `String` (`String` is not a superclass of `Integer`). However, the method call `aThing.toString()` is valid (and returns a string) because type `Object` has a `toString` method. (Which `toString` method would be called: `Object.toString` or `Integer.toString`?)

Using **instanceof** to Guard a Casting Operation

In the preceding Pitfall we mentioned that a ClassCastException occurs if we attempt an invalid casting operation. Java provides the **instanceof** *operator*, which you can use to guard against this kind of error.

EXAMPLE 3.5   The following array stuff can store 10 objects of any data type, because every object type is a subclass of Object.

```
Object[] stuff = new Object[10];
```

Assume that the array stuff has been loaded with data, and we want to find the sum of all numbers that are wrapped in objects. We can use the following loop to do so:

```
double sum = 0;
for (int i = 0; i < stuff.length; i++) {
    if (stuff[i] instanceof Number) {
        Number next = (Number) stuff[i];
        sum += next.doubleValue();
    }
}
```

The **if** condition (stuff[i] instanceof Number) is true if the object referenced by stuff[i] is a subclass of Number. It would be false if stuff[i] referenced a String or other nonnumeric object. The statement

```
Number next = (Number) stuff[i];
```

casts the object referenced by stuff[i] (type Object) to type Number and then references it through variable next (type Number). The variable next contains a reference to the same object as does stuff[i], but the type of the reference is different (type Number instead of type Object). Then the statement

```
sum += next.doubleValue();
```

invokes the appropriate doubleValue method to extract the numeric value and add it to sum. Rather than declare variable next, you could write the **if** statement as

```
if (stuff[i] instanceof Number)
    sum += ((Number) stuff[i]).doubleValue();
```

PROGRAM STYLE

Polymorphism Eliminates Nesting if Statements

If Java didn't support polymorphism, the **if** statement just shown would be much more complicated. You would need to write something like the following

```
// Inefficient code that does not take advantage of polymorphism
if (stuff[i] instanceof Integer)
    sum += ((Integer) stuff[i]).doubleValue();
else if (stuff[i] instanceof Double)
    sum += ((Double) stuff[i]).doubleValue();
else if (stuff[i] instanceof Float)
    sum += ((Float) stuff[i]).doubleValue();
    . . .
```

Each condition here uses the instanceof operator to determine the data type of the actual object referenced by stuff[i]. Once the type is known, we cast to that type and call its doubleValue method. Obviously this code is very cumbersome and is more likely to be flawed than the original **if** statement. More importantly, if a new wrapper class is defined for numbers, we would need to modify the **if** statement to process objects of this new class type. So be wary of selection statements like the one shown here—their presence often indicates that you are not taking advantage of polymorphism.

Downcasting an Interface Type

All that you have learned regarding superclass (general) and subclass (specific) references to objects applies to interfaces (general) and implementors of an interface (specific). An object whose type implements an interface must have all the methods declared in the interface, so you can reference such an object through a reference variable that is of the interface type:

```
PhoneDirectory directory = new ArrayBasedPD();
```

Because an object referenced through an interface variable must be an instance of one of the implementors of the interface, you can downcast the interface reference to the specific implementor type:

```
((ArrayBasedPD) directory).get("Jane")
```

The Method Object.equals

The Object.equals method has a parameter of type Object. It compares two objects to determine whether they are equal. The result depends on the contents of the objects, not their addresses. You must override the equals method if you want to be able to compare two objects of a class. For example, class String provides an equals method with the header

```
public boolean equals(Object obj)
```

that compares the character sequences contained in two String objects. We show how to write an equals method next.

EXAMPLE 3.6   Suppose we have a class `Employee` with the following data fields:

```
public class Employee {
    // Data Fields
    private String name;
    private double hours;
    private double rate;
    private Address address;
    ...
```

To determine whether two `Employee` objects are equal, we could compare all four data fields. However, it makes more sense to determine whether two objects are the same employee by comparing their `name` and `address` data fields. We now show a method `equals` that overrides the `equals` method defined in class `Object`. By overriding this method, we ensure that the `equals` method for class `Employee` will always be called when method `equals` is applied to an `Employee` object.

```
/** Determines whether the current object matches its argument.
    @param The object to be compared to the current object
    @return true if the objects have the same name and address;
            otherwise, return false.
*/
public boolean equals(Object obj) {
    if (obj instanceof Employee) {
        Employee other = (Employee) obj;
        return name.equals(other.name) &&
                address.equals(other.address);
    } else {
        return false;
    }
}
```

If the object referenced by `obj` is not type `Employee`, we return false. If it is type `Employee`, we downcast that object to type `Employee`. After the downcast, the `return` statement calls method `String.equals` to compare the `name` field of the current object to the `name` field of object `other`, and method `Address.equals` to compare the two `address` data fields. Therefore, method `equals` must also be defined in class `Address`. The method result is true if both the `name` and `address` fields match, and it is false if one or both fields do not match. The method result is also false if the downcast can't be performed because the argument is an incorrect type or **null**.

Cloning

The purpose of *cloning* in object-oriented programming is the same as cloning in biology: to create an independent copy of an object. A living clone will initially have the same attributes as the original because of heredity, but after its creation, what happens to the clone should not affect the original (and vice-versa). The same should be true in programming. Although both objects will initially store the same information, you should be able to change one without affecting the other. You might try to do that using the assignments

```
Address myOffice = new Address("Room 311", "Wachman Hall");

Employee e1 = new Employee("Sam", 40, 15.50, myOffice);
Employee e2 = e1;
```

However, what you get is two references to the same object (see Figure 3.6). Hence the statement

```
e1.setName("Jim");
```

would cause both e1.name and e2.name to reference "Jim". If the object referenced by e2 were a clone of object e1, then changing e1.name should not affect e2.name.

The Shallow Copy Problem

You could attempt to create a clone of an Employee object by constructing a new object that stores a copy of all the data field values of the current object. The following method does that.

```
public Object clone() {
    Object cloned = new Employee(name, hours, rate, address);
    return cloned;
}
```

The statement

```
Employee e2 = (Employee) e1.clone();
```

would cause e2 to reference the clone of e1. The downcast is necessary because e1.clone() returns a type Object reference and Employee is a subclass of Object. Figure 3.7 shows the objects referenced by e1 and e2.

FIGURE 3.6

Two **Employee** References to the Same Object

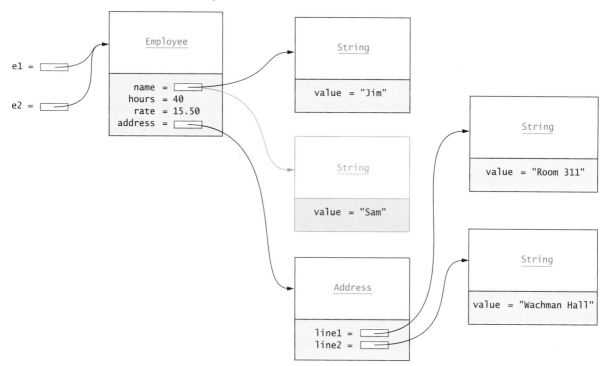

FIGURE 3.7

An **Employee** Object and a Shallow Copy

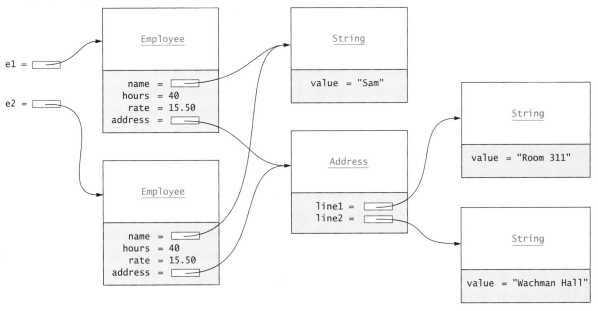

Although this clone method seems to work, it has one problem. Data field e2.rate has a copy of the value in the data field e1.rate, so you can change e2.rate without changing e1.rate. However, the data fields that are references in e2 (name and address) will reference the same objects as do e1's data fields. Because e1.address and e2.address reference the same object, e2 is considered a *shallow copy* of e1. The statement

```
e1.setAddressLine1("Room 224");
```

changes e1.address.line1, and it will also change the String referenced by e2.address.line1. What you need to do is construct a clone of e1.address as well.

It is not necessary to clone String components, because Strings are immutable. If you change e1.name, you will create a new object referenced by e1.name, and e2.name will continue to reference the original String object ("Sam").

The **Object.clone** Method

Java provides the Object.clone method to help solve the shallow copy problem. The statement

```
Employee cloned = (Employee) super.clone();
```

invokes the clone method for the superclass (method Object.clone in this case) to create the initial copy that is referenced by cloned. The initial copy is a shallow copy because the current object's data fields are copied to object cloned. To make a *deep copy* (see Figure 3.8), you must create cloned copies of all components (excluding Strings and primitive values) by invoking their respective clone methods. For class

Employee, you would need to clone data field address (type Address). In Figure 3.8, if you change e1.address.line1, it will reference a new string, but e2.address.line1 will continue to reference the string "Room 311".

Assuming class Address has a clone method, the statement

```
cloned.address = (Address) address.clone();
```

invokes it to create a clone of the object referenced by data field address. Therefore, you can successfully clone an Employee object only if both class Employee *and* class Address have a clone method.

The method Object.clone will generate a CloneNotSupportedException if it is called in a class that does not implement the Cloneable interface (part of java.lang). Therefore, the headings for class Employee and class Address must be

```
public class Employee implements Cloneable {
    . . .
}

public class Address implements Cloneable {
    . . .
}
```

Because CloneNotSupportedException is a checked exception class, the method clone must either catch a CloneNotSupportedException or declare that one can be thrown. Because the exception should never occur in a class that implements Cloneable, we place the call inside a **try-catch** sequence, and throw the exception InternalError (an unrecoverable error) in the **catch** block. We show the clone method for class Employee next.

```
/** Method clone for class Employee. Clones an Employee object.
    @return A clone of this object
*/
public Object clone() {
    try {
        Employee cloned = (Employee) super.clone();
        cloned.address = (Address) address.clone();
        return cloned;
    } catch (CloneNotSupportedException ex) {
        throw new InternalError();
    }
}
```

The class Address must have a clone method that is similar to the one shown for Employee. Because class Address contains only type String fields (immutable), it will not need to clone any of its components.

```
/** Method clone for class Address. Clones an Address object.
    @return A clone of this object
*/
public Object clone() {
    try {
        Address cloned = (Address) super.clone();
        return cloned;
    } catch (CloneNotSupportedException ex) {
        throw new InternalError();
    }
}
```

FIGURE 3.8
Deep Copy or Clone of an Object

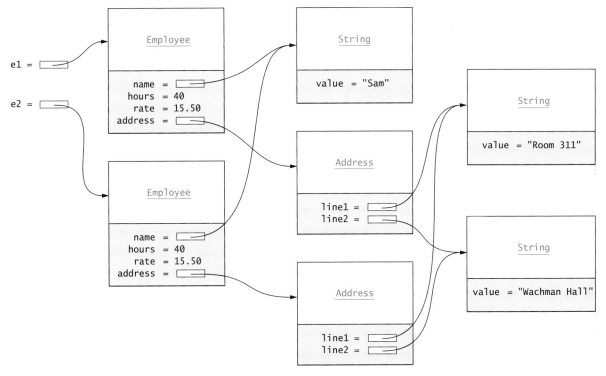

🚫 **PITFALL**

Improper Call to `Object.clone`

To help detect improper uses of `Object.clone`, Java has defined it to have protected visibility instead of public visibility. If you forget to define a `clone` method in class `Address`, for example, the call `address.clone()` will invoke the inherited method `Object.clone`. This will result in the syntax error `method clone() has protected access in class java.lang.Object`.

🚫 **PITFALL**

Failure to Declare `implements Cloneable`

If you override the `clone` method, but fail to declare that your class implements the `Cloneable` interface, when you call `super.clone()`, the `CloneNotSupported-Exception` will be thrown.

PROGRAM STYLE

Dealing with the CloneNotSupportedException

The CloneNotSupportedException is thrown by the Object.clone method if the object is not an instance of a class that implements Cloneable. If you have declared your class to implement Cloneable, this exception should not be thrown. However, it is a checked exception, so you must enclose it within a **try-catch** sequence anyway. You may then ask what you should put in the **catch** block. Many programmers leave it empty. The approach suggested by the designers of Java is to throw the exception InternalError. This exception indicates that there is some error in the Java Virtual Machine, which would be the case if this exception were to be thrown.

EXERCISES FOR SECTION 3.4

SELF-CHECK

1. What is the difference between a shallow copy and a deep copy?
2. Why is it not a problem to have a shallow copy of a String or primitive type data field?
3. Show what happens in Figure 3.7 (shallow copy) when the following statements exit.
   ```
   e2.setLine1("Room 345");
   e2.setLine2("College Hall");
   ```
   Contrast this with what happens when the following statement executes:
   ```
   e2.address = new Address("Room 345", "College Hall");
   ```
4. Answer Exercise 3 for Figure 3.8 (deep copy).

PROGRAMMING

1. Complete class Address.
2. Write a clone method for class LapTop (Listing 3.3) and class Computer (Listing 3.1). What other changes are needed to the class definitions?
3. Write a clone method for the following class. What other clone methods must be defined? *Hint:* When you clone data field wings, you should cast the result to type Wing[]. The clone operation is already implemented for arrays.
   ```
   public class Airplane {
       // Data Fields
       Engine eng;
       Rudder rud;
       Wing[] wings = new Wing[2];
   . . . }
   ```

3.5 Multiple Inheritance, Multiple Interfaces, and Delegation

The ability to extend more than one class is called *multiple inheritance*. Multiple inheritance can be a useful concept in some class hierarchies. For example, you could have a class Student and also a class Employee. A university would have many students who are full-time students and many employees who are full-time employees, but there would also be some student workers who are both students and employees. This suggests the hierarchy in Figure 3.9. In this diagram, the data fields shown for the three subclasses are all inherited from their superclasses.

Multiple inheritance is a language feature that is difficult to implement and can lead to ambiguity. If a class extends two classes, and each declares the same data field (for example, name and address in Student and Employee) or instance method, which one does the subclass inherit? For this reason, Java does not allow a class to extend more than one class.

Using Multiple Interfaces to Emulate Multiple Inheritance

If we define two interfaces StudentInt and EmployeeInt, a StudentWorker class can implement both these interfaces (there is no limit to the number of interfaces a class can implement). Figure 3.10 shows a new class hierarchy that includes these interfaces. Instead of extending class Student, class StudentWorker implements a StudentInt interface. Listing 3.5 shows the interfaces. Note that we declare abstract method getName in both interfaces. Because both declarations have the same signature and return type, they are considered to be the same method.

FIGURE 3.9
Class StudentWorker
Extends Student and
Employee

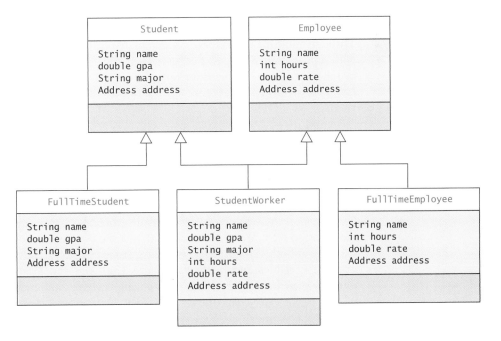

FIGURE 3.10

Class Hierarchy with Interfaces `StudentInt` and `EmployeeInt`

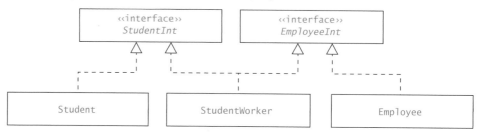

LISTING 3.5

Interfaces `StudentInt` and `EmployeeInt`

```
/** Interface StudentInt */
public interface StudentInt {
    String getName();
    double getGPA();
    String getMajor();
    Address getAddress();
}

/** Interface EmployeeInt */
public interface EmployeeInt {
    String getName();
    double getHours();
    double getRate();
    Address getAddress();
}
```

Through multiple interfaces, we get many of the benefits of multiple inheritance without the disadvantages. Because class `StudentWorker` implements both interfaces, instances of class `StudentWorker` can be referenced through variables of type `EmployeeInt` and `StudentInt`. For example, the three following declarations are valid:

```
StudentWorker sam = new StudentWorker("Sam", 3.8, "computer science",
                                      40.00, 20.0,
                                      new Address("room 25", "new dorm"));
StudentInt samStu = sam;
EmployeeInt samEmp = sam;
```

The variables `sam`, `samStu`, and `samEmp` all reference the same `StudentWorker` object.

Unfortunately, we cannot declare instance variables (or define actual methods) in an interface, so we will need to declare all instance variables and define all methods for students in both class `Student` and class `StudentWorker`. The same holds true for the instance variables and methods of class `Employee` and `StudentWorker`. We discuss one way to reduce the problem of duplicate variables and method declarations next.

PITFALL

If a class implements two interfaces that contain methods with the same signature, the methods must also have the same return type; otherwise a compiler error will occur. If these interfaces define constants with the same name and data type, you must refer to them using the interface name as a prefix.

Example:

```
interface RainbowColors {
    // Associate integers with colors.
    int RED = 1; int ORANGE = 2; int YELLOW = 3; int GREEN = 4;
    int BLUE = 5; int VIOLET = 6;
}
interface DisplayColors {
    // Associate RGB color values with colors.
    int RED = 0xff0000; int YELLOW = 0xffff00; int GREEN = 0x00ff00;
    int CYAN = 0x00ffff; int BLUE = 0x0000ff; int MAGENTA = 0xff00ff;
}
class UseColors implements RainbowColors, DisplayColors {
    int defaultColor = RED;    // Does not compile.
    int someRainbowColor = RainbowColors.RED;   // OK
    int someDisplayColor = DisplayColors.RED;   // OK
}
```

Implementing Reuse Through Delegation

In implementing class StudentWorker, we would need to define the data fields and methods (except for constructors) defined in class Student and class Employee. Besides the nuisance of typing in all the data fields and methods in more than one place, this leads to a problem of *version control*. If we make a change to a method in class Student, we have to remember to make the same change to the method in class StudentWorker. We can reduce this duplication by introducing the implementation technique known as *delegation* by which a method of one class accomplishes an operation by delegating it to a method in another class. To use delegation, we need to declare data fields of type Student and Employee in class StudentWorker. Figure 3.11 shows the modified UML diagrams. The filled-in diamonds represent class composition or the *has-a* relationship (that is, a StudentWorker *has* a Student component).

Declaring data fields student (type Student) and employee (type Employee) in class StudentWorker,

```
public class StudentWorker implements StudentInt, EmployeeInt {
    private Student student;
    private Employee employee;
. . . }
```

enables us to write method getGPA as follows:

```
public double getGPA() { return student.getGPA(); }
```

FIGURE 3.11
UML Diagram with
Delegation

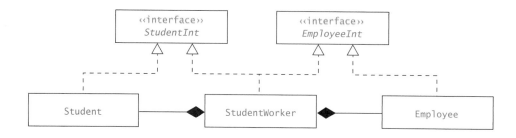

In other words, we have delegated the task of getting this student worker's GPA to
Student's getGPA method. Listing 3.6 shows class StudentWorker.

LISTING 3.6
Class StudentWorker with Delegation

```
/** Class to represent a student worker using delegation. */
public class StudentWorker implements StudentInt, EmployeeInt {
    private Student student;
    private Employee employee;

    public StudentWorker(String nam, double grade, String maj,
                         double hour, double rat, Address addr) {
        student = new Student(nam, grade, maj, addr);
        employee = new Employee(nam, hour, rat, addr);
    }

    public String getName() { return student.getName(); }
    public double getGPA() { return student.getGPA(); }
    public String getMajor() { return student.getMajor(); }
    public Address getAddress() { return student.getAddress(); }
    public double getHours() { return employee.getHours(); }
    public double getRate() { return employee.getRate(); }
}
```

EXERCISES FOR SECTION 3.5

SELF-CHECK

1. Explain how delegation solves the problem of version control.

PROGRAMMING

1. Write class Employee and class Student.
2. Write clone methods for class Student and class StudentWorker.

3.6 Packages and Visibility

Packages

You have already seen packages. The Java API is organized into packages such as `java.lang`, `java.util`, `java.io`, and `javax.swing`. The package to which a class belongs is declared by the first statement in the file in which the class is defined using the keyword **package** followed by the package name. For example, we could begin each class in the computer hierarchy (class `LapTop` and class `Computer`) with the line:

```
package computers;
```

All classes in the same package are stored in the same directory or folder. The directory must have the same name as the package. All the classes in the folder must declare themselves to be in the package.

Classes that are not part of a package may access only public members (data fields or methods) of classes in the package. If the application class is not in the package, it must reference the classes by their complete names. The complete name of a class is *packageName.className*. However, if the package is imported by the application class, then the prefix *packageName.* is not required. For example, we can reference the constant `GREEN` in class `java.awt.Color` as `Color.GREEN` if we import package `java.awt`. Otherwise, we would need to use the complete name `java.awt.Color.GREEN`.

The No-Package-Declared Environment

So far we have not specified packages, yet objects of one class could communicate with objects of another class. How does this work? Just as there is a default visibility, there is a default package. Files that do not specify a package are considered part of the default package. Therefore, if you don't declare packages, all your classes belong to the same package (the default package).

SYNTAX **Package Declaration**

FORM:

package *packageName*;

EXAMPLE:

package computers;

INTERPRETATION:

This declaration appears as the first line of the file in which a class is defined. The class is now considered part of the package. This file must be contained in a folder with the same name as the package.

PROGRAM STYLE

When to Package Classes

The default package facility is intended for use during the early stages of implementing classes or for small prototype programs. If you are developing an application that has several classes that are part of a hierarchy of classes, you should declare them all to be in the same package. The package declaration will keep you from accidentally referring to classes by their short names in other classes that are outside the package. It will also restrict visibility of protected members of a class to only its subclasses outside the package (and to other classes inside the package) as intended.

Package Visibility

So far, we have discussed three layers of visibility for classes and class members (data fields and methods): private, protected, and public. There is a fourth layer, called *package visibility*, that sits between private and protected. Classes, data fields, and methods with package visibility are accessible to all other methods of the same package but are not accessible to methods outside of the package. By contrast, classes, data fields, and methods that are declared protected are visible within subclasses that are declared outside the package, in addition to being visible to all members of the package.

We have used the visibility modifiers **private**, **public**, and **protected** to specify the visibility of a class member. If we do not use one of these visibility modifiers, then the class member has package visibility and it is visible in all classes of the same package, but not outside the package. Note that there is no visibility modifier **package**; package visibility is the default if no visibility modifier is specified.

Visibility Supports Encapsulation

The rules for visibility control how encapsulation occurs in a Java program. Table 3.3 summarizes the rules in order of decreasing protection.

Notice that private visibility is for members of a class that should not be accessible to anyone but the class, not even classes that extend it. Except for inner classes, it does not make sense for a class to be private. It would mean that no other class can use it.

Also notice that package visibility (the default if a visibility modifier is not given) allows the developer of a library to shield classes and class members from classes outside the package. Typically such classes perform tasks required by the public classes within the package.

Use of protected visibility allows the package developer to give control to other programmers who want to extend classes in the package. Protected data fields are typically essential to an object. Similarly, protected methods are those that are essential to an extending class.

Table 3.3 shows that public classes and members are universally visible. Within a package, the public classes are those that are essential to communicating with objects outside the package.

TABLE 3.3
Summary of Kinds of Visibility

Visibility	Applied to Classes	Applied to Class Members
`private`	Applicable to inner classes. Accessible only to members of the class in which it is declared.	Visible only within this class.
Default or package	Visible to classes in this package.	Visible to classes in this package.
`protected`	Applicable to inner classes. Visible to classes in this package and to classes outside the package that extend the class in which it is declared.	Visible to classes in this package and to classes outside the package that extend this class.
`public`	Visible to all classes.	Visible to all classes. The class defining the member must also be public.

 PITFALL

Protected Visibility Can Be Equivalent to Public Visibility

The intention of protected visibility is to enable a subclass to access a member (data field or method) of a superclass directly. However, protected members can also be accessed within any class that is in the same package. This is not a problem if the class with the protected members is declared to be in a package; however, if it is not, then it is in the default package. Protected members of a class in the default package are visible in all other classes you have defined that are not part of an actual package. This is generally not a desirable situation. You can avoid this dilemma by using protected visibility only with members of classes that are in explicitly declared packages. In all other classes, use either public or private visibility because protected visibility is virtually equivalent to public visibility.

EXERCISES FOR SECTION 3.6

SELF-CHECK

1. Consider the following declarations:

```
package pack1;
public class Class1 {
    private int v1;
    protected int v2;
    int v3;
    public int v4;
}

package pack1;
public class Class2 { . . . }

package pack2;
public class Class3 extends pack1.Class1 { . . . }

package pack2;
public class Class4 { . . . }
```

   a. What visibility must variables declared in pack1.Class1 have in order to be visible in pack1.Class2?
   b. What visibility must variables declared in pack1.Class1 have in order to be visible in pack2.Class3?
   c. What visibility must variables declared in pack1.Class1 have in order to be visible in pack2.Class4?

3.7 A Shape Class Hierarchy

In this section we illustrate some of the principles in this chapter. We will use a class hierarchy with several interfaces and simulate multiple inheritance using delegation.

CASE STUDY   Drawing Geometric Figures

Problem We would like to draw some standard geometric shapes on the screen. Each figure object will be one of three standard shapes (rectangle, circle, right triangle) and can appear anywhere on the screen with any interior color or border color. We would also like to be able to do standard computations, such as finding the area and perimeter, for any of these shapes.

Analysis For each of the shapes we can draw, we need a class that represents the shape and knows how to perform the standard computations on it (that is, find its area and perimeter). These classes will be `Rectangle`, `Circle`, and `RtTriangle`. To ensure that these shape classes all define the required computational methods, we will require them to implement an interface, `ShapeInt`. If the class does not have the required methods, we will get a syntax error when we attempt to compile it.

For each shape object, we also need a class that knows how to *draw* that shape object (`DrawableRectangle`, `DrawableCircle`, `DrawableTriangle`). To draw an object on the screen, we must know the object's position on the screen (x, y coordinates), dimensions, interior color, and border color. Except for the object's dimensions, these attributes are the same for all drawable objects, so we can create a class `Drawable` that stores these attributes, rather than storing them in each drawable object class.

FIGURE 3.12
Interface **ShapeInt** and Three Implementors

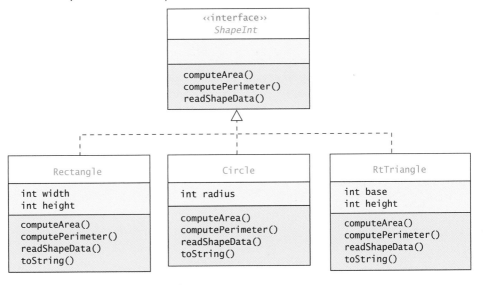

Class `DrawableRectangle` cannot be a subclass of both `Rectangle` and `Drawable`, because Java does not support multiple inheritance. However, we can define an abstract class `DrawableShape` that is a subclass of `Drawable` and implements the `ShapeInt` interface. The `DrawableShape` class will contain a reference to an object that implements the `ShapeInt` interface (`Rectangle`, `Circle`, `RtTriangle`) and will use delegation to implement its methods. Each subclass of `DrawableShape` (`DrawableRectangle`, `DrawableCircle`, `DrawableTriangle`) will, on instantiation, initialize this reference to the appropriate concrete `ShapeInt` object. Thus `DrawableRectangle` will initialize the reference to a `Rectangle`, `DrawableCircle` will initialize it to a `Circle`, and `DrawableTriangle` will initialize it to a `RtTriangle`.

To ensure that all the methods necessary for drawing and positioning objects are defined, we will also need an interface `DrawableInt` that declares these methods (`drawMe`, `setPos`, and so on). This is the interface that drawing applications will use to reference the family of drawable shapes. `DrawableShape` will implement both the `ShapeInt` and `DrawableInt` interfaces, but, because it is an abstract class, it does not need to implement the `drawMe` method. This method must be implemented by its subclasses because it will be different for each subclass. Figure 3.13 shows the class hierarchy.

Notice that `DrawableShape` inherits the methods from class `Drawable` required to implement the `DrawableInt` interface except for method `drawMe`, which is defined in each subclass (`DrawableRectangle` and so on). `DrawableShape` defines the methods needed to implement the `ShapeInt` interface, and these are inherited by each subclass.

Although `Rectangle` is shown as a component of `DrawableRectangle`, that is not really the case. As mentioned, `Rectangle` is a possible component of `DrawableShape` that would be initialized through `DrawableRectangle`.

Design We will focus on the top three actual classes in Figure 3.13: `Rectangle`, `Drawable`, and `DrawableRectangle`. Class `Rectangle` has data fields `width` and `height` and methods `computeArea`, `computePerimeter`, and `readShapeData`, which reads the figure's parameters. For the sake of brevity, we will not show all the accessor and modifier methods for these classes.

Table 3.4 shows class `Rectangle`. Class `Rectangle` has data fields `width` and `height`. It has methods to compute area and perimeter, to read in the attributes of a rectangular object (`readShapeData`), and a `toString` method. Although not shown in our class diagram, we will use class `JOptionPane` from the `javax.swing` API to read the shape data.

FIGURE 3.13
Drawable Shapes Hierarchy

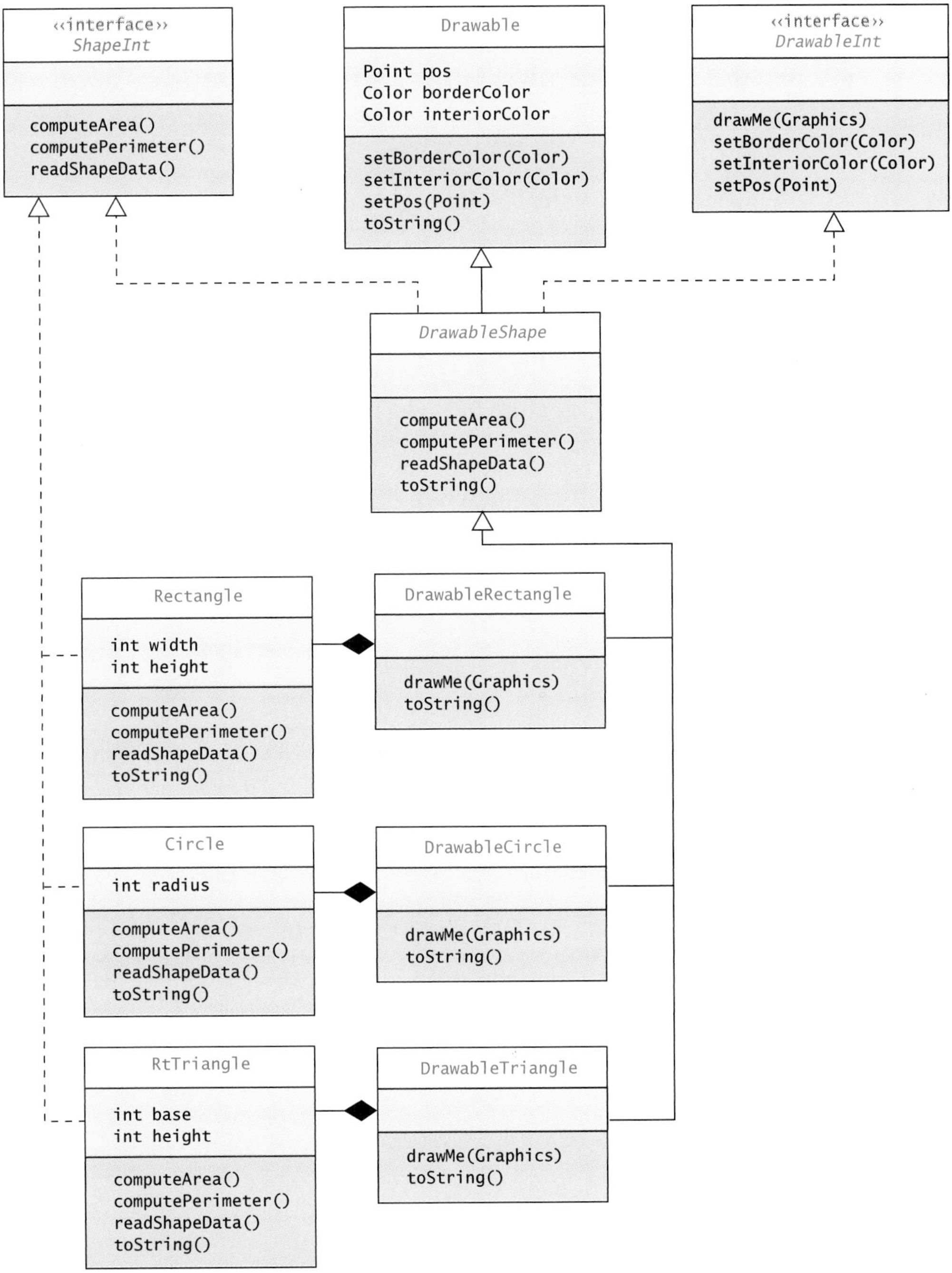

TABLE 3.4
Class `Rectangle`

Data Field	Attribute
`int width`	Width of a rectangle
`int height`	Height of a rectangle
Method	**Behavior**
`double computeArea()`	Computes the rectangle area (width × height).
`double computePerimeter()`	Computes the rectangle perimeter (2 × width + 2 × height).
`void readShapeData()`	Reads the width and height.
`String toString()`	Returns a string representing the state.

Class `Drawable` (see Table 3.5) has data fields that represent information needed to display an object on the screen. These are its position `pos` (type `Point`) and its `interiorColor` and `borderColor` (both type `Color`). Classes `Point`, `Color`, and `Graphics` are defined in the API `java.awt` (Abstract Window Toolkit), which contains some of the classes for drawing and graphics used in this case study.

TABLE 3.5
Class `Drawable`

Data Field	Attribute
`Point pos`	(x, y) position on screen
`Color borderColor`	Border color
`Color interiorColor`	Interior color
Methods	**Behavior**
`void setPos(Point p)`	Sets the (x, y) screen position.
`void setBorderColor(Color col)`	Sets the border color to its argument.
`void setInteriorColor(Color col)`	Sets the interior color to its argument.
`String toString()`	Returns a string representing the state.

TABLE 3.6
Class DrawableShape

Data Field	Attribute
ShapeInt theShape	Reference to an object that implements the ShapeInt interface
Method	**Behavior**
double computeArea()	Computes the area of the shape.
double computePerimeter()	Computes the perimeter of the shape.
void readShapeData()	Prompts for and reads the data that defines the size of the shape.
String toString()	Returns a string representation.

TABLE 3.7
Class DrawableRectangle

Method	Behavior
void drawMe(Graphics g)	Draws the rectangle on the screen.
String toString()	Returns a string representing the state.

Class DrawableShape (Table 3.6) has a data field theShape of type ShapeInt. The DrawableShape class will delegate tasks to this object.

Class DrawableRectangle (Table 3.7) is a subclass of DrawableShape. It defines a drawMe method for drawing rectangles. It has a single argument of type Graphics, which represents the device on which the image is created. We discuss class Graphics in detail in Appendix C, "Event-Oriented Programming". The descriptions of classes DrawableCircle and DrawableTriangle are similar to those of class DrawableRectangle.

Implementation   Listing 3.7 shows interfaces ShapeInt and DrawableInt. We declare them, and all of the other classes and interfaces in this case study, to be in the package drawableShapes.

....
LISTING 3.7
Interfaces ShapeInt (ShapeInt.java) and DrawableInt (DrawableInt.java)

```java
package drawableShapes;
/** ShapeInt.java */
public interface ShapeInt {
    double computeArea();
    double computePerimeter();
    void readShapeData();
}

package drawableShapes;
import java.awt.*;

/** DrawableInt.java */
public interface DrawableInt {
    void drawMe(Graphics g);
    void setBorderColor(Color border);
    void setInteriorColor(Color inter);
    void setPos(Point p);
}
```

Listing 3.8 shows class Drawable. It declares the data fields pos, borderColor, and
interiorColor. The constructor initializes these to specified values. Because these
fields are declared **protected**, they are accessible to other members of the
drawableShapes package. Code for the modifiers is not shown. The toString
method displays the values of the data fields. The format for the Color fields displays the primary color components (red, green, and blue).

LISTING 3.8
Class Drawable (Drawable.java)

```java
package drawableShapes;
import java.awt.*;

/** This class encapsulates the common attributes of drawable objects.
*/
public class Drawable {
    // Data Fields
    /** The position of the origin of the shape. */
    protected Point pos = new Point(0, 0);
    /** The border color. */
    protected Color borderColor = Color.black;
    /** The interior color. */
    protected Color interiorColor = Color.white;
```

```
        // Constructors
        /** Construct a Drawable with the specified parameters.
            @param poi The position of the origin
            @param border The border color
            @param inter The interior color
        */
        public Drawable(Point poi, Color border, Color inter) {
            pos = poi;
            borderColor = border;
            interiorColor = inter;
        }

        /** Create a string representation of this class.
            @return A string representation of this class
        */
        public String toString() {
            return "\nx coordinate is " + pos.x
                    + ", y coordinate is " + pos.y
                    + "\nborder color is " + borderColor
                    + "\ninterior color is " + interiorColor;
        }
    }
```

Listing 3.9 shows class `DrawableShape`. Its heading shows its relationship to its superclass and interfaces:

```
        public abstract class DrawableShape extends Drawable
                            implements ShapeInt, DrawableInt {
            // Data Fields
            /** Reference to the shape object. */
            private ShapeInt theShape;
```

Each constructor initializes data field `theShape` to reference the shape object specified by the constructor argument `aShape`. Because `DrawableShape` is abstract, you can't call its constructors to create new `DrawableShape` objects, but they can be invoked by a subclass constructor to initialize the inherited data field `theShape`.

```
        public DrawableShape(Point poi, Color border, Color inter,
                            ShapeInt aShape) {
            super(poi, border, inter);
            theShape = aShape;
        }
```

We use delegation to implement the instance methods.

```
        public double computeArea() {
            return theShape.computeArea();
        }
```

LISTING 3.9
Class DrawableShape (DrawableShape.java)

```java
package drawableShapes;
import java.awt.*;

/** DrawableShape.java */
public abstract class DrawableShape extends Drawable
        implements ShapeInt, DrawableInt {
    // Data Fields
    /** Reference to the shape object. */
    protected ShapeInt theShape;

    // Constructor
    /** Construct a DrawableShape with the given parameters.
        @param poi The position of the origin
        @param border The border color
        @param inter The interior color
        @param aShape The shape
    */
    public DrawableShape(Point poi, Color border, Color inter,
                         ShapeInt aShape) {
        super(poi, border, inter);
        theShape = aShape;
    }

    // Delegated Methods
    /** Compute the area.
        @return The area
    */
    public double computeArea() {
        return theShape.computeArea();
    }

    /** Compute the perimeter.
        @return The perimeter
    */
    public double computePerimeter() {
        return theShape.computePerimeter();
    }

    /** Read the size parameters from the user. */
    public void readShapeData() {
        theShape.readShapeData();
    }
}
```

Listing 3.10 shows class Rectangle.

LISTING 3.10
Class Rectangle (Rectangle.java)

```java
package drawableShapes;
import javax.swing.*;

/** Represents a rectangle.
    Implements ShapeInt.
*/
public class Rectangle implements ShapeInt {

    // Data Fields
    /** The width of the rectangle. */
    private int width = 0;
    /** The height of the rectangle. */
    private int height = 0;

    // Constructors
    /** Constructs a rectangle of the specified size.
        @param wid the width
        @param hei the height
    */
    public Rectangle(int wid, int hei) {
        width = wid;
        height = hei;
    }

    // Methods
    /** Get the width.
        @return The width
    */
    public int getWidth() {
        return width;
    }

    /** Get the height.
        @return The height
    */
    public int getHeight() {
        return height;
    }

    /** Compute the area.
        @return The area of the rectangle
    */
    public double computeArea() {
        return height * width;
    }

    /** Compute the perimeter.
        @return the perimeter of the rectangle
```

```
    */
    public double computePerimeter() {
        return 2 * (height + width);
    }

    /** Read the parameters of the rectangle. */
    public void readShapeData() {
        String widthStr = JOptionPane.showInputDialog
            ("Enter the width of the Rectangle");
        width = Integer.parseInt(widthStr);
        String heightStr = JOptionPane.showInputDialog
            ("Enter the height of the Rectangle");
        height = Integer.parseInt(heightStr);
    }


    /** Create a string representaion of the rectangle.
        @return A string representation of the rectangle
    */
    public String toString() {
        return "Rectangle: width is " + width + ", height is " + height;
    }

}
```

Listing 3.11 shows class `DrawableRectangle`:

```
public class DrawableRectangle extends DrawableShape {
```

The constructor in class `DrawableRectangle` calls its superclass constructor, passing a new `Rectangle` object to parameter aShape.

```
public DrawableRectangle(int wid, int hei,
                         Point poi, Color border, Color inter) {
    super(poi, border, inter, new Rectangle(wid, hei));
}
```

Method drawMe calls `Graphics` methods `fillRect` (fill rectangle) and `drawRect` (draw rectangle) to draw a rectangle on the screen whose top-left corner position, width, and height are specified as arguments.

```
g.fillRect(pos.x, pos.y,
           rectangle.getWidth(), rectangle.getHeight());
g.drawRect(pos.x, pos.y,
           rectangle.getWidth(), rectangle.getHeight());
```

···············

LISTING 3.11
Class `DrawableRectangle` (DrawableRectangle.java)

```
package drawableShapes;
import java.awt.*;

/** Represents a drawable rectangle.
    Implements ShapeInt and DrawableInt.
```

```
*/
public class DrawableRectangle extends DrawableShape {

    // Constructors
    /** Construct a rectangle of the given size, position, and color.
        @param wid The width
        @param hei The height
        @param poi The coordinates of the upper left corner
        @param border The border color
        @param inter The interior color
    */
    public DrawableRectangle(int wid, int hei,
                            Point poi, Color border, Color inter) {
        super(poi, border, inter, new Rectangle(wid, hei));
    }

    /** Draw the rectangle.
        @param g The graphics context (screen)
    */
    public void drawMe(Graphics g) {
        g.setColor(interiorColor);
        Rectangle rectangle = (Rectangle) theShape;
        g.fillRect(pos.x, pos.y,
                    rectangle.getWidth(), rectangle.getHeight());
        g.setColor(borderColor);
        g.drawRect(pos.x, pos.y,
                    rectangle.getWidth(), rectangle.getHeight());
    }

    public String toString() {
        return "Drawable " + theShape + super.toString();
    }
}
```

The method `toString` returns a string that starts with the characters "Drawable". Next, the method `Rectangle.toString` appends the characters that represent the width and height of the rectangle. Then method `Drawable.toString` appends characters that represent the *x*, *y* coordinates of the top-left corner of the rectangle and characters that represent the border color and interior color of the rectangle.

The statements

```
DrawableRectangle rect = new DrawableRectangle(10, 20,
                            new Point(0, 0), Color.GREEN, Color.RED);
JOptionPane.showMessageDialog(null, rect);
```

declare a `DrawableRectangle` object, rect, and display its string representation (see Figure 3.14). The color characters are returned by method `Color.toString` and consist of the RGB (red, green, blue) component values for a color. The border color is `Color.GREEN`, which has a green component value of 255 (maximum) and 0 (minimum) for the red and blue component values.

State of a `DrawableRectangle` object

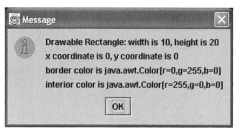

Drawable Rectangle: width is 10, height is 20
x coordinate is 0, y coordinate is 0
border color is java.awt.Color[r=0,g=255,b=0]
interior color is java.awt.Color[r=255,g=0,b=0]

OK

Listing 3.12 shows class `DrawableTriangle`. The `Graphics` class does not have a method for drawing triangles, but it does have methods for drawing polygons (`fillPolygon` and `drawPolygon`), which are called in method `drawMe` (a triangle is a polygon with three vertices). First, method `drawMe` creates a new `Polygon` `rtTri`. Next, it invokes method `addPoint` three times to add the triangle vertices to `rtTri`. Finally, methods `fillPolygon` and `drawPolygon` draw the `Polygon` `rtTri`, which is passed as an argument. We leave class `RtTriangle` as an exercise.

LISTING 3.12
Class `DrawableTriangle` (`DrawableTriangle.java`)

```
package drawableShapes;
import java.awt.*;

/** Represents a drawable triangle.
    Implements ShapeInt and DrawableInt.
*/
public class DrawableTriangle extends DrawableShape {

    // Constructor
    /** Construct a DrawableTriangle with the given color
        and position.
        @param bas The base
        @param hei The height
        @param poi The location of the lower left corner
        @param border The border color
        @param inter The interior color
    */
    public DrawableTriangle(int bas, int hei,
                            Point poi, Color border, Color inter) {
        super (poi, border, inter, new RtTriangle(bas, hei));
    }

    // Methods
    /** Draw the triangle using the given graphics context.
        @param g The graphics context
```

```
    */
    public void drawMe(Graphics g) {
        Polygon rtTri = new Polygon();
        RtTriangle triangle = (RtTriangle) theShape;
        rtTri.addPoint(pos.x, pos.y);
        rtTri.addPoint(pos.x, pos.y - triangle.getHeight());
        rtTri.addPoint(pos.x + triangle.getBase(), pos.y);
        g.setColor(interiorColor);
        g.fillPolygon(rtTri);
        g.setColor(borderColor);
        g.drawPolygon(rtTri);
    }

    /** Return a string representation of the triangle.
        @return A string representation of the triangle
    */
    public String toString() {
        return "Drawable " + theShape + super.toString();
    }
}
```

Listing 3.13 shows the class `DrawableCircle`. It invokes the method `fillOval` to draw a circle inside a square centered at point pos. The circle fits inside the square, so the square's side dimension is twice the circle radius. We leave class `Circle` as an exercise.

....
LISTING 3.13
Class `DrawableCircle` (`DrawableCircle.java`)

```
package drawableShapes;
import java.awt.*;

/** Represents a drawable circle
    Implements ShapeInt and DrawableInt.
*/
public class DrawableCircle extends DrawableShape {

    // Constructors
    /** Construct a DrawableCircle of the given radius,
        position, and color.
        @param rad The radius
        @param poi The coordinates of the center
        @param border The background color
        @param inter The interior color
    */
    public DrawableCircle(int rad,
                          Point poi, Color border, Color inter) {
        super(poi, border, inter, new Circle(rad));
    }
```

```
// Methods
/** Draw the circle.
    @param g The graphics context (screen)
*/
public void drawMe(Graphics g) {
    g.setColor(interiorColor);
    Circle circle = (Circle) theShape;
    g.fillOval(pos.x - circle.getRadius(),
            pos.y - circle.getRadius(),
            2 * circle.getRadius(), 2 * circle.getRadius());
    g.setColor(borderColor);
    g.drawOval(pos.x - circle.getRadius(),
            pos.y - circle.getRadius(),
            2 * circle.getRadius(), 2 * circle.getRadius());
}

/** Return a string representation of the circle.
    @return A string representation
*/
public String toString() {
    return "Drawable " + theShape + super.toString();
}
}
```

Testing   Listing 3.14 shows a class, `TestDrawFigures`, that tests our class hierarchy.

```
public class TestDrawFigures extends JPanel {
```

Various elements in Listing 3.14 are fully explained in Appendix C, "Event-Oriented Programming". Class `TestDrawFigures` extends class `JPanel`. `JPanel` and `JFrame` are Swing components. A `JFrame` object is a top-level window. A `JPanel` object is a container for graphics objects (buttons, and so on) that may be placed inside a `JFrame` object.

The data field `drawableShapes` (type `Object[]`) references an array that stores a collection of drawable figures:

```
Object[] drawableShapes;
```

The constructor declares a local variable `drawableShapes` to reference an array of shape objects. The constructor also creates a collection of shape objects that are referenced by the array elements. For example, the first array element references the object created by

```
new DrawableCircle(50, new Point(50, 50),
            Color.BLUE, Color.GREEN)
```

(a green drawable circle, with blue border, of radius 50 centered at (50, 50)) .

To perform a thorough test of our class, we will fill this array with many valid shape objects that will be displayed in a window. We will also try some invalid shape objects that can't be displayed.

The statement
```
this.drawableShapes = drawableShapes;
```
sets data field `drawableShapes` to reference the same array of shape objects as the local variable.

The **for** loop in the constructor displays each figure's area and perimeter in the console window, followed by its state. Note that each array element must be cast to type `ShapeInt` before method `computeArea` (an abstract method in `ShapeInt`) can be invoked.

The method `paintComponent` contains a **for** loop that draws each figure by invoking its `drawMe` method. Note that each array element must be cast to type `DrawableInt` before method `drawMe` can be invoked.

The `main` method statements
```
JFrame frame = new JFrame("Test Draw Figures");
frame.setSize(400, 450);
```
create a window (400 pixels by 450 pixels) with the title `Test Draw Figures`. The statement
```
frame.setContentPane(new TestDrawFigures());
```
calls method `setContentPane` to set the *content pane* (drawing surface) for the frame to be a new instance of class `TestDrawFigures`. The statement
```
frame.show();
```
makes visible what is drawn in the content pane. When this statement executes, the Windows Manager invokes method `paintComponent` of the class `TestDrawFigures` which draws the drawable shapes in the frame. (The class `JPanel` contains a method `paintComponent`; we override this method in `TestDrawFigures` to display the collection of figures.) The method `paintComponent` is called by the Windows Manager whenever the frame that contains a component is changed (e.g. it is moved, resized, or uncovered). The statement
```
frame.setDefaultCloseOperation(JFrame.EXIT_ON_CLOSE);
```
causes the program to terminate when the frame's close icon (**X**) is clicked.

LISTING 3.14
TestDrawFigures.java

```
package drawableShapes;
import java.awt.*;
import javax.swing.*;

/** Draws a collection of drawable objects stored in an array.
    Uses DrawableRectangle, DrawableCircle,
    DrawableTriangle, and awt.
```

```java
*/
public class TestDrawFigures extends JPanel {

    /** An array of DrawableShapes. */
    Object[] drawableShapes;

    /** Create some drawable shapes and compute their areas and
        perimeters.
    */
    private TestDrawFigures() {
        Object[] drawableShapes =  {
            new DrawableCircle(50, new Point (50, 50),
                                Color.BLUE, Color.GREEN),
            new DrawableRectangle(100, 200, new Point (100, 100),
                                Color.RED, Color.YELLOW),
            new DrawableTriangle(50, 100, new Point (250, 300),
                                Color.BLACK, Color.RED),
            new DrawableRectangle(60, 50, new Point(300, 200),
                                Color.ORANGE, Color.GRAY),
            new DrawableCircle(0, new Point(0, 0),
                                Color.BLACK, Color.WHITE),
            new DrawableRectangle(0, 0, new Point(0, 0),
                                Color.BLACK, Color.WHITE),
            new DrawableTriangle(0, 0, new Point(0, 0),
                                Color.BLACK, Color.WHITE),
            new DrawableCircle(-100, new Point(300, 350),
                                Color.BLACK, Color.WHITE),
            new DrawableRectangle(-50, 50, new Point(50, 400),
                                Color.GREEN, Color.RED)
        };

        // Save a reference to this array of objects.
        this.drawableShapes = drawableShapes;

        // Display three attributes of the drawable objects.
        for (int i = 0; i < drawableShapes.length; i++) {
            System.out.println("\n" + drawableShapes[i]);
            System.out.println
                ("Area: "
                + ((ShapeInt) drawableShapes[i]).computeArea()
                + ", perimeter: "
                + ((ShapeInt) drawableShapes[i]).computePerimeter());
        }
    }

    /** Main method. Create a frame and a TestDrawFigures object
        and place the TestDrawFigures into the frame.
        @param args The command line arguments - not used
```

```
    */
    public static void main(String[] args) {
        // Create a frame to display the figures.
        JFrame frame = new JFrame("Test Draw Figures");
        frame.setSize(400, 450);
        // Create a collection of figures in the content pane.
        frame.setContentPane(new TestDrawFigures());
        // Display the frame and draw the figures.
        frame.show();
        frame.setDefaultCloseOperation(JFrame.EXIT_ON_CLOSE);
    }

    /** Paint the drawable shapes.
        @param g The graphics environment
    */
    public void paintComponent(Graphics g) {
        // Paint the background.
        super.paintComponent(g);

        // Draw the drawable objects.
        for (int i = 0; i < drawableShapes.length; i++) {
            ((DrawableInt) drawableShapes[i]).drawMe(g);
        }
    }
}
```

Figure 3.15 shows the display resulting from running `TestDrawFigures`. It shows four figures: a circle, a large rectangle, a triangle, and a small rectangle. These four figures were created by

```
new DrawableCircle(50, new Point (50, 50),
                    Color.BLUE, Color.GREEN),
new DrawableRectangle(100, 200, new Point (100, 100),
                       Color.RED, Color.YELLOW),
new DrawableTriangle(50, 100, new Point (250, 300),
                      Color.BLACK, Color.RED),
new DrawableRectangle(60, 50, new Point(300, 200),
                       Color.ORANGE, Color.GRAY),
```

Observe that the circle is at the upper-left corner. This is as expected, because the center is at position (50, 50) and the radius is 50. The rightmost point of the circle should have an x-coordinate of 100, which corresponds to the x-coordinate of the left side of the large rectangle. The bottom point of the circle should have a y-coordinate of 100, which corresponds to the y-coordinate of the top side of the large rectangle. The bottom of the triangle has a y-coordinate of 300, which corresponds to the y-coordinate of the bottom of the large rectangle. The top corner of the triangle has a y-coordinate of 200, which corresponds to the y-coordinate of the top of the small rectangle. Finally, the right corner of the triangle has an x-coordinate of 300, which corresponds to the left side of the small rectangle.

FIGURE 3.15
Display of
`TestDrawFigures`

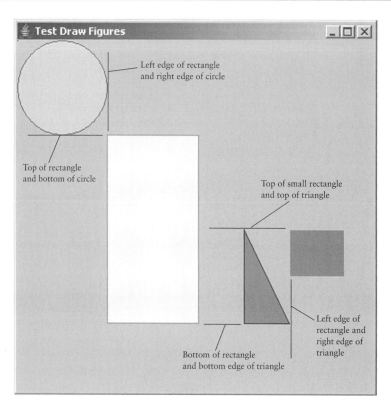

FIGURE 3.16
Console Window
from Running
`TestDrawFigures`
(first part)

```
Command Prompt - java drawableShapes.TestDrawFigures
Drawable Circle: radius is 50
x coordinate is 50, y coordinate is 50
border color is java.awt.Color[r=0,g=0,b=255]
interior color is java.awt.Color[r=0,g=255,b=0]
Area: 7853.981633974483, perimeter: 314.1592653589793

Drawable Rectangle: width is 100, height is 200
x coordinate is 100, y coordinate is 100
border color is java.awt.Color[r=255,g=0,b=0]
interior color is java.awt.Color[r=255,g=255,b=0]
Area: 20000.0, perimeter: 600.0

Drawable Right Triangle: base is 50, height is 100
x coordinate is 250, y coordinate is 300
border color is java.awt.Color[r=0,g=0,b=0]
interior color is java.awt.Color[r=255,g=0,b=0]
Area: 2500.0, perimeter: 261.8033988749895

Drawable Rectangle: width is 60, height is 50
x coordinate is 300, y coordinate is 200
border color is java.awt.Color[r=255,g=200,b=0]
interior color is java.awt.Color[r=128,g=128,b=128]
Area: 3000.0, perimeter: 220.0
```

FIGURE 3.17
Console Window
from Running
TestDrawFigures
(second part)

```
Command Prompt - java drawableShapes.TestDrawFigures                    _ □ ×
Drawable Circle: radius is 0
x coordinate is 0, y coordinate is 0
border color is java.awt.Color[r=0,g=0,b=0]
interior color is java.awt.Color[r=255,g=255,b=255]
Area: 0.0, perimeter: 0.0

Drawable Rectangle: width is 0, height is 0
x coordinate is 0, y coordinate is 0
border color is java.awt.Color[r=0,g=0,b=0]
interior color is java.awt.Color[r=255,g=255,b=255]
Area: 0.0, perimeter: 0.0

Drawable Right Triangle: base is 0, height is 0
x coordinate is 0, y coordinate is 0
border color is java.awt.Color[r=0,g=0,b=0]
interior color is java.awt.Color[r=255,g=255,b=255]
Area: 0.0, perimeter: 0.0

Drawable Circle: radius is -100
x coordinate is 300, y coordinate is 350
border color is java.awt.Color[r=0,g=0,b=0]
interior color is java.awt.Color[r=255,g=255,b=255]
Area: 31415.926535897932, perimeter: -628.3185307179587

Drawable Rectangle: width is -50, height is 50
x coordinate is 50, y coordinate is 400
border color is java.awt.Color[r=0,g=255,b=0]
interior color is java.awt.Color[r=255,g=0,b=0]
Area: -2500.0, perimeter: 0.0
```

Figure 3.16 shows the portion of the console window that displays the areas and perimeters of these four figures. Using a calculator, we can verify that the values displayed are correct.

The test program generates three additional figures that are not valid shape objects:

```
new DrawableCircle(0, new Point(0, 0),
                   Color.BLACK, Color.WHITE),
new DrawableRectangle(0, 0, new Point(0, 0),
                      Color.BLACK, Color.WHITE),
new DrawableTriangle(0, 0, new Point(0, 0),
                     Color.BLACK, Color.WHITE),
```

The first three are displayed as a single pixel in the upper left corner (0, 0), and may not be visible in Figure 3.15. Figure 3.17 shows the console output. The perimeters and areas for these are all zero, as expected.

Finally, two figures with negative size parameters are created:

```
new DrawableCircle(-100, new Point(300, 350),
                   Color.BLACK, Color.WHITE),
new DrawableRectangle(-50, 50, new Point(50, 400),
                      Color.GREEN, Color.RED)
```

These are not displayed in Figure 3.15. Also, as can be seen in Figure 3.17, the computation of area and perimeter is not correct.

This demonstrates the value of boundary condition testing, which was discussed in Chapter 2. The tests using negative sizes indicate that there is a defect either in our requirements or possibly in our implementation. The requirements did not specify that the sizes had to be positive, neither did they specify what to do with negative sizes. Correcting these defects is left as an exercise.

EXERCISES FOR SECTION 3.7

SELF-CHECK

1. Explain the role of delegation in the case study. Which class employs it? Why was it necessary?
2. Explain why it was necessary to cast elements of array `drawableShapes` to type `DrawableInt` before invoking method `drawMe` and to type `ShapeInt` before invoking method `computeArea`. Why was it not necessary to do this before displaying each element's state?
3. Why must class `DrawableShape` be an abstract class?
4. Modify the requirements to either specifically allow or specifically reject negative sizes. Also specify the action to take when presented with negative sizes.

PROGRAMMING

1. Write class `Circle`.
2. Write class `RtTriangle`.
3. Modify the classes as necessary to meet the modified requirements you developed in response to Self-Check Exercise 4.

3.8 Object Factories

An object factory is a method that creates instances of other classes. You might ask, "Doesn't the **new** operator do that already?" The answer is yes, it does, but when you use the **new** operator to invoke the constructor, you need to provide the parameters. Also, you can't instantiate interfaces or abstract classes, but you can declare a reference variable whose type is an interface or abstract class and have that variable reference an actual object (an implementation). However, you may not know which implementation of an interface or abstract class is appropriate. Object factories are useful under the following circumstances:

- The necessary parameters are not known or must be derived via computation.
- The appropriate implementation of an interface or abstract class should be selected as the result of some computation.

We illustrate the use of an object factory in the following case study.

CASE STUDY   Compute Areas and Perimeters of Geometric Shapes

Problem   We want to write a program that determines the area and perimeter for a variety of geometric shapes. The user should be prompted for the kind of shape and the parameters appropriate for that shape. The program should then display the area and perimeter.

Analysis   The interface `ShapeInt` requires that each class that implements that interface provide the methods `computeArea` and `computePerimeter`. We can use these classes to do the computation. We need to design a method to provide an appropriate instance of `ShapeInt` based on the response to the prompt for the kind of figure.

Design   Our program will be encapsulated in the class `ComputeAreaAndPerim`, which will contain static methods `main`, `getShape`, and `displayResult`. The `main` method calls `getShape` to prompt for the kind of shape. This method returns a reference to a `ShapeInt` object. The methods `computeArea` and `computePerimeter` are then called to obtain the values of the area and perimeter. Finally, `displayResult` is called to display the result.

The method `getShape` is an example of a *factory method*. The author of the `main` method has no awareness of the individual kinds of shapes. Knowledge of the available shapes is confined to the `getShape` method. This method must present a list of available shapes to the user and decode the user's response to return an instance of the desired shape.

Implementation   The code for `ComputeAreaAndPerim` is shown in Listing 3.15. The `main` method is very straightforward, and so is `displayResult`. The `main` method first calls `getShape`, which constructs a list of available shapes and prompts the user for the choice. The reply is expected to be a single character. The nested **if** statement determines which shape instance to return. For example, if the user's choice is C (for Circle), the statement

```
    return new Circle();
```

returns a new `Circle` object.

After the new shape instance is returned to `myShape` in `main`, the statement

```
    myShape.readShapeData();
```

invokes method `readShapeData` to read the shape object's parameter(s). This method must be declared in interface `ShapeInt` and defined in each class.

....
LISTING 3.15
Class `ComputeAreaAndPerim.java`

```
import javax.swing.JOptionPane;

/**
    Computes the area and perimeter of selected figures.
```

```java
*/
public class ComputeAreaAndPerim {

    /** The main program performs the following steps.
        1. It asks the user for the type of figure.
        2. It asks the user for the characteristics of that figure.
        3. It computes the perimeter.
        4. It computes the area.
        5. It displays the result.
        @param args The command line arguments -- not used
    */
    public static void main(String args[]) {
        ShapeInt myShape;
        double perimeter;
        double area;
        myShape = getShape();                         // Ask for figure type
        myShape.readShapeData();                      // Read the shape data
        perimeter = myShape.computePerimeter();  // Compute perimeter
        area = myShape.computeArea();                 // Compute the area
        displayResult(area, perimeter);               // Display the result
        System.exit(0);                               // Exit the program
    }

    /** Ask the user for the type of figure.
        @return An instance of the selected shape
    */
    public static ShapeInt getShape() {
        String figType = JOptionPane.showInputDialog(
            "Enter C for circle\nEnter R for Rectangle\n"
            + "Enter T for rightTriangle");
        if (figType.equalsIgnoreCase("c")) {
            return new Circle();
        } else if (figType.equalsIgnoreCase("r")) {
            return new Rectangle();
        } else if (figType.equalsIgnoreCase("t")) {
            return new RtTriangle();
        } else {
            return null;
        }
    }

    /** Display the result of the computation.
        @param area The area of the figure
        @param perim The perimeter of the figures
    */
    private static void displayResult(double area, double perim) {
        JOptionPane.showMessageDialog(null, "The area is " + area
                                    + "\nThe perimeter is " + perim);
    }
}
```

EXERCISES FOR SECTION 3.8

SELF-CHECK

1. Discuss how you might test the application in Listing 3.15 to make sure that it works properly.

PROGRAMMING

1. Write method readShapeData for class Rectangle and Circle.
2. Write an application that uses an object factory. Base it on the program in Listing 3.15.

Chapter Review

- Inheritance and class hierarchies enable you to capture the idea that one thing may be a refinement or extension of another. For example, a plant is a living thing. Such *is-a* relationships create the right balance between too much and too little structure. Think of inheritance as a means of creating a refinement of an abstraction. The entities farther down the hierarchy are more complex and less general than those higher up. The entities farther down the hierarchy may inherit data members (attributes) and methods from those farther up, but not vice versa. A class that inherits from another class **extends** that class.

- Encapsulation and inheritance impose structure on object abstractions. Polymorphism provides a degree of flexibility in defining methods. It loosens the structure a bit in order to make methods more accessible and useful. Polymorphism means "many forms." It captures the idea that methods may take on a variety of forms to suit different purposes.

- The keyword **interface** defines an interface. A class that realizes an interface **implements** the interface and must define the methods that the interface declares. Interfaces provide a substitute for multiple inheritance (which is unavailable in Java) because a class can implement more than one interface.

- The keyword **abstract** defines an abstract class or method. An abstract class is like an interface in that it leaves method implementations up to subclasses, but it can also have data fields and actual methods. You use an abstract class as the superclass/subclass for a group of classes in a hierarchy.

◆ Delegation is also a technique that can be used to gain some of the advantages of multiple inheritance. You can create a class that has objects of other classes as its members (the *has-a* relationship). You can access the data of the component classes in the new class. You can write methods for the new class by delegating tasks to methods that perform the same operation in its component classes.

◆ Visibility is influenced by the package in which a class is declared. You assign classes to a package by including the statement **package** *packageName*; at the top of the file. You can refer to classes within a package by their direct names when the package is imported through an `import` declaration.

Java Constructs Introduced in This Chapter

extends	abstract	private
super(...)	instanceof	protected
super.	package	
this(...)	public	

Java API Classes Introduced in This Chapter

java.awt.Color	java.lang.Byte	java.lang.Number
java.awt.Graphics	java.lang.Float	java.lang.Object
java.awt.Point	java.lang.Integer	java.lang.Short

User-Defined Interfaces and Classes in This Chapter

Computer	StudentWorker	DrawableShape
LapTop	Drawable	Triangle
Food	DrawableInt	DrawableTriangle
Employee	ShapeInt	DrawableCircle
Student	DrawableRectangle	TestDrawFigures
StudentInt	Rectangle	ComputeAreaAndPerim
EmployeeInt	RtTriangle	

Quick-Check Exercises

1. What does polymorphism mean, and how is it used in Java? What is method overriding? Method overloading?
2. What is a method signature? Describe how it is used in method overloading.
3. Describe the use of the keywords **super** and **this**.
4. When would you use an abstract class, and what should it contain?
5. When would you use an interface? Can a class implement more than one interface? What does an interface contain?
6. Describe the difference between *is-a* and *has-a* relationships.
7. Which can have more data fields and methods: the superclass or the subclass?
8. You can reference an object of a _____ type through a variable of a _____ type.
9. You cast an object referenced by a _____ type to an object of a _____ type in order to apply methods of the _____ type to the object. This is called a _____.
10. The four kinds of visibility in order of decreasing visibility are: _____, _____, _____, and _____.

Answers to Quick-Check Exercises

1. *Polymorphism* means "many forms." *Method overriding* means that the same method appears in a subclass and a superclass. *Method overloading* means that the same method appears with different signatures in the same class.

2. A signature is the form of a method determined by its name, and arguments. For example, `doIt(int, double)` is the signature for a method `doIt` that has one type `int` parameter and one type **double** parameter. If several methods in a class have the same name (method overloading), Java applies the one with the same signature as the method call.

3. The keyword **this** followed by a dot and a name means use the named member (data field or method) of the object to which the current method is applied rather than the member with the same name declared locally in the method. The keyword **super.** means use the method (or data field) with this name defined in the superclass of the object, not the one belonging to the object. Using **super(...)** as a method call in a constructor tells Java to call a constructor for the superclass of the object being created. Similarly, using **this(...)** as a method call in a constructor tells Java to call another constructor for the same class but with a different parameter list. The **super(...)** or **this(...)** call must be the first statement in a subclass constructor.

4. An abstract class is used as a parent class for a collection of related subclasses. An abstract class cannot be instantiated. The abstract methods (identified by modifier **abstract**) defined in the abstract class act as placeholders for the actual methods. Also, you should define data fields that are common to all the subclasses in the abstract class. An abstract class can have actual methods as well as abstract methods.

5. An interface is used to specify that a collection of classes has some common functionality. It allows the definition of abstract methods and constants (identified by the modifiers **static final**) for the subclasses of a hierarchy of classes. It provides all the advantages of using an abstract class without putting the classes that implement it in a subclass relationship. Therefore, a class can implement multiple interfaces; this capability is Java's answer to multiple inheritance.

6. An *is-a* relationship between classes means that one class is a subclass of a parent class. A *has-a* relationship means that a class has data members for representing the attribute being described.

7. Subclass

8. You can reference an object of a *subclass* type through a variable of a *superclass* type.

9. You cast an object referenced by a *superclass* type to an object of a *subclass* type in order to apply methods of the *subclass* type to the object. This is called a downcast.

10. The four kinds of visibility in order of decreasing visibility are *public*, *protected*, *package*, and *private*.

Review Questions

1. Which method is invoked in a particular class when a method definition is overridden in several classes that are part of an inheritance hierarchy? Answer the question for the case in which the class has a definition for the method and also for the case where it doesn't.

2. Like a rectangle, a parallelogram has opposite sides that are parallel, but it has a corner angle, theta, that is less than 90 degrees. Discuss how you would add parallelograms to the class hierarchy for geometric shapes (see Figure 3.12). Write a definition for class `Parallelogram`.

3. Explain what multiple inheritance means. How does Java support behavior that is similar to multiple inheritance?

4. Explain how assignments can be made within a class hierarchy and the role of casting in a class hierarchy. What is strong typing? Why is it an important language feature?

5. If Java encounters a method call of the following form:

   superclassVar.methodName()

   where *superclassVar* is a variable of a superclass that references an object whose type is a subclass, what is necessary for this statement to compile? During run time, will method *methodName* from the class that is the type of *superclassVar* always be invoked, or is it possible that a different method *methodName* will be invoked? Explain your answer.

6. Assume the situation in Question 5, but method *methodName* is not defined in the class that is the type of *superclassVar*, but it is defined in the subclass type. Rewrite the method call so that it will compile.

7. Explain the process of initializing an object that is a subclass type in the subclass constructor. What part of the object must be initialized first? How is this done?

8. Discuss when abstract classes are used. How do they differ from actual classes and from interfaces?

9. What is default or package visibility?

Programming Projects

1. A veterinary office wants to store information regarding the kinds of animals it treats. Data includes diet, whether the animal is nocturnal or not, whether its bite is poisonous (as for some snakes), whether it flies, and so on. Use a superclass `Pet` with abstract methods and create appropriate subclasses to support about 10 animals of your choice.

2. A student is a person, and so is an employee. Create a class `Person` that has the data attributes common to both students and employees (name, social security number, age, gender, address, and telephone number) and appropriate method definitions. A student has a grade-point average (GPA), major, and year of graduation. An employee has a department, job title, and year of hire. In addition, there are hourly employees (hourly rate, hours worked, and union dues) and salaried employees (annual salary). Define a class hierarchy and write an application class that you can use to first store the data for an array of people and then display that information in a meaningful way.

3. Create a pricing system for a company that makes individualized computers, such as you might see on a Web site. There are two kinds of computers: laptops and desktop computers. The customer can select the processor speed, the amount of memory, and the size of the disk drive. The customer can also choose either a CD drive (CD ROM, CD-RW), a DVD drive, or both. For laptops, there is a choice of screen size. Other options are a modem, a network card, or wireless network. You should have an abstract class `Computer` and subclasses `DeskTop` and `LapTop`. Each subclass should have methods for calculating the price of a computer given the base price plus the cost of the different options. You should have methods for calculating memory price, hard drive price, and so on. There should be a method to calculate shipping cost.

4. Write a banking program that simulates the operation of your local bank. You should declare the following collection of classes.

   Class Account

   Data fields: customer (type Customer), balance, accountNumber, transactions array (type Transaction[])

   Methods: getBalance(), getCustomer(), toString(), setCustomer(), setBalance(), toString()

   Class SavingsAccount extends Account

   Methods: deposit(), withdraw(), addInterest()

   Class CheckingAccount extends Account

   Methods: deposit(), withdraw(), addInterest()

   Class Customer

   Data fields: name, address, age, telephoneNumber, customerNumber

   Methods: Accessors and modifiers for data fields

   Classes Senior, Adult, Student, *all these classes extend* Customer

   Each has constant data fields, SAVINGS_INTEREST, CHECK_INTEREST, CHECK_CHARGE, and OVERDRAFT_PENALTY, that define these values for customers of that type.

   Class Bank

   Data field: accounts array (type Account[])

   Methods: addAccount(), makeDeposit(), makeWithdrawal(), getAccount()

   Class Transaction

   Data fields: customerNumber, transactionType, amount, fees (a string describing unusual fees)

   Methods: processTran()

   You need to write all these classes and an application class that interacts with the user. In the application, you should first open several accounts and then enter several transactions.

5. You have a sizeable collection of music and videos and want to develop a data-base for storing and processing information about this collection. You need to develop a class hierarchy for your media collection that will be helpful in designing the data-base. Try the class hierarchy shown in Figure 3.18, where Audio and Video are media categories. Then CDs and cassette tapes would be subclasses of Audio, and DVDs and VHS tapes would be subclasses of Video.

FIGURE 3.18
Media Class Hierarchy

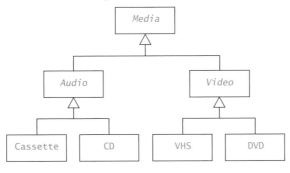

If you go to the video store to get a movie, you can rent or purchase only movies that are recorded on VHS tapes or DVDs. For this reason, class Video (and also classes Media and Audio) should be abstract classes, because there are no actual objects of these types. However, they are useful classes to help define the hierarchy.

Class Media should have data fields and methods common to all classes in the hierarchy. Every media object has a title, major artist, distributor, playing time, price, and so on. Class Video should have additional data fields for information describing movies recorded on DVDs and video tapes. This would include information about the supporting actors, the producer, the director, and the movie's rating. Class DVD would have specific information about DVD movies only, such as the format of the picture, special features on the disk, and so on. Figure 3.19 shows a possible class diagram for Media, Video, and subclasses of Video.

....
FIGURE 3.19
Class Video and Its Superclass and Subclasses

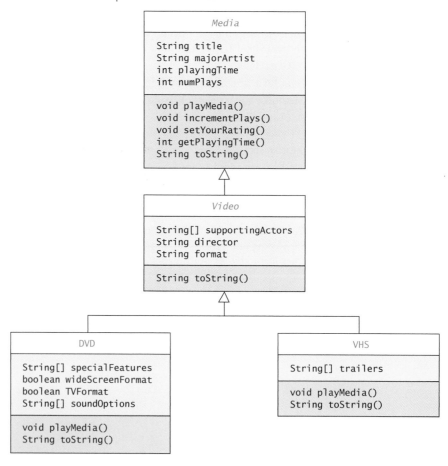

Provide methods to load the media collection from a file and write it back out to a file. Also provide a method to retrieve the information for a particular item identified by its title and a method to retrieve all your items for a particular artist.

6. Add shape classes `Square`, `DrawableSquare`, `EquilateralTriangle`, and `DrawableEquLatTri` to the figures hierarchy in Section 3.7. Modify class `TestDrawFigures` (Listing 3.14) to draw the new figures.

7. Add shape classes `Square`, `DrawableSquare`, `EquilateralTriangle`, and `DrawableEquLatTri` to the drawable shapes class hierarchy and to the object factory method in Section 3.8. Write an application to test your modifications.

8. Complete the `Food` class hierarchy in Section 3.3. Read and store a list of your favorite foods. Show the total calories for these foods and the overall percentages of fat, protein, and carbohydrates for this list. To find the overall percentage, if an item has 200 calories and 10 percent is fat calories, then that item contributes 20 fat calories. You need to find the totals for fat calories, protein calories, and carbohydrate calories, and then calculate the percentages.

9. A hospital has different kinds of patients who require different procedures for billing and approval of procedures. Some patients have insurance and some do not. Of the insured patients, some are on Medicare, some are in HMOs, and some have other health insurance plans. Develop a collection of classes to model these different kinds of patients.

10. A company has two different kinds of employees: professional and nonprofessional. Generally, professional employees have a monthly salary, whereas nonprofessional employees are paid an hourly rate. Similarly, professional employees have a certain number of days of vacation, whereas nonprofessional employees receive vacation hours based on the number of hours they have worked. The amount contributed for health insurance is also different for each kind of employee. Use an abstract class `Employee` to store information common to all employees and to declare methods for calculating weekly salary and computing health care contributions and vacation days earned that week. Define subclasses `Professional` and `NonProfessional`. Test your class hierarchy.

4

Lists and the Collection Interface

Chapter Objectives

- To become familiar with the List interface
- To understand how to write an array-based implementation of the List interface
- To study the differences between single-, double-, and circular linked list data structures
- To learn how to implement the List interface using a linked-list
- To understand the Iterator interface
- To learn how to implement the iterator for a linked list
- To become familiar with the Java Collection framework

So far we have one data structure that you can use in your programming—the array. Giving a programmer an array and asking her to develop software systems is like giving a carpenter a hammer and asking him to build a house. In both cases, more tools are needed. The Java developers attempted to supply those tools by providing a rich set of data structures written as Java classes. The classes are all part of a hierarchy called the Java Collection framework. We will discuss classes from this hierarchy in the rest of the book, starting in this chapter with the classes that are considered lists.

A list has the property that elements can be inserted or removed anywhere in the list, not just at the beginning or at the end. Some lists are *indexed*, which means their elements can be accessed in arbitrary order (called *random access*) using a subscript to select an element. For other lists you must always start at the beginning and process the elements in sequence. We will also discuss *iterators* and their role in facilitating sequential access to lists.

In this chapter we will discuss the ArrayList and Vector classes and linked lists (class LinkedList) and their similarities and differences. We will show that these classes are subclasses of the abstract class AbstractList and that they implement the List interface.

4.1 The List Interface and ArrayList Class

An *array* is an indexed data structure, which means you can select its elements in arbitrary order as determined by the subscript value. You can also access the elements in sequence using a loop that increments the subscript. However, you can't do the following with an array object:

- Increase or decrease its length, which is fixed
- Add an element at a specified position without shifting the other elements to make room
- Remove an element at a specified position without shifting the other elements to fill in the resulting gap

The classes that implement the Java List interface (part of Java API java.util) all provide methods to do these operations and more. Here are some other operations that can be performed:

- Find a specified target value
- Add an element at either end
- Remove an element from either end
- Traverse the list structure without having to manage a subscript

Although all of the classes we study in this chapter support these operations, they do not do them all with the same degree of efficiency. The kinds of operations you intend to perform in a particular application should influence your decision as to which List class to use for a particular application.

FIGURE 4.1
The `java.util.List`
Interface and Its
Implementers

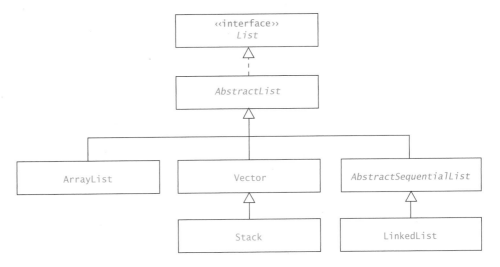

One feature that the array data structure provides that these classes don't is the ability to store primitive-type values. The List classes all store references to Objects, so all primitive-type values must be wrapped in Objects.

Figure 4.1 shows an overview of the List interface and the four actual classes that implement it. We will study the ArrayList, Vector, and LinkedList classes in this chapter; we will study the Stack class in the next chapter. We will briefly discuss the two abstract classes AbstractList and AbstractSequentialList in Section 4.8.

The ArrayList Class

The simplest class that implements the List interface is the ArrayList class. An ArrayList object is an improvement over an array object in that it supports all of the operations just listed. ArrayList objects are used most often when a programmer wants to be able to add new elements to the end of a list but still needs the capability to access the elements stored in the list in arbitrary order. These are the features we needed for our telephone directory application: New entries were added at the end, and we also needed to find numbers for entries already in the directory. The size of an ArrayList automatically increases as new elements are added to it, and the size decreases as elements are removed. An ArrayList object has an instance method size which returns its current size.

EXAMPLE 4.1   Figure 4.2 shows ArrayList object myList before and after the insertion of the String "Doc" at the element with subscript 2:

```
myList.add(2, "Doc");
```

The size before the insertion was 4, and the new size is 5. The strings formerly referenced by the elements with subscripts 2 and 3 are now referenced by the elements with subscripts 3 and 4. This is the same as what happens when someone cuts into a line of people waiting to buy tickets; everyone following the person who cuts in moves back one position in the line.

The last diagram in Figure 4.2 shows the effect of the statement

    myList.add("Dopey");

which adds "Dopey" to the end of the ArrayList. The size of myList is now 6.

···············

FIGURE 4.2

Insertion in the Middle and at the End of an ArrayList Object

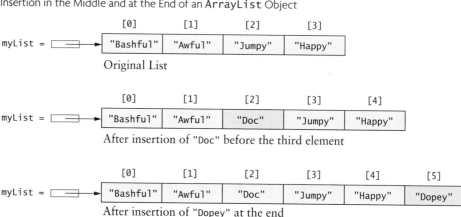

Similarly, if you remove an element from an ArrayList object, the size automatically decreases, and the elements following the one removed shift over to fill the vacated space. This is the same as when someone leaves a ticket line; the people in back all move forward. Here is object myList after removal of the element with subscript 1. Notice that the strings formerly referenced by subscripts 2 through 5 are now referenced by subscripts 1 through 4 (in the darker color), and the size has decreased by 1.

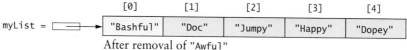

Even though an ArrayList is an indexed collection, you can't access its elements using a subscript. Instead, you use a get or set method to access its elements. For example, the method call

    myList.get(2)

returns the string "Jumpy". (It actually returns a type Object reference, so you must cast to type String if you want to apply the String methods.) Similarly, you would use the method call

    myList.set(2, "Sneezy")

to replace the reference to string "Jumpy" with a reference to string "Sneezy".

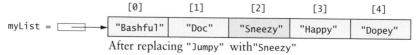

PITFALL

Using Subscripts with an ArrayList

If you use a subscript with an ArrayList (for example, myList[i]), you will get the syntax error array type required for [] but ArrayList found. This means that subscripts can be used only with arrays, not with indexed collections.

You can also search an ArrayList. The method call

      myList.indexOf("Jumpy")

would return −1 after "Jumpy" was removed. The method call

      myList.indexOf("Sneezy")

would return 2.

Specification of the ArrayList Class

The ArrayList class, part of the package java.util, implements the List interface. A selected subset of the methods from this Java API is shown in Table 4.1.

TABLE 4.1
Methods of Class java.util.ArrayList

Method	Behavior
public Object get(int index)	Returns a reference to the element at position index.
public Object set(int index, Object anEntry)	Sets the element at position index to reference anEntry. Returns the previous value.
public int size()	Gets the current size of the ArrayList.
public boolean add(Object anEntry)	Adds a reference to anEntry at the end of the ArrayList. Always returns true.
public void add(int index, Object anEntry)	Adds a reference to anEntry, inserting it before the item at position index.
int indexOf(Object target)	Searches for target and returns the position of the first occurrence, or −1 if it is not in the ArrayList.
public Object remove(int index)	Returns and removes the item at position index and shifts the items that follow it to fill the vacated space.

EXERCISES FOR SECTION 4.1

SELF-CHECK

1. Describe the effect of each of the following operations on object `myList` as shown at the end of this section. What is the value of `myList.size()` after each operation?

```
myList.add("Pokey");
myList.add("Campy");
int i = myList.indexOf("Happy");
myList.set(i, "Bouncy");
myList.remove(myList.size() - 2);
String temp = (String) myList.get(1);
myList.set(1, temp.toUpperCase());
```

PROGRAMMING

1. Write the following static method:

```
/** Replaces each occurrence of oldItem in aList with newItem. */
public static void replace(ArrayList aList, Object oldItem,
                           Object newItem)
```

2. Write the following static method:

```
/** Deletes the first occurrence of target in aList. */
public static void delete(ArrayList aList, Object target)
```

4.2 Application of ArrayList

The `ArrayList` gives you additional capability beyond what an array provides. However, there is a price paid for this. The `ArrayList` stores items of type `Object`. Thus, it can store an object of any class. The `add` and `set` methods will accept an object of any class as an argument. The `get` method will return the objects back to you, but you must cast them back to their original class type. Another limitation is that you cannot store values of the primitive types directly. Instead you must use the wrapper class for that type (see Appendix A to review wrapper classes). We show the use of the `ArrayList` to store some **int** values in the following example.

EXAMPLE 4.2   The following statements store a collection of **int** values in ArrayList `someInts`. Each **int** value is wrapped in an `Integer` object before it is stored.

```
ArrayList someInts = new ArrayList();
int[] nums = {5, 7, 2, 15};
for (int i = 0; i < nums.length; i++)
    someInts.add(new Integer(nums[i]));
```

Before we can process primitive type values that are stored in an `ArrayList`, we must "unwrap" them. The following loop finds the sum of the **int** values in `someInts`.

```
        int sum = 0;
        for (int i = 0; i < someInts.size(); i++) {
            int n = ((Integer) someInts.get(i)).intValue();
            sum += n;
        }
```

Although it may seem wasteful to carry out these operations when you already have an array of ints, the purpose of this example is to illustrate what steps would be needed to process a collection of Integer objects in an ArrayList.

 PITFALL

Forgetting to Cast an Item Retrieved from an ArrayList

Whenever an object is stored into an ArrayList, the programmer must remember the original type. When an object is retrieved (using get), it will be returned as type Object and must be cast back to the original type before it can be processed as the original type. Without the cast, you will get a syntax error when you attempt to apply a method that is not defined in class Object to the object returned by get.

The Phone Directory Application Revisited

In Chapter 1 we introduced a phone directory case study. Our solution involved building an array of phone directory entries that expanded as new directory entries were added. Basically we constructed an expandable array that was a data field of class ArrayBasedPD (see Listing 1.3). We could accomplish the same operations much more easily using an ArrayList to store the phone directory:

```
        private ArrayList theDirectory = new ArrayList();
```

We used method addOrChangeEntry to search for a name in the directory and change its number, if the name was in the directory, or add the name and number, if the name was not present. In method addOrChangeEntry in Listing 4.1, the statement

```
        int index = theDirectory.indexOf(new DirectoryEntry(name, ""));
```

uses method ArrayList.indexOf to search theDirectory for an entry selected by parameter name. Method indexOf applies the equals method for class DirectoryEntry to each element of theDirectory. Method DirectoryEntry.equals compares the name field of each element to the name field of the argument of indexOf (an anonymous object with the desired name). Next, if the name is found at position index, the statement

```
        DirectoryEntry de = (DirectoryEntry) theDirectory.get(index);
```

retrieves the directory entry (using ArrayList.get) and casts it to type DirectoryEntry. Otherwise, the statement

```
        theDirectory.add(new DirectoryEntry(name, newNumber));
```

uses method ArrayList.add to insert the new directory entry at the end.

LISTING 4.1
Method addOrChangeEntry

```
/** Add an entry or change an existing entry.
    @param name The name of the person being added or changed
    @param newNumber The new number to be assigned
    @return The old number, or if a new entry, null
*/
public String addOrChangeEntry(String name, String newNumber) {
    int index =
        theDirectory.indexOf(new DirectoryEntry(name, ""));
    String oldNumber = null;
    if (index != -1) {
        DirectoryEntry de =
            (DirectoryEntry) theDirectory.get(index);
        oldNumber = de.getNumber();
        de.setNumber(newNumber);
    } else {
        theDirectory.add(new DirectoryEntry(name,
                        newNumber));
    }
    modified = true;
    return oldNumber;
}
```

 DESIGN CONCEPT

Generic Types

A proposed change to the Java language, providing for *generic types,* will be part of the latest release of Java (J2SDK 1.5). Generic types allow us to define a collection such as an ArrayList of a specific type. This collection would then work like the array in that only objects of the specific (or compatible) type could be stored in it, and items retrieved would be of the specific type.

You would create a generic ArrayList using the following syntax:

    ArrayList<*ClassName*> *variable* = new ArrayList<*ClassName*>;

Example

    ArrayList<String> words = new ArrayList<String>;

The methods get and remove would return String objects, and the methods set and add would accept only String parameters.

Only class types (or interfaces) can be specified as the *ClassName.* Thus, primitive types must still be wrapped in their wrapper classes. An additional update to the Java language, also part of version 1.5, will make the wrapping and unwrapping of the primitive types automatic.

EXERCISES FOR SECTION 4.2

SELF-CHECK

1. What does the following code fragment do?

```
ArrayList myList = new ArrayList();
myList.add(new Double(3.456));
myList.add(new Integer(5));
double result = ((Integer) myList.get(1)).intValue()
                + ((Double) myList.get(0)).doubleValue();
System.out.println("Result is " + result);
```

PROGRAMMING

1. Write the lookupEntry method of the ArrayBasedPD class to use an ArrayList.
2. Write the removeEntry method of the ArrayBasedPD class to use an ArrayList.
3. Write the save method of the ArrayBasedPD class to use an ArrayList.

4.3 Implementation of an ArrayList Class

We will implement a simplified version of the ArrayList class called KWArrayList. We use a Java array internally to contain the data of a KWArrayList, as shown in Figure 4.3. The physical size of the array is indicated by the data field capacity. The number of data items is indicated by the data field size. The elements between size and capacity are available for the storage of new items.

We are assuming the following data fields in the discussion of our KWArrayList class. This is not exactly how it is done in Java, but it will give you a feel for how to write the class methods. The constructor shown in the following code allocates storage for the underlying array and initializes its capacity to 10. We will not provide a complete implementation, because we expect you to use the standard ArrayList class provided by the Java API (package java.util).

```
public class KWArrayList {
    // Data Fields
    /** The default initial capacity */
    private static final int INITIAL_CAPACITY = 10;

    /** The underlying data array */
    private Object[] theData;

    /** The current size */
    private int size = 0;

    /** The current capacity */
    private int capacity = 0;
```

```
// Methods
public KWArrayList() {
    theData = new Object[INITIAL_CAPACITY];
    capacity = INITIAL_CAPACITY
}
```

FIGURE 4.3
Internal Structure of
`ArrayList`

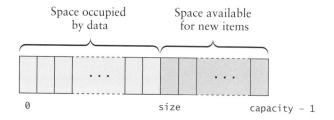

The add(Object obj) Method

We implement two add methods with different signatures. The first appends an item
to the end of a KWArraylist; the second inserts an item at a specified position. If size
is less than capacity, then to append a new item:

a. Insert the new item at the position indicated by the value of size.
b. Increment the value of size.
c. Return **true** to indicate successful insertion.

This sequence of operations is illustrated in Figure 4.4. The add method is specified
in the Collection interface, which is discussed in Section 4.8. The Collection interface is a superinterface to the List interface. The add method must return a **boolean**
to indicate whether or not the insertion is successful. For an ArrayList, this is
always true. The old value of size is in gray; its new value is in color.

If the size is already equal to the capacity, we must first allocate a new array to
hold the data and then copy the data to this new array. The method reallocate
(explained shortly) does this. The code for the add method follows.

```
public boolean add(Object theValue) {
    if (size == capacity) {
        reallocate();
    }
    theData[size] = theValue;
    size++;
    return true;
}
```

FIGURE 4.4
Adding an Element to
the End of an
`ArrayList`

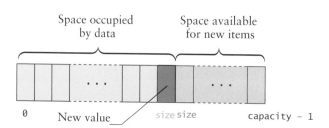

PROGRAM STYLE

Using the Postfix (or Prefix) Operator with a Subscript

Some programmers prefer to combine the two statements before return in the add method and write them as

```
theData[size++] = theValue;
```

This is perfectly valid. Java uses the current value of size as the subscript for array access and then increments it. The only difficulty is the fact that two operations are written in one statement and are carried out in a predetermined order. If you are unsure of the order, you might select prefix when you needed postfix, or vice versa.

The add(int index, Object theValue) Method

To insert an item into the middle of the array (anywhere but the end), the values that are at the insertion point and beyond must be shifted over to make room. In Figure 4.5, the arrow with label 1 shows the first element moved, the arrow with label 2 shows the next element moved, and so on. This data move is done using the following loop:

```
for (int i = size; i > index; i--) {
    theData[i] = theData[i - 1];
}
```

Notice that the array subscript starts at size and moves toward the beginning of the array (down to index + 1). If we had started the subscript at index + 1 instead, we would copy the value at index into each element of the array with a larger subscript. Before we execute this loop, we need to be sure that size is not equal to capacity. If it is, we must call reallocate.

After increasing the capacity (if necessary) and moving the other elements, we can then add the new item. The complete code is as follows:

```
public void add(int index, Object theValue) {
    if (index < 0 || index > size) {
        throw new ArrayIndexOutOfBoundsException(index);
    }
    if (size == capacity) {
        reallocate();
    }
    // Shift data in elements from index to size - 1
    for (int i = size; i > index; i--) {
        theData[i] = theData[i - 1];
    }
    // Insert the new item.
    theData[index] = theValue;
    size++;
}
```

FIGURE 4.5
Making Room to Insert an Item into an Array

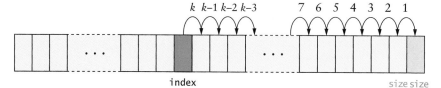

The remove Method

To remove an item, the items that follow it must be moved forward to close up the space. In Figure 4.6, the arrow with label 1 shows the first element moved, the arrow with label 2 shows the next element moved, and so on. This data move is done using the following loop:

```
for (int i = index + 1; i < size; i++) {
    theData[i - 1] = theData[i];
}
```

The complete code for the remove method follows. The item removed is returned as the method result.

```
public Object remove(int index) {
    if (index < 0 || index >= size) {
        throw new ArrayIndexOutOfBoundsException(index);
    }
    Object returnValue = theData[index];
    for (int i = index + 1; i < size; i++) {
        theData[i - 1] = theData[i];
    }
    size--;
    return returnValue;
}
```

FIGURE 4.6
Removing an Item from an Array

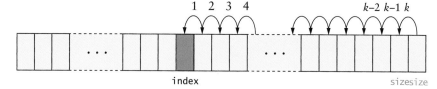

The reallocate Method

The reallocate method creates a new array that is twice the size of the current array and then copies the contents of the current array into the new one. The reference variable theData is then set to reference this new array. The code is as follows:

```
private void reallocate() {
    capacity = 2 * capacity;
    Object[] newData = new Object[capacity];
    System.arraycopy(theData, 0, newData, 0, size);
    theData = newData;
}
```

The reason for doubling is to spread out the cost of copying. Doubling an array of size n allows us to add n more items before we need to do another array copy. Therefore, we can add n new items after we have copied over n existing items. This averages out to 1 copy per add, so reallocation is effectively an O(1) operation. Recall that it will take only about 20 `reallocate` operations to create an array that can store over a million references (2^{20} is greater than 1,000,000).

Performance of the KWArrayList

The `set` and `get` methods (Programming Exercise 1) are each a few lines of code and contain no loops. Thus we say that these methods execute in constant time, or O(1).

If we insert into (or remove from) the middle of a `KWArrayList`, then at most n items have to be shifted. Therefore, the cost of inserting or removing an element is O(n). What if we have to reallocate before we can insert? Recall that we spread out the cost of copying so that effectively it is an O(1) operation, so the insertion is still O(n). Even if we don't spread out the cost of copying, the copy operation would still be O(n), so the worst case would just double the cost.

The Vector Class

The initial release of the Java API `java.util` contained the class `Vector`, which has similar functionality to the `ArrayList`. Because the `Vector` and `ArrayList` both implement the `List` interface, they both contain all the same methods. New applications should use the `ArrayList` rather than the `Vector`, but the `Vector` is retained for compatibility with older applications. Also, the class `Stack`, which we will study in the next chapter, is a subclass of `Vector`.

EXERCISES FOR SECTION 4.3

SELF CHECK

1. Trace the execution of the following:
   ```
   int[] anArray = {0, 1, 2, 3, 4, 5, 6, 7};
   for (int i = 3; i < anArray.length - 1; i++)
       anArray[i + 1] = anArray[i];
   ```
   and the following:
   ```
   int[] anArray = {0, 1, 2, 3, 4, 5, 6, 7};
   for (int i = anArray.length - 1; i > 3; i--)
       anArray[i] = anArray[i - 1];
   ```
   What are the contents of anArray after the execution of each loop?

2. Write statements to remove the middle object from a `KWArrayList` and place it at the end.

PROGRAMMING

1. Implement the get and set methods of the KWArrayList. Your methods should test the index and throw an ArrayIndexOutOfBoundsException when appropriate.
2. Implement the find method of the KWArrayList class.
3. Provide a constructor for class KWArrayList that accepts an **int** argument that represents the initial array capacity.

4.4 Single-Linked Lists and Double-Linked Lists

The ArrayList has the limitation that the add and remove methods operate in linear (**O**(*n*)) time because they require a loop to shift elements in the underlying array. In this section we introduce a data structure, the linked list, that overcomes this limitation by providing the ability to add or remove items anywhere in the list in constant (**O**(1)) time. A linked list is useful when you need to insert and remove elements at arbitrary locations (not just at the end) and when you will do frequent insertions and removals.

One example would be maintaining an alphabetized list of students in a course at the beginning of a semester while students are adding and dropping courses. If you were using an ArrayList, you would have to shift all names that follow the new person's name down one position before you could insert a new student's name. Figure 4.7 shows this process. The names in gray were all shifted down when Barbara added the course. Similarly, if a student drops the course, the names of all students after the one who dropped (in gray in Figure 4.8) would be shifted up one position to close up the space.

Another example would be maintaining a list of students who are waiting to register for a course. Instead of having the students waiting in an actual line, you can give each student a number, which is the student's position in the line. If someone drops out of the line, everyone with a higher number gets a new number that is 1 lower than before. If someone cuts into the line because they "need the course to graduate", everyone after this person gets a new number which is one higher than before. The person maintaining the list is responsible for giving everyone their new number after a change. Figure 4.9 illustrates what happens when Alice is inserted and given the number 1: Everyone whose number is ≥ 1 gets a new number. This

FIGURE 4.7
Inserting a Student into a Class List

Before adding Browniten, Barbara

Abidoye, Olandunni
Boado, Annabelle
Butler, James
Chee, Yong-Han
Debaggis, Tarra
⋮

After adding Browniten, Barbara

Abidoye, Olandunni
Boado, Annabelle
Browniten, Barbara
Butler, James
Chee, Yong-Han
Debaggis, Tarra
⋮

process is analogous to maintaining the names in an `ArrayList`; each person's number is that person's position in the list, and some names in the list are shifted after every change.

A better way to do this would be to give each person the name of the next person in line, instead of his or her own position in the line (which can change frequently). To start the registration process, the person who is registering students calls the person who is at the head of the line. After she finishes registration, the person at the head of the line calls the next person, and so on. Now what if person A lets person B cut into the line before him? Because B has taken A's position in line, A will register after B, so person B must have A's name. Also, the person in front of the new person must know to call B, instead of A. Figure 4.10 illustrates what happens when Alice is inserted in the list. Only the two entries shown in color need to be changed (Emily must call Alice instead of Phong, and Alice must call Phong). Although Alice is shown at the bottom of Figure 4.10, she is really the second student in the list. The first four students in the list are Emily Warner, Alice Franklin, Phong Dang, and Anna Feldman.

FIGURE 4.8
Removing a Student
Who Dropped

Before dropping `Boado, Annabelle`

Abidoye, Olandunni
Boado, Annabelle
Browniten, Barbara
Butler, James
Chee, Yong-Han
Debaggis, Tarra
⋮

After dropping `Boado, Annabelle`

Abidoye, Olandunni
Browniten, Barbara
Butler, James
Chee, Yong-Han
Debaggis, Tarra
⋮

FIGURE 4.9
Inserting into a
Numbered List of
Students Waiting to
Register

Before inserting `Alice` at position 1

0. Warner, Emily
1. Dang, Phong
2. Feldman, Anna
3. Barnes, Aaron
4. Torres, Kristopher
⋮

After inserting `Alice` at position 1

0. Warner, Emily
1. **Franklin, Alice**
2. Dang, Phong
3. Feldman, Anna
4. Barnes, Aaron
5. Torres, Kristopher
⋮

FIGURE 4.10
Inserting into a List
Where Each Student
Knows Who Is Next

Before inserting `Alice`

Person in line	Person to call
Warner, Emily	Dang, Phong
Dang, Phong	Feldman, Anna
Feldman, Anna	Barnes, Aaron
Barnes, Aaron	Torres, Kristopher
Torres, Kristopher	...
⋮	⋮

After inserting `Alice`

Person in line	Person to call
Warner, Emily	Franklin, Alice
Dang, Phong	Feldman, Anna
Feldman, Anna	Barnes, Aaron
Barnes, Aaron	Torres, Kristopher
Torres, Kristopher	...
⋮	⋮
Franklin, Alice	Dang, Phong

FIGURE 4.11
Removing a Student from a List Where Each Student Knows Who Is Next

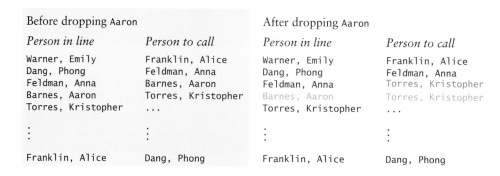

What happens if someone drops out of our line? In this case, the name of the person who follows the one that drops out must be given to the person who comes before the one who drops out. Figure 4.11 illustrates this. If Aaron drops out, only one entry needs to be changed (Anna must call Kristopher instead of Aaron).

Using a linked list is analogous to the process just discussed and illustrated in Figures 4.10 and 4.11 for storing our list of student names. Insertion and removal are done in constant time and no shifts are required. Each element in a linked list, called a *node*, stores information and a link to the next node in the list. For example, for our list of students in Figure 4.11, the information "Warner, Emily" would be stored in the first node, and the link to the next node would reference a node whose information part was "Franklin, Alice". Here are the first three nodes of this list:

"Warner, Emily" $\longrightarrow$ "Franklin, Alice" $\longrightarrow$ "Dang, Phong"

We discuss how to represent and manipulate a linked list next.

A List Node

FIGURE 4.12
Node and Link

A node is a data structure that contains a data item and one or more links. A *link* is a reference to a node. A UML diagram of this relationship is shown in Figure 4.12. This shows that a Node contains a data field named data of type Object and a reference (as indicated by the open diamond) to a Node. The name of the reference is next, as shown on the line from the Node to itself. Figure 4.13 shows four Nodes linked together to form the list [Tom, Dick, Harry, Sam]. In this figure we show that data references a String object. In subsequent figures we will show the string value inside the Node.

We can define a Node as a Java class as follows:

```
/** A Node is the building block for a single-linked list. */
private static class Node {
    // Data Fields
    /** The reference to the data. */
    private Object data;
    /** The reference to the next node. */
    private Node next;
```

```
// Constructors
/** Creates a new node with a null next field.
    @param dataItem The data stored
*/
private Node(Object dataItem) {
    data = dataItem;
    next = null;
}

/** Creates a new node that references another node.
    @param dataItem The data stored
    @param nodeRef The node referenced by new node
*/
private Node(Object dataItem, Node nodeRef) {
    data = dataItem;
    next = nodeRef;
}
}
```

A Node is generally defined inside of another class, making it an *inner class*. The keyword **static** indicates that the Node class will not reference its outer class. (It can't, because it has no methods other than constructors.) In the Java API documentation, inner classes are called *nested classes*.

Generally we want to keep the details of the Node class private. Thus the qualifier **private** is applied to the class as well as to the data fields and constructor. However, the data fields and methods of an inner class are visible anywhere within the parent class.

The first constructor stores the data passed to it in instance variable data of a new node. It also sets the next field to null. The second constructor sets the next field to reference the same node as its second argument. We didn't define a default constructor because none is needed.

FIGURE 4.13
Nodes in a Linked List

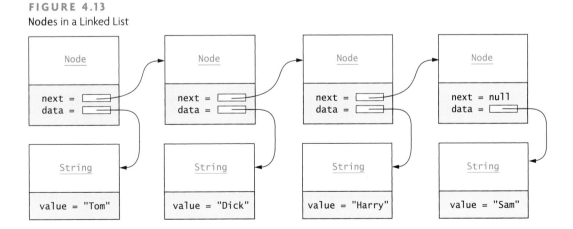

Connecting Nodes

We can construct the list shown in Figure 4.13 using the following sequence of statements:

```
Node tom = new Node("Tom");
Node dick = new Node("Dick");
Node harry = new Node("Harry");
Node sam = new Node("Sam");
tom.next = dick;
dick.next = harry;
harry.next = sam;
```

The statement

```
tom.next = dick;
```

stores a reference (link) to the node with data "Dick" in data field next of node tom.

Generally we do not have individual references to each of the nodes. Instead, we have a reference to the first node in the list and work from there. Thus we could build the list shown in Figure 4.13 as follows:

```
Node head = new Node("Tom");
head.next = new Node("Dick");
head.next.next = new Node("Harry");
head.next.next.next = new Node("Sam");
```

In the foregoing fragment, we grew the list by adding each new node to the end of the list so far. The node referenced by head was always the first node in the list (data is "Tom"). We can also grow a list by adding nodes to the front of the list. The following fragment creates the same list, but each new node is added to the front of the list so far. After each addition, head references a different node. The first node referenced by head (data is "Sam") will be the last node in the final list.

```
Node head = new Node("Sam");
head = new Node("Harry", head);
head = new Node("Dick", head);
head = new Node("Tom", head);
```

Each statement of the form

```
head = new Node(aName, head);
```

creates a new node, whose data component references *aName* and whose next component is the list so far. Then head is reset to reference this new node. This has the effect of adding the new node to the front of the existing list.

Inserting a Node in a List

We can insert a new node, "Bob", into the list after "Harry" as follows:

```
Node bob = new Node("Bob");
bob.next = harry.next;  // Step 1
harry.next = bob;       // Step 2
```

The linked list now is as shown in Figure 4.14. We show the number of the step that created each link alongside it.

Removing a Node

If we have a reference, tom, to the node that contains "Tom", we can remove the node that follows "Tom":

```
tom.next = tom.next.next;
```

The list is now as shown in Figure 4.15. Notice that we did not start with a reference to "Dick" but instead started with a reference to "Tom". To delete a node, we need a reference to the node that precedes it, not the node being deleted. (Recall from our registration list example that the person in front of the one dropping out of line must be told to call the person who follows the one who is dropping out.)

Traversing a Linked List

Traversing a linked list is a fairly simple process.

1. Set nodeRef to reference the first node.
2. **while** nodeRef is not **null**
3.   Do something with node referenced by nodeRef.
4.   Set nodeRef to nodeRef.next.

This is illustrated by the following loop (which displays the information in our example linked list) where variable tom references the first list node:

FIGURE 4.14
After Inserting **bob**

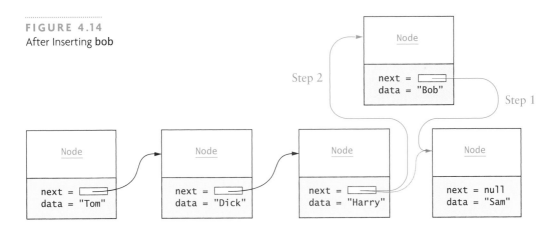

FIGURE 4.15
After Removing Node Following **tom**

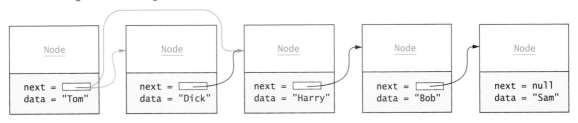

```
Node nodeRef = tom;
while (nodeRef != null) {
    System.out.print(nodeRef.data);
    if (nodeRef.next != null) {
        System.out.print (" ==> ");
    }
    nodeRef = nodeRef.next;  // Advance down the list.
}
```

As new values are assigned to variable nodeRef by the statement

```
nodeRef = nodeRef.next;   // Advance down the list.
```

nodeRef walks down the list, referencing each of the list nodes in turn. The value of nodeRef is **null** when the traversal is finished.

Traversing the list shown in Figure 4.15, the loop produces the following output:

```
Tom ==> Harry ==> Bob ==> Sam
```

Double-Linked Lists

Our single-linked list data structure has some limitations:

- We can insert a node only after a node we have a reference to. For example, to insert "Bob" in Figure 4.14 we needed a reference to the node containing "Harry". If we wanted to insert "Bob" before "Sam" but did not have a reference to "Harry", we would have to start at the beginning of the list and search until we found a node whose next node was "Sam".

- We can remove a node only if we have a reference to its predecessor node. For example, to remove "Dick" in Figure 4.15 we needed a reference to the node containing "Tom". If we wanted to remove "Dick" without having this reference, we would have to start at the beginning of the list and search until we found a node whose next node was "Dick".

- We can traverse the list only in the forward direction, whereas with an ArrayList we can move forward (or backward) by incrementing (or decrementing) the index.

We can overcome these limitations by adding a reference to the previous node in the Node class, as shown in the UML class diagram in Figure 4.16. The open diamond indicates that both prev and next are references whose values can be changed. Our *double-linked list* is shown in Figure 4.17.

 PITFALL

Falling Off the End of a List

If nodeRef is at the last list element and you execute the statement

```
nodeRef = nodeRef.next;
```

nodeRef will be set to **null**, and you will have fallen off the end of the list. This is not an error. However, if you execute this statement again, you will get a NullPointer-Exception, because nodeRef.next is undefined when nodeRef is **null**.

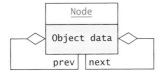

FIGURE 4.16
Double-Linked List
Node UML Diagram

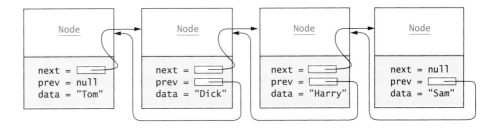

FIGURE 4.17
A Double-Linked List

The **Node** Class

The Node class for a double-linked list has references to the data and to the next and previous nodes. The declaration of this class follows.

```
/** A Node is the building block for a double-linked list. */
private static class Node {
    /** The data value. */
    private Object data;
    /** The link to the next node. */
    private Node next = null;
    /** The link to the previous node. */
    private Node prev = null;

    /** Construct a node with the given data value.
        @param dataItem The data value
    */
    private Node(Object dataItem) {
        data = dataItem;
    }
}
```

Inserting into a Double-Linked List

If sam is a reference to the node containing "Sam", we can insert a new node containing "Sharon" into the list before "Sam" using the following statements. Before the insertion, we can refer to the predecessor of sam as sam.prev. After the insertion, this node will be referenced by sharon.prev.

```
Node sharon = new Node("Sharon");
// Link new node to its neighbors.
sharon.next = sam;         // Step 1
sharon.prev = sam.prev;    // Step 2
// Link old predecessor of sam to new predecessor.
sam.prev.next = sharon;    // Step 3
// Link to new predecessor.
sam.prev = sharon;         // Step 4
```

FIGURE 4.18
Steps 1 and 2 in
Inserting **sharon**

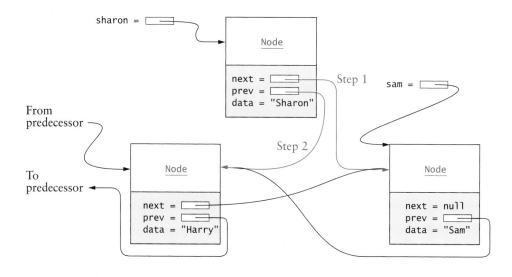

FIGURE 4.19
After Inserting **sharon**
before **sam**

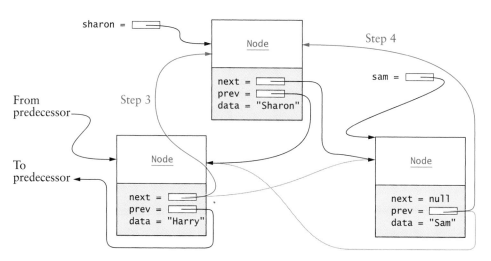

The three nodes affected by the insertion are shown in Figures 4.18 and 4.19. The old links are shown in gray, and the new links are shown in color. Next to each link we show the number of the step that creates it. Figure 4.18 shows the links after Steps 1 and 2, and Figure 4.19 shows the links after Steps 3 and 4.

Removing from a Double-Linked List

If we have a reference, harry, to the node that contains "Harry", we can remove that node without having a named reference to its predecessor:

```
harry.prev.next = harry.next;   // Step 1
harry.next.prev = harry.prev;   // Step 2
```

The list is now as shown in Figure 4.20.

FIGURE 4.20
Removing **harry** from a Double-Linked List

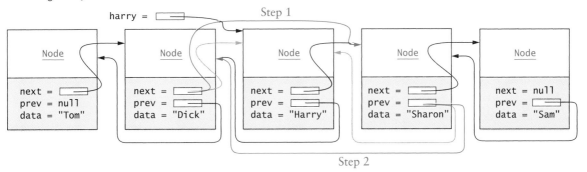

Creating a Double-Linked List Object

FIGURE 4.21
A Double-Linked
List Object

So far we have shown just the internal Nodes for a linked list. A double-linked list object would consist of a separate object with data fields head (a reference to the first list Node), tail (a reference to the last list Node), and size (the number of internal Nodes). See Figure 4.21.

Circular Lists

We can carry the development from the single-linked list to the double-linked list one step further and create a circular list by linking the last node to the first node (and the first node to the last one). If head references the first list node and tail references the last list node, the statements

```
head.prev = tail;
tail.next = head;
```

would accomplish this (Figure 4.22).

You could also create a circular list from a single-linked list by executing just the statement

```
tail.next = head;
```

This statement connects the last list element to the first list element. If you keep a reference to only the last list element, tail, you can access the last element and the first element (tail.next) in O(1) time.

FIGURE 4.22
Circular Linked List

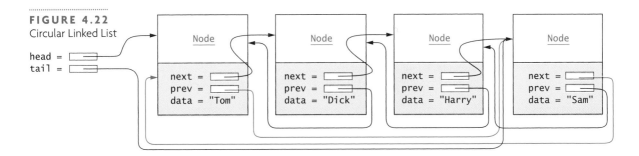

One advantage of a circular list is that you can continue to traverse in the forward (or reverse) direction even after you have passed the last (or first) list node. This enables you to visit all the list elements from any starting point. In a list that is not circular, you would have to start at the beginning or at the end if you wanted to visit all the list elements. A second advantage of a circular list is that you can never fall off the end of the list. There is a disadvantage: you must be careful not to set up an infinite loop.

EXERCISES FOR SECTION 4.4

SELF-CHECK

1. Draw a single-linked list of `Integer` objects containing the integers 5, 10, 7, and 30 and referenced by `head`. Complete the following fragment, which adds all `Integer` objects in a list. Your fragment should walk down the list, adding any integers to `sum` and ignoring any objects in the list that are not `Integer` objects.

```
int sum = 0;
Node nodeRef = _____;
while (nodeRef != null) {
    if (nodeRef._____ instanceof Integer) {
        int next = (Integer) _____;
        sum += next;
    }
    nodeRef = _____;
}
```

2. Answer the following questions about lists.
   a. Each node in a single-linked list has a reference to _____ and _____.
   b. In a double-linked list each node has a reference to _____, _____, and _____.
   c. To remove an item from a single-linked list you need a reference to _____.
   d. To remove an item from a double-linked list you need a reference to _____.

3. For the single-linked list in Figure 4.13, assume you have a reference variable head (type Node) that references the first node. Explain the effect of each statement in the following fragments.

   a. `head = new Node("Shakira", head.next);`

   b. ```
Node nodeRef = head.next;
nodeRef.next = nodeRef.next.next;
```

   c. ```
Node nodeRef = head;
while (nodeRef.next != null)
    nodeRef = nodeRef.next;
nodeRef.next = new Node("Tamika");
```

   d. ```
Node nodeRef = head;
while (nodeRef != null && !nodeRef.data.equals("Harry"))
    nodeRef = nodeRef.next;
if (nodeRef != null) {
    nodeRef.data = "Sally";
    nodeRef.next = new Node("Harry", nodeRef.next.next);
}
```
```

4. For the double-linked list in Figure 4.17, explain the effect of each statement in the fragments below.

a.
```
Node nodeRef = tail.prev;
nodeRef.prev.next = tail;
tail.prev = nodeRef.prev;
```

b.
```
Node nodeRef = head;
head = new Node("Tamika");
head.next = nodeRef;
nodeRef.prev = head;
```

c.
```
Node nodeRef = new Node("Shakira");
nodeRef.prev = head;
nodeRef.next = head.next;
head.next.prev = nodeRef;
head.next = nodeRef;
```

PROGRAMMING

1. Using the single-linked list shown in Figure 4.13, and assuming that head references the first Node and tail references the last Node, write statements to do each of the following.
   a. Insert "Bill" before "Tom".
   b. Remove "Sam".
   c. Insert "Bill" before "Tom".
   d. Remove "Sam".
2. Repeat Exercise 1 using the double-linked list shown in Figure 4.17.

4.5 The LinkedList Class and the Iterator and ListIterator Interfaces

The LinkedList Class

The LinkedList class, part of the Java API package java.util, implements the List interface using a double-linked list. A selected subset of the methods from this Java API is shown in Table 4.2. Because the LinkedList class, like the ArrayList class, implements the List interface, it contains many of the methods found in the ArrayList class as well as some additional methods.

The Iterator

Let's say we want to process each element in a LinkedList. We can use the following loop to access the list elements in sequence, starting with the one at index 0.

Selected Methods of the `java.util.LinkedList` Class

Method	Behavior
`public void add(int index, Object obj)`	Inserts object `obj` into the list at position `index`.
`public void addFirst(Object obj)`	Inserts object `obj` as the first element of the list.
`public void addLast(Object obj)`	Adds object `obj` to the end of the list.
`public Object get(int index)`	Returns the item at position `index`.
`public Object getFirst()`	Gets the first element in the list. Throws `NoSuchElementException` if list is empty.
`public Object getLast()`	Gets the last element in the list. Throws `NoSuchElementException` if list is empty.
`public boolean remove(Object obj)`	Removes the first occurrence of object `obj` from the list. Returns **true** if the list contained object `obj`; otherwise, returns **false**.
`public int size()`	Returns the number of objects contained in the list.

```
// Access each list element.
for (int index = 0; index < aList.size(); index++) {
    Object nextElement = aList.get(index);
    // Do something with the element at position index (nextElement)
    . . .
}
```

The loop is executed `aList.size()` times, thus it is linear. During each iteration we call method `get` to retrieve the element at position `index`.

If we assume that the `LinkedList` class stores only a reference to the first list node (head), each call to method `get` must advance a local reference (`nodeRef`) to the node at position `index` using a loop such as:

```
// Advance nodeRef to the element at position index.
Node nodeRef = head;
for (int j = 0; j < index; j++) {
    nodeRef = nodeRef.next;
}
```

This loop (in method `get`) executes `index` times. Since `index` ranges from 0 to `aList.size()` – 1 in the outer loop, the total execution time is 1 + 2 + … + `aList.size()` – 1. The value of this series is proportional to `aList.size()`^{2}, so the loop to process the list elements is $O(n^2)$ and is, therefore, very inefficient. We would like to have an alternative way to access the elements in a linked list sequentially.

We can use the concept of an *iterator* to accomplish this. Think of an iterator as a moving place marker that keeps track of the current position in a particular linked list. The `Iterator` object for a list starts at the first element in the list. The programmer can use the `Iterator` object's next method to retrieve the next element. Each time it does a retrieval, the `Iterator` object advances to the next list element, where it waits until it is needed again. We can also ask the Iterator object to determine whether the list has more elements left to process (method hasNext). If you are familiar with StringTokenizer objects (see Appendix A), you will recall that a StringTokenizer maintains a place marker that stops at delimiter characters in the string that it tokenizes. We can ask it to get the next token (method nextToken) and ask it to determine if there are more tokens left to process (method hasMoreTokens). Both Iterator and StringTokenizer objects throw a NoSuchElementException if they are asked to retrieve the next element (or next token) after all elements (or tokens) have been processed.

EXAMPLE 4.3   Assume iter is declared as an Iterator object for LinkedList myList. We can replace the fragment shown at the beginning of this section with the following one.

```
// Access each list element
while (iter.hasNext()) {
    Object nextElement = iter.next();
    // Do something with the next element (nextElement)
    . . .
}
```

This fragment is O(n) instead of O(n^2). All that remains is to determine how to declare iter as an Iterator for LinkedList object myList. We show how to do this in the next section and discuss Iterator a bit more formally.

The Iterator Interface

The interface Iterator is defined as part of API package java.util. Table 4.3 summarizes the methods declared by this interface.

The List interface declares the method iterator, which returns an Iterator object that will iterate over the elements of that list. (The requirement for the iterator method is actually in the Collection interface, which is the superinterface for the List interface. We discuss the Collection interface in Section 4.8.)

In the following loop, we process all items in a list through an Iterator; we use *ClassType* to represent the data type of the objects.

TABLE 4.3
The java.util.Iterator Interface

Method	Behavior
boolean hasNext()	Returns **true** if the next method returns a value.
Object next()	Returns the next element. If there are no more elements, throws the NoSuchElementException.
void remove()	Removes the last element returned by the next method from the list.

FIGURE 4.23
Advancing an `Iterator` via the `next` Method

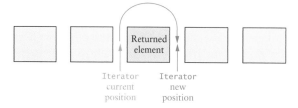

```
// Obtain an Iterator to the list aList.
Iterator itr = aList.iterator();
while (itr.hasNext() {
    ClassType value = (ClassType) itr.next();
    // Do something with value.
}
```

An `Iterator` does not refer to or point to a particular object at any given time. Rather you should think of an `Iterator` as pointing between objects within a list. The method `hasNext` tells us whether or not calling the `next` method will succeed. If `hasNext` returns **true**, then a call to `next` will return the next object in the list and advance the `Iterator` (see Figure 4.23). If `hasNext` returns false, a call to `next` will cause the `NoSuchElementException` to be thrown.

You can use the `Iterator` remove method to remove elements from a list as you access them. You can remove only the element that was most recently accessed by `next`. Each call to `remove` must be preceded by a call to `next` to retrieve the next element.

EXAMPLE 4.4   Assume that we have a `List` of `Integer` objects. We wish to remove all elements that are divisible by a particular value. The following method will accomplish this:

```
/** Remove items divisible by a given value.
    pre: LinkedList aList contains Integer objects.
    post: Elements divisible by div have been removed.
*/
public void removeDivisibleBy(LinkedList aList, int div) {
    Iterator iter = aList.iterator();
    while (iter.hasNext()) {
        int nextInt = ((Integer) iter.next()).intValue();
        if (nextInt % div == 0)
            iter.remove();
    }
}
```

The method call `iter.next` retrieves the next element in the list (an `Integer` object). If the value wrapped is divisible by `div`, the statement

```
iter.remove();
```

removes the element just retrieved from the list.

PITFALL

Improper Use of remove

If a call to remove is not preceded by a call to next, remove will throw an IllegalStateException. If you want to remove two consecutive elements in a list, a separate call to next must occur before each call to remove.

PROGRAM STYLE

Removal Using Iterator.remove Versus List.remove

You could also use method LinkedList.remove to remove elements from a list. However, it is more efficient to remove multiple elements from a list using Iterator.remove than it would be to use LinkedList.remove. The LinkedList remove method removes only one element at a time, so you would need to start at the beginning of the list each time and advance down the list to each element that you wanted to remove ($O(n^2)$ process). With the Iterator remove method, you can remove elements as they are accessed by the Iterator object without having to go back to the beginning of the list ($O(n)$ process).

The ListIterator Interface

The Iterator has some limitations. It can traverse the List only in the forward direction. It also provides only a remove method, not an add method. Also, to obtain an Iterator that starts somewhere other than the beginning, you must write your own loop to advance the iterator to the starting position.

The Java API also contains the ListIterator interface, which is an extension of the Iterator interface that overcomes these limitations. Like the Iterator, the ListIterator should be thought of as being positioned between elements of the linked list. The positions are assigned an index from 0 to size, where the position just before the first element has index 0 and the position just after the last element has index size. The next method moves the iterator forward and returns the element that was jumped over. The previous method moves the iterator backward and also returns the element that was jumped over. This is illustrated in Figure 4.24, where i is the currect position of the iterator. The methods defined by the ListIterator interface are shown in Table 4.4.

FIGURE 4.24

The ListIterator

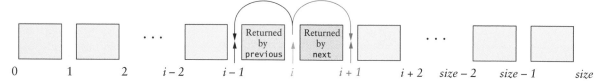

TABLE 4.4

The java.util.ListIterator Interface

Method	Behavior
void add(Object obj)	Inserts object obj into the list just before the item that would be returned by the next call to method next and after the item that would have been returned by method previous. If method previous is called after add, the newly inserted object will be returned.
boolean hasNext()	Returns **true** if next will not throw an exception.
boolean hasPrevious()	Returns **true** if previous will not throw an exception.
Object next()	Returns the next object and moves the iterator forward. If the iterator is at the end, the NoSuchElementException is thrown.
int nextIndex()	Returns the index of the item that will be returned by the next call to next. If the iterator is at the end, the list size is returned.
Object previous()	Returns the previous object and moves the iterator backward. If the iterator is at the beginning of the list, the NoSuchElementExcepton is thrown.
int previousIndex()	Returns the index of the item that will be returned by the next call to previous. If the iterator is at the beginning of the list, −1 is returned.
void remove()	Removes the last item returned from a call to next or previous. If a call to remove is not preceded by a call to next or previous, the IllegalStateException is thrown.
void set(Object obj)	Replaces the last item returned from a call to next or previous with obj. If a call to set is not preceded by a call to next or previous, the IllegalStateException is thrown.

To obtain a ListIterator, you call the listIterator method of the LinkedList class. This method has two forms, as shown in Table 4.5

TABLE 4.5
Methods in `java.util.LinkedList` That Return `ListIterators`

Method	Behavior
`public ListIterator listIterator()`	Returns a `ListIterator` that begins just before the first list element.
`public ListIterator listIterator(int index)`	Returns a `ListIterator` that begins just before position `index`.

EXAMPLE 4.5   The statement

```
ListIterator myIter = myList.listIterator(3);
```

would create a `ListIterator` object `myIter` positioned between the elements at positions 2 and 3 of the linked list. Assume that this is the position of the iterator before each of the following method calls. The method call

```
myIter.next()
```

would return a reference to the object at position 3; the method call

```
myIter.nextIndex()
```

would return 3. The method call

```
myIter.previous()
```

would return a reference to the object at position 2. The method call

```
myIter.previousIndex()
```

would return 2. The method calls

```
myIter.hasNext()
```

would return **true** if the list has at least 4 elements; the method call

```
myIter.hasPrevious()
```

would return **true**.

EXAMPLE 4.6   The fragment

```
ListIterator myIter = myList.listIterator();
while (myIter.hasNext()) {
    if (target.equals(myIter.next()) {
        myIter.set(newItem);
        break;  // Exit loop.
    }
}
```

searches for `target` in list `myList` and, if `target` is present, replaces it with `newItem`.

Comparison of `Iterator` and `ListIterator`

Since the `ListIterator` is a subinterface of `Iterator`, classes that implement `ListIterator` provide all of the capabilities of both. The `Iterator` interface requires fewer methods and can be used to iterate over more general data structures—that is, ones for which an index is not meaningful and ones for which traversing in only the forward direction is required. It is for this reason that the `Iterator` is required by the `Collection` interface (more general), whereas the `ListIterator` is required only by the `List` interface (more specialized). We will discuss the `Collection` interface in Section 4.8.

Conversion Between a `ListIterator` and an Index

The `ListIterator` has the methods `nextIndex` and `previousIndex`, which return the index values associated with the items that would be returned by a call to the `next` or `previous` methods. The `LinkedList` class has the method `listIterator(int index)`, which returns a `ListIterator` whose next call to `next` will return the item at position `index`. Thus you can convert between an index and a `ListIterator`. However, remember that the `listIterator(int index)` method creates the desired `ListIterator` by creating a new `ListIterator` that starts at the beginning and then walks along the list until the desired position is found. There is a special case where `index` is equal to `size()`, but all others are an O(n) operation.

EXERCISES FOR SECTION 4.5

SELF CHECK

1. The method `indexOf`, part of the `List` interface, returns the index of the first occurrence of an object in a `List`. What does the following code fragment do?
   ```
   int indexOfSam = myList.indexOf("Sam");
   ListIterator iteratorToSam = listIterator(indexOfSam);
   iteratorToSam.previous();
   iteratorToSam.remove();
   ```
   where `myList` is shown in the following figure:

   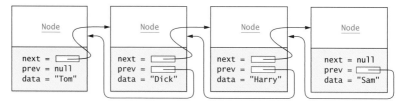

2. In Question 1, what if we change the statement
   ```
   iteratorToSam.previous();
   ```
   to
   ```
   iteratorToSam.next();
   ```

3. In Question 1, what if we omit the statement
   ```
   iteratorToSam.previous();
   ```

1. Write the method `indexOf` as specified in the `List` interface by adapting the code shown in Example 4.6 to return the index of the first occurrence of an object.
2. Write the method `lastIndexOf` specified in the `List` interface by adapting the code shown in Example 4.6 to return the index of the last occurrence of an object.
3. Write a method `indexOfMin` that returns the index of the minimum item in a `List`, assuming that each item in the list implements the `Comparable` interface.

4.6 Implementation of a Double-Linked List Class

In this section we will describe the class `KWLinkedList`, which implements some of the methods of the `List` interface using a double-linked list. We will not provide a complete implementation, because we expect you to use the standard `LinkedList` class provided by the Java API (in package `java.util`). The data fields for the `KWLinkedList` class are shown in Table 4.6.

Implementing the `KWLinkedList` Methods

We need to implement the methods shown earlier in Table 4.2 for the `LinkedList` class. The algorithm for the `add(int index, Object obj)` method is

1. Obtain a reference, `nodeRef`, to the node at position `index`.
2. Insert a new `Node` containing `obj` before the `Node` referenced by `nodeRef`.

Similarly the algorithm for the `get(int index)` method is

1. Obtain a reference, `nodeRef`, to the node at position `index`.
2. Return the contents of the `Node` referenced by `nodeRef`.

We also have the `listIterator(int index)` method with the following algorithm:

1. Obtain a reference, `nodeRef`, to the node at position `index`.
2. Return a `ListIterator` that is positioned just before the `Node` referenced by `nodeRef`.

TABLE 4.6
Data Fields for the `KWLinkedList` Class

Data Field	Attribute
`private Node head`	A reference to the first item in the list.
`private Node tail`	A reference to the last item in the list
`private int size`	A count of the number of items in the list.

These three methods all have the same first step. Therefore we want to use a common method to perform this step.

If we look at the requirements for the `ListIterator`, we see that it has an `add` method that inserts a new item before the current position of the iterator. Thus we can refine the algorithm for the `KWLinkedList.add(int, Object)` method to

1.   Obtain an iterator that is positioned just before the `Node` at position `index`.
2.   Insert a new `Node` containing `obj` before the `Node` currently referenced by this iterator.

Thus the `KWLinkedList` method add can be coded as

```
/** Add an item at the specified index.
    @param index The index at which the object is to be
            inserted
    @param obj The object to be inserted
    @throws IndexOutOfBoundsException if the index is out
            of range (i < 0 || i > size())
*/
public void add(int index, Object obj) {
    listIterator(index).add(obj);
}
```

Notice it was not necessary to declare a local `ListIterator` object in the `KWLinkedList` method add. The method call `listIterator(index)` returns an anonymous `ListIterator` object, to which we apply the `ListIterator.add` method.

Similarly, we can code the `get` method as

```
/** Get the first element in the list.
    @return The first element in the list
*/
public Object get(int index) {
    return listIterator(index).next();
}
```

Implementing the `ListIterator` Interface

We can implement most of the `KWLinkedList` methods by delegation to the class `KWListIter` which will implement the `ListIterator` interface (see Table 4.4). Because it is an inner class of `KWLinkedList`, its methods will be able to reference the data fields and members of the parent class (and also the other inner class, `Node`). The data fields for class `KWListIter` are shown in Table 4.7.

```
/** Inner class to implement the ListIterator interface. */
private class KWListIter implements ListIterator {
    /** A reference to the next item. */
    private Node nextItem;
    /** A reference to the last item returned. */
    private Node lastItemReturned;
    /** The index of the current item. */
    private int index = 0;
```

Figure 4.25 shows an example of a `KWLinkedList` object and a `KWListIter` object. The next method would return "Harry", and the previous method would return "Dick". The nextIndex method would return 2, and the previousIndex method would return 1.

TABLE 4.7
Data Fields of the `KWListIter` Class

Data Field	Attribute
private Node nextItem	A reference to the next item.
private Node lastItemReturned	A reference to the node that was last returned by next or previous.
private int index	The iterator is positioned just before the item at index.

FIGURE 4.25
Double-Linked List with `KWListIter`

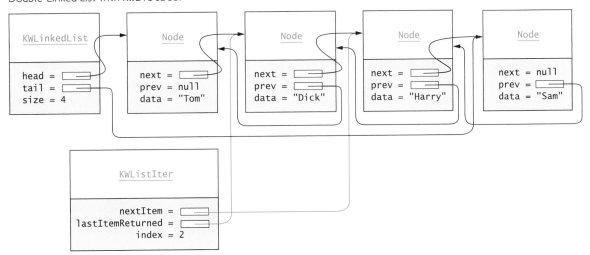

The Constructor

The `KWListIter` constructor takes as a parameter the index of the `Node` at which the iteration is to begin. A test is made for the special case where the index is equal to the size; in that case the iteration starts at the tail. Otherwise, a loop starting at the head walks along the list until the node at `index` is reached.

```
/** Construct a KWListIter that will reference the ith item.
    @param i The index of the item to be referenced
*/
public KWListIter(int i) {
    // Validate i parameter.
    if (i < 0 || i > size) {
        throw new IndexOutOfBoundsException(
            "Invalid index " + i);
    }
    lastItemReturned = null;   // No item returned yet.
```

```
            // Special case of last item.
            if (i == size) {
                index = size;
                nextItem = null;
            } else {    // Start at the beginning
                nextItem = head;
                for (index = 0; index < i; index++) {
                    nextItem = nextItem.next;
                }
            }
        }
```

The hasNext and next Methods

The data field nextItem will always reference the Node that will be returned by the next method. Therefore, the hasNext method merely tests to see whether nextItem is **null**.

```
/** Indicate whether movement forward is defined.
    @return true if call to next will not throw an exception
*/
public boolean hasNext() {
    return nextItem != null;
}
```

The next method begins by calling hasNext. If the result is **false**, the NoSuchElemenentException is thrown. Otherwise, lastItemReturned is set to nextItem, then nextItem is advanced to the next node, and index is incremented. The data field of the node referenced by lastItemReturned is returned. As shown in Figure 4.26, the previous iterator position is indicated by the gray arrows and the new position by the colored arrows.

```
/** Move the iterator forward and return the next item.
    @return the next item in the list
    @throws NoSuchElementException if there is no such object
*/
public Object next() {
    if (!hasNext()) {
        throw new NoSuchElementException();
    }
    lastItemReturned = nextItem;
    nextItem = nextItem.next;
    index++;
    return lastItemReturned.data;
}
```

The hasPrevious and previous Methods

The hasPrevious method is a little trickier. When the iterator is at the end of the list, nextItem is null. In this case, we can determine that there is a previous item by checking the size—a nonempty list will have a previous item when the iterator is at the end. If the iterator is not at the end, then nextItem is not null, and we can check for a previous item by examining nextItem.prev.

FIGURE 4.26

Advancing a `KWListIter`

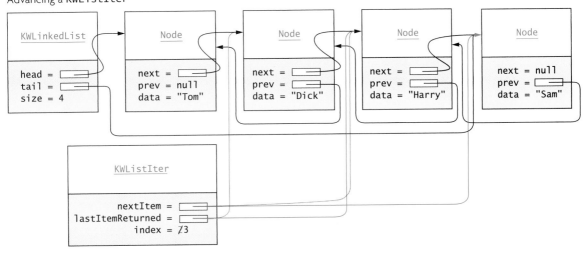

```
/** Indicate whether movement backward is defined.
    @return true if call to previous will not throw an exception
*/
public boolean hasPrevious() {
    return (nextItem == null && size != 0)
            || nextItem.prev != null;
}
```

The `previous` method begins by calling `hasPrevious`. If the result is **false**, the `NoSuchElementException` is thrown. Otherwise, if `nextItem` is **null**, the iterator is past the last element, so `nextItem` is set to `tail` because the previous element must be the last list element. If `nextItem` is not **null**, `nextItem` is set to `nextItem.prev`. Either way, `lastItemReturned` is set to `nextItem`, and `index` is decremented. The `data` field of the node referenced by `lastItemReturned` is returned.

```
/** Move the iterator backward and return the previous item.
    @return The previous item in the list
    @throws NoSuchElementException if there is no such object
*/
public Object previous() {
    if (!hasPrevious()) {
        throw new NoSuchElementException();
    }
    if (nextItem == null) {     // Iterator past the last element
        nextItem = tail;
    } else {
        nextItem = nextItem.prev;
    }
    lastItemReturned = nextItem;
    index--;
    return lastItemReturned.data;
}
```

FIGURE 4.27
Adding to an Empty List

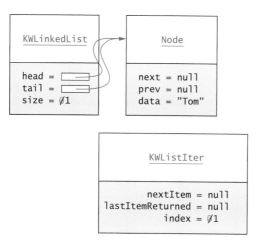

The **add** Method

The add method inserts a new node before the node referenced by nextItem. There are four cases: add to an empty list, add to the head of the list, add to the tail of the list, and add to the middle of the list. We next discuss each case separately; combine them to write the method.

An empty list is indicated by head equal to null. In this case, a new Node is created, and both head and tail are set to reference it. This is illustrated in Figure 4.27.

```
/** Add a new item between the item that will be returned.
    by next and the item that will be returned by previous.
    If previous is called after add, the element added is
    returned.
    @param obj The item to be inserted
 */
public void add(Object obj) {
    if (head == null) {    // Add to an empty list.
        head = new Node(obj);
        tail = head;
    ...
```

The KWListIter object shows a value of **null** for lastItemReturned and 1 for index. These data fields are set at the end of the method. In all cases, data field nextItem is not changed by the insertion. It must reference the successor of the item that was inserted, or **null** if there is no successor.

If nextItem equals head, then the insertion is at the head. The new Node is created and is linked to the beginning of the list.

```
    } else if (nextItem == head) {    // Insert at head.
        // Create a new node.
        Node newNode = new Node(obj);
        // Link it to the nextItem.
        newNode.next = nextItem;    // Step 1
        // Link nextItem to the new node.
        nextItem.prev = newNode;    // Step 2
        // The new node is now the head.
        head = newNode;             // Step 3
```

FIGURE 4.28
Adding to the Head of the List

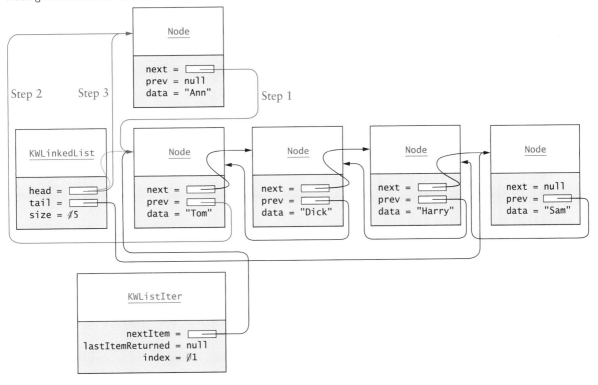

This is illustrated in Figure 4.28.

If nextItem is null, then the insertion is at the tail. The new node is created and linked to the tail.

```
    } else if (nextItem == null) {    // Insert at tail.
        // Create a new node.
        Node newNode = new Node(obj);
        // Link the tail to the new node.
        tail.next = newNode;         // Step 1
        // Link the new node to the tail.
        newNode.prev = tail;         // Step 2
        // The new node is the new tail.
        tail = newNode;              // Step 3
```

This is illustrated in Figure 4.29.

If none of the previous cases is true, then the addition is into the middle of the list. The new node is created and inserted before the node referenced by nextItem.

```
    } else {    // Insert into the middle.
        // Create a new node.
        Node newNode = new Node(obj);
```

```
                        // Link it to nextItem.prev.
                        newNode.prev = nextItem.prev;   // Step 1
                        nextItem.prev.next = newNode;   // Step 2
                        // Link it to the nextItem.
                        newNode.next = nextItem;        // Step 3
                        nextItem.prev = newNode;        // Step 4
                }
```

This is illustrated in Figure 4.30.

After the new node is inserted, both `size` and `index` are incremented and `lastItemReturned` is set to **null**.

```
                        // Increase size and index and set lastItemReturned.
                        size++;
                        index++;
                        lastItemReturned = null;
                } // End of method add.
```

FIGURE 4.29
Adding to the Tail of the List

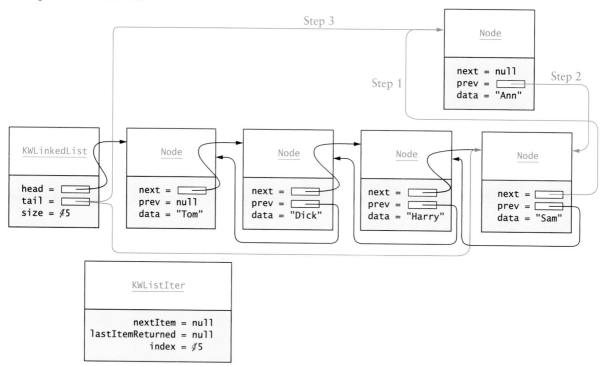

FIGURE 4.30
Adding to the Middle of the List

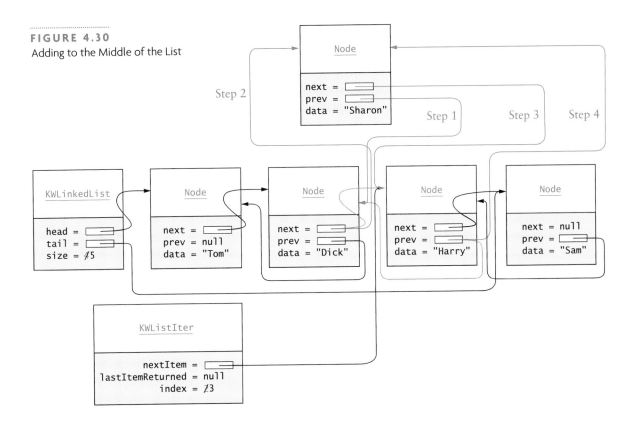

EXERCISES FOR SECTION 4.6

SELF CHECK

1. Why didn't we write the `hasPrevious` method as follows?
```
public boolean hasPrevious() {
    return nextItem.prev != null
            || (nextItem == null && size != 0);
}
```
2. Why must we call `next` or `previous` before we call `remove`?
3. What happens if we call `remove` after we call `add`? What does the Java API documentation say? What does our implementation do?

PROGRAMMING

1. Implement the `KWListIter.remove` method.
2. Implement the `KWListIter.set` method.
3. Implement the `KWLinkedList listIterator` and `iterator` methods.

4.7 Application of the LinkedList Class

In this section, we introduce a case study that uses the Java LinkedList class to solve a common problem: maintaining an ordered list.

CASE STUDY   Maintaining an Ordered list

Problem As discussed in Section 4.4, we can use a linked list to maintain a list of students who are registered for a course. We want to maintain this list so that it will be in alphabetical order even after students have added and dropped the course.

Analysis Instead of solving this problem just for a list of students, we will develop a general OrderedList class that can be used to store any group of objects that can be compared. Java classes whose object types can be compared implement the Comparable interface, which is defined as follows:

```
/** Instances of classes that realize this interface can be
    compared. */
public interface Comparable {
    /** Method to compare this object to the argument object.
        @param obj The argument object
        @return Returns a negative integer if this object < obj;
                zero if this object equals obj;
                a positive integer if this object > obj
    */
    int compareTo(Object obj);
}
```

Therefore, a class that implements the Comparable interface must provide a compareTo method that returns an **int** value that indicates the relative ordering of two instances of that class.

We can either extend the Java LinkedList class to create a new class OrderedList, or create an OrderedList class that uses a LinkedList to store the items. If we implement our OrderedList class as an extension of LinkedList, a client will be able to use methods in the List interface that can insert new elements or modify existing elements in such a way that the items are no longer in order. Therefore, we will use the LinkedList class as a component of the OrderedList class, and we will implement only those methods that preserve the order of the items.

Design The class diagram in Figure 4.31 shows the relationships among the OrderedList class, the LinkedList class, and the Comparable interface. The filled diamond indicates that the LinkedList is a component of the OrderedList, and the open diamond indicates that the LinkedList will contain Comparable objects.

FIGURE 4.31
OrderedList Class Diagram

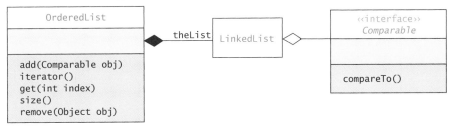

Because we want to be able to make insertions and deletions in the ordered linked list, we must implement add and remove methods. We also provide a get method, to access the element at a particular position, and an iterator method, to provide the user with the ability to access all of the elements in sequence efficiently. Table 4.8 describes the class.

Implementation   Let's say we have an ordered list that contains the data: "Alice", "Andrew", "Caryn", "Sharon" and we want to insert "Bill" (see Figure 4.32). If we start at the beginning of the list and access "Alice", we know that "Bill" must follow "Alice", but we can't insert "Bill" yet. If we access "Andrew", we know that "Bill" must follow "Andrew", but we can't insert "Bill" yet. However, when we access "Caryn", we know we must insert "Bill" before "Caryn". Therefore, to insert an element in an ordered list, we need to access the first element whose data is *larger* than the data in the element to be inserted. Once we have accessed the successor of our new node, we can insert a new node just before it. (Note that in order to access "Caryn" using method next, we have advanced the iterator just past "Caryn".)

TABLE 4.8
Class OrderedList

Data Field	Attribute
private LinkedList theList	A linked list to contain the data.
Method	**Behavior**
public void add(Comparable obj)	Inserts obj into the list preserving the list's order.
public Iterator iterator()	Returns an Iterator to the list.
public Object get(int index)	Returns the object at the specified position.
public int size()	Returns the size of the list.
public void remove(Object obj)	Removes obj from the list.

FIGURE 4.32
Inserting "Bill" before "Caryn" in an Ordered List

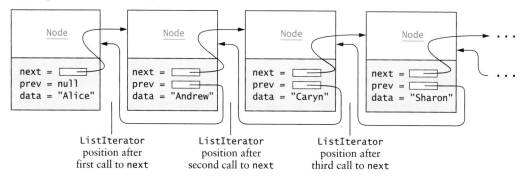

ListIterator
position after
first call to next

ListIterator
position after
second call to next

ListIterator
position after
third call to next

Algorithm for Insertion

The algorithm for insertion is

1.   Find the first item in the list that is greater than the item to be inserted.
2.   Insert the new item before this one.

We can refine this algorithm as follows:

1.1   Create a ListIterator that starts at the beginning of the list.
1.2   **while** the ListIterator is not at the end and the item to be inserted is greater than or equal to the next item
1.3   Advance the ListIterator.
2.   Insert the new item before the current ListIterator position.

The add Method

A straightforward coding of the insertion algorithm would be the following:

```
// Warning - This does not work.
ListIterator iter = theList.listIterator();
while (iter.hasNext()
       && obj.compareTo(iter.next()) >= 0) {
    // iter was advanced - check new position.
}
iter.add(obj);
```

Unfortunately, this does not work. When the **while** loop terminates, either we are at the end of the list, or the ListIterator has just skipped over the first item that is greater than the item to be inserted. In the first case, the add method will insert the item at the end of the list, just as we want, but in the second case it will insert the item just *after* the position where it belongs (see Figure 4.33). Therefore we must separate the two cases and code the add method as follows:

FIGURE 4.33
Attempted Insertion into an Ordered List

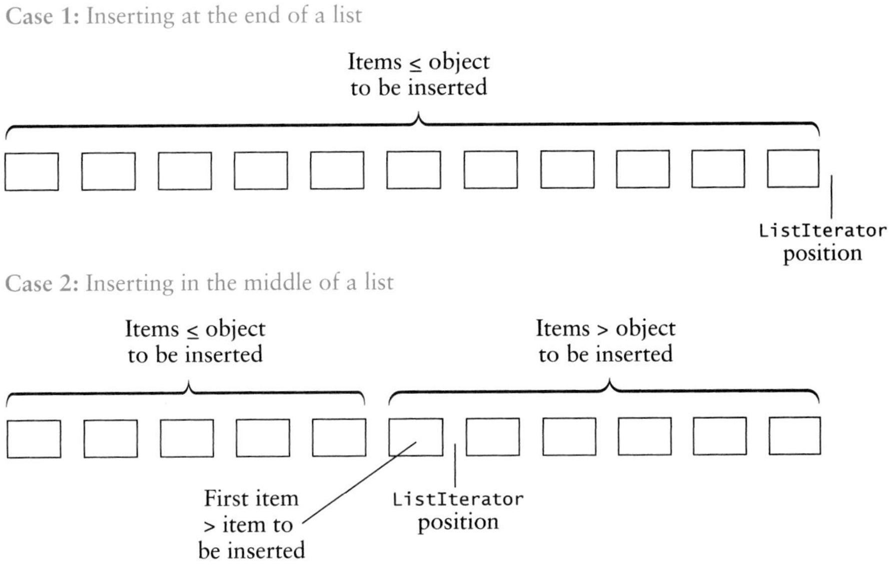

Case 1: Inserting at the end of a list

Case 2: Inserting in the middle of a list

```java
/** Insert obj into the list preserving the list's order.
    pre: The items in the list are ordered.
    post: obj has been inserted into the list
          such that the items are still in order.
    @param obj The item to be inserted
*/
public void add(Comparable obj) {
    ListIterator iter = theList.listIterator();
    // Find the insertion position and insert.
    while (iter.hasNext()) {
        if (obj.compareTo(iter.next()) < 0) {
            // Iterator has stepped over the first element
            // that is greater than the element to be inserted.
            // Move the iterator back one.
            iter.previous();
            // Insert the element.
            iter.add(obj);
            // Exit the loop and return.
            return;
        }
    }
    // assert: All items were examined and no item is larger than
    // the element to be inserted.
    // Add the new item to the end of the list.
    iter.add(obj);
}
```

The Other Methods

The other methods in Table 4.8 are implemented via delegation to the `LinkedList` class. They merely call the corresponding method in the `LinkedList`. For example, the `get` method is coded as follows.

```
/** Returns the element at the specified position.
    @param index The index of the specified position
*/
Object get(int index) {
    return theList.get(index);
}
```

Testing   You can test the `OrderedList` class by storing a collection of randomly generated positive integers in an `OrderedList`. You can then insert a negative integer and an integer larger than any integer in the list. This tests the two special cases of inserting at the beginning and at the end of the list. You can then create an iterator and use it to traverse the list, displaying an error message if the current integer is smaller than the previous integer. You can also display the list during the traversal so that you can inspect it to verify that it is in order. Finally, you can remove the first element, the last element, and an element in the middle and repeat the traversal. Listing 4.2 shows a program that performs this test.

Method `traverseAndShow` traverses an ordered list passed as an argument using iterator `aListIter` to access the list elements. The **if** statement displays an error message if the previous value is greater than the current value (`prevItem.compareTo (thisItem) > 0` is **true**). Method `main` calls `traverseAndShow` after all elements are inserted and after the three elements are removed. In method `main`, the loop

```
for (int i = 0; i < START_SIZE; i++) {
    Integer anInteger = new Integer(random.nextInt(MAX_INT));
    testList.add(anInteger);
}
```

fills the ordered list with randomly generated values between 0 and `MAX_INT - 1`. Variable `random` is an instance of class `Random` (in API java.util), which contains methods for generating pseudorandom numbers. Method `Random.nextInt` generates random integers between 0 and its argument.

LISTING 4.2
Class `TestOrderedList`

```
import java.util.*;

public class TestOrderedList {
    /** Traverses ordered list and displays each element.
        Displays an error message if an element is out of order.
        pre: The list elements are all positive and the list is not
            empty.
        @param An ordered list
```

```
    */
    public static void traverseAndShow(OrderedList testList) {
        ListIterator aListIter = (ListIterator) testList.iterator();
        Integer prevItem = (Integer) testList.get(0);

        // Traverse ordered list and display any value that
        // is out of order.
        while (aListIter.hasNext()) {
            Integer thisItem = (Integer) aListIter.next();
            System.out.println(thisItem);
            if (prevItem.compareTo(thisItem) > 0)
                System.out.println("*** FAILED, value is "
                                        + thisItem);
            prevItem = thisItem;
        }
    }

    public static void main(String[] args) {
        OrderedList testList = new OrderedList();
        final int MAX_INT = 500;
        final int START_SIZE = 100;

        // Create a random number generator.
        Random random = new Random();
        for (int i = 0; i < START_SIZE; i++) {
            Integer anInteger =
                new Integer(random.nextInt(MAX_INT));
            testList.add(anInteger);
        }

        // Add to beginning and end of list.
        testList.add(new Integer(-1));
        testList.add(new Integer(MAX_INT + 1));
        traverseAndShow(testList);  // Traverse and display.

        // Remove first, last, and middle elements.
        Integer first = (Integer) testList.get(0);
        testList.remove(first);
        Integer last =
                (Integer) testList.get(testList.size() - 1);
        testList.remove(last);
        Integer middle =
                (Integer) testList.get(testList.size() / 2);
        testList.remove(middle);
        traverseAndShow(testList);  // Traverse and display.
    }
}
```

EXERCISES FOR SECTION 4.7

SELF CHECK

1. Why don't we implement the OrderedList by extending LinkedList? What would happen if someone called the add method? How about the set method?
2. What other methods in the List interface could we include in the OrderedList class? See the Java API documentation for a complete list of methods.
3. If we implement the iterator method by delegating to the LinkedList, we will get a ListIterator that has been upcast to an Iterator. Is this a problem?

PROGRAMMING

1. Write the code for the other methods of the OrderedList class that are listed in Table 4.8.
2. Rewrite the OrderedList.add method to start at the end of the list and iterate using the ListIterator's previous method.

4.8 The Collection Hierarchy

The ArrayList and the LinkedList implement the List interface that we described in Section 4.1. Both the ArrayList and LinkedList represent a collection of objects that can be referenced by means of an index. But what if we removed the requirement that each object have an index?

The Collection interface models this more abstract concept. The Collection interface specifies a subset of the methods specified in the List interface. Specifically, the add(int, Object), get(int), remove(int), set(int, Object), and related methods (all of which have an **int** parameter that represents a position) are not in the Collection interface, but the add(Object) method and remove(Object) methods, which do not specify a position, are included. The iterator method is also included in the Collection interface; thus, you can use an Iterator to access all of the items in a Collection, but the order in which they are retrieved is not necessarily related to the order in which they were inserted.

The Collection interface is the root of the *collection hierarchy* as shown in Figure 4.34. This hierarchy has two branches: one rooted by the List interface and the other by the Set interface, which we will discuss in Chapter 9. The Java API does not provide any direct implementation of the Collection interface. The interface is used to pass collections of data as a method parameter in the most general way.

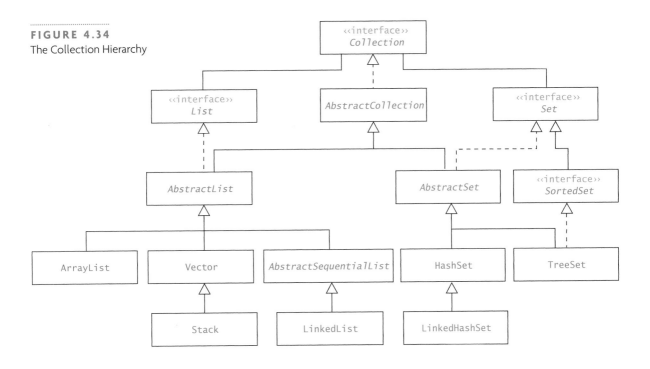

FIGURE 4.34
The Collection Hierarchy

Common Features of Collections

Because it is the root of the class hierarchy, the Collection interface specifies a set of common methods. If you look at the documentation for the Java API java.util.Collection, you will see that this is a fairly large set of methods and other requirements. There are a few features that can be considered fundamental:

- Collections grow as needed.
- Collections hold references to objects.
- Collections have at least two constructors: one to create an empty collection and one to make a copy of another collection.

Table 4.9 shows selected methods defined in the Collection interface. We have already seen and discussed these methods in the discussions of the ArrayList and LinkedList. The Iterator provides a common way to access all of the elements in a Collection. For collections implementing the List interface, the order of the elements is determined by the index of the elements. In the more general Collection, the order is not specified.

In the ArrayList and LinkedList, the add(Object) method always inserts the object at the end and always returns **true**. In the more general Collection, the position where the object is inserted is not specified. The Set interface extends the Collection by requiring that the add method not insert an object that is already present; instead, in that case it returns **false**. The Set interface is discussed in Chapter 9.

....
TABLE 4.9
Selected Methods of the `java.util.Collection` Interface

Method	Behavior
`boolean add(Object obj)`	Ensures that the collection contains the object `obj`. Returns **true** if the collection was modified.
`boolean contains(Object obj)`	Returns **true** if the collection contains the object `obj`.
`Iterator iterator()`	Returns an `Iterator` to the collection.
`int size()`	Returns the size of the collection.

The `AbstractCollection`, `AbstractList`, and `AbstractSequentialList` Classes

If you look at the Java API documentation, you will see that the `Collection` and `List` interfaces specify a large number of methods. To help implement these interfaces, the Java API includes the `AbstractCollection` and `AbstractList` classes. You can think of these classes as a kit (or as a cake mix) that can be used to build implementations of their corresponding interface. Most of the methods are provided, but you need to add a few to make it complete.

To implement the `Collection` interface completely, you need only extend the `AbstractCollection` class, provide an implementation of the add, size, and iterator methods, and provide an inner class to implement the `Iterator` interface. To implement the `List` interface, you can extend the `AbstractList` class and provide an implementation of the add(int, Object), get(int), remove(int), set(int, Object), and size() methods. Since we provided these methods in our `KWArrayList`, we can make it a complete implementation of the `List` interface by changing the class declaration to

```
public class KWArrayList extends AbstractList
```

Note that the `AbstractList` class implements the iterator and listIterator methods using the index associated with the elements.

Another way to implement the `List` interface is to extend the `AbstractSequentialList` class, implement the listIterator and size methods, and provide an inner class that implements the `ListIterator` interface. This was the approach we took in our `KWLinkedList`. Thus, by changing the class declaration to

```
public class KWLinkedList extends AbstractSequentialList
```

it becomes a complete implementation of the `List` interface. Our `KWLinkedList` class included the add, get, remove, and set methods. These are provided by the `AbstractSequentialList`, so we could remove them from our `KWLinkedList` class and still have a complete `List` implementation.

EXERCISES FOR SECTION 4.8

SELF-CHECK

1. Look at the AbstractCollection definition in the Java API documentation. What methods are abstract? Could we use the KWArrayList and extend the AbstractCollection, but not the AbstractList, to develop an implementation of the Collection interface? How about using the KWLinkedList and the AbstractCollection, but not the AbstractSequentialList?

PROGRAMMING

1. Using either the KWArrayList or KWLinkedList as the base, develop an implementation of the Collection interface by extending the AbstractCollection. Test it by ensuring that the following statement compiles:

   Collection testCollection = new *MyClass*();

   where *MyClass* is the name of your class.

Chapter Review

- ◆ The List is a generalization of the array. As in the array, elements of a List are accessed by means of an index. Unlike the array, the List can grow or shrink. Items may be inserted or removed from any position.

- ◆ The Java API provides the ArrayList class, which uses an array as the underlying structure to implement the List. We provided an example of how this might be implemented by allocating an array that is larger than the number of items in the list. As items are inserted into the list, the items with higher indices are moved up to make room for the inserted item, and as items are removed, the items with higher indices are moved down to fill in the emptied space. When the array capacity is reached, a new array is allocated that is twice the size and the old array is copied to the new one. By doubling the capacity, the cost of the copy is spread over each insertion, so that the copies can be considered to have a constant time contribution to the cost of each insertion.

- ◆ A linked list data structure consists of a set of nodes, each of which contains its data and a reference to the next node in the list. In a double-linked list, each node contains a reference to both the next and the previous node in the list. Insertion into and removal from a linked list is a constant-time operation.

◆ To access an item at a position indicated by an index in a linked list requires walking along the list from the beginning until the item at the specified index is reached. Thus, traversing a linked list using an index would be an $O(n^2)$ operation because we need to repeat the walk each time the index changes. The Iterator provides a general way to traverse a list so that traversing a linked list using an iterator is an $O(n)$ operation.

◆ An iterator provides us with the ability to access the items in a List sequentially. The Iterator interface defines the methods available to an iterator. The List interface defines the iterator method, which returns an Iterator to the list. The Iterator.hasNext method tells whether there is a next item, and the Iterator.next method returns the next item and advances the iterator. The Iterator also provides the remove method, which lets us remove the last item returned by the next method.

◆ The ListIterator interface is an extension of the Iterator interface. The ListIterator provides us with the ability to traverse the list either forward or backward. In addition to the hasNext and next methods, the ListIterator has the hasPrevious and previous methods. Also, in addition to the remove method, it has an add method that inserts a new item into the list just before the current iterator position.

◆ The Java API provides the LinkedList class, which uses a double-linked list to implement the List interface. We show an example of how this might be implemented. Because the class that realizes the ListIterator interface provides the add and remove operations, the corresponding methods in the linked list class can be implemented by constructing an iterator (using the listIterator(int) method) that references the desired position and then calling on the iterator to perform the insertion or removal.

◆ The Collection interface is the root of the Collection hierarchy. The Collection is more general than the List, because the items in a Collection are not indexed. The add method inserts an item into a Collection but does not specify where it is inserted. The Iterator is used to traverse the items in a Collection, but it does not specify the order of the items.

◆ The Collection interface and the List interface define a large number of methods that make these abstractions useful for many applications. In our discussion of both the ArrayList and LinkedList we showed how to implement only a few key methods. The Collection hierarchy includes the AbstractCollection, AbstractList, and AbstractSequentialList classes. These classes implement their corresponding interface except for a few key methods; these are the same methods for which we showed implementations.

Java API Interfaces and Classes Introduced in This Chapter

java.util.ArrayList
java.util.AbstractCollection
java.util.AbstractList
java.util.AbstractSequentialList
java.util.Collection

java.util.Iterator
java.util.LinkedList
java.util.List
java.util.ListIterator

User-Defined Interfaces and Classes in This Chapter

KWArrayList
KWLinkedList
KWListIter

Node
OrderedList

Quick-Check Exercises

1. Elements of a List are accessed by means of _____.
2. A List can _____ or _____ as items are added or removed.
3. When we allocate a new array for an ArrayList because the current capacity is exceeded, we make the new array at least _____. This allows us to _____.
4. In a single-linked list, if we want to remove a list element, which list element do we need to access? If nodeRef references this element, what statement removes the desired element?
5. Suppose a single-linked list contains three Nodes with data "him", "her", and "it" and head references the first element. What is the effect of the following fragment?

   ```
   Node nodeRef = head.next;
   nodeRef.data = "she";
   ```
6. Answer Question 5 for the following fragment.

   ```
   Node nodeRef = head.next;
   head.next = nodeRef.next;
   ```
7. Answer Question 5 for the following fragment.

   ```
   head = new Node("his", head);
   ```
8. An Iterator allows us to access items of a List _____.
9. A ListIterator allows us to access the elements _____.
10. The Java LinkedList class uses a _____ to implement the List interface.
11. The Collection is a _____ of the List.

Answers to Quick-Check Exercises

1. *an index*
2. *grow, shrink*
3. *twice the size, spread out the cost of the reallocation so that it is effectively a constant-time operation.*
4. The predecessor of this node. nodeRef.next = nodeRef.next.next;
5. Replaces "her" with "she".
6. Deletes the second list element ("she").
7. Insert a new first element containing "his".
8. *sequentially*
9. *both forward and backward*

10. *double-linked list*
11. *superinterface*

Review Questions

1. What is the difference between the size and the capacity of an `ArrayList`? Why do we have a constructor that lets us set the initial capacity?
2. What is the difference between the `remove(Object obj)` and `remove(int index)` methods?
3. When we insert an item into an `ArrayList`, why do we start copying from the end?
4. The `Vector` and `ArrayList` both provide the same methods, since they both implement the `List` interface. The `Vector` has some additional methods with the same functionality but different names. For example, the `Vector addElement` and `add` methods have the same functionality. There are some methods that are unique to `Vector`. Look at the Java API documentation and make a list of the methods that are in `Vector` that have equivalent methods in `ArrayList` and ones that are unique. Can the unique methods be implemented using the methods available in `ArrayList`?
5. What is the advantage of a double-linked list over a single-linked list? What is the disadvantage?
6. Why is it more efficient to use an iterator to traverse a linked list?
7. What is the difference between the `Iterator` and `ListIterator` interfaces?
8. How would you make a copy of a `ListIterator`? Consider the following:

```
ListIterator copyOfIter =
    myList.ListIterator(otherIterator.previousIndex());
```

Is this an efficient approach? How would you modify the `KWLinkedList` class to provide an efficient method to copy a `ListIterator`?
9. What is a `Collection`? Are there any classes in the Java API that completely implement the `Collection` interface?

Programming Projects

1. Develop a program to maintain a list of homework assignments. When an assignment is assigned, add it to the list, and when it is completed, remove it. You should keep track of the due date. Your program should provide the following services:
   - Add a new assignment.
   - Remove an assignment.
   - Provide a list of the assignments in the order they were assigned.
   - Find the assignment(s) with the earliest due date.
2. We can represent a polynomial as an ordered list of terms, where the terms are ordered by their exponents. To add two polynomials, you traverse both lists and examine the two terms at the current iterator position. If the exponent of one is smaller than the exponent of the other, then insert this one into the result and advance that list's iterator. If the exponents are equal, then create a new term with that exponent and the sum of the coefficients, and advance both iterators. For example:

   $3x^4 + 2x^2 + 3x + 7$ added to $2x^3 + 4x + 5$ is $3x^4 + 2x^3 + 2x^2 + 7x + 12$

   Write a program to read and add polynomials. You should define a class `Term` that contains the exponent and coefficient. This class should implement the `Comparable` interface by comparing the values of the exponents.

3. Write a program to manage a list of students waiting to register for a course as described in Section 4.4. Operations should include adding a new student at the end of the list, adding a new student at the beginning of the list, removing the student from the beginning of the list, and removing a student by name.

4. A circular linked list has no need of a head or tail. Instead, you need only a reference to a current node, which is the `nextNode` returned by the `Iterator`. Implement such a `CircularList` class. For a nonempty list, the `Iterator.hasNext` method will always return **true**.

5. The Josephus problem is named after the historian Flavius Josephus, who lived between the years 37 and 100 CE. Josephus was also a reluctant leader of the Jewish revolt against the Roman Empire. When it appeared that Josephus and his band were to be captured, they resolved to kill themselves. Josephus persuaded the group by saying, "Let us commit our mutual deaths to determination by lot. He to whom the first lot falls, let him be killed by him that hath the second lot, and thus fortune shall make its progress through us all; nor shall any of us perish by his own right hand, for it would be unfair if, when the rest are gone, somebody should repent and save himself," (Flavius Josephus, *The Wars of the Jews,* Book III, Chapter 8, Verse 7, tr. William Whiston, 1737). Yet that is exactly what happened; Josephus was left for last, and he and the person he was to kill surrendered to the Romans. Although Josephus does not describe how the lots were assigned, the following approach is generally believed to be the way it was done. People form a circle and count around the circle some predetermined number. When this number is reached, that person receives a lot and leaves the circle. The count starts over with the next person. Using the circular linked list developed in Exercise 4, simulate this problem. Your program should take two parameters: *n,* the number of people that start, and *m,* the number of counts. For example, try *n* = 20 and *m* = 12. Where does Josephus need to be in the original list so that he is the last one chosen?

6. To mimic the procedure used by Josephus and his band strictly, the person eliminated remains in the circle until the next one is chosen. Modify your program to take this into account. You may need to modify the circular linked list class to make a copy of an iterator. Does this change affect the outcome?

7. A two-dimensional shape can be defined by its boundary-polygon, which is simply a list of all coordinates ordered by a traversal of its outline. See the following figure for an example:

The left picture shows the original shape; the middle picture, the outline of the shape. The rightmost picture shows an abstracted boundary, using only the "most important" vertices. We can assign an importance measure to a vertex *P* by considering its neighbors *L* and *R.* We compute the distances *LP, PR,* and *LR.* Call these distances *l1, l2,* and *l3.* Define the importance as *l1 + l2 − l3.*

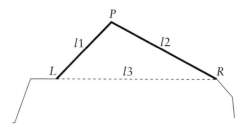

Use the following algorithm to find the *n* most important points.
1. **while** the number of points is greater than *n*
2.   Compute the importance of each point.
3.   Remove the least significant one.

Write a program to read a set of coordinates that form an outline and reduce the list to the *n* most significant ones, where *n* is an input value. Draw the initial and resulting shapes.

8. As an additional feature, add a slider to your application in Project 7, showing each step of the simplification. Because a slider can go back and forth, you have to store the results of each single simplification step. Consult the Java API documentation on how to use a slider.

Stacks

Chapter Objectives

- To learn about the stack data type and how to use its four methods: push, pop, peek, and empty
- To understand how Java implements a stack
- To learn how to implement a stack using an underlying array or a linked list
- To see how to use a stack to perform various applications, including finding palindromes, testing for balanced (properly nested) parentheses, and evaluating arithmetic expressions

In this chapter we illustrate how to use and implement an abstract data type known as a stack. A stack is more restrictive than the linked list data structure that we studied in the last chapter. A client can access any element in a linked list and can insert elements at any location. However, a client can access only a single element in a stack: the one that was most recently inserted in the stack. This may seem like a serious restriction that would make stacks not very useful, but it turns out that stacks are actually one of the most commonly used data structures in computer science. For example, during program execution, a stack is used to store information about the parameters and return points for all the methods that are currently executing (you will see how this is done in Chapter 7, "Recursion"). Compilers also use stacks to store information while evaluating expressions. Part of the reason for the widespread use of stacks is that a stack is relatively easy to implement. This was an important consideration for programming in languages that did not provide the capability for implementing ADTs as classes.

We will discuss several applications of stacks in this chapter. We will also show how to implement stacks using both arrays and linked lists.

5.1 Stack Abstract Data Type

In a cafeteria you can see stacks of dishes placed in spring-loaded containers. Usually several dishes are visible above the top of the container, and the rest are inside the container. You can access only the dish that is on top of the stack. If you want to place more dishes on the stack, you can place the dishes on top of those that are already there. The spring inside the stack container compresses under the weight of the additional dishes, adjusting the height of the stack so that only the top few dishes are always visible.

Another physical example of a stack is a Pez® dispenser (see Figure 5.1). A Pez dispenser is a toy that contains candies. There is also a spring inside the dispenser. The top of the dispenser is a character's head. When you open the dispenser, a single candy *pops* out. You can only extract one candy at a time. If you want to eat more than one candy, you have to open the dispenser multiple times.

FIGURE 5.1
A Pez Dispenser

In programming, a stack is a data structure with the property that only the top element of the stack is accessible. In a stack, the top element is the data value that was most recently stored in the stack. Sometimes this storage policy is known as Last-In, First-Out, or *LIFO*.

Next, we specify some of the operations that we might wish to perform on a stack.

Specification of the Stack Abstract Data Type

Because only the top element of a stack is visible, the operations performed by a stack are few in number. We need to be able to inspect the top element (method peek), retrieve the top element (method pop), push a new element onto the stack (method push), and test for an empty stack (method empty). Table 5.1 shows a specification for the Stack ADT which specifies the stack operators. We will write this as interface StackInt. We introduce this interface because we want to discuss different implementations of a stack. In the Java API, class java.util.Stack implements a stack; there is no stack interface.

TABLE 5.1
Specification of Stack ADT

Methods	Behavior
`boolean empty()`	Returns **true** if the stack is empty; otherwise, returns **false**.
`Object peek()`	Returns the object at the top of the stack without removing it.
`Object pop()`	Returns the object at the top of the stack and removes it.
`Object push(Object item)`	Pushes an item onto the top of the stack and returns the item pushed.

Listing 5.1 shows the Java interface `StackInt`, which declares the methods in the Stack ADT. The class `java.util.Stack` also implements the methods of this interface.

LISTING 5.1
StackInt.java

```java
/** A Stack is a data structure in which objects are inserted into
    and removed from the same end (i.e., Last-In, First-Out).
*/
public interface StackInt {

    /** Pushes an item onto the top of the stack and returns
        the item pushed.
        @param obj The object to be inserted
        @return The object inserted
    */
    Object push(Object obj);

    /** Returns the object at the top of the stack
        without removing it.
        post: The stack remains unchanged.
        @return The object at the top of the stack
        @throws EmptyStackException if stack is empty
    */
    Object peek();

    /** Returns the object at the top of the stack
        and removes it.
        post: The stack is one item smaller.
        @return The object at the top of the stack
        @throws EmptyStackException if stack is empty
    */
    Object pop();

    /** Returns true if the stack is empty; otherwise,
        returns false.
        @return true if the stack is empty
    */
    boolean empty();
}
```

A client program can allocate multiple stacks by declaring several variables of classes that implement StackInt. Because stacks that implement StackInt will store variables of type Object, objects of any class may be stored in a stack. We can even store primitive-type values in a stack, provided we wrap them in the appropriate wrapper class. The advantage of this approach is that we can build a stack of integers or a stack of characters using the same implementation of the Stack ADT. It is the programmer's responsibility to remember what an object's actual type is and to cast it back to that type when using either peek or pop.

EXAMPLE 5.1

A stack names of five strings is shown in Figure 5.2(a). The name "Rich" was placed on the stack before the other four names; "Jonathan" was the last element placed on the stack.

For stack names in Figure 5.2(a), the value of names.empty() is **false**. The statement

```
String last = (String) names.peek();
```

stores "Jonathan" in last without changing names. The statement

```
String temp = (String) names.pop();
```

removes "Jonathan" from names and stores a reference to it in temp. The stack names now contains four elements and is shown in Figure 5.2(b). The statement

```
names.push("Philip");
```

pushes "Philip" onto the stack; the stack names now contains five elements and is shown in Figure 5.2(c).

FIGURE 5.2
Stack names

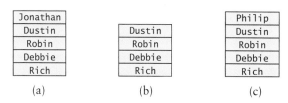

        (a)   (b)   (c)

EXERCISES FOR SECTION 5.1

SELF-CHECK

1. Assume that the stack names is defined as in Figure 5.2(c) and perform the following sequence of operations. Indicate the result of each operation and show the new stack if it is changed.

```
names.push(new String("Jane"));
names.push("Joseph");
String top = (String) names.pop();
String nextTop = (String) names.peek();
```

5.2 Stack Applications

In this section we will study two client programs that use stacks: a palindrome finder and a program that verifies that the parentheses in an expression are nested properly. We will use class `java.util.Stack`.

CASE STUDY   Finding Palindromes

Problem   A palindrome is a string that reads the same in either direction: left to right or right to left. For example, "kayak" is a palindrome, as is "I saw I was I". A well-known palindrome regarding Napoleon Bonaparte is "Able was I ere I saw Elba" (the island where he was sent in exile). We would like a program that reads a string and determines whether it is a palindrome.

Analysis   This problem can be solved in many different ways. For example, you could set up a loop in which you compare the characters at each end of a string as you work towards the middle. If any pair of characters is different, the string can't be a palindrome. Another approach would be to scan a string backward (from right to left) and append each character to the end of a new string, which would become the reverse of the original string. Then you could see whether the strings were equal. The approach we will study here uses a stack to assist in forming the reverse of a string. It is not the most efficient way to solve the problem, but it makes good use of a stack.

w	
a	
s	
I	

If we scan the input string from left to right and push each character in the input string onto a stack, we can form the reverse of the string by popping the characters and joining them together in the order that they come off the stack. For example, the stack at left contains the characters in the string `"I saw"`.

If we pop them off and join them together, we will get `"w" + "a" + "s" + " " + "I"`, or the string `"was I"`. When the stack is empty, we can compare the string we formed with the original. If they are the same, the original string is a palindrome. Because **char** is a primitive type, each character must be wrapped in a `Character` object before it can be pushed onto the stack.

Data Requirements

PROBLEM INPUTS

An input string to be tested

PROBLEM OUTPUTS

A message indicating whether the string is a palindrome

TABLE 5.2
Class `PalindromeFinder`

Data Fields	Attributes
`private String inputString`	The input string.
`private Stack charStack`	The stack where characters are stored.

Methods	Behavior
`public PalindromeFinder(String str)`	Initializes a new `PalindromeFinder` object, storing a reference to the parameter `str` in `inputString` and pushing each character onto the stack.
`private void fillStack()`	Fills the stack with the characters in `inputString`.
`private String buildReverse()`	Returns the string formed by popping each character from the stack and joining the characters. Empties the stack.
`public boolean isPalindrome()`	Returns **true** if `inputString` and the string built by `buildReverse` have the same contents, except for case. Otherwise, returns **false**.

Design   We can define a class called `PalindromeFinder` (Table 5.2) with data fields for storing the input string and the stack. The class needs methods to push all characters from the input string onto the stack (`fillStack`), to build a string by popping the characters off the stack and joining them (`buildReverse`), and to compare the strings to see whether they are palindromes (`isPalindrome`).

Implementation   Listing 5.2 shows the class. The constructor calls method `fillStack` to build the stack when a new `PalindromeFinder` object is created. The statement

```
charStack.push(new Character(nextChar));
```

wraps each character in a `Character` object before pushing it onto the stack.

In method `buildReverse`, the loop

```
while (!charStack.empty()) {
    // Remove top item from stack and append it to result
    result.append(charStack.pop());
}
```

pops each object off the stack and appends it to the result string. We don't need to extract the character wrapped in each `Character` object, because the `toString` method is implicitly called when an `Object` is appended to a string. The `toString` method for class `Character` returns a string whose contents is the stored character.

Method `isPalindrome` uses the `String` method `equalsIgnoreCase` to compare the original `String` with its reverse.

```
return inputString.equalsIgnoreCase(buildReverse());
```

LISTING 5.2
PalindromeFinder.java

```java
import java.util.*;

/** Class with methods to check whether a string is a palindrome. */
public class PalindromeFinder {

    /** String to store in stack. */
    private String inputString;
    /** Stack to hold characters. */
    private Stack charStack = new Stack();

    /** Store the argument string in a stack of characters.
        @param str String of characters to store in the stack
    */
    public PalindromeFinder(String str) {
        inputString = str;
        fillStack();
    }

    /** Method to fill a stack of characters from an input
        string. */
    private void fillStack() {
        for (int i = 0; i < inputString.length(); i++) {
            char nextChar = inputString.charAt(i);
            charStack.push(new Character(nextChar));
        }
    }

    /** Method to build a string
        containing the characters in a stack.
        post: The stack is empty.
        @return The string containing the words in the stack
    */
    private String buildReverse() {
        StringBuffer result = new StringBuffer();
        while (!charStack.empty()) {
            // Remove top item from stack and append it to result.
            result.append(charStack.pop());
        }
        return result.toString();
    }

    public boolean isPalindrome() {
        return inputString.equalsIgnoreCase(buildReverse());
    }
}
```

Testing   To test this class you should run it with several different strings, including both palindromes and nonpalindromes, as follows:

- A single character (always a palindrome)
- Multiple characters in one word
- Multiple words
- Different cases
- Even-length strings
- Odd-length strings
- An empty string (considered a palindrome)

CASE STUDY   Checking for Balanced Parentheses

Problem   When analyzing arithmetic expressions, it is important to determine whether an expression is balanced with respect to parentheses. For example, the expression

```
(a + b * (c / (d - e))) + (d / e)
```

is balanced. This problem is easy if all parentheses are the same kind—all we need to do is increment a counter each time we scan an opening parenthesis, and decrement the counter when we scan a closing parenthesis. If the counter is always greater than or equal to zero, and the final counter value is zero, the expression is balanced. However, if we can have different kinds of open and closing parentheses, the problem becomes more difficult. For example,

```
(a + b * {c / [d - e]}) + (d / e)
```

is balanced, but the expression

```
(a + b * {c / [d - e}}) + (d / e)
```

is not, because the subexpression [d - e} is incorrect. In this expression, the set of opening parentheses includes the symbols {, [, (, and the set of closing parentheses includes the matching symbols },],).

Analysis   An expression is balanced if each subexpression that starts with the symbol { ends with the symbol }, and the same statement is true for the other symbol pairs. Another way of saying this is that the unmatched opening parenthesis that is nearest to each closing parenthesis must have the correct shape. For example, if } is the closing parenthesis in question, then the nearest unmatched opening parenthesis must be the symbol {.

We can use a stack to determine whether the parentheses are balanced (or nested properly). We will scan the expression from left to right, ignoring all characters except for parentheses. We will push each open parenthesis onto a stack of characters. When we reach a closing parenthesis, we will see whether it matches the open parenthesis symbol on the top of the stack. If so, we will pop it off and continue the scan. If the characters don't match or the stack is empty, there is an error in the expression. If there are any characters left on the stack when we are finished, that also indicates an error.

Data Requirements

PROBLEM INPUTS

An expression string

PROBLEM OUTPUTS

A message indicating whether the expression has balanced parentheses

Design   We will write class `ParenChecker` to check for balanced parentheses. The class should define a method `isBalanced` that returns a **boolean** value indicating whether the expression is balanced. We also need methods `isOpen` and `isClose` to determine whether a character is an opening or closing parenthesis. Because `isBalanced` is the only method that processes the expression, we make it a **static** method with the expression as a parameter. Table 5.3 shows the class methods. Method `isBalanced` implements the following algorithm.

Algorithm for method `isBalanced`

1.   Create an empty stack of characters.
2.   Assume that the expression is balanced (`balanced` is **true**).
3.   Set index to 0.
4.   **while** `balanced` is **true** and index < the expression's length
5.   Get the next character in the data string.
6.   **if** the next character is an opening parenthesis
7.   Push it onto the stack.
8.   **else if** the next character is a closing parenthesis
9.   Pop the top of the stack.
10.   **if** stack was empty or its top does not match the closing parenthesis
11.   Set balanced to **false**.
12.   Increment index.
13.   Return **true** if `balanced` is **true** and the stack is empty.

The **if** statement at Step 5 tests each character in the expression, ignoring all characters except for opening and closing parentheses. If the next character is an opening parenthesis, it is pushed onto the stack. If the next character is a closing parenthesis, the nearest unmatched opening parenthesis is retrieved (by popping the stack) and compared to the closing parenthesis.

....
TABLE 5.3
Methods of Class `ParenChecker`

Method	Behavior
`public static boolean isBalanced(String expression)`	Returns **true** if expression is balanced with respect to parentheses and **false** if it is not.
`private static boolean isOpen(char ch)`	Returns **true** if ch is an opening parenthesis.
`private static boolean isClose(char ch)`	Returns **true** if ch is a closing parenthesis.

Implementation

Listing 5.3 shows the `ParenChecker` class. In the **try** block of method `isBalanced`, the **while** loop (Step 3 of the algorithm) begins by storing the next character (starting with the character at position 0) of `expression` in `nextCh`.

```
int index = 0;
while (balanced && index < expression.length()) {
    char nextCh = expression.charAt(index);
```

Method `isOpen` (`isClose`) returns **true** if its type char argument is in the string of opening parentheses, string `OPEN` (closing parentheses, string `CLOSE`). If `nextCh` stores an opening parenthesis, the statement

```
s.push(new Character(nextCh));
```

pushes `nextCh` onto the stack `s` (a local `Stack` object). We need to wrap `nextCh` in a `Character` object, because only objects can be placed on a `Stack`.

For each closing parenthesis, the pop method retrieves the nearest unmatched opening parenthesis from the stack:

```
char topCh = ((Character) s.pop()).charValue();
```

Each object popped off the stack must be cast to type `Character`; method `charValue` extracts its char value. Next, we see whether `topCh` is a corresponding opening parenthesis to the `nextCh` closing parenthesis. This is done by comparing their positions in the list of open and close parentheses using the expression

```
OPEN.indexOf(topCh) == CLOSE.indexOf(nextCh)
```

The method `String.indexOf` returns the position of the character argument in the string. Thus we must be careful when defining the list of opening (`OPEN`) and closing (`CLOSE`) parentheses that the corresponding parentheses are in the same position.

The **catch** block executes if an attempt is made to pop the stack of opening parentheses when it is empty. It sets `balanced` to `false`.

After the **try** or **catch** block finishes execution, the function result is returned. The result is **true** only when the expression is balanced and the stack is empty:

```
return balanced && s.empty();
```

LISTING 5.3

ParenChecker.java

```java
import java.util.Stack;
import java.util.EmptyStackException;
import javax.swing.JOptionPane;

/** Class to check for balanced parentheses. */
public class ParenChecker {

    // Constants
    /** Set of opening parenthesis characters. */
    private static final String OPEN = "([{";
    /** Set of closing parenthesis characters, matches OPEN. */
    private static final String CLOSE = ")]}";

    /** Test the input string to see that it contains balanced
        parentheses. This method tests an input string to see
        that each type of parenthesis is balanced. '(' is matched
        with ')', '[' is matched with ']', and
        '{' is matched with '}'.
        @param expression A String containing the expression to
               be examined
        @return true if all the parentheses match
    */
    public static boolean isBalanced(String expression) {
        Stack s = new Stack();  // Create an empty stack.
        boolean balanced = true;
        try {
            int index = 0;
            while (balanced && index < expression.length()) {
                char nextCh = expression.charAt(index);
                if (isOpen(nextCh)) {
                    s.push(new Character(nextCh));
                } else if (isClose(nextCh)) {
                    char topCh = ((Character) s.pop()).charValue();
                    balanced = OPEN.indexOf(topCh)
                               == CLOSE.indexOf(nextCh);

                }
                index++;
            }
        } catch (EmptyStackException ex) {
            balanced = false;
        }
        return (balanced && s.empty());
    }

    /** Method to determine whether a character is one of the
        opening parentheses.
        @param ch Character to be tested
        @return true if ch is one of the opening parentheses
    */
    private static boolean isOpen(char ch) {
        return OPEN.indexOf(ch) > -1;
    }
```

```
    /** Method to determine whether a character is one of the
        closing parentheses.
        @param ch Character to be tested
        @return true if ch is one of the closing parentheses
    */
    private static boolean isClose(char ch) {
        return CLOSE.indexOf(ch) > -1;
    }

    /** main method. Ask the user for a string and
        call the ParenChecker to see whether the parentheses
        are balanced.
        @param args Not used
    */
    public static void main(String args[]) {
        String expression = JOptionPane.showInputDialog(
            "Enter an expression containing parentheses");
        if (ParenChecker.isBalanced(expression)) {
            JOptionPane.showMessageDialog(null, expression
                                            + " is balanced");
        } else {
            JOptionPane.showMessageDialog(null, expression
                                            + " is not balanced");
        }
        System.exit(0);
    }
}
```

 PITFALL

Attempting to Pop an Empty Stack

If you attempt to pop an empty stack, your program will throw an EmptyStackException. You can guard against this error by testing for a nonempty stack before popping the stack. Alternatively, you can catch the error if it occurs and handle it as was done in method isBalanced (balanced is set to **false**). We chose this approach because attempting to pop an empty stack is a reasonable thing to do when an expression has more closing parentheses than opening parentheses.

 PROGRAM STYLE

Declaring Constants

We declared OPEN and CLOSE as class constants instead of declaring them locally in the methods where they are used (isOpen and isClose). There are two reasons for this. First, it is a more efficient use of memory to declare them as class constants instead of having to allocate storage for these constants each time the method is called. Also, if a new kind of parenthesis is introduced, it is easier to locate and update the class constants instead of having to find their declarations inside a method.

Testing A simple test driver is included in Listing 5.3. Test this program by providing a variety of input expressions and displaying the result (**true** or **false**). You should try expressions that have several levels of nested parentheses. Also, try expressions that would be properly nested if the parentheses were all of one type, but are not properly nested because a closing parenthesis does not match a particular opening parenthesis (for example, {x + y] is not balanced because] is not the correct closing parenthesis for {). Also check expressions that have too many opening or closing parentheses. Finally, test for some strange strings such as "{[}]", which should fail. The string "{[a * + b]}", which is not a valid expression, should pass because its parentheses are balanced.

EXERCISES FOR SECTION 5.2

SELF-CHECK

1. The result returned by the palindrome finder depends on all characters in a string, including spaces and punctuation. Discuss how you would modify the palindrome finder so that only the letters in the input string were used to determine whether the input string was a palindrome. You should ignore any other characters.
2. Trace the execution of function isBalanced for each of the following expressions. Your trace should show the stack after each push or pop operation. Also show the values of balanced, isOpen, and isClose after each closing parenthesis is processed.
   ```
   (a + b * {c / [d - e]}) + (d / e)
   (a + b * {c / [d - e}}) + (d / e)
   ```

PROGRAMMING

1. Write a method that reads a line and reverses the words in the line (not the characters) using a stack. For example, given the following input:
   ```
   The quick brown fox jumps over the lazy dog.
   ```
   you should get the following output:
   ```
   dog. lazy the over jumps fox brown quick The
   ```
2. Two different approaches to finding palindromes are discussed in the Analysis section of that case study. Code the first approach.
3. Code the second approach to finding palindromes.

5.3 Implementing a Stack

This section discusses how to implement the Stack ADT. You may have recognized that a stack is very similar to an ArrayList. In fact, in the Java Collections hierarchy, the class Stack extends class Vector, which is the historical predecessor of ArrayList.

Implementing a Stack as an Extension of Vector

The Java API includes a Stack class as part of the package java.util. This class is declared as follows:

```
public class Stack extends Vector
```

The Vector class implements a growable array of objects. Like an ArrayList, it contains components that can be accessed using an integer index. Also, the size of a Vector can grow or shrink as needed to accommodate adding and removing items after the Vector has been created. Figure 5.3 shows the characters of the string "Java" stored in a stack s, represented as a Vector where s[3], the last element of the Vector, references the Character object at the top of the stack. To implement interface StackInt, all we need to do is write methods that perform the required operations. For example, push can be implemented as follows:

```
public Object push(Object item) {
    add(item);
    return item;
}
```

FIGURE 5.3
Characters of "Java"
stored in Stack s
(a Vector)

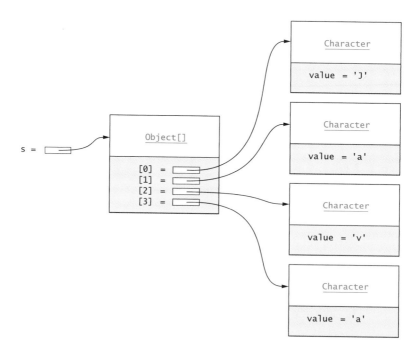

PITFALL

Accessing a Stack Element That Is Out of Bounds

Because Java implements a Stack as an extension of Vector, you can use the methods defined in the Vector class with a Stack object. This means that you may get an ArrayIndexOutOfBoundsException if you attempt to access a Vector element with an invalid index (for example, using Vector method get). This is another reason to restrict yourself to using just the methods described in the Stack specification (push, pop, peek, empty).

Similarly, pop can be coded as:

```java
public Object pop() throws EmptyStackException {
    try {
        return remove(size() - 1);
    } catch (ArrayIndexOutOfBoundsException ex) {
        throw new EmptyStackException();
    }
}
```

There is a drawback to the approach taken by the Java developers, however. Because their implementation states that a Stack *is a* Vector, all of the operations for a Vector can be applied. Therefore, the entire stack can be displayed (using Vector.toString) or searched (using Vector.indexOf), which violates the principle of information hiding (only the top element of a stack should be accessible). We discuss a better way to do this in the next section.

Implementing a Stack with a List Component

An alternative to implementing a stack as an extension of Vector is to write a class, which we will call ListStack, that has a List component. We can use either the ArrayList, the Vector, or the LinkedList for this component (all of them implement the List interface). We will call this component theData, and it will contain the stack data.

The code for the public methods of the ListStack class and the java.util.Stack class are essentially the same. For example in java.util.Stack, the push method is coded as:

```java
public Object push(Object item) {
    add(item);
    return item;
}
```

and we code the ListStack.push method as:

```java
public Object push(Object item) {
    theData.add(item);
    return item;
}
```

The ListStack class is said to be an *adapter class* because it adapts the methods available in another class (List) to the interface its clients expect by giving different names to essentially the same operations (for example, push instead of add). This is an example of delegation (see Section 3.5).

Listing 5.4 shows the ListStack class. Note that the statements that manipulate the stack explicitly refer to the stack data field. For example, in push we use the statement

```
theData.add(item);
```

instead of the java.util.stack statement

```
add(item);
```

which was used when the stack was considered an extension of a Vector object.

LISTING 5.4
ListStack.java

```java
import java.util.*;

/** The ListStack implements the Stack Abstract Data Type as
    an adapter to the List. This implementation is functionally
    equivalent to that given in java.util.Stack except that the
    underlying List is not publicly exposed.
*/
public class ListStack implements StackInt {

    /** The List containing the data */
    private List theData;

    /** Construct an empty stack using an ArrayList as the
        container. */
    public ListStack() {
        theData = new ArrayList();
    }

    /** Push an object onto the stack.
        post: The object is at the top of the stack.
        @param obj The object to be pushed
        @return The object pushed
    */
    public Object push(Object obj) {
        theData.add(obj);
        return obj;
    }

    /** Peek at the top object on the stack.
        @return The top object on the stack
        @throws EmptyStackException if the stack is empty
    */
    public Object peek() {
        if (empty()) {
            throw new EmptyStackException();
        }
        return theData.get(theData.size() - 1);
    }
```

```
/** Pop the top object off the stack.
    post: The object at the top of the stack is removed.
    @return The top object, which is removed
    @throws EmptyStackException if the stack is empty
*/
public Object pop() {
    if (empty()) {
        throw new EmptyStackException();
    }
    return theData.remove(theData.size() - 1);
}

/** See whether the stack is empty.
    @return true if the stack is empty
*/
boolean empty() {
    return theData.size() == 0;
}
}
```

 DESIGN CONCEPT

Using an ArrayList Object as a Stack Component

In Listing 5.4 we used an ArrayList object to store the ListStack data. We could use any of the implementers of List, but an ArrayList is the best choice, because a Vector is not recommended for new applications and a LinkedList would require more storage. Regardless of the container used, all stack operations would be performed in $O(1)$ time.

Implementing a Stack Using an Array

We can also use an array data field for storage of a stack instead of using Java's ArrayList class. In that case, however, we need to allocate storage for an array with an initial default capacity when we create a new stack object. We also need to keep track of the top of the stack (topOfStack), because the array size does not grow and shrink after each push and pop. Also, there is no size method (as there is for an ArrayList) to tell us how many elements are currently in the stack. The value of topOfStack is the subscript of the element at the top of the stack; for an empty stack, topOfStack should be −1. The data field declarations follow.

```
import java.util.EmptyStackException;

/** Implementation of the StackInt interface using
    an array.
*/
public class ArrayStack implements StackInt {
    // Data Fields
    /** Storage for stack. */
    Object[] theData;
```

```
        /** Index to top of stack. */
        int topOfStack = -1;      // Initially empty stack
...
```

Figure 5.4 shows an `ArrayStack` of characters after pushing the individual letters of the string `"Java"`, where the last character in the string is at the top of the stack. The value of `topOfStack` is 3. If we pop a character (the `'a'` at position 3), `topOfStack` decreases to 2; if we push a character onto the stack, `topOfStack` increases to 4 and the new character is stored at `theData[4]`.

The `push` method needs to reallocate additional storage space when the array becomes filled, as was done for class `KWArrayList` in Section 4.3. Then `topOfStack` is incremented and the item is inserted at the element with subscript `topOfStack`.

```
    /** Insert a new item on top of the stack.
        post: The new item is the top item on the stack.
              All other items are one position lower.
        @param item The item to be inserted
        @return The item that was inserted
    */
    public Object push(Object item) {
        if (topOfStack == theData.length - 1) {
            reallocate();
        }
        topOfStack++
        theData[topOfStack] = item;
        return item;
    }
```

FIGURE 5.4

Stack of **Character** Objects in an Array

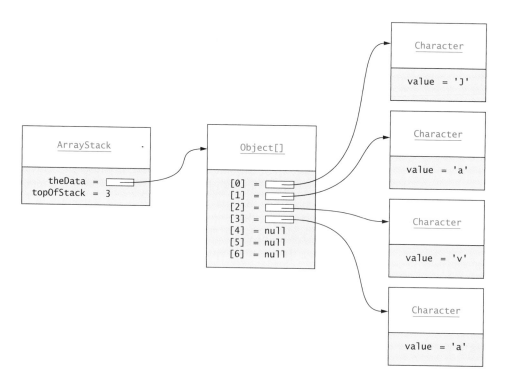

Method pop is shown next. The return statement gets the element at the top of the stack and then decrements topOfStack. Method peek is the same, except that topOfStack is not decremented. Method empty (not shown) would test for a value of topOfStack equal to −1.

```
/** Remove and return the top item on the stack.
    pre: The stack is not empty.
    post: The top item on the stack has been
          removed and the stack is one item smaller.
    @return The top item on the stack
    @throws EmptyStackException if the stack is empty
*/
public Object pop() {
    if (empty()) {
        throw new EmptyStackException();
    }
    return theData[topOfStack--];
}
```

Implementing a Stack as a Linked Data Structure

We can also implement a stack using a linked list of nodes. We show the stack containing the characters in "Java" in Figure 5.5, with the last character in the string stored in the node at the top of the stack. Class LinkedStack contains a collection of Node objects (see Section 4.4). Recall that inner class Node has attributes data (type Object) and next (type Node).

Reference variable topOfStackRef (type Node) references the last element placed on the stack (see Section 4.4). Because it is easier to insert and delete from the head of a linked list, we will have topOfStackRef reference the node at the head of the list.

Method push inserts a node at the head of the list. The statement

```
    topOfStackRef = new Node(item, topOfStackRef);
```

sets topOfStackRef to reference the new node; topOfStackRef.next references the old top of the stack. When the stack is empty, topOfStackRef is **null**, so the attribute next for the first item pushed onto the stack (the item at the bottom) will be **null**.

Method peek will be very similar to method getFirst. Method empty tests for a value of topOfStackRef equal to **null**. Method pop simply resets topOfStackRef to the value stored in the next field of the list head and returns the old topOfStackRef data. Listing 5.5 shows class LinkedStack.

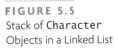

FIGURE 5.5
Stack of **Character** Objects in a Linked List

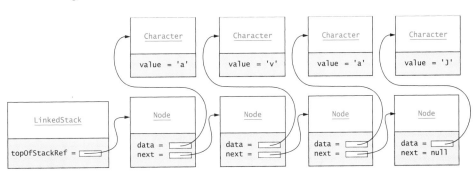

....
LISTING 5.5
Class LinkedStack

```java
import java.util.EmptyStackException;

/** Class to implement a stack as a linked list. */
public class LinkedStack implements StackInt {

    // Insert inner class Node here. (See Section 4.4)

    // Data Fields
    /** The reference to the first stack node. */
    private Node topOfStackRef = null;

    /** Insert a new item on top of the stack.
        post: The new item is the top item on the stack.
              All other items are one position lower.
        @param item The item to be inserted
        @return The item that was inserted
    */
    public Object push(Object item) {
        topOfStackRef = new Node(item, topOfStackRef);
        return item;
    }

    /** Remove and return the top item on the stack.
        pre: The stack is not empty.
        post: The top item on the stack has been
              removed and the stack is one item smaller.
        @return The top item on the stack
        @throws EmptyStackException if the stack is empty
    */
    public Object pop() {
        if (empty()) {
            throw new EmptyStackException();
        }
        else {
            Object result = topOfStackRef.data;
            topOfStackRef = topOfStackRef.next;
            return result;
        }
    }

    /** Return the top item on the stack.
        pre: The stack is not empty.
        post: The stack remains unchanged.
        @return The top item on the stack
        @throws EmptyStackException if the stack is empty
    */
    public Object peek() {
        if (empty()) {
            throw new EmptyStackException();
        }
        else {
            return topOfStackRef.data;
        }
    }
```

```
        /** Return true if the stack is empty.
            @return true if the stack is empty
        */
        public boolean empty() {
            return topOfStackRef == null;
        }
    }
```

Comparison of Stack Implementations

As stated earlier, the implementation of the Stack ADT as an extension of Vector is a poor choice because all the Vector methods are accessible. The easiest approach to implementing a stack in Java would be to give it an ArrayList component for storing the data. Since all insertions and deletions are at one end, the stack operations would all be O(1) operations. You could use an object of another class that implements the List interface to store the stack data, but the ArrayList is the simplest.

Alternatively, you could use an underlying array data structure, but this would be slightly more difficult to implement, as you would have to update the index to the top of the stack after each insertion or deletion. You would also have to reallocate storage when the stack became filled. All stack operations using an underlying array would be O(1).

Finally, you could also use your own linked data structure. This has the advantage of using exactly as much storage as is needed for the stack. However, you would also need to allocate storage for the links. Because all insertions and deletions are at one end, the flexibility provided by a linked data structure is not utilized. All stack operations using a linked data structure would be O(1).

EXERCISES FOR SECTION 5.3

SELF-CHECK

1. For the implementation of stack s using an array as the underlying data structure (see Figure 5.4), show how the underlying data structure changes after each statement below executes. What is the value of topOfStack? Assume the initial capacity of the stack is 7 and the characters in "Java" are stored on the stack (J pushed on first).
   ```
   s.push('i');
   s.push('s');
   Character ch1 = (Character) s.pop();
   s.pop();
   s.push(' ');
   Character ch2 = (Character) s.peek();
   ```

2. How do your answers to Question 1 change if the initial capacity is 5 instead of 7?

3. For the implementation of stack s using a linked list of nodes as the underlying data structure (see Figure 5.5), show how the underlying data structure changes after each statement in Question 1 executes. Assume the characters in "Java" are stored on the stack (J pushed on first).

PROGRAMMING

1. Write a method `size` for class `LinkedStack` that returns the number of elements currently on a `LinkedStack`.
2. Complete the implementation of `ArrayStack`. Provide two constructors. The no-parameter constructor should initialize the array to the default initial capacity (a constant). The constructor with an **int** argument should initialize the array to the argument value. Also write methods `reallocate` and `empty`.

5.4 Additional Stack Applications

In this section we consider two case studies that relate to evaluating arithmetic expressions. The first problem is slightly easier, and it involves evaluating expressions that are in postfix form. The second problem discusses how to convert from *infix notation* (common mathematics notation) to postfix form.

Normally we write expressions using infix notation, in which binary operators (*, +, and so forth) are inserted between their operands. Infix expressions present no special problem to humans, because we can easily scan left and right to find the operands of a particular operator. A calculator (or computer), on the other hand, normally scans an expression string in the order that it is input (left to right). Therefore, it is easier to evaluate an expression if the user types the operands for each operator in before typing the operator *(postfix notation)*. Table 5.4 shows some examples of expressions in postfix and infix form. The braces under each postfix expression will help you visualize the operands for each operator.

The advantage of the postfix form is that there is no need to group subexpressions in parentheses or even to consider operator precedence. (We talk more about postfix form in the second case study in this section.) The braces in Table 5.4 are for our convenience and are not required. The next case study develops a program that evaluates a postfix expression.

TABLE 5.4
Postfix Expressions

Postfix Expression	Infix Expression	Value
5 6 *	5 * 6	30
5 6 1 + *	5 * (6 + 1)	35
5 6 * 10 –	(5 * 6) – 10	20
4 5 6 * 3 / +	4 + ((5 * 6) / 3)	14

CASE STUDY   Evaluating Postfix Expressions

Problem   Write a class that evaluates a postfix expression. The postfix expression will be a string containing digit characters and operator characters from the set +, -, *, /. The space character will be used as a delimiter between tokens (integers and operators).

Analysis   In a postfix expression the operands precede the operators. A stack is the perfect place to save the operands until the operator is scanned. When the operator is scanned, its operands can be popped off the stack (the last operand scanned, the right operand, will be popped first). Therefore, our program will push each integer operand onto the stack. When an operator is read, the top two operands are popped, the operation is performed on its operands, and the result is pushed back onto the stack. The final result should be the only value remaining on the stack when the end of the expression is reached.

Design   We will write class `PostfixEvaluator` to evaluate postfix expressions. The class should define a method `eval`, which scans a postfix expression and processes each of its tokens, where a token is either an operand (an integer) or an operator. We also need a method `evalOp`, which evaluates each operator when it is scanned, and a method `isOperator`, which determines whether a character is an operator. Table 5.5 describes the class.

The algorithm for `eval` follows. The stack operators perform algorithm steps 1, 5, 7, 8, and 10.

Table 5.6 shows the evaluation of the third expression in Table 5.4 using this algorithm. The arrow under the expression points to the character being processed; the stack diagram shows the stack after this character is processed.

TABLE 5.5
Class `PostfixEvaluator`

Data Field	Attribute
Stack operandStack	The stack of operands (`Integer` objects).
Method	**Behavior**
`public int eval(String expression)`	Returns the value of `expression`.
`private int evalOp(char op)`	Pops two operands and applies operator op to its operands, returning the result.
`private boolean isOperator(char ch)`	Returns **true** if ch is an operator symbol.

TABLE 5.6
Evaluating a Postfix
Expression

Expression	Action	Stack
5 6 * 10 – ↑	Push 5	5
5 6 * 10 – ↑	Push 6	6 5
5 6 * 10 – ↑	Pop 6 and 5 Evaluate 5 * 6 Push 30	30
5 6 * 10 – ↑	Push 10	10 30
5 6 * 10 – ↑	Pop 10 and 30 Evaluate 30 – 10 Push 20	20
5 6 * 10 – ↑	Pop 20 Stack is empty Result is 20	⌴

Algorithm for method eval

1. Create an empty stack of integers.
2. **while** there are more tokens
3.   Get the next token.
4.   **if** the first character of the token is a digit
5.   Push the integer onto the stack.
6.   **else if** the token is an operator
7.   Pop the right operand off the stack
8.   Pop the left operand off the stack.
9.   Evaluate the operation.
10.   Push the result onto the stack.
11. Pop the stack and return the result.

Implementation   Listing 5.6 shows the implementation of class `PostfixEvaluator`. The only data field is the operand stack. There is an inner class that defines the exception `SyntaxErrorException`.

Method eval implements the algorithm shown in the design section. We assume that there are spaces between operands and operators, so eval uses the `StringTokenizer` object `tokens` to extract the individual tokens. If you are unfamiliar with class `StringTokenizer`, see Appendix A.

If an `EmptyStackException` is thrown when an item is popped off the `operandStack`, this indicates a syntax error in the expression. Therefore, the body of method eval is enclosed within a **try-catch** sequence. An EmptyStackException, thrown either as a result of a pop operation in eval or by a pop operation in a method called by eval, will be caught by the **catch** clause. In either case, a SyntaxErrorException is thrown.

Private method isOperator determines whether a character is an operator. When an operator is encountered, private method evalOp is called to evaluate it. This method pops the top two operands from the stack. The first item popped is the right-hand operand, and the second is the left-hand operand. When a value is popped from the stack, it must be cast from the Object class back to the original class, in this case Integer.

```
Integer rhs = (Integer) operandStack.pop();
Integer lhs = (Integer) operandStack.pop();
```

To perform the arithmetic operations, the **int** value must be extracted from the Integer object. A **switch** statement is then used to select the appropriate expression to evaluate for the given operator. For example, the following **case** processes the addition operator and returns the sum of the integers in Integer objects lhs and rhs.

```
case '+' : result = lhs.intValue() + rhs.intValue();
           break;
```

LISTING 5.6

PostfixEvaluator.java

```java
import java.util.*;

/** Class that can evaluate a postfix expression. */
public class PostfixEvaluator {

    // Nested Class
    /** Class to report a syntax error. */
    public static class SyntaxErrorException extends Exception {
        /** Construct a SyntaxErrorException with the specified
            message.
            @param message The message
        */
        SyntaxErrorException(String message) {
            super(message);
        }
    }

    // Constant
    /** A list of operators. */
    private static final String OPERATORS = "+-*/";

    // Data Field
    /** The operand stack. */
    private Stack operandStack;
```

```java
// Methods
/** Evaluates the current operation.
    This function pops the two operands off the operand
    stack and applies the operator.
    @param op A character representing the operator
    @return The result of applying the operator
    @throws EmptyStackException if pop is attempted on
            an empty stack.
*/
private int evalOp(char op) {
    // Pop the two operands off the stack.
    Integer rhs = (Integer) operandStack.pop();
    Integer lhs = (Integer) operandStack.pop();
    int result = 0;
    // Evaluate the operator.
    switch (op) {
        case '+' : result = lhs.intValue() + rhs.intValue();
                   break;
        case '-' : result = lhs.intValue() - rhs.intValue();
                   break;
        case '/' : result = lhs.intValue() / rhs.intValue();
                   break;
        case '*' : result = lhs.intValue() * rhs.intValue();
                   break;
    }
    return result;
}

/** Determines whether a character is an operator.
    @param op The character to be tested
    @return true if the character is an operator
*/
private boolean isOperator(char ch) {
    return OPERATORS.indexOf(ch) != -1;
}

/** Evaluates a postfix expression.
    @param expression The expression to be evaluated
    @return The value of the expression
    @throws SyntaxErrorException if a syntax error is detected
*/
public int eval(String expression) throws SyntaxErrorException {
    // Create an empty stack.
    operandStack = new Stack();

    // Process each token.
    StringTokenizer tokens = new StringTokenizer(expression);
    try {
        while (tokens.hasMoreTokens()) {
            String nextToken = tokens.nextToken();
            // Does it start with a digit?
            if (Character.isDigit(nextToken.charAt(0))) {
```

```
                            // Get the integer value.
                            int value = Integer.parseInt(nextToken);
                            // Push value onto operand stack.
                            operandStack.push(new Integer(value));
                        } // Is it an operator?
                        else if (isOperator(nextToken.charAt(0))) {
                            // Evaluate the operator.
                            int result = evalOp(nextToken.charAt(0));
                            // Push result onto the operand stack.
                            operandStack.push(new Integer(result));
                        }
                        else {
                            // Invalid character.
                            throw new SyntaxErrorException(
                                "Invalid character encountered");
                        }
                    }    // End while.

                    // No more tokens - pop result from operand stack.
                    Integer answer = (Integer) operandStack.pop();
                    // Operand stack should be empty.
                    if (operandStack.empty()) {
                        return answer.intValue();
                    } else {
                        // Indicate syntax error.
                        throw new SyntaxErrorException(
                            "Syntax Error: Stack should be empty");
                    }
                } catch (EmptyStackException ex) {
                    // Pop was attempted on an empty stack.
                    throw new SyntaxErrorException(
                        "Syntax Error: The stack is empty");
                }
            }
        }
```

 PROGRAM STYLE

Creating Your Own Exception Class

The program would work just the same if we did not bother to declare the SyntaxError Exception class and just threw a new Exception object each time an error occurred. However, we feel that this approach gives the user a more meaningful description of the cause of an error. Also, if other errors are possible in a client of this class, any SyntaxErrorException can be caught and handled in a separate **catch** clause.

Testing You will need to write a driver for the `PostfixEvaluator` class. This driver should create a `PostfixEvaluator` object, read one or more expressions, and report the result. It will also have to catch the exception `PostfixEvaluator.SyntaxErrorException`. A white-box approach to testing would lead you to consider the following test cases. First, you want to exercise each path in the `evalOp` method by entering a simple expression that uses each operator. Then you need to exercise the paths through `eval` by trying different orderings and multiple occurrences of the operators. These tests exercise the normal cases, so you next need to test for possible syntax errors. Consider the following cases: an operator without any operands, a single operand, an extra operand, an extra operator, a variable name, and finally an empty string.

CASE STUDY   Converting from Infix to Postfix

We normally write expressions in infix notation. Therefore, one approach to evaluating expressions in infix notation is first to convert it to postfix and then to apply the evaluation technique just discussed. We will show in this case study how to accomplish this conversion using a stack. An infix expression can also be evaluated directly using two stacks. This is left as a programming project.

Problem To complete the design of an expression evaluator, we need a set of methods that convert infix expressions to postfix form. We will assume that the expression will consist only of spaces, operands, and operators, where the space is a delimiter character between tokens. All operands that are identifiers begin with a letter or underscore character; all operands that are numbers begin with a digit. (Although we are allowing for identifiers, our postfix evaluator can't really handle them.)

Analysis Table 5.4 showed the infix and postfix forms of four expressions. For each expression pair, the operands are in the same sequence; however, the placement of the operators changes in going from infix to postfix. For example, in converting

```
x1 + 2.5 * count / 3
```

to its postfix form

```
x1 2.5 count * 3 / +
```

we see that the four operands (the tokens `x1`, `2.5`, `count`, `3`) retain their relative ordering from the infix expression, but the order of the operators is changed. The first operator in the infix expression, `+`, is the last operator in the postfix expression. Therefore, we can insert the operands in the output expression (`postfix`) as soon as they are scanned in the input expression (`infix`), but each operator should be inserted in the postfix string after its operands and in the order in which they should be evaluated, not the order in which they were scanned. For expressions without parentheses, there are two criteria that determine the order of operator evaluation:

- Operators are evaluated according to their *precedence* or rank. Higher-precedence operators are evaluated before lower-precedence operators. For example, *, /, and % (the *multiplicative* operators) are evaluated before +, -.
- Operators with the same precedence are evaluated in left-to-right order (left-associative rule).

If we temporarily store the operators on a stack, we can pop them whenever we need to and insert them in the postfix string in an order that indicates when they should be evaluated, rather than when they were scanned. For example, if we have the first two operators from the string "x1 + 2.5 * count / 3" stored on a stack as follows,

the operator * (scanned second) must come off the stack and be placed in the postfix string before the operator + (scanned first). If we have the stack as just shown and the next operator is /, we need to pop the * off the stack and insert it in the postfix string before /, because the multiplicative operator scanned earlier (*) should be evaluated before the multiplicative operator (/) scanned later (the left-associative rule).

Design   Class InfixToPostfix contains methods needed for the conversion. The class should have a data field operatorStack, which stores the operators. It should also have a method convert, which does the initial processing of all tokens (operands and operators). Method convert needs to get each token (using a StringTokenizer object) and process it. Each token that is an operand should be appended to the postfix string. Method processOperator will process each operator token. Method isOperator determines whether a token is an operator, and method precedence returns the precedence of an operator. Table 5.6 describes class InfixToPostfix.

TABLE 5.6
Class InfixToPostfix

Data Field	Attribute
private Stack operatorStack	Stack of operators.
private StringBuffer postfix	The postfix string being formed.
Method	**Behavior**
public String convert(String infix)	Extracts and processes each token in infix and returns the equivalent postfix string.
private void processOperator(char op)	Processes operator op by updating operatorStack.
private int precedence(char op)	Returns the precedence of operator op.
private boolean isOperator(char ch)	Returns **true** if ch is an operator symbol.

The algorithm for method convert follows. The while loop extracts and processes each token, calling processOperator to process each operator token. After all tokens are extracted from the infix string and processed, any operators remaining on the stack should be popped and appended to the postfix string. They are appended to the end because they have lower precedence than those operators inserted earlier.

Algorithm for Method convert

1. Initialize postfix to an empty StringBuffer.
2. Initialize the operator stack to an empty stack.
3. while there are more tokens in the infix string
4.   Get the next token.
5.   if the next token is an operand
6.   Append it to postfix.
7.   else if the next token is an operator
8.   Call processOperator to process the operator.
9.   else
10.   Indicate a syntax error.
11. Pop remaining operators off the operator stack and append them to postfix.

Method processOperator

The real decision making happens in method processOperator. By pushing operators onto the stack or popping them off the stack (and into the postfix string), this method controls the order in which the operators will be evaluated.

Each operator will eventually be pushed onto the stack. However, before doing this, processOperator compares the operator's precedence with that of the stacked operators, starting with the operator at the top of the stack. If the current operator has higher precedence than the operator at the top of the stack, it is pushed onto the stack immediately. This will ensure that none of the stacked operators can be inserted into the postfix string before it.

However, if the operator at the top of the stack has higher precedence than the current operator, it is popped off the stack and inserted in the postfix string, because it should be performed before the current operator according to the precedence rule. Also, if the operator at the top of the stack has the same precedence as the current operator, it is popped off the stack and inserted into the postfix string, because it should be performed before the current operator according to the left-associative rule. After an operator is popped off the stack, we repeat the process of comparing the precedence of the operator currently at the top of the stack with the precedence of the current operator until the current operator is pushed onto the stack.

A special case is an empty operator stack. In this case, there are no stacked operators to compare with the new one, so we will simply push the current operator onto the stack. We use method peek to access the operator at the top of the stack without removing it.

Algorithm for Method processOperator

1. **if** the operator stack is empty
2.   Push the current operator onto the stack.
   else
3.   Peek the operator stack and let topOp be the top operator.
4.   **if** the precedence of the current operator is greater than the precedence of topOp
5.   Push the current operator onto the stack.
      else
6.   **while** the stack is not empty and the precedence of the current operator is less than or equal to the precedence of topOp
7.   Pop topOp off the stack and append it to postfix.
8.   **if** the operator stack is not empty
9.   Peek the operator stack and let topOp be the top operator.
10.   Push the current operator onto the stack.

Table 5.7 shows a trace of the conversion of the infix expression x1 + 2.5 * count / 3 to the postfix expression x1 2.5 count * 3 / +. The final value of postfix shows that * is performed first (operands 2.5 and count), / is performed next (operands 2.5 * count and 3), and + is performed last.

TABLE 5.7
Conversion of x1 + 2.5 * count / 3

Next Token	Action	Effect on operatorStack	Effect on postfix
x1	Append x1 to postfix.		x1
+	The stack is empty Push + onto the stack	+	x1
2.5	Append 2.5 to postfix	+	x1 2.5
*	precedence(*) > precedence(+), Push * onto the stack	* +	x1 2.5
count	Append count to postfix	* +	x1 2.5 count
/	precedence(/) equals precedence(*) Pop * off of stack and append to postfix	+	x1 2.5 count *

TABLE 5.7 (continued)

Next Token	Action	Effect on operatorStack	Effect on postfix
/	precedence(/) > precedence(+), Push / onto the stack	/ +	x1 2.5 count *
3	Append 3 to postfix	/ +	x1 2.5 count * 3
End of input	Stack is not empty, Pop / off the stack and append to postfix	+	x1 2.5 count * 3 /
End of input	Stack is not empty, Pop + off the stack and append to postfix	(empty)	x1 2.5 count * 3 / +

Although the algorithm will correctly convert a well-formed expression and will detect some expressions with invalid syntax, it doesn't do all the syntax checking required. For example, an expression with extra operands would not be detected. We discuss this further in the testing section.

Implementation   Listing 5.7 shows the InfixToPostfix class. The convert method begins by initializing postfix and the operatorStack and creating a StringTokenizer object infixTokens. The tokens are extracted and processed within a **try** block. The condition

```
(Character.isJavaIdentifierStart(firstChar)
        || Character.isDigit(firstChar))
```

tests the first character (firstChar) of the next token to see whether the next token is an operand (identifier or number). Method isJavaIdentifierStart returns **true** if the next token is an identifier; method isDigit returns **true** if the next token is a number (starts with a digit). If this condition is true, the token is appended to postfix followed by a space character. The next condition,

```
(isOperator(firstChar))
```

is true if nextToken is an operator. If so, method processOperator is called. If the next token is not an operand or an operator, the exception SyntaxErrorException is thrown.

Once the end of the expression is reached, the remaining operators are popped off the stack and appended to postfix. Finally, postfix is converted to a String and returned.

Method `processOperator` uses private method `precedence` to determine the precedence of an operator (2 for *, /; 1 for +, -.). If the stack is empty or the condition

```
(precedence(op) > precedence(topOp))
```

is true, the current operator, op, is pushed onto the stack. Otherwise, the **while** loop executes, popping all operators off the stack that have the same or greater precedence than op and appending them to the `postfix` string.

```
while (!operatorStack.empty()
        && precedence(op) <= precedence(topOp)) {
    operatorStack.pop();
    postfix.append(topOp);
    postfix.append(' ');
```

After loop exit, the statement

```
operatorStack.push(new Character(op));
```

pushes the current operator onto the stack.

In method `precedence`, the statement

```
return PRECEDENCE[OPERATORS.indexOf(op)];
```

returns the element of **int**[] array `PRECEDENCE` selected by the method call `OPERATORS.indexOf(op)`. The precedence value returned will be 1 or 2.

LISTING 5.7
InfixToPostfix.java

```java
import java.util.*;

/** Translates an infix expression to a postfix expression. */
public class InfixToPostfix {

    /** Insert nested class SyntaxErrorException here. */

    // Data Fields
    /** The operator stack */
    private Stack operatorStack;
    /** The operators */
    private static final String OPERATORS = "+-*/";
    /** The precedence of the operators, matches order in OPERATORS. */
    private static final int[] PRECEDENCE = {1, 1, 2, 2};
    /** The postfix string */
    private StringBuffer postfix;

    /** Convert a string from infix to postfix.
        @param expression The infix expression
        @throws SyntaxErrorException
    */
    public String convert(String infix)
            throws SyntaxErrorException {
        operatorStack = new Stack();
        postfix = new StringBuffer();
```

```
                    StringTokenizer infixTokens = new StringTokenizer(infix);
                    try {
                        // Process each token in the infix string.
                        while (infixTokens.hasMoreTokens()) {
                            String nextToken = infixTokens.nextToken();
                            char firstChar = nextToken.charAt(0);
                            // Is it an operand?
                            if (Character.isJavaIdentifierStart(firstChar)
                                    || Character.isDigit(firstChar)) {
                                postfix.append(nextToken);
                                postfix.append(' ');
                            } // Is it an operator?
                            else if(isOperator(firstChar)) {
                                processOperator(firstChar);
                            }
                            else {
                                throw new SyntaxErrorException
                                    ("Unexpected Character Encountered: "
                                     + firstChar);
                            }
                        }   // End while.

                        // Pop any remaining operators and
                        // append them to postfix.
                        while (!operatorStack.empty()) {
                            Character op = (Character) operatorStack.pop();
                            postfix.append(op);
                            postfix.append(' ');
                        }
                        // assert: Stack is empty, return result.
                        return postfix.toString();
                    } catch (EmptyStackException ex) {
                        throw new SyntaxErrorException
                            ("Syntax Error: The stack is empty");
                    }
                }

                /** Method to process operators.
                    @param op The operator
                    @throws EmptyStackException
                */
                private void processOperator(char op) {
                    if (operatorStack.empty()) {
                        operatorStack.push(new Character(op));
                    } else {
                        // Peek the operator stack and
                        // let topOp be top operator.
                        char topOp =
                            ((Character) operatorStack.peek()).charValue();
                        if (precedence(op) > precedence(topOp)) {
                            operatorStack.push(new Character(op));
                        }
```

```
        else {
            // Pop all stacked operators with equal
            // or higher precedence than op.
            while (!operatorStack.empty()
                    && precedence(op) <= precedence(topOp)) {
                operatorStack.pop();
                postfix.append(topOp);
                postfix.append(' ');
                if (!operatorStack.empty()) {
                    // Reset topOp.
                    topOp = ((Character)
                            operatorStack.peek()).charValue();
                }
            }
            // assert: Operator stack is empty or
            //         current operator precedence >
            //         top of stack operator precedence.
            operatorStack.push(new Character(op));
        }
    }
}

/** Determine whether a character is an operator.
    @param ch The character to be tested
    @return true if ch is an operator
*/
private boolean isOperator(char ch) {
    return OPERATORS.indexOf(ch) != -1;
}

/** Determine the precedence of an operator.
    @param op The operator
    @return the precedence
*/
private int precedence(char op) {
    return PRECEDENCE[OPERATORS.indexOf(op)] ;
}
}
```

 PITFALL

Forgetting the Actual Type of the Item Stored in a Stack

The client programs in this chapter used instances of the java.util.Stack class to store Objects. It is important to remember the actual type of the item stored in the stack and to cast it back to that type when popping or peeking. Also, if you want to store primitive types (for example, **int** in class PostfixEvaluator, **char** in class InfixToPostfix), you must use the wrapper classes (for example, Integer in class PostfixEvaluator or Character in class InfixToPostfix).

PROGRAM STYLE

Updating a StringBuffer is an Efficient Operation

We used a `StringBuffer` object for `postfix` because we knew that `postfix` was going to be continually updated. Because `String` objects are immutable, it would have been less efficient to use a `String` object for `postfix`. A new `String` object would have to be allocated each time `postfix` changed.

Testing   Listing 5.8 shows a main method that tests the `InfixToPostfix` class. When entering a test expression, be careful to type a space character between operands and operators.

Use enough test expressions to satisfy yourself that the conversion is correct for properly formed input expressions. For example, try different orderings and multiple occurrences of the operators. You should also try infix expressions where all operators have the same precedence (for example, all multiplicative).

If `convert` detects a syntax error, it will throw the exception `InfixToPostfix.Syntax ErrorException`. The driver will catch this exception and display an error message. If an exception is not thrown, the driver will display the result. Unfortunately, not all possible errors are detected. For example, an adjacent pair of operators or operands is not detected. To detect this error, we would need to add a **boolean** flag whose value indicates whether the last token was an operand. If the flag is **true**, the next token must be an operator; if the flag is **false**, the next token must be an operand. This modification is left as an exercise.

LISTING 5.8
Main Method to Test `InfixToPostfix`

```java
public static void main(String args[]) {
    InfixToPostfix inToPost = new InfixToPostfix();
    String infix = JOptionPane.showInputDialog
                    ("Enter an infix expression");
    try {
        String postfix = inToPost.convert(infix);
        JOptionPane.showMessageDialog(null,
                "Infix expression " + infix +
                "\nconverts to " + postfix);
    } catch (SyntaxErrorException e) {
        JOptionPane.showMessageDialog(null, e.getMessage());
    }
    System.exit(0);
}
```

CASE STUDY   Part 2: Converting Expressions with Parentheses

Problem   The ability to convert expressions with parentheses is an important (and necessary) addition. Parentheses are used to separate an expression into subexpressions.

Analysis   We can think of an opening parenthesis on an operator stack as a boundary or fence between operators. Whenever we encounter an opening parenthesis, we want to push it onto the stack. A closing parenthesis is the terminator symbol for a subexpression. Whenever we encounter a closing parenthesis, we want to pop off all operators on the stack until we pop the matching opening parenthesis. Neither opening nor closing parentheses should appear in the postfix expression. Because operators scanned after the opening parenthesis should be evaluated before the opening parenthesis, the precedence of the opening parenthesis must be smaller than any other operator. We also give a closing parenthesis the lowest precedence. This ensures that a "(" can only be popped by a ")".

Design   We should modify method `processOperator()` to push each opening parenthesis onto the stack as soon as it is scanned. Therefore, the method should begin with the following new condition:

```
if (operatorStack.empty() || op == '(') {
    operatorStack.push(new Character(op));
```

When a closing parenthesis is scanned, we want to pop all operators up to and including the matching opening parenthesis, inserting all operators popped (except for the opening parenthesis) in the postfix string. This will happen automatically in the `while` statement if the precedence of the closing parenthesis is smaller than that of any other operator except for the opening parenthesis:

```
while (!operatorStack.empty()
        && precedence(op) <= precedence(topOp)) {
    operatorStack.pop();
    if (topOp == '(') {
        // Matching '(' popped - exit loop.
        break;
    }
    postfix.append(topOp);
```

A closing parenthesis is considered processed when an opening parenthesis is popped from the stack, and the closing parenthesis is not placed on the stack. The following `if` statement executes after the `while` loop exit:

```
if (op != ')')
    operatorStack.push(new Character(op));
```

Implementation   Listing 5.9 shows class `InfixToPostfixParens`, modified to handle parentheses. The additions are shown in color. We have omitted parts that do not change.

LISTING 5.9
InfixToPostfixParens.java

```java
import java.util.*;

/** Translates an infix expression with parentheses
    to a postfix expression.
*/
public class InfixToPostfixParens {

    // Insert nested class SyntaxErrorException here.

    // Data Fields
    /** The operator stack */
    private Stack operatorStack;
    /** The operators */
    private static final String OPERATORS = "+-*/()";
    /** The precedence of the operators, matches order of OPERATORS. */
    private static final int[] PRECEDENCE = {1, 1, 2, 2, -1, -1};
    /** The postfix string */
    private StringBuffer postfix;

    /** Convert a string from infix to postfix.
        @param expression The infix expression
        @throws SyntaxErrorException
    */
    public String convert(String infix)
            throws SyntaxErrorException {
        operatorStack = new Stack();
        postfix = new StringBuffer();
        StringTokenizer infixTokens = new StringTokenizer(infix);
        try {
            // Process each token in the infix string
            // (same as for class InfixToPostfix)
            ...
            // Pop any remaining operators
            // and append them to postfix.
            while (!operatorStack.empty()) {
                Character op = (Character) operatorStack.pop();
                // Any '(' on the stack is not matched.
                if (op.charValue() == '(')
                    throw new SyntaxErrorException(
                            "Unmatched opening parenthesis");
                postfix.append(op);
                postfix.append(' ');
            }
            // assert: Stack is empty, return result.
            return postfix.toString();
        } catch (EmptyStackException ex) {
            throw new SyntaxErrorException
                    ("Syntax Error: The stack is empty");
        }
    }
}
```

```java
/** Method to process operators.
    @param op The operator
    @throws EmptyStackException
*/
private void processOperator(char op) {
    if (operatorStack.empty() || op == '(') {
        operatorStack.push(new Character(op));
    } else {
        // Peek the operator stack and
        // let topOp be the top operator.
        char topOp =
            ((Character) operatorStack.peek()).charValue();
        if (precedence(op) > precedence(topOp)) {
            operatorStack.push(new Character(op));
        }
        else {
            // Pop all stacked operators with equal
            // or higher precedence than op.
            while (!operatorStack.empty()
                    && precedence(op) <= precedence(topOp)) {
                operatorStack.pop();
                if (topOp == '(') {
                    // Matching '(' popped - exit loop.
                    break;
                }
                postfix.append(topOp);
                postfix.append(' ');
                if (!operatorStack.empty()) {
                    // Reset topOp.
                    topOp =
                        ((Character)
                            operatorStack.peek()).charValue();
                }
            }

            // assert: Operator stack is empty or
            //         current operator precedence >
            //         top of stack operator precedence.
            if (op != ')')
                operatorStack.push(new Character(op));
        }
    }
}
```

Tying Both Case Studies Together

You can use the classes developed for the prior case studies to evaluate infix expressions with integer operands and nested parentheses. Your driver program will need to create instances of both classes, and apply method `convert` to the `InfixToPostfixParens` object. The argument for `convert` will be the infix expression. The result will be its postfix form. Next it will apply method `eval` of the `PostfixEvaluator` object. The argument for `eval` will be the postfix expression returned by `convert`.

EXERCISES FOR SECTION 5.4

SELF-CHECK

1. Trace the evaluation of the following expression using class `PostfixEvaluator`. Show the operand stack each time it is modified.

   `10 2 * 5 / 6 2 5 * + −`

2. Trace the conversion of the following expressions to postfix using class `InfixToPostfix` or `InfixToPostfixParens`. Show the operator stack each time it is modified.

   `y − 7 * 35 + 4 / 6 − 10`
   `( x + 15 ) * ( 3 * ( 4 − (5 + 7 / 2 ) ) )`

PROGRAMMING

1. Modify class `InfixToPostfix` to handle the exponentiation operator, indicated by the symbol ∧. The first operand is raised to the power indicated by the second operand. Assume that a sequence of ∧ operators will not occur and that `precedence('∧')` is greater than `precedence('*')`.

2. Discuss how you would modify the infix-to-postfix `convert` method to detect a sequence of two operators or two operands.

Chapter Review

- A stack is a last-in, first-out data structure *(LIFO)*. This means that the last item added to a stack is the first one removed.

- A stack is a simple but powerful data structure. It has only four operators: empty, peek, pop, and push.

- Stacks are useful when we want to process information in the reverse of the order that it is encountered. For this reason, a stack was used to implement the balanced parenthesis checker and the palindrome finder.

◆ `java.util.Stack` is implemented as an extension of the `Vector` class. The problem with this approach is that it allows a client to invoke other methods from the `Vector` class.

◆ We showed three different ways to implement stacks: using an object of a class that implements the `List` interface as a container, using an array as a container, and using a linked list as a container.

◆ Stacks can be applied in algorithms for evaluating arithmetic expressions. We showed how to evaluate postfix expressions and how to translate infix expressions with and without parentheses to postfix.

Java API Interfaces and Classes Introduced in This Chapter

`java.util.Stack`
`java.util.EmptyStackException`

User-Defined Interfaces and Classes in This Chapter

ArrayStack   ListStack
InfixToPostfix   PalindromeFinder
InfixToPostfixParens   ParenChecker
IsPalindrome   PostfixEvaluator
LinkedStack   SyntaxErrorException

Quick-Check Exercises

1. A stack is a _____-in, _____-out data structure.

2. Draw this stack `s` as an object of type `ArrayStack`. What is the value of data field `topOfStack`?

   > $
   > *
   > &

3. What is the value of `s.size()` for the stack shown in Question 2?

4. What is returned by `s.pop()` for the stack shown in Question 2?

5. Answer Question 2 for a stack `s` implemented as a linked list (type `LinkedStack`).

6. Why should the statement `s.remove(i)`, where `s` is of type `StackInt` and `i` is an integer index, not appear in a client program? Can you use this statement with an object of the `Stack` class defined in `java.util`? Can you use it with an object of class `ArrayStack` or `LinkedStack`?

7. What would be the postfix form of the following expression?

   `x + y - 24  *  zone - ace /  25 + c1`

   Show the contents of the operator stack just before each operator is processed and just after all tokens are scanned using method `InfixToPostfix.convert`.

8. Answer Question 7 for the following expression

   `( x + y - 24 ) * ( zone - ace / ( 25 + c1 ) )`

9. The value of the expression `20 35 - 5 / 10 7 * + is _____`. Show the contents of the operand stack just before each operator is processed and just after all tokens are scanned.

Answers to Quick-Check Exercises

1. A stack is a *last*-in, *first*-out data structure.
2. Each character in the following array should be wrapped in a `Character` object. The value of `topOfStack` should be 2.

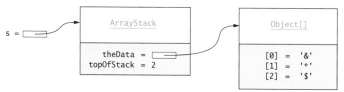

3. Method `size` returns 3.
4. `pop` returns a reference to the `Character` object that wraps `'$'`.

5.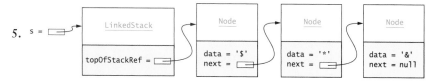

6. Method `remove(int i)` is not defined for classes that implement interface `StackInt`. The `Stack` class defined in API `java.util` would permit its use. Classes `ArrayStack` and `LinkedStack` would not.
7. Infix: `x + y - 24 * zone - ace / 25 + c1`
   Postfix: `x y + 24 zone * - ace 25 / - c1 +`

Operator stack before first + :	| Empty stack (vertical bar is bottom of stack)
Operator stack before first - :	| +
Operator stack before first * :	| -
Operator stack before second - :	| -, *
Operator stack before first / :	| -
Operator stack before second + :	| -, /
Operator stack after all tokens scanned:	| +

8. Infix: `( x + y - 24 ) * ( zone - ace / ( 25 + c1 ) )`
   Postfix: `x y + 24 - zone ace 25 c1 + / - *`

Operator stack before first (:	| Empty stack (vertical bar is bottom of stack)
Operator stack before first + :	| (
Operator stack before first - :	| (, +
Operator stack before first) :	| (, -
Operator stack before first * :	| Empty stack
Operator stack before second (:	| *
Operator stack before second - :	| *, (
Operator stack before second / :	| *, (, -
Operator stack before third (:	| *, (, -, /
Operator stack before second + :	| *, (, -, /, (
Operator stack before second) :	| *, (, -, /, (, +
Operator stack before third) :	| *, (, -, /
Operator stack after all tokens scanned:	| *

9. 20 35 − 5 / 10 7 * + is 67 (−3 + 70)

Operand stack just before − :	| 20, 35
Operand stack just before / :	| −15, 5
Operand stack just before * :	| −3, 10, 7
Operand stack just before + :	| −3, 70
Operand stack after all tokens :	| 67

Review Questions

1. Show the effect of each of the following operations on stack s. Assume that y (type Character) contains the character '&'. What are the final values of x and success and the contents of the stack s?

```
s = new Stack();
Object x;
push(new Character('+'));
try {
    x = s.pop();
    success = true;
}
catch (EmptyStackException e) {
    success = false;
}
try {
    x = s.pop();
    success = true;
}
catch (EmptyStackException e) {
    success = false;
}
push(new Character('('));
push(y);
try {
    x = s.pop();
    success = true;
}
catch (EmptyStackException e) {
    success = false;
}
```

2. Write a clone method for class ArrayStack.
3. Write a toString method for class LinkedStack.
4. Write a clone method for class LinkedStack.
5. Write an infix expression that would convert to the postfix expression in Quick-Check Question 9.
6. Write a constructor for class LinkedStack that loads the stack from an array parameter. The last array element should be at the top of the stack.
7. Write a client that removes all negative numbers from a stack of Integer objects. If the original stack contained the integers 30, −15, 20, −25 (top of stack), the new stack should contain the integers 30, 20.
8. Write a method peekNextToTop that allows you to retrieve the element just below the one at the top of the stack without removing it. Write this method for both ArrayStack and LinkedStack. It should return **null** if the stack has just one element, and it should throw an exception if the stack is empty.

Programming Projects

1. Add a method `isPalindromeLettersOnly` to the `PalindromeFinder` class that bases its findings only on the letters in a string (ignoring spaces and other characters that are not letters).

2. Provide a complete implementation of class `LinkedStack` and test it on each of the applications in this chapter.

3. Provide a complete implementation of class `ArrayStack` and test it on each of the applications in this chapter.

4. Develop an Expression Manager that can do the following operations:

   Balanced Symbols Check

   - Read a mathematical expression from the user.
   - Check and report whether the expression is balanced or not.
   - {, }, (,), [,] are the only symbols considered for the check. All other characters can be ignored.

   Infix to Postfix Conversion

   - Read an infix expression from the user.
   - Perform the Balanced Symbols Check on the expression read.
   - If the expression fails the Balanced Symbols Check, report a message to the user that the expression is invalid.
   - If the expression passes the Balanced Symbols Check, convert the infix expression into a postfix expression and display it to the user.
   - Operators to be considered are +, -, *, /, %.

   Postfix to Infix Conversion

   - Read a postfix expression from the user.
   - Convert the postfix expression into an infix expression and display it to the user.
   - Display an appropriate message if the postfix expression is not valid.
   - Operators to be considered are +, -, *, /, %.

   Evaluating a Postfix Expression

   - Read the postfix expression from the user.
   - Evaluate the postfix expression and display the result.
   - Display an appropriate message if the postfix expression is not valid.
   - Operators to be considered are +, -, *, /, %.
   - Operands should be only integers.

   Implementation

   - Design a menu that has buttons or requests user input to select from all the aforementioned operations.

5. Write a client program that uses the Stack abstract data type to simulate a session with a bank teller. Unlike most banks, this one has decided that the last customer to arrive will always be the first to be served. Create classes that represent information about a bank customer and a transaction. For each customer you need to store a name, current balance, and a reference to the transaction. For each transaction, you need to store the transaction type (deposit or withdrawal) and the amount of the transaction. After every five customers are processed, display the size of the stack and the name of the customer who will be served next.

6. Write a program to handle the flow of widgets into and out of a warehouse. The warehouse will have numerous deliveries of new widgets and orders for widgets. The widgets in a filled order are billed at a profit of 50 percent over their cost. Each delivery of new widgets may have a different cost associated with it. The accountants for the firm have instituted a last-in, first-out system for filling orders. This means that the newest widgets are the first ones sent out to fill an order. Also, the most recent orders are filled first. This method of inventory can be represented using two stacks: orders-to-be-filled and widgets-on-hand. When a delivery of new widgets is received, any unfilled orders (on the orders-to-be-filled stack) are processed and filled. After all orders are filled, if there are widgets remaining in the new delivery, a new element is pushed onto the widgets-on-hand stack. When an order for new widgets is received, one or more objects are popped from the widgets-on-hand stack until the order has been filled. If the order is completely filled and there are widgets left over in the last object popped, a modified object with the quantity updated is pushed onto the widgets-on-hand stack. If the order is not completely filled, the order is pushed onto the orders-to-be-filled stack with an updated quantity of widgets to be sent out later. If an order is completely filled, it is not pushed onto the stack.

Write a class with methods to process the shipments received and to process orders. After an order is filled, display the quantity sent out and the total cost for all widgets in the order. Also indicate whether there are any widgets remaining to be sent out at a later time. After a delivery is processed, display information about each order that was filled with this delivery and indicate how many widgets, if any, were stored in the object pushed onto the widgets-on-hand stack.

7. You can combine the algorithms for converting between infix to postfix and for evaluating postfix to evaluate an infix expression directly. To do so you need two stacks: one to contain operators and the other to contain operands. When an operand is encountered, it is pushed onto the operand stack. When an operator is encountered, it is processed as described in the infix to postfix algorithm. When an operator is popped off the operator stack, it is processed as described in the postfix evaluation algorithm: The top two operands are popped off the operand stack, the operation is performed, and the result is pushed back onto the operand stack. Write a program to evaluate infix expressions directly using this combined algorithm.

8. Write a client program that uses the Stack abstract data type to compile a simple arithmetic expression without parentheses. For example, the expression

a + b * c - d

should be compiled according to the following table

Operator	Operand 1	Operand 2	Result
*	b	c	z
+	a	z	y
−	y	d	x

The table shows the order in which the operations are performed (*, +, −) and operands for each operator. The result column gives the name of an identifier (working backward from z) chosen to hold each result. Assume the operands are the letters a through m and the operators are (+, −, *, /). Your program should read each character and process it as follows: If the character is blank, ignore it. If the character is neither blank nor an operand nor an operator, display an error message and terminate the program. If it is an operand, push it onto the operand stack. If it is an operator, compare its precedence to that of the operator on top of the operator stack. If the current operator has higher precedence than the one currently on top of the stack (or stack is empty), it should be pushed onto the operator stack. If the current operator has the same or lower precedence, the operator on top of the operator stack must be evaluated next. This is done by popping that operator off the operator stack along with a pair of operands from the operand stack and writing a new line in the output table. The character selected to hold the result should then be pushed onto the operand stack. Next, the current operator should be compared to the new top of the operator stack. Continue to generate output lines until the top of the operator stack has lower precedence than the current operator or until it is empty. At this point, push the current operator onto the top of the stack and examine the next character in the data string. When the end of the string is reached, pop any remaining operator along with its operand pair just described. Remember to push the result character onto the operand stack after each table line is generated.

Queues

Chapter Objectives

Chapter Objectives

◆ To learn how to represent a waiting line (queue) and how to use the five methods in the Queue interface: insert, retrieve, peek, getSize, and isEmpty

◆ To understand how to implement the Queue interface using a single-linked list, a circular array, and a double-linked list

◆ To understand how to simulate the operation of a physical system that has one or more waiting lines using Queues and random number generators

I n this chapter we study an abstract data type, Queue, that is widely used like the stack but differs from it in one important way. A stack is a LIFO (last-in, first-out) list, because the last element pushed onto a stack will be the first element popped off. A queue, on the other hand, is a FIFO (first-in, first-out) list, because the first element inserted in the queue will be the first element removed.

You will learn how to use a queue to store items (for example, customers) that will be accessed on a first-come, first-served basis. We will also show you how to implement queues. Finally, you will also learn how to use simulation to estimate the amount of time customers will spend waiting in a queue.

6.1 Queue Abstract Data Type

The easiest way to visualize a queue is to think of a line of customers waiting for service, as shown in Figure 6.1. Usually, the next person to be served is the one who has been waiting the longest, and latecomers are added to the end of the line. The Queue ADT gets its name from the fact that such a waiting line is called a queue in English-speaking countries other than the United States.

A Print Queue

In computer science, queues are used in operating systems to keep track of tasks waiting for a scarce resource and to ensure that the tasks are carried out in the order that they were generated. One example is a print queue. A Web surfer may select several pages to be printed in a few seconds. Because a printer is relatively slow device (approximately 10 pages per minute), you will often select new pages to print faster than they can be printed. Rather than require you to wait until the current page is finished before you can select a new one, the operating system stores docu-

FIGURE 6.1
Customers Waiting in a
Line or Queue

FIGURE 6.2
A Print Queue in the Windows Operating System

Document Name	Status	Owner	Pages	Size	Submitted	P.
Microsoft Word - Queues_Paul_1007.doc		Paul Wolfgang	52	9.75 MB	1:53:18 PM 10/7/2003	
Microsoft Word - Stacks.doc		Paul Wolfgang	46	9.05 MB	1:53:57 PM 10/7/2003	
Microsoft Word - Trees2.doc		Paul Wolfgang	54	38.4 MB	1:54:41 PM 10/7/2003	

HP LaserJet 4050 Series PS – Use Printer Offline
Printer Document View Help
3 document(s) in queue

ments to be printed in a print queue (see Figure 6.2). Because they are stored in a queue, the pages will be printed in the same order as they were selected (first-in, first-out). The document first inserted in the queue will be the first one printed.

The Unsuitability of a "Print Stack"

Suppose your operating system used a stack (last-in, first-out) instead of a queue to store documents waiting to print. Then the most recently selected Web page would be the next page to print. This may not matter if only one person is using the printer. However, if the printer is connected to a computer network, this would be a big problem. Unless the print queue was empty when you selected a page to print (and the page printed immediately), that page would not print until all pages selected after it (by yourself or any other person on the network) were printed. If you were waiting by the printer for your page to print before going to your next class, you would have no way of knowing how long your wait might be. You would also be very unhappy if people who started after you had their documents printed before yours. So a print queue is a much more sensible alternative than a print stack.

A Queue of Customers

A queue of three customers waiting to buy concert tickets is shown in Figure 6.3. The name of the customer who has been waiting the longest is Thome; the name of the most recent arrival is Jones. Customer Thome will be the first customer removed from the queue (and able to buy tickets) when a ticket agent becomes available, and customer Abreu will then become the first one in the queue. Any new customers will be inserted in the queue after customer Jones.

FIGURE 6.3
A Queue of Customers

Ticket agent

Thome
Abreu
Jones

Using a Queue for Traversing a Multi-Branch Data Structure

In Chapter 12, you will see a data structure, called a graph, that models a *network* of *nodes,* with many links connecting each node to other nodes in the network (see Figure 6.4). Unlike a linked list, in which each node has only one successor, a node in a graph may have several successors. For example, node 0 in Figure 6.4 has nodes 1 and 3 as its successors. Consequently, it is not a simple matter to visit the nodes in a systematic way and to ensure that each node is visited only once. Programmers

FIGURE 6.4

A Network of Nodes

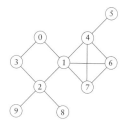

often use a queue to ensure that nodes closer to the starting point are visited before nodes that are farther away. We will not go into the details here because we cover them later, but the idea is to put nodes that have not yet been visited into the queue when they are first encountered. After visiting the current node, the next node to visit is taken from the queue. This ensures that nodes are visited in the same order that they were encountered. Such a traversal is called a *breadth-first traversal* because the nodes visited spread out from the starting point. If we use a stack to hold the new nodes that are encountered and take the next node to visit from the stack, we will follow one path to the end before embarking on a new path. This kind of traversal is called a *depth-first traversal*.

Specification for a Queue Interface

A specification for a `Queue` interface follows. We used method names `insert` and `remove` for the `Queue` methods that perform these operations; other common names for these methods are `enqueue` and `dequeue`. We provided a `peek` method because the `Stack` class has one.

We define a `Queue` interface (Listing 6.1) because the Java API does not provide a `Queue` class. Each implementation of this interface must define at least the methods shown in Table 6.1.

TABLE 6.1

Specification of Abstract Data Type Queue

Method	Behavior
`Object insert(Object item)`	Inserts `item` at the rear of the queue.
`Object peek()`	Returns the `Object` at the front of the queue if the queue is not empty. If the queue is empty, throws an `EmptyQueueException`.
`Object remove()`	Removes the `Object` at the front of the queue and returns it if the queue is not empty. If the queue is empty, throws an `EmptyQueueException`.
`int getSize()`	Returns the number of items in the queue.
`boolean isEmpty()`	Returns **true** if the queue is empty, otherwise returns **false**.

LISTING 6.1

Queue.java

```
/** A Queue is a data structure in which objects are inserted at one
    end and removed from the other (i.e., first in-first out).
*/
public interface Queue {

    /** Insert an item into the queue.
        @param obj The object to be inserted
        @return The object inserted
    */
    Object insert(Object obj);
```

```
/** Peek at the first item in the queue.
    @return The object at the front of the queue
    @throws EmptyQueueException
*/
Object peek();

/** Remove the first item in the queue.
 *  @return The object at the front of the queue
    @throws EmptyQueueException
*/
Object remove();

/** Return the size of the queue.
    @return The number of items in the queue
*/
int getSize();

/** Determine whether the queue is empty.
    @return true if the queue is empty
*/
boolean isEmpty();
}
```

Class EmptyQueueException

Because there is no Queue class defined in the Java API, there is no exception class associated with the action of attempting to remove an item from an empty queue. Listing 6.2 shows the definition of the EmptyQueueException. This exception class is defined to be an extension of RuntimeException, the same as EmptyStackException. We will describe three implementations of the Queue interface later in this chapter.

....
LISTING 6.2
EmptyQueueException.java

```
/** EmptyQueueException is thrown by classes that implement
    the Queue interface whenever a peek or remove operation
    is performed on an empty Queue. This is an unchecked
    exception, like EmptyStackException.
*/
public class EmptyQueueException extends RuntimeException {
    /** Constructs a new EmptyQueueException with null
        as its error message string. */
    public EmptyQueueException() {
    }
}
```

EXERCISES FOR SECTION 6.1

SELF-CHECK

1. Draw the queue in Figure 6.3 as it will appear after the insertion of customer Harris and the removal of one customer from the queue. Which customer is removed? How many customers are left?

2. Assume that myQueue is an instance of a class that implements Queue and myQueue is an empty queue. Explain the effect of each of the following operations.

```
myQueue.insert("Hello");
myQueue.insert("Bye");
System.out.println(myQueue.peek());
myQueue.remove();
myQueue.insert("Welcome");
if (!myQueue.isEmpty()) {
    System.out.println(myQueue.remove()
        + ", new size is " + myQueue.getSize());
    System.out.println("Item in front is " + myQueue.peek());
}
```

6.2 Maintaining a Queue of Customers

In this section we present an application that maintains a queue of Strings representing the names of customers waiting for service. We include a factory method that will create an instance of a specified implementation. In the next section, we will show three different classes that implement the Queue interface.

CASE STUDY   Maintaining a Queue

Problem Write a menu-driven program that maintains a list of customers waiting for service. The program user should be able to insert a new customer in the line, display the customer who is next in line, remove the customer who is next in line, and display the length of the line.

Analysis As discussed earlier, a queue is a good data structure for storing a list of customers waiting for service because they would expect to be served in the order in which they arrived. We can display the menu (using the JOptionPane.showOptionDialog method) and then perform the requested operation by calling the appropriate Queue method to update the customer list. We will use JOptionPane dialog windows to enter new customer names and to display results.

Problem Inputs

The operation to be performed

The name of a new customer to insert

Problem Outputs

The effect of each operation

TABLE 6.2
Class MaintainQueue

Data Field	Attribute
private Queue customers	A queue of customers.
Method	**Behavior**
private static Queue getQueue()	Returns a Queue object.
public static void processCustomers()	Accepts and processes each user's selection.

Design We will write a class MaintainQueue to store the queue and control its processing. Class MaintainQueue has a Queue component customers. We will use a factory method to create the actual Queue object based on the user's selection. In the next section, we describe the classes ArrayQueue, ListQueue (single-linked list), and LinkedListQueue (double-linked list) that implement the Queue interface.

Method processCustomers displays a menu of choices and processes the user selection by calling the appropriate Queue method. Table 6.2 shows class MaintainQueue.

The algorithm for method processCustomers follows.

Algorithm for processCustomers

1. **while** the user is not finished
2.   Display the menu and get the operation selected.
3.   Perform the operation selected.

Implementation Listing 6.3 shows the data field declarations and the constructor. The constructor calls the factory method, getQueue, to return an instance of the Queue implementation selected by the program user. If the user enters "a" (for "array"), the statement

```
return new ArrayQueue();
```

returns an empty queue using the ArrayQueue implementation of the Queue interface. We will discuss all three implementation in the next section. They can be downloaded from the textbook Web site.

LISTING 6.3
Constructor and Method getQueue in Class MaintainQueue

```
import javax.swing.*;

/** Class to maintain a queue of customers. */
public class MaintainQueue {
```

```
        // Data Field
        Queue customers;

        // Methods
        /** Create an empty queue. */
        public MaintainQueue() {
            customers = getQueue();
        }

        /** Factory method returns an instance of the implementation
            selected by the user.
            @return An instance of the selected Queue implementation
        */
        private static Queue getQueue() {
            do {
                String queueType = JOptionPane.showInputDialog(
                                    "Select kind of queue:"
                                    + "\nEnter a for array"
                                    + "\nEnter d for double-linked list"
                                    + "\nEnter s for single-linked list");
                if (queueType.equalsIgnoreCase("a")) {
                    return new ArrayQueue();
                } else if (queueType.equalsIgnoreCase("d")) {
                    return new LinkedListQueue();
                } else if (queueType.equalsIgnoreCase("s")) {
                    return new ListQueue();
                }
            } while (true);    // Repeat until queue created.
        }
    ...
    }
```

In method processCustomers (Listing 6.4), the call to method showOptionDialog displays the menu shown in Figure 6.5. After the selection is returned to choiceNum, the switch statement calls a Queue method to perform the selected operation. For example, if the user clicks the *insert* button, the statements

```
    String name = JOptionPane.showInputDialog
            ("Enter new customer name");
    customers.insert(name);
```

read the customer name and insert it into in the queue. The **switch** statement is inside a **try-catch** sequence that handles an EmptyQueueException by displaying an error message window.

FIGURE 6.5
Menu Displayed by MaintainQueue

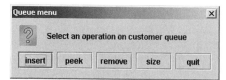

LISTING 6.4
Method processCustomers in Class MaintainQueue

```java
/** Performs the operations selected on queue customers.
    pre:  customers has been created.
    post: customers is modified based on user selections.
*/
public void processCustomers() {
    int choiceNum = 0;
    String[] choices =
            {"insert", "peek", "remove", "size", "quit"};

    // Perform all operations selected by user.
    while (choiceNum < choices.length - 1) {
        // Select the next operation.
        choiceNum = JOptionPane.showOptionDialog(null,
                "Select an operation on customer queue",
                "Queue menu", JOptionPane.YES_NO_CANCEL_OPTION,
                JOptionPane.QUESTION_MESSAGE, null,
                choices, choices[0]);

        // Process the current choice.
        try {
            switch (choiceNum) {
              case 0 :
                  String name = JOptionPane.showInputDialog
                          ("Enter new customer name");
                  customers.insert(name);
                  JOptionPane.showMessageDialog(null,
                          "Customer " + name
                          + " added to line");
                  break;
              case 1 :
                  JOptionPane.showMessageDialog(null,
                          "Customer " + customers.peek()
                          + " is next in line");
                  break;
              case 2 :
                  JOptionPane.showMessageDialog(null,
                          "Customer " + customers.remove()
                          + " removed from line");
                  break;
              case 3 :
                  JOptionPane.showMessageDialog(null,
                          "Size of line is "
                          + customers.getSize());
                  break;
              case 4:
                  JOptionPane.showMessageDialog(null,
                          "Leaving customer queue. "
                          + "\nNumber of customers in queue is "
                          + customers.getSize());
                  break;
```

```
            default :
                JOptionPane.showMessageDialog(null,
                        "Invalid selection");
                break;
        }
    }
    catch (EmptyQueueException ex) {
        JOptionPane.showMessageDialog(null,
                "The Queue is empty", "",
                JOptionPane.ERROR_MESSAGE);
    }
}    // End while.
}
```

Testing   You can use class MaintainQueue to test each of the different Queue implementations discussed in the next section. You should verify that all customers are stored and retrieved in first-in, first-out order. You should also verify that an EmptyQueueException is thrown if you attempt to remove a customer from an empty queue. You can thoroughly test the queue by selecting different sequences of queue operations.

EXERCISES FOR SECTION 6.2

SELF-CHECK

1. Write an algorithm to display all the elements in a queue using just the queue operations. How would your algorithm change the queue?

2. Trace the following fragment for a stack s and an empty queue q.
```
while (!s.empty()) {
    Object item = s.pop();
    q.insert(item);
}
while (!q.isEmpty()) {
    item = q.remove();
    s.push(item);
}
```
   a. What is stored in stack s after the first loop executes? What is stored in queue q after the first loop executes?
   b. What is stored in stack s after the second loop executes? What is stored in queue q after the second loop executes?

PROGRAMMING

1. Write a static method that takes a `Queue` parameter and returns a string that shows the contents of the queue using the `Queue` operators.

   `public static String toString(Queue q)`

   What happens to the queue that is passed as an argument? How can you prevent this from happening?

6.3 Implementing the Queue Interface

In this section we will discuss three approaches to implementing a queue: using a single-linked list, using the Java `LinkedList` class, and using an array. We begin with using a single-linked list.

Using a Single-Linked List to Implement a Queue

We can implement a queue using a single-linked list like the one shown in Figure 6.6. Class `ListQueue` contains a collection of `Node` objects (see Section 4.4). Recall that class `Node` has attributes `data` (type `Object`) and `next` (type `Node`).

Insertions are at the rear of a queue, and removals are from the front. We need a reference to the last list node so that insertions can be performed in O(1) time; otherwise, we would have to start at the list head and traverse all the way down the list to do an insertion. There is a reference variable `front` to the first list node (the list head) and a reference variable `rear` to the last list node. There is also a data field `size`. Notice that we can't exchange the references `front` and `rear`, because if we did, we would have to traverse the list to find the predecessor to `front` before we could remove the queue element referenced by `front`.

The number of elements in the queue is changed by methods `insert` and `remove`, so `size` must be incremented by one in `insert` and decremented by one in `remove`. The value of `size` is tested in `isEmpty` to determine the status of the queue. The method `getSize` simply returns the value of `size`.

Listing 6.5 shows class `ListQueue`. Method `insert` treats insertion into an empty queue as a special case, because both `front` and `rear` should both reference the new node after the insertion.

FIGURE 6.6

A Queue as a
Single-Linked List

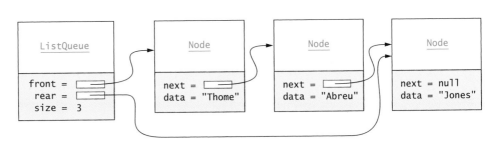

```
rear = new Node(item, null);
front = rear;
```

If we insert into a queue that is not empty, the new node must be linked to the old rear of the queue, but front is unchanged.

```
rear.next = new Node(item, null);
rear = rear.next;
```

If the queue is empty, method peek throws an EmptyQueueException. Otherwise, it returns the element at the front of the queue:

```
return front.data;
```

Method remove calls method peek and returns its result. However, before returning, it disconnects the node at the front of the queue and decrements size.

```
front = front.next;
size--;
```

LISTING 6.5
Class ListQueue

```
/** Class to implement Queue using a single-linked list. */
public class ListQueue implements Queue {

    // Data Fields
    /** Reference to front of queue. */
    private Node front;
    /** Reference to rear of queue. */
    private Node rear;
    /** Size of queue. */
    private int size;

    // Insert inner class Node here.

    // Methods
    /** Insert an item into the queue.
        pre: front references first item or is null,
            rear references last item or is null.
        post: rear references new item that is inserted.
        @param item The item to be inserted
        @return The item inserted
    */
    public Object insert(Object item) {
        // Check for empty queue.
        if (front == null) {
            rear = new Node(item);
            front = rear;
        } else {
            // Allocate a new node at end, store item in it, and
            // link it to old end of queue.
            rear.next = new Node(item);
            rear = rear.next;
        }
        size++;
        return item;
    }
```

```
/** Remove the item at the front of the queue.
    pre: front references first item or is null,
         rear references last item or is null.
    post: front references item that was second in the queue,
          rear references last item in the queue.
          size is decremented.
    @return The object at the front of the queue
    @throws EmptyQueueException
*/
public Object remove() {
    Object item = peek();      // Retrieve item at front.
    // Remove item at front.
    front = front.next;
    size--;
    return item;    // Return data at front of queue.
}

/** Peek at the item at the front of the queue.
    @return The object at the front of the queue
    @throws EmptyQueueException
*/
public Object peek() {
    if (isEmpty())
        throw new EmptyQueueException();
    return front.data;
}

/** Return the size of the queue.
    @return The number of items in the queue */
public int getSize() {
    return size;
}

/** Determine whether the queue is empty.
    @return true if queue is empty; false if it isn't
*/
public boolean isEmpty() {
    return size == 0;
}
}
```

Implementing a Queue Using Java's LinkedList

The queue can be implemented as an adapter of any class that implements the List interface (such as ArrayList, Vector, or LinkedList). The insert method can be implemented using the add method to add the new item to the end of the list as follows:

```
Object insert (Object obj) {
    theData.add(obj);
    return obj;
}
```

The remove method can be implemented to remove the element at the front of the list (position 0) as follows:

```
Object remove() {
    return theData.remove(0);
}
```

This works, but it is not very efficient unless we use a `LinkedList` for `theData`. Removal from the front of a queue stored in an `ArrayList` or `Vector` component is an O(n) operation because all elements that follow the first one have to be shifted to fill the vacated space. However, if we use a `LinkedList`, removal is an O(1) operation.

The authors of the Java API included additional methods such as `removeFirst()`, `removeLast()`, `addFirst()`, and `addLast()` to facilitate using a `LinkedList` as a queue. Listing 6.6 shows a queue implementation that uses an instance of Java's `LinkedList` (a double-linked list) for storage of the queue.

....

LISTING 6.6
LinkedListQueue.java

```java
import java.util.LinkedList;

/** Implements the Queue interface using Java's LinkedList.
*/
public class LinkedListQueue implements Queue {

    // Data Fields
    /** List to hold the data. */
    private LinkedList theData;

    // Methods
    /** Construct an empty queue. */
    public LinkedListQueue() {
        theData = new LinkedList();
    }

    /** Insert an item into the queue.
        @param obj The object to be inserted
        @return The object inserted
    */
    public Object insert(Object obj) {
        theData.addLast(obj);
        return obj;
    }

    /** Peek at the first item in the queue.
        @return The object at the front of the queue
        @throws EmptyQueueException
    */
    public Object peek() {
        if (isEmpty()) {
            throw new EmptyQueueException();
        }
        return theData.getFirst();
    }
```

```
/** Remove the first item in the queue.
    @return The object at the front of the queue
    @throws EmptyQueueException
*/
public Object remove() {
    if (isEmpty()) {
        throw new EmptyQueueException();
    }
    return theData.removeFirst();
}

/** Return the size of the queue.
    @return The number of items in the queue
*/
public int getSize() {
    return theData.size();
}

/** Determine whether the queue is empty.
    @return true if the queue is empty
*/
public boolean isEmpty() {
    return theData.size() == 0;
}
}
```

Implementing a Queue Using a Circular Array

While the time efficiency of using a single- or double-linked list to implement the Queue is acceptable, there is some space inefficiency. Each node of a single-linked list contains a reference to its successor, and each node of a double-linked list contains references to its predecessor and successor. These additional references will increase the storage space required.

An alternative is to use an array. If we use an array, we can do an insertion at the rear of the array in $O(1)$ time. However, a removal from the front will be an $O(n)$ process if we shift all the elements that follow the first one over to fill the space vacated. Similarly, removal from the rear is $O(1)$, but insertion at the front is $O(n)$. We next discuss how to avoid this inefficiency.

Overview of the Design

To represent a queue, we will use an object with four **int** data members (front, rear, size, capacity), and an array data member, theData, which provides storage for the queue elements.

```
/** Index of the front of the queue. */
private int front;
/** Index of the rear of the queue. */
private int rear;
/** Current size of the queue. */
private int size;
/** Current capacity of the queue. */
private int capacity;
```

```
/** Default capacity of the queue. */
private static final int DEFAULT = 10;

/** Array to hold the data. */
private Object[] theData;
```

The **int** fields front and rear are indices to the queue elements at the front and rear of the queue, respectively. The **int** field size keeps track of the actual number of items in the queue and allows us to determine easily whether the queue is empty (size is 0) or full (size is capacity).

It makes sense to store the first queue item in element 0, the second queue item in element 1, and so on. So we should set front to 0 and rear to –1 when we create an initially empty queue. Each time we do an insertion, we should increment size and rear by 1 so that front and rear will both be 0 if a queue has one element. Figure 6.7 shows an instance of a queue that is filled to its capacity (size is capacity). The queue contains the symbols &, *, +, /, –, inserted in that order.

Because the queue in Figure 6.7 is filled to capacity, we cannot insert a new character without allocating more storage. However, we can remove a queue element by decrementing size and incrementing front to 1, thereby removing theData[0] (the symbol &) from the queue. Figure 6.8 shows the queue after removing the first element (it is still in the array, but not part of the queue). The queue contains the symbols *, +, /, –, in that order.

Although the queue in Figure 6.8 is no longer filled, we cannot insert a new character, because rear is at its maximum value. One way to solve this problem is to shift the elements in array theData so that the empty cells come after rear and then adjust front and rear accordingly. This array shifting must be done very carefully to avoid losing track of active array elements. It is also an $O(n)$ operation.

A better way to solve this problem is to represent the array field theData as a *circular array*. In a circular array, the elements wrap around so that the first element actually follows the last. This is like counting modulo size; the array subscripts take on the values 0, 1, . . . , size – 1, 0, 1, and so on. This allows us to "increment" rear to 0 and store a new character in theData[0]. Figure 6.9 shows the queue after inserting a new element (the character A). After the insertion, front is still 1 but rear becomes 0. The contents of theData[0] changes from & to A. The queue now contains the symbols *, +, /, –, A, in that order.

FIGURE 6.7
A Queue Filled with Characters

FIGURE 6.8
The Queue after Deletion of the First Element

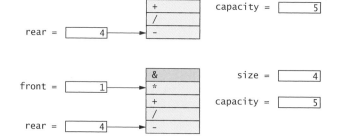

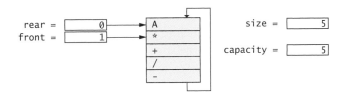

FIGURE 6.9
A Queue as a
Circular Array

EXAMPLE 6.1   The upper half of Figure 6.10 shows the effect of removing two elements from the queue just described. There are currently three characters in this queue (stored in `theData[3]`, `theData[4]`, and `theData[0]`). The queue now contains the symbols /, -, A, in that order.

The lower half of Figure 6.10 shows the queue after insertion of a new character (B). The value of `rear` is incremented to 1 and the next element is inserted in `theData[1]`. This queue element follows the character A in `theData[0]`. The value of `front` is still 3 because the character / at `theData[3]` has been in the queue the longest. `theData[2]` is now the only queue element that is unused. The queue now contains the symbols /, -, A, B in that order.

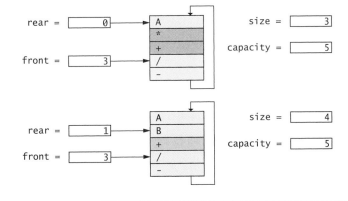

FIGURE 6.10
The Effect of Two
Deletions . . .

and One Insertion

Implementing **ArrayQueue**

Listing 6.7 shows the implementation of the class `ArrayQueue`.

The constructors set `size` to 0 and `front` to 0 because array element `theData[0]` is considered the front of the empty queue, and `rear` is initialized to `capacity` - 1 (instead of −1) because the queue is circular.

In method `insert`, the statement

```
rear = (rear + 1) % capacity;
```

is used to increment the value of `rear` modulo `capacity`. When `rear` is less than `capacity`, this statement simply increments its value by one. But when `rear` becomes equal to `capacity` - 1, the next value of `rear` will be 0 (capacity mod capacity is 0), thereby wrapping the last element of the queue around to the first element. Because the constructor initializes `rear` to `capacity` - 1, the first queue element will be placed in `theData[0]` as desired.

In method `remove`, the element currently stored in `theData[front]` is copied into `result` before `front` is incremented modulo capacity; `result` is then returned. In method `peek`, the element at `theData[front]` is returned, but `front` is not changed.

When the capacity is reached, we double the capacity and copy the array into the new one, as was done for the `ArrayList`. However, we can't simply use the `reallocate` method we developed for the `ArrayList` because of the circular nature of the array. We can't copy over elements from the original array to the first half of the expanded array; we must first copy the elements from position `front` through the end of the original array to the beginning of the expanded array; then copy the elements from the beginning of the original array through `rear` to follow those in the expanded array (see Figure 6.11).

We begin by creating an array `newData`, whose capacity is double that of `theData`. The loop

```
int j = front;
for (int i = 0; i < size; i++) {
    newData[i] = theData[j];
    j = (j + 1) % capacity;
}
```

copies `size` elements over from `theData` to the first half of `newData`. In the copy operation

```
newData[i] = theData[j]
```

subscript `i` for `newData` goes from 0 to `size - 1` (the first half of `newData`). Subscript `j` for `theData` starts at `front`. The statement

```
j = (j + 1) % capacity;
```

increments the subscript for array `theData`. Therefore, subscript `j` goes from `front` to `capacity - 1` (in increments of 1) and then back to 0. So the elements are copied from `theData` in the sequence `theData[front]`, . . . , `theData[capacity - 1]`, `theData[0]`, . . . , `theData[rear]`, where `theData[front]` is stored in `newData[0]` and `theData[rear]` is stored in `newData[size - 1]`. After the copy loop, `front` is reset to 0 and `rear` is reset to `size - 1` (see Figure 6.11).

By choosing a new capacity that is twice the current capacity, the cost of the reallocation is amortized across each insert, just as for an `ArrayList`. Thus, insertion is still considered an O(1) operation.

 PITFALL

Using System.arraycopy

You might consider using the statement

```
System.arraycopy(theData, 0, newData, 0, capacity)
```

to copy all of the elements over from array `theData` to the first half of array `newData`. The problem, however, is that in circular array `theData`, element `theData[0]` follows element `theData[capacity - 1]`, but this is not the case in array `newData`, because its capacity is double that of `theData`.

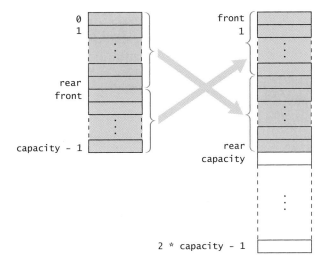

FIGURE 6.11
Reallocating a Circular
Array

LISTING 6.7
ArrayQueue.java

```java
/** Implements the Queue interface using a circular array. */
public class ArrayQueue implements Queue {

    // Data Fields
    /** Index of the front of the queue. */
    private int front;
    /** Index of the rear of the queue. */
    private int rear;
    /** Current size of the queue. */
    private int size;
    /** Current capacity of the queue. */
    private int capacity;
    /** Default capacity of the queue. */
    private static final int DEFAULT = 10;
    /** Array to hold the data. */
    private Object[] theData;

    // Constructors
    /** Construct a queue with the default initial capacity.
    */
    public ArrayQueue() {
        this(DEFAULT);
    }

    /** Construct a queue with the specified initial capacity.
        @param initCapacity The initial capacity
    */
    public ArrayQueue(int initCapacity) {
        capacity = initCapacity;
        theData = new Object[capacity];
        front = 0;
        rear = capacity - 1;
        size = 0;
    }
```

```
// Public Methods
/** Insert an item into the queue.
    @param obj The object to be inserted
    @return The object inserted
*/
public Object insert(Object obj) {
    if (size == capacity) {
        reallocate();
    }
    size++;
    rear = (rear + 1) % capacity;
    theData[rear] = obj;
    return obj;
}

/** Peek at the first item in the queue.
    @return The object at the front of the queue
    @throws EmptyQueueException
*/
public Object peek() {
    if (isEmpty()) {
        throw new EmptyQueueException();
    }
    return theData[front];
}

/** Remove the first item in the queue.
    @return The object at the front of the queue
    @throws EmptyQueueException
*/
public Object remove() {
    if (isEmpty()) {
        throw new EmptyQueueException();
    }
    Object result = theData[front];
    front = (front + 1) % capacity;
    size--;
    return result;
}

/** Return the size of the queue.
    @return The number of items in the queue
*/
public int getSize() {
    return size;
}

/** Determine whether the queue is empty.
    @return true if the queue is empty
*/
public boolean isEmpty() {
    return size == 0;
}
```

```
// Private Methods
/** Double the capacity and reallocate the data.
    pre: The array is filled to capacity.
    post: The capacity is doubled and the first half of the
          expanded array is filled with data.
*/
private void reallocate() {
    int newCapacity = 2 * capacity;
    Object[] newData = new Object[newCapacity];
    int j = front;
    for (int i = 0; i < size; i++) {
        newData[i] = theData[j];
        j = (j + 1) % capacity;
    }
    front = 0;
    rear = size - 1;
    capacity = newCapacity;
    theData = newData;
}
}
```

Comparing the Three Implementations

As mentioned earlier, all three implementations of the Queue interface are comparable in terms of computation time. All operations are O(1) regardless of the implementation. Although reallocating an array is an O(n) operation, it is amortized over n items, so the cost per item is O(1).

In terms of storage requirements, both linked-list implementations require more storage because of the extra space required for links. To perform an analysis of the storage requirements, you need to know that Java stores a reference to the data for a queue element in each node in addition to the links. Therefore, each node for a single-linked list would store a total of two references (one for the data and one for the link), a node for a double-linked list would store a total of three references, and a node for a circular array would store just one reference. Therefore, a double-linked list would require 1.5 times the storage required for a single-linked list with the same number of elements. A circular array that is filled to capacity would require half the storage of a single-linked list to store the same number of elements. However, if the array were just reallocated, half the array would be empty, so it would require the same storage as a single-linked list.

EXERCISES FOR SECTION 6.3

SELF-CHECK

1. Show the new array for the queue in Figure 6.9 after the array size is doubled.
2. Provide the algorithm for the method in Programming Exercise 1 below.
3. Redraw the queue in Figure 6.6 so that rear references the list head and front references the list tail. Show the queue after an element is inserted and an element is removed. Explain why the approach used in the book is better.

PROGRAMMING

1. Write a new method for ListQueue that displays the entire queue contents (from front to rear, inclusive).
2. Do Programming Exercise 1 for LinkedListQueue.
3. Do Programming Exercise 1 for ArrayQueue.
4. Replace the loop in method reallocate with two calls to System.arraycopy.
5. For Self-Check Exercise 3, write methods insert and remove.

6.4 Simulating Waiting Lines Using Queues

Simulation is a technique used to study the performance of a physical system by using a physical, mathematical, or computer model of the system. Through simulation, the designers of a new system can estimate the expected performance of the system before they actually build it. The use of simulation can lead to changes in the design that will improve the expected performance of the new system. Simulation is especially useful when the actual system would be too expensive to build or too dangerous to experiment with after its construction.

System designers often use computer models to simulate physical systems. In this section we will implement and test a computer model of an airline check-in counter in order to compare various strategies for improving service and reducing the waiting time for each passenger. We will use a queue to simulate the passenger waiting line. A special branch of mathematics called *queuing theory* has been developed to study these kinds of problems using mathematical models (systems of equations) instead of computer models.

CASE STUDY   Simulate a Strategy for Serving Airline Passengers

Problem   We Fly Anywhere Airlines (WFAA) is considering redesigning its ticket counters for airline passengers. The company would like to have two separate waiting lines: one for regular customers and one for frequent flyers. Assuming there is only one ticket agent available to serve all passengers, the company would like to determine the average waiting time for both types of passengers using various strategies for taking passengers from the waiting lines (see Figure 6.12).

A "democratic" strategy for serving passengers would be to take turns serving passengers from both lines (that is, one frequent flyer, one regular passenger, one frequent flyer, and so on). Another "democratic" strategy would be to serve the passenger who has been waiting in line the longest, but this would be the same as having a single queue. (Why?) An "elitist" strategy would be to serve any frequent flyer waiting in line before serving the regular passengers.

Analysis   Running a computer simulation is a good way to investigate the effect of different serving strategies. To run a computer simulation, we must keep track of the current time by maintaining a clock that is set to an initial time of zero. This clock will increase by one time unit until the simulation is finished. During each time interval, one or more of the following events may occur.

1. A new frequent flyer passenger arrives in line.
2. A new regular passenger arrives in line.
3. The ticket agent finishes serving a passenger and begins to serve a passenger from the frequent flyer line.

FIGURE 6.12
Passenger Waiting
Lines

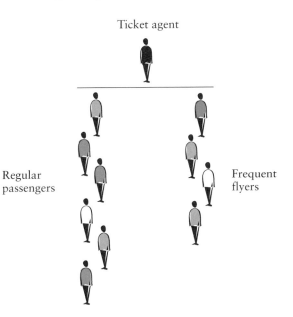

Ticket agent

Regular
passengers

Frequent
flyers

4. The ticket agent finishes serving a passenger and begins to serve a passenger from the regular passenger line.

5. The ticket agent is idle because there are no passengers in either line to serve.

The purpose of running the simulation is to determine statistics about the waiting times for frequent flyers and for regular passengers. Besides the priority given to frequent flyers, the waiting times depend on the arrival rate of each type of passenger (number of passengers arriving per minute) and the time required to serve a passenger. There are different arrival rates for each kind of passenger. In addition to statistics on waiting times, we can display a minute-by-minute trace of events occurring during each minute of the simulation.

We can simulate different serving strategies by introducing a simulation variable `frequentFlyerMax`, which must be a positive integer. This will represent the number of consecutive frequent flyer passengers served between regular passengers. When `frequentFlyerMax` is 1, every other passenger served will be a regular passenger (the "democratic" strategy). When `frequentFlyerMax` is 2, every third passenger served will be a regular passenger. When `frequentFlyerMax` is a very large number, any frequent flyer passenger will be served before a regular passenger (the "elitist" strategy).

Design   To begin an object-oriented design, we look at the problem description and identify the classes. We can use the nouns in the problem statement as a starting point. Doing this we see that we have an *agent*, *passengers*, and two *passenger queues*. These are part of the *simulation*. This leads to the initial UML class diagram shown in Figure 6.13. The diagram shows that `PassengerQueue` is a subclass of `ArrayQueue` and is also a component (filled diamond) of `AirlineCheckinSim`—the class that runs the simulation. Also, a `PassengerQueue` stores objects of type `Passenger` (open diamond).

Next we develop a sequence diagram to see how the data flows between the objects and to identify the messages passed between them. In object-oriented design, when one object sends a message to another, this implies that the receiving object's class must have a method to respond to the message. The objects involved in the simulation are the `AirlineCheckinSim` instance, the two passenger queues, and `Passenger` objects.

FIGURE 6.13
Airline Check-In
Simulation: Initial
UML Class Diagram

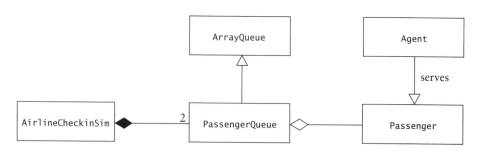

Figure 6.14 shows the sequence diagram that is based on the events described in the analysis phase. The comments in the colored boxes show conditions that must be true before a message is sent. We will explain these conditions shortly. First the AirlineCheckinSim object checks to see whether a new frequent flyer passenger has arrived, by sending the checkNewArrival message to the frequentFlyerQueue. If a new passenger has arrived (random() < arrivalRate is **true**), the frequentFlyer Queue then creates a Passenger object (sending the new message) and inserts it into the queue (by sending itself an insert message). Then the AirlineCheckinSim object checks to see whether a regular passenger has arrived, and the same process is performed with the regularPassengerQueue.

....
FIGURE 6.14
Airline Check-In Simulation: Sequence Diagram

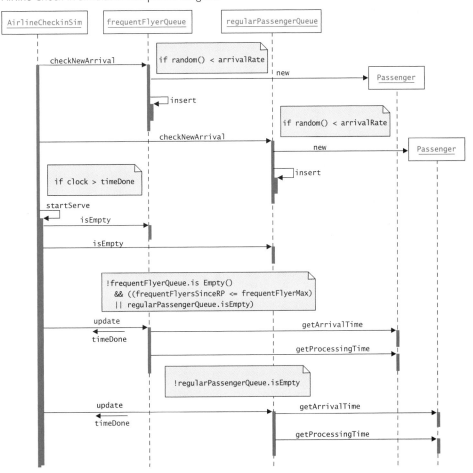

Then, if the Agent is free (`clock > timeDone`), the `AirlineCheckinSim` instance determines the next passenger to be served by the Agent. To see whether either or both of the passenger queues have passengers waiting, it sends the `isEmpty` message to the queues. If there is a frequent flyer waiting and the number of frequent flyers between regular passengers has not been exceeded, or if there are no regular passengers waiting, then we simulate the agent serving the next frequent flyer by sending the `update` message to the frequent flyer queue. Otherwise, if there is a regular passenger waiting, we simulate the agent serving the next regular passenger in the queue by sending the `update` message to the regular passenger queue. The response to this message (the return value from the method) is the time at which the agent will next be free.

This sequence diagram tells us two things. First, that the agent doesn't participate in the simulation. For the purposes of the simulation, the agent is either busy or idle and can thus be represented by a **boolean** expression. Second, the sequence diagram has identified the methods that we need in each class. This leads to the revised UML class diagram shown in Figure 6.15.

FIGURE 6.15
Airline Check-In Simulation:
Updated Class Diagram

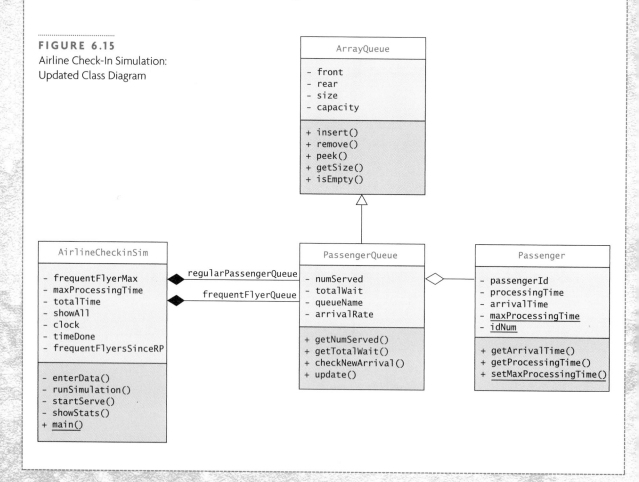

Class `AirlineCheckinSim`

The sequence diagram shown in Figure 6.14 represents the `runSimulation` method shown in Figure 6.15 for class `AirlineCheckinSim`. Table 6.3 shows its data fields and methods. Methods `main`, `enterData`, and `showStats` are fairly straightforward and will be discussed briefly in the implementation. As an aid to testing our implementation, we want to have the option of printing a minute-by-minute state of the simulation and to track individual passengers. Thus, we add a `showAll` attribute to the `AirlineCheckinSim` class. If the value of `showAll` is **true**, we will essentially trace each action taken by the program through a call to `println`.

TABLE 6.3
Class `AirlineCheckinSim`

Data Field	Attribute
private PassengerQueue frequentFlyerQueue	The queue of frequent flyers.
private PassengerQueue regularPassengerQueue	The queue of regular passengers.
private int frequentFlyerMax	The maximum number of frequent flyers to serve between regular passengers.
private int maxProcessingTime	The maximum time to serve a passenger.
private boolean showAll	A flag indicating whether to trace the simulation.
private int totalTime	The total time to run the simulation.
private int clock	The current clock time (initially zero).
private int timeDone	The time that the current passenger will be finished.
private int frequentFlyersSinceRP	The number of frequent flyers served since the last regular passenger.
Method	**Behavior**
public static void main(String[] args)	Starts the execution of the simulation by calling enterData and runSimulation.
private void runSimulation()	Controls the simulation. Executes the steps shown in Figure 6.14.
private void enterData()	Reads in the data for the simulation.
private void startServe()	Initiates service for a passenger.
private void showStats()	Displays the summary statistics.

Class **PassengerQueue**

The PassengerQueue class extends the ArrayQueue class and contains the summary data about the queue (see Table 6.4). By encapsulating the queue within this class and having its methods manipulate both the queue and the summary data, we ensure that the summary data is always maintained. Specifically, when the method checkNewArrival determines that a new passenger has arrived, it inserts the passenger into the queue. When the update method removes a passenger, it updates the number of passengers served and the total wait time.

TABLE 6.4
Class PassengerQueue

Data Field	Attribute
private int numServed	The number from this queue that were served.
private int totalWait	The total time spent waiting by passengers that were in this queue.
private String queueName	The name of this queue.
private double arrivalRate	The arrival rate for this queue.
Method	**Behavior**
public PassengerQueue(String queueName)	Constructs a new queue with the specified name.
private void checkNewArrival(int clock, boolean showAll)	Checks whether there was a new arrival for this queue and, if so, inserts the passenger into the queue.
private int update(int clock, boolean showAll)	Updates the total waiting time and number of passengers served when a passenger from this queue is served.

The **Passenger** Class

The passenger class stores the following information about a passenger:

- A unique ID number
- The time the passenger arrived
- The actual processing time
- The maximum processing time

The ID number is used to identify passengers when the simulation is traced. It starts at 0 and is incremented by 1 each time a new Passenger object is created. Table 6.5 shows the class methods.

TABLE 6.5
Methods of the **Passenger** Class

Method	Behavior
public Passenger(int arrivalTime)	Constructs a new passenger, assigns it a unique ID and the specified arrival time. Computes a random processing time in the range 1 to maxProcessingTime.
public int getArrivalTime()	Returns the value of arrivalTime.
public int getProcessingTime()	Returns the value of processingTime.
public static void setMaxProcessingTime(int maxProcessingTime)	Sets the maxProcessingTime used to generate the random processing time.

Implementation   Coding the **AirlineCheckinSim** Class

The class and data field declarations follow:

```java
import javax.swing.*;

/** Simulate the check-in process of an airline.
*/
public class AirlineCheckinSim {

    // Data Fields
    /** Queue of frequent flyers. */
    private PassengerQueue frequentFlyerQueue =
            new PassengerQueue("Frequent Flyer");
    /** Queue of regular passengers. */
    private PassengerQueue regularPassengerQueue =
            new PassengerQueue("Regular Passenger");
    /** Maximum number of frequent flyers to be served
        before a regular passenger gets served. */
    private int frequentFlyerMax;
    /** Maximum time to service a passenger. */
    private int maxProcessingTime;
    /** Total simulated time. */
    private int totalTime;
    /** If set true, print additional output. */
    private boolean showAll;
    /** Simulated clock. */
    private int clock = 0;
    /** Time that the agent will be done with the current passenger.*/
    private int timeDone;
    /** Number of frequent flyers served since the
        last regular passenger was served. */
    private int frequentFlyersSinceRP;

    ...
}
```

THE main METHOD

The main method constructs an AirlineCheckinSim object, calls enterData to read the input data, and then calls runSimulation to perform the simulation. After the simulation is complete, the showStats method displays the summary results.

```
/** Main method.
    @param args Not used
*/
public static void main(String args[]) {
    AirlineCheckinSim sim = new AirlineCheckinSim();
    sim.enterData();
    sim.runSimulation();
    sim.showStats();
    System.exit(0);
}
```

THE enterData METHOD

The enterData method (not shown) gets the input values shown in Table 6.6. It could use dialog windows or a GUI or the console. If it uses dialog windows or a GUI, it should echo the input to the console so that the trace and summary statistics can be interpreted.

THE runSimulation METHOD

The runSimulation method executes a loop once for each minute of simulated time. During each iteration, it calls method checkNewArrival on both the frequentFlyerQueue and the regularPassengerQueue to see whether any new passengers have arrived. Variable showAll is passed in both method calls. If the clock has advanced past the value of timeDone, then the current passenger is finished with

TABLE 6.6
Airline Simulation Input Parameters

Internal Variable	Attribute	Conversion
frequentFlyerQueue.arrivalRate	Expected number of frequent flyer arrivals per hour.	Divide input by 60 to obtain arrivals per minute.
regularPassengerQueue.arrivalRate	Expected number of regular passenger arrivals per hour.	Divide input by 60 to obtain arrivals per minute.
maxProcessingTime	Maximum service time in minutes.	None.
totalTime	Total simulation time in minutes.	None.
showAll	Flag. If **true**, display minute-by-minute trace of simulation.	Input beginning with 'Y' or 'y' will set this to **true**; other inputs will set it to **false**.

the ticket agent, so method `startServe` is called to start the next passenger. Data field `timeDone` is reset to the time the current passenger will be finished, which is the current clock time plus the service time.

```java
private void runSimulation() {
    for (clock = 0; clock < totalTime; clock++) {
        frequentFlyerQueue.checkNewArrival(clock, showAll);
        regularPassengerQueue.checkNewArrival(clock, showAll);
        if (clock >= timeDone) {
            startServe();
        }
    }
}
```

THE `startServe` METHOD

The `startServe` method selects a queue and then calls that queue's `update` method to remove the next passenger and update the simulation variables.

If the frequent flyer queue is not empty, it is selected if either of the two following conditions is true:

- The number of frequent flyers who have been served since the last regular passenger is less than or equal to `frequentFlyerMax`.
- The regular passenger queue is empty.

Otherwise, `startServe` selects the regular passenger queue. If both queues are empty, `startServe` prints a message that the agent is idle if `showAll` is **true**.

After selecting a queue, `startServe` increments `frequentFlyersSinceRP` or sets it to zero, depending upon the passenger type being served.

```java
private void startServe() {
    if (!frequentFlyerQueue.isEmpty()
            && ((frequentFlyersSinceRP <= frequentFlyerMax)
            || regularPassengerQueue.isEmpty())) {
        // Serve the next frequent flyer.
        frequentFlyersSinceRP++;
        timeDone = frequentFlyerQueue.update(clock, showAll);
    } else if (!regularPassengerQueue.isEmpty()) {
        // Serve the next regular passenger.
        frequentFlyersSinceRP = 0;
        timeDone = regularPassengerQueue.update(clock, showAll);
    } else if (showAll) {
        System.out.println("Time is " + clock
                            + " server is idle");
    }
}
```

THE `showStats` METHOD

The `showStats` method displays the total number of each kind of passenger and their average waiting time. It also displays the number of passengers left in each queue at the end of the simulation.

```java
/** Method to show the statistics. */
private void showStats() {
    System.out.println
            ("\nThe number of regular passengers served was "
            + regularPassengerQueue.getNumServed());
    double averageWaitingTime =
            (double) regularPassengerQueue.getTotalWait()
            / (double) regularPassengerQueue.getNumServed();
    System.out.println(" with an average waiting time of "
                    + averageWaitingTime);
    System.out.println("The number of frequent flyers served was "
                    + frequentFlyerQueue.getNumServed());
    double averageWaitingTime =
                    (double) frequentFlyerQueue.getTotalWait()
                    / (double) frequentFlyerQueue.getNumServed();
    System.out.println(" with an average waiting time of "
                    + averageWaitingTime);
    System.out.println("Passengers in frequent flyer queue: "
                    + frequentFlyerQueue.getSize());
    System.out.println("Passengers in regular passenger queue: "
                    + regularPassengerQueue.getSize());
}
```

Coding Class **PassengerQueue**

The data field declarations and constructor for PassengerQueue follow. The constructor saves the name of the queue. This is used to display the name of the queue when the showAll flag is set to show the minute-by-minute trace of the simulation.

```java
/** Class to simulate a queue of passengers. */
public class PassengerQueue extends ArrayQueue {
    // Data Fields
    /** The number of passengers served. */
    private int numServed;
    /** The total time passengers were waiting. */
    private int totalWait;
    /** The name of this queue. */
    private String queueName;
    /** The average arrival rate. */
    private double arrivalRate;

    // Constructor
    /** Construct a PassengerQueue with the given name.
        @param queueName The name of this queue
    */
    public PassengerQueue(String queueName) {
        numServed = 0;
        totalWait = 0;
        this.queueName = queueName;
    }
    ...
}
```

The method checkNewArrival is the most interesting part of the simulation program. Its purpose is to determine whether a new arrival occurs during a given time unit and, if so, to update the appropriate passenger queue. During each time unit, checkNewArrival is applied to each passenger queue.

```java
/** Check if a new arrival has occurred.
    @param clock The current simulated time
    @param showAll Flag to indicate that detailed
                   data should be output
*/
public void checkNewArrival(int clock, boolean showAll) {
    if (Math.random() < arrivalRate) {
        insert(new Passenger(clock));
        if (showAll) {
            System.out.println("Time is "
                            + clock + ": "
                            + queueName
                            + " arrival, new queue size is "
                            + getSize());
        }
    }
}
```

The arrival of passengers is considered a "random event" because we cannot predict with certainty the time at which passengers arrive. The arrival rate tells us the average rate at which passengers will arrive. For example, an arrival rate of 0.25 means that on average 0.25 passengers will arrive every minute or, stated another way, one passenger will arrive every four minutes. However, this does not mean that passengers will arrive precisely at clock times 0, 4, 8, 12, and so on. A group of passengers may arrive in consecutive time units, and then we may not see another arrival for several more minutes. All we know is that if the simulation runs long enough, the number of passenger arrivals should be pretty close to the total simulation length times 0.25. In statistical terms, an arrival rate of 0.25 means that the probability of a passenger arrival in any given minute is 0.25, or 25 percent. To obtain the arrival rate, we divide the number of passengers expected per hour (a data item) by 60 because our clock increments every minute. If we expect more than 60 passengers per hour, we need to run the simulation with a smaller clock increment so that the arrival rate used by checkNewArrival is less than one.

We can use a pseudorandom number generator to determine whether a passenger has arrived in a given minute of the simulation. The Java API function Math.random is a function that generates a pseudorandom number between 0 and 1. The condition

```java
Math.random() < arrivalRate
```

compares the pseudorandom number generated to the value of arrivalRate. Because the values being compared are in the range 0.0–1.0, the probability that this condition will be true is proportional to the value of arrivalRate, as desired. If arrivalRate is 0.25, this condition should be true 25 percent of the time.

The `update` method removes a passenger from the queue, computes that passenger's waiting time (clock time – arrival time), and adds it to the total wait time. Next, `update` increments the count of passengers from this queue who have been served since the simulation began. Method `update` also computes the time that the agent will be finished with this passenger and returns the time to the caller.

```
/** Update statistics.
    @param clock The current simulated time
    @param showAll Flag to indicate whether to show detail
    @return Time passenger is done being served
*/
public int update(int clock, boolean showAll) {
    Passenger nextPassenger = (Passenger) remove();
    int timeStamp = nextPassenger.getArrivalTime();
    int wait = clock - timeStamp;
    totalWait += wait;
    numServed++;
    if (showAll) {
        System.out.println("Time is " + clock
                        + ": Serving "
                        + queueName
                        + " with time stamp "
                        + timeStamp);
    }
    return clock + nextPassenger.getProcessingTime();
}
```

Coding the **Passenger** Class

Data field `idNum` is the passenger sequence number. It is `static` because the same variable is used for all passengers and we don't want it reset to zero when a new passenger is created. Since the `maxProcessingTime` applies to all instances of `Passenger`, this is a `static` attribute and the method `setMaxProcessingTime` is also `static`.

We will assume that the processing time is uniformly distributed between 1 and the `maxProcessingTime`. We call method `Random.nextInt` to generate a random `int` value between 0 and `maxProcessingTime - 1`. We compute the `processingTime` in the constructor. Listing 6.8 shows the `Passenger` class.

LISTING 6.8
Passenger.java

```
/** A class to represent a passenger. */
public class Passenger {

    // Data Fields
    /** The ID number for this passenger. */
    private int passengerId;
    /** The time needed to process this passenger. */
    private int processingTime;
```

```
/** The time this passenger arrives. */
private int arrivalTime;
/** The maximum time to process a passenger. */
private static int maxProcessingTime;
/** The sequence number for passengers. */
private static int idNum = 0;

/** Create a new passenger.
    @param arrivalTime The time this passenger arrives */
public Passenger(int arrivalTime) {
    this.arrivalTime = arrivalTime;
    processingTime = 1 + Random.nextInt(maxProcessingTime);
    passengerId = idNum++;
}

/** Get the arrival time.
    @return The arrival time */
public int getArrivalTime() {
    return arrivalTime;
}

/** Get the processing time.
    @return The processing time */
public int getProcessingTime() {
    return processingTime;
}

/** Get the passenger ID.
    @return The passenger ID */
public int getId() {
    return passengerId;
}

/** Set the maximum processing time
    @param maxProcessingTime The new value */
public static void setMaxProcessingTime(int maxProcessTime) {
    maxProcessingTime = maxProcessTime;
}
}
```

Testing Figure 6.16 shows a sample run of the simulation program with the trace turned on. To test the simulation program, you should run it a number of times with the trace turned on and verify that passengers in the frequent flyer queue have the specified priority over regular passengers. Method enterData should display the data values so that you can interpret the simulation results in a meaningful way. Also, make sure that the "server is idle" message is displayed only when both queues are empty. If both arrival rates are the same, check that the waiting times reflect the priority given to frequent flyers. Also see what happens when both kinds of passengers are treated equally (frequentFlyerSinceRP is 1).

When running the program, make sure that you use integer values for the total simulation time and for the service time. It is also a good idea to choose values for arrival rates and service time that keep the system from becoming saturated. The system will become saturated if the arrival rates are too large and passengers arrive more quickly than they can be served. This will result in very long queues and large waiting times. The system will become saturated if the total number of arrivals per minute (frequent flyer arrival rate + regular passenger arrival rate) is greater than the number of passengers being served in a minute: [1 / (maxProcessingTime / 2)].

After you are certain that the program runs correctly, you should turn off the trace and focus on the summary statistics. It is interesting to see how these values change for a particular set of arrival rates and service times. Remember, passenger arrivals are a random event, so the results should vary from one run to the next even if all input data stay the same.

 DESIGN CONCEPT

Pseudorandom Numbers

When you need a random number, as when playing a game, you can perform some procedure, such as spinning a wheel, in which imperceptibly small variations in the physical circumstances (hand position and force, condition of the bearings) all have large enough effects on the result to make it unpredictable.

When a computer needs a random number, it uses a mathematical process that is analogous to spinning a wheel, but because the computer is a machine designed to produce consistent results regardless of variations in its physical circumstances, the "wheel" is spun a controlled number of clicks each time, so the results are not truly random. However, if the size of the "wheel" and the algorithms for determining the number of clicks are chosen properly, the results can be made to appear to be random. We say that they appear to be random because they pass statistical tests. Such numbers are *pseudorandom* numbers, though they are often called "random".

The Java API includes the Random class. Objects of this class generate random (pseudorandom) numbers in different numerical types (**int**, **long**, **float**, **double**, and so forth). The class also provides a method to set the *seed* (the initial wheel position). By default the seed is set to the date and time of day (in milliseconds). Thus, each time you run the program, you will get different random values.

When you are debugging, you can set the seed to a fixed value, thus ensuring that the same sequence of numbers will be generated for each test run. When you are finished debugging, you can remove the fixed seed.

The Math.random method creates a Random object when it is first called. It then uses that object's nextDouble method to return a random number in the range 0 to 1.

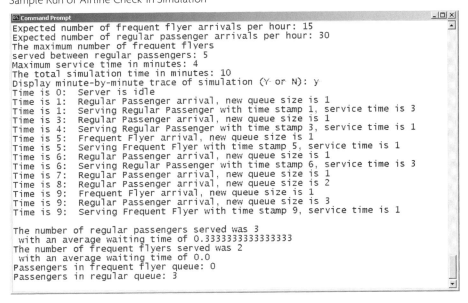

FIGURE 6.16
Sample Run of Airline Check-In Simulation

EXERCISES FOR SECTION 6.4

SELF-CHECK

1. Show the output that would be generated by running the simulation program for 20 minutes with the following passenger arrivals when showAll is **true** and frequentFlyerMax is 1.

    A frequent flyer passenger arrives at clock = 0 and service time is 2
    A frequent flyer passenger arrives at clock = 1 and service time is 1
    A frequent flyer passenger arrives at clock = 3 and service time is 3
    A frequent flyer passenger arrives at clock = 5 and service time is 2
    A regular passenger arrives at clock = 0 and service time is 1
    A regular passenger arrives at clock = 1 and service time is 1
    A regular passenger arrives at clock = 2 and service time is 1
    A regular passenger arrives at clock = 3 and service time is 1
    A regular passenger arrives at clock = 4 and service time is 2

2. Answer Self-Check Exercise 1 when frequentFlyerMax is 2.

3. Method `runSimulation` begins with the statements
```
frequentFlyerQueue.checkNewArrival(clock, showAll);
regularPassengerQueue.checkNewArrival(clock, showAll);
```
Would exchanging the order of these statements change the result? Explain your answer.

PROGRAMMING

1. Run the `AirlineCheckInSim` program with a variety of inputs to determine the maximum passenger arrival rate for a given average processing time and the effect of the frequent flyer service policy.
2. Modify the `AirlineCheckInSim` program to simulate every second of simulated time. Does this affect the results?
3. Write method `enterData` using class `JOptionPane` for data entry.

Chapter Review

♦ The queue is an abstract data type with a first-in, first-out, or FIFO, structure. This means that the item that has been in the queue the longest will be the first one removed. Queues can be used to represent reservation lists and waiting lines (from which the data structure gets its name "queue").

♦ The `Queue` interface declares methods `insert` (or `enqueue`), `remove` (or `dequeue`), `peek`, `size`, and `isEmpty`.

♦ We discussed three ways to implement the `Queue` interface: as a single-linked list, as a circular array, and as an adapter of the `LinkedList` class (a double-linked list). All three implementations support insertion and removal in $O(1)$ time; however, there will be a need for reallocation in the circular array implementation (amortized $O(1)$ time). The array implementation requires the smallest amount of storage when it is close to capacity. The adapter of the `LinkedList` class requires the most storage.

♦ To avoid the cost of building a physical system or running an actual experiment, computer simulation can be used to evaluate the expected performance of a system or operational strategy. We showed how to do this using a pair of queues to simulate passengers waiting for service at an airline ticket counter. We used pseudorandom numbers to determine whether a particular event occurs.

Java API Classes Introduced in This Chapter

`java.util.Random`

User-Defined Interfaces and Classes in This Chapter

Queue
EmptyQueueException
MaintainQueue
ListQueue
LinkedListQueue

ArrayQueue
AirlineCheckinSim
PassengerQueue
Passenger

Quick-Check Exercises

1. A queue is a _____-in, _____-out data structure.
2. Would a compiler use a stack or a queue in a program that converts infix expressions to postfix?
3. Would an operating system use a stack or a queue to determine which print job should be handled next?
4. Assume that a queue q of capacity 6 (circular array representation) contains the five characters +, *, −, &, and # (all wrapped in Character objects), where + is the first character inserted. Assume that + is stored in the first position in the array. What is the value of q.front? What is the value of q.rear?
5. Remove the first element from the queue in Exercise 4 and insert the characters \ then %. Draw the new queue. What is the value of q.front? What is the value of q.rear?
6. If a single-linked list were used to implement the queue in Question 5, the character _____ would be at the head of the list and the character _____ would be at the rear of the list.
7. For a nonempty queue implemented as a single-linked list, the statement _____ would be used inside method insert to store a new Node whose data field is referenced by item in the queue; the statement _____ would be used to disconnect a Node after its data was retrieved from the queue.
8. Pick the queue implementation (circular array, single-linked list, double-linked list) that is most appropriate for each of the following conditions.
   a. Storage must be reallocated when the queue is full.
   b. This implementation is normally most efficient in use of storage.
   c. This is an adapter of an existing class in the Java API.
9. Write an if statement that uses a pseudorandom number to assign "heads" or "tails" to a variable coinFlip. The probability of each should be 0.5.
10. Write a statement that uses a pseudorandom number to assign a value of 1 through 6 to a variable die, where each number is equally likely.

Answers to Quick-Check Exercises

1. *first, first*
2. stack
3. queue
4. q.front is 0; q.rear is 4
5.
q.rear →	%
q.front →	*
	−
	&
	#
	\

q.front is 1; q.rear is 0.

6. `'*'`, `'%'`

7. For insertion: `rear.next = new Node(item);`

    To disconnect the node removed: `front = front.next;`

8. **a.** circular array
    b. single-linked list
    c. double-linked list

9. ```
   if (Math.random() < 0.5)
         coinFlip = "heads";
   else
         coinFlip = "tails";
   ```

10. `die = 1 + (int) (6 * Math.random());`

    The expression `6 * Math.random()` generates a real number that is between 0 and 6.0 (not including 6.0). Hence the casting operation will yield an **int** value between 0 and 5, where each integer is equally likely.

Review Questions

1. Show the effect of each of the following operations on queue q. Assume that y (type Character) contains the character `'&'`. What are the final values of x and success (type **boolean**) and the contents of queue q?
   ```
   Queue q = new ArrayQueue();
   boolean success = true;
   Object x;
   q.insert(new Character('+'));
   try {
         x = q.remove();
         x = q.remove();
         success = true;
   } catch(EmptyQueueException e) {
         success = false;
   }
   q.insert(new Character('('));
   q.insert(y);
   try {
         x = q.remove();
         success = true;
   } catch(EmptyQueueException e) {
         success = false;
   }
   ```

2. Write a new queue method called `moveToRear` that moves the element currently at the front of the queue to the rear of the queue. The element that was second in line will be the new front element. Do this using methods `Queue.insert` and `Queue.remove`.

3. Answer Question 2 without using methods `Queue.insert` or `Queue.remove` for a single-linked list implementation of `Queue`. You will need to manipulate the queue internal data fields directly.

4. Answer Question 2 without using methods `Queue.insert` or `Queue.remove` for a circular array implementation of `Queue`. You will need to manipulate the queue internal data fields directly.

5. Write a new queue method called `moveToFront` that moves the element at the rear of the queue to the front of the queue, while the other queue elements maintain their relative positions behind the old front element. Do this using methods `Queue.insert` and `Queue.remove`.
   ```

6. Answer Question 5 without using `Queue.insert` and `Queue.remove` for a single-linked list implementation of `Queue`.

7. Answer Question 5 without using methods `Queue.insert` or `Queue.remove` for a circular array implementation of `Queue`.

Programming Projects

1. Redo Project 6 from Chapter 5, assuming that widgets are shipped using a first-in, first-out inventory system.

2. A *deque* is a double-ended queue, that is, a structure in which elements may be inserted or removed at either end. Define an interface `Deque` as an extension of `Queue` and a class `ArrayDeque` as an extension of `ArrayQueue`.

3. Write a program that simulates the operation of a busy airport that has only two runways to handle all takeoffs and landings. You may assume that each takeoff or landing takes 15 minutes to complete. One runway request is made during each five-minute time interval, and the likelihood of a landing request is the same as for a takeoff request. Priority is given to planes requesting a landing. If a request cannot be honored, it is added to a takeoff or landing queue.

   Your program should simulate 120 minutes of activity at the airport. Each request for runway clearance should be time-stamped and added to the appropriate queue. The output from your program should include the final queue contents, the number of takeoffs completed, the number of landings completed, and the average number of minutes spent in each queue.

4. An operating system assigns jobs to print queues based on the number of pages to be printed (less than 10 pages, less than 20 pages, or more than 20 pages but less than 50 pages). You may assume that the system printers are able to print 10 pages per minute. Smaller print jobs are printed before larger print jobs, and print jobs of the same priority are queued up in the order in which they are received. The system administrators would like to compare the time required to process a set of print jobs using 1, 2, or 3 system printers.

   Write a program that simulates processing 100 print jobs of varying lengths using 1, 2, or 3 printers. Assume that a print request is made every minute and that the number of pages to print varies from 1 to 50 pages.

   The output from your program should indicate the order in which the jobs were received, the order in which they were printed, and the time required to process the set of print jobs. If more than one printer is being used, indicate which printer each job was printed on.

5. Write a menu-driven program that uses an array of queues to keep track of a group of executives as they are transferred from one department to another, get paid, or become unemployed. Executives within a department are paid based on their seniority; with the person who has been in the department the longest receiving the most money. Each person in the department receives $1000 in salary for each person in her department having less seniority than she has. Persons who are unemployed receive no compensation.

   Your program should be able to process the following set of commands:

Join *<person> <department>*	*<person>* is added to *<department>*.
Quit *<person>*	*<person>* is removed from his or her department.
Change *<person> <department>*	*<person>* is moved from old department to *<department>*.
Payroll	Each executive's salary is computed and displayed by department in decreasing order of seniority.

Hint: You might want to include a table that contains each executive's name and information and the location of the queue that contains his or her name, to make searching more efficient.

6. Simulate the operation of a bank. Customers enter the bank, and there are one or more tellers. If a teller is free, that teller serves the customer. Otherwise the customer enters the queue and waits until a teller is free. Your program should accept the following inputs:
   - The arrival rate for the customers
   - The average processing time
   - The number of tellers

   Use your program to determine how many tellers are required for a given arrival rate and average processing time.

7. Simulate a checkout area of a supermarket consisting of one super-express counter, two express counters, and numStandLines standard counters. All customers with numSuper or fewer items proceed to a super-express counter with the fewest customers, unless there is a free express or regular line, and those with between numSuper and numExp proceed to the express counter with the shortest line unless there is a free standard line. Customers with more than numExp go to the standard counter with the shortest standard line.

   The number of items bought will be a random number in the range 1 to maxItems. The time to process a customer is 5 seconds per item.

   Calculate the following statistics:
   - Average waiting time for each of the lines
   - Overall average waiting time
   - Maximum length of each line
   - Number of customers per hour for each line and overall
   - Number of items processed per hour for each line and overall
   - Average free time of each counter
   - Overall free time

   Note: The average waiting time for a line is the total of the customer waiting times divided by the number of customers. A customer's waiting time is the time from when he (or she) enters the queue for a given checkout line until the checkout processing begins. If the customer can find a free line, then the wait time is zero.

   Your program should read the following data:

numSuper	The number of items allowed in the super-express line.
numExp	The number of items allowed in the express line.
numStandLines	The number of regular lines.
arrivalRate	The arrival rate of customers per hour.
maxItems	The maximum number of items.
maxSimTime	The simulation time.

   It may be that some lines do not get any business. In that case you must be sure, in calculating the average, *not* to divide by zero.

Chapter 7

Recursion

Chapter Objectives

- ◆ To understand how to think recursively
- ◆ To learn how to trace a recursive method
- ◆ To learn how to write recursive algorithms and methods for searching arrays
- ◆ To learn about recursive data structures and recursive methods for a LinkedList class
- ◆ To understand how to use recursion to solve the Towers of Hanoi problem
- ◆ To understand how to use recursion to process two-dimensional images
- ◆ To learn how to apply backtracking to solve search problems such as finding a path through a maze

This chapter introduces a programming technique called recursion and shows you how to think recursively. You can use recursion to solve many kinds of programming problems that would be very difficult to conceptualize and solve without recursion. Computer scientists in the field of artificial intelligence (AI) often use recursion to write programs that exhibit intelligent behavior: playing games such as chess, proving mathematical theorems, recognizing patterns, and so on.

In the beginning of the chapter you will be introduced to recursive thinking and how to design a recursive algorithm and prove that it is correct. You will also learn how to trace a recursive method and use activation frames for this purpose.

Recursive algorithms and methods can be used to perform common mathematical operations such as computing a factorial or a greatest common divisor. Recursion can be used to process familiar data structures such as strings, arrays, and linked lists, and to design a very efficient array search technique called binary search. You will also see that a linked list is a recursive data structure, and how to write recursive methods that perform common list-processing tasks.

Recursion can be used to solve a variety of other problems. The case studies in this chapter use recursion to solve a game, to search for "blobs" in a two-dimensional image, and to find a path through a maze.

7.1 Recursive Thinking

Recursion is a problem-solving approach that can be used to generate simple solutions to certain kinds of problems that would be difficult to solve in other ways. In a recursive algorithm the original problem is split into one or more simpler versions of itself. For example, if the solution to the original problem involved n items, recursive thinking might split it into two problems: one involving $n - 1$ items and one involving just a single item. Then the problem with $n - 1$ items could be split again into one involving $n - 2$ items and one involving just a single item, and so on. If the solution to all the one-item problems is "trivial," we can build up the solution to the original problem from the solutions to the simpler problems.

As an example of how this might work, consider a collection of nested wooden figures as shown in Figure 7.1. If you wanted to write an algorithm to "process" this collection in some way (such as counting the figures or painting a face on each figure), you would have difficulty doing it, because you don't know how many objects are in the nest. But you could use recursion to solve the problem in the following way:

Recursive Algorithm to Process Nested Figures

1.   **if** there is one figure in the nest
2.   Do whatever is required to the figure.
    else
3.   Do whatever is required to the outer figure in the nest.
4.   Process the nest of figures inside the outer figure in the same way.

FIGURE 7.1
A Set of Nested Wooden Figures

FIGURE 7.1
A Set of Nested Wooden Figures

In this recursive algorithm, the solution is trivial if there is only one figure: Perform Step 2. If there is more than one figure, perform Step 3 to process the outer figure. Step 4 is the recursive operation—recursively process the nest of figures inside the outer figure. This nest will, of course, have one less figure than before, so it is a simpler version of the original problem.

As another example, let's consider searching for a target value in an array. Assume that the array elements are sorted and are in increasing order. A recursive approach, which we will study in detail in Section 7.3, involves replacing the problem of searching an array of *n* elements with one of searching an array of *n*/2 elements. How do we do that? We compare the target value to the value of the element in the middle of the sorted array. If there is a match, we have found the target. If not, based on the result of the comparison, we either search the elements that come before the middle one or the elements that come after the middle one. So we have replaced the problem of searching an array with *n* elements to one that involves searching a smaller array with only *n*/2 elements. The recursive algorithm follows.

Recursive Algorithm to Search an Array

1.   **if** the array is empty
2.   Return −1 as the search result.
      else if the middle element matches the target
3.   Return the subscript of the middle element as the result.
      else if the target is less than the middle element
4.   Recursively search the array elements before the middle element
           and return the result.
      else
5.   Recursively search the array elements after the middle element and
           return the result.

The condition in Step 1 is true when there are no elements left to search. Step 2 returns −1 to indicate that the search failed. Step 3 executes when the middle element matches the target. Otherwise, we recursively apply the search algorithm (Steps 4 and 5), thereby searching a smaller array (approximately half the size), and return the result. For each recursive search, the region of the array being searched will be different, so the middle element will also be different.

The two recursive algorithms we showed so far follow this general approach:

General Recursive Algorithm

1.   `if` the problem can be solved for the current value of n
2.   Solve it.
     `else`
3.   Recursively apply the algorithm to one or more problems involving smaller values of n.
4.   Combine the solutions to the smaller problems to get the solution to the original.

Step 1 involves a test for what is called the *base case:* the value of n for which the problem can be solved easily. Step 3 is the *recursive case* because we recursively apply the algorithm. Because the value of n for each recursive case is smaller than the original value of n, each recursive case makes progress towards the base case. Whenever a split occurs, we revisit Step 1 for each new problem to see whether it is a base case or a recursive case.

Steps to Design a Recursive Algorithm

From what we have seen so far, we can summarize the characteristics of a recursive solution:

- There must be at least one case (the base case), for a small value of n, that can be solved directly.
- A problem of a given size (say, n) can be split into one or more smaller versions of the same problem (the recursive case).

Therefore, to design a recursive algorithm, we must

- Recognize the base case and provide a solution to it.
- Devise a strategy to split the problem into smaller versions of itself. Each recursive case must make progress toward the base case.
- Combine the solutions to the smaller problems in such a way that each larger problem is solved correctly.

Next we look at a recursive algorithm for a common programming problem. We will also provide a Java method that solves this problem. All of the methods in this section and in the next will be found in class `RecursiveMethods.java` on this textbook's Web site.

EXAMPLE 7.1   Let's see how we could write our own recursive method for finding string length. How would you go about doing this? If there is a special character that marks the end of a string, then you can count all the characters that precede this special character. But if there is no special character, you might try a recursive approach. The base case is an empty string—its length is 0. For the recursive case, consider that each string has two parts: the first character and the "rest of the string." If you can find the length of the "rest of the string," you can then add 1 (for the first character) to get the length of the larger string. For example, the length of "abcde" is 1 + the length of "bcde".

Recursive Algorithm for Finding the Length of a String

1.   **if** the string is empty (has no characters)
2.   The length is 0.
    else
3.   The length is 1 plus the length of the string that excludes the first character.

We can implement this algorithm as a `static` method with a `String` argument. The test for the base case is a string reference of `null` or a string that contains no characters (""). In either case, the length is 0. In the recursive case,

```
return 1 + length(str.substring(1));
```

the method call `str.substring(1)` returns a reference to a string containing all characters in string `str` except for the character at position 0. Then we call method `length` again with this substring as its argument. The method result is one more than the value returned from the next call to `length`. Each time we reenter method `length`, the **if** statement executes with `str` referencing a string containing all but the first character in the previous call. Method `length` is called a *recursive method* because it calls itself.

```
/** Recursive method length (in RecursiveMethods.java).
    @param str The string
    @return The length of the string
*/
public static int length(String str) {
    if (str == null || str.equals(""))
        return 0;
    else
        return 1 + length(str.substring(1));
}
```

EXAMPLE 7.2   Method `printChars` is a recursive method that displays each character in its string argument on a separate line. In the base case (an empty or non-existent string), the method return occurs immediately and nothing is displayed. In the recursive case, `printChars` displays the first character of its string argument and then calls itself to display the characters in the rest of the string. If the initial call is `printChars("hat")`, the method will display the lines

```
h
a
t
```

Unlike method `length` in Example 7.1, `printChars` is a **void** method. However, both methods follow the format for the general recursive algorithm shown earlier.

```
/** Recursive method printChars (in RecursiveMethods.java).
    post: The argument string is displayed, one character
          per line.
    @param str The string
```

```
*/
public static void printChars(String str) {
    if (str == null || str.equals("")) {
        return;
    } else {
        System.out.println(str.charAt(0));
        printChars(str.substring(1));
    }
}
```

You get an interesting result if you reverse the two statements in the recursive case.

```
/** Recursive method printCharsReverse (in RecursiveMethods.java).
    post: The argument string is displayed in reverse,
          one character per line.
    @param str The string
*/
public static void printCharsReverse(String str) {
    if (str == null || str.equals("")) {
        return;
    } else {
        printCharsReverse(str.substring(1));
        System.out.println(str.charAt(0));
    }
}
```

Method printCharsReverse calls itself to display the rest of the string before displaying the first character in the current string argument. The effect will be to delay displaying the first character in the current string until all characters in the rest of the string are displayed. Consequently, the characters in the string will be displayed in reverse order. If the initial call is printCharsReverse("hat"), the method will display the lines

```
t
a
h
```

Proving That a Recursive Method Is Correct

To prove that a recursive method is correct, you must verify that you have performed correctly the design steps listed earlier. You can use a technique that mathematicians use to prove that a theorem is true for all values of n. A *proof by induction* works the following way:

- Prove the theorem is true for the base case of (usually) $n = 0$ or $n = 1$.
- Show that if the theorem is assumed true for n, then it must be true for $n + 1$.

We can extend the notion of an inductive proof and use it as the basis for proving that a recursive algorithm is correct. To do this:

- Verify that the base case is recognized and solved correctly.
- Verify that each recursive case makes progress toward the base case.
- Verify that if all smaller problems are solved correctly, then the original problem is also solved correctly.

If you can show that your algorithm satisfies these three requirements, then your algorithm will be correct.

EXAMPLE 7.3   To prove that the `length` method is correct, we know that the base case is an empty string, and its length is correctly set at 0. The recursive case involves a call to `length` with a smaller string, so it is making progress toward the base case. Finally, if we know the length of the rest of the string, adding 1 gives us the length of the longer string consisting of the first character and the rest of the string.

Tracing a Recursive Method

Figure 7.2 traces the execution of the method call `length("ace")`. The diagram shows a sequence of recursive calls to method `length`. After returning from each call to `length`, we complete execution of the statement `return 1 + length( . . . );` by adding 1 to the result so far and then returning from the current call. The final result, 3, would be returned from the original call. The arrow alongside each word `return` shows which call to `length` is associated with that result. For example, `0` is the result of the method call `length("")`. After adding 1, we return 1, which is the result of the call `length("e")`, and so on. This process of returning from the recursive calls and computing the partial results is called *unwinding the recursion*.

The Run-Time Stack and Activation Frames

You can also trace a recursive method by showing what Java does when one method calls another. Java maintains a run-time stack, on which it saves new information in the form of an *activation frame*. The activation frame contains storage for the method arguments and any local variables as well as the return address of the instruction that called the method. Whenever a method is called, Java pushes a new activation frame onto the run-time stack and saves this information on the stack. This is done whether the method is recursive or not.

The left side of Figure 7.3 shows the activation frames on the run-time stack after the last recursive call (corresponding to `length("")`) resulting from an initial call to `length("ace")`. At any given time, only the frame at the top of the stack is accessible, so its argument values will be used when the method instructions execute. When the `return` statement executes, control will be passed to the instruction at the specified return address, and this frame will be popped from the stack (Figure 7.3, right).

FIGURE 7.2
Trace of
`length("ace")`

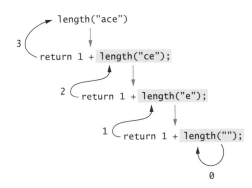

FIGURE 7.3
Run-time Stack Before and After Removal of Frame for `length("")`

Frame for length("")	str: "" return address in length("e")
Frame for length("e")	str: "e" return address in length("ce")
Frame for length("ce")	str: "ce" return address in length("ace")
Frame for length("ace")	str: "ace" return address in caller

Frame for length("e")	str: "e" return address in length("ce")
Frame for length("ce")	str: "ce" return address in length("ace")
Frame for length("ace")	str: "ace" return address in caller

Run-time stack after all calls   Run-time stack after return from last call

The activation frame corresponding to the next-to-last call (`length("e")`) is now accessible.

You can think of the run-time stack for a sequence of calls to a recursive method as an office tower in which an employee on each floor has the same list of instructions.[1] The employee in the bottom office carries out part of the instructions on the list, calls the employee in the office above, and is put on hold. The employee in the office above starts to carry out the list of instructions, calls the employee in the next higher office, is put on hold, and so on. When the employee on the top floor is called, that employee carries out the list of instructions to completion and then returns an answer to the employee below. The employee below then resumes carrying out the list of instructions and returns an answer to the employee on the next lower floor, and so on, until an answer is returned to the employee in the bottom office, who then resumes carrying out the list of instructions.

To make the flow of control easier to visualize, we will draw the activation frames from the top of the page down (see Figure 7.4). For example, the activation frame at the top, which would actually be at the bottom of the run-time stack, represents the first call to the recursive method. The downward-pointing arrows connect each statement that calls a method with the frame for that particular execution of the method. The upward-pointing arrows show the return point from each lower-level call with the value returned alongside the arrow. For each frame, the return point is to the addition operator in the statement `return 1 + length(...)`; For each frame, the code in the color screen is executed prior to the creation of the next activation frame; the rest of the code shown is executed after the return.

[1]Analogy suggested by Richard Pattis, Carnegie-Mellon University.

FIGURE 7.4
Trace of
`length("ace")`
Using Activation Frames

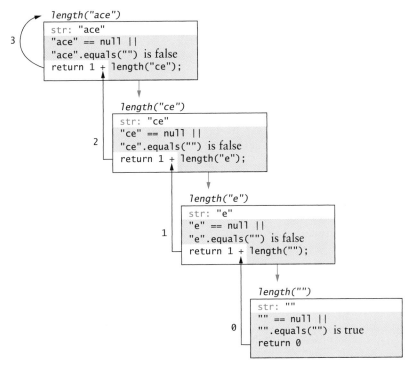

EXERCISES FOR SECTION 7.1

SELF-CHECK

1. Trace the execution of the call `mystery(4)` for the following recursive method using the technique shown in Figure 7.2. What does this method do?
   ```
   public static mystery(int n) {
       if (n == 0)
           return 0;
       else
           return n * n + mystery(n - 1);
   }
   ```

2. Answer Exercise 1 using activation frames.

3. Trace the execution of `printChars("tic")` (Example 7.2) using activation frames.

4. Trace the execution of `printCharsReverse("toc")` using activation frames.

5. Prove that the `printChars` method is correct.

PROGRAMMING

1. Write a recursive method `toNumber` that forms the integer sum of all digit characters in a string. For example, the result of `toNumber("3ac4")` would be 7. *Hint:* If next is a digit character ('0' through '9'), `Character.isDigit(next)` is true and the numeric value of next is `Character.digit(next, 10)`.

2. Write a recursive method `stutter` that returns a string with each character in its argument repeated. For example, if the string passed to `stutter` is "hello", stutter will return the string "hheelllloo".

7.2 Recursive Definitions of Mathematical Formulas

Mathematicians often use recursive definitions of formulas. These definitions lead very naturally to recursive algorithms.

EXAMPLE 7.4   The factorial of n, or $n!$, is defined as follows:

$$0! = 1$$
$$n! = n \times (n - 1)!$$

The first formula identifies the base case: n equal to 0. The second formula is a recursive definition. It leads to the following algorithm for computing $n!$.

Recursive Algorithm for Computing n!

1.   **if** n equals 0
2. $n!$ is 1.

   else

3. $n! = n \times (n - 1)!$

To verify the correctness of this algorithm, we see that the base case is solved correctly ($0!$ is 1). The recursive case makes progress toward the base case, because it involves the calculation of a smaller factorial. Also, if we can calculate $(n - 1)!$, the recursive case gives us the correct formula for calculating $n!$.

The recursive method follows. The statement

```
return n * factorial(n - 1);
```

implements the recursive case. Each time `factorial` calls itself, the method body executes again with a different argument value. An initial method call such as `factorial(4)` will generate four recursive calls, as shown in Figure 7.5.

```
/** Recursive factorial method (in RecursiveMethods.java).
    pre: n >= 0
    @param n The integer whose factorial is being computed
    @return n!
*/
public static int factorial(int n) {
    if (n == 0)
        return 1;
    else
        return n * factorial(n - 1);
}
```

FIGURE 7.5
Trace of
`factorial(4)`

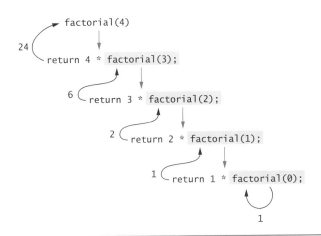

 PITFALL

Infinite Recursion and Stack Overflow

If you call method `factorial` with a negative argument, you will see that the recursion does not terminate. It will continue forever, because the stopping case, n equals 0, can never be reached, as n gets more negative with each call. For example, if the original value of n is −4, you will make method calls `factorial(-5)`, `factorial(-6)`, `factorial(-7)`, and so on. You should make sure that your recursive methods are constructed so that a stopping case is always reached. One way to prevent the infinite recursion in this case would be to change the terminating condition to n <= 0. However, this would incorrectly return a value of 1 for n! if n is negative. A better solution would be to throw an `IllegalArgumentException` if n is negative.

If your program does not terminate properly, you may see an extremely long display on the console (if the console is being used to display its results). Eventually the exception `StackOverflowError` will be thrown. This means that the memory area used to store information about method calls (the run-time stack) has been used up because there have been too many calls to the recursive method. Because there is no memory available for this purpose, your program can't execute any more method calls.

EXAMPLE 7.5   Let's develop a recursive method that raises a number x to a power n, where n is positive or zero. You can raise a number to a power by repeatedly multiplying that number by itself. So if we know x^k, we can get x^{k+1} by multiplying x^k by x. The recursive definition is

$$x^n = x \times x^{n-1}$$

This gives us the recursive case. You should know that any number raised to the power 0 is 1, so the base case is

$$x^0 = 1$$

Recursive Algorithm for Calculating x^n ($n \geq 0$)

1.   **if** n is 0
2.   The result is 1.
    else
3.   The result is $x \times x^{n-1}$.

We show the method next.

```
/** Recursive power method (in RecursiveMethods.java).
    pre: n >= 0
    @param x The number being raised to a power
    @param n The exponent
    @return x raised to the power n
*/
public static double power(double x, int n) {
    if (n == 0)
        return 1;
    else
        return x * power(x, n - 1);
}
```

EXAMPLE 7.6   The greatest common divisor (gcd) of two numbers is the largest integer that divides both numbers. For example, the gcd of 20, 15 is 5; the gcd of 36, 24 is 12; the gcd of 36, 18 is 18. The mathematician Euclid devised an algorithm for finding the greatest common divisor of two integers, m and n, based on the following definition:

Definition of gcd(m, n) for $m > n$

gcd(m, n) = n if n is a divisor of m

gcd(m, n) = gcd(n, m % n) if n isn't a divisor of m

This definition states that gcd(m, n) is n if n divides m. This is correct, because no number larger than n can divide n. Otherwise, the definition states that gcd(m, n) is the same as gcd(n, m % n), where m % n is the integer remainder of m divided by n. Therefore, gcd(20, **15**) is the same as gcd(**15**, 5), or 5, because 5 divides 15. This recursive definition leads naturally to a recursive algorithm.

Recursive Algorithm for Calculating gcd(m, n) for $m > n$

1.   **if** n is a divisor of m
2.   The result is n.
    else
3.   The result is gcd(n, m % n).

To verify that this is correct, we need to make sure that there is a base case and that it is solved correctly. The base case is "n is a divisor of m." If so, the solution is n (n is the greatest common divisor), which is correct. Does the recursive case make progress to the base case? It must, because both arguments in each recursive call are smaller than in the previous call, and the new second argument is always smaller than the new first argument (*m* % *n* must be less than *n*). Eventually a divisor will be found or the second argument will become 1. Since 1 is a base case (1 divides every integer), we have verified that the recursive case makes progress towards the base case.

Next, we show method gcd. Notice that the method introduces a new recursive case that transposes m and n if the initial value of n happens to be larger than m:

```
else if (m < n)
    return gcd(n, m);
```

This clause allows us to handle arguments that initially are not in the correct sequence.

```
/** Recursive gcd method (in RecursiveMethods.java).
    pre: m > 0 and n > 0
    @param m The larger number
    @param n The smaller number
    @return Greatest common divisor of m and n
*/
public static double gcd(int m, int n) {
    if (m % n == 0)
        return n;
    else if (m < n)
        return gcd(n, m);    // Transpose arguments.
    else
        return gcd(n, m % n);
}
```

Recursion Versus Iteration

You may have noticed that there are some similarities between recursion and iteration. Both techniques enable us to repeat a compound statement. In iteration, a loop repetition condition in the loop header determines whether we repeat the loop body or exit from the loop. We repeat the loop body while the repetition condition is true. In recursion, the condition usually tests for a base case. We stop the recursion when the base case is reached (the condition is true), and we execute the method body again when the condition is false. We can always write an iterative solution to a problem that is solvable by recursion. However, the recursive algorithm may be easier to conceptualize and may, therefore, lead to a method that is easier to write, read, and debug—all of which are very desirable attributes of code.

Tail Recursion or Last-Line Recursion

Most of the recursive algorithms and methods you have seen so far have are examples of *tail recursion* or *last-line recursion*. In these algorithms, there is a single recursive call and it is the last line of the method. An example is the factorial method in Example 7.4.

```
public static int factorial(int n) {
    if (n == 0)
        return 1;
    else
        return n * factorial(n - 1);
}
```

It is a straightforward process to turn such a method into an iterative one, replacing the `if` statement with a loop, as we show next.

EXAMPLE 7.7   An iterative version of the `factorial` method follows.

```
/** Iterative factorial method.
    pre: n >= 0
    @param n The integer whose factorial is being computed
    @return n!
*/
public static int factorialIter(int n) {
    int result = 1;
    for (int k = 1; k <= n; k++)
        result = result * k;
    return result;
}
```

Efficiency of Recursion

The iterative method `factorialIter` multiplies all integers between 1 and n to compute $n!$. It may be slightly less readable than the recursive method `factorial`, but not much. In terms of efficiency, both algorithms are $O(n)$, because the number of loop repetitions or recursive calls increases linearly with n. However, the iterative version is probably faster, because the overhead for a method call and return would be greater than the overhead for loop repetition (testing and incrementing the loop control variable). The difference, though, would not be significant. Generally, if it is easier to conceptualize an algorithm using recursion, then you should code it as a recursive method, because the reduction in efficiency does not outweigh the advantage of readable code that is easy to debug.

EXAMPLE 7.8   The Fibonacci numbers fib_n are a sequence of numbers that were invented to model the growth of a rabbit colony. Therefore, we would expect this sequence to grow very quickly, and it does. For example, fib_{10} is 55, fib_{15} is 610, fib_{20} is 6765, and fib_{25} is 75025 (that's a lot of rabbits!). The definition of this sequence follows:

$$fib_1 = 1$$
$$fib_2 = 1$$
$$fib_n = fib_{n-1} + fib_{n-2}$$

Next, we show a method that calculates the nth Fibonacci number. The last line codes the recursive case.

```
/** Recursive method to calculate Fibonacci numbers
    (in RecursiveMethods.java).
    pre: n >= 1
    @param n The position of the Fibonacci number being calculated
    @return The Fibonacci number
```

```
*/
public static int fibonacci(int n) {
    if (n <= 2)
        return 1;
    else
        return fibonacci(n - 1) + fibonacci(n - 2);
}
```

Unfortunately, this solution is very inefficient because of multiple calls to `fibonacci` with the same argument. For example, calculating `fibonacci(5)` results in calls to `fibonacci(4)` and `fibonacci(3)`. Calculating `fibonacci(4)` results in calls to `fibonacci(3)` (second call) and also `fibonacci(2)`. Calculating `fibonacci(3)` twice results in two more calls to `fibonacci(2)` (three calls total), and so on (see Figure 7.6).

Because of the redundant method calls, the time required to calculate `fibonacci(n)` increases exponentially with n. For example, if n is 100, there are approximately 2^{100} activation frames. This number is approximately 10^{30}. If you could process one million activation frames per second, it would still take 10^{24} seconds, which is approximately 3×10^{16} years. However, it is possible to write recursive methods for computing Fibonacci numbers that have $O(n)$ performance. We show one such method next.

```
/** Recursive O(n) method to calculate Fibonacci numbers
    (in RecursiveMethods.java).
    pre: n >= 1
    @param fibCurrent The current Fibonacci number
    @param fibPrevious The previous Fibonacci number
    @param n The count of Fibonacci numbers left to calculate
    @return The value of the Fibonacci number calculated so far
*/
private static int fibo(int fibCurrent, int fibPrevious, int n) {
    if (n == 1)
        return fibCurrent;
    else
        return fibo(fibCurrent + fibPrevious, fibCurrent, n - 1);
}
```

FIGURE 7.6
Method Calls Resulting
from `fibonacci(5)`

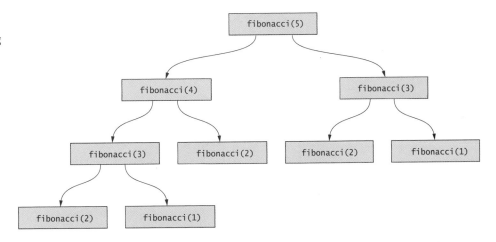

Unlike method `fibonacci`, method `fibo` does not follow naturally from the recursive definition of the Fibonacci sequence. In method `fibo` the first argument is always the current Fibonacci number, and the second argument is the previous one. We update these values for each new call. When n is 1 (the base case), we have calculated the required Fibonacci number, so we return its value (`fibCurrent`). The recursive case,

```
return fibo(fibCurrent + fibPrevious, fibCurrent, n - 1);
```

passes the sum of the current Fibonacci number and the previous Fibonacci number to the first parameter (the new value of `fibCurrent`); it passes the current Fibonacci number to the second parameter (the new value of `fibPrevious`); and it decrements n, making progress toward the base case.

To start this method executing, we need the following *wrapper method*, which is not recursive. This method is called a wrapper method because its only purpose it to call the recursive method and return its result. Its parameter, n, specifies the position in the Fibonacci sequence of the number we want to calculate. It calls the recursive method `fibo`, passing the first Fibonacci number as its first argument and n as its third.

```
/** Wrapper method for calculating Fibonacci numbers
    (in RecursiveMethods.java).
    pre: n >= 1
    @param n The position of the desired Fibonacci number
    @return The value of the nth Fibonacci number
*/
public static int fibonacciStart(int n) {
    return fibo(1, 0, n);
}
```

Figure 7.7 traces the execution of the method call `fibonacciStart(5)`. Notice that the first arguments for the method calls to `fibo` form the sequence 1, 1, 2, 3, 5, which is the Fibonacci sequence. Also notice that the result of the first return (5) is simply passed on by each successive return. That is because the recursive case does not specify any operations other than returning the result of the next call.

FIGURE 7.7

Trace of
fibonacciStart(5)

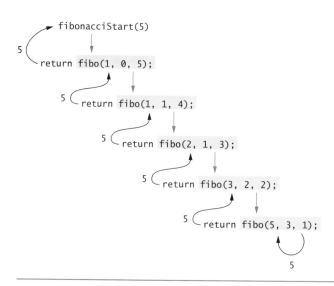

EXERCISES FOR SECTION 7.2

SELF-CHECK

1. Does the recursive algorithm for raising x to the power n work for negative values of n? Does it work for negative values of x? Indicate what happens if it is called for each of these cases.
2. Trace the execution of `fibonacciStart(5)` using activation frames.
3. For each of the following method calls, show the argument values in the activation frames that would be pushed onto the run-time stack.
    a. `gcd(6, 21)`
    b. `factorial(5)`
    c. `gcd(31, 7)`
    d. `fibonacci(6)`
    e. `fibonacciStart(7)`
4. See for what value of n method `fibonacci` begins to take a long time to run on your computer (over 1 minute). Compare the performance of `fibonacciStart` and `fibo` for this same value.

PROGRAMMING

1. Write a recursive method for raising x to the power n that works for negative n as well as positive n. Use the fact that $x^{-n} = \dfrac{1}{x^n}$.
2. Modify the factorial method to throw an `IllegalArgumentException` if n is negative.
3. Write a class that has an iterative method for calculating Fibonacci numbers. Use an array that saves each Fibonacci number as it is calculated. Your method should take advantage of the existence of this array so that subsequent calls to the method simply retrieve the desired Fibonacci number if it has been calculated. If not, start with the largest Fibonacci number in the array rather than repeating all calculations.

7.3 Recursive Array Search

Searching an array is an activity that can be accomplished using recursion. The simplest way to search an array is a *linear search*. In a linear search, we examine one array element at a time, starting with the first element or the last element, to see whether it matches the target. The array element we are seeking may be anywhere in the array, so on average we will examine $\dfrac{n}{2}$ items to find the target if it is in the array. If it is not in the array, we will have to examine all n elements (the worst case). This means linear search is an $O(n)$ algorithm.

Design of a Recursive Linear Search Algorithm

Let's consider how we might write a recursive algorithm that returns the subscript of a target item.

The base case would be an empty array. If the array is empty, the target cannot be there, so the result should be –1. If the array is not empty, we will assume that we can examine just one element, so another base case would be *when the array element being examined matches the target*. If so, the result should be the subscript of that array element.

The recursive step would be to search the rest of the array, excluding the element we just examined. One way to get the rest of an array is to exclude the last element from the list of candidates in the next recursive call. Therefore, to determine whether we have reached the stopping case *when the array element being examined matches the target*, we need to examine the last element. The algorithm follows.

Algorithm for Recursive Linear Array Search

1. **if** the array is empty
2.   The result is –1.
    else if the last element matches the target
3.   The result is the subscript of the last element.
    else
4.   Search the array excluding the last element and return the result.

Implementation of Linear Search

The following method, `linearSearch` (part of class `RecursiveMethods`), shows the linear search algorithm.

```java
/** Recursive linear search method (in RecursiveMethods.java).
    @param items The array being searched
    @param target The object being searched for
    @param size The number of candidates left in the array
    @return The subscript of target if found; otherwise -1
*/
private static int linearSearch(Object[] items,
                               Object target, int size) {
    if (size == 0)
        return -1;
    else if (target.equals(items[size - 1]))
        return size - 1;
    else
        return linearSearch(items, target, size - 1);
}
```

The method parameter `size` represents the number of candidates that can match the target. The first condition tests whether the pool of candidates is empty. The condition `(target.equals(items[size - 1]))` tests whether the current last candidate matches the target. The statement

```java
return linearSearch(items, target, size - 1);
```

implements the recursive step; it decrements `size` to exclude the current candidate from the next search. Notice that the array `items` is not shrinking, just the pool of candidates.

To search an array `x` (type `Object[]`) in a client class, you could use the method call

```
RecursiveMethods.linearSearch(x, target, x.length)
```

However, it is unnecessary to pass the declared length of the array as an argument. For this reason, we define a nonrecursive wrapper method (also called `linearSearch`) that has just two parameters: `x` and `target`.

```
/** Wrapper for recursive linear search method (in
    RecursiveMethods.java).
    @param items The array being searched
    @param target The object being searched for
    @return The subscript of target if found; otherwise -1
*/
public static int linearSearch(Object[] items, Object target) {
    return linearSearch(items, target, items.length);
}
```

The sole purpose of this method is to call the recursive method and return its result. This method definition overloads the previous one. When a client calls `linearSearch`, the arguments used in the call will determine which method executes. Also, the recursive method has private visibility, so it can't be accessed outside of class `RecursiveMethods`.

Figure 7.8 traces the execution of the call to `linearSearch` in the second statement.

```
String[] greetings = {"Hi", "Hello", "Shalom"};
int posHello = linearSearch(greetings, "Hello");
```

The value returned to `posHello` will be 1.

Design of a Binary Search Algorithm

A second approach to searching an array is called *binary search*. Binary search can be performed only on an array that has been sorted. In binary search, the stopping cases are the same as for linear search:

- When the array is empty
- When the array element being examined matches the target

However, rather than examining the last array element, binary search compares the "middle" element of the array to the target. If there is a match, it returns the position of the middle element. Otherwise, because the array has been sorted, we know with certainty which half of the array must be searched to find the target. We then can exclude the other half of the array (not just one element as with linear search). The binary search algorithm (first introduced in Section 7.1) follows.

Binary Search Algorithm

1. **if** the array is empty
2.   Return −1 as the search result.
        else if the middle element matches the target

3.   Return the subscript of the middle element as the result.

    else if the target is less than the middle element

4.   Recursively search the array elements before the middle element and return the result.

  else

5.   Recursively search the array elements after the middle element and return the result.

Figure 7.9 illustrates binary search for an array with seven elements. The shaded array elements in color are the ones that are being searched each time. The array element in color is the one that is being compared to the target. In the first call, we compare "Dustin" to "Elliot". Because "Dustin" is smaller, we need to search only the part of the array before "Elliot" (consisting of just 3 candidates). In the second call, we compare "Dustin" to "Debbie". Because "Dustin" is larger, we need to search only the part of the array in color after "Debbie" (consisting of just 1 candidate). In the third call, we compare "Dustin" to "Dustin", and the subscript of "Dustin" (2) is our result. If there were no match at this point (for example, the array contained "Duncan" instead of "Dustin"), the array of candidates to search would become an empty array.

FIGURE 7.8

Trace of `linearSearch(greetings, "Hello")`

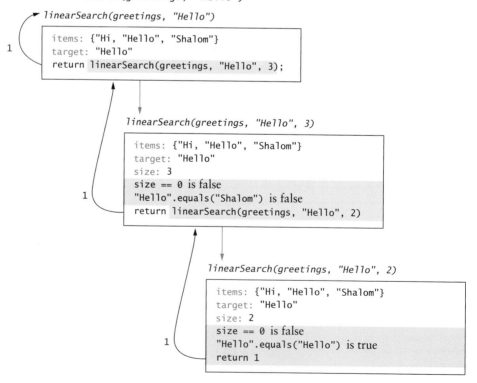

FIGURE 7.9
Binary Search for "Dustin"

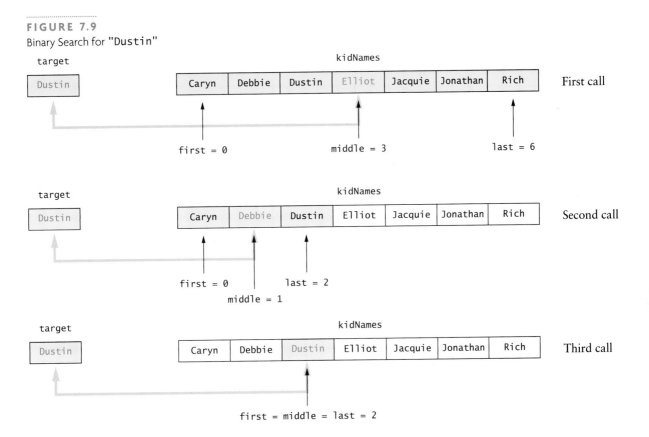

Efficiency of Binary Search

Because we eliminate at least half of the array elements from consideration with each recursive call, binary search is an O(log n) algorithm. To verify this, an unsuccessful search of an array of size 16 could result in our searching arrays of size 16, 8, 4, 2, and 1 to determine that the target was not present. Thus an array of size 16 requires a total of 5 probes in the worst case (16 is 2^4, so 5 is $\log_2 16 + 1$). If we double the array size, we would need to make only 6 probes for an array of size 32 in the worst case (32 is 2^5, so 6 is $\log_2 32 + 1$). The advantages of binary search become even more apparent for larger arrays. For an array with 32,768 elements, the maximum number of probes required would be 16 ($\log_2 32{,}768$ is 15), and if we expand the array to 65,536 elements, we would increase the number of probes required only to 17.

The Comparable Interface

We introduced the Comparable interface in Section 4.7. Classes that implement this interface must define a compareTo method that enables its objects to be compared in a standard way. Method compareTo returns an integer whose value indicates the relative ordering of the two objects being compared (as described in the @return tag below). If the target is type `Comparable`, we can apply its `compareTo` method to compare the target to the objects stored in the array.

```
/** Instances of classes that realize this interface can be
    compared.
*/
public interface Comparable {
    /** Method to compare this object to the argument object.
        @param obj The argument object
        @return Returns a negative integer if this object < obj;
                zero if this object equals obj;
                a positive integer if this object > obj
    */
    int compareTo(Object obj);
}
```

Implementation of Binary Search

Listing 7.1 shows a recursive implementation of the binary search algorithm and its nonrecursive wrapper method. The parameters `first` and `last` are the subscripts of the first element and last element in the array being searched. For the initial call to the recursive method from the wrapper method, `first` is 0 and `last` is `items.length - 1`. The parameter `target` is type `Comparable`.

The condition (`first > last`) becomes true when the list of candidates is empty. The statement

```
int middle = (first + last) / 2;
```

computes the subscript of the "middle" element in the current array (midway between `first` and `last`).

The statement

```
int compResult = target.compareTo(items[middle]);
```

saves the result of comparing the target to the middle element of the array. If the result is 0 (a match), the subscript `middle` is returned. If the result is negative, the recursive step

```
return binarySearch(items, target, first, middle - 1);
```

returns the result of searching the part of the current array before the middle item (with subscripts `first` through `middle - 1`). If the result is positive, the recursive step

```
return binarySearch(items, target, middle + 1, last);
```

returns the result of searching the part of the current array after the middle item (with subscripts `middle + 1` through `last`).

....

LISTING 7.1
Methods `binarySearch`

```
/** Recursive binary search method (in RecursiveMethods.java).
    @param items The array being searched
    @param target The object being searched for
    @param first The subscript of the first element
    @param last The subscript of the last element
    @return The subscript of target if found; otherwise -1.
```

```
*/
private static int binarySearch(Object[] items, Comparable target,
                                int first, int last) {
    if (first > last)
        return -1;      // Base case for unsuccessful search.
    else {
        int middle = (first + last) / 2;  // Next probe index.
        int compResult = target.compareTo(items[middle]);
        if (compResult == 0)
            return middle;   // Base case for successful search.
        else if (compResult < 0)
            return binarySearch(items, target, first, middle - 1);
        else
            return binarySearch(items, target, middle + 1, last);
    }
}

/** Wrapper for recursive binary search method (in RecursiveMethods.java).
    @param items The array being searched
    @param target The object being searched for
    @return The subscript of target if found; otherwise -1.
*/
public static int binarySearch(Object[] items, Comparable target) {
    return binarySearch(items, target, 0, items.length - 1);
}
```

Figure 7.10 traces the execution of binarySearch for the array shown in Figure 7.9. The parameter items always references the same array; however, the pool of candidates changes with each call.

Testing Binary Search

To test the binary search algorithm, you must test arrays with an even number of elements and arrays with an odd number of elements. You must also test arrays that have duplicate items. Each array must be tested for the following cases:

- The target is the element at each position of the array, starting with the first position and ending with the last position.
- The target is less than the smallest array element.
- The target is greater than the largest array element
- The target is a value between each pair of items in the array.

Method Arrays.binarySearch

The Java API class Arrays contains a binarySearch method. It can be called with sorted arrays of primitive types or with sorted arrays of objects. If the objects in the array are not mutually comparable or if the array is not sorted, the results are undefined. If there are multiple copies of the target value in the array, there is no guarantee as to which one will be found. This is the same as for our binarySearch method. The method throws a ClassCastException if the target is not comparable to the array elements (for example, if the target is type Integer and the array elements are type String).

FIGURE 7.10
Trace of binarySearch(kidNames, "Dustin")

binarySearch(kidNames, "Dustin")

2

items: kidNames
target: "Dustin"
return binarySearch(kidNames, "Dustin", 0, 6);

binarySearch(kidNames, "Dustin", 0, 6)

items: kidNames
target: "Dustin"
first: 0
last: 6
middle = (0 + 6) / 2 = 3
(0 > 6) is false
compResult is negative
return binarySearch(kidNames, "Dustin", 0, 2);

2

binarySearch(kidNames, "Dustin", 0, 2)

items: kidNames
target: "Dustin"
first: 0
last: 2
middle = (0 + 2) / 2 = 1
(0 > 2) is false
compResult is positive
return binarySearch(kidNames, "Dustin", 2, 2);

2

binarySearch(kidNames, "Dustin", 2, 2)

items: kidNames
target: "Dustin"
first: 2
last: 2
middle = (2 + 2) / 2 = 2
(2 > 2) is false
compResult is zero
return 2

2

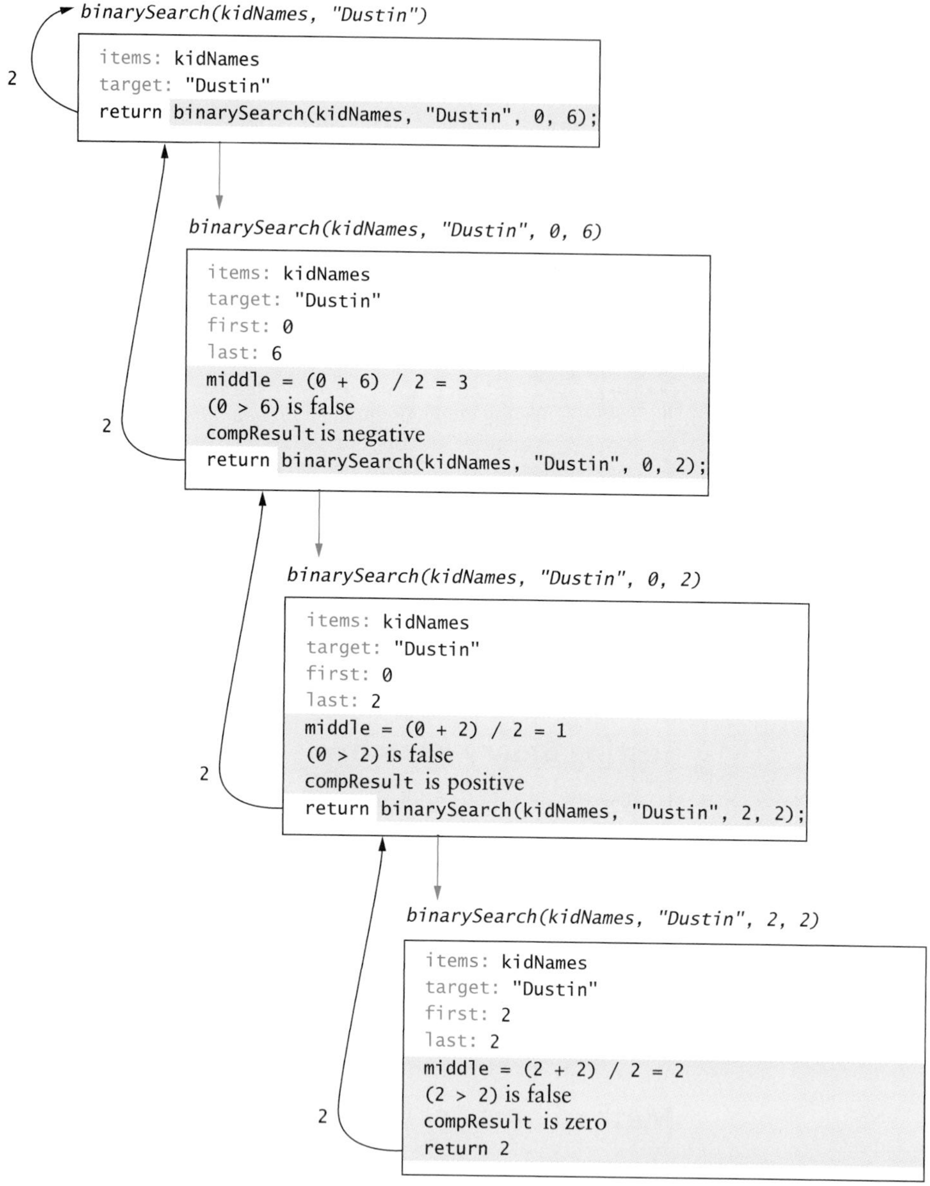

EXERCISES FOR SECTION 7.3

SELF-CHECK

1. For the array shown in Figure 7.9, show the values of first, last, middle, and compResult in successive frames when searching for a target of "Rich"; when searching for a target of "Alice"; when searching for a target of "Daryn".
2. How many elements will be compared to target for an unsuccessful binary search in an array of 1000 items? What is the answer for 2000 items?
3. If there are multiple occurrences of the target item in an array, what can you say about the subscript value that will be returned by linearSearch? Answer the same question for binarySearch.

PROGRAMMING

1. Write a recursive algorithm to find the sum of all values stored in an array of integers.
2. Write a recursive linear search method with a recursive step that finds the last occurrence of a target in an array, not the first. You will need to modify the linear search method so that the last element of the array is always tested, not the first. You will need to pass the current length of the array as an argument.

7.4 Recursive Data Structures

Computer scientists often encounter data structures that are defined recursively. A *recursive data structure* is one that has another version of itself as a component. We will define the tree data structure as a recursive data structure in Chapter 8, but we can also define a linked list, described in Chapter 4, as a recursive data structure. In this section we demonstrate that recursive methods provide a very natural mechanism for processing recursive data structures. The first language developed for artificial intelligence research was a recursive language designed expressly for LISt Processing and therefore called LISP.

Recursive Definition of a Linked List

The following definition implies that a non-empty linked list is a collection of nodes such that each node references another linked list consisting of the nodes that follow it in the list. The last node references an empty list.

A linked list is empty, or it consists of a node, called the list head, that stores data and a reference to a linked list.

Class LinkedListRec

We will define a class LinkedListRec that implements several list operations using recursive methods. The class LinkedListRec has a single data field head and a private inner class called Node, which has the structure defined in Chapter 4. A Node has attributes data (type Object) and next (type Node).

```
/** A recursive linked list class with recursive methods. */
public class LinkedListRec {

    /** The list head */
    private Node head;

    // Insert inner class Node here.
    ...
}
```

We will write the following recursive methods: size (returns the size), toString (represents the list contents as a string), add (adds an element to the end of the list), and replace (replaces one object in a list with another). We code each operation using a pair of methods: a public wrapper method that calls a private recursive method. To perform a list operation, you apply a wrapper method to an instance of class LinkedListRec.

Method size

The method size returns the size of a linked list and is similar to the method length defined earlier for a string. The recursive method returns 0 if the list is empty (head == null is true). Otherwise, the statement

```
return 1 + size(head.next);
```

returns 1 plus the size of the rest of the list which is referenced by head.next.

The wrapper method calls the recursive method, passing the list head as an argument, and returns the value returned by the recursive method. In the initial call to the recursive method, head will reference the first list node. In each subsequent call, head will reference the successor of the node that it currently references.

```
/** Finds the size of a list.
    @param head The head of the current list
    @return The size of the current list
*/
private int size(Node head) {
    if (head == null)
        return 0;
    else
        return 1 + size(head.next);
}

/** Wrapper method for finding the size of a list.
    @return The size of the list
*/
public int size() {
    return size(head);
}
```

Method `toString`

The method `toString` returns a string representation of a linked list. The recursive method is very similar to method `size`. The statement

```
return head.data + "\n" + toString(head.next);
```

appends the data in the current list head to the string representation of the rest of the list. The line space character is inserted after each list item. If the list contains the elements "hat", Integer(55), "dog", the string result would be "hat\n55\ndog\n".

```
/** Returns the string representation of a list.
    @param head The head of the current list
    @return The state of the current list
*/
private String toString(Node head) {
    if (head == null)
        return "";
    else
        return head.data + "\n" + toString(head.next);
}

/** Wrapper method for returning the string representation of a list.
    @return The string representation of the list
*/
public String toString() {
    return toString(head);
}
```

Method `replace`

The method `replace` replaces each occurrence of an object in a list (parameter `oldObj`) with a different object (parameter `newObj`). The **if** statement in the recursive method is different from what we are used to. The method does nothing for the base case of an empty list. If the list is not empty, the **if** statement

```
if (oldObj.equals(head.data))
    head.data = newObj;
```

tests whether the item in the current list head matches `oldObj`. If so, it stores `newObj` in the current list head. Regardless of whether a replacement is performed, method `replace` is called recursively to process the rest of the list.

```
/** Replaces all occurrences of oldObj with newObj.
    post: Each occurrence of oldObj has been replaced by newObj.
    @param head The head of the current list
    @param oldObj The object being removed
    @param newObj The object being inserted
*/
private void replace(Node head, Object oldObj, Object newObj) {
    if (head != null) {
        if (oldObj.equals(head.data))
            head.data = newObj;
        replace(head.next, oldObj, newObj);
    }
}
```

```
/*  Wrapper method for replacing oldObj with newObj.
    post: Each occurrence of oldObj has been replaced by newObj.
    @param oldObj The object being removed
    @param newObj The object being inserted
*/
public void replace(Object oldObj, Object newObj) {
    replace(head, oldObj, newObj);
}
```

Method add

You can use the add method to add nodes to an existing list. You can also use it to build a list by adding new nodes to the end of an initially empty list.

The add methods have two features that are different from what we have seen before. The wrapper method tests for an empty list (head == null is true), and it calls the recursive add method only if the list is not empty. If the list is empty, the wrapper add method creates a new node, which is referenced by the data field head, and stores the first list item in this node.

```
/** Adds a new node to the end of a list.
    @param head The head of the current list
    @param data The data for the new node
*/
private void add(Node head, Object data) {
    // If the list has just one element, add to it.
    if (head.next == null)
        head.next = new Node(data);
    else
        add(head.next, data);
}


/** Wrapper method for adding a new node to the end of a list.
    @param data The data for the new node
*/
public void add(Object data) {
    if (head == null)
        head = new Node(data);
    else
        add(head, data);
}
```

For each node referenced by argument head, the recursive method tests to see whether the node referenced by argument head is the last node in the list (head.next is null). If so, method add then resets head.next to reference a new node that contains the data being inserted.

PITFALL

Testing for an Empty List Instead of Testing for the Last List Node

In recursive method add, we test whether head.next is null. This condition is true when head references a list with just one node. We then reset its next field to reference a new node. If we tested whether head was null (an empty list), and then executed the statement

```
head = new Node(data);
```

this would have no effect on the original list. The local reference head would be changed to reference the new node, but this node would not be connected to a node in the original list.

Removing a List Node

One of the reasons for using linked lists is that they enable easy insertion and removal of nodes. We show how to do removal next and leave insertion as an exercise. In the following recursive method remove, the first base case returns **false** if the list is empty. The second base case determines whether the list head should be removed by comparing its data field to outData. If there is a match, the assignment statement removes the list head by connecting its predecessor (referenced by pred) to the successor of the list head. For this case, method remove returns **true**. The recursive case applies remove to the rest of the list. In the next execution of the recursive method, the current list head will be referenced by pred, and the successor of the current list head will be referenced by head.

```
/** Removes a node from a list.
    post: The first occurrence of outData is removed.
    @param head The head of the current list
    @param pred The predecessor of the list head
    @param outData The data to be removed
    @return true if the item is removed
            and false otherwise
*/
private boolean remove(Node head, Node pred, Object outData) {
    if (head == null)  // Base case - empty list.
        return false;
    else if (head.data.equals(outData)) {  // 2nd base case.
        pred.next = head.next;  // Remove head.
        return true;
    } else
        return remove(head.next, head, outData);
}
```

The following wrapper method takes care of the special case where the node to be removed is at the head of the list. The first condition returns **false** if the list is empty. The second condition removes the list head and returns **true** if the list head contains the data to be removed. The **else** clause calls the recursive remove method.

In the first execution of the recursive method, head will reference the actual second node, and pred will reference the actual first node.

```
/** Wrapper method for removing a node (in LinkedListRec).
    post: The first occurrence of outData is removed.
    @param outData The data to be removed
    @return true if the item is removed,
            and false otherwise
*/
public boolean remove(Object outData) {
    if (head == null)
        return false;
    else if (head.data.equals(outData)) {
        head = head.next;
        return true;
    } else
        return remove(head.next, head, outData);
}
```

EXERCISES FOR SECTION 7.4

SELF-CHECK

1. Describe the result of executing each of the following statements.
```
LinkedListRec aList = new LinkedListRec();
aList.add(new Integer(25));
aList.add("hello");
Double num = new Double(3.14);
aList.add(num);
System.out.println(aList.size() + ", " + aList.toString());
aList.replace("hello", "bye");
aList.remove(num);
aList.remove("hello");
System.out.println(aList.size() + ", " + aList.toString());
```

2. Trace each call to a LinkedListRec method in Exercise 1.

3. Write a recursive algorithm for method insert(Object obj, int index) where index is the position of the insertion.

4. Write a recursive algorithm for method remove(int index) where index is the position of the item to be removed.

PROGRAMMING

1. Write an equals method for the LinkedListRec class that compares this LinkedListRc object to one specified by its argument. Two lists are equal if they have the same number of nodes and store the same information at each node. Don't use the size method.

2. Write a search method that returns **true** if its argument is stored as the data field of a LinkedListRec node and returns **false** if its argument is not stored in any node.

3. Write a recursive method insertBefore that inserts a specified data object before the first occurrence of another specified data object. For example, the method call

`aList.insertBefore(target, inData)` would insert the object referenced by `inData` in a new node just before the first node of `aList` that stores a reference to `target` as its data.

4. Write a recursive method `reverse` which reverses the elements in a linked list.

5. Code method `insert` in Self-check Exercise 3.

6. Code method `remove` in Self-check Exercise 4.

7.5 Problem Solving with Recursion

In this section we discuss recursive solutions to two problems. Our recursive solutions will break each problem up into multiple smaller versions of the original problem. Both problems are easier to solve using recursion because recursive thinking enables us to split each problem into more manageable subproblems. They would both be much more difficult to solve without recursion.

CASE STUDY   Towers of Hanoi

Problem   You may be familiar with a version of this problem that is sold as a child's puzzle. There is a board with three pegs and three disks of different sizes (see Figure 7.11). The goal of the game is to move the three disks from the peg where they have been placed (largest disk on the bottom, smallest disk on the top) to one of the empty pegs, subject to the following constraints:

- Only the top disk on a peg can be moved to another peg.
- A larger disk cannot be placed on top of a smaller disk.

Analysis   We can solve this problem by displaying a list of moves to be made. The problem inputs will be the number of disks to move, the starting peg, the destination peg, and the temporary peg. We will write a class `Tower` that contains a method `showMoves` that builds a string with all the moves.

FIGURE 7.11
Children's Version of Towers of Hanoi

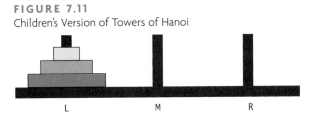

....
TABLE 7.1
Inputs and Outputs for Towers of Hanoi Problem

Problem Inputs
Number of disks (an integer)
Letter of starting peg: L (left), M (middle), or R (right)
Letter of destination peg (L, M, or R), but different from starting peg
Letter of temporary peg (L, M, or R), but different from starting peg and destination peg
Problem Outputs
A list of moves

Design   We still need to determine a strategy for making a move. If we examine the situation in Figure 7.11 (all three disks on the L peg) we can derive a strategy to solve it. If we can figure out how to move the top two disks to the M peg (a two-disk version of the original problem), we can then place the bottom disk on the R peg (see Figure 7.12). Now all we need to do is move the two disks on the M peg to the R peg. If we can solve both of these two-disk problems, then the three-disk problem is also solved:

Solution to 3-Disk Problem: Move 3 Disks from Peg L to Peg R

1. Move the top two disks from peg L to peg M.
2. Move the bottom disk from peg L to peg R.
3. Move the top two disks from peg M to peg R.

....
FIGURE 7.12
Towers of Hanoi After the First Two Steps in Solution of the Three-Disk Problem

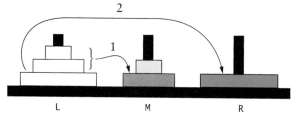

We can split the solution to each two-disk problem into three problems involving single disks. We solve the second two-disk problem next; the solution to the first one (move the top two disks from peg L to peg M) is quite similar.

Solution to 2-Disk Problem: Move Top 2 Disks from Peg M to Peg R

1. Move the top disk from peg M to peg L.
2. Move the bottom disk from peg M to peg R.
3. Move the top disk from peg L to peg R.

In Figure 7.13 we show the pegs after steps 1 and 2. When step 3 is completed, the three pegs will be on peg R.

FIGURE 7.13
Towers of Hanoi After First Two Steps in Solution of Two-Disk Problem

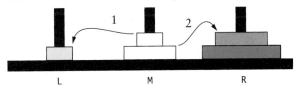

In a similar way, we can split a four-disk problem into two three-disk problems. Figure 7.14 shows the pegs after the top three disks have been moved from peg L to peg M. Because we know how to solve three-disk problems, we can also solve four-disk problems.

Solution to 4-Disk Problem: Move 4 Disks from Peg L to Peg R

1. Move the top three disks from peg L to peg M.
2. Move the bottom disk from peg L to peg R.
3. Move the top three disks from peg M to peg R.

FIGURE 7.14
Towers of Hanoi After the First Two Steps in Solution of the Four-Disk Problem

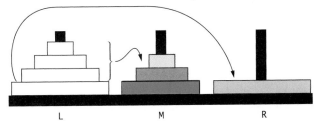

Next, we show a general recursive algorithm for moving *n* disks from one of the three pegs to a different peg.

Recursive Algorithm for *n*-Disk Problem: Move *n* Disks from the Starting Peg to the Destination Peg

1. **if** *n* is 1
2. Move disk 1 (the smallest disk) from the starting peg to the destination peg.
3. **else**
4. Move the top *n* − 1 disks from the starting peg to the temporary peg (neither starting nor destination peg).
5. Move disk *n* (the disk at the bottom) from the starting peg to the destination peg.
6. Move the top *n* − 1 disks from the temporary peg to the destination peg.

The stopping case is the one-disk problem. The recursive step enables us to split the *n*-disk problem into two (*n* − 1)-disk problems and a single-disk problem. Each problem has a different starting peg and destination peg.

Our recursive solution method showMoves will display the solution as a list of disk moves. For each move, we show the number of the disk being moved and its starting and destination pegs. For example, for the two-disk problem shown earlier (move two disks from the middle peg, M, to the right peg, R), the list of moves would be

```
Move disk 1 from peg M to peg L
Move disk 2 from peg M to peg R
Move disk 1 from peg L to peg R
```

The method showMoves must have the number of disks, the starting peg, the destination peg, and the temporary peg as its parameters. If there are *n* disks, the bottom disk has number *n* (the top disk has number 1). Table 7.2 describes the method required for class TowersOfHanoi.

Implementation Listing 7.2 shows class TowersOfHanoi. In method showMoves, the recursive step

```
return showMoves(n - 1, startPeg, tempPeg, destPeg)
       + "Move disk " + n + " from peg " + startPeg
       + " to peg " + destPeg + "\n"
       + showMoves(n - 1, tempPeg, destPeg, startPeg);
```

TABLE 7.2
Class TowersOfHanoi

Method	Behavior
public String showMoves(int n, char startPeg, char destPeg, char tempPeg)	Builds a string containing all moves for a game with n disks on startPeg that will be moved to destPeg using tempPeg for temporary storage of disks being moved.

returns the string formed by concatenating the list of moves for the first (n − 1)-disk problem (the recursive call after `return`), the move required for the bottom disk (disk n), and the list of moves for the second (n − 1)-disk problem.

LISTING 7.2
Class TowersOfHanoi

```java
import javax.swing.*;

/** Class that solves Towers of Hanoi problem. */
public class TowersOfHanoi {
    /** Recursive method for "moving" disks.
        pre: startPeg, destPeg, tempPeg are different.
        @param n is the number of disks
        @param startPeg is the starting peg
        @param destPeg is the destination peg
        @param tempPeg is the temporary peg
        @return A string with all the required disk moves
    */
    public static String showMoves(int n, char startPeg,
                                   char destPeg, char tempPeg) {
        if (n == 1) {
            return "Move disk 1 from peg " + startPeg +
                    " to peg " + destPeg + "\n";
        } else {  // Recursive step
            return showMoves(n - 1, startPeg, tempPeg, destPeg)
                    + "Move disk " + n + " from peg " + startPeg
                    + " to peg " + destPeg + "\n"
                    + showMoves(n - 1, tempPeg, destPeg, startPeg);
        }
    }
}
```

Testing Figure 7.15 shows the result of executing the following `main` method for the data 3, L, R ("move 3 disks from peg L to peg R"). The first three lines are the solution to the problem "move 2 disks from peg L to peg M," and the last three lines are the solution to the problem "move 2 disks from peg M to peg R."

```java
public static void main(String[] args) {
    String nDisks =
        JOptionPane.showInputDialog("Enter number of disks");
    String startPeg =
        JOptionPane.showInputDialog("Enter start peg (L, M, R)");
    String destPeg =
        JOptionPane.showInputDialog("Enter destination peg "
                                    + "(L, M, R), "
                                    + "but not " + startPeg);
```

```
        String tempPeg =
            JOptionPane.showInputDialog("Enter temporary peg "
                                        + "(L, M, R), "
                                        + "but not " + startPeg
                                        + " or " + destPeg);
        String moves = showMoves(Integer.parseInt(nDisks),
                                 startPeg.toUpperCase().charAt(0),
                                 destPeg.toUpperCase().charAt(0),
                                 tempPeg.toUpperCase().charAt(0));
        JOptionPane.showMessageDialog(null, moves);
    }
```

FIGURE 7.15
Solution to "Move 3
Disks from Peg L to
Peg R"

Visualization of Towers of Hanoi

We have provided a graphical visualization that you can use to observe the movement of disks in a solution to the Towers of Hanoi. You can access it through the companion Web site for this book.

CASE STUDY　Counting Cells in a Blob

In this case study we consider how we might process an image that is presented as a two-dimensional array of color values. The information in the two-dimensional array might come from a variety of sources. For example, it could be an image of part of a person's body that comes from an X-ray or an MRI, or it could be a picture of part of the earth's surface taken by a satellite. Our goal in this case study is to determine the size of any area in the image that is considered abnormal because of its color values.

Problem You have a two-dimensional grid of cells, and each cell contains either a normal background color or a second color, which indicates the presence of an abnormality. The user wants to know the size of a *blob*, where a blob is a collection of contiguous abnormal cells. The user will enter the x, y coordinates of a cell in the blob, and the count of all cells in that blob will be determined.

Analysis Data Requirements

PROBLEM INPUTS

- The two-dimensional grid of cells
- The coordinates of a cell in a blob

PROBLEM OUTPUTS

- The count of cells in the blob

Classes

We will have two classes. Class TwoDimGrid will manage the two-dimensional grid of cells. You can find the discussion of the design and implementation of this class on the Web site for this book. Here we will focus on the design of class Blob, which contains the recursive method that counts the number of cells in a blob.

Design Table 7.3 describes the public methods of class TwoDimGrid, and Table 7.4 describes class Blob.

Method countCells in class Blob is a recursive method that is applied to a TwoDimGrid object. Its parameters are the (x, y) position of a cell. The algorithm follows.

TABLE 7.3
Class TwoDimGrid

Method	Behavior
void recolor(int x, int y, Color aColor)	Resets the color of the cell at position (x, y) to aColor.
Color getColor(int x, int y)	Retrieves the color of the cell at position (x, y).
int getNRows()	Returns the number of cells in the y-axis.
int getNCols()	Returns the number of cells in the x-axis.

TABLE 7.4
Class Blob

Method	Behavior
int countCells(int x, int y)	Returns the number of cells in the blob at (x, y).

Algorithm for countCells(x, y)

1. **if** the cell at (x, y) is outside the grid
2.   The result is 0.

    else if the color of the cell at (x, y) is not the abnormal color
3.   The result is 0.

    else
4.   Set the color of the cell at (x, y) to a temporary color.
5.   The result is 1 plus the number of cells in each piece of the blob that includes a nearest neighbor.

The two stopping cases are reached if the coordinates of the cell are out of bounds or if the cell does not have the abnormal color and, therefore, can't be part of a blob. The recursive step involves counting 1 for a cell that has the abnormal color and adding the counts for the blobs that include each immediate neighbor cell. Each cell has eight immediate neighbors: two in the horizontal direction, two in the vertical direction, and four in the diagonal directions.

If no neighbor has the abnormal color, then the result will be just 1. If any neighbor cell has the abnormal color, then it will be counted along with all its neighbor cells that have the abnormal color, and so on until no neighboring cells with abnormal color are encountered (or the edge of the grid is reached). The reason for setting the color of the cell at (x, y) to a temporary color is to prevent it from being counted again when its neighbors' blobs are counted.

Implementation Listing 7.3 shows class `Blob`. The interface `GridColors` defines the three constants: `BACKGROUND`, `ABNORMAL`, and `TEMP_COLOR`. The first terminating condition,

```
(x < 0 || x >= grid.getNCols() || y < 0 || y >= grid.getNRows())
```

compares x to 0 and the value returned by `getNCols()`, the number of columns in the grid. Because x is plotted along the horizontal axis, it is compared to the number of columns, not the number of rows. The same test is applied to y and the number of rows. The second terminating condition,

```
(!grid.getColor(x, y).equals(ABNORMAL))
```

is true if the cell at (x, y) has either the background color or the temporary color.

The recursive step is implemented by the statement

```
return 1
    + countCells(x - 1, y + 1) + countCells(x, y + 1)
    + countCells(x + 1, y + 1) + countCells(x - 1, y)
    + countCells(x + 1, y) + countCells(x - 1, y - 1)
    + countCells(x, y - 1) + countCells(x + 1, y - 1);
```

Each recursive call to `countCells` has as its arguments the coordinates of a neighbor of the cell at (x, y). The value returned by each call will be the number of cells in the blob it belongs to, excluding the cell at (x, y) and any other cells that may have been counted already.

LISTING 7.3
Class Blob

```java
import java.awt.*;

/** Class that solves problem of counting abnormal cells. */
public class Blob implements GridColors {

    /** The grid */
    private TwoDimGrid grid;

    /** Constructors */
    public Blob(TwoDimGrid grid) {
        this.grid = grid;
    }

    /** Finds the number of cells in the blob at (x,y).
        pre: Abnormal cells are in ABNORMAL color;
             Other cells are in BACKGROUND color.
        post: All cells in the block are in the TEMPORARY color.
        @param x The x-coordinate of a blob cell
        @param y The y-coordinate of a blob cell
        @return The number of cells in the blob that contains (x, y)
     */
    public int countCells(int x, int y) {
        int result;

        if (x < 0 || x >= grid.getNCols()
                || y < 0 || y >= grid.getNRows())
            return 0;
        else if (!grid.getColor(x, y).equals(ABNORMAL))
            return 0;
        else {
            grid.recolor(x, y, TEMPORARY);
            return 1
                + countCells(x - 1, y + 1) + countCells(x, y + 1)
                + countCells(x + 1, y + 1) + countCells(x - 1, y)
                + countCells(x + 1, y) + countCells(x - 1, y - 1)
                + countCells(x, y - 1) + countCells(x + 1, y - 1);
        }
    }
}
```

Testing   To test the recursive algorithm in this case study and the one in the next section, we will need to implement class TwoDimGrid. To make the program interactive and easy to use, we implemented TwoDimGrid as a two-dimensional grid of buttons placed in a panel. When the button panel is placed in a frame and displayed, the user can toggle the color of a button (from normal to abnormal and back to normal) by clicking it. Similarly, the program can change the color of a button by applying the recolor method to the button. Information about the design of class TwoDimGrid is on the companion Web site for this book, as is the class itself.

We also provide a class `BlobTest` on the Web site. This class allows the user to load the colors for the button panel from a file that contains a representation of the image as lines of 0s and 1s, where 0 is the background color and 1 is the abnormal color. Alternatively, the user can set the dimensions of the grid and then enter the abnormal cells by clicking on each button that represents an abnormal cell. When the grid has been finalized, the user clicks twice on one of the abnormal cells (to change its color to normal and then back to abnormal) and then clicks the button labeled Solve. This invokes method `countCells` with the coordinates of the last button clicked as its arguments. Figure 7.16 shows a sample grid of buttons with the x, y coordinate of each button shown as the button label. The background cells are dark gray, and the abnormal cells are light gray. Invoking `countCells` with a starting point of (x = 4, y = 1) should return a count of 7. Figure 7.17 shows the blob cells in the temporary color (black) after the execution of method `countCells`.

When you test this program, make sure you verify that it works for the following cases:

- A starting cell that is on the edge of the grid
- A starting cell that has no neighboring abnormal cells
- A starting cell whose only abnormal neighbor cells are diagonally connected to it
- A "bull's-eye": a starting cell whose neighbors are all normal but their neighbors are abnormal
- A starting cell that is normal
- A grid that contains all abnormal cells
- A grid that contains all normal cells

FIGURE 7.16
A Sample Grid for Counting Cells in a Blob

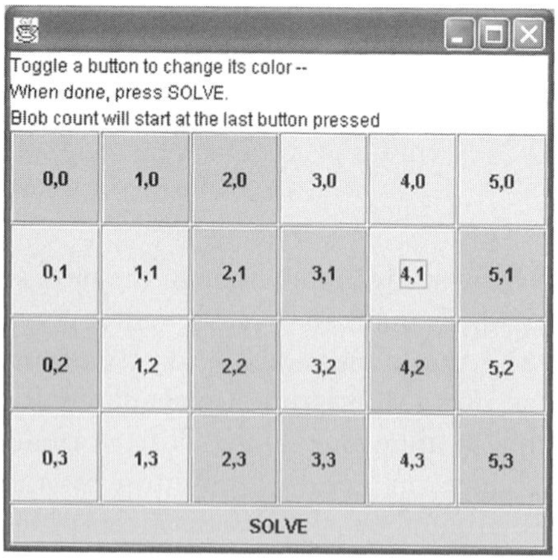

FIGURE 7.17
Blob Cells (in Black) After Execution of `countCells`

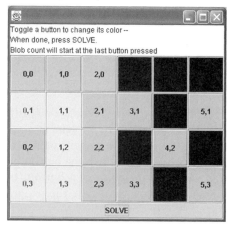

EXERCISES FOR SECTION 7.5

SELF-CHECK

1. What is the big-O for the Towers of Hanoi as a function of n, where n represents the number of disks? Compare it to the function 2^n.
2. How many moves would be required to solve the five-disk problem?
3. Provide a "trace" of the solution to a four-disk problem by showing all the calls to showMoves that would be generated.
4. Explain why the first condition of method countCells must precede the second condition.

PROGRAMMING

1. Modify method countCells, assuming that cells must have a common side in order to be counted in the same blob. This means that they must be connected horizontally or vertically but not diagonally. Under this condition, the value of the method call aBlob.countCells(4, 1) would be 4 for the grid in Figure 7.16.
2. Write a method Blob.restore that restores the grid back to its original state. You will need to reset the color of each cell that is in the temporary color back to its original color.

7.6 Backtracking

In this section we consider the problem-solving technique called *backtracking*. Backtracking is an approach to implementing systematic trial and error in a search for a solution. An application of backtracking is finding a path through a maze.

If you are attempting to walk through a maze, you will probably follow the general approach of walking down a path as far as you can go. Eventually either you will reach your destination and exit the maze, or you won't be able to go any further. If you exit the maze, you are done. Otherwise, you need to retrace your steps (backtrack) until you reach a fork in the path. At each fork, if there is a branch you did not follow, you will follow that branch hoping to reach your destination. If not, you will retrace your steps again, and so on.

What makes backtracking different from random trial and error is that backtracking provides a systematic approach to trying alternative paths and eliminating them if they don't work out. You will never try the exact same path more than once, and you will eventually find a solution path if one exists.

Problems that are solved by backtracking can be described as a set of choices made by some method. If at some point, it turns out that a solution is not possible with the current set of choices, the most recent choice is identified and removed. If there is an untried alternative choice, it is added to the set of choices, and search continues. If there is no untried alternative choice, then the next most recent choice is removed, and an alternative is sought for it. This process continues until either we reach a choice with an untried alternative and can continue our search for a solution, or we determine that there are no more alternative choices to try. Recursion allows us to implement backtracking in a relatively straightforward manner, because we can use each activation frame to remember the choice that was made at that particular decision point.

We will show how to use backtracking to find a path through a maze, but it can be applied to many other kinds of problems that involve a search for a solution. For example, a program that plays chess may use a kind of backtracking. If a sequence of moves it is considering does not lead to a favorable position, it will backtrack and try another sequence.

CASE STUDY   Finding a Path Through a Maze

Problem   Use backtracking to find and display the path through a maze. From each point in a maze, you can move to the next cell in the horizontal or vertical direction, if that cell is not blocked. So there are at most four possible moves from each point.

Analysis   Our maze will consist of a grid of colored cells like the grid used in the previous case study. The starting point is the cell at the top left corner (0, 0), and the exit point is the cell at the bottom right corner (getNCols() - 1, getNRows() - 1). All cells that can be part of a path will be in the BACKGROUND color. All cells that represent barriers and cannot be part of a path will be in the ABNORMAL color. To keep track of a cell that we have visited, we will set it to the TEMPORARY color. If we find a path, all cells on the path will be reset to the PATH color (a new color for a button defined in GridColors). So there are a total of four possible colors for a cell.

Design   The following recursive algorithm returns **true** if a path is found. It changes the color of all cells that are visited, but found not to be on the path, to the temporary color. In the recursive algorithm, each cell (x, y) being tested is reachable from the starting point. We can use recursion to simplify the problem of finding a path from cell (x, y) to the exit. We know that we can reach any unblocked neighbor cell that is in the horizontal or vertical direction from cell (x, y). So a path exists from cell (x, y) to the maze exit if there is a path from a neighbor cell of (x, y) to the maze exit. If there is no path from any neighbor cell, we must backtrack and replace (x, y) with an alternative that has not yet been tried. That is done automatically through recursion. If there is a path, it will eventually be found and findMazePath will return **true**.

Recursive Algorithm for `findMazePath(x, y)`

1.   **if** the current cell is outside the maze
2.   Return **false** (you are out of bounds).
     else if the current cell is part of the barrier or has already been visited
3.   Return **false** (you are off the path or in a cycle).
     else if the current cell is the maze exit
4.   Recolor it to the path color and return **true** (you have successfully completed the maze).
     else // *Try to find a path from the current path to the exit:*
5.   Mark the current cell as on the path by recoloring it to the path color.
6.   **for** each neighbor of the current cell
7.   **if** a path exists from the neighbor to the maze exit
8.   Return **true**.
     // *No neighbor of the current cell is on the path.*
9.   Recolor the current cell to the temporary color (visited) and return **false**.

If no stopping case is reached (Steps 2, 3, or 4), the recursive case (the **else** clause) marks the current cell as being on the path and then tests whether there is a path from any neighbor of the current cell to the exit. If a path is found, we return **true** and begin unwinding from the recursion. During the process of unwinding from the recursion, the method will continue to return **true**. However, if all neighbors of the current cell are tested without finding a path, this means that the current cell cannot be on the path, so we recolor it to the temporary color and return **false** (Step 9). Next, we backtrack to a previous call and try to find a path through a cell that is an alternative to the cell just tested. The cell just tested will have been marked as visited (the temporary color), so we won't try using it again.

Notice there is no attempt to find the shortest path through the maze. We just show the first path that is found.

Implementation   Listing 7.4 shows class Maze with data field maze (type TwoDimGrid). There is a wrapper method that calls recursive method findMazePath with its argument values set to the coordinates of the starting point (0, 0). The wrapper method returns the result of this call (**true** or **false**).

The recursive version of findMazePath begins with three stopping cases: two unsuccessful and one successful ((x, y) is the exit point). The recursive case contains an **if** condition with four recursive calls. Because of short-circuit evaluation, if any call returns **true**, the rest are not executed. The arguments for each call are the coordinates of a neighbor cell. If a path exists from a neighbor to the maze exit, then the neighbor is part of the solution path, so we return **true**. If a neighbor cell is not on the solution path, we try the next neighbor until all four neighbors have been tested.

If there is no path from any neighbor, we recolor the current cell to the temporary color and return **false**.

....

LISTING 7.4
Class Maze

```java
import java.awt.*;

/** Class that solves maze problems with backtracking. */
public class Maze implements GridColors {

    /** The maze */
    private TwoDimGrid maze;

    public Maze(TwoDimGrid m) {
        maze = m;
    }

    /** Wrapper method. */
    public boolean findMazePath() {
        return findMazePath(0, 0);    // (0, 0) is the start point.
    }

    /** Attempts to find a path through point (x, y).
        pre: Possible path cells are in BACKGROUND color;
             barrier cells are in ABNORMAL color.
        post: If a path is found, all cells on it are set to the
              PATH color; all cells that were visited but are
              not on the path are in the TEMPORARY color.
        @param x The x-coordinate of current point
        @param y The y-coordinate of current point
        @return If a path through (x, y) is found, true;
                otherwise, false
    */
    public boolean findMazePath(int x, int y) {
        if (x < 0 || y < 0
            || x >= maze.getNCols() || y >= maze.getNRows())
            return false;        // Cell is out of bounds.
        else if (!maze.getColor(x, y).equals(BACKGROUND))
            return false;        // Cell is on barrier or dead end.
        else if (x == maze.getNCols() - 1
                 && y == maze.getNRows() - 1) {
            maze.recolor(x, y, PATH);   // Cell is on path
            return true;                // and is maze exit.
        } else {                        // Recursive case.
            // Attempt to find a path from each neighbor.
            // Tentatively mark cell as on path.
            maze.recolor(x, y, PATH);
            if (findMazePath(x - 1, y)
                || findMazePath(x + 1, y)
                || findMazePath(x, y - 1)
```

```
                        || findMazePath(x, y + 1 ) ) {
                    return true;
                } else {
                    maze.recolor(x, y, TEMPORARY);  // Dead end.
                    return false;
                }
            }
        }
    }
```

The Effect of Marking a Cell as Visited

If a path can't be found from a neighbor of the current cell to the maze exit, the current cell is considered a "dead end" and is recolored to the temporary color. You may be wondering whether the program would still work if we just recolored it to the background color. The answer is "Yes". In this case, cells that turned out to be dead ends or cells that were not visited would be in the background color after the program terminated. This would not affect the ability of the algorithm to find a path or to determine that none exists; however, it would affect the algorithm's efficiency. After backtracking, the method could try to place on the path a cell that had been found to be a dead end. The cell would be classified once again as a dead end. Marking it as a dead end (color TEMPORARY) the first time prevents this from happening.

To demonstrate the efficiency of this approach, we tested the program on a maze with 4 rows and 6 columns that had a single barrier cell at the maze exit. When we recolored each dead end cell in the TEMPORARY color, it took 93 recursive calls to findMazePath to determine that a path did not exist. When we recolored each tested cell in the BACKGROUND color, it took 177,313 recursive calls to determine that a path did not exist.

Testing We will use class TwoDimGrid and class MazeTest (from the companion Web site) to test the maze. The MazeTest class is very similar to BlobTest. The main method prompts for the grid dimensions and creates a new TwoDimGrid object with those dimensions. The class constructor builds the GUI for the maze solver, including the button panel, and registers a listener for each button. When the SOLVE button is clicked, method MazeTest.actionPerformed calls findMazePath and displays its result. Figure 7.18 shows the GUI before the SOLVE button is clicked (barrier cells are in light gray, other cells are in dark gray), and Figure 7.19 shows it after the SOLVE button is clicked and the final path is displayed. In Figure 7.19 the barrier cells are in light gray (ABNORMAL color), the cells on the final path are in white (PATH color), and the cells that were visited but then rejected (not on the path) are in black (TEMPORARY color).

You should test this with a variety of mazes, some that can be solved and some that can't (no path exists). You should also try a maze that has no barrier cells and one that has a single barrier cell at the exit point. In the latter case, no path exists.

FIGURE 7.18
Maze as Grid of Buttons Before SOLVE Is Clicked

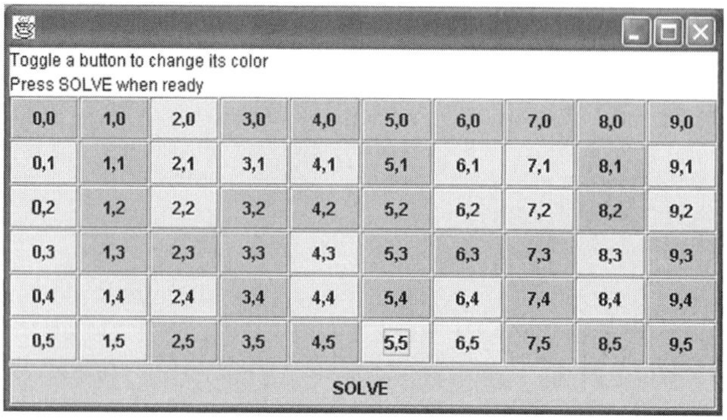

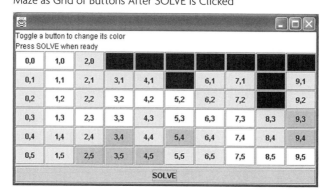

FIGURE 7.19
Maze as Grid of Buttons After SOLVE Is Clicked

EXERCISES FOR SECTION 7.6

SELF-CHECK

1. The terminating conditions in findMazePath must be performed in the order specified. What could happen if the second or third condition were evaluated before the first? If the third condition were evaluated before the second condition?

2. Does it matter in which order the neighbor cells are tested in findMazePath? How could this order affect the path that is found?

3. Is the path shown in Figure 7.19 the shortest path to the exit? If not, list the cells on the shortest path.

PROGRAMMING

1. Show the interface `GridColors`.
2. Write a `Maze.resetTemp` method that recolors the cells that are in the TEMPORARY color to the BACKGROUND color.
3. Write a `Maze.restore` method that restores the maze to its initial state.

Chapter Review

♦ A recursive method has the following form, where Step 2 is the base case, and Steps 3 and 4 are the recursive case:

1.   `if` the problem can be solved for the current value of n
2.   Solve it.
       `else`
3.   Recursively apply the algorithm to one or more problems involving smaller values of n.
4.   Combine the solutions to the smaller problems to get the solution to the original.

♦ To prove that a recursive algorithm is correct, you must
—Verify that the base case is recognized and solved correctly.
—Verify that each recursive case makes progress toward the base case.
—Verify that if all smaller problems are solved correctly, then the original problem must also be solved correctly.

♦ The run-time stack uses activation frames to keep track of argument values and return points during recursive method calls. Activation frames can be used to trace the execution of a sequence of recursive method calls.

♦ Mathematical sequences and formulas that are defined recursively can be implemented naturally as recursive methods.

♦ Recursive data structures are data structures that have a component that is the same data structure. A linked list can be considered a recursive data structure because each node consists of a data field and a reference to a linked list. Recursion can make it easier to write methods that process a linked list.

♦ Two problems that can be solved using recursion were investigated: the Towers of Hanoi problem and counting cells in a blob.

♦ Backtracking is a technique that enables you to write programs that can be used to explore different alternative paths in a search for a solution.

User-Defined Classes in This Chapter

RecursiveMethods

LinkedListRec

TowersOfHanoi

Blob

TwoDimGrid

BlobTest

Maze

MazeTest

Quick-Check Exercises

1. A recursive method has two cases: _____ and _____.
2. Each recursive call of a recursive method must lead to a situation that is _____ to the _____ case.
3. The control statement used in a recursive method is the _____ statement.
4. What three things are stored in an activation frame? Where are the activation frames stored?
5. You can sometimes substitute _____ for recursion.
6. Explain how a recursive method might cause a stack overflow exception.
7. If you have a recursive and iterative method that calculate the same result, which do you think would be more efficient? Explain your answer.
8. Binary search is an O(___) algorithm, and linear search is an O(___) algorithm.
9. Towers of Hanoi is an O(___) algorithm. Explain your answer.
10. Why did you need to provide a wrapper method for recursive methods linearSearch and binarySearch?
11. Why did you need to provide a wrapper method for recursive methods in the LinkedListRec class?

Answers to Quick-Check Exercises

1. A recursive method has two cases: *base case* and *recursive case*.
2. Each recursive call of a recursive method must lead to a situation that is *closer* to the *base* case.
3. The control statement used in a recursive method is the *if* statement.
4. An activation frame stores the following information on the run-time stack: the method argument values, the method local variable values, and the address of the return point in the caller of the method.
5. You can sometimes substitute *iteration* for recursion.
6. A recursive method that doesn't stop would continue to call itself, eventually pushing so many activation frames onto the run-time stack that a stack overflow exception would occur.
7. An *iterative* method would generally be more efficient, because there is more overhead associated with multiple method calls.
8. Binary search is an $O(\log_2 n)$ algorithm, and linear search is an $O(n)$ algorithm.
9. Towers of Hanoi is an $O(2^n)$ algorithm, because each problem splits into two problems at the next lower level.

10. Both search methods should be called with the array name and target as arguments. However, the recursive linear search method needs the subscript of the element to be compared to the target. The binary search method needs the search array bounds.

11. The wrapper method should be applied to a `LinkedListRec` object. The recursive method needs the current list head as an argument.

Review Questions

1. Explain the use of the run-time stack and activation frames in processing recursive method calls.

2. What is a recursive data structure? Give an example of one.

3. For class `LinkedListRec`, write a recursive search method that returns **true** if its target argument is found and **false** otherwise. If you need a wrapper method, provide one.

4. For class `LinkedListRec`, write a recursive `replaceFirst` method that replaces the first occurrence of a reference to its first argument with a reference to its second argument. If you need a wrapper method, provide one.

5. For Towers of Hanoi, show the output string that would be created by the method call `showMoves(3, 'R', 'M', 'L')`. Also, show the sequence of method calls.

6. For the counting cells in a blob problem, show the activation frames in the first 10 recursive calls to `countCells` following `countCells(4, 1)`.

7. For the maze path found in Figure 7.19, explain why cells (3, 4), (2, 5), (3, 5), (4, 5) were never visited and why cells (5, 1) and (3, 0) through (9, 0) were visited and rejected. Show the activation frames for the first 10 recursive calls in solving the maze.

Programming Projects

1. Download and run class `BlobTest`. Try running it with a data file made up of lines consisting of 0s and 1s with no spaces between them. Also run it without a data file.

2. Download and run class `MazeTest`. Try running it with a data file made up of lines consisting of 0s and 1s with no spaces between them. Also run it without a data file.

3. Write a recursive method that converts a decimal integer to a binary string. Write a recursive method that converts a binary string to a decimal integer.

4. Write a `LinkedListRec` class that has the following methods: `size`, `empty`, `insertBefore`, `insertAfter`, `addAtHead`, `addAtEnd`, `remove`, `replace`, `peekFront`, `peekEnd`, `removeFront`, `removeEnd`, `toString`. Use recursion to implement most of these methods.

5. As discussed in Chapter 5, a palindrome is a word that reads the same left to right as right to left. Write a recursive method that determines whether its argument string is a palindrome.

6. Write a program that will read a list of numbers and a desired sum, then determine the subset of numbers in the list that yield that sum if such a subset exists.

7. Write a recursive method that will dispense change for a given amount of money. The method will display all combinations of quarters, dimes, nickels, and pennies that equal the desired amount.

8. Produce the Sierpinski fractal. Start by drawing an equilateral triangle that faces upward. Then draw an equilateral triangle inside it that faces downward.

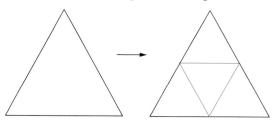

Continue this process on each of the four smaller triangles. Stop when the side dimension for a triangle to be drawn is smaller than a specified minimum size.

9. Write a recursive method for placing eight queens on a chessboard. The eight queens should be placed so that no queen can capture another. Recall that a queen can move in the horizontal, vertical, or diagonal direction.

Chapter 8

Trees

Chapter Objectives

- To learn how to use a tree to represent a hierarchical organization of information
- To learn how to use recursion to process trees
- To understand the different ways of traversing a tree
- To understand the difference between binary trees, binary search trees, and heaps
- To learn how to implement binary trees, binary search trees, and heaps using linked data structures and arrays
- To learn how to use a binary search tree to store information so that it can be retrieved in an efficient manner
- To learn how to use a Huffman tree to encode characters using fewer bits than ASCII or Unicode, resulting in smaller files and reduced storage requirements

The data organizations you studied so far are linear in that each element has only one predecessor or successor. Accessing all the elements in sequence is an $O(n)$ process. In this chapter we begin our discussion of a data organization that is nonlinear or hierarchical: the tree. Instead of having just one successor, a node in a tree can have multiple successors; but it has just one predecessor. A tree in computer science is like a natural tree, which has a single trunk that may split off into two or more main branches. The predecessor of each main branch is the trunk. Each main branch may spawn several secondary branches (successors of the main branches). The predecessor of each secondary branch is a main branch. In computer science, we draw a tree from the top down, so the root of the tree is at the top of the diagram instead of the bottom.

Because trees have a hierarchical structure, we use them to represent hierarchical organizations of information, such as a class hierarchy, a disk directory and its subdirectories (see Figure 8.1), or a family tree. You will see that trees are recursive data structures, because they can be defined recursively. For this reason, many of the methods used to process tress are written as recursive methods.

FIGURE 8.1
Part of the Programs
Directory

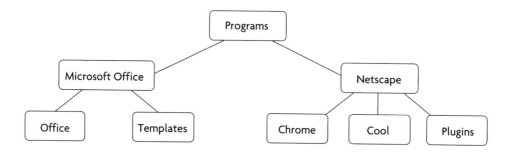

This chapter will focus on a restricted tree structure, a binary tree, in which each element has, at most, two successors. You will learn how to use linked data structures and arrays to represent binary trees. You will also learn how to use a special kind of binary tree called a binary search tree to store information (for example, the words in a dictionary) in an ordered way. Because each element of a binary tree can have two successors, you will see that searching for an item stored in a binary search tree is much more efficient than searching for an item in a linear data structure: (generally $O(\log n)$ for a binary tree versus $O(n)$ for a list).

You also will learn about other kinds of binary trees. Expression trees are used to represent arithmetic expressions. The heap is an ordered tree structure that is used as the basis for a very efficient sorting algorithm and for a special kind of queue called the priority queue. The Huffman tree is used for encoding information and compressing files.

Trees

8.1 Tree Terminology and Applications

Tree Terminology

We use the same terminology to describe trees in computer science as we do trees in nature. A computer science tree consists of a collection of elements or nodes, with each node linked to its successors. The node at the top of a tree is called its *root* because computer science trees grow from the top-down. The links from a node to its successors are called *branches*. The successors of a node are called its *children*. The predecessor of a node is called its *parent*. Each node in a tree has exactly one parent except for the root node, which has no parent. Nodes that have the same parent are *siblings*. A node that has no children is a *leaf node*. Leaf nodes are also known as *external* nodes, and nonleaf nodes are known as *internal* nodes.

A generalization of the parent-child relationship is the *ancestor-descendant relationship*. If node A is the parent of node B, which is the parent of node C, node A is node C's *ancestor*, and node C is node A's *descendant*. Sometimes we say that node A and node C are a grandparent and grandchild, respectively. The root node is an ancestor of every other node in a tree, and every other node in a tree is a descendant of the root node.

Figure 8.2 illustrates these features in a tree that stores a collection of words. The branches are the lines connecting a parent to its children. In discussing this tree, we will refer to a node by the string that it stores. For example, we will refer to the node that stores the string "dog" as node *dog*.

FIGURE 8.2
A Tree of Words

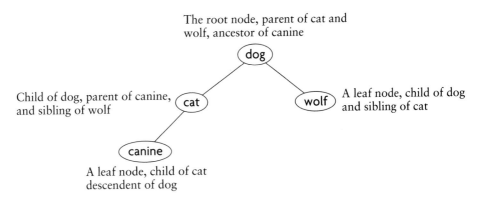

A *subtree of a node* is a tree whose root is a child of that node. For example, the nodes *cat* and *canine* and the branch connecting them are a subtree of node *dog*. The other subtree of node *dog* is the tree consisting of the single node *wolf*. The subtree consisting of the single node *canine* is a subtree of node *cat*.

The *level of a node* is a measure of its distance from the root. It is defined recursively as follows:

- If node *n* is the root of tree T, its level is 1.
- If node *n* is not the root of tree T, its level is 1 + the level of its parent.

For the tree in Figure 8.2, node *dog* is at level 1, nodes *cat* and *wolf* are at level 2, and node *canine* is at level 3. Since nodes are below the root, we sometimes use the term *depth* as an alternative term for level. The two have the same meaning.

The *height of a tree* is the number of nodes in the longest path from the root node to a leaf node. The height of the tree in Figure 8.2 is 3 (the longest path goes through the nodes *dog*, *cat*, and *canine*). Another way of saying this is as follows:

- If T is empty, its height is 0.
- If T is not empty, its height is the maximum depth of its nodes.

An alternate definition of the height of a tree is the number of branches in the longest path from the root node to a leaf node plus one.

Binary Trees

The tree in Figure 8.2 is a *binary tree*. Informally, this is a binary tree because each node has at most two subtrees. A more formal definition for a binary tree follows:

A set of nodes T is a binary tree if either of the following is true:

- T is empty.
- If T is not empty, its root node has two subtrees, T_L and T_R, such that T_L and T_R are binary trees.

We refer to T_L as the left subtree and T_R as the right subtree. For the tree in Figure 8.2, the right subtree of node *cat* is empty. The leaf nodes (*wolf* and *canine*) have empty left and right subtrees. This is illustrated in Figure 8.3, where the empty subtrees are indicated by the squares. Generally the empty subtrees are represented by **null** references, but another value may be chosen. From now on, we will consistently use a **null** reference, and we will not draw the squares for the empty subtrees.

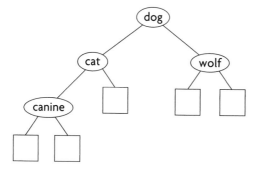

Some Types of Binary Trees

Next we discuss three different types of binary trees that are common in computer science.

An Expression Tree

Figure 8.4 shows a binary tree that stores an expression. Each node contains an operator (+, −, *, /, %) or an operand. The expression in Figure 8.4 corresponds to (x + y) * ((a + b) / c). Operands are stored in leaf nodes. Parentheses are not stored in the tree, because the tree structure dictates the order of operator evaluation. Operators in nodes at higher levels are evaluated after operators in nodes at lower levels, so the operator * in the root node is evaluated last. If a node contains a binary operator, its left subtree represents the operator's left operand and its right subtree represents the operator's right operand. The left subtree of the root represents the expression x + y, and the right subtree of the root represents the expression (a + b) / c.

FIGURE 8.4
Expression Tree

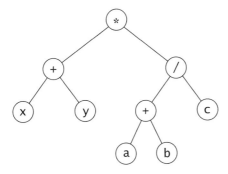

A Huffman Tree

Another use of a binary tree is to represent *Huffman codes* for characters that might appear in a text file. Unlike ASCII or Unicode encoding, which use the same number of bits to encode each character, a Huffman code uses different numbers of bits to encode the letters. It uses fewer bits for the more common letters (for example, space, *e*, *a*, and *t*) and more bits for the less common letters (for example, *q*, *x*, and *z*). On average, using Huffman codes to encode text files should give you files with fewer bits than you would get using other codes. Many programs that compress files use Huffman encoding to generate smaller files in order to save disk space or to reduce the time spent sending the files over the Internet.

Figure 8.5 shows the Huffman encoding tree for an alphabet consisting of the lowercase letters and the space character. All the characters are at leaf nodes. The data stored at nonleaf nodes is not shown. To determine the code for a letter, you form a binary string by tracing the path from the root node to that letter. Each time you go left, append a 0, and each time you go right, append a 1. To reach the space character, you go right three times, so the code is 111. The code for the letter *d* is 10110 (right, left, right, right, left).

The two characters shown at level 4 of the tree (space, *e*) are the most common and, therefore, have the shortest codes (111, 010). The next most common characters (*a*, *o*, *i*, and so forth) are at level 5 of the tree.

You can store the code for each letter in an array. For example, the code for the space ' ' would be at position 0, the letter 'a' would be at position 1 and the code for letter 'z' would be at position 26. You can *encode* each letter in a file by looking up its code in the array.

FIGURE 8.5
Huffman Code Tree

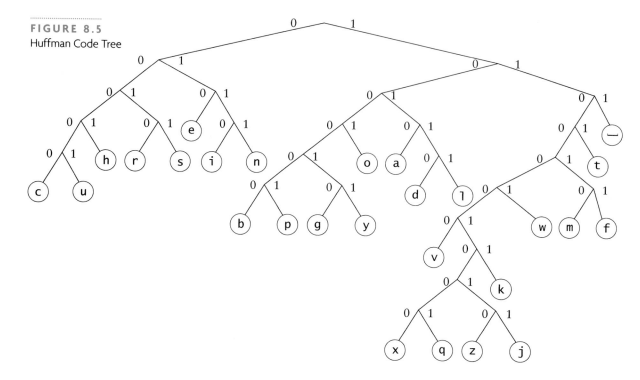

FIGURE 8.5
Huffman Code Tree

However, to *decode* a file of letters and spaces, you walk down the Huffman tree, starting at the root, until you reach a letter and then append that letter to the output text. Once you have reached a letter, go back to the root. Here is an example. The substrings that represent the individual letters are shown in alternate colors to help you follow the process. The underscore in the second line represents a space character (code is 111).

```
100010100111101010101000101011101100011
    g    o    _  e   a    g    l   e  s
```

Huffman trees are discussed further in Section 8.6.

Binary Search Trees

The tree in Figure 8.2 is a *binary search tree* because, for each node, all words in its left subtree precede the word in that node, and all words in its right subtree follow the word in that node. For example, for the root node *dog*, all words in its left subtree *(cat, canine)* precede dog in the dictionary, and all words in its right subtree *(wolf)* follow *dog*. Similarly, for the node *cat*, the word in its left subtree *(canine)* precedes it. There are no duplicate entries in a binary search tree.

More formally, we define a binary search tree as follows:

A set of nodes T is a binary search tree if either of the following is true:

- T is empty.
- If T is not empty, its root node has two subtrees, T_L and T_R, such that T_L and T_R are binary search trees and the value in the root node of T is greater than all values in T_L and is less than all values in T_R.

The order relations in a binary search tree expedite searching the tree. A recursive algorithm for searching a binary search tree follows:

1.   **if** the tree is empty
2.   Return **null**   *(target is not found)*.
          else if the target matches the root node's data
3.   Return the data stored at the root node.
          else if the target is less than the root node's data
4.   Return the result of searching the left subtree of the root.

      else
5.   Return the result of searching the right subtree of the root.

The first two cases are base cases and self-explanatory. In the first recursive case, if the target is less than the root node's data, we search only the left subtree (T_L) because all data items in T_R are larger than the root node's data and, therefore, larger than the target. Likewise we execute the second recursive step (search the right subtree) if the target is greater than the root node's data.

Just as with a binary search of an array, each probe into the binary search tree has the potential of eliminating half the elements in the tree. If the binary search tree is relatively balanced (that is, the depths of the leaves are approximately the same), searching a binary search tree is an O(log n) process, just like a binary search of an ordered array.

What is the advantage of using a binary search tree instead of just storing elements in an array and then sorting it? A binary search tree never has to be sorted, because its elements always satisfy the required order relations. When new elements are inserted (or removed), the binary search tree property can be maintained. In contrast, an array must be expanded whenever new elements are added, and it must be compacted whenever elements are removed. Both expanding and contracting involve shifting items and are thus O(n) operations.

Fullness and Completeness

Trees grow from the top down, and each new value is inserted in a new leaf node. Trees have different shapes depending on how the values are inserted. The tree on the left in Figure 8.6 is called a *full binary tree* of height 3 because the leaf nodes are all at level 3, the height of the tree. A binary tree is a full binary tree if every node has two children except for the leaves, which are all at the bottom.

FIGURE 8.6
Full Binary Tree (Left) and
Complete Binary Tree
(Right) of Height 3

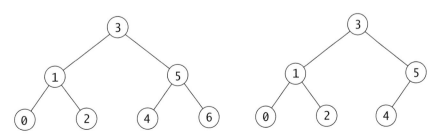

If a tree is not full, it may still be a *complete binary tree* of height *h* if it is filled up to level *h* – 1 and, at level *h*, any unfilled nodes are on the right (see Figure 8.6, right). A node is *filled* if it has a value stored in it. More formally, a binary tree of height *h* is complete if:

- All nodes at level *h* – 2 and above have two children.
- When a node at level *h* – 1 has children, all nodes to the left of it have two children.
- If a node at level *h* – 1 has one child, it is a left child.

General Trees

A general tree is a tree that does not have the restriction that each node of a tree has at most two subtrees. So nodes in a general tree can have any number of subtrees. Figure 8.7 shows a general tree that represents a family tree showing the descendants of King William I (the Conqueror) of England.

We will not discuss general trees in this chapter. However, it is worth mentioning that a general tree can be represented using a binary tree. Figure 8.8 shows a binary tree representation of the family tree in Figure 8.7. We obtained it by connecting the left branch from a node to the oldest child (if any). Each right branch from a node is connected to the next younger sibling (if any).

The names of the men who became kings are in boldface type. You would expect the eldest son to succeed his father as king; however, this would not be the case if the eldest male died before his father. For example, Robert died before William I, so William II became king instead. Starting with King John (near the bottom of the tree), the eldest son of each king did become King of England.

FIGURE 8.7
Family Tree for the Descendants of William I of England

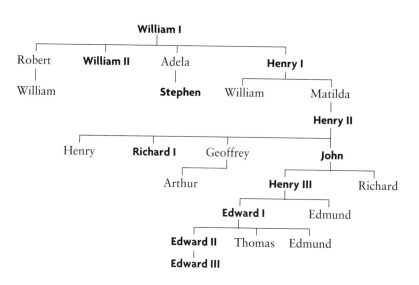

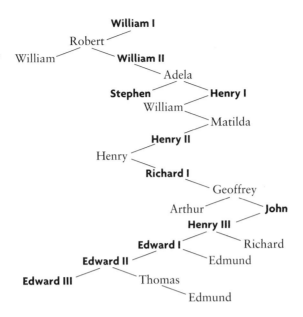

FIGURE 8.8
Binary Tree Equivalent
of King William's Family
Tree

EXERCISES FOR SECTION 8.1

SELF-CHECK

1. Draw binary expression trees for the following infix expressions. Your trees should enforce the Java rules for operator evaluation (higher-precedence operators before lower-precedence operators and left associativity).

   a. x / y + a − b * c
   b. (x * a) − y / b * (c + d)

2. Using the Huffman tree in Figure 8.5,

   a. Write the binary string for the message "scissors cuts paper".
   b. Decode the following binary string:

   110001000101000100101110110001111111000110101011110101101001

3. For each tree shown below, answer these questions. What is its height? Is it a full tree? Is it a complete tree? Is it a binary search tree? If not, make it a binary search tree.

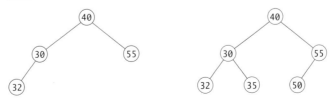

4. Represent the general tree in Figure 8.1 as a binary tree.

8.2 Tree Traversals

Often we want to determine the nodes of a tree and their relationship. We can do this by walking through the tree in a prescribed order and visiting the nodes (processing the information in the nodes) as they are encountered. This process is known as *tree traversal*. We will discuss three kinds of traversal in this section: inorder, preorder, and postorder. These three methods are characterized by when they visit a node in relation to the nodes in its subtrees (T_L and T_R).

- Preorder: Visit root node, traverse T_L, traverse T_R.
- Inorder: Traverse T_L, visit root node, traverse T_R.
- Postorder: Traverse T_L, traverse T_R, visit root node.

Because trees are recursive data structures, we can write similar recursive algorithms for all three techniques. The difference in the algorithms is whether the root is visited before the children are traversed (pre), in between traversing the left and right children (in), or after the children are traversed (post).

Algorithm for Preorder Traversal	Algorithm for Inorder Traversal	Algorithm for Postorder Traversal
1. **if** the tree is empty	1. **if** the tree is empty	1. **if** the tree is empty
2. Return.	2. Return.	2. Return.
else	**else**	**else**
3. Visit the root.	3. Inorder traverse the left subtree.	3. Postorder traverse the left subtree.
4. Preorder traverse the left subtree.	4. Visit the root.	4. Postorder traverse the right subtree.
5. Preorder traverse the right subtree.	5. Inorder traverse the right subtree.	5. Visit the root.

Visualizing Tree Traversals

You can visualize a tree traversal by imagining a mouse that walks along the edge of the tree. If the mouse always keeps the tree to the left (from the mouse's point of view) it will trace the route shown in color around the tree shown in Figure 8.9. This is known as an *Euler tour*.

If we record each node as the mouse first encounters it (indicated by the arrows pointing down in Figure 8.9), we get the following sequence:

    a b d g e h c f i j

This is a preorder traversal, because the mouse visits each node before traversing its subtrees. The mouse also walks down the left branch (if it exists) of each node before going down the right branch, so the mouse visits a node, traverses its left subtree, and traverses its right subtree.

If we record each node as the mouse returns from traversing its left subtree (indicated by the arrows pointing to the right in Figure 8.9), we get the following sequence:

d g b h e a i f j c

This is an inorder traversal. The mouse traverses the left subtree, visits the root, and then traverses the right subtree. Node *d* is visited first because it has no left subtree.

If we record each node as the mouse last encounters it (indicated by the arrows pointing up in Figure 8.9), we get the following sequence:

g d h e b i j f c a

This is a postorder traversal, because we visit the node after traversing both its subtrees. The mouse traverses the left subtree, traverses the right subtree, and then visits the node.

FIGURE 8.9
Traversal of a Binary
Tree

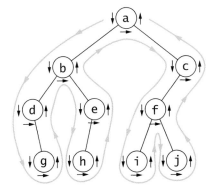

Traversals of Binary Search Trees and Expression Trees

An inorder traversal of a binary search tree results in the nodes being visited in sequence by increasing data value. For example, for the binary search tree shown earlier in Figure 8.2, the inorder traversal would visit the nodes in the sequence:

canine, cat, dog, wolf

Traversals of expression trees give interesting results. If we perform an inorder traversal of the expression tree first shown in Figure 8.4 and repeated here, we visit the nodes in the sequence x + y * a + b / c. If we insert parentheses where they belong, we get the infix expression

(x + y) * ((a + b) / c)

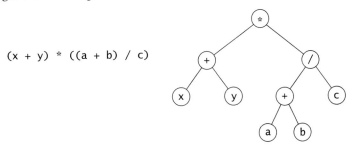

The postorder traversal of this tree would visit the nodes in the sequence

x y + a b + c / *

which is the postfix form of the expression. To illustrate this, we show the *operand-operand-operator* groupings under the expression.

The preorder traversal visits the nodes in the sequence

* + x y / + a b c

which is the prefix form of the expression. To illustrate this, we show the *operator-operand-operand* groupings under the expression.

EXERCISES FOR SECTION 8.2

SELF-CHECK

1. For the following trees:

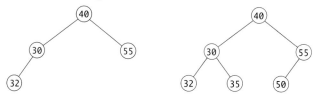

   If visiting a node displays the integer value stored, show the inorder, preorder, and postorder traversal of each tree.
2. Draw an expression tree corresponding to each of the following:
   a. Inorder traversal is x / y + 3 * b / c (Your tree should represent the Java meaning of the expression.)
   b. Postorder traversal is x y z + a b – c * / –
   c. Preorder traversal is * + a – x y / c d
3. Explain why the statement "Your tree should represent the Java meaning of the expression," was not needed for parts b and c of Exercise 2.

8.3 Implementing a BinaryTree Class

In this section we show how to use linked data structures to represent binary trees and binary tree nodes. We begin by focusing on the structure of a binary tree node.

The Node Class

Just as for a linked list, a node consists of a data part and links (references) to successor nodes. So that we can store any kind of data in a tree node, we will make the

FIGURE 8.10
Linked Structure to
Represent a Node

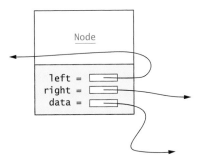

data part a reference of type Object. Instead of having a single link (reference) to a successor node as in a list, a binary tree node must have links (references) to both its left and right subtrees. Figure 8.10 shows the structure of a binary tree node; Listing 8.1 shows its implementation.

Class Node will be nested within class BinaryTree. Notice that it is declared **protected** and its data fields are all **protected**. Later, we will use the BinaryTree and Node classes as superclasses. By declaring the nested Node class and its data fields protected, we make them accessible in the subclasses of BinaryTree and Node.

The constructor for class Node creates a leaf node (both left and right are **null**). The toString method for the class just displays the data part of the node.

Both the BinaryTree class and the Node class are declared to implement the Serializable interface. The Serializable interface defines no methods; it is used to provide a marker for classes that can be written to a binary file using the ObjectOutputStream and read using the ObjectInputStream. We clarify what this means later in the section.

LISTING 8.1
Nested Class Node

```
/** Class to encapsulate a tree node. */
protected static class Node implements Serializable {
    // Data Fields
    /** The information stored in this node. */
    protected Object data;
    /** Reference to the left child. */
    protected Node left;
    /** Reference to the right child. */
    protected Node right;

    // Constructors
    /** Construct a node with given data and no children.
        @param data The data to store in this node
    */
    public Node(Object data) {
        this.data = data;
        left = null;
        right = null;
    }
```

```
            // Methods
            /** Return a string representation of the node.
                @return A string representation of the data fields
            */
            public String toString () {
                return data.toString();
            }
}
```

The BinaryTree Class

Table 8.1 shows the design of the BinaryTree class. The single data field root references the root node of a BinaryTree object. It has protected visibility because we will need to access it in subclass BinarySearchTree, discussed later in this chapter. In Figure 8.11, we draw the expression tree for ((x + y) * (a / b)) using our Node representation. Each character shown as tree data would be stored in a Character object.

EXAMPLE 8.1   Assume the tree drawn in Figure 8.11 is referenced by variable bT (type BinaryTree).

- bT.root.data references the Character object storing '*'
- bT.root.left references the left subtree of the root (the root node of tree x + y).
- bT.root.right references the right subtree of the root (the root node of tree a / b).
- bT.root.right.data references the Character object storing '/'.

FIGURE 8.11
Linked Representation
of Expression Tree
((x + y) * (a / b))

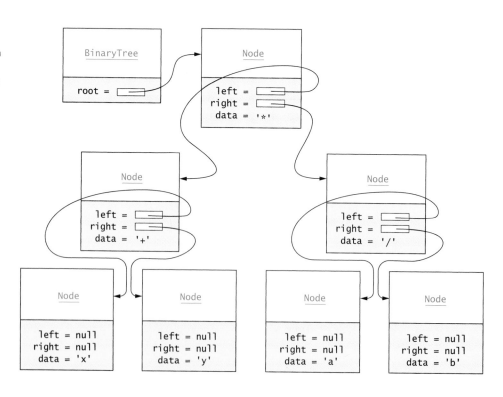

TABLE 8.1
Design of the BinaryTree Class

Data Field	Attribute
protected Node root	Reference to the root of the tree.
Constructor	**Behavior**
public BinaryTree()	Constructs an empty binary tree.
protected BinaryTree(Node root)	Constructs a binary tree with the given node as the root.
public BinaryTree(Object data, BinaryTree left, BinaryTree right)	Constructs a binary tree with the given data at the root and the two given subtrees.
Method	**Behavior**
public BinaryTree getLeftSubtree()	Returns the left subtree.
public BinaryTree getRightSubtree()	Returns the right subtree.
public Object getData()	Returns the data in the root.
public boolean isLeaf()	Returns **true** if this tree is a leaf, **false** otherwise.
public String toString()	Returns a String representation of the tree.
private void preOrderTraverse(Node node, int depth, StringBuffer sb)	Performs a preorder traversal of the subtree whose root is node. Appends the representation to the StringBuffer. Increments the value of depth (the current tree level).
public static BinaryTree readBinaryTree(BufferedReader bR)	Constructs a binary tree by reading its data from stream bR.

The class heading and data field declarations follow.

```
import java.io.Serializable;

/** Class for a binary tree that stores Object objects. */
public class BinaryTree implements Serializable {

    // Insert inner class Node here.

    // Data Field
    /** The root of the binary tree */
    protected Node root;
    . . .
}
```

The Constructors

There are three constructors: a no-parameter constructor, a constructor that creates a tree with a given node as its root, and a constructor that builds a tree from a data value and two trees.

The no-parameter constructor merely sets the data field root to **null**.

```
public BinaryTree() {
    root = null;
}
```

The constructor that takes a `Node` as a parameter is a protected constructor. This is because client classes do not know about the `Node` class. This constructor can be used only by methods internal to the `BinaryTree` class and its subclasses.

```
protected BinaryTree(Node root) {
    this.root = root;
}
```

The third constructor takes three parameters: data to be referenced by the root node, and two `BinaryTrees` that will become its left and right subtrees. If `leftTree` is not **null**, the statement

```
root.left = leftTree.root;
```

executes. After its execution, the root node of the tree referenced by `leftTree` (`leftTree.root`) is referenced by `root.left`, making `leftTree` the left subtree of the new root node. If `lT.root` references the root node of binary tree x + y and `rT.root` references the root node of binary tree a / b, the statement

```
BinaryTree bT = new BinaryTree(new Character('*'), lT, rT);
```

would cause bT to reference the tree shown in Figure 8.12.

```
/** Constructs a new binary tree with data in its root,
    leftTree as its left subtree and rightTree as its
    right subtree.
*/
public BinaryTree(Object data, BinaryTree leftTree,
                  BinaryTree rightTree) {
    root = new Node(data);
    if (leftTree != null) {
        root.left = leftTree.root;
    } else {
        root.left = null;
    }
    if (rightTree != null) {
        root.right = rightTree.root;
    } else {
        root.right = null;
    }
}
```

The getLeftSubtree and getRightSubtree Methods

The `getLeftSubtree` method returns a binary tree whose root is the left subtree of the object on which the method is called. It uses the protected constructor discussed above to construct a new `BinaryTree` object whose root references the left subtree of this tree. The `getRightSubtree` method is symmetric.

FIGURE 8.12
The Expression Tree
(x + y) * (a / b)

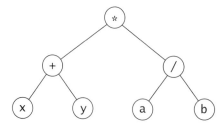

```
/** Return the left subtree.
    @return The left subtree or
            null if either the root or the
            left subtree is null
*/
public BinaryTree getLeftSubtree() {
    if (root != null && root.left != null) {
        return new BinaryTree(root.left);
    } else {
        return null;
    }
}
```

The `isLeaf` Method

The `isLeaf` method tests to see whether this tree has any subtrees. If there are no subtrees, then **true** is returned.

```
/** Determine whether this tree is a leaf.
    @return true if the root has no children
*/
boolean isLeaf() {
    return (root.left == null && root.right == null);
}
```

The `toString` Method

The `toString` method generates a string representation of the `BinaryTree` for display purposes. The string representation is a preorder traversal in which each local root is displayed indented a distance proportional to its depth. Also, if a subtree is empty, the string "null" is displayed. For example, the expression tree in Figure 8.12 would be displayed as follows:

```
*
  +
    x
      null
      null
    y
      null
      null
  /
    a
      null
      null
    b
      null
      null
```

The `toString` method creates a `StringBuffer` and then calls the recursive `preOrderTraverse` method (described next) with the root and a depth of one.

```
public String toString() {
    StringBuffer sb = new StringBuffer();
    preOrderTraverse(root, 1, sb);
    return sb.toString();
}
```

The preOrderTraverse Method

This method follows the preorder traversal algorithm given in Section 8.2. It begins by appending a string of spaces proportional to the level so that all nodes at a particular level will be indented to the same point in the tree display. Then, if the node is **null**, the string "null\n" is appended to the string buffer. Otherwise the string representation of the node is appended to the StringBuffer and the method is recursively called on the left and right subtrees.

```
/** Perform a preorder traversal.
    @param node The local root
    @param depth The depth
    @param sb The string buffer to save the output
 */
private void preOrderTraverse(Node node, int depth,
                                StringBuffer sb) {
    for (int i = 1; i < depth; i++) {
        sb.append("  ");
    }
    if (node == null) {
        sb.append("null\n");
    } else {
        sb.append(node.toString());
        sb.append("\n");
        preOrderTraverse(node.left, depth + 1, sb);
        preOrderTraverse(node.right, depth + 1, sb);
    }
}
```

Reading a Binary Tree

If we use a BufferedReader to read the individual lines created by the toString and preOrderTraverse methods previously discussed, we can reconstruct the binary tree using the algorithm:

1. Read a line that represents information at the root.
2. Remove the leading and trailing spaces using the String.trim method.
3. **if** it is "null"
4.   Return **null**.

   else

5.   Recursively read the left child.
6.   Recursively read the right child.
7.   Return a tree consisting of the root and the two children.

The code for a method that implements this algorithm is shown in Listing 8.2.

···
LISTING 8.2
Method to Read a
Binary Tree

```
/** Method to read a binary tree.
    pre: The input consists of a preorder traversal
        of the binary tree. The line "null" indicates a null tree.
    @param bR The input file
```

```
      @return The binary tree
      @throws IOException If there is an input error
  */
  public static BinaryTree readBinaryTree(BufferedReader bR)
      throws IOException {
      // Read a line and trim leading and trailing spaces.
      String data = bR.readLine().trim();
      if (data.equals("null")) {
          return null;
      } else {
          BinaryTree left = readBinaryTree(bR);
          BinaryTree right = readBinaryTree(bR);
          return new BinaryTree(data, left, right);
      }
  }
}
```

Using an `ObjectOutputStream` and `ObjectInputStream`

The Java API includes the class `ObjectOutputStream` that will write any object that is declared to be `Serializable`. You declare that an object is `Serializable` by adding the declaration

```
      implements Serializable
```

to the class declaration. The `Serializable` interface (in java.io) contains no methods, but it serves to mark the class as being `Serializable`. This gives you control over whether or not you want your class to be written to an external file. Generally you will want to have this capability.

To write an object of a `Serializable` class to a file, you do the following:

```
      try {
          ObjectOutputStream out =
              new ObjectOutputStream(new FileOutputStream(nameOfFile));
          out.writeObject(nameOfObject);
      } catch (Exception ex) {
          ex.printStackTrace();
          System.exit(1);
      }
```

The `writeObject` method performs a traversal of whatever data structure is referenced by the object being written. Thus, if the object is a binary tree, a deep copy of all of the nodes of the binary tree will be written to the file.

To read a `Serializable` class from a file, you do the following:

```
      try {
          ObjectInputStream in =
              new ObjectInputStream(new FileInputStream(nameOfFile));
          objectName = (objectClass) in.readObject();
      } catch (Exception ex) {
          ex.printStackTrace();
          System.exit(1);
      }
```

This code will reconstruct the object that was saved to the file, including any referenced objects. Thus, if a `BinaryTree` is written to an `ObjectOutputStream`, this method will read it back and restore it completely.

PITFALL

Modifying the Class File of a Serialized Object

When an object is serialized, a unique class signature is recorded with the data. If you recompile the Java source file for the class to recreate the .class file, even though you did not make any changes, the resulting .class file will have a different class signature. When you attempt to read the object, you will get an exception.

EXERCISES FOR SECTION 8.3

SELF-CHECK

1. Draw the linked representation of the two trees below.

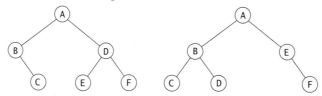

2. Show the tree that would be built by the following input string:

```
30
  15
    4
      null
      null
    20
      18
        null
        19
          null
          null
      null
  35
    32
      null
      null
    38
      null
      null
```

3. What can you say about this tree?
4. Write the strings that would be displayed for the two binary trees in Figure 8.6.

PROGRAMMING

1. Write a method that is not a member of the `BinaryTree` class to display the pre-order traversal of a binary tree as a sequence of strings each separated by a space.

Use the expression getData().toString() to obtain the string representation of the data in the root.

2. Write a method to display the postorder traversal of a binary tree in the same form as Programming Exercise 1.

3. Write a method to display the inorder traversal of a binary tree in the same form as Programming Exercise 1, except place a left parenthesis before each subtree and a right parenthesis after each subtree. Don't display anything for an empty subtree. For example the expression tree shown in Figure 8.12 would be represented as (((x) + (y)) * ((a) / (b))), and the tree on the left side of the figure in Self-Check Exercise 1 would be represented as (((C) B (D)) A (E (F))).

8.4 Binary Search Trees

Overview of a Binary Search Tree

In Section 8.1 we provided the following recursive definition of a binary search tree:

A set of nodes T is a binary search tree if either of the following is true:

- T is empty
- If T is not empty, its root node has two subtrees, T_L and T_R, such that T_L and T_R are binary search trees and the value in the root node of T is greater than all values in T_L and is less than all values in T_R.

Figure 8.13 shows a binary search tree that contains the words in lowercase from the nursery rhyme "The House That Jack Built." We can use the following algorithm to find an object in a binary search tree.

FIGURE 8.13
Binary Search Tree Containing All of the Words from "The House That Jack Built"

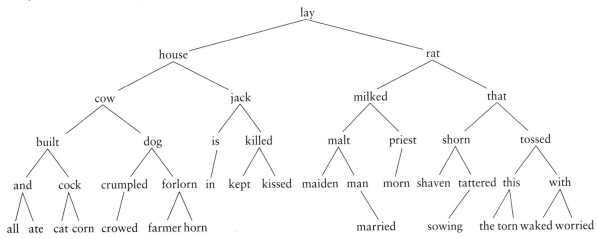

Recursive Algorithm for Searching a Binary Search Tree

1. **if** the root is **null**
2.   The item is not in the tree; return **null**.
3. Compare the value of **target**, the item being sought, with `root.data`.
4. **if** they are equal
5.   The target has been found, return the data at the root.
    else if `target` is less than `root.data`
6.   Return the result of searching the left subtree.
    else
7.   Return the result of searching the right subtree.

EXAMPLE 8.2 Suppose we wish to find *jill* in Figure 8.13. We first compare *jill* with *lay*. Because *jill* is less than *lay*, we continue the search with the left subtree and compare *jill* with *house*. Because *jill* is greater than *house*, we continue with the right subtree and compare *jill* with *jack*. Because *jill* is greater than *jack*, we continue with *killed* followed by *kept*. Now *kept* has no left child, and *jill* is less than *kept*, so we conclude that *jill* is not in this binary search tree. (She's in a different nursery rhyme.) Follow the entire path marked in color in Figure 8.14.

FIGURE 8.14
Looking for Jill

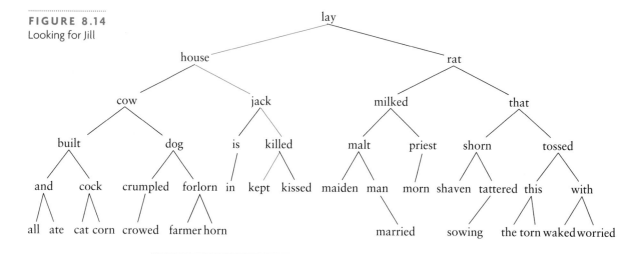

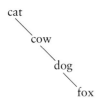

Performance

Searching the tree in Figure 8.14 is O(log *n*). However, if a tree is not very full, performance will be worse. The tree in the figure at left has only right subtrees, so searching it is O(*n*).

TABLE 8.2
The SearchTree interface

Method	Behavior
boolean add(Object item)	Inserts item where it belongs in the tree. Returns **true** if item is inserted; **false** if it isn't (already in tree).
boolean contains(Object target)	Returns **true** if target is found in the tree.
Object find(Object target)	Returns a reference to the node with target as its data if target is found. Otherwise, returns **null**.
Object delete(Object target)	Removes target (if found) from tree and returns it; otherwise, returns **null**.
boolean remove(Object target)	Removes target (if found) from tree and returns **true**; otherwise, returns **false**. Uses delete.

Class TreeSet and Interface SearchTree

The Java API provides a class TreeSet that is an implementation of a binary search tree. It provides methods add (for inserting in a tree), contains (for searching a tree), and remove (for deleting a node). Table 8.2 shows a SearchTree interface that includes these methods. We use the TreeSet class in the Case Study at the end of this section.

The BinarySearchTree Class

Next we implement class BinarySearchTree. Table 8.3 shows the data fields declared in the class. These data fields are used to store a second result from the add and delete methods. Neither result can be returned directly from the recursive add and delete methods because they return a reference to a tree node.

The class heading and data field declarations follow. Notice that class BinarySearchTree extends class BinaryTree and also implements the SearchTree interface (see Figure 8.15). Besides the data fields shown, class BinarySearchTree inherits the data field root from class BinaryTree (declared as **protected**) and also inherits the inner class Node.

TABLE 8.3
Data Fields of Class BinarySearchTree

Data Field	Attribute
protected boolean addReturn	Stores a second return value from the recursive add method that indicates whether the item has been inserted.
protected Object deleteReturn	Stores a second return value from the recursive delete method that references the item that was stored in the tree.

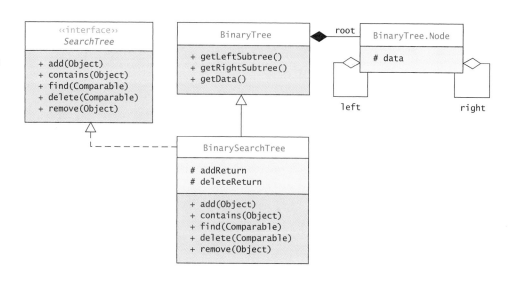

```
public class BinarySearchTree extends BinaryTree
                                    implements SearchTree {
    // Data Fields
    /** Return value from the public add method. */
    protected boolean addReturn;
    /** Return value from the public delete method. */
    protected Object deleteReturn;
...
}
```

Implementing the **find** Methods

Earlier we showed a recursive algorithm for searching a binary search tree. Next we
show how to implement this algorithm and a non-recursive starter method for the
algorithm. Our method find will return a reference to the node that contains the
information we are seeking.

Listing 8.3 shows the code for method find. The starter method calls the recursive
method with the tree root and the object being sought as its parameters. In the
starter method, the parameter target is type Object, so it must be cast to type
Comparable when the recursive find method is called. If bST is a reference to a
BinarySearchTree, the method call bST.find(target) invokes the starter method.

The recursive method first tests the local root for **null**. If it is **null**, the object is not
in the tree, so **null** is returned. If the local root is not **null**, the statement

```
int compResult = target.compareTo(localRoot.data);
```

compares target to the data at the local root. Recall that method compareTo returns
an **int** value that is either negative, zero, or positive depending on whether the
object (target) is less than, equal to, or greater than the argument (localRoot.data).

If the objects are equal, we return the data at the local root. If target is smaller, we
recursively call method find, passing the left subtree root as the parameter.

```
        return find(localRoot.left, target);
```

Otherwise, we call find to search the right subtree.

```
        return find(localRoot.right, target);
```

....

LISTING 8.3
BinarySearchTree find Method

```
/** Starter method find.
    pre: The target object must implement
         the Comparable interface.
    @param target The Comparable object being sought
    @return The object, if found, otherwise null
*/
public Object find(Object target) {
    return find(root, (Comparable) target);
}

/** Recursive find method.
    @param localRoot The local subtree's root
    @param target The object being sought
    @return The object, if found, otherwise null
*/
private Object find(Node localRoot, Comparable target) {
    if (localRoot == null)
        return null;

    // Compare the target with the data field at the root.
    int compResult = target.compareTo(localRoot.data);
    if (compResult == 0)
        return localRoot.data;
    else if (compResult < 0)
        return find(localRoot.left, target);
    else
        return find(localRoot.right, target);
}
```

 PITFALL

target is not Comparable

In the SearchTree interface (and in class TreeSet), the parameter target is declared as type Object, so it must be declared as such in the starter method. However, the recursive find method uses method compareTo, which can be applied only to Comparable objects. For this reason, we declared the parameter target as type Comparable in the recursive find method. You must cast target to type Comparable before calling the recursive find method. If target is not Comparable, you will get a ClassCastException.

Insertion into a Binary Search Tree

Inserting an item into a binary search tree follows a similar algorithm as searching for the item, because we are trying to find where in the tree the item would be, if it were there. In searching, a result of **null** is an indicator of failure; in inserting, we replace this **null** with a new leaf that contains the new item. If we reach a node that contains the object we are trying to insert, then we can't insert it (duplicates are not allowed), so we return **false** to indicate that we were unable to perform the insertion. The insertion algorithm follows.

Recursive Algorithm for Insertion in a Binary Search Tree

1.   **if** the root is **null**
2.   Replace empty tree with a new tree with the item at the root and return **true**.
3.   **else if** the item is equal to root.data
4.   The item is already in the tree; return **false**.
5.   **else if** the item is less than root.data
6.   Recursively insert the item in the left subtree.
7.   **else**
8.   Recursively insert the item in the right subtree.

The algorithm returns **true** when the new object is inserted and **false** if it is a duplicate (the second stopping case). The first stopping case tests for an empty tree. If so, a new BinarySearchTree is created and the new item is stored in its root node (Step 2).

EXAMPLE 8.3   To insert *jill* into Figure 8.13, we would follow the steps shown in Example 8.2 except that when we reached *kept* we would insert *jill* as the left child of the node that contains *kept* (see Figure 8.16).

FIGURE 8.16
Inserting Jill

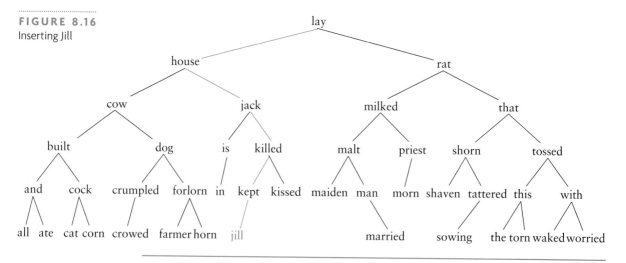

Implementing the **add** Methods

Listing 8.4 shows the code for the starter and recursive add methods. The recursive add follows the algorithm presented earlier, except that the return value is the new (sub)tree that contains the inserted item. The data field addReturn is set to **true** if the item is inserted and to **false** if the item already exists. The starter method calls the recursive method with the root as its argument. The root is set to the value returned by the recursive method (the modified tree). The value of addReturn is then returned to the caller.

In the recursive method, the statements

```
addReturn = true;
return new Node(item);
```

execute when a **null** branch is reached. The first statement sets the insertion result to **true**; the second returns a new node containing item as its data.

The statements

```
addReturn = false;
return localRoot;
```

execute when item is reached. The first statement sets the insertion result to **false**; the second returns a reference to the subtree that contains item in its root.

If item is less than the root's data, the statement

```
localRoot.left = add(localRoot.left, item);
```

attempts to insert item in the left subtree of the local root. After returning from the call, this left subtree is set to reference the modified subtree, or the original subtree if there is no insertion. The statement

```
localRoot.right = add(localRoot.right, item);
```

affects the right subtree of localRoot in a similar way.

....
LISTING 8.4
BinarySearchTree add Methods

```
/** Starter method add.
    pre: The object to insert must implement the
         Comparable interface.
    @param item The Comparable object being inserted
    @return true if the object is inserted, false
            if the object already exists in the tree
*/
public boolean add(Object item) {
    root = add(root, (Comparable) item);
    return addReturn;
}

/** Recursive add method.
    post: The data field addReturn is set true if
          the item is added to the tree, false if the
          item is already in the tree.
    @param localRoot The local root of the subtree
    @param item The object to be inserted
    @return The new local root that now contains the
            inserted item
```

```
*/
private Node add(Node localRoot, Comparable item) {
    if (localRoot == null) {
        // item is not in the tree – insert it.
        addReturn = true;
        return new Node(item);
    } else if (item.compareTo(localRoot.data) == 0) {
        // item is equal to localRoot.data
        addReturn = false;
        return localRoot;
    } else if (item.compareTo(localRoot.data) < 0) {
        // item is less than localRoot.data
        localRoot.left = add(localRoot.left, item);
        return localRoot;
    } else {
        // item is greater than localRoot.data
        localRoot.right = add(localRoot.right, item);
        return localRoot;
    }
}
```

 PROGRAM STYLE

Multiple calls to compareTo

Method add has two calls to method compareTo. We wrote it this way so that the code mirrors the algorithm. However, it would be more efficient to call compareTo once and save the result in a local variable as we did for method find. Depending on the number and type of the data fields being compared, the extra call to method compareTo could be costly.

 PROGRAM STYLE

Comment on Insertion Algorithm and add Methods

Notice as we return along the search path, the statement

```
    localRoot.left = add(localRoot.left, item);
```

or

```
    localRoot.right = add(localRoot.right, item);
```

resets each local root to reference the modified tree below it. You may wonder whether this is necessary. The answer is "No". In fact, it is only really necessary to reset the reference from the parent of the new node to the new node; all references above the parent remain the same. We can modify the insertion algorithm to do this by checking for a leaf node before making the recursive call to add:

5.1.   **else if** the item is less than root.data
5.2.   **if** the local root is a leaf node.
5.3.   Reset the left subtree to reference a new node with the item as its data.
               else
5.4.   Recursively insert the item in the left subtree.

A similar change should be made for the case where item is greater than the local root's data. You would also have to modify the starter add method to check for an empty tree and insert the new item in the root node if the tree is empty instead of calling the recursive add method.

One reason we did not write the algorithm this way is that we will want to be able to adjust the tree if the insertion makes it unbalanced. This involves resetting one or more branches above the insertion point. We discuss how this is done in Chapter 11.

Removal from a Binary Search Tree

Removal also follows the search algorithm except that when the item is found, it is removed. If the item is a leaf node, then its parent's reference to it is set to **null**, thereby removing the leaf node. If the item has only a left or right child, then the grandparent references the remaining child instead of the child's parent (the node we want to remove).

EXAMPLE 8.4   If we remove *is* from Figure 8.13, we can replace it with *in*. This is accomplished by changing the left child reference in *jack* (the grandparent) to reference *in* (see Figure 8.17).

FIGURE 8.17
Removing *is*

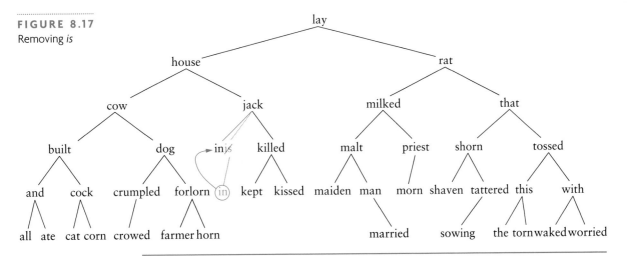

A complication arises when the item we wish to remove has two children. In this case we need to find a replacement parent for the children. Remember that the parent must be larger than all of the data fields in the left subtree and smaller than all of the data fields in the right subtree. If we take the largest item in the left subtree and promote it to be the parent, then all of the remaining items in the left subtree will be smaller. This item is also less than the items in the right subtree. This item is also known as the *inorder predecessor* of the item being removed. (We could use the inorder successor instead; this is discussed in the exercises.)

EXAMPLE 8.5   If we remove *house* from Figure 8.13, we look in the left subtree (root contains *cow*) for the largest item, *horn*. We then replace *house* with *horn* and remove the node containing *horn* (see Figure 8.18).

FIGURE 8.18
Removing *house*

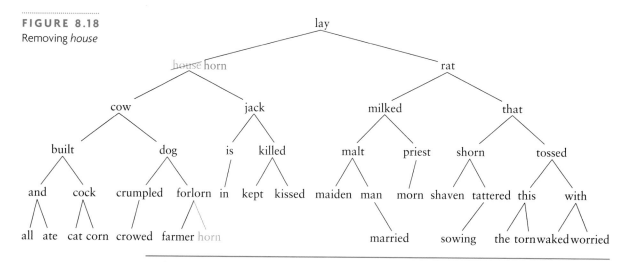

EXAMPLE 8.6   If we want to remove *rat* from the tree in Figure 8.13, we would start the search for the inorder successor at *milked* and see that it has a right child, *priest*. If we now look at *priest*, we see that it does not have a right child, but it does have a left child. We would then replace *rat* with *priest* and replace the reference to *priest* in *milked* with a reference to *morn* (the left subtree of the node containing *priest*). See Figure 8.19.

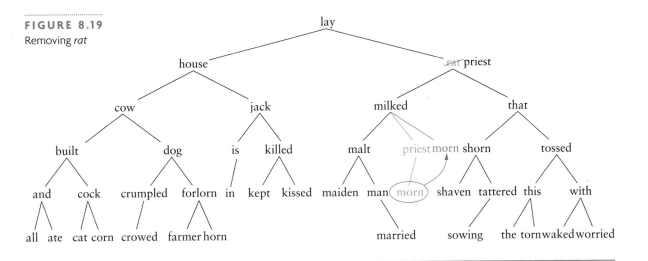

FIGURE 8.19
Removing *rat*

Recursive Algorithm for Removal from a Binary Search Tree

1. **if** the root is null
2.   The item is not in tree – return **null**.
3.   Compare the item to the data at the local root.
4. **if** the item is less than the data at the local root
5.   Return the result of deleting from the left subtree.
6. **else if** the item is greater than the local root
7.   Return the result of deleting from the right subtree.
8. **else** // *The item is in the local root*
9.   Store the data in the local root in `deletedReturn`.
10.   **if** the local root has no children
11.   Set the parent of the local root to reference **null**.
12.   **else if** the local root has one child
13.   Set the parent of the local root to reference that child.
14.   **else** // *Find the inorder predecessor*
15.   **if** the left child has no right child it is the inorder predecessor
16.   Set the parent of the local root to reference the left child.
17.   **else**
18.   Find the rightmost node in the right subtree of the left child.
19.   Copy its data into the local root's data and remove it by setting its parent to reference its left child.

Implementing the **delete** Methods

Listing 8.5 shows both the starter and the recursive delete methods. As with the add method, the recursive delete method returns a reference to a modified tree that, in this case, no longer contains the item. The public starter method is expected to return the item removed. Thus the recursive method saves this value in the data field deleteReturn before removing it from the tree. The starter method then returns this value.

LISTING 8.5

BinarySearchTree delete Methods

```java
/** Starter method delete.
    pre:  The object being deleted must be Comparable.
    post: The object is not in the tree.
    @param target The object to be deleted
    @return The object deleted from the tree
            or null if the object was not in the tree
    @throws ClassCastException if target does not implement
            Comparable
*/
public Object delete(Object target) {
    root = delete(root, (Comparable) target);
    return deleteReturn;
}

/** Recursive delete method.
    post: The item is not in the tree;
          deleteReturn is equal to the deleted item
          as it was stored in the tree or null
          if the item was not found.
    @param localRoot The root of the current subtree
    @param item The item to be deleted
    @return The modified local root that does not contain
            the item
*/
private Node delete(Node localRoot, Comparable item) {
    if (localRoot == null) {
        // item is not in the tree.
        deleteReturn = null;
        return localRoot;
    }

    // Search for item to delete.
    int compResult = item.compareTo(localRoot.data);
    if (compResult < 0) {
        // item is smaller than localRoot.data.
        localRoot.left = delete(localRoot.left, item);
        return localRoot;
    } else if (compResult > 0) {
        // item is larger than localRoot.data.
        localRoot.right = delete(localRoot.right, item);
        return localRoot;
```

```
        } else {
            // item is at local root.
            deleteReturn = localRoot.data;
            if (localRoot.left == null) {
                // If there is no left child, return right child
                // which can also be null.
                return localRoot.right;
            } else if (localRoot.right == null) {
                // If there is no right child, return left child.
                return localRoot.left;
            } else {
                // Node being deleted has 2 children, replace the data
                // with inorder predecessor.
                if (localRoot.left.right == null) {
                    // The left child has no right child.
                    // Replace the data with the data in the
                    // left child.
                    localRoot.data = localRoot.left.data;
                    // Replace the left child with its left child.
                    localRoot.left = localRoot.left.left;
                    return localRoot;
                } else {
                    // Search for the inorder predecessor (ip) and
                    // replace deleted node's data with ip.
                    localRoot.data = findLargestChild(localRoot.left);
                    return localRoot;
                }
            }
        }
    }
}
```

For the recursive method the two stopping cases are an empty tree and a tree whose root contains the item being removed. We first test to see whether the tree is empty (local root is **null**). If so, then the item sought is not in the tree. The deleteReturn data field is set to **null**, and the local root is returned to the caller.

Next localRoot.data is compared to the item to be deleted. If the item to be deleted is less than localRoot.data, it must be in the left subtree if it is in the tree at all, so we set localRoot.left to the value returned by recursively calling this method.

```
        localRoot.left = delete(localRoot.left, item);
```

If the item to be deleted is greater than localRoot.data, the statement

```
        localRoot.right = delete(localRoot.right, item);
```

affects the right subtree of localRoot in a similar way.

If localRoot.data is the item to be deleted, we have reached the second stopping case which begins with the lines

```
        } else {
            // item is at local root.
            deleteReturn = localRoot.data;
        ...
```

The value of localRoot.data is saved in deleteReturn. If the node to be deleted has one child (or zero children), we return a reference to the only child (or **null**), so the parent of the deleted node will reference its only grandchild (or **null**).

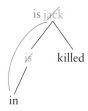

If the node to be deleted (*jack* in the figure at left) has two children, we need to find the replacement for this node. If its left child has no right subtree, the left child (*is*) is the inorder predecessor. The first statement below

```
localRoot.data = localRoot.left.data;
// Replace the left child with its left child.
localRoot.left = localRoot.left.left;
```

copies the left child's data into the local node's data (*is* to *jack*); the second resets the local node's left branch to reference its left child's left subtree (*in*).

If the left child of the node to be deleted has a right subtree, the statement

```
localRoot.data = findLargestChild(localRoot.left);
```

calls `findLargestChild` to find the largest child and to remove it. The largest child's data is referenced by `localRoot.data`. This is illustrated in Figure 8.19. The left child *milked* of the node to be deleted (*rat*) has a right child *priest*, which is its largest child. Therefore, *priest* becomes referenced by `localRoot.data` (replacing *rat*) and *morn* (the left child of *priest*) becomes the new right child of *milked*.

Method `findLargestChild`

Method `findLargestChild` (see Listing 8.6) takes the parent of a node as its argument. It then follows the chain of rightmost children until it finds a node whose right child does not itself have a right child. This is done via tail recursion.

When a parent node is found whose right child has no right child, the right child is the inorder predecessor of the node being deleted, so the data value from the right child is saved.

```
Object returnValue = parent.right.data;
parent.right = parent.right.left;
```

The right child is then removed from the tree by replacing it with its left child (if any).

LISTING 8.6
BinarySearchTree findLargestChild Method

```
/** Find the node that is the
    inorder predecessor and replace it
    with its left child (if any).
    post: The inorder predecessor is removed from the tree.
    @param parent The parent of possible inorder
                  predecessor (ip)
    @return The data in the ip
*/
private Object findLargestChild(Node parent) {
    // If the right child has no right child, it is
    // the inorder predecessor.
    if (parent.right.right == null) {
        Object returnValue = parent.right.data;
        parent.right = parent.right.left;
        return returnValue;
    } else {
        return findLargestChild(parent.right);
    }
}
```

CASE STUDY   Writing an Index for a Term Paper

Problem   You would like to write an index for a term paper. The index should show each word in the paper followed by the line number in which it occurred. The words should be displayed in alphabetical order. If a word occurs on multiple lines, the line numbers should be listed in ascending order. For example, the three lines

```
a, 3
a, 13
are, 3
```

show that the word *a* occurred on lines 3 and 13 and the word *are* occurred on line 3.

Analysis   A binary search tree is an ideal data structure to use for storing the index entries. We can store each word and its line number as a string in a tree node. For example, the two occurrences of the word *Java* on lines 5 and 10 could be stored as the strings "java, 005" and "java, 010". Each word will be stored in lowercase to ensure that it appears in its proper position in the index. The leading zeros are necessary so that the string "java, 005" is considered less than the string "java, 010". If the leading zeros were removed, this would not be the case ("java, 5" is greater than "java, 10"). After all the strings are stored in the search tree, we can display them in ascending order by performing an inorder traversal. Storing each word in a search tree is an $O(\log n)$ process where n is the number of words currently in the tree. Storing each word in an ordered list would be an $O(n)$ process.

Design   Our binary search tree will be an instance of class TreeSet, part of the java.util API. We will use class DecimalFormat, part of the java.text API, to format the line numbers. We will write a class IndexGenerator (see Table 8.4) with a TreeSet data field. Method buildIndex will read each word from a data file and store it in the search tree. Method showIndex will display the index.

TABLE 8.4
Data Fields and Methods of Class IndexGenerator

Data Field	Attribute
`private TreeSet index`	The search tree used to store the index.
Method	**Behavior**
`public void buildIndex(BufferedReader bR)`	Reads each word from the file referenced by bR and stores it in tree index.
`public void showIndex()`	Performs an inorder traversal of tree index.

Implementation   Listing 8.7 shows class IndexGenerator. In method buildIndex, the outer **while** loop reads each data line into nextLine. After incrementing lineNum, a new StringTokenizer object is created for the current data line. The inner **while** loop processes each token. The statement

```
index.add(tokens.nextToken().toLowerCase()
             + ", " + threeDigits.format(lineNum));
```

inserts in tree index a string consisting of the next word in lowercase followed by the current line number formatted with the necessary leading zeros.

In method showIndex, the statement

```
Iterator indexIt = index.iterator();
```

creates an iterator, indexIt, to tree index. A TreeSet iterator accesses the tree nodes in ascending order. Thus the **while** loop performs an inorder traversal of tree index, displaying each node's data on a separate line.

LISTING 8.7
Class IndexGenerator.java

```java
import java.io.*;
import java.util.*;
import java.text.*;

/** Class to build an index. */
public class IndexGenerator {

    // Data Fields
    /** Tree for storing the index. */
    private TreeSet index = new TreeSet();
    /** String for formatting numbers as 3 digits with leading zeros. */
    private static String LEADING_ZEROS = "000";

    // Methods
    /** Reads each word in data file bR and stores it in search tree
        along with its line number.
        post: Lowercase form of each word with line
              number stored in index.
        @param bR A reference to the data file
        @throws IOException
    */
    public void buildIndex(BufferedReader bR)
            throws IOException {
        DecimalFormat threeDigits = new DecimalFormat(LEADING_ZEROS);
        int lineNum = 0;        // Line number
        String nextLine;        // Each data line
        // Keep reading lines until done.
        while ((nextLine = bR.readLine()) != null) {
            lineNum++;
            // Create a StringTokenizer for the current data line
            // using punctuation and white space as delimiters.
```

```
                StringTokenizer tokens =
                        new StringTokenizer(nextLine, " ,.:-!?/%");
                // Insert each token in the index.
                while (tokens.hasMoreTokens()) {
                    index.add(tokens.nextToken().toLowerCase()
                            + ", " + threeDigits.format(lineNum));
                }
            }
        }

        /** Displays the index, one word per line. */
        public void showIndex() {
            Iterator indexIt = index.iterator();
            // Use iterator indexIt to access and display tree data.
            while (indexIt.hasNext()) {
                System.out.println(indexIt.next());
            }
        }
    }
```

Testing To test class IndexGenerator, write a main method that declares new BufferedReader and IndexGenerator objects. The BufferedReader can reference any text file stored on your hard drive. Make sure that duplicate words are handled properly (including duplicates on the same line), that words at the end of each line are stored in the index, that empty lines are processed correctly, and that the last line of the document is also part of the index.

EXERCISES FOR SECTION 8.4

SELF-CHECK

1. Show the tree that would be formed for the following data items. Exchange the first and last items in each list, and rebuild the tree that would be formed if the items were inserted in the new order.
   a. happy, depressed, manic, sad, ecstatic
   b. 45, 30, 15, 50, 60, 20, 25, 90
2. Explain how the tree shown in Figure 8.13 would be changed if you inserted *mother*. If you inserted *jane*? Does either of these insertions change the height of the tree?
3. Show or explain the effect of removing the nodes *kept, cow* from the tree in Figure 8.13.

4. In Exercise 3, a replacement value must be chosen for the node *cow* because it has two children. What is the relationship between the replacement word and the word *cow*? What other word in the tree could also be used as a replacement for *cow*? What is the relationship between that word and the word *cow*?

5. The algorithm for deleting a node does not explicitly test for the situation where the node being deleted has no children. Explain why this is not necessary.

6. In Step 19 of the algorithm for deleting a node, when we replace the reference to a node that we are removing with a reference to its left child, why is it not a concern that we might lose the right subtree of the node that we are removing?

PROGRAMMING

1. Write methods `contains` and `remove` for the `BinarySearchTree` class. Use methods `find` and `delete` to do the work.

2. Self-check Exercise 4 indicates that there are two items that can be used to replace a data item in a binary search tree. Rewrite method `delete` so that it retrieves the leftmost element in the right subtree instead. You will also need to provide a method `findSmallestChild`.

3. In the comment after the `add` method, we discuss how to modify the algorithm to check for a leaf node before calling the recursive `add` method. Write and test the modified methods.

8.5 Heaps and Priority Queues

In this section, we discuss a binary tree that is ordered but in a different way than a binary search tree. At each level of a heap, the value in a node is less than all values in its two subtrees. Figure 8.20 shows an example of a heap. Observe that 6 is the smallest value. Observe that each parent is smaller than its children, and that each parent has two children, with the exception of node 39 at level 3 and the leaves. Furthermore, with the exception of 66, all leaves are at the lowest level. Also, 39 is the next-to-last node at level 3, and 66 is the last (rightmost) node at level 3.

More formally, a heap is a complete binary tree with the following properties:

- The value in the root is the smallest item in the tree.
- Every subtree is a heap.

FIGURE 8.20
Example of a Heap

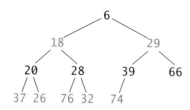

Inserting an Item into a Heap

We use the following algorithm for inserting an item into a heap. Our approach is to place each item initially in the bottom row of the heap and then move it up until it reaches the position where it belongs.

Algorithm for Inserting in a Heap

1. Insert the new item in the next position at the bottom of the heap.
2. `while` new item is not at the root and new item is smaller than its parent
3. Swap the new item with its parent, moving the new item up the heap.

New items are added to the last row (level) of a heap. If a new item is larger than or equal to its parent, nothing more need be done. If we insert 89 in the heap in Figure 8.20, 89 would become the right child of 39 and we are done. However, if the new item is smaller than its parent, the new item and its parent are swapped. This is repeated up the tree until the new item is in a position where it is no longer smaller than its parent. For example, let's add 8 to the heap shown in Figure 8.21. Since 8 is smaller than 66, these values are swapped as shown in Figure 8.22. Also, 8 is smaller than 29, so these values are swapped resulting in the updated heap shown in Figure 8.23. But 8 is greater than 6, so we are done.

Removing an Item from a Heap

Removal from a heap is always from the top. The top item is first replaced with the last item in the heap (at the lower right-hand position), so that the heap remains a complete tree. If we used any other value, there would be a "hole" in the tree where that value used to be. Then the new item at the top is moved down the heap until it is in its proper position.

Algorithm for Removal from a Heap

1. Remove the item in the root node by replacing it with the last item in the heap (LIH).
2. `while` item LIH has children and item LIH is larger than either of its children
3. Swap item LIH with its smaller child, moving LIH down the heap.

As an example, if we remove 6 from the heap shown in Figure 8.23, 66 replaces it as shown in Figure 8.24. Since 66 is larger than both of its children, it is swapped

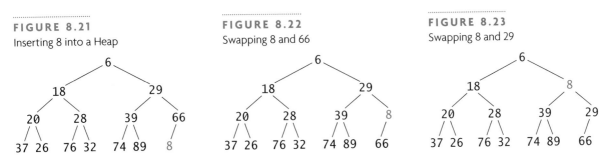

FIGURE 8.21
Inserting 8 into a Heap

FIGURE 8.22
Swapping 8 and 66

FIGURE 8.23
Swapping 8 and 29

FIGURE 8.24

After Removal of 6

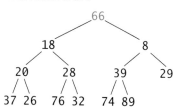

FIGURE 8.25

Swapping 66 and 8

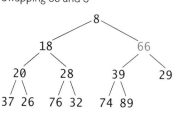

FIGURE 8.26

Swapping 66 and 29

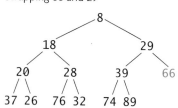

with the smaller of the two, 8, as shown in Figure 8.25. The result is still not a heap because 66 is larger than both its children. Swapping 66 with its smaller child, 29, restores the heap as shown in Figure 8.26.

Implementing a Heap

Because a heap is a complete binary tree, we can implement it efficiently using an array (or `ArrayList`) instead of a linked data structure. We can use the first element (subscript 0) for storing a reference to the root data. We can use the next two elements (subscripts 1 and 2) for storing the two children of the root. We can use elements with subscripts 3, 4, 5, and 6 for storing the four children of these two nodes, and so on. Therefore, we can view a heap as a sequence of rows; each row is twice as long as the previous row. The first row (the root) has one item, the second row two, the third four, and so on. All of the rows are full except for the last one (see Figure 8.27.)

Observe that the root, 6, is at position 0. The root's two children, 18 and 29, are at positions 1 and 2. For a node at position p, the left child is at $2p + 1$ and the right child is at $2p + 2$. A node at position c can find its parent at $(c - 1) / 2$. Thus, as shown in Figure 8.27, children of 28 (at position 4) are at positions 9 and 10.

Insertion into a Heap Implemented as an `ArrayList`

We will use an `ArrayList` for storing our heap because it is easier to expand and contract than an array is. Figure 8.28 shows the heap after it is expanded by inserting 8 into position 13. This corresponds to inserting the new value into the lower right position as shown in the figure, right. Now we need to move 8 up the heap, by comparing it to the values stored in its ancestor nodes. The parent (66) is in position 6 (13 minus 1 is 12, divided by 2 is 6). Since 66 is larger than 8, we need to swap as shown in Figure 8.29.

FIGURE 8.27

Internal Representation of the Heap

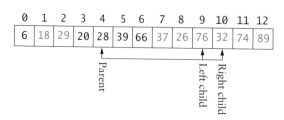

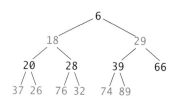

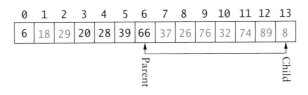
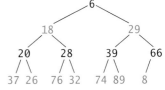

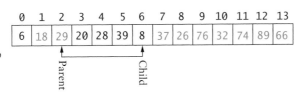
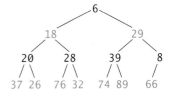

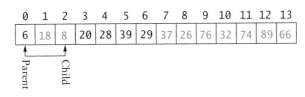
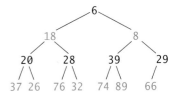

Now the child is at position 6 and the parent is at position 2 (6 minus 1 is 5, divided by 2 is 2). Since the parent, 29, is larger than the child, 8, we must swap again as shown in Figure 8.30.

The child is now at position 2 and the parent at position 0. Since the parent is smaller than the child, the heap property is restored. In the heap insertion and removal algorithms that follow, we will use `table` to reference the `ArrayList` that stores the heap. We will use `table[index]` to represent the element at position `index` of `table`. In the actual code, a subscript cannot be used with an `ArrayList`.

Insertion of an Element into a Heap Implemented as an `ArrayList`

1. Insert the new element at the end of the `ArrayList` and set `child` to `table.size() - 1`.
2. Set `parent` to `(child - 1) / 2`.
3. **while** (`parent >= 0 and table[parent] > table[child]`)
4.   Swap `table[parent]` and `table[child]`.
5.   Set `child` equal to `parent`.
6.   Set `parent` equal to `(child - 1) / 2`.

Removal from a Heap Implemented as an `ArrayList`

In removing elements from a heap, we must always remove and save the element at the top of the heap, which is the smallest element. We start with an `ArrayList` that has been organized to form a heap. To remove the first item (6), we begin by replacing the first item with the last item, and then removing the last item. This is illustrated in Figure 8.31. The new value of the root (position 0) is larger than both of

FIGURE 8.31
Internal Representation of Heap After 6 Is Removed

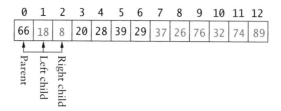

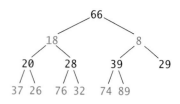

FIGURE 8.32
Internal Representation of Heap After 8 and 66 Are Swapped

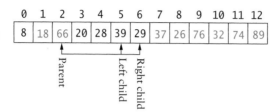

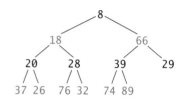

FIGURE 8.33
Internal Representation of Heap After Swap of 66 and 29

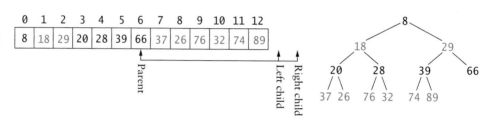

its children (18 in position 1, and 8 in position 2). The smaller of the two children (8 in position 2) is swapped with the parent as shown in Figure 8.32. Next, 66 is swapped with the smaller of its two new children (29) and the heap is restored (Figure 8.33).

The algorithm for removal from a heap implemented as an `ArrayList` follows:

Removing an Element from a Heap Implemented as an `ArrayList`

1. Remove the last element (that is, the one at `size() - 1`) and set the item at 0 to this value.
2. Set parent to 0.
3. **while (true)**
4.   Set `leftChild` to `(2 * parent) + 1` and `rightChild` to `leftChild + 1`.
5.   **if** `leftChild >= table.size()`
6.   Break out of loop.
7.   Assume `minChild` (the smaller child) is `leftChild`.
8.   **if** `rightChild < table.size()` and `table[rightChild] < table[leftChild]`
9.   Set `minChild` to `rightChild`.
10.   **if** `table[parent] > table[minChild]`
11.   Swap `table[parent]` and `table[minChild]`.

12.   Set parent to minChild.
               else
13.   Break out of loop.

The loop (Step 3) is terminated under one of two circumstances: Either the item has moved down the tree so that it has no children (line 5 is true), or it is smaller than both its children (line 10 is false). In these cases, the loop terminates (line 6 or 13). This is shown in Figure 8.33. At this point the heap property is restored, and the next smallest item can be removed from the heap.

Performance of the Heap

Method `remove` traces a path from the root to a leaf, and method `insert` traces a path from a leaf to the root. This requires at most h steps, where h is the height of the tree. The largest heap of height h is a full tree of height h. This tree has $2^h - 1$ nodes. The smallest heap of height h is a complete tree of height h, consisting of a full tree of height $h - 1$, with a single node as the left child of the leftmost child at height $h - 1$. Thus, this tree has $2^{(h-1)}$ nodes. Therefore, both `insert` and `remove` are O($\log n$) where n is the number of items in the heap.

Priority Queues

In computer science, a heap is used as the basis of a very efficient algorithm for sorting arrays, called Heapsort, which you will study in Chapter 10. The heap is also used to implement a special kind of queue called a priority queue. However, the heap is not very useful as an ADT on its own. Consequently, we will not create a Heap interface or code a class that implements it. Instead we will incorporate its algorithms when we implement a priority queue class and Heapsort.

Sometimes a FIFO (First-In-First-Out) queue may not be the best way to implement a waiting line. In a print queue you might want to print a short document before some longer documents that were ahead of the short document in the queue. For example, if you were waiting by the printer for a single page to print, it would be very frustrating to have to wait until several documents of 50 pages or more were printed just because they entered the queue before yours did. Therefore, a better way to implement a print queue would be to use a priority queue. A *priority queue* is a data structure in which only the highest-priority item is accessible. During insertion, the position of an item in the queue is based on its priority relative to the priorities of other items in the queue. If a new item has higher priority than all items currently in the queue, it will be placed at the front of the queue and, therefore, will be removed before any of the other items inserted in the queue at an earlier time. This violates the FIFO property of an ordinary queue.

EXAMPLE 8.7   Figure 8.34 sketches a print queue that at first (top of diagram) contains two documents. We will assume that each document's priority is inversely proportional to its page count (priority is $\dfrac{1}{\text{page count}}$). The middle queue shows the effect of inserting a document 3 pages long. The bottom queue shows the effect of inserting a second one-page document: It follows the earlier document with that page length.

FIGURE 8.34
Insertion into a Priority Queue

```
pages = 1            pages = 4
title = "web page 1" title = "history paper"
```

After inserting document with 3 pages

```
pages = 1             pages = 3        pages = 4
title = "web page 1"  title = "Lab1"   title = "history paper"
```

After inserting document with 1 page

```
pages = 1             pages = 1          pages = 3        pages = 4
title = "web page 1"  title = "receipt"  title = "Lab1"   title = "history paper"
```

The PriorityQueue Interface

The PriorityQueue interface is effectively the same as the Queue interface given in Chapter 6. The differences are in the specification for the peek and remove methods. These are defined to return the smallest item in the queue rather than the oldest item in the queue. Table 8.5 summarizes the PriorityQueue interface, and the complete definition is shown in Listing 8.8.

TABLE 8.5
Specification of the PriorityQueue Interface

Method	Behavior
void insert(Object item)	Inserts an item into the queue based on its priority.
Object peek()	Peeks at the smallest item in the queue.
Object remove()	Removes the smallest item in the queue.
int getSize()	Returns the size of the queue.
boolean isEmpty()	Determines whether the queue is empty.

LISTING 8.8
Interface PriorityQueue

```
/** Interface that defines a priority queue. A priority queue
    is similar to a queue, except that items are removed in
    priority order, where the smallest value is considered
    the highest priority.
*/
public interface PriorityQueue {
```

```
/** Insert an item into the queue based on its priority.
    post: The item is inserted into the priority queue.
    @param item The item to be inserted
*/
void insert(Object item);

/** Peek at the smallest item in the queue.
    post: The priority queue remains unchanged.
    @return The item with the smallest priority value
    @throws EmptyQueueException if the queue is empty
*/
Object peek();

/** Remove the smallest item in the queue.
    post: The item is no longer in the queue.
    @return The item with the smallest priority value
    @throws EmptyQueueException if the queue is empty
*/
Object remove();

/** Return the size of the queue.
    @return The number of items in the queue
*/
int getSize();

/** Determine whether the queue is empty.
    @return true if the queue is empty
*/
boolean isEmpty();
}
```

Observe that we specify the insert method to take a parameter of type Object and not of type Comparable. In many cases we will insert objects that implement Comparable into PriorityQueues, but, as we will see later, we may need to insert objects that do not implement Comparable, and we may want to specify a different ordering from that defined by the object's compareTo method. We discuss how this is done after we complete the implementation.

Classes that implement the PriorityQueue interface are free to require that the objects that are inserted implement Comparable by documenting that an exception will be thrown if they do not. This will be the case with the implementation we describe next.

Using a Heap as the Basis of a Priority Queue

The smallest item is always removed first from a priority queue (the smallest item has the highest priority) just as it is for a heap. Because insertion into and removal from a heap is $O(\log n)$, a heap can be the basis for an efficient implementation of a priority queue.

We will use an ArrayList for storage of the heap, because the size of an ArrayList automatically adjusts as elements are inserted and removed. To insert an item into the priority queue, we first insert the item at the end of the ArrayList. Then, following the algorithm described earlier, we move this item up the heap until it is smaller than its parent.

TABLE 8.6
Design of HeapPriorityQueue Class

Data Field	Attribute
ArrayList theData	An ArrayList to hold the data.

Method	Behavior
HeapPriorityQueue()	Constructs a HeapPriorityQueue that uses the objects' natural ordering.
protected int compare(Object left, Object right)	Compares two objects and returns a negative number if object left is less than object right, zero if they are equal, and a positive number if object left is greater than object right.
private void swap(int i, int j)	Exchanges the object references in theData at indexes i and j.

To remove an item from the priority queue, we take the first item from the ArrayList; this is the smallest item. We then remove the last item from the ArrayList and put it into the first position of the ArrayList, overwriting the value currently there. Then following the algorithm described earlier, we move this item down until it is smaller than its children or it has no children.

Design of **HeapPriorityQueue** Class

The design of the HeapPriorityQueue class is shown in Table 8.6. The data field theData is used to store the heap. We have added methods compare and swap to those shown earlier in Table 8.5. The class heading and data field declarations follow.

```
import java.util.*;

/** The HeapPriorityQueue implements the PriorityQueue interface
    by building a heap in an ArrayList. The heap is structured
    so that the "smallest" item is at the top.
*/
public class HeapPriorityQueue implements PriorityQueue {

    // Data Fields
    /** The ArrayList to hold the data */
    private ArrayList theData = new ArrayList();
    ...
}
```

The **compare** Method

Because the objects being compared are Comparable, method compare uses compareTo to perform the comparison.

```
/** Compare two items using their natural ordering.
    pre: Both left and right implement Comparable.
    @param left One item
    @param right The other item
    @return Negative int if left less than right,
            0 if left equals right,
```

```
            positive int if left > right
        @throws ClassCastException if items are not Comparable
    */
    protected int compare(Object left, Object right) {
        Comparable comparable = (Comparable) left;
        return comparable.compareTo(right);
    }
```

 DESIGN CONCEPT

Need to Declare compare as protected

Normally we would declare a method such as compare to be a private method because a user of the HeapPriorityQueue class would have no need to call it. However, we expect that subclasses of HeapPriorityQueue will want to override method compare, so we have given it more visibility by declaring it to be protected. This will enable it to be overridden in a subclass, which it could not be if it had private visibility. Note that protected methods still cannot be called by a user or client of the class.

The **insert** Method

The insert method appends the new item to the ArrayList theData. It then moves this item up the heap until the ArrayList is restored to a heap.

```
/** Insert an item into the priority queue.
    pre: The item to be inserted implements Comparable
        and the ArrayList theData is in heap order.
    post: The item is in the priority queue and
        theData is is heap order.
    @param item The Object to be inserted
*/
public void insert(Object item) {
    // Add the item to the heap.
    theData.add(item);
    // child is newly inserted item.
    int child = theData.size() - 1;
    int parent = (child - 1) / 2;  // Find child's parent.
    // Reheap
    while (parent >= 0 && compare(theData.get(parent),
                                theData.get(child)) > 0) {
        swap(parent, child);
        child = parent;
        parent = (child - 1) / 2;
    }
    return item;
}
```

The **remove** Method

The remove method first saves the item at the top of the heap. If there is more than one item in the heap, the method then removes the last item from the heap and places it at the top. Then it moves the item at the top down the heap until the heap property is restored. It then returns the original top of the heap.

```java
/** Remove an item from the priority queue
    pre: The ArrayList theData is in heap order.
    post: The ArrayList theData is in heap order.
    @return The item with the smallest priority value
    @throws queue.EmptyQueueException if the queue is empty
*/
public Object remove() {
    if (isEmpty()) {
        throw new queue.EmptyQueueExeption();
    }
    // Save the top of the heap.
    Object result = theData.get(0);
    // If only one item then remove it.
    if (theData.size() == 1) {
        theData.remove(0);
        return result;
    }
    /* Remove the last item from the ArrayList and place it into
       the first position. */
    theData.set(0, theData.remove(theData.size() - 1));
    // The parent starts at the top.
    int parent = 0;
    while (true) {
        int leftChild = 2 * parent + 1;
        if (leftChild >= theData.size()) {
            break; // Out of heap.
        }
        int rightChild = leftChild + 1;
        int minChild = leftChild;  // Assume leftChild is smaller.
        // See whether rightChild is smaller.
        if (rightChild < theData.size()
            && compare(theData.get(leftChild),
                    theData.get(rightChild)) > 0) {
            minChild = rightChild;
        }
        // assert: minChild is the index of the smaller child.
        // Move smaller child up heap if necessary.
        if (compare(theData.get(parent),
                theData.get(minChild)) > 0) {
            swap(parent, minChild);
            parent = minChild;
        } else { // Heap property is restored.
            break;
        }
    }
    return result;
}
```

Using a Comparator

The objects that we want to store in a priority queue may not implement Comparable, or we may want to order the objects in a different way than what is prescribed by the compareTo method. For example, files to be printed may be ordered

TABLE 8.7
The **Comparator** Interface

Method	Behavior
`int compare(Object left, Object right)`	Returns a negative value if `left` less than `right`, a positive value if `left` greater than `right`, and zero if `left` equals `right`.

by their name using the `compareTo` method, but we may want to assign priority based on their length. The Java API contains the `Comparator` interface, which allows us to specify alternative ways to compare objects. An implementation of the `Comparator` interface must implement a `compare` method that is similar to `compareTo` except that it has two parameters (see Table 8.7).

We can extend the `HeapPriorityQueue` to create the class `HeapPQwithComparator` that includes a constructor that accepts a `Comparator` object (see Figure 8.35). The class has a data field `comparator` of type `Comparator` (shown by the line with the open diamond). The `HeapPriorityQueue` method `compare` is overridden to call the `comparator.compare` method. Listing 8.9 shows the listing for the class `HeapPQwith Comparator`.

FIGURE 8.35
UML Class Diagram of
HeapPQwithComparator

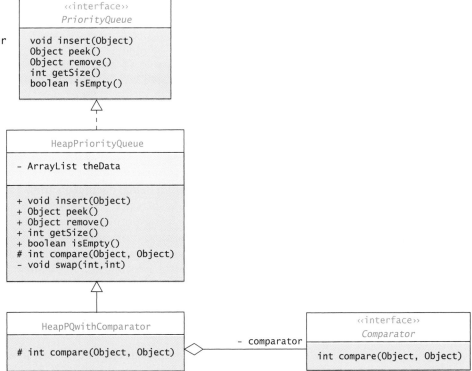

LISTING 8.9
HeapPQwithComparator.java

```java
import java.util.*;

/** The HeapPQwithComparator extends the HeapPriorityQueue
    by providing for a Comparator object that overrides the
    natural ordering of the items or provides an ordering for
    items that do not implement Comparable.
*/
public class HeapPQwithComparator extends HeapPriorityQueue {

    // Data Fields
    /** The Comparator object to define the ordering. */
    private Comparator comparator;

    // Methods
    /** Construct a HeapPQwithComparator that uses the provided
        Comparator to define the ordering.
        @param comparator The comparator to use
    */
    public HeapPQwithComparator(Comparator comparator) {
        this.comparator = comparator;
    }

    /** Compare two items using
        the ordering defined by the Comparator.
        @param left One item
        @param right The other item
        @return a negative number if left < right,
                zero if left == right,
                a positive number if left > right
        @throws NullPointerException if comparator is null
    */
    protected int compare(Object left, Object right) {
        return comparator.compare(left, right);
    }
}
```

EXAMPLE 8.8   The class PrintDocument is used to define documents to be printed on a printer. This class implements the Comparable interface, but the result of its compareTo method is based on the name of the file being printed. The class also has a getSize method that gives the number of bytes to be transmitted to the printer, and a getTimeStamp which gets the time that the print job was submitted. Instead of basing the ordering on file names, we want to order the documents by a value that is a function of both size and time submitted. If we were to use either time or size alone, small documents could be delayed while big ones are printed, or the big documents would never be printed. By using a priority value that is a combination, we achieve a balanced usage of the printer.

We define the Comparator for our PrintDocument class as shown in Listing 8.10. The method orderValue computes the weighted sum of the size and timeStamp using the weighting factors P1 and P2. The method `Double.compare` is defined by the Java API. It compares two `double` values and returns −1, 0, or +1 depending on whether its left argument is less than, equal to, or greater than its right argument.

In a client program, we can use the statement

```
PriorityQueue printQueue =
    new HeapPQwithComparator(new ComparePrintDocuments());
```

to create a print queue (referenced by `printQueue`). The argument expression `new ComparePrintDocuments()` creates a new object that implements the `Comparator` interface. This object will be referenced by data field `comparator` in the priority queue.

LISTING 8.10
ComparePrintDocuments.java

```
import java.util.Comparator;

/** Class to compare PrintDocuments based on both
    their size and time stamp.
*/
public class ComparePrintDocuments implements Comparator {
    /** Weight factor for size. */
    private static final double P1 = 0.8;
    /** Weight factor for time. */
    private static final double P2 = 0.2;

    /** Compare two PrintDocuments.
        @param left The left-hand side of the comparison
        @param right The right-hand side of the comparison
        @return -1 if left < right; 0 if left == right;
                and +1 if left > right
        @throws ClassCastException if left or right is not
                a PrintDocument
    */
    public int compare(Object left, Object right) {
        PrintDocument leftPD = (PrintDocument) left;
        PrintDocument rightPD = (PrintDocument) right;
        return Double.compare(orderValue(leftPD), orderValue(rightPD));
    }

    /** Compute the order value for a print document.
        @param pd The PrintDocument
        @return The order value based on the size and time stamp
    */
    private double orderValue(PrintDocument pd) {
        return P1 * pd.getSize() + P2 * pd.getTimeStamp();
    }
}
```

EXERCISES FOR SECTION 8.5

SELF-CHECK

1. Show the heap that would be used to store the words *this, is, the, house, that, jack, built,* assuming they are inserted in that sequence. Exchange the order of arrival of the first and last words and build the new heap.

2. Draw the heaps for Exercise 1 as arrays.

3. Show the result of removing the number 18 from the heap in Figure 8.26. Show the new heap and its array representation.

PROGRAMMING

1. Complete the implementation of the `HeapPriorityQueue` class. Write method `swap`. Also write methods `peek`, `isEmpty`, and `getSize`.

8.6 Huffman Trees

In Section 8.1 we showed the Huffman coding tree and how it can be used to decode a message. We will now implement some of the methods needed to build a tree and decode a message. We will do this using a binary tree and a `PriorityQueue` (which also uses a binary tree).

A straight binary coding of an alphabet assigns a unique binary number k to each symbol in the alphabet a_k. An example of such a coding is Unicode, which is used by Java for the **char** data type. There are 65,536 possible characters and they are assigned a number between 0 and 65,535, which is a string of 16 binary digit ones. Therefore, the length of a message would be $16 \times n$, where n is the total number of characters in the message. For example, the message "go eagles" contains 9 characters and would require 9×16 or 144 bits. As shown in the example in Section 8.1, a Huffman coding of this message requires just 38 bits.

Table 8.8, based on data published in Donald Knuth, *The Art of Computer Programming, Vol 3: Sorting and Searching* (Addison-Wesley, 1973), p. 441, represents the relative frequencies of the letters in English text and is the basis of the tree shown in Figure 8.36. The letter *e* occurs an average of 103 times every 1,000 letters, or 10.3% of the letters are *e*'s. (This is a useful table to know if you are a fan of *Wheel of Fortune*.) We can use this Huffman tree to encode and decode a file of English text. However, files may contain other symbols or may contain these symbols in different frequencies than what is found in normal English. For this reason, you may want to build a custom Huffman tree based on the contents of the file you are encoding. You would then attach this tree to the encoded file so that it can be used to decode the file. We discuss how to build a Huffman tree in the next case study.

TABLE 8.8
Frequency of Letters in English Text

Symbol	Frequency	Symbol	Frequency	Symbol	Frequency
⎵	186	h	47	g	15
e	103	d	32	p	15
t	80	l	32	b	13
a	64	u	23	v	8
o	63	c	22	k	5
i	57	f	21	j	1
n	57	m	20	q	1
s	51	w	18	x	1
r	48	y	16	z	1

FIGURE 8.36
Huffman Tree Based on Frequency of Letters in English Text

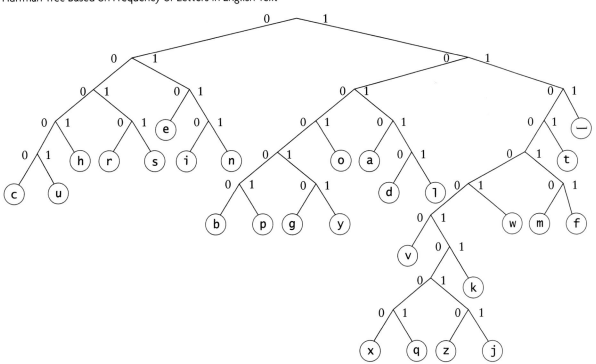

CASE STUDY   Building a Custom Huffman Tree

Problem You want to build a custom Huffman tree for a particular file. Your input will consist of an array of objects such that each object contains a reference to a symbol occurring in that file and the frequency of occurrence (weight) for the symbol in that file.

Analysis Each node of a Huffman tree has storage for two data items: the weight of the node and the symbol associated with that node. All symbols will be stored at leaf nodes. For nodes that are not leaf nodes, the symbol part has no meaning. The weight of a leaf node will be the frequency of the symbol stored at that node. The weight of an interior node will be the sum of frequencies of all nodes in the subtree rooted at the interior node. For example, the interior node with leaf nodes *c* and *u* (on the left of Figure 8.36), would have a weight of 45 (22 + 23).

We will use a priority queue as the key data structure in constructing the Huffman tree. We will store individual symbols and subtrees of multiple symbols in order by their priority (frequency of occurrence). We want to remove symbols that occur less frequently first because they should be lower down in the Huffman tree we are constructing. We discuss how this is done next.

FIGURE 8.37
Priority Queue with the Symbols *a, b, c, d,* and *e*

13	22	32	64	103
b	c	d	a	e

To build a Huffman tree, we start by inserting references to trees with just leaf nodes in a priority queue. Each leaf node will store a symbol and its weight. The queue elements will be ordered so that the leaf node with smallest weight (lowest frequency) is removed first. Figure 8.37 shows a priority queue, containing just the symbols *a, b, c, d, e*, that uses the weights shown in Table 8.8. The item at the front of the queue stores a reference to a tree with a root node that is a leaf node containing the symbol *b* with a weight (frequency) of 13. To represent the tree referenced by a queue element, we list the root node information for that tree. The queue elements are shown in priority order.

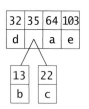

Now we start to build the Huffman tree. We build it from the bottom up. The first step is to remove the first two tree references from the priority queue and combine them to form a new tree. The weight of the root node for this tree will be the sum of the weights of its left and right subtrees. We insert the new tree back into the priority queue. The priority queue now contains references to four binary trees instead of five. The tree referenced by the second element of the queue has a combined weight of 35 (13 + 22) as shown at left.

Again we remove the first two tree references and combine them. The new binary tree will have a weight of 67 in its root node. We put this tree back in the queue, and it will be referenced by the second element of the queue.

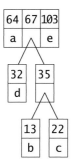

We repeat this process again. The new queue follows:

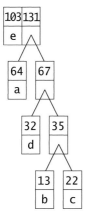

Finally we combine the last two elements into a new tree and put a reference to it in the priority queue. Now there is only one tree in the queue, so we have finished building the Huffman tree (see Figure 8.38). Table 8.9 shows the codes for this tree.

FIGURE 8.38
Huffman Tree of *a, b, c, d, e*

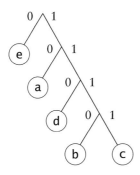

TABLE 8.9
Huffman Code for *a, b, c, d, e*

Symbol	Code
a	10
b	1110
c	1111
d	110
e	0

TABLE 8.10
Data Fields and Methods of Class `HuffmanTree`

Data Field	Attribute
`BinaryTree huffTree`	A reference to the Huffman tree.

Method	Behavior
`buildTree(HuffData[] input)`	Builds the Huffman tree using the given alphabet and weights.
`String decode(String message)`	Decodes a message using the generated Huffman tree.
`printCode(PrintStream out)`	Outputs the resulting code.

Design The class `HuffData` will represent the data to be stored in each node of the Huffman binary tree. For a leaf, a `HuffData` object will contain the symbol and the weight.

Our class `HuffmanTree` will have the methods and attributes listed in Table 8.10.

Algorithm for Building a Huffman Tree

1. Construct a set of trees with root nodes that contain each of the individual symbols and their weights.
2. Place the set of trees into a priority queue.
3. **while** the priority queue has more than one item
4.   Remove the two trees with the smallest weights.
5.   Combine them into a new binary tree in which the weight of the tree root is the sum of the weights of its children.
6.   Insert the newly created tree back into the priority queue.

Each time through the **while** loop, two nodes are removed from the priority queue and one is inserted. Thus, effectively one tree is removed, and the queue gets smaller with each pass through the loop.

Implementation Listing 8.11 shows the `HuffmanTree` class. The `Comparator` class and the methods are discussed in following subsections.

LISTING 8.11
Class `HuffmanTree`

```
/** Class to represent and build a Huffman tree. */
public class HuffmanTree implements Serializable {

    // Nested classes
    /** A datum in the Huffman tree. */
    public static class HuffData implements Serializable {
```

```
        // Data Fields
        /** The weight or probability assigned to this HuffData. */
        private double weight;
        /** The alphabet symbol if this is a leaf. */
        private Object symbol;

        public HuffData(double weight, Object symbol) {
            this.weight = weight;
            this.symbol = symbol;
        }
    }

    /** Insert a nested Comparator class for Huffman trees. */
    // See CompareHuffmanTrees below.

    // Data Fields
    /** A reference to the Huffman tree. */
    private BinaryTree huffTree;

    // Methods
    // Methods are discussed in the text and in separate listings.
}
```

The Comparator

Since the `BinaryTree` class does not implement `Comparable`, we need to define a comparator for use with our `HeapPriorityQueue`. This `CompareHuffmanTrees` class will compare the weights in the `HuffData` objects stored in each node of the `BinaryTree`.

```
/** A Comparator for Huffman trees; nested class. */
private static class CompareHuffmanTrees implements Comparator {
    /** Compare two objects.
        @param left The left-hand object
        @param right The right-hand object
        @return -1 if left less than right,
                0 if left equals right,
                and +1 if left greater than right
    */
    public int compare(Object left, Object right) {
        BinaryTree treeLeft = (BinaryTree) left;
        BinaryTree treeRight = (BinaryTree) right;
        double wLeft = ((HuffData) treeLeft.getData()).weight;
        double wRight = ((HuffData) treeRight.getData()).weight;
        return Double.compare(wLeft, wRight);
    }
}
```

The **buildTree** Method

Method `buildTree` (see Listing 8.12) takes an array of `HuffData` objects. The **for** loop loads the priority queue with trees consisting of just leaf nodes. Each leaf node contains a `HuffData` object with the weight and alphabet symbol.

The **while** loop builds the tree. Each time through this loop, the trees with the smallest weights are removed and referenced by left and right. The statements

```
HuffData sum = new HuffData(wl + wr, null);
BinaryTree newTree = new BinaryTree(sum, left, right);
```

combine them to form a new BinaryTree with a root node whose weight is the sum of the weights of its children. This new tree is then inserted into the priority queue. The number of trees in the queue decreases by 1 each time we do this. Eventually there will only be one tree in the queue, and that will be the Huffman tree. The final statement sets the variable huffTree to reference this tree.

LISTING 8.12
The buildTree Method (HuffmanTree.java)

```
/** Builds the Huffman tree using the given alphabet and weights.
    post:  huffTree contains a reference to the Huffman tree.
    @param symbols An array of HuffData objects
*/
public void buildTree(HuffData[] symbols) {
    HeapPriorityQueue theQueue
            = new HeapPriorityQueue(new CompareHuffmanTrees());
    // Load the queue with the leaves.
    for (int i = 0; i < symbols.length; i++) {
        BinaryTree aBinaryTree =
                new BinaryTree(symbols[i], null, null);
        theQueue.insert(aBinaryTree);
    }

    // Build the tree.
    while (theQueue.getSize() > 1) {
        BinaryTree left = (BinaryTree) theQueue.remove();
        BinaryTree right = (BinaryTree) theQueue.remove();
        double wl = ((HuffData) left.getData()).weight;
        double wr = ((HuffData) right.getData()).weight;
        HuffData sum = new HuffData(wl + wr, null);
        BinaryTree newTree = new BinaryTree(sum, left, right);
        theQueue.insert(newTree);
    }

    // The queue should now contain only one item.
    huffTree = (BinaryTree) theQueue.remove();
}
```

Testing   Methods printCode and decode can be used to test the custom Huffman tree. Method printCode displays the tree, so you can examine it and verify that the Huffman tree is correct based on the input data.

Method decode will decode a message that has been encoded using the code stored in the Huffman tree and displayed by printCode. So you can pass it a message string that consists of binary digits only and see whether it can be transformed back to the original symbols.

We will discuss testing the Huffman tree further in the next chapter when we continue the case study.

The `printCode` Method

To display the code for each alphabet symbol, we perform a preorder traversal of the final tree. The code so far is passed as a parameter, along with the current node. If the current node is a leaf, as indicated by the symbol not being **null**, then the code is output. Otherwise the left and right subtrees are traversed. When we traverse the left subtree, we append a 0 to the code, and when we traverse the right subtree, we append a 1 to the code. Recall that at each level in the recursion there is a new copy of the parameters and local variables.

```
/** Outputs the resulting code.
    @param out A PrintStream to write the output to
    @param code The code up to this node
    @param tree The current node in the tree
*/
private void printCode(PrintStream out, String code,
                       BinaryTree tree) {
    Datum datum = (Datum) tree.getData();
    if (datum.symbol != null) {
        out.println(datum.symbol + ": " + code);
    } else {
        printCode(out, code + "0", tree.getLeftSubtree());
        printCode(out, code + "1", tree.getRightSubtree());
    }
}
```

The `decode` Method

To illustrate the decode process we will show a method that takes a String that contains a sequence of the digit characters '0' and '1' and decodes it into a message that is also a String. Method decode starts by setting currentTree to the Huffman tree. It then loops through the coded message one character at a time. If the character is a '1' then currentTree is set to the right subtree; otherwise it is set to the left subtree. If the currentTree is now a leaf, the symbol is appended to the result, and currentTree is reset to the Huffman tree (see Listing 8.13). Note that this method is for testing purposes only. In actual usage, a message would be coded as a string of bits (not digit characters) and would be decoded one bit at a time.

LISTING 8.13

The decode Method (HuffmanTree.java)

```
/** Method to decode a message that is input as a string of
    digit characters '0' and '1'.
    @param codedMessage The input message as a String of
                        zeros and ones.
    @return The decoded message as a String
*/
```

```
public String decode(String codedMessage) {
    StringBuffer result = new StringBuffer();
    BinaryTree currentTree = huffTree;
    for (int i = 0; i < codedMessage.length(); i++) {
        if (codedMessage.charAt(i) == '1') {
            currentTree = currentTree.getRightSubtree();
        } else {
            currentTree = currentTree.getLeftSubtree();
        }
        if (currentTree.isLeaf()) {
            HuffData datum = (HuffData) currentTree.getData();
            result.append(datum.symbol);
            currentTree = huffTree;
        }
    }
    return result.toString();
}
```

EXERCISES FOR SECTION 8.6

SELF-CHECK

1. What is the Huffman code for the letters *a, j, k, l, s, t, v* using Figure 8.36?
2. Create the Huffman code tree for the following frequency table:

Symbol	Frequency
*	50
+	30
–	25
/	10
%	5

3. What would the Huffman code look like if all symbols in the alphabet had equal frequency?

PROGRAMMING

1. Write a method encode for the HuffmanTree class that encodes a String of letters that is passed as its first argument. Assume that a second argument, codes (type String []), contains the code strings (binary digits) for the symbols (space at position 0, *a* at position 1, *b* at position 2, and so on).

Chapter Review

- A tree is a recursive, nonlinear data structure that is used to represent data that is organized as a hierarchy.

- A binary tree is a collection of nodes with three components: a reference to a data object, a reference to a left subtree, and a reference to a right subtree. A binary tree object has a single data field, which references the root node of the tree.

- In a binary tree used to represent arithmetic expressions, the root node should store the operator that is evaluated last. All interior nodes store operators, and the leaf nodes store operands. An inorder traversal (traverse left subtree, visit root, traverse right subtree) of an expression tree yields an infix expression, a preorder traversal (visit root, traverse left subtree, traverse right subtree) yields a prefix expression, and a postorder traversal (traverse left subtree, traverse right subtree, visit root) yields a postfix expression.

- A binary search tree is a tree in which the data stored in the left subtree of every node is less than the data stored in the root node, and the data stored in the right subtree of every node is greater than the data stored in the root node. The performance depends on the fullness of the tree and can range from $O(n)$ (for trees that resemble linked lists) to $O(\log n)$ if the tree is full. An inorder traversal visits the nodes in increasing order.

- A heap is a complete binary tree in which the data in each node is less than the data in both its subtrees. A heap can be implemented very effectively as an array. The children of the node at subscript p are at subscripts $2p + 1$ and $2p + 2$. The parent of child c is at $(c - 1) / 2$. The item at the top of a heap is the smallest item.

- Insertion and removal in a heap are both $O(\log n)$. For this reason, a heap can be used to efficiently implement a priority queue. A priority queue is a data structure in which the item with the highest priority (indicated by the smallest value) is removed next. The item with the highest priority is at the top of a heap and is always removed next.

- A Huffman tree is a binary tree used to store a code that facilitates file compression. The length of the bit string corresponding to a symbol in the file is inversely proportional to its frequency, so the symbol with the highest frequency of occurrence has the shortest length. In building a Huffman tree, a priority queue is used to store the symbols and trees formed so far. Each step in building the Huffman tree consists of removing two items and forming a new tree with these two items as the left and right subtrees of the new tree's root node. A reference to each new tree is inserted in the priority queue.

Java API Interfaces and Classes Introduced in This Chapter

```
java.util.Comparator
java.text.DecimalFormat
java.util.TreeSet
```

User-Defined Interfaces and Classes in This Chapter

BinaryTree   HuffData
BinarySearchTree   PriorityQueue
Node   HeapPriorityQueue
IndexGenerator   HeapPQWithComparator
HuffmanTree   ComparePrintDocuments

Quick-Check Exercises

1. For the following expression tree

   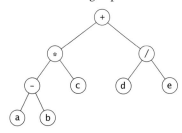

   a. Is the tree full? _____ Is the tree complete? _____
   b. List the order in which the nodes would be visited in a preorder traversal.
   c. List the order in which the nodes would be visited in an inorder traversal.
   d. List the order in which the nodes would be visited in a postorder traversal.
2. Searching a full binary search tree is O(____).
3. A heap is a binary tree that is a (full / complete) tree.
4. Show the binary search tree that would result from inserting the items 35, 20, 30, 50, 45, 60, 18, 25 in this sequence.
5. Show the binary search tree in Exercise 4 after 35 is removed.
6. Show the heap that would result from inserting the items from Exercise 4 in the order given.
7. Draw the heap from Exercise 6 as an array.
8. Show the heap in Exercise 7 after 18 is removed.
9. In a Huffman tree, the item with the highest frequency of occurrence will have the _____ code.
10. List the code for each symbol shown in the following Huffman tree.

    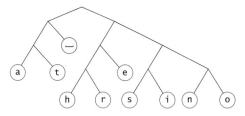

Answers to Quick-Check Exercises

1. **a.** Not full, complete
   b. + * – a b c / d e
   c. a – b * c + d / e
   d. a b – c * d e / +
2. $O(\log n)$.
3. A heap is a binary tree that is a *complete* tree.
4.

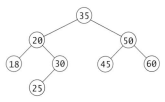

5.

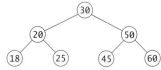

6.

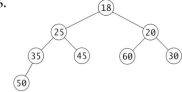

7. 18, 25, 20, 35, 45, 60, 30, 50, where 18 is at position 0 and 50 is at position 7.
8.

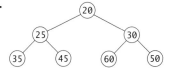

9. In a Huffman tree, the item with the highest frequency of occurrence will have the *shortest* code.
10.

Symbol	Code	Symbol	Code
Space	01	n	1110
a	000	o	1111
e	101	r	1001
h	1000	s	1100
i	1101	t	001

Review Questions

1. Draw the tree that would be formed by inserting the words in this question into a binary search tree. Use lowercase letters.
2. Show all 3 traversals of this tree.
3. Show the tree from Question 1 after removing *draw, by,* and *letters* in that order.
4. Answer Question 1, but store the words in a heap instead of a binary search tree.
5. Given the following frequency table, construct a Huffman code tree. Show the initial priority queue and all changes in its state as the tree is constructed.

Symbol	Frequency
x	34
y	28
w	20
a	10
b	8
c	5

Programming Projects

1. Assume that a class `ExpressionTree` has a data field that is a `BinaryTree`. Write an instance method to evaluate an expression stored in a binary tree whose nodes contain either integer values (stored in `Integer` objects) or operators (stored in `Character` objects). Your method should implement the following algorithm:

Algorithm to Evaluate an Expression Tree

```
1.    if the root node is an Integer object
2.        Return the integer value.
3.    else if the root node is a Character object
4.        Let leftVal be the value obtained by recursively applying this algorithm to
          the left subtree.
5.        Let rightVal be the value obtained by recursively applying this algorithm
          to the right subtree.
6.        Return the value obtained by applying the operator in the root node to
          leftVal and rightVal.
```

Use method `readBinaryTree` to read the expression tree in.

2. Write an application to test the `HuffmanTree` class. Your application will need to read a text file and build a frequency table for the characters occurring in that file. Once that table is built, create a Huffman code tree and then a string consisting of `'0'` and `'1'` digit characters that represents the code string for that file. Read that string back in and recreate the contents of the original file.

3. Solve Programming Project 4 in Chapter 6, "Queues", using the class `HeapPriorityQueue`.

4. In a breadth-first traversal of a binary tree, the nodes are visited in an order prescribed by their level. First visit the node at level 1, the root node. Then visit the nodes at level 2, in left-to-right order, and so on. You can use a queue to implement a breadth-first traversal of a binary tree:

Algorithm for Breadth-First Traversal of a Binary Tree

1.   Insert the root node in the queue.
2.   **while** the queue is not empty
3.   Remove a node from the queue and visit it.
4.   Place references to its left and right subtrees in the queue.

Code this algorithm and test it on several binary trees.

5. Define an `IndexTree` class by extending the `BinarySearchTree` class. Class `IndexTree` should have additional data fields to store the count of occurrences of each word in the tree and the line number for each occurrence. Use an `ArrayList` to store the line numbers. Use an `IndexTree` object to store an index of words appearing in a text file and then display the index by performing an inorder traversal of this tree.

6. The Morse code (see Table 8.11) is a common code that is used to encode messages consisting of letters and digits. Each letter consists of a series of dots and dashes; for example, the code for the letter *a* is ·- and the code for the letter *b* is -··· . Store each letter of the alphabet in a node of a binary tree of level 5. The root node is at level 1 and stores no letter. The left node at level 2 stores the letter *e* (code is ·) and the right node stores the letter *t* (code is –). The 4 nodes at level 3 store the letters with codes (··, ·-, -·, --). To build the tree (see Figure 8.39), read a file in which each line consists of a letter followed by its code. The letters should be ordered by tree level. To find the position for a letter in the tree, scan the code and branch left for a dot and branch right for a dash. Encode a message by replacing each letter by its code symbol. Then decode the message using the Morse code tree. Make sure you use a delimiter symbol between coded letters.

TABLE 8.11
Morse Code for Letters

a	·-	b	-···	c	-·-·
d	-··	e	·	f	··-·
g	--·	h	····	i	··
j	·---	k	-·-	l	·-··
m	--	n	-·	o	---
p	·--·	q	--·-	r	·-·
s	···	t	-	u	··-
v	···-	w	·--	x	-··-
y	-·--	z	--··		

FIGURE 8.39
Morse Code Tree

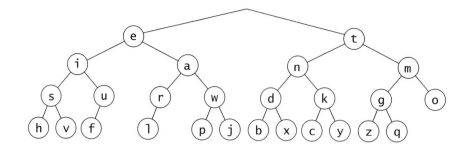

Sets and Maps

In Chapter 4 we introduced the Java Collection interface, focusing on the List interface and the classes that implement it (ArrayList and LinkedList). The classes that implement the List interface are all indexed collections. That is, there is an index or subscript associated with each member (element) of an object of these classes. Often an element's index reflects the relative order of its insertion in the List object. Searching for a particular value in a List object is generally an O(n) process. The exception is a binary search of a sorted object, which is an O(log n) process.

In this chapter we consider the other part of the Collection hierarchy: the Set interface and the classes that implement it. Set objects are not indexed, and the order of insertion of items is not known. Their main purpose is to enable efficient search and retrieval of information. It is also possible to remove elements from these collections without moving other elements around. By contrast, if an element is removed from the collection in an ArrayList object, the elements that follow it are normally shifted over to fill the vacated space.

A second, related interface is the Map. Map objects provide efficient search and retrieval of entries that consist of pairs of objects. The first object in each pair is the key (used for search and retrieval), and the second object is the information associated with that key.

We also study the hash table data structure. The hash table is a very important data structure that has been used very effectively in compilers and in building dictionaries. It can be used as the underlying data structure for a Map or Set implementation. It stores objects at arbitrary locations and offers an average constant time for insertion, removal, and searching.

We will see two ways to implement a hash table and how to use it as the basis for a class that implements the Map or Set. We will not show you the complete implementation of an object that implements Map or Set, because we expect that you will use the ones provided by the Java API. However, we will certainly give you a head start on what you need to know to implement these interfaces.

Sets and Maps

9.1 Sets and the Set Interface

We introduced the Collection hierarchy in Chapter 4. We covered the part of that hierarchy that focuses on the List interface and its implementers. In this section we explore the Set interface and its implementers.

Figure 9.1 shows the part of the Collection hierarchy that relates to sets. It includes three interfaces, two abstract classes, and two actual classes: HashSet and TreeSet. The HashSet is a set that is implemented using a hash table (discussed later). The TreeSet is implemented using a special kind of binary search tree, called the Red-Black tree (discussed in Chapter 11). In Section 8.4, we showed how to use a TreeSet to store an index for a term paper.

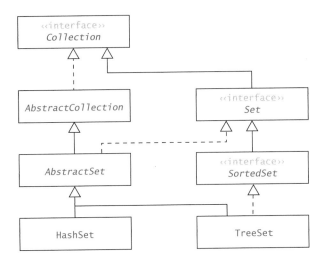

The Set Abstraction

The Java API documentation for the interface java.util.Set describes the Set as follows:

> A collection that contains no duplicate elements. More formally, sets contain no pair of elements e1 and e2 such that e1.equals(e2), and at most one null element. As implied by its name, this interface models the mathematical *set* abstraction.

What mathematicians call a *set* can be thought of as a collection of objects. There is the additional requirement that the elements contained in the set are unique. For example, if we have the set of fruits {"apples", "oranges", and "pineapples"} and add "apples" to it, we still have the same set. Also, we usually want to know whether or not a particular object is a member of the set rather than where in the set it is located. Thus, if s is a set, we would be interested in the expression

    s.contains("apples")

which returns the value **true** if "apples" is in set s and **false** if it is not. We would have no need to use a method such as

    s.indexOf("apples")

which might return the location or position of "apples" in set s. Nor would we have a need to use the expression

    s.get(i)

where i is the position (index) of an object in set s.

We assume that you are familiar with sets from a course in discrete mathematics. Just as a review, however, the operations that are performed on a mathematical set are testing for membership (method contains), adding elements, and removing elements. Other common operations on a mathematical set are *set union* $(A \cup B)$, *set intersection* $(A \cap B)$, and *set difference* $(A - B)$. There is also a *subset operator* $(A \subset B)$. These operations are defined as follows:

- The union of two sets A, B is a set whose elements belong either to A or B or to both A and B. Example: {1, 3, 5, 7} ∪ {2, 3, 4, 5} is {1, 2, 3, 4, 5, 7}
- The intersection of sets A, B is the set whose elements belong to both A and B. Example: {1, 3, 5, 7} ∩ {2, 3, 4, 5} is {3, 5}.
- The difference of sets A, B is the set whose elements belong to A but not to B. Examples: {1, 3, 5, 7} – {2, 3, 4, 5} is {1, 7}; {2, 3, 4, 5} – {1, 3, 5, 7} is {2, 4}
- Set A is a subset of set B if every element of set A is also an element of set B. Example: {1, 3, 5, 7} ⊂ {1, 2, 3, 4, 5, 7} is true.

The Set Interface and Methods

A `Set` has required methods for testing for set membership (`contains`), testing for an empty set (`isEmpty`), determining the set size (`size`), and creating an iterator over the set (`iterator`). It has optional methods for adding an element (`add`) and removing an element (`remove`). It provides the additional restriction on constructors that all sets they create must contain no duplicate elements. It also puts the additional restriction on the `add` method that a duplicate item cannot be inserted. Table 9.1 shows the commonly used methods of the `Set` interface. The `Set` interface also has methods that support the mathematical set operations. The required method `containsAll` tests the subset relationship. There are optional methods for set union (`addAll`), set intersection (`retainAll`), and set difference (`removeAll`). We show the methods that are used to implement the mathematical set operations in italics in Table 9.1.

Calling a method "optional" means just that: An implementer of the `Set` interface is not required to provide it. However, a method that matches the signature must be provided. This method should throw the `UnsupportedOperationException` whenever it is called. This gives the class designer some flexibility. For example, if a class instance is intended to provide efficient search and retrieval of the items stored, the class designer may decide to omit the optional mathematical set operations.

TABLE 9.1

Some `java.util.Set` Methods (with Mathematical Set Operations in Italics)

Method	Behavior
`boolean add(Object obj)`	Adds object `obj` to this set if it is not already present (optional operation) and returns **true**. Returns false if `obj` is already in the set.
`boolean addAll(Collection coll)`	*Adds all of the elements in collection `coll` to this set if they're not already present (optional operation). Returns **true** if the set is changed. Implements set union if `coll` is a `Set`.*
`boolean contains(Object obj)`	Returns **true** if this set contains object `obj`. Implements a test for set membership.
`boolean containsAll(Collection coll)`	*Returns **true** if this set contains all of the elements of collection `coll`. If `coll` is a set, returns **true** if this set is a **subset** of `coll`.*

TABLE 9.1 (continued)

Method	Behavior
`boolean isEmpty()`	Returns **true** if this set contains no elements.
`Iterator iterator()`	Returns an iterator over the elements in this set.
`boolean remove(Object obj)`	Removes object `obj` from this set if it is present (optional operation). Returns **true** if the object was removed.
`boolean removeAll(Collection coll)`	*Removes from this set all of its elements that are contained in collection* `coll` *(optional operation). Returns* **true** *if this set is changed. If* `coll` *is a set, performs the set difference operation.*
`boolean retainAll(Collection coll)`	*Retains only the elements in this set that are contained in collection* `coll` *(optional operation). Returns* **true** *if this set is changed. If* `coll` *is a set, performs the set intersection operation.*
`int size()`	Returns the number of elements in this set (its cardinality).

EXAMPLE 9.1

Listing 9.1 contains a main method that creates three sets: setA, setAcopy, and setB. It loads these sets from two arrays and then forms their union in setA and their intersection in setAcopy, using the statements

```
setA.addAll(setB);         // Set union
setAcopy.retainAll(setB);  // Set intersection
```

Running this method generates the output lines below. The brackets and commas are inserted by method toString.

```
The 2 sets are:
[Jill, Ann, Sally]
[Bill, Jill, Ann, Bob]
Items in set union are: [Bill, Jill, Ann, Sally, Bob]
Items in set intersection are: [Jill, Ann]
```

LISTING 9.1
Illustrating the Use of Sets

```java
public static void main(String[] args) {

    // Create the sets.
    String[] listA = {"Ann", "Sally", "Jill", "Sally"};
    String[] listB = {"Bob", "Bill", "Ann", "Jill"};
    Set setA = new HashSet();
    Set setAcopy = new HashSet();  // Copy of setA
    Set setB = new HashSet();

    // Load sets from arrays.
    for (int i = 0; i < listA.length; i++) {
        setA.add(listA[i]);
        setAcopy.add(listA[i]);
    }
```

```
        for (int i = 0; i < listB.length; i++) {
            setB.add(listB[i]);
        }
        System.out.println("The 2 sets are: " + "\n" + setA
                           + "\n" + setB);

        // Display the union and intersection.
        setA.addAll(setB);          // Set union
        setAcopy.retainAll(setB);  // Set intersection
        System.out.println("Items in set union are: " + setA);
        System.out.println("Items in set intersection are: "
                           + setAcopy);
    }
```

Comparison of Lists and Sets

Collections implementing the `Set` interface must contain unique elements. Unlike the `List.add` method, the `Set.add` method will return **`false`** if you attempt to insert a duplicate item.

Unlike a `List`, a `Set` does not have a `get` method. Therefore, elements cannot be accessed by index. So if `setA` is a `Set` object, the method call `setA.get(0)` would cause the syntax error `method get(int) not found.`

Although you can't reference a specific element of a `Set`, you can iterate through all its elements using an `Iterator` object. The loop below accesses each element of `Set` object `setA`. However, the elements will be accessed in arbitrary order. This means that they will not necessarily be accessed in the order in which they were inserted.

```
Iterator setAIter = setA.iterator();   // Create an iterator to aSet.
while (setAIter.hasNext()) {
    Object nextItem = setAIter.next();
    // Do something with nextItem
    . . .
}
```

EXERCISES FOR SECTION 9.1

SELF-CHECK

1. Explain the effect of the following method calls.

```
Set s = new HashSet();
s.add("hello");
s.add("bye");
s.addAll(s);
Set t = new TreeSet();
t.add("123");
s.addAll(t);
System.out.println(s.containsAll(t));
System.out.println(t.containsAll(s));
System.out.println(s.contains("ace"));
```

```
System.out.println(s.contains("123"));
s.retainAll(t);
System.out.println(s.contains("123"));
t.retainAll(s);
System.out.println(t.contains("123"));
```

2. What is the relationship between the `Set` interface and the `Collection` interface?
3. What are the differences between the `Set` interface and the `List` interface?
4. In Example 9.1, why is `setAcopy` needed? What would happen if you used the statement

```
setAcopy = setA;
```

to define `setAcopy`?

PROGRAMMING

1. Assume you have declared three sets a, b, and c and that sets a and b store objects. Write statements that use methods from the `Set` interface to perform the following operations:

   a. c = (a ∪ b)

   b. c = (a ∩ b)

   c. c = (a – b)

   d. `if (a ⊂ b)`
   ```
            c = a;
        else
            c = b;
   ```

2. Write a `toString` method for a class that implements the `Set` interface and displays the set elements in the form shown in Example 9.1

9.2 Maps and the Map Interface

The `Map` is related to the `Set`. Mathematically a `Map` is a set of ordered pairs whose elements are known as the key and the value. The key is required to be unique, as are the elements of a set, but the value is not necessarily unique. For example, the following would be a map:

{(J, Jane), (B, Bill), (S, Sam), (B1, Bob), {B2, Bill)}

The keys in this example are strings consisting of one or two characters, and each value is a person's name. The keys are unique but not the values (there are two Bills). The key is based on the first letter of the person's name. The keys **B1** and **B2** are the keys for the second and third person whose name begins with the letter B.

You can think of each key as "mapping" to a particular value (hence the name *map*). For example, the key **J** maps to the value Jane. The keys **B** and **B2** map to the value Bill. You can also think of the keys as forming a set (keySet) and the values as

FIGURE 9.2
Example of Mapping

keySet   valueSet

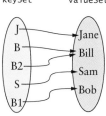

forming a set (valueSet). Each element of keySet maps to a particular element of valueSet, as shown in Figure 9.2. In mathematical set terminology, this is a *many-to-one mapping* (that is, more than one element of keySet may map to a particular element of valueSet). For example, both keys **B** and **B2** map to the value Bill. This is also an *onto mapping* in that all elements of valueSet have a corresponding member in keySet.

A Map can be used to enable efficient storage and retrieval of information in a table. The key is a unique identification value associated with each item stored in a table. As you will see, each key value has an easily computed numeric code value.

EXAMPLE 9.2   When information about an item is stored in a table, the information stored may consist of a unique ID (identification code, which may or may not be a number) as well as descriptive data. The unique ID would be the key, and the rest of the information would represent the value associated with that key. Some examples follow:

Type of Item	Key	Value
University student	Student ID number	Student name, address, major, grade-point average
Customer for on-line store	E-mail address	Customer name, address, credit card information, shopping cart
Inventory item	Part ID	Description, quantity, manufacturer, cost, price

In the above examples, the student ID number may be assigned by the university, or it may be the student's social security number. The e-mail address is a unique address for each customer, but it is not numeric. Similarly, a part ID could consist of a combination of letters and digits.

In comparing maps to indexed collections, you can think of the keys as selecting the elements of a map, just as indexes select elements in a List object. The keys for a map, however, can have arbitrary values (not restricted to 0, 1, and so on as for indexes). As you will see later, an implementation of the Map interface should have methods of the form

```
Object get(Object key)
Object put(Object key, Object value)
```

The get method retrieves the value corresponding to a specified key; the put method stores a key-value pair in a map.

The Map Hierarchy

Figure 9.3 shows part of the Map hierarchy in the Java API. Although not strictly part of the Collection hierarchy, the Map interface defines a structure that relates elements in one set to elements in another set. The first set, called the *keys,* must imple-

FIGURE 9.3
The Map Hierarchy

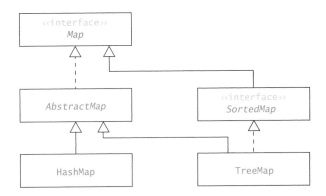

ment the Set interface, that is, the *keys* are unique. The second set is not strictly a Set, but an arbitrary Collection known as the *values*. These are not required to be unique.

The Map is a more useful structure than the Set. In fact, the Java API implements the Set using a Map.

The TreeMap uses a Red-Black binary search tree (discussed in Chapter 11) as its underlying data structure. We will focus on the HashMap and show how to implement it later in the chapter.

The Map Interface

Methods of the Map interface (in Java API java.util) are shown in Table 9.2. The put method either inserts a new mapping or changes the value associated with an existing mapping. The get method returns the current value associated with a given key. The remove method deletes an existing mapping. Both put and remove return the previous value (or **null**, if there was none) of the mapping that is changed or deleted.

TABLE 9.2
Some java.util.Map Methods

Method	Behavior
Object get(Object key)	Returns the value associated with the specified key. Returns **null** if the key is not present.
boolean isEmpty()	Returns **true** if this map contains no key-value mappings.
Object put(Object key, Object value)	Associates the specified value with the specified key in this map (optional operation). Returns the previous value associated with the specified key, or **null** if there was no mapping for the key.
Object remove(Object key)	Removes the mapping for this key from this map if it is present (optional operation). Returns the previous value associated with the specified key, or **null** if there was no mapping for the key.
int size()	Returns the number of key-value mappings in this map.

EXAMPLE 9.3 The following statements build a Map object that contains the mapping shown in Figure 9.2.

```
Map aMap = new HashMap();    // HashMap implements Map
aMap.put("J", "Jane");
aMap.put("B", "Bill");
aMap.put("S", "Sam");
aMap.put("B1", "Bob");
aMap.put("B2", "Bill");
```

The statement

```
System.out.println("B1 maps to " + aMap.get("B1"));
```

would display B1 maps to Bob. The statements

```
System.out.println("Bill maps to " + aMap.get("Bill"));
```

would display "Bill maps to null" because "Bill" is a value, not a key.

EXAMPLE 9.4 In Section 8.4, we used a binary search tree to store an index of words occurring in a term paper. Each data element in the tree was a string consisting of a word followed by a 3-digit line number.

Although this is one approach to storing an index, it would be more useful to store each word and all the line numbers for that word as a single index entry. We could do this by storing the index in a Map in which each word is a key and its associated value is a list of all the line numbers at which the word occurs. While building the index, each time a word is encountered, its list of line numbers would be retrieved (using the word as a key) and the most recent line number would be appended to this list (an ArrayList). For example, if the word *fire* has already occurred on lines 4 and 8 and we encounter it again on line 20, the ArrayList associated with *fire* would reference three Integer objects wrapping the numbers 4, 8, and 20.

Listing 9.2 shows method buildIndexAllLines (adapted from buildIndex in Listing 8.7). Data field index is a Map. The statement

```
ArrayList lines = (ArrayList) index.get(word);    // Get the list.
```

retrieves the value (an ArrayList or **null**) associated with the next word. The **if** statement sets lines to an empty ArrayList if this is the first occurrence of word (lines is **null**). The statements

```
lines.add(new Integer(lineNum));
index.put(word, lines);                // Store the list.
```

add the new line number to the ArrayList and store it back in the Map. In Section 9.5, we show how to display the final index.

....

LISTING 9.2
Method `buildIndexAllLines`

```
/** Reads each word (a key) in data file bR and stores it in a Map
    along with an ArrayList of line numbers (a value).
    pre:  index is an empty Map.
    post: Lowercase form of each word with all its line
          numbers is stored in index.
    @param bR A reference to the data file
    @throws IOException
*/
public void buildIndexAllLines(BufferedReader bR)
            throws IOException {
    int lineNum = 0;        // Line number
    String nextLine;        // Each data line
    // Keep reading lines until done.
    while ((nextLine = bR.readLine()) != null) {
        lineNum++;
        // Create a StringTokenizer for the current data line
        // using punctuation and white space as delimiters.
        StringTokenizer tokens =
                new StringTokenizer(nextLine, " ,.:-!?/%");
        // Insert each token in the index.
        while (tokens.hasMoreTokens()) {
            String word = tokens.nextToken();
            ArrayList lines = (ArrayList) index.get(word);
            // Get the list.
            if (lines == null) {
                lines = new ArrayList();
            }
            lines.add(new Integer(lineNum));
            index.put(word, lines);          // Store new list.
        }
    }
}
```

EXERCISES FOR SECTION 9.2

SELF-CHECK

1. If you were using a Map to store the following lists of items, which data field would you select as the key and why?
   a. textbook title, author, ISBN (International Standard Book Number), year, publisher
   b. player's name, uniform number, team, position
   c. computer manufacturer, model number, processor, memory, disk size
   d. department, course title, course ID, section number, days, time, room

PROGRAMMING

1. Write statements to create a Map object that stores each word occurring in a term paper along with the number of times the word occurs.

9.3 Hash Tables

Before we discuss the details of implementing the required methods of the Set and Map interfaces, we will describe a data structure, the *hash table*, that can be used as the basis for such an implementation. The goal behind the hash table is to be able to access an entry based on its key value, not its location. In other words, we want to be able to access an element directly through its key value, rather than having to determine its location first by searching for the key value in an array. (This is why the Set interface has method contains(obj) instead of get(index).) Using a hash table enables us to retrieve an item in constant time (expected O(1)). We say expected O(1) rather than just O(1) because there will be some cases where the performance will be much worse than O(1) and may even be O(*n*), but on the average, we expect that it will be O(1). Contrast this with the time required for linear search of an array, O(*n*), and the time to access an element in a binary search tree, O(log *n*).

Hash Codes and Index Calculation

The basis of hashing (and hash tables) is to transform the item's key value to an integer value (its *hash code*) which will then be transformed into a table index. Figure 9.4 illustrates this process for a table of size *n*. We discuss how this might be done in the next few examples.

EXAMPLE 9.5   Consider the Huffman code problem discussed in Section 8.6. To build the Huffman tree, you needed to know the number of occurrences of each character in the text being encoded. Let's assume that the text contained only the ASCII characters (the first 128 Unicode values starting with \u0000). We could use a table of size 128, one element for each possible character, and let the Unicode for each character be its location in the table. Using this approach, table element 65 would give us the number of occurrences of the letter A, table element 66 would give us the number of occurrences of the letter B, and so on. The hash code for each character is its Unicode value (a number), which is also its index in the table. In this case, we could calculate the table index for character asciiChar using the following assignment statement, where asciiChar represents the character we are seeking in the table.

```
int index = asciiChar;
```

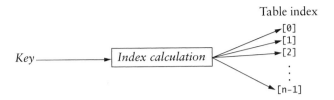

FIGURE 9.4
Index Calculation for
a Key

EXAMPLE 9.6 Let's consider a slightly harder problem: Assume that any of the Unicode characters can occur in the text, and we want to know the number of occurrences of each character. There are over 65,000 Unicode characters, however. For any file, let's assume that at most 100 different characters actually appear. So, rather than use a table with 65,536 elements, it would make sense to try to store these items in a much smaller table (say 200 elements). If the hash code for each character is its Unicode value, we need to convert this value (between 0 and 65,536) to an array index between 0 and 199. We can calculate the array index for character uniChar as:

```
int index = uniChar % 200
```

Because the range of Unicode values (the key range) is much larger than the index range, it is likely that some characters in our text will have the same index value. Because we can store only one key-value pair in a given array element, a situation known as a *collision* results. We discuss how to deal with collisions shortly.

Methods for Generating Hash Codes

In most applications, the keys that we will want to store in a table will consist of strings of letters or digits rather than a single character (for example, a social security number, a person's name, or a part ID). We need a way to map each string to a particular table index. Again, we have a situation in which the number of possible key values is much larger than the table size. For example, if a string can store up to 10 letters or digits, the number of possible strings is 36^{10} (approximately 3.7×10^{15}), assuming the English alphabet with 26 letters.

Generating good hash codes for arbitrary strings or arbitrary objects is somewhat of an experimental process. Simple algorithms tend to generate a lot of collisions. For example, simply summing the **int** values for all characters in a string would generate the same hash code for words that contained the same letters, but in different orders, such as "sign" and "sing", which would have the same hash code using this algorithm ('s' + 'i' + 'n' + 'g'). The algorithm used by the Java API accounts for the position of the characters in the string as well as the character values.

The String.hashCode() method returns the integer calculated by the formula

$$s_0 \times 31^{(n-1)} + s_1 \times 31^{(n-2)} + \cdots + s_{n-1}$$

where s_i is the ith character of the string, and n is the length of the string. For example, the string "Cat" would have a hash code of $'C' \times 31^2 + 'a' \times 31 + 't'$. This is the number 67,510. (The number 31 is a prime number that generates relatively few collisions.)

As previously discussed, the integer value returned by method `String.hashCode` can't be unique, because there are too many possible strings. However, the probability of two strings having the same hash code value is relatively small, because the `String.hashCode` method distributes the hash code values fairly evenly throughout the range of **int** values.

Because the hash codes are distributed evenly throughout the range of **int** values, method `String.hashCode` will appear to produce a random value, as will the expressions `s.hashCode() % table.length`, which selects the initial value of `index` for `String s`. If the object is not already present in the table, the probability that this expression does not yield an empty slot in the table is proportional to how full the table is.

One additional criterion for a good hash function, besides a random distribution for its values, is that it be relatively simple and efficient to compute. It doesn't make much sense to use a hash function whose computation is an $O(n)$ process to avoid doing an $O(n)$ search.

Open Addressing

Next we consider two ways to organize hash tables: open addressing and chaining. In open addressing, each hash table element (type `Object`) references a single key-value pair. We can use the following simple approach (called *linear probing*) to access an item in a hash table. If the index calculated for an item's key is occupied by an item with that key, we have found the item. If that element contains an item with a different key, we increment the index by one. We keep incrementing the index (modulo the table length) until either we find the key we are seeking or we reach a **null** entry. A **null** entry indicates that the key is not in the table.

Algorithm for Accessing an Item in a Hash Table

1. Compute the index by taking the item's `hashCode() % table.length`.
2.   **if** `table[index]` is **null**
3.   The item is not in the table.
4.   **else if** `table[index]` is equal to the item
5.   The item is in the table.

   else

6.   Continue to search the table by incrementing the index until either the item is found or a **null** entry is found.

Step 1 ensures that the `index` is within the table range (0 through `table.length − 1`). If the condition in Step 2 is true, the table index does not reference an object, so the item is not in the table. The condition in Step 4 is true if the item being sought is at position `index`, in which case the item is located. Steps 1 through 5 can be done in $O(1)$ expected time.

Step 6 is necessary for two reasons. The values returned by method `hashCode` are not unique, so the item being sought can have the same hash code as another one in the table. Also the remainder calculated in Step 1 can yield the same index for different hash code values. Both of these cases are examples of collisions.

Table Wraparound and Search Termination

Notice that as you increment the table index, your table should wrap around (as in a circular array), so that the element with subscript 0 "follows" the element with subscript `table.length − 1`. This enables you to use the entire table, not just the part with subscripts larger than the hash code value, but it leads to the potential for an infinite loop in Step 6 of the algorithm. If the table is full and the objects examined so far do not match the one you are seeking, how do you know when to stop? One approach would be to stop when the index value for the next probe is the same as the hash code value for the object. This means that you have come full-circle to the starting value for the index. A second approach would be to ensure that the table is never full by increasing its size after an insertion if its occupancy rate exceeds a specified threshold. This is the approach that we take in our implementation.

EXAMPLE 9.7   We illustrate insertion of five names in a table of size 5 and in a table of size 11. Table 9.3 shows the names, the corresponding hash code, the hash code modulo 5, and the hash code modulo 11. We picked prime numbers (5 and 11) because empirical tests have shown that hash tables with a size that is a prime number often give better results.

For a table of size 5 (an occupancy rate of 100 percent), `"Tom"`, `"Dick"`, and `"Sam"` have hash indexes of 4, and `"Harry"` and `"Pete"` have hash indexes of 3; whereas for a table length of 11 (an occupancy rate of 45 percent), `"Dick"` and `"Sam"` have hash indexes of 5, but the others have hash indexes that are unique. We see how the insertion process works next.

For a table of size 5, if `"Tom"` and `"Dick"` are the first two entries, `"Tom"` would be stored at the element with index 4, the last element in the table. Consequently, when `"Dick"` is inserted, because element 4 is already occupied, the hash index is incremented to 0 (the table wraps around to the beginning), where `"Dick"` is stored.

TABLE 9.3
Names and `hashCode` Values for Table Sizes 5 and 11

Name	hashCode()	hashCode()%5	hashCode()%11
"Tom"	84274	4	3
"Dick"	2129869	4	5
"Harry"	69496448	3	10
"Sam"	82879	4	5
"Pete"	2484038	3	7

```
[0]  "Dick"
[1]  null
[2]  null
[3]  null
[4]  "Tom"
```

"Harry" is stored in position 3 (the hash index), and "Sam" is stored in position 1, because its hash index is 4 but the elements at 4 and 0 are already filled.

```
[0]  "Dick"
[1]  "Sam"
[2]  null
[3]  "Harry"
[4]  "Tom"
```

Finally, "Pete" is stored in position 2, because its hash index is 3 but the elements at positions 3, 4, 0, 1 are filled.

```
[0]  "Dick"
[1]  "Sam"
[2]  "Pete"
[3]  "Harry"
[4]  "Tom"
```

For the table of size 11, the entries would be stored as shown in the following table, assuming that they were inserted in the order "Tom", "Dick", "Harry", "Sam", and finally "Pete". Insertions go more smoothly for the table of size 11. The first collision occurs when "Sam" is stored, so "Sam" is stored at position 6 instead of position 5.

```
[0]   null
[1]   null
[2]   null
[3]   "Tom"
[4]   null
[5]   "Dick"
[6]   "Sam"
[7]   "Pete"
[8]   null
[9]   null
[10]  "Harry"
```

For the table of size 5, retrieval of "Tom" can be done in one step. Retrieval of all of the others would require a linear search because of collisions that occurred when they were inserted. For the table of size 11, retrieval of all but "Sam" can be done in one step, and retrieval of "Sam" requires only two steps. This example illustrates that the best way to reduce the probability of a collision is to increase the table size.

Traversing a Hash Table

One thing that you cannot do is traverse a hash table in a meaningful way. If you visit the hash table elements in sequence and display the objects stored, you would display the strings "Dick", "Sam", "Pete", "Harry", "Tom" for the table of length 5 and the strings "Tom", "Dick", "Sam", "Pete", "Harry" for a table of length 11. In either case, the list of names is in arbitrary order.

Deleting an Item Using Open Addressing

When an item is deleted, we cannot just set its table entry to **null**. If we do, then when we search for an item that may have collided with the deleted item, we may incorrectly conclude that the item is not in the table. (Because the item that collided was inserted after the deleted item, we will have stopped our search prematurely.) By storing a dummy value when an item is deleted, we force the search algorithm to keep looking until either the desired item is found or a **null** value, representing a free cell, is located.

Although the use of a dummy value solves the problem, keep in mind that it can lead to search inefficiency, particularly when there are many deletions. Removing items from the table does not reduce the search time, because the dummy value is still in the table and is part of a search chain. In fact, you cannot even replace a deleted value with a new item, because you still need to go to the end of the search chain to ensure that the new item is not already present in the table. So deleted items waste storage space and reduce search efficiency. In the worst case, if the table is almost full and then most of the items are deleted, you will have O(n) performance when searching for the few items remaining in the table.

Reducing Collisions by Expanding the Table Size

Even with a good hashing function, there is still the problem of collisions resulting from taking the hash value modulo the table size. The first step in reducing these collisions is to use a prime number for the size of the table.

Additionally, the probability of a collision is proportional to how full the table is. Therefore, when the hash table becomes sufficiently full, a larger table should be allocated and the entries re-inserted.

We previously saw examples of expanding the size of an array. Generally, what we did was to allocate a new array with twice the capacity of the original, copy the values in the original array to the new array, and then reference the new array instead of the original. This approach will not work with hash tables. If you use it, some search chains will be broken because the new table does not wrap around in the same way as the original table. The last element in the original table will be in the middle of the new table, and it does not wrap-around to the first element of the new table. Therefore, you expand a hash table (called *rehashing*) using the following algorithm:

Algorithm for Rehashing

1. Allocate a new hash table with twice the capacity of the original.
2. Reinsert each old table entry that has not been deleted into the new hash table.
3. Reference the new table instead of the original.

Step 2 reinserts each item from the old table into the new table instead of copying it over to the same location. We illustrate this in the hash table implementation. Notice that deleted items are not reinserted into the new table, thereby saving space and reducing the length of some search chains.

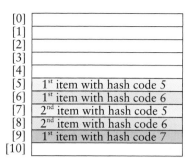

Reducing Collisions Using Quadratic Probing

The problem with linear probing is that it tends to form clusters of keys in the table, causing longer search chains. For example, if the table already has keys with hash codes of 5 and 6, a new item that collides with either of these keys will be placed at index 7. An item that collides with any of these three items will be placed at index 8, and so on. Figure 9.5 shows a hash table of size 11 after inserting elements with hash codes in the sequence 5, 6, 5, 6, 7. Each new collision expands the cluster by one element, thereby increasing the length of the search chain for each element in that cluster. For example, if another element is inserted with any hash code in the range 5 through 9, it will be placed at position 10, and the search chain for items with hash codes of 5 and 6 would include the elements at indexes 7, 8, 9, and 10.

One approach to reduce the effect of clustering is to use *quadratic probing* instead of linear probing. In quadratic probing, the increments form a quadratic series ($1 + 2^2 + 3^2 + \cdots$). Therefore, the next value of index is calculated using the steps:

```
probeNum++;
index = (startIndex + probeNum * probeNum) % table.length
```

where startIndex is the index calculated using method hashCode and probeNum starts at 0. Ignoring wraparound, if an item has a hash code of 5, successive values of index will be 6 (5 + 1), 9 (5 + 4), 14 (5 + 9), . . . , instead of 6, 7, 8, ... Similarly, if the hash code is 6, successive values of index will be 7, 10, 15, and so on. Unlike linear probing, these two search chains have only one table element in common (at index 6).

Figure 9.6 illustrates the hash table after elements with hash codes in the same sequence as in the preceding table (5, 6, 5, 6, 7) have been inserted with quadratic probing. Although the cluster of elements looks similar, their search chains do not overlap as much as before. Now the search chain for an item with a hash code of 5 consists of the elements at 5, 6, and 9, and the search chain for an item with a hash code of 6 consists of the elements at positions 6 and 7.

Problems with Quadratic Probing

One disadvantage of quadratic probing is that the next index calculation is a bit time consuming as it involves a multiplication, an addition, and a modulo division. A more efficient way to calculate the next index follows:

FIGURE 9.6

Insertion with Quadratic Probing

[0]	
[1]	
[2]	
[3]	
[4]	
[5]	1st item with hash code 5
[6]	1st item with hash code 6
[7]	2nd item with hash code 6
[8]	1st item with hash code 7
[9]	2nd item with hash code 5
[10]	

```
k += 2;
index = (index + k) % table.length;
```

which replaces the multiplication with an addition. If the initial value of k is –1, successive values of k will be 1, 3, 5, 7, ... If the hash code is 5, successive values of index will be 5, 6 (5 + 1), 9 (5 + 1 + 3), 14 (5 + 1 + 3 + 5), ... The proof of the equality of these two approaches to calculating index is based on the following mathematical series:

$$n^2 = 1 + 3 + 5 + \cdots + 2n - 1$$

A more serious problem with quadratic probing is that not all table elements are examined when looking for an insertion index, so it is possible that an item can't be inserted even when the table is not full. It is also possible that your program can get stuck in an infinite loop while searching for an empty slot. It can be proved that if the table size is a prime number and the table is never more than half-full, this can't happen. However, requiring that the table be half-empty at all times wastes quite a bit of memory. For these reasons, we will use linear probing in our implementation.

Chaining

An alternative to open addressing is a technique called *chaining,* in which each table element references a linked list that contains all the items that hash to the same table index. This linked list is often called a *bucket,* and this approach is sometimes called *bucket hashing.* Figure 9.7 shows the result of chaining for our earlier example with a table of size 5. Each new element with a particular hash index can be placed at the beginning or the end of the associated linked list. The algorithm for accessing such a table is the same as for open addressing, except for the step for resolving collisions. Instead of incrementing the table index to access the next item with a particular hash code value, you traverse the linked list referenced by the table element with index hashCode() % table.length.

One advantage of chaining is that only items that have the same value for hashCode() % table.length will be examined when looking for an object. In open addressing, search chains can overlap, so a search chain may include items in the table that have different starting index values.

FIGURE 9.7
Example of Chaining

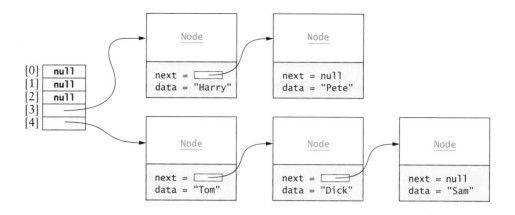

A second advantage is that you can store more elements in the table than the number of table slots (indexes), which is not the case for open addressing. If each table index already references a linked list, additional items can be inserted in an existing list without increasing the table size (number of indexes).

Once you have determined that an item is not present, you can insert it either at the beginning or at the end of the list. To delete an item, simply remove it from the list. In contrast to open addressing, removing an item actually deletes it, so it will not be part of future search chains.

Performance of Hash Tables

The *load factor* for a hash table is the number of filled cells divided by table size. The load factor has the greatest effect on hash table performance. The lower the load factor, the better the performance, because there is less chance of a collision when a table is sparsely populated. If there are no collisions, the performance for search and retrieval is $O(1)$, regardless of the table size.

Performance of Open Addressing Versus Chaining

Donald Knuth (D.E. Knuth, *Searching and Sorting*, vol. 3 of *The Art of Computer Programming*, Addison-Wesley, 1973) derived the following formula for the expected number of comparisons, c, required for finding an item that is in a hash table using open addressing with linear probing and a load factor L:

$$c = \frac{1}{2}\left(1 + \frac{1}{1-L}\right)$$

Table 9.4 (second column) shows the value of c for different values of load factor (L). It shows that if L is 0.5 (half-full), the expected number of comparisons required is 1.5. If L increases to 0.75, the expected number of comparisons is 2.5 which is still very respectable. If L increases to 0.9 (90% full), the expected number of comparisons is 5.5. This is true regardless of the size of the table.

TABLE 9.4
Number of Probes for Different Values of Load Factor (*L*)

L	Number of Probes with Linear Probing	Number of Probes with Chaining
0	1.00	1.00
0.25	1.17	1.13
0.5	1.50	1.25
0.75	2.50	1.38
0.85	3.83	1.43
0.9	5.50	1.45
0.95	10.50	1.48

Using chaining, if an item is in the table, on average we have to examine the table element corresponding to the item's hash code and then half of the items in each list. The average number of items in a list is *L*, the number of items divided by the table size. Therefore, we get the formula

$$c = 1 + \frac{L}{2}$$

for a successful search. Table 9.4 (third column) shows the results for chaining. For values of *L* between 0.0 and 0.75, the results are similar to those of linear probing, but chaining gives better performance than linear probing for higher load factors. Quadratic probing (not shown) gives performance that is between those of linear probing and chaining.

Performance of Hash Tables Versus Sorted Arrays and Binary Search Trees

If we compare hash table performance with binary search of a sorted array, the number of comparisons required by binary search is $O(\log n)$, so the number of comparisons increases with table size. A sorted array of size 128 would require up to 7 probes (2^7 is 128), which is more than for a hash table of any size that is 90 percent full. A sorted array of size 1024 would require up to 10 probes (2^{10} is 1024). A binary search tree would yield the same results.

You can insert into or remove elements from a hash table in $O(1)$ expected time. Insertion or removal from a binary search tree is $O(\log n)$, but insertion or removal from a sorted array is $O(n)$ (you need to shift the larger elements over). (Worst case performance for a hash table or a binary search tree is $O(n)$.)

Storage Requirements for Hash Tables, Sorted Arrays, and Trees

The performance of hashing is certainly preferable to that of binary search of an array (or a binary search tree), particularly if *L* is less than 0.75. However, the tradeoff is that the lower the load factor, the more unfilled storage cells there are in a hash table, whereas there are no empty cells in a sorted array. Because a binary search tree requires three references per node (the item, the left subtree, and the right subtrees), more storage would be required for a binary search tree than for a hash table with a load factor of 0.75.

EXAMPLE 9.8   A hash table of size 100 with open addressing could store 75 items with a load factor of 0.75. This would require storage for 100 references. Storage would be required for 225 references to store the 75 items in a binary search tree, but only for 75 references to store the items in a sorted array.

Storage Requirements for Open Addressing and Chaining

Next, we consider the effect of chaining on storage requirements. For a table with a load factor of L, the number of table elements required is n (the size of the table). For open addressing, the number of references to an item (a key-value pair) is n. For chaining, the average number of nodes in a list is L. If we use the Java API LinkedList, there will be three references in each node (the item, the next list element, and the previous element). However, we could use our own single-linked list and eliminate the previous-element reference (at some time cost for deletions). Therefore, we will require storage for $n + 2L$ references.

EXAMPLE 9.9   If we have 60,000 items in our hash table and use open addressing, we would need a table size of 80,000 to have a load factor of 0.75 and an expected number of comparisons of 2.5. Next, we calculate the table size, n, needed to get similar performance using chaining:

$$2.5 = 1 + L / 2$$
$$5.0 = 2 + L$$
$$3.0 = 60,000 / n$$
$$n = 20,000$$

A hash table of size 20,000 requires storage space for 20,000 references to lists. There will be 60,000 nodes in the table (one for each dictionary word). If we use linked lists of nodes, we will need storage for 140,000 references (2 references per node plus the 20,000 table references). This is almost twice the storage needed for open addressing.

EXERCISES FOR SECTION 9.3

SELF-CHECK

1. For the hash table search algorithm shown in this section, why was it unnecessary to test whether all table entries had been examined as part of Step 5?
2. For the items in the 5-element table of Table 9.3, compute hashCode() % table.length for lengths of 7 and 13. What would be the position of each word

in tables of these sizes using open addressing and linear probing? Answer the same question for chaining.

3. The following table stores `Integer` keys with the **int** values shown. Show one sequence of insertions that would store the keys as shown. Which elements were placed in their current position because of collisions? Show the table that would be formed by chaining.

Index	Key
[0]	24
[1]	6
[2]	20
[3]	
[4]	14

4. For Table 9.3 and the table size of 5 shown in Example 9.7, discuss the effect of deleting the entry for Dick and replacing it with a **null** value. How would this affect the search for Sam, Pete, and Harry? Answer both questions if you replace the entry for Dick with the string "deleted" instead of **null**.

5. Explain what is wrong with the following strategy to reclaim space that is filled with deleted items in a hash table: When attempting to insert a new item in the table, if you encounter an item that has been deleted, replace the deleted item with the new item.

6. Compare the storage requirement for a hash table with open addressing, a table size of 500, and a load factor of 0.5 with a hash table that uses chaining and gives the same performance.

PROGRAMMING

1. Code the following algorithm for finding the location of an object as a static method. Assume a hash table array and an object to be located in the table are passed as arguments. Return the object's position if it is found; return −1 if the object is not found.

1. Compute the index by taking the `hashCode()` % `table.length`.
2. **if** `table[index]` is **null**
3.   The object is not in the table.
   else if `table[index]` is equal to the object
4.   The object is in the table.
   else
5.   Continue to search the table (by incrementing `index`) until either the object is found or a **null** entry is found.

9.4 Implementing the Hash Table

In this section, we discuss how to implement a hash table. We will show implementations for hash tables using open addressing and chaining.

Interface KWHashMap

Because we want to show more than one way to implement a hash table, we introduce an interface KWHashMap in Table 9.5. The methods for interface KWHashMap (get, put, isEmpty, remove, and size) are similar to the ones shown earlier for the Map interface (see Table 9.2). There is a class Hashtable in the Java API java.util; however, it has been superseded by the class HashMap. Our interface KWHashMap doesn't include all the methods of class HashMap.

Class Entry

A hash table stores key-value pairs, so we will use an inner class Entry in each hash table implementation with data fields key and value (see Table 9.6). The implementation of inner class Entry is straightforward and we show it in Listing 9.3.

TABLE 9.5
Interface KWHashMap

Method	Behavior
Object get(Object key)	Returns the value associated with the specified key. Returns **null** if the key is not present.
boolean isEmpty()	Returns **true** if this table contains no key-value mappings.
Object put(Object key, Object value)	Associates the specified value with the specified key. Returns the previous value associated with the specified key, or **null** if there was no mapping for the key.
Object remove(Object key)	Removes the mapping for this key from this table if it is present (optional operation). Returns the previous value associated with the specified key, or **null** if there was no mapping.
int size()	Returns the size of the table.

TABLE 9.6
The Inner Class Entry

Data Field	Attribute
private Object key	The key.
private Object value	The value.

TABLE 9.6 (continued)

Constructor	Behavior
public Entry(Object key, Object value)	Constructs an Entry with the given values.

Method	Behavior
public Object getKey()	Retrieves the key.
public Object getValue()	Retrieves the value.
public Object setValue(Object val)	Sets the value.

LISTING 9.3
Inner Class Entry

```java
/** Contains key-value pairs for a hash table. */
private static class Entry {

    /** The key */
    private Object key;
    /** The value */
    private Object value;

    /** Creates a new key-value pair.
        @param key The key
        @param value The value
    */
    public Entry(Object key, Object value) {
        this.key = key;
        this.value = value;
    }

    /** Retrieves the key.
        @return The key
    */
    public Object getKey() {
        return key;
    }

    /** Retrieves the value.
        @return The value
    */
    public Object getValue() {
        return value;
    }

    /** Sets the value.
        @param val The new value
    */
    public Object setValue(Object val) {
        Object oldVal = value;
        value = val;
        return oldVal;
    }
}
```

TABLE 9.7
Data Fields for Class `HashtableOpen`

Data Field	Attribute
`private Entry[] table`	The hash table array.
`private static final int START_CAPACITY`	The initial capacity.
`private double LOAD_THRESHOLD`	The maximum load factor.
`private int numKeys`	The number of keys in the table excluding keys that were deleted.
`private int numDeletes`	The number of deleted keys.
`private static final Entry DELETED`	A special object to indicate that an entry has been deleted.

Class `HashtableOpen`

In a hash table that uses open addressing, we represent the hash table as an array of Entry objects (initial size is START_CAPACITY). We describe the data fields in Table 9.7. The Entry object DELETED is used to indicate that the Entry at a particular table element has been deleted.

The class and data field declarations for HashtableOpen follow.

```
/** Hash table implementation using open addressing. */
public class HashtableOpen implements KWHashMap {
    // Data Fields
    private Entry[] table;
    private static final int START_CAPACITY = 101;
    private double LOAD_THRESHOLD = 0.75;
    private int numKeys;
    private int numDeletes;
    private static final Entry DELETED =
                new Entry("*****", "*****");

    // Insert inner class Entry here.
    ...
}
```

Several methods for class HashtableOpen use a private method find that searches the table (using linear probing) until it finds either the target key or an empty slot. By expanding the table when its load factor exceeds the LOAD_THRESHOLD, we ensure that there will always be an empty slot in the table. Table 9.8 summarizes these private methods.

The algorithm for method find follows. Listing 9.4 shows the method.

TABLE 9.8
Private Methods for Class HashtableOpen

Method	Behavior
private int find(Object key)	Returns the index of the specified key if present in the table; otherwise, returns the index of the first available slot.
private void rehash()	Doubles the capacity of the table and permanently removes deleted items.

Algorithm for HashtableOpen.find(Object key)

1. Set index to key.hashCode() % table.length.
2. **if** index is negative, add table.length.
3. **while** table[index] is not empty and table[index] does not contain the key
4.   Increment index.
5.   **if** index is greater than or equal to table.length
6.   Set index to 0.
7. Return the index.

LISTING 9.4
Method HashtableOpen.find

```
/** Finds either the target key or the first empty slot in the
    search chain using linear probing.
    pre: The table is not full.
    @param key The key of the target object
    @return The position of the target or the first empty slot if
            the target is not in the table.
*/
private int find(Object key) {
    // Calculate the starting index.
    int index = key.hashCode() % table.length;
    if (index < 0)
        index += table.length;     // Make it positive.

    // Increment index until an empty slot is reached
    // or the key is found.
    while ((table[index] != null)
            && (!table[index].key.equals(key))) {
        index++;
        // Check for wraparound.
        if (index >= table.length)
            index = 0;     // Wrap around.
    }
    return index;
}
```

Notice that the method call key.hashCode() calls key's hashCode. The condition (!table[index].key.equals(key)) compares the key at table[index] with the key being sought (the method parameter). Notice that it is not necessary to use getKey with table[index], because the key field is defined in an inner class. Therefore, when key is used with a prefix of type Entry, it refers to the data field key; when key is used without a prefix, it refers to the parameter key.

Next we discuss the public methods: get and put. The get algorithm follows; Listing 9.5 shows the code.

Algorithm for get(Object key)

1. Find the first table element that is empty or the table element that contains the key.
2. **if** the table element found contains the key
       Return the value at this table element.
3. **else**
4.   Return **null**.

LISTING 9.5
Method HashtableOpen.get

```
/** Method get for class HashtableOpen.
    @param key The key being sought
    @return the value associated with this key if found;
            otherwise, null
*/
public Object get(Object key) {
    // Find the first table element that is empty
    // or the table element that contains the key.
    int index = find(key);

    // If the search is successful, return the value.
    if (table[index] != null)
        return table[index].value;
    else
        return null;  // key not found.
}
```

Next we write the algorithm for method put. After inserting a new entry, the method checks to see whether the load factor exceeds the LOAD_THRESHOLD. If so, it calls method rehash to expand the table and reinsert the entries. Listing 9.6 shows the code for method put.

Algorithm for HashtableOpen.put(Object key, Object value)

1. Find the first table element that is empty or the table element that contains the key.
2. **if** an empty element was found
3.   Insert the new item and increment numKeys.
4.   Check for need to rehash.
5.   Return **null**.
6. The key was found. Replace the value associated with this table element and return the old value.

LISTING 9.6
Method `HashtableOpen.put`

```
/** Method put for class HashtableOpen.
    post: This key-value pair is inserted in the
          table and numKeys is incremented. If the key is already
          in the table, its value is changed to the argument
          value and numKeys is not changed. If the LOAD_THRESHOLD
          is exceeded, the table is expanded.
    @param key The key of item being inserted
    @param value The value for this key
    @return Old value associated with this key if found;
            otherwise, null
*/
public Object put(Object key, Object value)  {
    // Find the first table element that is empty
    // or the table element that contains the key.
    int index = find(key);

    // If an empty element was found, insert new entry.
    if (table[index] == null) {
        table[index] = new Entry(key, value);
        numKeys++;
        // Check whether rehash is needed.
        double loadFactor =
                (double) (numKeys + numDeletes) / table.length;
        if (loadFactor > LOAD_THRESHOLD)
            rehash();
        return null;
    }

    // assert: table element that contains the key was found.
    // Replace value for this key.
    Object oldVal = table[index].value;
    table[index].value = value;
    return oldVal;
}
```

 PITFALL

Integer Division for Calculating Load Factor

Before calling method rehash, method put calculates the load factor by dividing the number of filled slots by the table size. This is a simple computation, but if you forget to cast the numerator or denominator to **double**, the load factor will be zero (because of integer division), and the table will not be expanded. This will slow down the performance of the table when it becomes nearly full, and it will cause an infinite loop (in method `find`) when the table is completely filled.

Next, we write the algorithm for method `remove`. Note that we "remove" a table element by setting it to reference object DELETED. We leave the implementation as an exercise.

Algorithm for `remove(Object key)`

1. Find the first table element that is empty or the table element that contains the key.
2. **if** an empty element was found
3.   Return **null**.
4. Key was found. Remove this table element, increment `numDeletes`, and decrement numKeys.
5. Return the value associated with this key.

Finally, we write the algorithm for private method `rehash`. Listing 9.7 shows the method. Although we do not take the effort to make the table size a prime number, we do make it an odd number.

Algorithm for `HashtableOpen.rehash`

1. Allocate a new hash table that is double the size and has an odd length.
2. Reset the number of keys and number of deletions to 0.
3. Reinsert each table entry that has not been deleted in the new hash table.

....

LISTING 9.7
Method `HashtableOpen.rehash`

```
/** Expands table size when loadFactor exceeds LOAD_THRESHOLD
    post: The size of table is doubled and is an odd integer.
          Each nondeleted entry from the original table is
          reinserted into the expanded table.
          The value of numKeys is reset to the number of items
          actually inserted; numDeletes is reset to 0.
*/
private void rehash() {
    // Save a reference to oldTable.
    Entry[] oldTable = table;
    // Double capacity of this table.
    table = new Entry[2 * oldTable.length + 1];

    // Reinsert all items in oldTable into expanded table.
    numKeys = 0;
    numDeletes = 0;
    for (int i = 0; i < oldTable.length; i++) {
        if ((oldTable[i] != null) && (oldTable[i] != DELETED)) {
            // Insert entry in expanded table
            put(oldTable[i].key, oldTable[i].value);
            numKeys++;
        }
    }
}
```

Data Fields for Class `HashtableChain`

Data Field	Attribute
`private LinkedList[] table`	A table of references to linked lists.
`private int numKeys`	The number of keys (entries) in the table.
`private static final int CAPACITY`	The size of the table.
`private static final int LOAD_THRESHOLD`	The maximum load factor.

Class `HashtableChain`

Next we turn our attention to class `HashtableChain` that implements `KWHashMap` using chaining. We will represent the hash table as an array of linked lists as shown in Table 9.9. Even though a hash table that uses chaining can store any number of elements in the same slot, we will expand the table if the number of entries becomes three times the number of slots (`LOAD_THRESHOLD` is 3.0) to keep the performance at a reasonable level.

Listing 9.8 shows the data fields and the constructor for class `HashtableChain`.

LISTING 9.8
Data Fields and Constructor for `HashtableChain.java`

```java
/** Hash table implementation using chaining. */
public class HashtableChain implements KWHashMap {
    /** The table */
    private LinkedList[] table;
    /** The number of keys */
    private int numKeys;
    /** The capacity */
    private static final int CAPACITY = 101;
    /** The maximum load factor */
    private static final int LOAD_THRESHOLD = 3.0;

    // Insert inner class Entry here.

    // Constructor
    public HashtableChain() {
        table = new LinkedList[CAPACITY];
    }
    ...
}
```

Next we discuss the three methods `get`, `put`, and `remove`. Instead of introducing a `find` method to search a list for the key, we will include a search loop in each method. We will create a `ListIterator` object and use that object to access each list element.

We begin with the algorithm for get. Listing 9.9 shows its code. We didn't use methods getKey and getValue to access an item's key and value because those private data fields of class Entry are visible in the class that contains it.

Algorithm for HashtableChain.get(Object key)

1. Set index to key.hashCode() % table.length.
2. **if** index is negative
3.   Add table.length.
4. **if** table[index] is **null**
5.   key is not in the table; return **null**.
6. For each element in the list at table[index]
7.   **if** that element's key matches the search key
8.   Return that element's value.
9. key is not in the table; return **null**.

LISTING 9.9
Method HashtableChain.get

```
/** Method get for class HashtableChain.
    @param key The key being sought
    @return The value associated with this key if found;
            otherwise, null
*/
public Object get(Object key) {
    int index = key.hashCode() % table.length;
    if (index < 0)
        index += table.length;
    if (table[index] == null)
        return null;  // key is not in the table.

    // Search the list at table[index] to find the key.
    Iterator listIter = table[index].iterator();
    while (listIter.hasNext()) {
        Entry nextItem = (Entry) listIter.next();
        // If the search is successful, return the value.
        if (nextItem.key.equals(key))
            return nextItem.value;
    }

    // assert: key is not in the table.
    return null;
}
```

Next we write the algorithm for method put. Listing 9.10 shows its code.

Algorithm for `HashtableChain.put(Object key, Object value)`

1. Set index to `key.hashCode() % table.length`.
2. **if** index is negative, add `table.length`.
3. **if** `table[index]` is **null**
4.   Create a new linked list at `table[index]`.
5. Search the list at `table[index]` to find the key.
6. **if** the search is successful
7.   Replace the value associated with this key.
8.   Return the old value.
9. **else**
10.   Insert the new key-value pair in the linked list at `table[index]`.
11.   Increment numKeys.
12.   **if** the load factor exceeds the `LOAD_THRESHOLD`
13.   Rehash.
14.   Return **null**.

....
LISTING 9.9
Method `HashtableChain.put`

```
/** Method put for class HashtableChain.
    post: This key-value pair is inserted in the
          table and numKeys is incremented. If the key is already
          in the table, its value is changed to the argument
          value and numKeys is not changed.
    @param key The key of item being inserted
    @param value The value for this key
    @return The old value associated with this key if
            found; otherwise, null
*/
public Object put(Object key, Object value) {
    int index = key.hashCode() % table.length;
    if (index < 0)
        index += table.length;
    if (table[index] == null) {
        // Create a new linked list at table[index].
        table[index] = new LinkedList();
    }

    // Search the list at table[index] to find the key.
    Iterator listIter = table[index].iterator();
    while (listIter.hasNext()) {
        Entry nextItem = (Entry) listIter.next();
        // If the search is successful, replace the old value.
        if (nextItem.key.equals(key)) {
            // Replace value for this key
            Object oldVal = nextItem.value;
            nextItem.setValue(value);
            return oldVal;
        }
    }
```

```
        // assert: key is not in the table, add new item.
        table[index].addFirst(new Entry(key, value));
        numKeys++;
        if (numKeys > (LOAD_THRESHOLD * table.length))
            rehash();
        return null;
}
```

Last, we write the algorithm for method remove. We leave the implementation of rehash and reemove as an exercise.

Algorithm for HashtableChain.remove(Object key)

1. Set index to key.hashCode() % table.length.
2. **if** index is negative, add table.length.
3. **if** table[index] is **null**
4.   key is not in the table; return **null**.
5. Search the list at table[index] to find the key.
6. **if** the search is successful
7.   Remove the entry with this key and decrement numKeys.
8.   **if** the list at table[index] is empty
9.   Set table[index] to **null**.
10.   Return the value associated with this key.
11. key is not in the table; return **null**.

Testing the Hash Table Implementations

We discuss two approaches to testing the hash table implementations. One way is to create a file of key-value pairs and then read each key-value pair and insert it in the hash table, observing how the table is filled. To do this, you need to write a toString method for the table that captures the index of each table element that is not **null** and then the contents of that table element. For open addressing, the contents would be the string representation of the key-value pair. For chaining, you could use a list iterator to traverse the linked list at that table element and append each key-value pair to the result string (see the Programming exercises for this section).

If you use a data file, you can carefully test different situations. The following are some of the cases you should examine:

- Does the array index wrap around as it should?
- Are collisions resolved correctly?
- Are duplicate keys handled appropriately? Is the new value retrieved instead of the original value?
- Are deleted keys retained in the table, but no longer accessible via a get?
- Does rehashing occur when the load factor reaches 0.75 (3.0 for chaining)?

By stepping through the get and put methods you can observe how the table is probed and the search chain that is followed to access or retrieve a key.

An alternative to creating a data file is to insert randomly generated integers in the hash table. This will allow you to create a very large table with little effort. The following loop generates SIZE key-value pairs. Each key is an integer between 0 and 32,000 and is wrapped in an Integer object. For each table entry, the value is the same as the key. The Integer.hashCode method returns the **int** value wrapped inside the object it is applied to.

```
for (int i = 0; i < SIZE; i++) {
    Integer nextInt =
            new Integer((int) (32000 * Math.random()));
    Object found = hashTable.put(nextInt, nextInt);
}
```

Because the keys are generated randomly, you can't investigate the effect of duplicate keys as you can with a data file. However, you can build arbitrarily large tables and observe how the elements are placed in the table. After the table is complete, you can interactively enter items to retrieve, delete, and insert and verify that they are handled properly.

If you are using open addressing, you can add statements to count the number of items probed each time an insertion is made. You can accumulate these totals and display the average search chain length. If you are using chaining, you can also count the number of probes made and display the average. After all items have been inserted, you can calculate the average length of each linked list and compare that with the number predicted by the formula provided in the discussion of performance in Section 9.3.

EXERCISES FOR SECTION 9.4

SELF CHECK

1. The following table stores Integer keys with the **int** values shown. Where would each key be placed in the new table resulting from rehashing the current table?

Index	Key
0	24
1	6
2	20
3	
4	14

PROGRAMMING

1. Write a remove method for class HashtableOpen.
2. Write rehash and remove methods for class HashtableChain.
3. Write a toString method for class HashtableOpen.
4. Write a toString method for class HashtableChain.

5. Write a method size for both hash table implementations.

6. Modify method find to count and display the number of probes made each time it is called. Accumulate these in a data field numProbes and count the number of times find is called in another data field. Provide a method that returns the average number of probes per call to find.

9.5 Implementation Considerations for Maps and Sets

Methods hashCode and equals

Class Object implements methods hashCode and equals, so every class can access these methods unless it overrides them. Method Object.equals compares two objects based on their addresses, not their contents. Similarly, method Object.hashCode calculates an object's hash code based on its address, not its contents. If you want to compare two objects for equality, you must implement an equals method for that class. In doing so, you should override the equals method for class Object by providing an equals method with the form

```
public boolean equals(Object obj) {...}
```

Most predefined classes (for example, String and Integer) override method equals and method hashCode. If you override the equals method, Java recommends you also override the hashCode method. Otherwise, your class will violate the Java contract for hashCode, which states the following:

If obj1.equals(obj2) is true, then obj1.hashCode() == obj2.hashCode().

Consequently, you should make sure that your hashCode method uses the same data field(s) as your equals method. We provide an example next.

EXAMPLE 9.10   Class Person has data field IDNumber, which is used to determine whether two Person objects are equal. The equals method returns true only if the objects' IDNumber fields have the same contents.

```
public boolean equals(Object obj) {
    if (obj instanceof Person)
        return IDNumber.equals(((Person) obj).IDNumber);
    else
        return false;
}
```

To satisfy its contract, method Object.hashCode must also be overridden as follows. Now two objects that are considered equal will also have the same hash code.

```
public int hashCode() {
    return IDNumber.hashCode();
}
```

TABLE 9.10
Corresponding Map and Set Methods

Map Method	Set Method
`Object get(Object key)`	`boolean contains(Object key)`
`Object put(Object key, Object value)`	`boolean add(Object key)`
`Object remove(Object key)`	`boolean remove(Object key)`

Implementing HashSetOpen

We can modify the hash table methods from Section 9.4 to implement a hash set.
Table 9.10 compares corresponding Map and Set methods.

The set `contains` method performs a test for set membership instead of retrieving a
value, so it is type **boolean**. Similarly, each of the other Set methods in Table 9.10
returns a **boolean** value that indicates whether the method was able to perform its
task. The process of searching the hash table elements would be done the same way
in each Set method as it is done in the corresponding Map method.

For open-addressing, method put uses the statement

```
table[index] = new Entry(key, value);
```

to store a reference to a new Entry object in the hash table. The corresponding statement in method add would be

```
table[index] = key;
```

because the key is the actual item that is stored.

Writing HashSetOpen as an Adapter Class

Instead of writing new methods from scratch, we can implement HashSetOpen as an
adapter class with the private data field

```
private KWHashMap setMap = new HashtableOpen();
```

We can write methods contains, add, and remove as follows. Because the map stores
key-value pairs, we will have each set element reference an Entry object with the
same key and value.

```
/** A hash table for storing set elements using open addressing. */
public class HashSetOpen {
    private KWHashMap setMap = new HashtableOpen();

    /** Adapter method contains.
        @return true if the key is found in setMap
    */
    public boolean contains(Object key) {
        // HashtableOpen.get returns null if the key is not found.
        return (setMap.get(key) != null);
    }
```

```
    /** Adapter method add.
        post: Adds a new Entry object (key, key)
             if key is not a duplicate.
        @return true if the key is not a duplicate
    */
    public boolean add(Object key) {
        /* HashtableOpen.put returns null if the
           key is not a duplicate. */
        return (setMap.put(key, key) == null);
    }

    /** Adapter method remove.
        post: Removes the key-value pair (key, key).
        @return true if the key is found and removed
    */
    public boolean remove(Object key) {
        /* HashtableOpen.remove returns null if the
           key is not removed. */
        return (setMap.remove() != null);
    }
}
}
```

Implementing the Java Map and Set Interfaces

Our goal in this chapter was to show you how to implement the operators in our hash table interface, not to implement the Map or Set interface fully. However, the Java API uses a hash table to implement both the Map and Set interfaces (class HashMap and class HashSet). You may be wondering what additional work would be required to implement the Map and Set interfaces using the classes we have developed so far.

The task of implementing these interfaces is simplified by the inclusion of abstract classes AbstractMap and AbstractSet in the Collection hierarchy (see Figures 9.1 and 9.3). These classes provide implementations of several methods for the Map and Set interfaces. So if class HashtableOpen extends class AbstractMap, we can reduce the amount of additional work we need to do.

The AbstractMap provides relatively inefficient ($O(n)$) implementations of the get and put methods. Because we overrode these methods in both our implementations (HashtableOpen and HashtableChain), we will get $O(1)$ expected performance. There are other, less critical methods that we don't need to provide because they are implemented in AbstractMap or its superclasses, such as clear, isEmpty, putAll, equals, hashCode, and toString.

Nested Interface Map.Entry

One requirement on the key-value pairs for a Map object is that they implement the interface Map.Entry, which is an inner interface of interface Map. This may sound a bit confusing, but what it means is that an implementer of the Map interface must contain an inner class that provides code for the methods described in Table 9.11. The inner class definition would be similar to the definition of inner class Entry in Listing 9.3, except it would end with the clause implements Map.Entry.

TABLE 9.11
The `java.util.Map.Entry` Interface

Method	Behavior
`Object getKey()`	Returns the key corresponding to this entry.
`Object getValue()`	Returns the value corresponding to this entry.
`Object setValue(Object val)`	Resets the value field for this entry to `val`. Returns its previous value field.

Creating a Set View of a Map

Method `entrySet` creates a set view of the entries in a `Map`. This means that method `entrySet` returns an object that implements the `Set` interface—that is, a set. The members of the set returned are the key-value pairs defined for that `Map` object. For example, if a key is `"0123"` and the corresponding value is `"Jane Doe"`, the pair (`"0123"`, `"Jane Doe"`) would be an element of the set view. This is called a view because it provides an alternative way to access the contents of the `Map`, but there is only a single copy of the underlying `Map` object.

We usually call method `entrySet` via a statement of the form:

```
Iterator iter = myMap.entrySet().iterator();
```

The method call `myMap.entrySet()` creates a set view of `myMap`; next, we apply method `iterator` to that set, thereby returning an `Iterator` object for it. We can access all the elements in the set through `Iterator` `iter`'s methods `hasNext` and `next`, but the elements are in arbitrary order. The objects returned by the iterator's `next` method are `Map.Entry` objects.

Method `entrySet` and Classes `EntrySet` and `SetIterator`

Method `entrySet` returns a set view of the underlying hash table (its key-value pairs) by returning an instance of inner class `EntrySet`. We define method `entrySet` next and then class `EntrySet`.

```
/** Creates a set view of a map.
    @return a set view of all key-value pairs in this map
*/
public Set entrySet() {
    return new EntrySet();
}
```

We show the inner class `EntrySet` in Listing 9.11. This class is an extension of the `AbstractSet`, which provides a complete implementation of the `Set` interface except for the `size` and `iterator` methods. The other methods required by the `Set` interface are defined using these methods. Most methods are implemented by using the `Iterator` object that is returned by the `EntrySet.iterator` method to access the contents of the hash table through its set view. You can also use such an `Iterator` object to access the elements of the set view.

```
..................................
LISTING 9.11
```
The Inner Class EntrySet

```
/** Inner class to implement the set view. */
private class EntrySet extends AbstractSet {

    /** Return the size of the set. */
    public int size() {
        return numKeys;
    }

    /** Return an iterator over the set. */
    public Iterator iterator() {
        return new SetIterator();
    }
}
```

The final step is to write class `SetIterator`, which implements the `Iterator` interface. The inner class `SetIterator` enables access to the entries in the hash table. The `SetIterator` class implements the `java.util.Iterator` interface and provides methods `hasNext`, `next`, and `remove`. Its implementation is left to a Programming Project (see Project 6).

Classes TreeMap and TreeSet

Besides `HashMap` and `HashSet`, the `Java Collection` hierarchy provides classes `TreeMap` and `TreeSet` that implement the `Map` and `Set` interfaces. These classes use a Red-Black tree (Section 11.3), which is a balanced binary search tree. We discussed earlier that the performances for search, retrieval, insertion, and removal operations are better for a hash table than for a binary search tree (expected $O(1)$ versus $O(\log n)$). However, the primary advantage of a binary search tree is that it can be traversed in sorted order. Hash tables, on the other hand, can't be traversed in any meaningful way. Also, subsets based on a range of key values can be selected using a `TreeMap` but not by using a `HashMap`.

EXAMPLE 9.11   In Example 9.4 we showed how to use a `Map` to build an index for a term paper. Because we want to display the words of the index in alphabetical order, we must store the index in a `TreeMap`. Method `showIndex` below displays the string representation of each index entry in the form

key =value

If the word *fire* appears on lines 4, 8, and 20, the corresponding output line would be

```
fire =[4, 8, 20]
```

It would be relatively easy to display this in the more common form: `fire, 4, 8, 20` (see Programming Exercise 4).

```
/** Displays the index, one word per line. */
public void showIndex() {
    // Create a set view of the index and an iterator to it.
    Iterator indexIt = index.entrySet().iterator();
```

```
        // Use iterator indexIt to access the tree data.
        while (indexIt.hasNext()) {
            Map.Entry entry = (Map.Entry) indexIt.next();
            System.out.println(entry);
        }
    }
}
```

EXERCISES FOR SECTION 9.5

SELF-CHECK

1. Explain why the nested interface Map.Entry is needed.

PROGRAMMING

1. Write statements to display all key, value pairs in Map object m, one pair per line. You will need to create an iterator to access the map entries. *Hint:* Create the iterator using the statement

   ```
   Iterator itr = m.entrySet().iterator();
   ```

2. Assume a Person has data fields lastName and firstName. Write an equals method that returns true if two Person objects have the same first and last names. Write a hashCode method that satisfies the hashCode contract. Make sure that your hashCode method does not return the same value for Henry James and James Henry. Your equals method should return a value of **false** for these two people.

3. Assume class HashSetOpen is written using an array table for storage instead of a HashMap object. Write method contains.

4. Modify method showIndex so each output line displays a word followed by a comma and a list of line numbers separated by commas. You can either edit the string corresponding to each Map entry before displaying it or use methods Map.Entry.getKey and Map.Entry.getValue to build a different string.

9.6 Additional Applications of Maps

In this section we will consider two case studies that use a Map object. We take another look at the telephone directory case first presented in Chapter 1 and revisited in Chapter 4.

CASE STUDY   Implementing the Phone Directory Using a Map

Problem

In Section 1.4 we introduced the PhoneDirectory interface (see Listing 1.2), which contained methods (loadData, lookupEntry, addOrChangeEntry, removeEntry, save) for processing a phone directory consisting of name-number pairs.

Initially we implemented this interface using an array (Section 1.7) and later an ArrayList (Section 4.2) to store DirectoryEntry objects. To look up a name or to change an existing name, we performed a linear search of the array, which is an $O(n)$ operation. By using a Map we can obtain a more efficient implementation.

Analysis

The PhoneDirectory is essentially a map. It relates names (which must be unique) to phone numbers. For the entries shown in the following table, the name is the key field and the phone number is the value field.

Index	Value
Jane Smith	215-555-1234
John Smith	215-555-1234
Bill Jones	508-555-6123

Thus, we can implement the PhoneDirectory interface by using a Map object for the phone directory. The Map object would contain the key-value pairs { ("Jane Smith", "215-555-1234"), ("John Smith", "215-555-1234"), ("Bill Jones", "508-555-6123") }.

Design

We need to design the class MapBasedPhoneDirectory, which implements the Phone-Directory interface. Table 9.12 shows the methods required by the PhoneDirectory interface and the corresponding method or methods in the Map interface. Three of these methods have direct correspondents, whereas the other two do not.

Implementation

In the following methods, data field theDirectory is type Map. Method addOrChange-Entry uses the Map.put method to either change or add a new name-number pair to the directory.

```
public String addOrChangeEntry(String name, String newNumber) {
    String oldNumber = (String) theDirectory.put(name,
                                                 newNumber);
    modified = true;
    return oldNumber;
}
```

Method put inserts the new name and number pair (method arguments) for a Map entry and returns the old value for that name (the number) if it was previously stored. We cast the result (type Object) to type String. If an entry with the given name was not previously stored, **null** is returned.

PhoneDirectory Interface versus Map Interface

PhoneDirectory Interface	Map Interface
addOrChangeEntry	put
lookupEntry	get
removeEntry	remove
loadData	None
save	None

The lookupEntry method uses the Map.get method to retrieve the directory entry. The entry key field (name) is passed as an argument.

```
public String lookupEntry(String name) {
    return (String) theDirectory.get(name);
}
```

The removeEntry method uses the Map.remove method to delete a directory entry. The data field modified is set to **true** only if the item was found and removed.

```
public String removeEntry(String name) {
    String returnValue = (String) theDirectory.remove(name);
    if (returnValue != null) {
        modified = true;
    }
    return returnValue;
}
```

The loadData method reads the entries from a data file and stores them in a Map. We will write the loop that does the read and store operations. It uses the Map.put method to add an entry with the given name and number.

```
while ((name = ins.readLine()) != null) {
    // Read name and number from successive lines.
    if ((number = ins.readLine()) == null) {
        break;    // No number - end of data reached.
    }
    // Add an entry for this name and number.
    theDirectory.put(name, number);
}
```

To save the directory, we need to extract each name-number pair sequentially from the list and write it out. We can use the Map.entrySet() method to obtain a view of the Map's contents as a Set of Map.Entry objects. We can use an Iterator to access the objects in this Set. The statement

```
Iterator iter = theDirectory.entrySet().iterator();
```

creates an Iterator, iter, to this set. Using this Iterator, we can write out the contents of the map as a sequence of consecutive lines containing the name-number pairs:

```
        while (iter.hasNext()) {
            // Get an entry.
            Map.Entry current = (Map.Entry) iter.next();
            // Write the name.
            outs.println(current.getKey());
            // Write the number.
            outs.println(current.getValue());
        }
```

The statement

```
    Map.Entry current = (Map.Entry) iter.next();
```

retrieves each entry, casting it to type `Map.Entry`. Method `getKey` returns the key field (the person's name) for each directory entry, and method `getValue` returns the value field (the person's phone number).

Testing   To test the `MapBasedPhoneDirectory`, you must change the line that declares the `phoneDirectory` object, initializing it with the new implementing class.

```
    PhoneDirectory phoneDirectory = new MapBasedPhoneDirectory();
```

The rest of the `main` method used to test the application would be the same.

CASE STUDY   Completing the Huffman Coding Problem

Problem   In Chapter 8 we showed how to compress a file by using a Huffman tree to encode the symbols occurring in the file so that the most frequently occurring characters had the shortest binary codes. The input to method `buildTree` of class `HuffmanTree` was a `HuffData` array consisting of (weight, symbol) pairs, where the weight in each pair was the frequency of occurrence of the corresponding symbol. We need a method to build this array for any data file so that we can create the Huffman tree. Once the tree is built, we need to encode each symbol in the input file by writing the corresponding bit string for that symbol to the output file.

Analysis   A `Map` is a very useful data structure for both these tasks: creating the array of `HuffData` elements and replacing each input character by its bit string code in the output file. For either situation we need to look up a symbol in a table. Using a `Map` ensures that the table lookup is an expected O(1) process.

To build the frequency table, we need to read a file and count the number of occurrences of each symbol in the file. The symbol will be the key for each entry in a `Map`, and the corresponding value will be the count of occurrences so far. As each symbol is read, we retrieve its `Map` entry and increment the corresponding count. If the symbol is not yet in the frequency table, we insert it with a count of 1.

Once we have the frequency table, we can construct the Huffman tree using a priority queue as explained in Section 8.6. Then we need to build a code table that stores the bit string code associated with each symbol to facilitate encoding the data file. Storing the code table in a Map as well makes the encoding process more efficient, because we can look up the symbol and retrieve its bit string code (expected $O(1)$ process). To build the code table, we do a preorder traversal of the Huffman tree.

Design   The algorithm for building the frequency table follows. After all characters are read, we create a set view of the map and traverse it using an iterator. We retrieve each Map.Entry and transpose its fields to create the corresponding HuffData item, a (weight, symbol) pair.

Algorithm for buildFreqTable

1.   **while** there are more characters in the input file
2.   Read a character and retrieve its corresponding entry in frequencies.
3.   **if** the value field is **null**
4.   Set value to 1.
5.   **else**
6.   Increment value.
7.   Create a set view of frequencies.
8.   **while** there are more entries in the set
9.   Store its data as a weight-symbol pair in the HuffData array.
10. Return the HuffData array.

We can use another Map which stores each symbol and its corresponding bit code string (a string of 0s and 1s) to encode the file.

Method buildCodeTable builds the code table by performing a preorder traversal of the Huffman tree. As we traverse the tree, we keep track of the bit code string so far. When we traverse left, we append a 0 to the bit string, and when we traverse right, we append a 1 to the bit string. If we encounter a symbol in a node, we insert that symbol along with a copy of the code so far (a new entry) in the code table. Because all symbols are stored in leaf nodes, we return immediately without going deeper in the tree.

Algorithm for Method buildCodeTable

1.   Get the data at the current root.
2.   **if** a symbol is stored in the current root (reached a leaf node)
3.   Insert the symbol and bit string code so far as a new code table entry.
4.   **else**
5.   Append a 0 to the bit string code so far.
6.   Apply the method recursively to the left subtree.
7.   Append a 1 to the bit string code.
8.   Apply the method recursively to the right subtree.

Finally, to encode the file, we read each character, look up its bit string code in the code table Map, and then write it to the output file.

Algorithm for encode

1.   **while** there are more characters in the input file
2.   Read a character and get its corresponding bit string code.
3.   Write its bit string to the output file.

Implementation

Listing 9.12 shows the code for method buildFreqTable. The **while** loop inside the **try** block builds the frequency table (Map frequencies). Because a Map stores references to objects, we wrap each character in a Character object (the key) and its count in an Integer object (the value). Once the table is built, we create an Iterator iter to the set view of frequencies. In the second **while** loop, we traverse the set view, retrieving each entry from the map and using its data to create a new HuffData element for array freqTable. When we finish, we return freqTable as the method result.

LISTING 9.12
Method buildFreqTable

```java
public static HuffData[] buildFreqTable(BufferedReader ins) {
    Map frequencies = new HashMap();  // Map of frequencies.
    try {
        int nextChar;    // For storing the next character as an int
        while ((nextChar = ins.read()) != -1) {  // Test for more data
            // Create a Character object for the data character.
            Character next = new Character((char) nextChar);
            // Get the current count and increment it.
            Integer count = (Integer) frequencies.get(next);
            Integer newCount;    // count after incrementing.
            if (count == null)
                newCount = new Integer(1);   // First occurrence.
            else
                newCount = new Integer(count.intValue() + 1);

            // Store updated count.
            frequencies.put(next, newCount);
        }
        ins.close();
    } catch (IOException ex) {
        ex.printStackTrace();
    }

    // Copy Map entries to a HuffData[] array.
    HuffData[] freqTable = new HuffData[frequencies.size()];
    int i = 0;      // Start at beginning of array.
    // Create an iterator to a set view of the Map.
    Iterator iter = frequencies.entrySet().iterator();
    // Get each map entry and store it in the array
    // as a weight-symbol pair.
    while (iter.hasNext()) {
```

```
                Map.Entry entry = (Map.Entry) iter.next();
                freqTable[i] =
                        new HuffData(((Integer) entry.getValue()).doubleValue(),
                                        entry.getKey());
                i++;
        }
        return freqTable;      // Return the array.
}
```

Next, we show method `buildCodeTable`. We provide a starter method and the recursive method that implements the algorithm discussed in the Design section.

```
/** Starter method to build the code table.
    post: The table is built.
*/
public void buildCodeTable() {
    // Call recursive method with empty bit string for code so far.
    buildCodeTable(huffTree, new BitString());
}

/** Recursive method to perform breadth-first traversal
    of the Huffman tree and build the code table.
    @param tree The current tree root
    @param code The code string so far
*/
private void buildCodeTable(BinaryTree tree, BitString code) {
    // Get data at local root.
    HuffData datum = (HuffData) tree.getData();
    if (datum.symbol != null) {  // Test for leaf node.
        // Found a symbol, insert its code in the map.
        codeMap.put(datum.symbol, code);
    } else {
        // Append 0 to code so far and traverse left.
        BitString leftCode = (BitString) code.clone();
        leftCode.append(false);
        buildCodeTable(tree.getLeftSubtree(), leftCode);
        // Append 1 to code so far and traverse right.
        BitString rightCode = (BitString) code.clone();
        rightCode.append(true);
        buildCodeTable(tree.getRightSubtree(), rightCode);
    }
}
```

Method encode reads each character again, looks up its bit code string, and writes it to the output file. We assume that the code table is in Map `codeTable` (a data field).

```
/** The Map to store the code table. */
private Map codeTable = new HashMap();
```

We use a class `BitString` whose instances store a sequence of 0 and 1 bits. (Class `BitString` may be downloaded from the Web site for this textbook.)

```
/** Encodes a data file by writing it in compressed bit string form.
    @param ins The input stream
    @param outs The output stream
```

```
     */
     public BitString encode(BufferedReader ins,
                             PrintWriter outs) {
         BitString result = new BitString();   // The complete bit string.
         try {
             int nextChar;
             while ((nextChar = ins.read()) != -1) {   // More data?
                 Character next = new Character((char) nextChar);

                 // Get bit string corresponding to symbol nextChar.
                 BitString nextChunk = (BitString) codeMap.get(next);
                 result.append(nextChunk);   // Append to result string.
             }

             // Write result to output file and close files.
             outs.print(result);
             ins.close();
             outs.close();
         } catch (IOException ex) {
             ex.printStackTrace();
         }
     }
```

Testing   To test these methods completely, you need to download class BitString (see Project 1) and write a main method that calls them in the proper sequence. For interim testing, you can read a data file and display the frequency table that is constructed to verify that it is correct. You can also use the StringBuffer class instead of class BitString in methods buildCodeTable and encode. The code would consist of a sequence of digit characters '0' and '1' instead of a sequence of bits 0 and 1. But this would enable you to verify that the program works correctly.

EXERCISES FOR SECTION 9.6

SELF-CHECK

1. Why did we make clones of the bit string code in recursive method buildCodeTable? What would happen if we didn't?

PROGRAMMING

1. Complete method loadData for class MapBasedPhoneDirectory.
2. Complete method save for class MapBasedPhoneDirectory.

Chapter Review

♦ The Set interface describes an abstract data type that supports the same operations as a mathematical set. We use Set objects to store a collection of elements that are not ordered by position. Each element in the collection is unique. Sets are useful for determining whether or not a particular element is in the collection, not its position or relative order.

♦ The Map interface describes an abstract data type that enables a user to access information (a value) corresponding to a specified key. Each key is unique and is mapped to a value that may or may not be unique. Maps are useful for retrieving or updating the value corresponding to a given key.

♦ A hash table uses hashing to transform an item's key into a table index so that insertions, retrievals, and deletions can be performed in expected O(1) time. When the hashCode method is applied to a key, it should return an integer value that appears to be a random number. A good hashCode method should be easy to compute and should distribute its values evenly throughout the range of **int** values. We use modulo division to transform the hash code value to a table index. Best performance occurs when the table size is a prime number.

♦ A collision occurs when two keys hash to the same table index. Collisions are expected, and hash tables utilize either open addressing or chaining to resolve collisions. In open addressing, each table element references a key-value pair, or **null** if it is empty. During insertion, a new entry is stored at the table element corresponding to its hash index if it is empty; otherwise, it is stored in the next empty location following the one selected by its hash index. In chaining, each table element references a linked list of key-value pairs with that hash index or **null** if none do. During insertion, a new entry is stored in the linked list of key-value pairs for its hash index.

♦ In open addressing, linear probing is often used to resolve collisions. In linear probing, finding a target or an empty table location involves incrementing the table index by 1 after each probe. This approach may cause clusters of keys to occur in the table, leading to overlapping search chains and poor performance. To minimize the harmful effect of clustering, quadratic probing increments the index by the square of the probe number. Quadratic probing can, however, cause a table to appear to be full when there is still space available, and it can lead to an infinite loop.

♦ The best way to avoid collisions is to keep the table load factor relatively low by rehashing when the load factor reaches a value such as 0.75 (75 percent full). To rehash, you increase the table size and reinsert each table element.

♦ In open addressing, you can't remove an element from the table when you delete it, but you must mark it as deleted. In chaining, you can remove a table element when you delete it. In either case, traversal of a hash table visits its entries in an arbitrary order.

◆ A set view of a Map can be obtained through method entrySet. You can create an Iterator object for this set view and use it to access the elements in the set view.

◆ Two Java API implementations of the Map (Set) interface are HashMap (HashSet) and TreeMap (TreeSet). The HashMap (and HashSet) implementation uses an underlying hash table; the TreeMap (and TreeSet) implementations use a Red-Black tree. Search and retrieval operations are more efficient using the underlying hash table (expected $O(1)$ versus $O(\log n)$). The tree implementation, however, enables you to traverse the key-value pairs in a meaningful way and allows for subsets based on a range of key values.

Java API Interfaces and Classes Introduced in This Chapter

java.util.Map
java.util.Set
java.util.TreeMap
java.util.TreeSet
java.util.HashMap

java.util.HashSet
java.util.AbstractMap
java.util.AbstractSet
java.util.Map.Entry

User-Defined Interfaces and Classes in This Chapter

KWHashMap
Entry
HashtableOpen
HashtableChain

HashSetOpen
EntrySet
SetIterator
BitString

Quick-Check Exercises

1. If s is a set that contains the characters 'a', 'b', 'c', write a statement to insert the character 'd'.

2. What is the effect of each of the following method calls, given the set in Exercise 1, and what does it return?

    ```
    s.add(new Character('a'));
    s.add(new Character('A'));
    next = 'b';
    s.contains(new Character(next));
    ```

    For questions 3 through 7, a Map, m, contains the following entries: (1234, "Jane Doe"), (1999, "John Smith"), (1250, "Ace Ventura"), (2000, "Bill Smythe"), (2999, "Nomar Garciaparra").

3. What is the effect of the statement m.put(new Integer(1234), "Jane Smith")? What is returned?

4. What is returned by the statement m.get(new Integer(1234))? What is returned by the statement m.get(new Integer(1500))?

5. If the entries for Map m are stored in a hash table of size 1000 with open addressing and linear probing, where would each of the items be stored?

6. Answer Question 5 for the case where the entries were stored using quadratic probing.

7. Answer Question 5 for the case where the entries were stored using chaining.

8. What class does the Java API provide that facilitates coding an implementer of the Map interface? Of the Set interface?

9. List two classes that the Java API provides that implement the `Map` interface. List two that implement the `Set` interface.

10. You apply method _____ to a `Map` to create a set view. You apply method _____ to this set view to get an object that facilitates sequential access to the `Map` elements.

Answers to Quick-Check Exercises

1. `s.add(new Character('d'));`

2. `s.add(new Character('a'));`   `// add 'a', duplicate - returns false`
   `s.add(new Character('A'));`   `// add 'A', returns true`
   `next = 'b';`
   `s.contains(new Character(next));`   `// 'b' is in the set, returns true`

3. The value associated with key 1234 is changed to `"Jane Smith"`. The string `"Jane Doe"` is returned.

4. The string `"Jane Doe"`, and then **null**.

5. 1234 at 234, 1999 at 999, 1250 at 250, 2000 at 000, 3999 at 001.

6. 1234 at 234, 1999 at 999, 1250 at 250, 2000 at 000, 3999 at 003.

7. 2000 in a linked list at 000, 1234 in a linked list at 234, 1250 in a linked list at 250, 1999 and 3999 in a linked list at 999.

8. `AbstractMap, AbstractSet`

9. `HashMap and TreeMap, HashSet and TreeSet`

10. `entrySet, iterator`

Review Questions

1. Show where the following keys would be placed in a hash table of size 5 using open addressing: 1000, 1002, 1007, 1003. Where would these keys be after rehashing to a table of size 11?

2. Answer Question 1 for a hash table that uses chaining.

3. Write a `toString` method for class `HashtableOpen`. This method should display each table element that is not **null** and is not deleted.

4. Class `HashtableChain` uses the class `LinkedList`, which is implemented as a double-linked list. Write the `put` method using a single-linked list to hold elements that hash to the same index.

5. Write the `get` method for the class in Question 4.

6. Write the `remove` method for the class in Question 4.

7. Write inner class `EntrySet` for the class in Question 4 (see Listing. 9.11).

Programming Projects

1. Complete all methods of class `HuffmanTree` and test them out using a document file and a Java source file on your computer. You can download class `BitString` from the Web site for this textbook.

2. Use a `HashMap` to store the frequency counts for all the words in a large text document. When you are done, display the contents of this `HashMap`. Next, create a set view of the `Map` and store its contents in an array. Then sort the array based on key value and display it. Finally, sort the array in decreasing order by frequency and display it.

3. Solve Project 2 using a `TreeMap`. You can display the words in key sequence without performing a sort.

4. Modify Project 2 to save the line numbers for every occurrence of a word as well as the count.

5. (Based on example in Brian W. Kernighan and Rob Pike, *The Practice of Programming,* Addison Wesley, 1999) We want to generate "random text" in the style of another author. Your first task is to collect a group of prefix strings of two words that occur in a text file and associate them with a list of suffix strings using a Map. For example, the text for Charles Dickens' *A Christmas Carol* contains the four phrases:

> Marley was dead: to begin with.
> Marley was as dead as a door-nail.
> Marley was as dead as a door-nail.
> Marley was dead.

The prefix string "Marley was" would be associated with the ArrayList containing the four suffix strings "dead:", "as", "as", "dead.". You must go through the text and examine each successive pair of two-word strings to see whether that pair is already in the map as a key. If so, add the next word to the ArrayList that is the value for that prefix string. For example, in examining the first two sentences shown, you would first add to the entry ("Marley was", ArrayList "dead:"). Next you would add the entry ("was dead", ArrayList "as"). Next you would add the entry ("dead as", ArrayList "a"), and so on. When you retrieve the prefix "Marley was" again, you would modify the ArrayList that is its value, and the entry would become ("Marley was", ArrayList "dead:", "as"). When you are all finished, add the entry "THE_END" to the suffix list for the last prefix placed in the Map.

   Once you have scanned the complete text, it is time to use the Map to begin generating new text that is in the same style as the old text. Output the first prefix you placed in the Map: "Marley was". Then retrieve the ArrayList that is the value for this prefix. Randomly select one of the suffixes, and then output the suffix. For example, the output text so far might be "Marley was dead" if the suffix "dead" was selected from the ArrayList of suffixes for "Marley was". Now continue with the two-word sequence consisting of the second word from the previous prefix and the suffix (that would be the string "was dead"). Look it up in the map, randomly select one of the suffixes, and output it. Continue this process until the suffix "THE_END" is selected.

6. Complete class HashtableOpen so that it fully implements the Map interface described in Section 9.2. As part of this, write method entrySet and classes EntrySet and SetIterator as described in Section 9.5. Class SetIterator provides methods hasNext and next. Use data field index to keep track of the next value of the iterator (initially 0). Data field lastItemReturned keeps track of the index of the last item returned by next; this is used by the remove method. The remove method removes the last item returned by the next method from the Set. It may only be called once for each call to next. Thus, the remove method checks to see that lastItemReturned has a valid value (not −1) and then sets it to an invalid value (−1) just before returning to the caller.

7. Complete class HashtableOpen so that it fully implements the Map interface, and test it out. Method hasNext determines whether there is a next element. Complete class SetIterator as described in Project 6.

8. Complete the implementation of class HashSetOpen, writing it as an adapter class of HashtableOpen.

9. Complete the implementation of class HashSetChain, writing it as an adapter class of HashtableChain.

10. Revise method put for HashtableOpen to place a new item into an already deleted spot in the search chain. Don't forget to check the scenario where the key has already been inserted.

Chapter 10

Sorting

Chapter Objectives

- ◆ To learn how to use the standard sorting methods in the Java API
- ◆ To learn how to implement the following sorting algorithms: selection sort, bubble sort, insertion sort, Shell sort, merge sort, heapsort, and quicksort
- ◆ To understand the difference in performance of these algorithms, and which to use for small arrays, which to use for medium arrays, and which to use for large arrays

B ecause sorting is done so frequently, computer scientists have devoted much time and effort to developing efficient algorithms for sorting arrays. Even though many languages (including Java) provide sorting utilities, it is still very important to study these algorithms, because they illustrate several well-known ways to solve the sorting problem, each with its own merits. You should know how they are written so that you can duplicate them if you need to use them with languages that don't have sorting utilities.

This chapter discusses several techniques for sorting an array and compares these algorithms with respect to their efficiency. We will cover three quadratic ($O(n^2)$) sorting algorithms that are fairly simple and appropriate for sorting small arrays but are not recommended for large arrays. We will also discuss three sorting algorithms that give improved performance ($O(n\ log\ n)$) on large arrays and one that gives performance that is much better than $O(n^2)$, but not as good as $O(n\ log\ n)$.

Our goal is to provide a sufficient selection of quadratic sorts and faster sorts. A few other sorting algorithms are described in the programming projects. Our expectation is that your instructor will select which algorithms you should study.

10.1 Using Java Sorting Methods

The Java API `java.util` provides a class `Arrays` with several overloaded `sort` methods for different array types. In addition, the class `Collections` (also part of the API `java.util`) contains similar sorting methods for `Lists`. The methods for arrays of primitive types are based on the quicksort algorithm (Section 10.9), and the methods for arrays of `Objects` and for `Lists` are based on the mergesort algorithm (Section 10.7). Both algorithms are O($n \log n$).

Method `Arrays.sort` is defined as a **public static void** method and is overloaded (see Table 10.1). The first argument in a call can be an array of any primitive type (although we have just shown **int[]**) or an array of objects. If the first argument is an array of objects, then either the class type of the array must implement the `Comparable` interface or a `Comparator` object must be passed as the last argument (see Section 8.5). A class that implements the `Comparable` interface must define a `compareTo` method that determines the natural ordering of its objects. If a `Comparator` is passed, its `compare` method will be used to determine the ordering.

For method `Collections.sort` (see Table 10.1), the first argument must be a collection of objects that implement the `List` interface (for example, an `ArrayList` or a `LinkedList`). If only one argument is provided, the objects in the `List` must implement the `Comparable` interface. Method `compareTo` is called by the sorting method to determine the relative ordering of two objects. Optionally, a `Comparator` can be passed as a second argument. Using a `Comparator`, you can compare objects based on some other information rather than using their natural ordering (as determined by method `compareTo`). The `Comparator` object must be the last argument in the call to the sorting method. Rather than rearranging the elements in the `List`, method `sort` first copies the `List` elements to an array, sorts the array using `Arrays.sort`, and then copies them back to the `List`.

TABLE 10.1
Methods `sort` in Classes `java.util.Arrays` and `java.util.Collections`

Method sort in Class Arrays	Behavior
`public static void sort(int[] items)`	Sorts the array `items` in ascending order.
`public static void sort(int[] items, int fromIndex, int toIndex)`	Sorts array elements `items[fromIndex]` to `items[toIndex]` in ascending order.
`public static void sort(Object[] items)`	Sorts the objects in array `items` in ascending order using their natural ordering (defined by method `compareTo`). All objects in `items` must implement the `Comparable` interface and must be mutually comparable.
`public static void sort(Object[] items, int fromIndex, int toIndex)`	Sorts array elements `items[fromIndex]` to `items[toIndex]` in ascending order using their natural ordering (defined by method `compareTo`). All objects must implement the `Comparable` interface and must be mutually comparable.
`public static void sort(Object[] items, Comparator comp)`	Sorts the objects in `items` in ascending order as defined by method `comp.compare`. All objects in `items` must be mutually comparable using method `comp.compare`.
`public static void sort(Object[] items, int fromIndex, int toIndex, Comparator comp)`	Sorts the objects in `items[fromIndex]` to `items[toIndex]` in ascending order as defined by method `comp.compare`. All objects in `items` must be mutually comparable using method `comp.compare`.
Method sort in Class Collections	**Behavior**
`public static void sort(List list)`	Sorts the objects in `list` in ascending order using their natural ordering (defined by method `compareTo`). All objects in `list` must implement the `Comparable` interface and must be mutually comparable.
`public static void sort(List list, Comparator comp)`	Sorts the objects in `list` in ascending order as defined by method `comp.compare`. All objects must be mutually comparable.

EXAMPLE 10.1 If array `items` stores a collection of integers, the method call

```
Arrays.sort(items, 0, items.length / 2) ;
```

sorts the integers in the first half of the array, leaving the second half of the array unchanged.

EXAMPLE 10.2 Let's assume class Person is defined as follows:

```
public class Person implements Comparable {
    // Data Fields
    /* The last name */
    private String lastName;
    /* The first name */
    private String firstName;
    /* Birthday represented by an integer from 1 to 366 */
    private int birthDay;

    // Methods
    /** Compares two Person objects based on names. The result
        is based on the last names if they are different;
        otherwise, it is based on the first names.
        @param obj The other Person object
        @return A negative integer if this person's name
                precedes the other person's name;
                0 if the names are the same;
                a positive integer if this person's name follows
                the other person's name.
        @throws ClassCastException if obj is not Person
    */
    public int compareTo(Object obj) {
        Person other = (Person) obj;
        // Compare this Person to other using last names.
        int result = lastName.compareTo(other.lastName);
        // Compare first names if last names are the same.
        if (result == 0)
            return firstName.compareTo(other.firstName);
        else
            return result;
    }

    // Other methods
    ...
}
```

Method Person.compareTo compares two Person objects based on their names using the last name as the primary key and the first name as the secondary key (the natural ordering). If people is an array of Person objects, the statement

```
Arrays.sort(people);
```

places the elements in array people in ascending order based on their names. Although the sort operation is $O(n \log n)$, the comparison of two names is $O(k)$ where k is the length of the shorter name.

EXAMPLE 10.3 You can also use a class that implements Comparator to compare Person objects. As an example, method compare in class ComparePerson compares two Person objects based on their birthdays, not their names.

```
import java.util.Comparator;

public class ComparePerson implements Comparator {
    /** Compare two Person objects based on birth date.
        @param left The left-hand side of the comparison
        @param right The right-hand side of the comparison
        @return A negative integer if the left person's birthday
                precedes the right person's birthday;
                0 if the birthdays are the same;
                a positive integer if the left person's birthday
                follows the right person's birthday.
        @throws ClassCastException if left or right is not a
                Person
    */
    public int compare(Object left, Object right) {
        Person leftPer = (Person) left;
        Person rightPer = (Person) right;
        return leftPer.getBirthDay() - rightPer.getBirthDay();
    }
}
```

If `peopleList` is a `List` of `Person` objects, the statement

```
Collections.sort(peopleList, new ComparePerson());
```

places the elements in `peopleList` in ascending order based on their birthdays. Comparing two birthdays is an **O**(1) operation.

EXERCISES FOR SECTION 10.1

SELF-CHECK

1. Indicate whether each method call below is valid. Describe why it isn't valid or, if it is valid, describe what it does. Assume `people` is an array of `Person` objects and `peopleList` is a `List` of `Person` objects.

   a. `people.sort();`
   b. `Arrays.sort(people, 0, people.length - 3);`
   c. `Arrays.sort(peopleList, 0, peopleList.length - 3);`
   d. `Collections.sort(people);`
   e. `Collections.sort(peopleList, new ComparePerson());`
   f. `Collections.sort(peopleList, 0, peopleList.size() - 3);`

PROGRAMMING

1. Write a method call to sort the last half of array `people` using the natural ordering.
2. Write a method call to sort the last half of array `people` using the ordering determined by class `ComparePerson`.
3. Write a method call to sort `peopleList` using the natural ordering.

10.2 Selection Sort

Selection sort is a relatively easy-to-understand algorithm that sorts an array by making several passes through the array, *selecting* the next smallest item in the array each time and placing it where it belongs in the array. We illustrate all sorting algorithms using an array of integer values for simplicity. However, each algorithm sorts an array of Comparable objects, so the **int** values must be wrapped in Integer objects.

We show the algorithm next, where *n* is the number of elements in an array with subscripts 0 through *n* – 1, and fill is the subscript of the element that will store the next smallest item in the array.

Selection Sort Algorithm

1.   **for** fill = 0 to n – 2 do
2.   Set posMin to the subscript of the smallest item in the subarray starting at subscript fill.
3.   Exchange the item at posMin with the one at fill.

Step 2 involves a search for the smallest item in each subarray. It requires a loop in which we compare each element in the subarray, starting with the one at position fill + 1, with the smallest value found so far. In the refinement of Step 2 shown in the following algorithm (Steps 2.1 through 2.4), we use posMin to store the subscript of the smallest value found so far. We assume that its initial position is fill.

Refinement of Selection Sort Algorithm (Step 2)

2.1   Initialize posMin to fill.
2.2   **for** next = fill + 1 to n – 1
2.3   **if** the item at next is less than the item at posMin
2.4   Reset posMin to next.

First the selection sort algorithm finds the smallest item in the array (smallest is 20) and moves it to position 0 by exchanging it with the element currently at position 0. At this point, the sorted part of the array consists of the new element at position 0. The values to be exchanged are shaded dark in all diagrams.

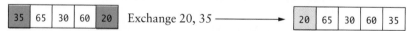

Next the algorithm finds the smallest item in the subarray starting at position 1 (next smallest is 30) and exchanges it with the element currently at position 1:

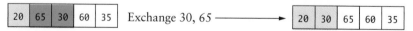

At this point, the sorted portion of the array consists of the elements at positions 0 and 1. Next the algorithm selects the smallest item in the subarray starting at position 2 (next smallest is 35) and exchanges it with the element currently at position 2:

| 20 | 30 | 65 | 60 | 35 | Exchange 35, 65 ⟶ | 20 | 30 | 35 | 60 | 65 |

At this point, the sorted portion of the array consists of the elements at positions 0, 1, and 2. Next the algorithm selects the smallest item in the subarray starting at position 3 (next smallest is 60) and exchanges it with the element currently at position 3:

| 20 | 30 | 35 | 60 | 65 | Exchange 60 with itself ⟶ | 20 | 30 | 35 | 60 | 65 |

The element at position 4, the last position in the array, must store the largest value (largest is 65), so the array is sorted.

Analysis of Selection Sort

Steps 2 and 3 are performed $n - 1$ times. Step 3 performs an exchange of items; consequently, there are $n - 1$ exchanges.

Step 2.3 involves a comparison of items and is performed $(n - 1 - fill)$ times for each value of *fill*. Since *fill* takes on all values between 0 and $n - 2$, the following series computes the number of executions of Step 2.3:

$$(n - 1) + (n - 2) + \cdots + 3 + 2 + 1$$

This is a well-known series that can be written in closed form as

$$\frac{n \times (n - 1)}{2} = \frac{n^2}{2} - \frac{n}{2}$$

For very large n we can ignore all but the most significant term in this expression, so the number of comparisons is $O(n^2)$, and the number of exchanges is $O(n)$. Because the number of comparisons increases with the square of n, the selection sort is called a *quadratic sort*.

Code for Selection Sort

Listing 10.1 shows the code for selection sort. The code follows the algorithm just given.

LISTING 10.1
SelectionSort.java

```java
/** Implements the selection sort algorithm. */
public class SelectionSort {

    /** Sort the array using selection sort algorithm.
        pre:  table contains Comparable objects.
        post: table is sorted.
        @param table The array to be sorted
```

```
        */
        public static void sort(Comparable[] table) {
            int n = table.length;
            for (int fill = 0; fill < n - 1; fill++) {
                // Invariant: table[0 ... fill - 1] is sorted.
                int posMin = fill;
                for (int next = fill + 1; next < n; next++) {
                    // Invariant: table[posMin] is the smallest item in
                    // table[fill ... next - 1].
                    if (table[next].compareTo(table[posMin]) < 0) {
                        posMin = next;
                    }
                }
                // assert: table[posMin] is the smallest item in
                // table[fill ... n - 1].
                // Exchange table[fill] and table[posMin].
                Comparable temp = table[fill];
                table[fill] = table[posMin];
                table[posMin] = temp;
                // assert: table[fill] is the smallest item in
                // table[fill ... n - 1].
            }
            // assert: table[0 ... n - 1] is sorted.
        }
    }
```

EXERCISES FOR SECTION 10.2

SELF-CHECK

1. Show the progress of each pass of the selection sort for the following array. How many passes are needed? How many comparisons are performed? How many exchanges? Show the array after each pass.

   40 35 80 75 60 90 70 75

2. How would you modify selection sort to arrange an array of values in decreasing sequence?

3. It is not really necessary to perform an exchange if the next smallest element is already at position fill. Modify the selection sort algorithm to eliminate the exchange of an element with itself. How does this affect big-O for exchanges? Discuss whether the time saved by eliminating unnecessary exchanges would exceed the cost of these extra steps.

PROGRAMMING

1. Modify the selection sort method to sort the elements in decreasing order and to incorporate the change in Self-Check Exercise 3.

2. Add statements to trace the progress of selection sort. Display the array contents after each exchange.

10.3 Bubble Sort

The next quadratic sorting algorithm, *bubble sort*, compares adjacent array elements and exchanges their values if they are out of order. In this way the smaller values *bubble* up to the top of the array (toward the first element) while the larger values sink to the bottom of the array; hence the name.

Bubble Sort Algorithm

1. Repeat
2.   **for** each pair of adjacent array elements
3.   **if** the values in a pair are out of order
4.   Exchange the values
5. Until the array is sorted.

As an example, we will trace through one execution of Step 2, or one pass through an array being sorted. By scanning the diagrams of Figure 10.1 from left to right, you can see the effect of each comparison. The pair of array elements being compared is shown in a darker color in each diagram. The first pair of values (table[0] is 60, table[1] is 42) is out of order, so the values are exchanged. The next pair of values (table[1] is now 60, table[2] is 75) is compared in the second array shown in Figure 10.1; this pair is in order, and so is the next pair (table[2] is 75, table[3] is 83). The last pair (table[3] is 83, table[4] is 27) is out of order, so the values are exchanged as shown is the last diagram, and 83 has sunk to the bottom of the array.

FIGURE 10.1
One Pass of Bubble Sort

The last array shown in Figure 10.1 is closer to being sorted than is the original. The only value that is out of order is the number 27 in table[3]. Unfortunately, it will be necessary to complete three more passes through the array before this value bubbles up to the top of the array. In each of these passes only one pair of values will be out of order, so only one exchange will be made. The contents of array table after the completion of each pass is shown in Figure 10.2; the portion that is sorted is shown in color.

FIGURE 10.2
Array After Completion of Each Pass

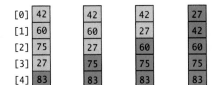

At the end of pass 1 only the last array element must be in its correct place, at the end of pass 2 the last two array elements must be in their correct places, and so on. There is no need to examine array elements that are already in place, so there is one less pair to test in the next pass. Only one pair will be tested during the last pass.

After the completion of four passes ($n - 1$ is 4), the array is now sorted. Sometimes an array will become sorted before $n - 1$ passes. This situation can be detected if a pass is made through the array without doing any exchanges. This is the reason for the **boolean** flag exchanges in the following refined bubble sort algorithm: to keep track of whether any exchanges were made during the current pass (exchanges is set to **false** when the pass begins and is reset to **true** after an exchange).

Refinement of Bubble Sort Algorithm (Step 2)

2.1   Initialize exchanges to **false**. // *No exchanges yet—array may be sorted*

2.2   **for** each pair of adjacent array elements

2.3   **if** the values in a pair are out of order

2.4   Exchange the values.

2.4   Set exchanges to **true**. // *Made an exchange, array not sorted*

Analysis of Bubble Sort

Because the actual numbers of comparisons and exchanges performed depend on the array being sorted, the bubble sort algorithm provides excellent performance in some cases and very poor performance in other cases. It works best when an array is nearly sorted to begin with.

Because all adjacent pairs of elements in the unsorted region are compared in each pass and there may be $n - 1$ passes, the number of comparisons is represented by the series

$$(n - 1) + (n - 2) + \cdots + 3 + 2 + 1$$

However, if the array becomes sorted early, the later phases and comparisons are not performed. In the worst case the number of comparisons is $O(n^2)$. Unfortunately, each comparison can lead to an exchange if the array is badly out of order. The worst case occurs when the array is *inverted* (that is, the array elements are in descending order as defined by the compareTo method), and the number of exchanges is $O(n^2)$.

The best case occurs when the array is already sorted. Only one pass will be required, in which there are $n - 1$ comparisons ($O(n)$ comparisons). If the array is sorted, there will be no exchanges, so the number of exchanges is 0 ($O(1)$ exchanges).

In estimating the worst-case performance of a sorting algorithm on a large array whose initial element values are determined arbitrarily, the definition of big-O requires us to be pessimistic. For this reason, bubble sort is considered a quadratic sort, and its performance is usually worse than selection sort (O(n)) because the number of exchanges can be O(n^2).

Code for Bubble Sort

Listing 10.2 shows the code for the BubbleSort class. Notice that the outer **do-while** loop terminates when the condition (exchanges) is false. This indicates the array is sorted, because no exchanges occurred during the pass just completed. If the array does not become sorted until all n - 1 passes are completed, then an extra pass will be required. However, the inner loop will be exited immediately, because table.length - pass will be equal to 0.

The inner loop control variable, i, is the subscript of the first element of each pair; consequently, i + 1 is the subscript of the second element of each pair. The initial value of i is 0. The final value must be one less than the last subscript in the unsorted region. For an array of n elements the final value of i is n - pass - 1, where pass is the number of the current pass, starting at 1 for the first pass.

LISTING 10.2
BubbleSort.java

```java
/** Implements the bubble sort algorithm. */
public class BubbleSort {

    /** Sort the array using bubble sort algorithm.
        pre:  table contains Comparable objects.
        post: table is sorted.
        @param table The array to be sorted
    */
    public static void sort(Comparable table[]) {
        int pass = 1;
        boolean exchanges = false;
        do {
            // Invariant: Elements after table.length - pass + 1
            // are in place.
            exchanges = false;  // No exchanges yet.
            // Compare each pair of adjacent elements.
            for (int i = 0; i < table.length - pass; i++) {
                if (table[i].compareTo(table[i + 1]) > 0) {
                    // Exchange pair.
                    Comparable temp = table[i];
                    table[i] = table[i + 1];
                    table[i + 1] = temp;
                    exchanges = true;  // Set flag.
                }
            }
            pass++;
        } while (exchanges);
        // assert: Array is sorted.
    }
}
```

EXERCISES FOR SECTION 10.3

SELF-CHECK

1. How many passes of bubble sort are needed to sort the following array of integers? How many comparisons are performed? How many exchanges? Show the array after each pass.

   40 35 80 75 60 90 70 75

2. How would you modify bubble sort to arrange an array of values in decreasing sequence?

PROGRAMMING

1. Add statements to trace the progress of bubble sort. Display the array contents after each pass is completed.

10.4 Insertion Sort

Our next quadratic sorting algorithm, *insertion sort*, is based on the technique used by card players to arrange a hand of cards. The player keeps the cards that have been picked up so far in sorted order. When the player picks up a new card, the player makes room for the new card and then *inserts* in its proper place.

The left diagram of Figure 10.3 shows a hand of cards (ignoring suits) after three cards have been picked up. If the next card is an 8, it should be inserted between the 6 and 10, maintaining the numerical order (middle diagram). If the next card is a 7, it should be inserted between the 6 and 8 as shown in the right diagram of Figure 10.3.

To adapt this insertion algorithm to an array that has been filled with data, we start with a sorted subarray consisting of the first element only. For example, in the leftmost array of Figure 10.4, the initial sorted subarray consists of only the first value 30 (in element 0). The array element(s) that are in order after each pass are in color, and the elements waiting to be inserted are in gray. We first *insert* the second element (25). Because it is smaller than the element in the sorted subarray, we insert it

FIGURE 10.3
Picking Up a Hand of Cards

FIGURE 10.4
An Insertion Sort

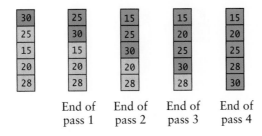

End of pass 1   End of pass 2   End of pass 3   End of pass 4

before the old first element (30), and the sorted subarray has two elements (25, 30 in second diagram). Next, we *insert* the third element (15). It is also smaller than all the elements in the sorted subarray, so we insert it before the old first element (25), and the sorted subarray has three elements (15, 25, 30 in third diagram). Next, we *insert* the fourth element (20). It is smaller than the second and third elements in the sorted subarray so we insert it before the old second element (25), and the sorted subarray has four elements (15, 20, 25, 30 in the fourth diagram). Finally we insert the last element (28). It is smaller than the last element in the sorted subarray, so we insert it before the old last element (30) and the array is sorted. The algorithm follows.

Insertion Sort Algorithm

1. **for** each array element from the second (nextPos = 1) to the last
2.   Insert the element at nextPos where it belongs in the array, increasing the length of the sorted subarray by 1 element.

To accomplish Step 2, the insertion step, we need to make room for the element to be inserted (saved in nextVal) by shifting all values that are larger than it, starting with the last value in the sorted subarray.

Refinement of Insertion Sort Algorithm (Step 2)

2.1   nextPos is the position of the element to insert.
2.2   Save the value of the element to insert in nextVal.
2.3   **while** nextPos > 0 and the element at nextPos - 1 > nextVal
2.4   Shift the element at nextPos - 1 to position nextPos.
2.5   Decrement nextPos by 1.
2.6   Insert nextVal at nextPos.

We illustrate these steps in Figure 10.5. For the array shown on the left, the first three elements (positions 0, 1, and 2) are in the sorted subarray, and the next element to insert is 20. First we save 20 in nextVal and 3 in nextPos. Then we shift the value in position 2 (30) down one position (see the second array in Figure 10.5), and then we shift the value in position 1 (25) down one position (see third array in Figure 10.5). After these shifts (third array), there will temporarily be two copies of the last value shifted (25). The first of these (shown in gray in Figure 10.5) is overwritten when the value in nextVal is moved into its correct position (nextPos is 1). The four-element sorted subarray is shown in color on the right of Figure 10.5.

FIGURE 10.5
Inserting the Fourth
Array Element

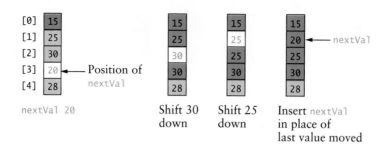

Analysis of Insertion Sort

The insertion step is performed $n - 1$ times. In the worst case, all elements in the sorted subarray are compared to nextVal for each insertion, so the maximum number of comparisons is represented by the series

$$1 + 2 + 3 + \cdots + (n - 2) + (n - 1)$$

which is $O(n^2)$. In the best case (when the array is already sorted), only one comparison is required for each insertion, so the number of comparisons is $O(n)$. The number of shifts performed during an insertion is one less than the number of comparisons or, when the new value is the smallest so far, the same as the number of comparisons. However, a shift in an insertion sort requires the movement of only one item, whereas in a bubble sort or a selection sort an exchange involves a temporary item and requires the movement of three items. A Java array of objects contains references to the actual objects, and it is these references that are changed. The actual objects remain in the physical locations where they were first created.

Code for Insertion Sort

Listing 10.3 shows the InsertionSort. We use method insert to perform the insertion step shown earlier. It would be more efficient to insert this code inside the **for** statement; however, using a method will make it easier later to implement the Shell sort algorithm.

The **while** statement in method insert compares and shifts all values greater than nextVal in the subarray table[0 ... nextPos - 1]. The **while** condition

```
((nextPos > 0) && (nextVal.compareTo(table[nextPos - 1]) < 0))
```

causes loop exit if the first element has been moved, or if nextVal is not less than the next element to move. It could lead to an out-of-range subscript error if the order of the conditions were reversed. Recall that Java performs short-circuit evaluation. If the left-hand operand of an && operation is false, the right-hand operand is not evaluated. If this were not the case, when nextPos becomes 0, the array subscript would be –1, which is outside the subscript range. Because nextPos is a value parameter, variable nextPos in sort is unchanged.

LISTING 10.3
InsertionSort.java

```java
/** Implements the insertion sort algorithm. */
public class InsertionSort {
    /** Sort the table using insertion sort algorithm.
        pre:  table contains Comparable objects.
        post: table is sorted.
        @param table The array to be sorted
     */
    public static void sort(Comparable table[]) {
        for (int nextPos = 1; nextPos < table.length; nextPos++) {
            // Invariant: table[0 ... nextPos - 1] is sorted.
            // Insert element at position nextPos
            // in the sorted subarray.
            insert(table, nextPos);
        } // End for.
    } // End sort.

    /** Insert the element at nextPos where it belongs
        in the array.
        pre:  table[0 ... nextPos - 1] is sorted.
        post: table[0 ... nextPos] is sorted.
        @param table The array being sorted
        @param nextPos The position of the element to insert
     */
    private static void insert(Comparable[] table, int nextPos) {
        Comparable nextVal = table[nextPos];  // Element to insert.
        while (nextPos > 0
                 && nextVal.compareTo(table[nextPos - 1]) < 0) {
            table[nextPos] = table[nextPos - 1]; // Shift down.
            nextPos--;               // Check next smaller element.
        }
        // Insert nextVal at nextPos.
        table[nextPos] = nextVal;
    }
}
```

EXERCISES FOR SECTION 10.4

SELF-CHECK

1. Sort the following array using insertion sort. How many passes are needed? How many comparisons are performed? How many exchanges? Show the array after each pass.

   40 35 80 75 60 90 70 75

PROGRAMMING

1. Eliminate method insert in Listing 10.3 and write its code inside the **for** statement.
2. Add statements to trace the progress of insertion sort. Display the array contents after the insertion of each value.

10.5 Comparison of Quadratic Sorts

Table 10.2 summarizes the performance of the three quadratic sorts. To give you some idea as to what these numbers mean, Table 10.3 shows some values of n and n^2. If n is small (say, 100 or less), it really doesn't matter which sorting algorithm you use. Of the three, insertion sort gives the best performance for most arrays, and bubble sort generally gives the worst performance. Insertion sort is better because it takes advantage of any partial sorting that is in the array and uses less costly shifts instead of exchanges to rearrange array elements. Unless the array is nearly sorted, bubble sort's performance usually exhibits its worst case behavior, $O(n^2)$. For this reason, bubble sort performs much worse than the others unless the initial array is nearly sorted. In the next section, we discuss a variation on insertion sort, known as Shell sort, that has $O(n^{3/2})$ or better performance.

Since the time to sort an array of n elements is proportional to n^2, none of these algorithms is particularly good for large arrays (that is, $n > 100$). The best sorting algorithms provide $n \log n$ average-case behavior and are considerably faster for large arrays. In fact, one of the algorithms that we will discuss has $n \log n$ worst-case behavior. You can get a feel for the difference in behavior by comparing the last column of Table 10.3 with the middle column.

TABLE 10.2
Comparison of Quadratic Sorts

	Number of Comparisons		Number of Exchanges	
	Best	Worst	Best	Worst
Selection sort	$O(n^2)$	$O(n^2)$	$O(n)$	$O(n)$
Bubble sort	$O(n)$	$O(n^2)$	$O(1)$	$O(n^2)$
Insertion sort	$O(n)$	$O(n^2)$	$O(n)$	$O(n^2)$

TABLE 10.3
Comparison of Rates of Growth

n	n^2	$n \log n$
8	64	24
16	256	64
32	1,024	160
64	4,096	384
128	16,384	896
256	65,536	2,048
512	262,144	4,608

Recall from Chapter 2 that big-O analysis ignores any constants that might be involved or any overhead that might occur from method calls needed to perform an exchange or comparison. However, the tables give you an estimate of the relative performance of the different sorting algorithms.

We haven't talked about storage usage for these algorithms. All the quadratic sorts require storage for the array being sorted. However, there is only one copy of this array, so the array is sorted in place. There are also requirements for variables that store references to particular elements, loop control variables, and temporary variables. However, for large n, the size of the array dominates these other storage considerations, so the extra space usage is proportional to $O(1)$.

Comparisons versus Exchanges

We have analyzed comparisons and exchanges separately, but you may be wondering whether one is more costly (in terms of computer time) than the other. In Java, an exchange requires your computer to switch two object references using a third object reference as an intermediary. A comparison requires your computer to execute a compareTo method. The cost of a comparison depends on its complexity, but it will probably be more costly than an exchange because of the overhead to call and execute method compareTo. In some programming languages (but not Java), an exchange may require physically moving the information in each object, rather than simply swapping object references. For these languages, the cost of an exchange would be proportional to the size of the objects being exchanged and may be more costly than a comparison.

EXERCISES FOR SECTION 10.5

SELF-CHECK

1. Complete Table 10.3 for $n = 1024$ and $n = 2048$.
2. What do the new rows of Table 10.3 tell us about the increase in time required to process an array of 1024 elements versus an array of 2048 elements for $O(n)$, $O(n^2)$, and $O(n \log n)$ algorithms?

10.6 Shell Sort: A Better Insertion Sort

Next we describe the *Shell sort*, which is a type of insertion sort, but with $O(n^{3/2})$ or better performance. Unlike the other algorithms, Shell sort is named after its discoverer, Donald Shell (D. L. Shell, "A High-Speed Sorting Procedure," *Communications of the ACM*, Vol. 2, No. 7 [1959], pp. 30–32). You can think of the Shell sort as a divide-and-conquer approach to insertion sort. Instead of sorting the entire array at the start, the idea behind Shell sort is to sort many smaller subarrays using insertion sort before sorting the entire array. The initial subarrays will contain two or three elements, so the insertion sorts will go very quickly. After each collection of subarrays is sorted, a new collection of subarrays with approximately twice as many elements as before will be sorted. The last step is to perform an insertion sort on the entire array, which has been presorted by the earlier sorts.

As an example, let's sort the following array using initial subarrays with only two and three elements. We determine the elements in each subarray by setting a gap value between the subscripts in each subarray. We will explain how we pick the gap values later. We will use an initial gap of 7.

[0]	[1]	[2]	[3]	[4]	[5]	[6]	[7]	[8]	[9]	[10]	[11]	[12]	[13]	[14]	[15]
40	35	80	75	60	90	70	75	55	90	85	34	45	62	57	65

A gap of 7 means the first subarray has subscripts 0, 7, 14 (element values 40, 75, 57, shown in light blue); the second subarray has subscripts 1, 8, 15 (element values 35, 55, 65, shown in dark blue); the third subarray has subscripts 2, 9 (element values 80, 90, shown in gray); and so on. There are seven subarrays. We start the process by inserting the value at position 7 (value of gap) into its subarray (elements at 0 and 7). Next, we insert the element at position 8 into its subarray (elements at 1 and 8). We continue until we have inserted the last element (at position 15) in its subarray (elements at 1, 8, and 15). The result of performing insertion sort on all seven subarrays with two or three elements follows.

[0]	[1]	[2]	[3]	[4]	[5]	[6]	[7]	[8]	[9]	[10]	[11]	[12]	[13]	[14]	[15]
40	35	80	75	34	45	62	57	55	90	85	60	90	70	75	65

Next we use a gap of 3. There are only three subarrays, and the longest one has six elements. The first subarray has subscripts 0, 3, 6, 9, 12, 15; the second subarray has subscripts 1, 4, 7, 10, 13; the third subarray has subscripts 2, 5, 8, 11, 14.

[0]	[1]	[2]	[3]	[4]	[5]	[6]	[7]	[8]	[9]	[10]	[11]	[12]	[13]	[14]	[15]
40	35	80	75	34	45	62	57	55	90	85	60	90	70	75	65

We start the process by inserting the element at position 3 (value of gap) into its subarray. Next, we insert the element at position 4, and so on. The result of all insertions is as follows.

[0]	[1]	[2]	[3]	[4]	[5]	[6]	[7]	[8]	[9]	[10]	[11]	[12]	[13]	[14]	[15]
40	34	45	60	35	55	62	57	60	65	70	75	75	85	80	90

Finally, we use a gap of 1, which performs an insertion sort on the entire array. Because of the presorting, it will require 1 comparison to insert 34, 1 comparison to insert 45 and 60, 3 comparisons to insert 35, 2 comparisons to insert 55, 1 comparison to insert 62, 2 comparisons to insert 57, 2 comparisons to insert 60, and only 1 comparison to insert each of the remaining values.

The algorithm for Shell sort follows. Steps 2 through 4 correspond to the insertion sort algorithm shown earlier. Because the elements with subscripts 0 through gap - 1 are the first elements in their subarrays, we begin Step 4 by inserting the element at position gap instead of at position 1 as we did for the insertion sort. Step 1 sets the initial gap between subscripts to n / 2 where n is the number of array elements. To get the next gap value, Step 7 divides the current gap value by 2.2 (chosen by experimentation). We want the gap to be 1 during the last insertion sort so that the entire array will be sorted. Step 5 ensures this by resetting gap to 1 if it is 2.

Shell Sort Algorithm

1.   Set the initial value of gap to n / 2.
2.   **while** gap > 0
3.   **for** each array element from position gap to the last element
4.   Insert this element where it belongs in its subarray.
5.   **if** gap is 2, set it to 1.
7.   **else** gap = gap/2.2.

Refinement of Step 4, the Insertion Step

4.1   nextPos is the position of the element to insert.
4.2   Save the value of the element to insert in nextVal.
4.3   **while** nextPos > gap and the element at nextPos – gap > nextVal
4.4   Shift the element at nextPos – gap to position nextPos.
4.5   Decrement nextPos by gap.
4.6   Insert nextVal at nextPos.

Analysis of Shell Sort

You may wonder why Shell sort is an improvement over regular insertion sort, because it ends with an insertion sort of the entire array. Each later sort (including the last one) will be performed on an array whose elements have been presorted by the earlier sorts. Because the behavior of insertion sort is closer to $O(n)$ than $O(n^2)$ when an array is nearly sorted, the presorting will make the later sorts, which involve larger subarrays, go more quickly. As a result of presorting, only 19 comparisons were required to perform an insertion sort on the last 15-element array shown in the previous section. This is critical, because it is precisely for larger arrays where $O(n^2)$ behavior would have the most negative impact. For the same reason, the improvement of Shell sort over insertion sort is much more significant for large arrays.

A general analysis of Shell sort is an open research problem in computer science. The performance depends on how the decreasing sequence of values for gap is chosen. It is known that Shell sort is $O(n^2)$ if successive powers of 2 are used for gap (that is, 32, 16, 8, 4, 2, 1). If successive values for gap are of the form $2^k - 1$ (that is, 31, 15, 7, 3, 1), however, it can be proven that the performance is $O(n^{3/2})$. This sequence is known as *Hibbard's sequence*. There are other sequences that give similar or better performance.

We have presented an algorithm that selects the initial value of gap as $\frac{n}{2}$ and then divides by 2.2 and truncates to the next lowest integer. Empirical studies of this approach show that the performance is $O(n^{5/4})$ or maybe even $O(n^{7/6})$, but there is no theoretical basis for this result (M. A. Weiss, *Data Structures and Problem Solving Using Java* [Addison Wesley, 1998], p. 230.).

Code for Shell Sort

Listing 10.4 shows the code for Shell sort. Method insert has a third parameter, gap. The expression after &&

```
((nextPos > gap - 1)
  && (nextVal.compareTo(table[nextPos - gap]) < 0))
```

compares elements that are separated by the value of gap instead of by 1. The expression before && is false if nextPos is the subscript of the first element in a sub-array. The statements in the **while** loop shift the element at nextPos down by gap (one position in the subarray) and reset nextPos to the subscript of the element just moved.

LISTING 10.4
ShellSort.java

```java
/** Implements the Shell sort algorithm. */
public class ShellSort {
    /** Sort the table using Shell sort algorithm.
        pre:  table contains Comparable objects.
        post: table is sorted.
        @param table The array to be sorted
    */
    public static void sort(Comparable table[]) {
        // Gap between adjacent elements.
        int gap = table.length / 2;
        while (gap > 0) {
            for (int nextPos = gap; nextPos < table.length;
                 nextPos++) {
                // Insert element at nextPos in its subarray.
                insert(table, nextPos, gap);
            }  // End for.

            // Reset gap for next pass.
            if (gap == 2) {
                gap = 1;
            } else {
                gap = (int) (gap / 2.2);
            }
        } // End while.
    } // End sort.

    /** Inserts element at nextPos where it belongs in array.
        pre:  Elements through nextPos - gap in subarray are sorted.
        post: Elements through nextPos in subarray are sorted.
        @param table The array being sorted
        @param nextPos The position of element to insert
        @param gap The gap between elements in the subarray
    */
```

```
      private static void insert(Comparable[] table,
                                 int nextPos, int gap) {
         Comparable nextVal = table[nextPos]; // Element to insert.
         // Shift all values > nextVal in subarray down by gap.
         while ((nextPos > gap - 1)  // First element not shifted.
                && (nextVal.compareTo(table[nextPos - gap]) < 0)) {
            table[nextPos] = table[nextPos - gap];    // Shift down.
            nextPos -= gap;        // Check next position in subarray.
         }
         table[nextPos] = nextVal;  // Insert nextVal.
      }
   }
```

EXERCISES FOR SECTION 10.6

SELF-CHECK

1. Trace the execution of Shell sort on the following array. Show the array after all sorts when the gap is 3 and after the final sort when the gap is 1. List the number of comparisons and exchanges required when the gap is 3 and when the gap is 1. Compare this with the number of comparisons and exchanges that would be required for a regular insertion sort.

   40 35 80 75 60 90 70 65

2. For the example of Shell sort shown in this section, determine how many comparisons and exchanges are required to insert all the elements for each gap value. Compare this with the number of comparisons and exchanges that would be required for a regular insertion sort.

PROGRAMMING

1. Eliminate method insert in Listing 10.4 and write its code inside the **for** statement.

2. Add statements to trace the progress of Shell sort. Display each value of gap and display the array contents after all subarrays for that gap value have been sorted.

10.7 Merge Sort

The next algorithm that we will consider is called *merge sort*. A *merge* is a common data processing operation that is performed on two sequences of data (or data files) with the following characteristics:

• Both sequences contain items with a common compareTo method.

• The objects in both sequences are ordered in accordance with this compareTo method (that is, both sequences are sorted).

The result of the merge operation is to create a third sequence that contains all of the objects from the first two sorted sequences. For example, if the first sequence is 3, 5, 8, 15 and the second sequence is 4, 9, 12, 20, the final sequence will be 3, 4, 5, 8, 9, 12, 15, 20. The algorithm for merging the two sequences is as follows:

Merge Algorithm

1. Access the first item from both sequences.
2. **while** not finished with either sequence
3.   Compare the current items from the two sequences, copy the smaller current item to the output sequence, and access the next item from the input sequence whose item was copied.
4. Copy any remaining items from the first sequence to the output sequence.
5. Copy any remaining items from the second sequence to the output sequence.

The **while** loop (Step 2) merges items from both input sequences to the output sequence. The current item from each sequence is the one that has been most recently accessed but not yet copied to the output sequence. Step 3 compares the two current items and copies the smaller one to the output sequence. If input sequence A's current item is the smaller one, the next item is accessed from sequence A and becomes its current item. If input sequence B's current item is the smaller one, the next item is accessed from sequence B and becomes its current item. After the end of either sequence is reached, Step 4 or Step 5 copies the items from the other sequence to the output sequence. Note that either Step 4 or Step 5 is executed, but not both.

As an example, consider the sequences shown in Figure 10.6. Steps 2 and 3 will first copy the items from sequence A with the values **244** and **311** to the output sequence; then items from sequence B with values 324 and 415 will be copied; and then the item from sequence A with value **478** will be copied. At this point, we have copied all items in sequence A, so we exit loop 2 and copy the remaining items from sequence B (499, 505) to the output (Steps 4 and 5).

Analysis of Merge

For two input sequences that contain a total of n elements, we need to move each element from its input sequence to its output sequence, so the time required for a merge is $O(n)$. How about the space requirements? We need to be able to store both initial sequences and the output sequence. So the array cannot be merged in place, and the *additional* space usage is $O(n)$.

FIGURE 10.6

Merge Operation

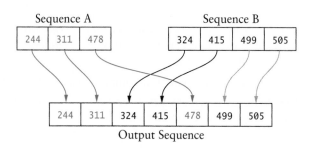

Output Sequence

Code for Merge

Listing 10.5 shows the merge algorithm applied to arrays of Comparable objects. Algorithm Steps 4 and 5 are implemented as **while** loops at the end of the method.

LISTING 10.5
Merge Method

```
/** Merge two sequences.
     pre: leftSequence and rightSequence are sorted.
     post: outputSequence is the merged result and is sorted.
     @param outputSequence The destination
     @param leftSequence The left input
     @param rightSequence The right input
*/
private static void merge(Comparable outputSequence[],
                          Comparable leftSequence[],
                          Comparable rightSequence[]) {
    int i = 0; // Index into the left input sequence.
    int j = 0; // Index into the right input sequence.
    int k = 0; // Index into the output sequence.
    // While there is data in both input sequences
    while (i < leftSequence.length && j < rightSequence.length) {
        // Find the smaller and
        // insert it into the output sequence.
        if (leftSequence[i].compareTo(rightSequence[j]) < 0) {
            outputSequence[k++] = leftSequence[i++];
        } else {
            outputSequence[k++] = rightSequence[j++];
        }
    }
    // assert: one of the sequences has more items to copy.
    // Copy remaining input from left sequence into the output.
    while (i < leftSequence.length) {
        outputSequence[k++] = leftSequence[i++];
    }
    // Copy remaining input from right sequence into output.
    while (j < rightSequence.length) {
        outputSequence[k++] = rightSequence[j++];
    }
}
```

 PROGRAM STYLE

By using the post-increment operator on the index variables, you can both extract the current item from one sequence and append it to the end of the output sequence in one statement. The statement:

```
outputSequence[k++] = leftSequence[i++];
```

is equivalent to the following three statements, executed in the order shown:

```
outputSequence[k] = leftSequence[i];
k++;
i++;
```

Both the single statement and the group of three statements maintain the invariant that the indexes reference the current item.

Algorithm for Merge Sort

We can modify merging to serve as an approach to sorting a single, unsorted array as follows:

1. Split the array into two halves.
2. Sort the left half.
3. Sort the right half.
4. Merge the two.

What sort algorithm should we use to do Steps 2 and 3? We can use the merge sort algorithm we are developing! The base case will be a table of size 1, which is already sorted, so there is nothing to do for the base case. We write the algorithm next, showing its recursive step.

Algorithm for Merge Sort

1. **if** the `tableSize` is > 1
2.   Set `halfSize` to `tableSize` divided by 2.
3.   Allocate a table called `leftTable` of size `halfSize`.
4.   Allocate a table called `rightTable` of size `tableSize - halfSize`.
5.   Copy the elements from `table[0 ... halfSize - 1]` into `leftTable`.
6.   Copy the elements from `table[halfSize ... tableSize]` into `rightTable`.
7.   Recursively apply the merge sort algorithm to `leftTable`.
8.   Recursively apply the merge sort algorithm to `rightTable`.
9.   Apply the merge method using `leftTable` and `rightTable` as the input and the original table as the output.

Trace of Merge Sort Algorithm

Each recursive call to method `sort` with an array argument that has more than one element splits the array argument into a left array and a right array, where each new array is approximately half the size of the array argument. We then sort each of these arrays, beginning with the left half, by recursively calling method `sort` with the left array and right array as arguments. After returning from the sort of the left array and right array at each level, we merge these two halves together back into the space occupied by the array that was split. Figure 10.7 illustrates this process. The left subarray in each recursive call (in gray) will be sorted before the processing of its corresponding right subarray (in color) begins. Lines 4 and 6 merge two one-element arrays to form a sorted two-element array. At line 7, the two sorted two-element arrays (50, 60 and 30, 45) are merged into a sorted four-element array. Next the right subarray in color on line 1 would be sorted in the same way. When done, the sorted subarray (15, 20, 80, 90) will be merged with the sorted subarray on line 7.

FIGURE 10.7
Trace of Merge Sort

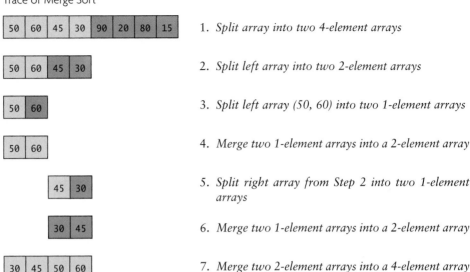

1. *Split array into two 4-element arrays*

2. *Split left array into two 2-element arrays*

3. *Split left array (50, 60) into two 1-element arrays*

4. *Merge two 1-element arrays into a 2-element array*

5. *Split right array from Step 2 into two 1-element arrays*

6. *Merge two 1-element arrays into a 2-element array*

7. *Merge two 2-element arrays into a 4-element array*

Analysis of Merge Sort

In Figure 10.7, the size of the arrays being sorted decreases from 8 to 4 (line 1) to 2 (line 2) to 1 (line 3). After each pair of subarrays is sorted, the pair will be merged to form a larger sorted array. Rather than showing a time sequence of the splitting and merging operations, we summarize them as follows.

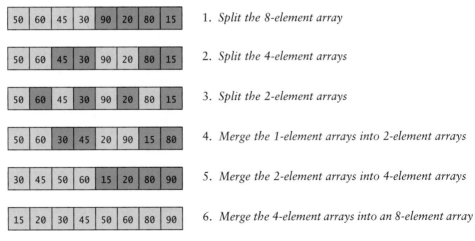

1. *Split the 8-element array*

2. *Split the 4-element arrays*

3. *Split the 2-element arrays*

4. *Merge the 1-element arrays into 2-element arrays*

5. *Merge the 2-element arrays into 4-element arrays*

6. *Merge the 4-element arrays into an 8-element array*

Lines 1 through 3 show the splitting operations, and lines 4 through 6 show the merge operations. Line 4 shows the two-element arrays formed by merging two-element pairs, line 5 shows the four-element arrays formed by merging 2-element pairs, and line 6 shows the sorted array. Because each of these lines involves a movement of n elements from smaller-size arrays to larger arrays, the effort to do each merge is $O(n)$. The number of lines that require merging (three in this case) is $\log n$ because each recursive step splits the array in half. So the total effort to reconstruct the sorted array through merging is $O(n \log n)$.

Recall from our discussion of recursion that whenever a recursive method is called, a copy of the local variables is saved on the run-time stack. Thus, as we go down the recursion chain sorting the leftTables, a sequence of rightTables of size $\frac{n}{2}$, $\frac{n}{4}, \ldots, \frac{n}{2^k}$ is allocated. Since $\frac{n}{2} + \frac{n}{4} + \ldots + 2 + 1 = n - 1$, a total of n addtional storage locations are required.

Code for Merge Sort

Listing 10.6 shows the MergeSort class.

LISTING 10.6
MergeSort.java

```java
/** Implements the recursive merge sort algorithm. In this version, copies
        of the subtables are made, sorted, and then merged.
*/
public class MergeSort {
    /** Sort the array using the merge sort algorithm.
        pre: table contains Comparable objects.
        post: table is sorted.
        @param table The array to be sorted
    */
    public static void sort(Comparable table[]) {
        // A table with one element is sorted already.
        if (table.length > 1) {
            // Split table into halves.
            int halfSize = table.length / 2;
            Comparable[] leftTable = new Comparable[halfSize];
            Comparable[] rightTable =
                    new Comparable[table.length - halfSize];
            System.arraycopy(table, 0, leftTable, 0, halfSize);
            System.arraycopy(table, halfSize, rightTable, 0,
                            table.length - halfSize);

            // Sort the halves.
            sort(leftTable);
            sort(rightTable);

            // Merge the halves.
            merge(table, leftTable, rightTable);
        }
    }
    // See Listing 10.5 for the merge method.
    ...
}
```

EXERCISES FOR SECTION 10.7

SELF-CHECK

1. Trace the execution of the merge sort on the following array, providing a figure similar to Figure 10.7.

55 50 10 40 80 90 60 100 70 80 20

2. For the array in Question 1, show the value of halfSize and arrays leftTable and rightTable for each recursive call to method sort in Listing 10.5 and show the array elements after returning from each call to merge. How many times is sort called, and how many times is merge called?

PROGRAMMING

1. Add statements that trace the progress of method sort by displaying the array table after each merge operation. Also display the arrays referenced by leftTable and rightTable.

10.8 Heapsort

The merge sort algorithm has the virtue that its time is $O(n \log n)$, but it still requires, at least temporarily, n extra storage locations. This next algorithm can be implemented without requiring any additional storage. It uses a heap to store the array and so is called *heapsort*.

First Version of a Heapsort Algorithm

We introduced the heap in Section 8.5. When used as a priority queue, a heap is a data structure that maintains the smallest value at the top. The following algorithm first places an array's data into a heap. Then it removes each heap item (an $O(\log n)$ process) and moves it back into the array.

Heapsort Algorithm: First Version

1. Insert each value from the array to be sorted into a priority queue (heap).
2. Set i to 0.
3. **while** the priority queue is not empty
4.   Remove an item from the queue and insert it back into the array at position i.
5.   Increment i.

Although this algorithm can be shown to be $O(n \log n)$, it does require n extra storage locations (the array and heap are both size n). We address this problem next.

Revising the Heapsort Algorithm

In the heaps we have used so far, each parent node value was less than the values of its children. We can also build the heap so that each parent is larger than its children. Figure 10.8 shows an example of such a heap.

Once we have such a heap, we can remove one item at a time from the heap. The item removed is always the top element, and it will end up at the bottom of the heap. When we reheap, we move the larger of a node's two children up the heap, instead of the smaller, so the next largest item is then at the top of the heap. Figure 10.9 shows the heap after we have removed one item and Figure 10.10 shows the heap after we have removed two items. In both figures, the items in color have been removed from the heap. As we continue to remove items from the heap, the heap size shrinks as the number of the removed items increases. Figure 10.11 shows the heap after we have emptied it.

If we implement the heap using an array, each element removed will be placed at the end of the array, but in front of the elements that were removed earlier. After we remove the last element, the array will be sorted. We illustrate this next.

Figure 10.12 shows the array representation of the original heap. As before, the root, 89, is at position 0. The root's two children, 76 and 74, are at positions 1 and 2. For a node at position p, the left child is at $2p + 1$ and the right child is at $2p + 2$. A node at position c can find its parent at $(c - 1) / 2$.

Figure 10.13 shows the array representation of the heaps in Figures 10.9 through 10.11. The items in color have been removed from the heap and are sorted. Each time an item is removed, the heap part of the array decreases by one element and

FIGURE 10.8

Example of a Heap with Largest Value in Root

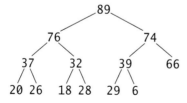

FIGURE 10.9

Heap After Removal of Largest Item

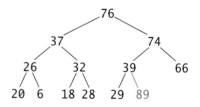

FIGURE 10.10

Heap After Removal of Two Largest Items

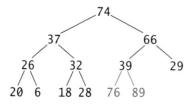

FIGURE 10.11

Heap After Removal of All Its Items

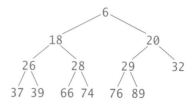

FIGURE 10.12

Internal Representation of the Heap Shown in Figure 10.8

[0]	[1]	[2]	[3]	[4]	[5]	[6]	[7]	[8]	[9]	[10]	[11]	[12]
89	76	74	37	32	39	66	20	26	18	28	29	6

FIGURE 10.13

Internal Representation of the Heaps Shown in Figures 10.9 through 10.11

[0]	[1]	[2]	[3]	[4]	[5]	[6]	[7]	[8]	[9]	[10]	[11]	[12]
76	37	74	26	32	39	66	20	6	18	28	29	89

[0]	[1]	[2]	[3]	[4]	[5]	[6]	[7]	[8]	[9]	[10]	[11]	[12]
74	37	66	26	32	39	29	20	6	18	28	76	89

:
:

[0]	[1]	[2]	[3]	[4]	[5]	[6]	[7]	[8]	[9]	[10]	[11]	[12]
6	18	20	26	28	29	32	37	39	66	74	76	89

the sorted part of the array increases by one element. In the array at the bottom of Figure 10.13, all items have been removed from the heap and the array is sorted.

From our foregoing observations, we can sort the array that represents a heap in the following way.

Algorithm for In-Place Heapsort

1. Build a heap by rearranging the elements in an unsorted array.
2. `while` the heap is not empty
3. Remove the first item from the heap by swapping it with the last item in the heap and restoring the heap property.

Each time through the loop (Steps 2 and 3), the largest item remaining in the heap is placed at the end of the heap, just before the previously removed items. Thus, when the loop terminates, the items in the array are sorted. In Section 8.5 we discussed how to remove an item from a heap and restore the heap property. We also implemented a `remove` method for a heap in an `ArrayList`.

Algorithm to Build a Heap

Step 1 of the algorithm builds a heap. If we start with an array, `table`, of length `table.length`, we can consider the first item (index 0) to be a heap of one item. We now consider the general case where the items in array `table` from 0 through n - 1 form a heap; the items from n through `table.length` - 1 are not in the heap. As each is inserted, we must "reheap" to restore the heap property.

Refinement of Step 1 for In-Place Heapsort

1.1.   `while` n is less than `table.length`

1.2.   Increment n by 1. This inserts a new item into the heap.

1.3.   Restore the heap property.

Analysis of Revised Heapsort Algorithm

From our knowledge of binary trees, we know that a heap of size n has $\log n$ levels. Building a heap requires finding the correct location for an item in a heap with $\log n$ levels. Because we have n items to insert and each insert (or remove) is $O(\log n)$, the `buildHeap` operation is $O(n \log n)$. Similarly, we have n items to remove from the heap, so that is also $O(n \log n)$. Because we are storing the heap in the original array, no extra storage is required.

Code for Heapsort

Listing 10.7 shows the `HeapSort` class. The `sort` method merely calls the `buildHeap` method followed by the `shrinkHeap` method which is based on the earlier `remove` method shown in Section 8.5. Method `swap` swaps the items in the table.

LISTING 10.7
HeapSort.java

```java
/** Implementaton of the heapsort algorithm. */
public class HeapSort {
    /** Sort the array using heap sort algorithm.
        pre: table contains Comparable items.
        post: table is sorted.
        @param table The array to be sorted
    */
    public static void sort (Comparable table[]) {
        buildHeap(table);
        shrinkHeap(table);
    }

    /** buildHeap transforms the table into a heap.
        pre:  The array contains at least one item.
        post: All items in the array are in heap order.
        @param table The array to be transformed into a heap
    */
    private static void buildHeap(Comparable table[]) {
        int n = 1;
        // Invariant: table[0 ... n-1] is a heap.
        while (n < table.length) {
            n++;  // Add a new item to the heap and reheap.
            int child = n - 1;
            int parent = (child - 1) / 2;  // Find parent.
            while (parent >= 0
                    && table[parent].compareTo(table[child]) < 0) {
                swap(table, parent, child);
                child = parent;
                parent = (child - 1) / 2;
```

```
                }
            }
        }

    /** shrinkHeap transforms a heap into a sorted array.
        pre: All items in the array are in heap order.
        post: The array is sorted.
        @param table The array to be sorted
    */
    private static void shrinkHeap(Comparable table[]) {
        int n = table.length;
        // Invariant: table[0 ... n - 1] forms a heap.
        // table[n .. table.length - 1] is sorted.
        while (n > 0) {
            n--;
            swap(table, 0, n);
            // table[1 ... n - 1] form a heap.
            // table[n ... table.length - 1] is sorted.
            int parent = 0;
            while (true) {
                int leftChild = 2 * parent + 1;
                if (leftChild >= n) {
                    break;          // No more children.
                }
                int rightChild = leftChild + 1;
                // Find the larger of the two children.
                int maxChild = leftChild;
                if (rightChild < n    // There is a right child.
                    && table[leftChild].compareTo(table[rightChild]) < 0) {
                    maxChild = rightChild;
                }
                // If the parent is smaller than the larger child,
                if (table[parent].compareTo(table[maxChild]) < 0) {
                    // Swap the parent and child.
                    swap(table, parent, maxChild);
                    // Continue at the child level.
                    parent = maxChild;
                } else {   // Heap property is restored.
                    break; // Exit the loop.
                }
            }
        }
    }

    /** Swap the items in table[i] and table[j].
        @param table The array that contains the items
        @param i The index of one item
        @param j The index of the other item
    */
    private static void swap(Comparable table[], int i, int j) {
        Comparable temp = table[i];
        table[i] = table[j];
        table[j] = temp;
    }
}
```

EXERCISES FOR SECTION 10.8

SELF-CHECK

1. Build the heap from the numbers in the following list. How many exchanges were required? How many comparisons?

   55 50 10 40 80 90 60 100 70 80 20

2. Shrink the heap from Question 1 to create the array in sorted order. How many exchanges were required? How many comparisons?

10.9 Quicksort

The next algorithm we will study is called *quicksort*. Developed by C. A. R. Hoare in 1962, it works in the following way: Given an array with subscripts first . . . last to sort, quicksort rearranges this array into two parts so that all the elements in the left subarray are less than or equal to a specified value (called the *pivot*) and all the elements in the right subarray are greater than the pivot. The pivot is placed between the two parts. Thus all of the elements on the left of the pivot value are smaller than all elements on the right of the pivot value, so the pivot value is in its correct position. By repeating this process on the two halves, the whole array becomes sorted.

As an example of this process, let's sort the following array.

44	75	23	43	55	12	64	77	33

We will assume that the first array element (44) is arbitrarily selected as the pivot value. A possible result of rearranging, or *partitioning*, the element values follows.

12	33	23	43	44	55	64	77	75

After the partitioning process, the pivot value, 44, is at its correct position. All values less than 44 are in the left subarray, and all values larger than 44 are in the right subarray, as desired. The next step would be to apply quicksort recursively to the two subarrays on either side of the pivot value, beginning with the left subarray (12, 33, 23, 43). Here is the result when 12 is the pivot value:

12	33	23	43

The pivot value is in the first position. Because the left subarray does not exist, the right subarray (33, 23, 43) is sorted next, resulting in the following situation shown below.

12	23	33	43

The pivot value 33 is in its correct place, and the left subarray (23) and right sub-array (43) have single elements, so they are sorted. At this point, we are finished sorting the left part of the original subarray, and quicksort is applied to the right subarray (55, 64, 77, 75). In the following array, all the elements that have been placed in their proper position are in dark blue.

If we use 55 for the pivot, its left subarray will be empty after the partitioning process and the right subarray 64, 77, 75 will be sorted next. If 64 is the pivot, the situation will be as follows, and we sort the right subarray (77, 75) next.

If 77 is the pivot and we move it where it belongs, we end up with the following array. Because the left subarray (75) has a single element, it is sorted and we are done.

75 | 77

Algorithm for Quicksort

The algorithm for quicksort follows. We will describe how to do the partitioning later. We assume that the indexes `first` and `last` are the end points of the array being sorted and that the index of the pivot after partitioning is `pivIndex`.

Algorithm for Quicksort

1.   **if** `first` < `last` then
2.   Partition the elements in the subarray `first . . . last` so that the pivot value is in its correct place (subscript `pivIndex`).
3.   Recursively apply quicksort to the subarray `first . . . pivIndex - 1`.
4.   Recursively apply quicksort to the subarray `pivIndex + 1 . . . last`.

Analysis of Quicksort

If the pivot value is a random value selected from the current subarray, then statis-tically it is expected that half of the items in the subarray will be less than the pivot and half will be greater than the pivot. If both subarrays always have the same num-ber of elements (the best case), there will be log n levels of recursion. At each level, the partitioning process involves moving every element into its correct partition, so quicksort is $O(n \log n)$, just like merge sort.

But what if the split is not 50-50? Let us consider the case where each split is 90-10. Instead of a 100-element array being split into two 50-element arrays, there will be one array with 90 elements and one with just 10. The 90-element array may be split 50-50, or it may also be split 90-10. In the latter case, there would be one array with 81 elements and one with just 9 elements. Generally, for random input, the splits will not be exactly 50-50, but neither will they all be 90-10. An exact analysis is dif-ficult and beyond the scope of this book, but the running time will be bound by a constant $\times n \log n$.

There is one situation, however, where quicksort gives very poor behavior. If, each time we partition the array, we end up with a subarray that is empty, the other subarray will have one less element than the one just split (only the pivot value will be removed). Therefore, we will have n levels of recursive calls (instead of log n), and the algorithm will be $O(n^2)$. Because of the overhead of recursive method calls (versus iteration), quicksort will take longer and require more extra storage on the runtime stack than any of the earlier quadratic algorithms. We will discuss a way to handle this situation later.

Code for Quicksort

Listing 10.8 shows the QuickSort class. The public method sort calls the recursive quickSort method, giving it the bounds of the table as the initial values of first and last. The two recursive calls in quickSort will cause the procedure to be applied to the subarrays that are separated by the value at pivIndex. If any subarray contains just one element (or zero elements), an immediate return will occur.

LISTING 10.8
QuickSort.java

```java
/** Implements the quicksort algorithm. */
public class QuickSort {

    /** Sort the table using the quicksort algorithm.
        pre: table contains Comparable objects.
        post: table is sorted.
        @param table The array to be sorted
    */
    public static void sort(Comparable[] table) {
        // Sort the whole table.
        quickSort(table, 0, table.length - 1);
    }

    /** Sort a part of the table using the quicksort algorithm.
        post: The part of table from first through last is sorted.
        @param table The array to be sorted
        @param first The index of the low bound
        @param last The index of the high bound
    */
    private static void quickSort(Comparable[] table,
                                  int first, int last) {
        if (first < last) {  // There is data to be sorted.
            // Partition the table.
            int pivIndex = partition(table, first, last);
            // Sort the left half.
            quickSort(table, first, pivIndex - 1);
            // Sort the right half.
            quickSort(table, pivIndex + 1, last);
        }
    }

    // Insert partition method. See Listing 10.9
    ...
}
```

Algorithm for Partitioning

The partition method selects the pivot and performs the partitioning operation. When we are selecting the pivot, it does not really matter which element is the pivot value (if the arrays are randomly ordered to begin with). For simplicity we chose the element with subscript first. We then begin searching for the first value at the left end of the subarray that is greater than the pivot value. When we find it, we search for the first value at the right end of the subarray that is less than or equal to the pivot value. These two values are exchanged, and we repeat the search and exchange operations. This is illustrated in Figure 10.14, where up points to the first value greater than the pivot and down points to the first value less than or equal to the pivot value. The elements less than the pivot are in light blue and the elements greater than the pivot are in gray.

The value 75 is the first value at the left end of the array that is larger than 44, and 33 is the first value at the right end that is less than or equal to 44, so these two values are exchanged. The indices up and down are advanced again, as shown in Figure 10.15.

The value 55 is the next value at the left end that is larger than 44, and 12 is the next value at the right end that is less than or equal to 44, so these two values are exchanged, and up and down are advanced again, as shown in Figure 10.16.

After the second exchange, the first five array elements contain the pivot value and all values less than or equal to the pivot; the last four elements contain all values larger than the pivot. The value 55 is selected once again by up as the next element larger than the pivot; 12 is selected by down as the next element less than or equal to the pivot. Since up has now "passed" down, these values are not exchanged. Instead, the pivot value (subscript first) and the value at position down are exchanged. This puts the pivot value in its proper position (the new subscript is down) as shown in Figure 10.17.

FIGURE 10.14
Locating First Values to Exchange

FIGURE 10.15
Array After the First Exchange

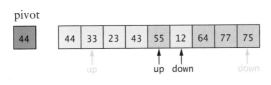

FIGURE 10.16
Array After the Second Exchange

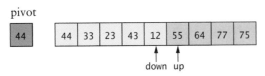

FIGURE 10.17
Array After Pivot Is
Inserted

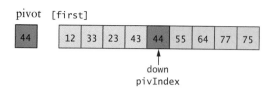

pivot [first]

The partition process is now complete, and the value of down is returned to the pivot index pivIndex. Method quickSort will be called recursively to sort the left subarray and the right subarray. The algorithm for partition follows.

Algorithm for partition Method

1. Define the pivot value as the contents of table[first].
2. Initialize up to first and down to last.
3. **do**
4.   Increment up until up selects the first element greater than the pivot value or up has reached last.
5.   Decrement down until down selects the first element less than or equal to the pivot value or down has reached first.
6.   **if** up < down then
7.   Exchange table[up] and table[down].
8.   **while** up is to the left of down
9.   Exchange table[first] and table[down].
10.   Return the value of down to pivIndex.

Code for partition

The code for partition is shown in Listing 10.9. The **while** statement:

```
while ((up < last) && (pivot.compareTo(table[up]) >= 0)) {
    up++;
}
```

advances the index up until it is equal to last or until it references an item in table that is greater than the pivot value. Similarly, the **while** statement:

```
while (pivot.compareTo(table[down]) < 0)) {
    down--;
}
```

moves the index down until it references an item in table that is less than or equal to the pivot value. The **do-while** condition

```
(up < down)
```

ensures that the partitioning process will continue while up is to the left of down.

What happens if there is a value in the array that is the same as the pivot value? The index down will stop at such a value. If up has stopped prior to reaching that value, table[up] and table[down] will be exchanged, and the value equal to the pivot will be in the left partition. If up has passed this value, and therefore passed down, table[first] will be exchanged with table[down] (same value as table[first]), and the value equal to the pivot will still be in the left partition.

FIGURE 10.18
Values of **up**, **down**, and
`pivIndex` if the Pivot
is the Smallest Value

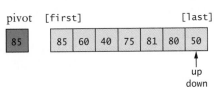

FIGURE 10.19
Values of **up**, **down**, and
`pivIndex` if the Pivot
Is the Largest Value

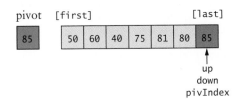

What happens if the pivot value is the smallest value in the array? Since the pivot value is at `table[first]`, the loop will terminate with down equal to `first`. In this case, the left partition is empty. Figure 10.18 shows an array for which this is the case.

By similar reasoning we can show that up will stop at `last` if there is no element in the array larger than the pivot. In this case, down will also stay at `last`, and the pivot value (`table[first]`) will be swapped with the last value in the array, so the right partition will be empty. Figure 10.19 shows an array for which this is the case.

LISTING 10.9
Quicksort `partition` Method (First Version)

```
/** Partition the table so that values from first to pivIndex
    are less than or equal to the pivot value, and values from
    pivIndex to last are greater than the pivot value.
    @param table The table to be partitioned
    @param first The index of the low bound
    @param last  The index of the high bound
    @return The location of the pivot value
*/
private static int partition(Comparable[] table,
                             int first, int last) {
    // Select the first item as the pivot value.
    Comparable pivot = table[first];
    int up = first;
    int down = last;
    do {
```

```
            /* Invariant:
                All items in table[first ... up - 1] <= pivot
                All items in table[down + 1 ... last] > pivot
            */
            while ((up < last) && (pivot.compareTo(table[up]) >= 0)) {
                up++;
            }
            // assert: up equals last or table[up] > pivot.
            while (pivot.compareTo(table[down]) < 0) {
                down--;
            }
            // assert: down equals first or table[down] <= pivot.
            if (up < down) {    // if up is to the left of down.
                // Exchange table[up] and table[down].
                swap(table, up, down);
            }
        } while (up < down); // Repeat while up is left of down.
        // Exchange table[first] and table[down] thus putting the
        // pivot value where it belongs.
        swap(table, first, down);
        // Return the index of the pivot value.
        return down;
    }
```

A Revised Partition Algorithm

We stated earlier that quicksort is $O(n^2)$ when each split yields one empty subarray. Unfortunately, that would be the case if the array was sorted. So the worst possible performance occurs for a sorted array, which is not very desirable.

A better solution is to pick the pivot value in a way that is less likely to lead to a bad split. One approach is to examine the first, middle, and last elements in the array and select the median of these three values as the pivot. We can do this by sorting the three-element subarray (in color in Figure 10.20). After sorting, the smallest of the three values is in position first, the median is in position middle, and the largest of the three is at position last.

At this point, we can exchange the first element with the middle element (the median) and use the partition algorithm shown earlier, which uses the first element (now the median) as the pivot value. When we exit the partitioning loop, table[first] and table[down] are exchanged, moving the pivot value where it belongs (back to the middle position). This revised partition algorithm follows.

FIGURE 10.20
Sorting First, Middle, and Last Elements in Array

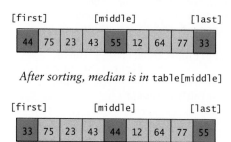

After sorting, median is in table[middle]

Algorithm for Revised partition Method

1. Sort `table[first]`, `table[middle]`, and `table[last]`.
2. Move the median value to `table[first]` (the pivot value) by exchanging `table[first]` and `table[middle]`.
3. Initialize up to `first` and down to `last`.
4. **do**
5.   Increment up until up selects the first element greater than the pivot value or up has reached `last`.
6.   Decrement down until down selects the first element less than or equal to the pivot value or down has reached `first`.
7.   **if** up < down **then**
8.   Exchange `table[up]` and `table[down]`.
9. **while** up is to the left of down.
10. Exchange `table[first]` and `table[down]`.
11. Return the value of down to `pivIndex`.

You may be wondering whether you can avoid the double shift (Steps 2 and 10) and just leave the pivot value at `table[middle]`, where it belongs. The answer is "Yes", but you would also need to modify the partition algorithm further if you did this. Programming Project 6 addresses this issue and the construction of an industrial-strength quicksort method.

Code for Revised partition Method

Listing 10.10 shows the revised version of method `partition` with method `bubbleSort3`, which applies the bubble sort algorithm to the three selected items in `table` so that

     `table[first] <= table[middle] <= table[last]`

Method `partition` begins with a call to method `bubbleSort3` and then calls `swap` to make the median the pivot. The rest of the method is unchanged.

....
LISTING 10.10
Revised partition Method and `bubbleSort3`

```
private static int partition(Comparable[] table,
                             int first, int last) {
    /* Put the median of table[first], table[middle], table[last]
       into table[first], and use this value as the pivot.
    */
    bubbleSort3(table, first, last);
    // Swap first element with median.
    swap(table, first, (first + last) / 2);

    // Continue as in Listing 10.9
    // . . .

/** Sort table[first], table[middle], and table[last].
    @param table The table to be sorted
    @param first Index of the first element
    @param last Index of the last element
```

```
*/
private static void bubbleSort3(Comparable[] table,
                                int first, int last) {
    int middle = (first + last) / 2;
    /* Perform bubble sort on table[first], table[middle],
       table[last].
    */
    if (table[middle].compareTo(table[first]) < 0) {
        swap(table, first, middle);
    }
    // assert: table[first] <= table[middle]
    if (table[last].compareTo(table[middle]) < 0) {
        swap(table, middle, last);
    }
    // assert: table[last] is the largest value of the three.
    if (table[middle].compareTo(table[first]) < 0) {
        swap(table, first, middle);
    }
    // assert: table[first] <= table[middle] <= table[last].
}
```

 PITFALL

Falling Off Either End of the Array

A common problem when incrementing up or down during the partition process is falling off either end of the array. This will be indicated by an `ArrayIndexOutOfBoundsException`. We used the condition

```
((up < last) && (pivot.compareTo(table[up]) >= 0))
```

to keep up from falling off the right end of the array. Self-Check Exercise 3 asks why we don't need to write similar code to avoid falling off the left end of the array.

EXERCISES FOR SECTION 10.9

SELF-CHECK

1. Trace the execution of quicksort on the following array, assuming that the first item in each subarray is the pivot value. Show the values of `first` and `last` for each recursive call and the array elements after returning from each call. Also, show the value of `pivot` during each call and the value returned through `pivIndex`. How many times is sort called, and how many times is `partition` called?

   55 50 10 40 80 90 60 100 70 80 20

2. Redo Question 1 using the revised partition algorithm, which does a preliminary sort of three elements and selects their median as the pivot value.

3. Explain why the condition (down > first) is not necessary in the loop that decrements down.

1. Insert statements to trace the quicksort algorithm. After each call to `partition`, display the values of `first`, `pivIndex`, and `last` and the array.

10.10 Testing the Sort Algorithms

To test the sorting algorithms, we need to exercise them with a variety of test cases. We want to make sure that they work, and we also want to get some idea of their relative performance when sorting the same array. We should test the methods with small arrays, large arrays, arrays whose elements are in random order, arrays that are already sorted, and arrays with duplicate copies of the same value. For performance comparisons to be meaningful, the methods must sort the same arrays.

Listing 10.11 shows a driver program that tests methods `Arrays.Sort` (from the API `java.util`) and `QuickSort.sort` on the same array of random integer values. Method `System.currentTimeMillis` returns the current time in milliseconds. This method is called just before a sort begins and just after the return from a sort. The elapsed time between calls is displayed in the console window. Although the numbers shown will not be precise, they give a good indication of the relative performance of two sorting algorithms if this is the only application currently executing.

Method `verify` verifies that the array elements are sorted by checking that each element in the array is not greater than its successor. Method `dumpTable` (not shown) should display the first 10 elements and last 10 elements of an array (or the entire array if the array has 20 or fewer elements).

LISTING 10.11
Driver to Test Sort Algorithms

```java
/** Driver program to test sorting methods.
    @param args Not used
*/
public static void main(String[] args) {
    int size = Integer.parseInt(
            JOptionPane.showInputDialog("Enter Array size:"));
    Integer[] items = new Integer[size];   // Array to sort.
    Integer[] copy = new Integer[size];    // Copy of array.
    Random rInt = new Random();   // For random number generation

    // Fill the array and copy with random Integers.
    for (int i = 0; i < items.length; i++) {
        items[i] = new Integer(rInt.nextInt());
        copy[i] = items[i];
    }

    // Sort with utility method.
    long startTime = System.currentTimeMillis();
    Arrays.sort(items);
    System.out.println("Utility sort time is "
                    + (System.currentTimeMillis()
                    - startTime) + "ms");
```

```
            JOptionPane.showMessageDialog(null,
                    "Utility sort successful (true/false): "
                    + verify(items));

            // Reload array items from array copy.
            for (int i = 0; i < items.length; i++) {
                items[i] = copy[i];
            }

            // Sort with quicksort.
            startTime = System.currentTimeMillis();
            QuickSort.sort(items);
            System.out.println("QuickSort time is "
                            + (System.currentTimeMillis()
                            - startTime) + " ms");
            JOptionPane.showMessageDialog(null,
                    "QuickSort successful (true/false): "
                    + verify(items));

            dumpTable(items);      // Display part of the array.
        }

    /** Verifies that the elements in array test are
        in increasing order.
        @param test The array to verify
        @return true if the elements are in increasing order;
                false if any 2 elements are not in increasing order
    */
    private static boolean verify(Comparable[] test) {
        boolean ok = true;
        int i = 0;
        while (ok && i < test.length - 1) {
            ok = test[i].compareTo(test[i + 1]) <= 0;
            i++;
        }
        return ok;
    }
}
```

EXERCISES FOR SECTION 10.10

SELF-CHECK

1. Explain why method verify will always determine whether an array is sorted. Does verify work if an array contains duplicate values?
2. Explain the effect of removing the second for statement in the main method.

PROGRAMMING

1. Write method dumpTable.
2. Modify the driver method to fill array items with a collection of integers read from a file when args[0] is not **null**.
3. Extend the driver to test all $O(n \log n)$ sorts and collect statistics on the different sorting algorithms. Test the sorts using an array of random numbers and also a data file processed by the solution to Programming Exercise 2.

10.11 The Dutch National Flag Problem (Optional Topic)

A variety of partitioning algorithms for quicksort have been published. Most are variations on the one presented in this text. There is another popular variation that uses a single left-to-right scan of the array (instead of scanning left and scanning right as we did). The following case study illustrates a partitioning algorithm that combines both scanning techniques to partition an array into three segments. The famous computer scientist Edsger W. Dijkstra described this problem in his book *A Discipline of Programming* (Prentice-Hall, 1976).

CASE STUDY   The Problem of the Dutch National Flag

Problem   The Dutch national flag consists of three stripes that are colored (from top to bottom) red, white, and blue as shown in Figure 10.21. Because we only have 2 colors, we use gray for red. Unfortunately, when the flag arrived, it looked like Figure 10.22; threads of each of the colors were all scrambled together! Fortunately, we have a machine that can unscramble it, but it needs software.

Analysis   Our unscrambling machine has the following abilities:

• It can look at one thread in the flag and determine its color.
• It can swap the position of two threads in the flag.

Our machine can also execute **while** loops and **if** statements.

FIGURE 10.21
The Dutch National Flag

FIGURE 10.22
Scrambled Dutch National Flag

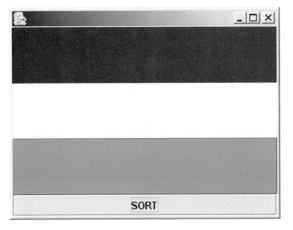

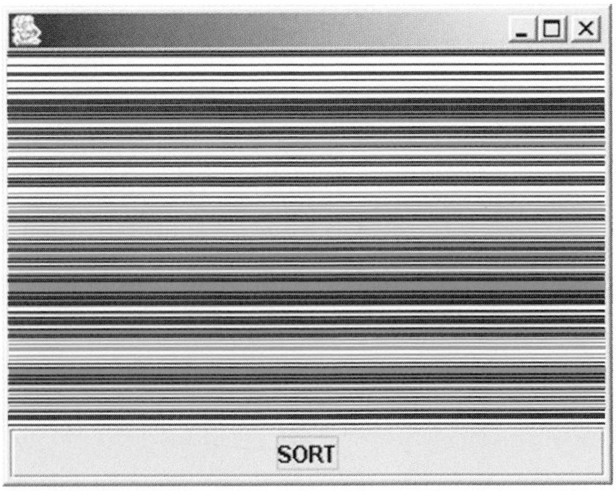

Loop Invariant

When we partitioned the array in quicksort, we split the array into three regions. Values between first and up were less than or equal to the pivot; values between down and last were greater than the pivot, and values between up and down were unknown. We started with the unknown region containing the whole array (first == up, and down == last). The partitioning algorithm preserves this invariant while shrinking the unknown region. The loop terminates when the unknown region becomes empty (up > down).

Since our goal is to have three regions when we are done, let us define four regions: the red region, the white region, the blue region, and the unknown region. Now initially the whole flag is unknown. When we get done, however, we would like the red region on top, the white region in the middle, and the blue region on the bottom. The unknown region must be empty.

Let us assume that the threads are stored in an array threads and that the total number of threads is HEIGHT. Let us define red to be the upper bound of the red region, white to be the lower bound of the white region, and blue to be the lower bound of the blue region. Then, if our flag is complete, we can say the following:

- If $0 \leq i <$ red, then threads[i] is red.
- If white $< i \leq$ blue, then threads[i] is white.
- If blue $< i <$ HEIGHT, then threads[i] is blue.

What about the case where red $\leq i \leq$ white? When the flag is all sorted, red should equal white, so this region should not exist. However, when we start, everything is in this region, so a thread in that region can have any color.

Thus we can define the following loop invariant:

- If $0 \leq i <$ red, then threads[i] is red.
- If red $\leq i \leq$ white, then the color is unknown.
- If white $< i \leq$ blue, then threads[i] is white.
- If blue $< i <$ HEIGHT, then threads[i] is blue.

This is illustrated in Figure 10.23.

FIGURE 10.23
Dutch National Flag
Loop Invariant

[0]

[red]

[white]

[blue]

[HEIGHT]

Algorithm   We can solve our problem by establishing the loop invariant and then executing a loop that both preserves the loop invariant and shrinks the unknown region.

1.   Set red to 0, white to HEIGHT - 1, and blue to HEIGHT - 1. This establishes our loop invariant with the unknown region the whole flag and the red, white, and blue regions empty.

2.   **while** red < white

3.   Shrink the distance between red and white while preserving the loop invariant.

Preserving the Loop Invariant

Let us assume that we now know the color of threads[white] (the thread at position white). Our goal is to either leave threads[white] where it is (in the white region if it is white) or "move it" to the region where it belongs. There are three cases to consider:

Case 1: The color of threads[white] is white. In this case we merely decrement the value of white to restore the invariant. By doing so, we increase the size of the white region by one thread.

Case 2: The color of threads[white] is red. We know from our invariant that the color of threads[red] is unknown. Therefore, if we swap the thread at threads[red] with the one at threads[white], we can then increment the value of red and preserve the invariant. By doing this, we add the thread to the end of the red region and reduce the size of the unknown region by one thread.

Case 3: The color of threads[white] is blue. We know from our invariant that the color of threads[blue] is white. Thus, if we swap the thread at threads[white] with the thread at threads[blue] and then decrement both white and blue, we preserve the invariant. By doing this, we insert the thread at the beginning of the blue region and reduce the size of the unknown region by one thread.

Implementation   A complete implementation of this program is left as a programming project. We show the coding of the sort algorithm in Listing 10.12.

LISTING 10.12
Dutch National Flag Sort

```
public void sort() {
    int red = 0;
    int white = height - 1;
    int blue = height - 1;
    /* Invariant:
       0 <= i < red      ==>threads[i].getColor() == Color.RED
       red <= i <= white ==>threads[i].getColor() is unknown
       white < i < blue  ==>threads[i].getColor() == Color.WHITE
       blue < i < height ==>threads[i].getColor() == Color.BLUE
    */
    while (red <= white) {
        if (threads[white].getColor() == Color.WHITE) {
            white--;
        } else if (threads[white].getColor() == Color.RED) {
            swap(red, white, g);
            red++;
        } else {  // threads[white].getColor() == Color.BLUE
            swap(white, blue, g);
            white--;
            blue--;
        }
    }
    // assert: red == white so unknown region is now empty.
}
```

EXERCISES FOR SECTION 10.11

PROGRAMMING

1. Adapt the Dutch National Flag algorithm to do the quicksort partitioning. Consider the red region to be those values less than the pivot, the white region to be those values equal to the pivot, and the blue region to be those values equal to the pivot. You should initially sort the first, middle, and last items and use the middle value as the pivot value.

Chapter Review

◆ We analyzed several sorting algorithms; their performance is summarized in Table 10.4.

◆ The three quadratic algorithms, $O(n^2)$, are selection sort, bubble sort, and insertion sort. They give satisfactory performance for small arrays (up to 100 elements). Generally, insertion sort is considered to be the best of the quadratic sorts. Bubble sort is a good choice when the array is likely to be nearly sorted but should be avoided otherwise.

◆ Shell sort, $O(n^{5/4})$, gives satisfactory performance for arrays up to 5000 elements.

◆ Quicksort has average-case performance of $O(n \log n)$, but if the pivot is picked poorly, the worst-case performance is $O(n^2)$.

◆ Merge sort and heapsort have $O(n \log n)$ performance.

◆ The Java API contains "industrial strength" sort algorithms in the classes `java.util.Arrays` and `java.util.Collections`. The methods in `Arrays` use a mixture of quicksort and insertion sort for sorting arrays of primitive type values and merge sort for sorting arrays of objects. For primitive types, quicksort is used until the size of the subarray reaches the point where insertion sort is quicker (7 elements or less). The sort method in `Collections` merely copies the list into an array and then calls `Arrays.sort`.

TABLE 10.4
Comparison of Sort Algorithms

	Number of Comparisons		
	Best	**Average**	**Worst**
Selection sort	$O(n^2)$	$O(n^2)$	$O(n^2)$
Bubble sort	$O(n)$	$O(n^2)$	$O(n^2)$
Insertion sort	$O(n)$	$O(n^2)$	$O(n^2)$
Shell sort	$O(n^{7/6})$	$O(n^{5/4})$	$O(n^2)$
Merge sort	$O(n \log n)$	$O(n \log n)$	$O(n \log n)$
Heapsort	$O(n \log n)$	$O(n \log n)$	$O(n \log n)$
Quicksort	$O(n \log n)$	$O(n \log n)$	$O(n^2)$

Java Classes Introduced in This Chapter

```
java.util.Arrays
java.util.Collections
```

User-Defined Interfaces and Classes in This Chapter

Person   SelectionSort
ComparePerson   ShellSort
BubbleSort   MergeSort
InsertionSort   QuickSort

Quick-Check Exercises

1. Name three quadratic sorts.
2. Name two sorts with $n \log n$ worst-case behavior.
3. Which algorithm is particularly good for an array that is already sorted? Which is particularly bad? Explain your answers.
4. What determines whether you should use a quadratic sort or a logarithmic sort?
5. Which quadratic sort's performance is least affected by the ordering of the array elements? Which is most affected?
6. What is a good all-purpose sorting algorithm for medium-sized arrays?

Answers to Quick-Check Exercises

1. Selection sort, insertion sort, bubble sort
2. Merge sort, heapsort
3. Bubble sort—it requires $n - 1$ comparisons with no exchanges. Quicksort can be bad if the first element is picked as the pivot value, because the partitioning process always creates one subarray with a single element.
4. Array size
5. Selection sort, bubble sort
6. Shell sort or any $O(n \log n)$ sort

Review Questions

1. When does quicksort work best, and when does it work worst?
2. Write a recursive procedure to implement the insertion sort algorithm.
3. What is the purpose of the pivot value in quicksort? How did we first select it in the text, and what is wrong with that approach for choosing a pivot value?
4. For the following array
   30 40 20 15 60 80 75 4 20
   show the new array after each pass of insertion sort, bubble sort, and selection sort. How many comparisons and exchanges are performed by each?
5. For the array in Question 4, trace the execution of Shell sort.
6. For the array in Question 4, trace the execution of merge sort.
7. For the array in Question 4, trace the execution of quicksort.
8. For the array in Question 4, trace the execution of heapsort.
9. The shaker sort is an adaptation of the bubble sort that alternates the direction in which the array elements are scanned during each pass. The first pass starts its scan with the first element, moving the larger element in each pair down the array. The second pass starts its scan with the next-to-last element, moving the smaller element in each pair up the array, and so on. Indicate what the advantage of the shaker sort might be.

Programming Projects

1. Use the random number function to store a list of 1000 pseudorandom integer values in an array. Apply each of the sort classes described in this chapter to the array and determine the number of comparisons and exchanges. Make sure the same array is passed to each sort method.

2. Investigate the effect of array size and initial element order on the number of comparisons and exchanges required by each of the sorting algorithms described in this chapter. Use arrays with 100 and 10,000 integers. Use three initial orderings of each array (randomly ordered, inversely ordered, and ordered). Be certain to sort the same six arrays with each sort method.

3. Implement the shaker sort algorithm described in Review Question 9.

4. A variation of the merge sort algorithm can be used to sort large sequential data files. The basic strategy is to take the initial data file, read in several (say 10) data records, sort these records using an efficient array-sorting algorithm, and then write these sorted groups of records (runs) alternately to one of two output files. After all records from the initial data file have been distributed to the two output files, the runs on these output files are merged one pair of runs at time and written to the original data file. After all runs from the output file have been merged, the records on the original data file are redistributed to the output files, and the merging process is repeated. Runs no longer need to be sorted after the first distribution to the temporary output files.

   Each time runs are distributed to the output files, they contain twice as many records as the time before. The process stops when the length of the runs exceeds the number of records in the data file. Write a program which implements merge sort for sequential data files. Test your program on a file with several thousand data values.

5. Write a method that sorts a linked list.

6. Write an industrial-strength quicksort method with the following enhancements:

   a. If an array segment contains 20 elements or fewer, sort it using insertion sort.

   b. After sorting the first, middle, and last elements, use the median as the pivot, instead of swapping the median with the first element. Because the first and last elements are in the correct partitions, it is not necessary to test them before advancing up and down. This is also the case after each exchange, so increment up and decrement down at the beginning of the **do-while** loop. Also, it is not necessary to test whether up is less than last before incrementing up, because the condition `pivot.compareTo(last) > 0` is false when up equals last (the median must be ≤ the last element in the array).

7. In the early days of data processing (before computers), data was stored on punched cards. A machine to sort these cards contained 12 bins (one for each digit value and + and −). A stack of cards was fed into the machine, and the cards were placed into the appropriate bin, depending on the value of the selected column. By restacking the cards so that all zeros were first, followed by the ones, followed by the twos, and so forth, and then sorting on the next column, the whole deck of cards could be sorted. This process, known as *radix sort*, requires $c \times n$ passes, where c is the number of columns and n is the number of cards.

   We can simulate the action of this machine using an array of queues. During the first pass, the least significant digit (the ones digit) of each number is examined and the number is added to the queue whose subscript matches that digit. After all numbers have been processed, the elements of each queue are added to an eleventh queue, starting with queue[0], followed by queue[1], and so forth. The process is then repeated for the next significant digit, taking the numbers out of the eleventh queue. After all the digits have been processed, the eleventh queue will contain the numbers in sorted order.

Write a program that implements radix sort on an array of **int** values. You will need to make 10 passes, because an **int** can store numbers up to 2,147,483,648.

8. Complete the Dutch National Flag case study. You will need to develop the following classes:

a. A main class that extends JFrame to contain the flag and a control button (Sort).

b. A class to represent the flag; an extension of JPanel is suggested. This class will contain the array of threads and the sort method.

c. A class to represent a thread. Each thread should have a color and a method to draw the thread.

Self-Balancing Search Trees

In Chapter 8 we introduced the binary search tree. The performance (time required to find, insert, or remove an item) of a binary search tree is proportional to the total *height of the tree,* where we define the height of a tree as the maximum number of nodes along a path from the root to a leaf. A full binary tree of height k can hold $2^k - 1$ items. Thus, if the binary search tree were full and contained n items, the expected performance would be $O(\log n)$.

Unfortunately, if we build the binary search tree as described in Chapter 8, the resulting tree is not necessarily full or close to being full. Thus the actual performance is worse than expected. In this chapter we explore two algorithms for building binary search trees so that they are as full as possible. We call these trees *self-balancing* because they attempt to achieve a balance so that the height of each left subtree and right subtree are equal or nearly equal.

Finally we look at the B-tree and its specializations, the 2-3 and 2-3-4 trees. These are not binary search trees, but they achieve and maintain balance.

In this chapter we focus on algorithms and methods for search and insertion. We also discuss removing an item, but we have left the details of removal to the programming projects.

11.1 Tree Balance and Rotation

Why Balance Is Important

Figure 11.1 shows an example of a valid, but extremely unbalanced, binary search tree. Searches or inserts into this tree would be $O(n)$, not $O(\log n)$. Figure 11.2 shows the binary search tree resulting from inserting the words of the sentence "The quick brown fox jumps over the lazy dog." It too is not well balanced, having a height of 7 but containing only nine words. (Note that the string "The" is the smallest, because it begins with an uppercase letter.)

FIGURE 11.1
Very Unbalanced
Binary Search Tree

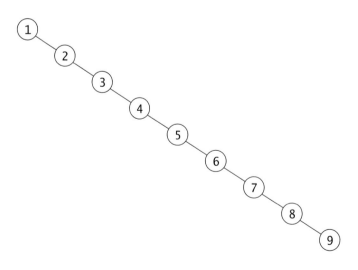

FIGURE 11.2

Realistic Example of
an Unbalanced Binary
Search Tree

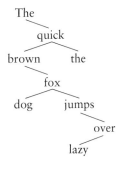

Rotation

To achieve self-adjusting capability, we need an operation on a binary search tree that will change the relative heights of left and right subtrees but preserve the binary search tree property—that is, the items in each left subtree are less than the item at the root, and the items in each right subtree are greater than the item in the root. In Figure 11.3 we show an unbalanced binary search tree with a height of 4 right after the insertion of node 7. The height of the left subtree of the root (20) is 3, and the height of the right subtree is 1.

We can transform the tree in Figure 11.3 by doing a *right rotation* around node 20, making 10 the root and 20 the root of the right subtree of the new root (10). Because 20 is now the right subtree of 10, we need to move node 10's old right subtree (root is 15). We will make it the left subtree of 20, as shown in Figure 11.4.

After these changes the new binary search tree has a height of 3 (one less than before), and the left and right subtrees of the new root (10) have a height of 2, as shown in Figure 11.5. Note that the binary search tree property is maintained for all the nodes of the tree.

This result can be generalized. If node 15 had children, its children would have to be greater than 10 and less than 20 in the original tree. The left and right subtrees of node 15 would not change when node 15 was moved, so the binary search tree property would still be maintained for all children of node 15 in the new tree (> 10 and < 20). We can make a similar statement for any of the other leaf nodes in the original tree.

Algorithm for Rotation

Figure 11.6 illustrates the internal representation of the nodes of our original binary search tree whose branches (indicated by arrows in color) will be changed by rotation. Initially, root references node 20. Rotation right is achieved by the following algorithm.

Algorithm for Rotation Right

1. Remember the value of root.left (temp = root.left).
2. Set root.left to the value of temp.right.
3. Set temp.right to root.
4. Set root to temp.

FIGURE 11.3
Unbalanced Tree Before Rotation

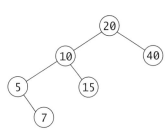

FIGURE 11.4
Right Rotation

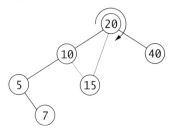

FIGURE 11.5
More Balanced Tree After Rotation

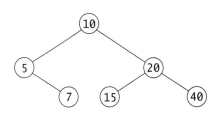

Figure 11.7 shows the rotated tree. Step 1 sets `temp` to reference the left subtree (node 10) of the original root. Step 2 resets the original root's left subtree to reference node 15. Step 3 resets node `temp`'s right subtree to reference the original root. Then Step 4 sets `root` to reference node `temp`. The internal representation corresponds to the tree shown in Figure 11.5.

The algorithm for rotation left is symmetric to rotation right and is left as an exercise.

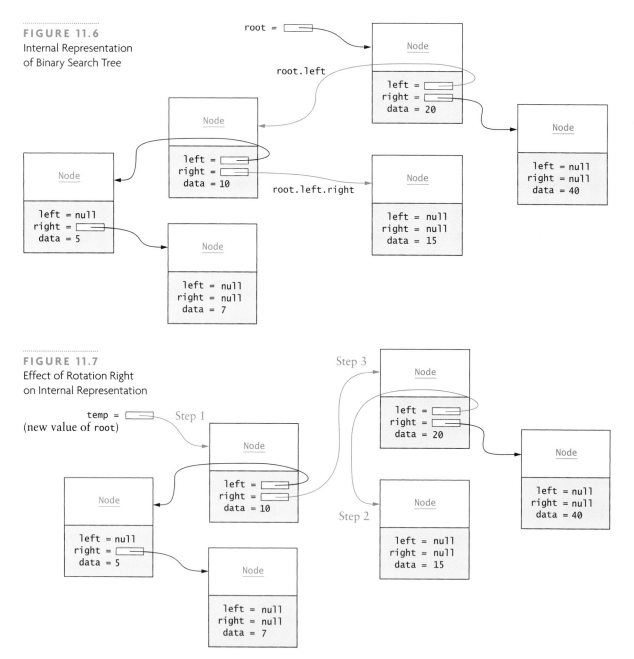

FIGURE 11.6
Internal Representation
of Binary Search Tree

FIGURE 11.7
Effect of Rotation Right
on Internal Representation

Implementing Rotation

Listing 11.1 shows class BinarySearchTreeWithRotate. This class is an extension of the BinarySearchTree class described in Chapter 8, and it will be used as the base class for the other search trees discussed in this chapter. It contains the methods rotateLeft and rotateRight. These methods take a reference to a Node that is the root of a subtree and return a reference to the root of the rotated tree. Figure 11.8 is a UML class diagram that shows the relationships between BinarySearchTreeWithRotate and the other classes in the hierarchy. BinarySearchTreeWithRotate is a subclass of BinaryTree as well as BinarySearchTree. Class BinaryTree has the static inner class Node and the data field root, which references the Node that is the root of the tree. The figure shows that a Node contains a data field named data of type Object and two references (as indicated by the open diamond) to a Node. The names of the reference are left and right, as shown on the line from the Node to itself.

....
FIGURE 11.8
UML Diagram of BinarySearchTreeWithRotate

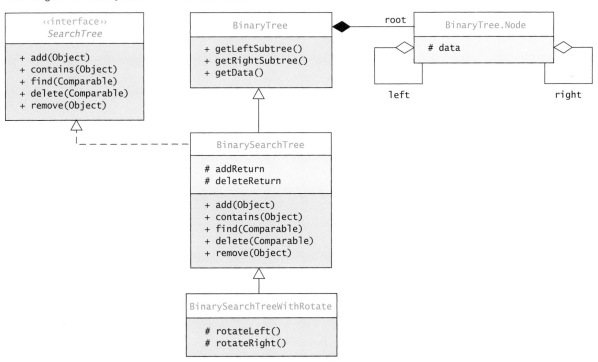

···················

LISTING 11.1

`BinarySearchTreeWithRotate.java`

```java
/**
    This class extends the BinarySearchTree by adding the rotate
    operations. Rotation will change the balance of a search
    tree while preserving the search tree property.
    Used as a common base class for self-balancing trees.
*/
public class BinarySearchTreeWithRotate extends BinarySearchTree {
    // Methods
    /** Method to perform a right rotation.
        pre:  root is the root of a binary search tree.
        post: root.right is the root of a binary search tree,
              root.right.right is raised one level,
              root.right.left does not change levels,
              root.left is lowered one level,
              the new root is returned.
        @param root The root of the binary tree to be rotated
        @return The new root of the rotated tree
    */
    protected Node rotateRight(Node root) {
        Node temp = root.left;
        root.left = temp.right;
        temp.right = root;
        return temp;
    }

    /** Method to perform a left rotation (rotateLeft).
        // See Programming Exercise 1
    */
}
```

▬▬▬▬▬▬▬▬▬▬▬▬▬▬▬▬▬▬▬▬▬

EXERCISES FOR SECTION 11.1

SELF-CHECK

1. Draw the binary search tree that results from inserting the words of the sentence "Now is the time for all good men to come to the aid of the party." What is its height? Compare this with 4, the smallest integer greater than $\log_2 13$, where 13 is the number of distinct words in this sentence.

2. Try to construct a binary search tree that contains the same words as in Question 1, but has a maximum height of 4.

3. Describe the algorithm for rotation left.

PROGRAMMING

1. Add the `rotateLeft` method to the `BinarySearchTreeWithRotate` class.

11.2 AVL Tree

Two Russian mathematicians, G. M. Adel'son-Vel'skiî and E. M. Landis, published a paper in 1962 that describes an algorithm for maintaining overall balance of a binary search tree. Their algorithm keeps track of the difference in height of each subtree. As items are added to (or removed from) the tree, the balance (that is, the difference in the heights of the subtrees) of each subtree from the insertion point up to the root is updated. If the balance ever gets out of the range –1 . . . +1, the subtree is rotated to bring it back into balance. Trees using this approach are known as *AVL trees* after the initials of the inventors. As before, we define the height of a tree as the number of nodes in the longest path from the root to a leaf node, including the root.

Balancing a Left-Left Tree

Figure 11.9 shows a binary search tree with a balance of –2 caused by an insert into its left-left subtree. Each white triangle with label a, b, or c represents a tree of height *k*; the shaded area at the bottom of the left-left triangle (tree a) indicates an insertion into this tree (its height is now *k* + 1). We use the formula

$$h_R - h_L$$

to calculate the balance for each node, where h_L and h_R are the heights of the left and right subtrees, respectively. The actual heights are not important; it is their relative difference that matters. The right subtree (b) of node 25 has a height of *k*; its left subtree (a) has a height of *k* + 1, so its balance is –1. The right subtree (of node 50) has a height of *k*; its left subtree has a height of *k* + 2, so its factor is –2. Such a tree is called a Left-Left tree because its root and the left subtree of the root are both left-heavy.

Figure 11.10 shows this same tree after a rotation right. The new tree root is node 25. Its right subtree (root 50) now has tree b as its left subtree. Notice that balance has now been achieved. Also, the overall height has not increased. Before the insertion, the tree height was *k* + 2; after the rotation, the tree height is still *k* + 2.

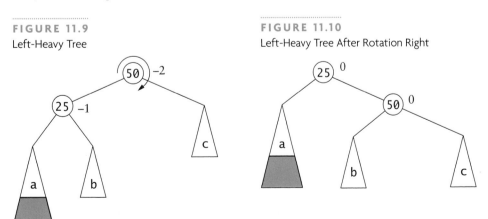

FIGURE 11.9
Left-Heavy Tree

FIGURE 11.10
Left-Heavy Tree After Rotation Right

Balancing a Left-Right Tree

Figure 11.11 shows a left-heavy tree caused by an insert into the left-right subtree. This tree is called a Left-Right tree because its root is left-heavy but the left-subtree of the root is right-heavy. We cannot fix this with a simple rotation right as in the Left-Left case. (See Self-Check Exercise 2 at the end of this section.)

FIGURE 11.11
Left-Right Tree

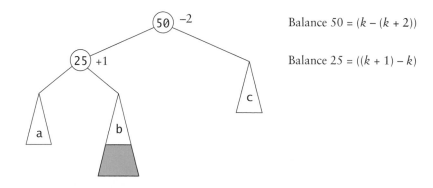

Balance $50 = (k - (k + 2))$

Balance $25 = ((k + 1) - k)$

Figure 11.12 shows a general Left-Right tree. Node 40, the root of the Left-Right subtree, is expanded into its subtrees b_L and b_R. Figure 11.12 shows the effect of an insertion into b_L, making node 40 left-heavy. If the left subtree is rotated left, as shown in Figure 11.13, the overall tree is now a Left-Left tree, similar to the case of Figure 11.9. Now if the modified tree is rotated right, overall balance is achieved, as shown in Figure 11.14. Figures 11.15–11.17 illustrate the effect of these double rotations after insertion into b_R.

In both cases, the new tree root is 40; its left subtree has node 25 as its root, and its right subtree has node 50 as its root. The balance of the root is 0. If the critically unbalanced situation was due to an insertion into subtree b_L, the balance of the root's left child is 0 and the balance of the root's right child is +1 (Figure 11.14). For insertion into subtree b_R, the balance of the root's left child is –1 and the balance of the root's right child is 0 (Figure 11.17).

FIGURE 11.12
Insertion into b_L

FIGURE 11.13
Left Subtree After Rotate Left

FIGURE 11.14
Tree After Rotate Right

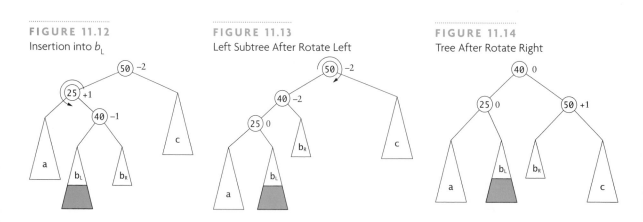

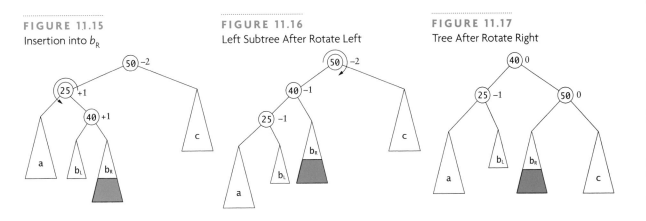

Four Kinds of Critically Unbalanced Trees

How do we recognize unbalanced trees and determine what to do to balance them? For the Left-Left tree shown in Figure 11.9 (parent and child nodes are both left-heavy, parent balance is –2, child balance is –1), the remedy is to rotate right around the parent.

For the Left-Right example shown in Figure 11.11 (parent is left-heavy with balance –2, child is right-heavy with balance +1), the remedy is to rotate left around child and then rotate right around parent. We list the four cases that need rebalancing and their remedies next.

- Left-Left (parent balance is –2, left child balance is –1): Rotate right around parent.
- Left-Right (parent balance is –2, left child balance is +1): Rotate left around child, then rotate right around parent.
- Right-Right (parent balance is +2, right child balance is +1): Rotate left around parent.
- Right-Left (parent balance is +2, right child balance is –1): Rotate right around child, then rotate left around parent.

EXAMPLE 11.1   We will build an AVL tree from the words in the sentence "The quick brown fox jumps over the lazy dog."

After inserting the words *The, quick,* and *brown,* we get the following tree.

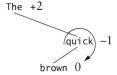

The subtree with the root *quick* is left-heavy by 1, but the overall tree with the root of *The* is right-heavy by 2 (Right-Left case). We must first rotate the subtree around *quick* to the right:

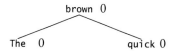

Then rotate left about *The:*

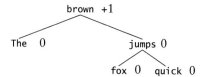

We now proceed to insert *fox* and *jumps:*

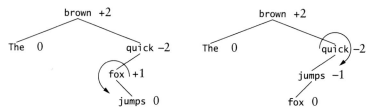

The subtree rooted about *quick* is now left-heavy by 2 (Left-Right case). Because this case is symmetric with the previous one, we rotate left about *fox* and then right about *quick,* giving the following result.

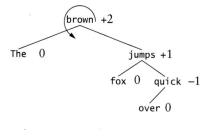

We now insert *over.*

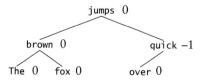

The subtrees at *quick* and *jumps* are unbalanced by 1. The subtree at *brown,* however, is right-heavy by 2 (Right-Right case), so a rotation left solves the problem.

jumps 0
```
       brown  0          quick −1
      /      \          /      \
  The 0   fox 0     over 0
```

We can now insert *the, lazy,* and *dog* without any additional rotations being necessary.

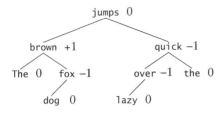

Implementing an AVL Tree

We begin by deriving the class `AVLTree` from `BinarySearchTreeWithRotate` (see Listing 11.1). Figure 11.18 is a UML class diagram showing the relationship between `AVLTree` and `BinarySearchTreeWithRotate`. The `AVLTree` class contains the **boolean** data field `increase` which indicates whether the current subtree height has increased as a result of the insertion. We override the methods `add` and `delete` but inherit method `find`, because searching a balanced tree is no different from searching an unbalanced tree. We also extend the inner class `BinaryTree.Node` with `AVLNode`. Within this class we add the additional field `balance`.

FIGURE 11.18
UML Class Diagram of AVLTree

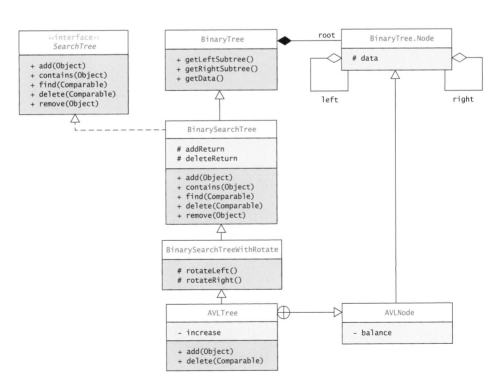

SYNTAX   **UML Syntax**

The line from the AVLTree class to the AVLNode class in the diagram in Figure 11.18 indicates that methods in the AVLTree class can access the private data field balance. The symbol ⊕ next to the AVLTree class indicates that the AVLNode class is an inner class of AVLTree. The arrow pointing to AVLNode indicates that methods in AVLTree access the contents of AVLNode, but methods in AVLNode do not access the contents of AVLTree.

Note that the Node class is an inner class of the BinaryTree class, but we do not show the ⊕. This is because an object of type Node, called root, is a component of the BinaryTree class, as indicated by the filled diamond next to the BinaryTree class. Showing both the ⊕ and the filled diamond would tend to clutter the diagram, so only the filled diamond is shown.

```
/**
    Self-balancing binary search tree using the algorithm defined
    by Adelson-Velskii and Landis.
*/
public class AVLTree extends BinarySearchTreeWithRotate {

    // Insert nested class AVLNode here.

    // Data Fields
    /** Flag to indicate that height of tree has increased. */
    private boolean increase;
    ...
}
```

The AVLNode Class

The AVLNode class is shown in Listing 11.2. It is an extension of the BinaryTree.Node class. It adds the data field balance and the constants LEFT_HEAVY, BALANCED, and RIGHT_HEAVY.

....
LISTING 11.2
The AVLNode Class

```
/** Class to represent an AVL Node. It extends the
    BinaryTree.Node by adding the balance field. */
private static class AVLNode extends Node {
    /** Constant to indicate left-heavy */
    public static final int LEFT_HEAVY = -1;
    /** Constant to indicate balanced */
    public static final int BALANCED = 0;
    /** Constant to indicate right-heavy */
    public static final int RIGHT_HEAVY = 1;
    /** balance is right subtree height - left subtree height */
    private int balance;

    // Methods
    /** Construct a node with the given item as the data field.
        @param item The data field
```

```
    */
    public AVLNode(Object item) {
        super(item);
        balance = BALANCED;
    }

    /** Return a string representation of this object.
        The balance value is appended to the contents.
        @return String representation of this object
    */
    public String toString() {
        return balance + ": " + super.toString();
    }
}
```

Inserting into an AVL Tree

The easiest way to keep a tree balanced is never to let it become unbalanced. If any node becomes critical and needs rebalancing, rebalance immediately. You can identify critical nodes by checking the balance at the root node of a subtree as you return to each parent node along the insertion path. If the insertion was in the left subtree and the left subtree height has increased, you must check to see whether the balance for the root node of the left subtree has become critical (–2 or +2). If so, we need to fix it by calling rebalanceLeft (rebalance a left-heavy tree when balance is –2) or rebalanceRight (rebalance a right-heavy tree when balance is +2). A symmetric strategy should be followed after returning from an insertion into the right subtree. The **boolean** variable increase is set before return from recursion to indicate to the next higher level that the height of the subtree has increased. This information is then used to adjust the balance of the next level in the tree. The following algorithm is based on the algorithm for inserting into a binary search tree, described in Chapter 8.

Algorithm for Insertion into an AVL Tree

1.   **if** the root is **null**
2.   Create a new tree with the item at the root and return **true**.
          else if the item is equal to root.data
3.   The item is already in the tree; return **false**.
          else if the item is less than root.data
4.   Recursively insert the item in the left subtree.
5.   **if** the height of the left subtree has increased (increase is **true**)
6.   Decrement balance.
7.   **if** balance is zero, reset increase to **false**.
8.   **if** balance is less than –1
9.   Reset increase to **false**.
10.   Perform a rebalanceLeft.
          else if the item is greater than root.data
11.   The processing is symmetric to Steps 4 through 10. Note that balance is incremented if increase is true.

After returning from the recursion (Step 4), examine the global data field `increase` to see whether the left subtree has increased in height. If it did, then decrement the balance. If the balance had been +1 (current subtree was right-heavy), it is now zero, so the overall height of the current subtree is not changed. Therefore, reset `increase` to **false** (Steps 5–7).

If the balance was −1 (current subtree was left-heavy), it is now −2, and a `rebalanceLeft` must be performed. The rebalance operation reduces the overall height of the tree by 1, so `increase` is reset to **false**. Therefore, no more rebalancing operations will occur, so we can fix the tree by either a single rotation (Left-Left case) or a double rotation (Left-Right case) (Steps 8–10).

add Starter Method

We are now ready to implement the insertion algorithm. The `add` starter method merely calls the recursive `add` method with the root as its argument. The returned `AVLNode` is the new root.

```
/** add starter method.
    pre: the item to insert implements the Comparable interface.
    @param item The item being inserted.
    @return true if the object is inserted; false
            if the object already exists in the tree
    @throws ClassCastException if item is not Comparable
*/
public boolean add(Object item) {
    increase = false;
    root = add((AVLNode) root, (Comparable) item);
    return addReturn;
}
```

As for the `BinarySearchTree` in Chapter 8, the recursive `add` method will set the data field `addReturn` to **true** (inherited from class `BinarySearchTree`) if the item is inserted and **false** if the item is already in the tree.

Recursive add Method

The declaration for the recursive add method begins as follows:

```
/** Recursive add method. Inserts the given object into the tree.
    post: addReturn is set true if the item is inserted,
          false if the item is already in the tree.
    @param localRoot The local root of the subtree
    @param item The object to be inserted
    @return The new local root of the subtree with the item
            inserted
*/
private AVLNode add(AVLNode localRoot, Comparable item)
```

We begin by seeing whether the `localRoot` is **null**. If it is, then we set `addReturn` and `increase` to **true** and return a new `AVLNode`, which contains the item to be inserted.

```
if (localRoot == null) {
    addReturn = true;
    increase = true;
    return new AVLNode(item);
}
```

Next we compare the inserted item with the data field of the current node. If it is equal, we set addReturn and increase to **false** and return the localRoot unchanged.

```
if (item.compareTo(localRoot.data) == 0) {
    // Item is already in the tree.
    increase = false;
    addReturn = false;
    return localRoot;
}
```

If it is less than this value, we recursively call the add method (Step 4 of the insertion algorithm), passing localRoot.left as the parameter and replacing the value of localRoot.left with the returned value.

```
else if (item.compareTo(localRoot.data) < 0) {
    // item < data
    localRoot.left = add((AVLNode) localRoot.left, item);
    ...
```

Upon return from the recursion, we examine the global data field increase. If increase is **true**, then the height of the left subtree has increased, so we decrement the balance by calling the decrementBalance method. If the balance is now less than -1, we reset increase to **false** and call the rebalanceLeft method. The return value from the rebalanceLeft method is the return value from this call to add. If the balance is not less than -1, or if the left subtree height did not increase, then the return from this recursive call is the same local root that was passed as the parameter.

```
if (increase) {
    decrementBalance(localRoot);
    if (localRoot.balance < AVLNode.LEFT_HEAVY) {
        increase = false;
        return rebalanceLeft(localRoot);
    } else {
        return localRoot;
    }
} else {
    return localRoot;
}
```

If the item is not equal to localRoot.data and not less than localRoot.data, then it must be greater than localRoot.data. The processing is symmetric with the less-than case and is left as an exercise.

Initial Algorithm for **rebalanceLeft**

Method rebalanceLeft rebalances a left-heavy tree. Such a tree can be a Left-Left tree (fixed by a single right rotation) or a Left-Right tree (fixed by a left rotation followed by a right rotation). If its left subtree is right-heavy, we have a Left-Right case, so we first rotate left around the left subtree. Finally we rotate the tree right.

1. **if** the left subtree has positive balance (Left-Right case)
2.   Rotate left around left subtree root.
3. Rotate right.

The algorithm for rebalanceRight is left as an exercise.

The Effect of Rotations on Balance

The rebalancing algorithm just presented is incomplete. So far we have focused on changes to the root reference and to the internal branches of the tree being balanced, but we have not adjusted the balances of the nodes. In the beginning of this section we showed that for a Left-Left tree, the balances of the new root node and of its right child are 0 after a right rotation; the balances of all other nodes are unchanged (see Figure 11.10).

The Left-Right case is more complicated. We made the following observation after studying the different cases.

The balance of the root is 0. If the critically unbalanced situation was due to an insertion into subtree b_L, the balance of the root's left child is 0 and the balance of the root's right child is +1 (Figure 11.14). For insertion into subtree b_R, the balance of the root's left child is −1, and the balance of the root's right child is 0 (Figure 11.17). So we need to change the balances of the new root node and both its left and right children; all other balances are unchanged. We will call insertion into subtree b_L the Left-Right-Left case and insertion into subtree b_R the Left-Right-Right case.

Revised Algorithm for **rebalanceLeft**

Based on the foregoing discussion we can now develop the complete algorithm for `rebalanceLeft`, including the required balance changes. It is easier to store the new balance for each node before the rotation than after.

1. **if** the left subtree has a positive balance (Left-Right case)
2.   **if** the left-left subtree has a negative balance (Left-Right-Left case)
3.   Set the left subtree (new left subtree) balance to 0.
4.   Set the left-left subtree (new root) balance to 0.
5.   Set the local root (new right subtree) balance to +1.
        else (Left-Right-Right case)
6.   Set the left subtree (new left subtree) balance to −1.
7.   Set the left-left subtree (new root) balance to 0.
8.   Set the local root (new right subtree) balance to 0.
9.   Rotate the left subtree left.
    else (Left-Left case)
10.   Set the left subtree balance to 0.
11.   Set the local root balance to 0.
12. Rotate the local root right.

The algorithm for `rebalanceRight` is left as an exercise.

Method **rebalanceLeft**

The code for `rebalanceLeft` is shown in Listing 11.3. First we test to see whether the left subtree is right-heavy (Left-Right case). If so, the Left-Right subtree is examined.

Depending on its balance, the balances of the left subtree and local root are set as previously described in the algorithm. The rotations will reduce the overall height of the tree by 1, so increase is now set to **false**. The left subtree is then rotated left, and then the tree is rotated right.

If the left child is LEFT_HEAVY, the rotation process will restore the balance to both the tree and its left subtree and reduce the overall height by 1; the balance for the left subtree and local root are both set to BALANCED, and increase is now set to **false**. The tree is then rotated right to correct the imbalance.

LISTING 11.3
The rebalanceLeft Method

```
/** Method to rebalance left.
    pre: localRoot is the root of an AVL subtree that is
        critically left-heavy.
    post: balance is restored.
    @param localRoot Root of the AVL subtree
        that needs rebalancing
    @return a new localRoot
*/
private AVLNode rebalanceLeft(AVLNode localRoot) {
    // Obtain reference to left child.
    AVLNode leftChild = (AVLNode) localRoot.left;
    // See whether left-right heavy.
    if (leftChild.balance > AVLNode.BALANCED) {
        // Obtain reference to left-right child.
        AVLNode leftRightChild = (AVLNode) leftChild.right;
        /** Adjust the balances to be their new values after
            the rotations are performed.
        */
        if (leftRightChild.balance < AVLNode.BALANCED) {
            leftChild.balance = AVLNode.BALANCED;
            leftRightChild.balance = AVLNode.BALANCED;
            localRoot.balance = AVLNode.RIGHT_HEAVY;
        } else {
            leftChild.balance = AVLNode.LEFT_HEAVY;
            leftRightChild.balance = AVLNode.BALANCED;
            localRoot.balance = AVLNode.BALANCED;
        }
        // Perform left rotation.
        localRoot.left = rotateLeft(leftChild);
    } else {    Left-Left case
        /** In this case the leftChild (the new root)
            and the root (new right child) will both be balanced
            after the rotation.
        */
        leftChild.balance = AVLNode.BALANCED;
        localRoot.balance = AVLNode.BALANCED;
    }
    // Now rotate the local root right.
    return (AVLNode) rotateRight(localRoot);
}
```

We also need a `rebalanceRight` method that is symmetric with `rebalanceLeft` (that is, all `left`s are changed to `right`s and all `right`s are changed to `left`s). Coding of this method is left as an exercise.

The `decrementBalance` Method

As we return from an insertion into a node's left subtree, we need to decrement the balance of the node. We also need to indicate whether the subtree height at that node has not increased, by setting `increase` (currently **true**) to **false**. There are two cases to consider: a node that is balanced and a node that is right-heavy. If a node is balanced, insertion into its left subtree will cause it to become left-heavy, and its height will also increase by 1 (see Figure 11.19). If a node is right-heavy, insertion into its left subtree will cause it to become balanced, and its height will not increase (see Figure 11.20).

```
private void decrementBalance(AVLNode node) {
    // Decrement the balance.
    node.balance--;
    if (node.balance == AVLNode.BALANCED) {
        /** If now balanced, overall height has not increased. */
        increase = false;
    }
}
```

Step 11 of the insertion algorithm performs insertion into a right subtree. This can cause the height of the right subtree to increase, so we will also need an `incrementBalance` method that increments the balance and resets `increase` to **false** if the balance changes from left-heavy to balanced. Coding this method is left as an exercise.

FIGURE 11.19
Decrement of `balance` by Insert on Left (Height Increases)

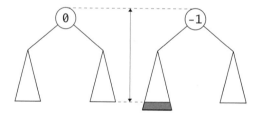

balance before insert is 0

balance is decreased due to insert; Overall height increased

FIGURE 11.20
Decrement of `balance` by Insert on Left (Height Does Not Change)

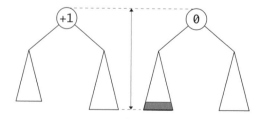

balance before insert is +1

balance is decreased due to insert; Overall height remains the same

Removal from an AVL Tree

When we remove an item from a left subtree, the balance of the local root is increased, and when we remove an item from the right subtree, the balance of the local root is decreased. We can adapt the algorithm for removal from a binary search tree to become an algorithm for removal from an AVL tree. We need to maintain a data field `decrease` that tells the previous level in the recursion that there was a decrease in the height of the subtree that was just returned from. (This data field is analogous to the data field `increase`, which is used in the insertion to indicate that the height of the subtree has increased.) We can then increment or decrement the local root balance. If the balance is outside the threshold, then the rebalance methods (`rebalanceLeft` or `rebalanceRight`) are used to restore the balance.

We need to modify methods `decrementBalance`, `incrementBalance`, `rebalanceLeft`, and `rebalanceRight` so that they set the value of `decrease` (as well as `increase`) after a node's balance has been decremented. When a subtree changes from either left-heavy or right-heavy to balanced, then the height has decreased, and `decrease` should be set **true**; when the subtree changes from balanced to either left-heavy or right-heavy, then `decrease` should be reset to **false**. We also need to provide methods similar to the ones needed for removal in a binary search tree. Implementing removal is left as a programming project.

Also, observe that the effect of rotations is not only to restore balance but to decrease the height of the subtree being rotated. Thus, while only one `rebalanceLeft` or `rebalanceRight` was required for insertion, during removal each recursive return could result in a further need to rebalance.

Performance of the AVL Tree

Since each subtree is kept as close to balanced as possible, one would expect that the AVL tree provides the expected $O(\log n)$ performance. Each subtree is allowed to be out of balance by ±1. Thus, the tree may contain some holes.

It can be shown that in the worst case, the height of an AVL tree can be 1.44 times the height of a full binary tree that contains the same number of items. However, this would still yield $O(\log n)$ performance, because we ignore constants.

The worst-case performance is very rare. Empirical tests (see, for example, Donald Knuth, *The Art of Computer Programming, Vol 3: Searching and Sorting*, [Addison-Wesley, 1973], p. 460) show that, on the average, $\log_2 n + 0.25$ comparisons are required to insert the nth item into an AVL tree. Thus the average performance is very close to that of the corresponding complete binary search tree.

EXERCISES FOR SECTION 11.2

SELF-CHECK

1. Show how the final AVL tree for the "The quick brown fox" changes as you insert "apple", "cat", and "hat" in that order.

2. Show the effect of just rotating right on the tree in Figure 11.11. Why doesn't this fix the problem?

3. Build an AVL tree that inserts the integers 30, 40, 15, 25, 90, 80, 70, 85, 15, 72 in the given order.

4. Build the AVL tree from the sentence "Now is the time for all good men to come to the aid of the party."

PROGRAMMING

1. Program the `rebalanceRight` method.

2. Program the code in the add method for the case where `item.compareTo(localRoot.data) > 0`.

3. Program the `incrementBalance` method.

11.3 Red-Black Trees

We discuss another approach to keeping a tree balanced, called the *Red-Black tree*. Rudolf Bayer developed the Red-Black tree as a special case of his B-tree (the topic of Section 11.4); Leo Guibas and Robert Sedgewick refined the concept and introduced the color convention. A Red-Black tree maintains the following invariants:

1. A node is either red or black.

2. The root is always black.

3. A red node always has black children. (A **null** reference is considered to refer to a black node.)

4. The number of black nodes in any path from the root to a leaf is the same.

Figure 11.21 shows an example of a Red-Black tree. Invariant 4 states that a Red-Black tree is always balanced because the root node's left and right subtrees must be the same height where the height is determined by counting just black nodes. Notice that by the standards of the AVL tree this tree is out of balance and would be considered a Left-Right tree. However, by the standards of the Red-Black tree it is balanced because there are two black nodes (counting the root) in any path from the root to a leaf. (We have one color in this textbook other than black, so we will use that color to indicate a red node.)

FIGURE 11.21
Red-Black Tree

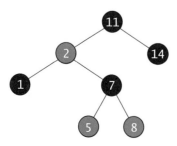

Insertion into a Red-Black Tree

The algorithm for insertion follows the same recursive search process used for all binary search trees to reach the insertion point. When a leaf is found, the new item is inserted, and it is initially given the color red, so invariant 4 will be maintained. If the parent is black, we are done.

However, if the parent is also red, then invariant 3 has been violated. Figure 11.22(a) shows the insertion of 35 as a red child of 30. If the parent's sibling is also red, then we can change the grandparent's color to red and change both the parent and parent's sibling to black. This restores invariant 3 but does not violate invariant 4. (See Figure 11.22(b).) If the root of the overall tree is now red, we can change it to black to restore invariant 2, and still maintain invariant 4 (the heights of all paths to a leaf are increased by 1). (See Figure 11.22(c).)

If we insert a value with a red parent, but that parent does not have a red sibling (see Figure 11.23(a)), then we change the color of the grandparent to red and the parent to black (see Figure 11.23(b)). Now we have violated invariant 4, as there are more black nodes on the side of the parent. We correct this by rotating about the grandparent so that the parent moves into the position where the grandparent was, thus restoring invariant 4 (see Figure 11.23(c)).

The preceding maneuver works only if the inserted value is on the same side of its parent as the parent is to the grandparent. Figure 11.24(a) shows 25 inserted as the left child of 30, which is the right child of 20. If we change the color of the grandparent (20) to red and the parent (30) to black (see Figure 11.24(b)) and then rotate (see Figure 11.24(c)), we are still left with a red parent–red child combination. Before changing the color and rotating about the grandparent level, we must first rotate about the parent so that the red child is on the same side of its parent as the parent is to the grandparent (see Figure 11.25(b)). We can then change the colors (see Figure 11.25(c)) and rotate (see Figure 11.25 (d)).

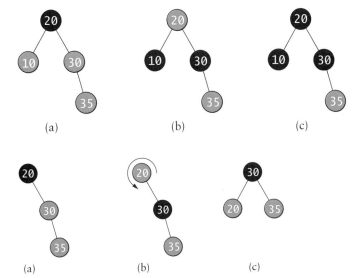

FIGURE 11.22
Insertion into a Red-Black Tree, Case 1

(a)   (b)   (c)

FIGURE 11.23
Insertion into a Red-Black Tree, Case 2

(a)   (b)   (c)

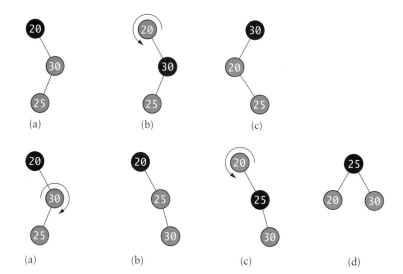

More than one of these cases can occur. Figure 11.26 shows the insertion of the value 4 into the Red-Black tree of Figure 11.21. Upon return from the insertion to the parent (node 5), it may be discovered that a red node now has a red child, which is a violation of invariant 3. If this node's sibling (node 8) is also red (case 1), then they must have a black parent. If we make the parent red (node 7) and both of the parent's children black, invariant 4 is preserved, and the problem is shifted up, as shown in Figure 11.27.

Looking at Figure 11.27 we see that 7 is red and that its parent, 2, is also red. However, we can't simply change 2's color as we did before, because 2's sibling, 14, is black. This problem will require one or two rotations to correct.

Because the red child (7) is not on the same side of its parent (2) as the parent is to the grandparent (11), this is an example of Case 3. We rotate the tree left (around node 2) so that the red node 2 is on the same side of red node 7 as node 7 is to the grandparent (11) (see Figure 11.28). We now change node 7 to black and node 11 to red (Figure 11.29) and rotate right around node 11, restoring the balance of black nodes as shown in Figure 11.30.

FIGURE 11.26
Red-Black Tree After Insertion of 4

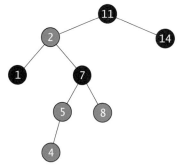

FIGURE 11.27
Moving Black Down and Red Up

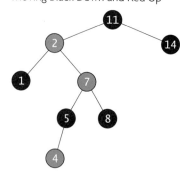

FIGURE 11.28
Rotating Red Node to Outside

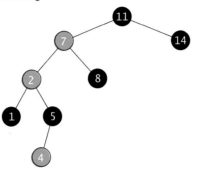

FIGURE 11.29
Changing Colors of Parent and Grandparent Nodes

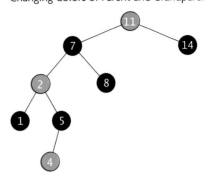

FIGURE 11.30
Final Red-Black Tree After Insert

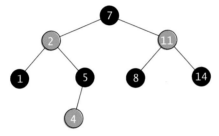

EXAMPLE 11.2

We will now build the Red-Black tree for the sentence "The quick brown fox jumps over the lazy dog."

We start by inserting *The*, *quick*, and *brown*.

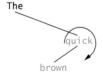

The parent of *brown (quick)* is red, but the sibling of *quick* is black (null nodes are considered black), so we have an example of Case 2 or Case 3. Because the child is not on the same side of the parent as the parent is to the grandparent, this is Case 3. We first rotate right about *quick* to get the child on the same side of the parent as the parent is to the grandparent.

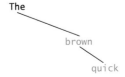

We then change the colors of *The* and *brown*.

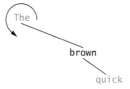

Then we rotate left about *The*.

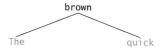

Next we insert *fox*.

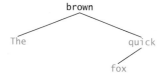

We see that *fox* has a red parent *(quick)* whose sibling is also red *(The)*. This is a Case 1 insertion, so we can change the color of the parent and its sibling to black and the grandparent to red.

Since the root is red, we can change it to black without violating the rule of balanced black nodes.

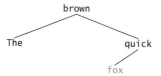

Now we add *jumps*, which gives us another Case 3 insertion.

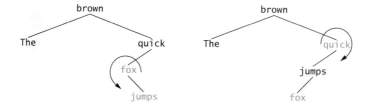

This triggers a double rotation. First rotate left about *fox* and change the color of its parent *jumps* to black and its grandparent *quick* to red. Next, rotate right about *quick*.

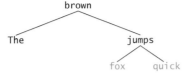

Next we insert *over.*

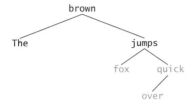

Because *quick* and *fox* are red, we have a Case 1 insertion, so we can move the black in *jumps* down, changing the color of *jumps* to red and *fox* and *quick* to black.

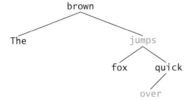

Next we add *the.* No changes are required, because its parent is black.

When compared to the corresponding AVL tree, this tree looks out of balance. But the black nodes are in balance (2 in each path).

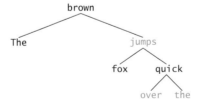

Now we insert *lazy.*

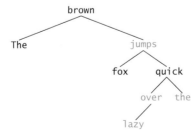

Because *over* and *the* are both red, we can move the black at *quick* down (Case 1).

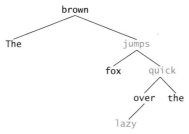

But now *quick* is a red node with a red parent *(jumps)*, but whose sibling is black *(The)*. Because *quick* and *jumps* are both right children, this is an example of Case 2. This triggers a rotate left around *brown*.

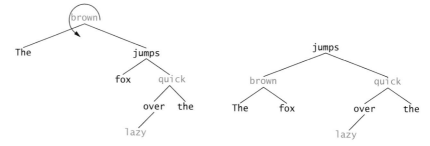

Finally we can insert *dog*.

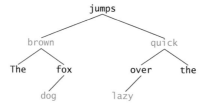

Surprisingly, the result is identical to the AVL tree for the same input, but the intermediate steps were very different.

Implementation of Red-Black Tree Class

We begin by deriving the class `RedBlackTree` from `BinarySearchTreeWithRotate` (see Listing 11.1). Figure 11.31 is a UML class diagram showing the relationship between `RedBlackTree` and `BinarySearchTreeWithRotate`. The `RedBlackTree` class overrides the add and delete methods. The nested class `BinaryTree.Node` is extended with the `RedBlackNode` class. This class has the additional data field `isRed` to indicate red nodes. Listing 11.4 shows the `RedBlackNode` class.

LISTING 11.4
The `RedBlackTree` and `RedBlackNode` Classes

```
/** Class to represent Red-Black tree. */
public class RedBlackTree extends BinarySearchTreeWithRotate {

    /** Nested class to represent a Red-Black node. */
    private static class RedBlackNode extends Node {
        // Additional data members
        /** Color indicator. True if red, false if black. */
        private boolean isRed;

        // Constructor
        /** Create a RedBlackNode with the default color of red
            and the given data field.
            @param item The data field
        */
        public RedBlackNode(Object item) {
            super(item);
            isRed = true;
        }

        // Methods
        /** Return a string representation of this object.
            The color (red or black) is appended to the
            node's contents.
            @return String representation of this object
        */
        public String toString() {
            if (isRed) {
                return "Red  : " + super.toString();
            } else {
                return "Black: " + super.toString();
            }
        }
    }
    ...
}
```

Algorithm for Red-Black Tree Insertion

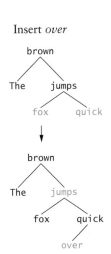

Insert *over*

The foregoing outline of the Red-Black tree insertion algorithm is from the point of view of the node being inserted. It can be, and has been, implemented using a data structure that has a reference to the parent of each node stored in it so that, given a reference to a node, one can access the parent, grandparent, and the parent's sibling (the node's aunt or uncle).

We are going to present a recursive algorithm where the need for fix-ups is detected from the grandparent level. This algorithm has one additional difference from the algorithm as presented in the foregoing examples: Whenever a black node with two red children is detected on the way down the tree, it is changed to red and the children are changed to black (for example, *jumps* and its children in the figure at left). If this change causes a problem, it is fixed on the way back up. This modification simplifies the logic a bit and improves the performance of the algorithm. This algorithm is also based on the algorithm for inserting into a binary search tree that was described in Chapter 8.

FIGURE 11.31

UML Class Diagram of `RedBlackTree`

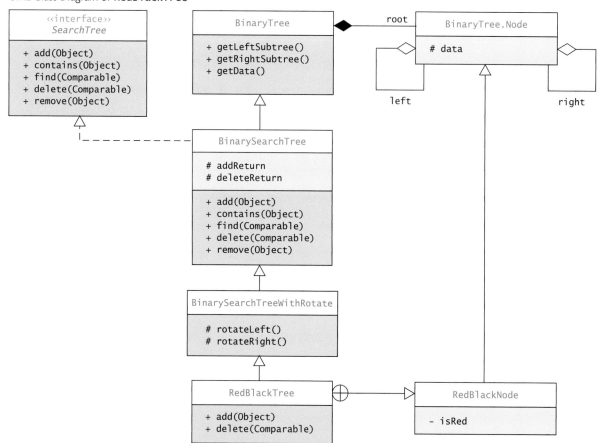

Algorithm for Red-Black Tree Insertion

1.   **if** the root is **null**
2.   Insert a new Red-Black node and color it black.
3.   Return **true**.
4.   **else if** the item is equal to `root.data`
5.   The item is already in the tree; return **false**.
6.   **else if** the item is less than `root.data`
7.   **if** the left subtree is **null**
8.   Insert a new Red-Black node as the left subtree and color it red.
9.   Return **true**.
10.   **else**
11.   **if** both the left child and the right child are red

12.		Change the color of the children to black and change local root to red.
13.		Recursively insert the item into the left subtree.
14.		**if** the left child is now red
15.			**if** the left grandchild is now red (grandchild is an "outside" node)
16.				Change the color of the left child to black and change the local root to red.
17.				Rotate the local root right.
18.			**else if** the right grandchild is now red (grandchild is an "inside" node)
19.				Rotate the left child left.
20.				Change the color of the left child to black and change the local root to red.
21.				Rotate the local root right.
22.	**else**	
23.		Item is greater than `root.data`; process is symmetric and is left as an exercise.
24.		**if** the local root is the root of the tree
25.			Force its color to be black.

Because Java passes the value of a reference, we have to work with a node that is a local root of a Red-Black tree. Thus, in Step 8, we replace the **null** reference to the left subtree with the inserted node.

If the left subtree is not **null** (Step 10), we recursively apply the algorithm (Step 13). But before we do so, we see whether both children are red. If they are, we change the local root to red and change the children to black (Steps 11 and 12). (If the local root's parent was red, this condition will be detected at that level during the return from the recursion.)

Upon return from the recursion (Step 14), we see whether the local root's left child is now red. If it is, we need to check its children (the local root's grandchildren). If one of them is red, then we have a red parent with a red child, and a rotation is necessary. If the left grandchild is red, a single rotation will solve the problem (Steps 15 through 17). If the right grandchild is red, a double rotation is necessary (Steps 18 through 21). Note that there may be only one grandchild or no grandchildren. However, if there are two grandchildren, they cannot both be red, because they would have been changed to black by Steps 11 and 12, as described in the previous paragraph.

The **add** Starter Method

As with the other binary search trees we have studied, the add starter method checks for a **null** root, and inserts a single new node. Since the root of a Red-Black tree is always black, we set the newly inserted node to black. The cast is necessary because root is a data field that was inherited from `BinaryTree` and is therefore of type `Node`.

```
public boolean add(Object item) {
    if (root == null) {
        root = new RedBlackNode(item);
        ((RedBlackNode) root).isRed = false; // root is black.
        return true;
    }
    ...
```

Otherwise the recursive add method is called. This method takes two parameters: the node that is the local root of the subtree into which the item is to be inserted, and the item to be inserted. The return value is the node that is the root of the subtree that now contains the inserted item. The data field addReturn is set to **true** if the insert method succeeded and to **false** if the item is already in the subtree.

The root is replaced by the return value from the recursive add method, the color of the root is set to black, and the data field addReturn is returned to the caller of the add starter method.

```
    else {
        root = add((RedBlackNode) root, (Comparable) item);
        ((RedBlackNode) root).isRed = false; // root is always black.
        return addReturn;
    }
```

The Recursive add Method

The recursive add method begins by comparing the item to be inserted with the data field of the local root. If they are equal, then the item is already in the tree; addReturn is set to **false** and the localRoot is returned (algorithm Step 5).

```
private Node add(RedBlackNode localRoot, Comparable item) {
    if (item.compareTo(localRoot.data) == 0) {
        // item already in the tree.
        addReturn = false;
        return localRoot;
    }
    ...
```

If it is less, then localRoot.left is checked to see whether it is **null**. If so, then we insert a new node and return (Steps 7 through 9).

```
    else if (item.compareTo(localRoot.data) < 0) {
        // item < localRoot.data.
        if (localRoot.left == null) {
            // Create new left child.
            localRoot.left = new RedBlackNode(item);
            addReturn = true;
            return localRoot;
        }
        ...
```

Otherwise, check to see whether both children are red. If so, we make them black and change the local root to red. This is done by the method moveBlackDown. Then we recursively call the add method, using root.left as the new local root (Steps 11–13).

```
    else {   // Need to search.
        // Check for two red children, swap colors if found.
        moveBlackDown(localRoot);
```

```
// Recursively add on the left.
localRoot.left = add((RedBlackNode) localRoot.left, item);
...
```

It is upon return from the recursive add that things get interesting. Upon return from the recursive call, `localRoot.left` refers to the parent of a Red-Black sub-tree that may be violating the rule against adjacent red nodes. Therefore we check the left child to see whether it is red (Step 14).

```
// See whether the left child is now red
    if (((RedBlackNode) localRoot.left).isRed) {
...
```

If the left child is red, then we need to check its two children. First we check the left grandchild (Step 15).

```
if (localRoot.left.left != null
    && ((RedBlackNode) localRoot.left.left).isRed) {
    // Left-left grandchild is also red.
...
```

If the left-left grandchild is red, we have detected a violation of invariant 3 (no consecutive red children), and we have a left-left case. Thus we change colors and perform a single rotation, returning the resulting local root to the caller (Steps 16–17).

```
// Single rotation is necessary.
((RedBlackNode) localRoot.left).isRed = false;
localRoot.isRed = true;
return rotateRight(localRoot);
```

If the left grandchild is not red, we then check the right grandchild. If it is red, the process is symmetric to the preceding case, except that a double rotation will be required (Steps 18–21).

```
else if (localRoot.left.right != null
        && ((RedBlackNode) localRoot.left.right).isRed) {
    // Left-right grandchild is also red.
    // Double rotation is necessary.
    localRoot.left = rotateLeft(localRoot.left);
    ((RedBlackNode) localRoot.left).isRed = false;
    localRoot.isRed = true;
    return rotateRight(localRoot);
}
```

If upon return from the recursive call the left child is black, the return is immediate, and all of this complicated logic is skipped. Similarly, if neither the left nor right grandchild is also red, nothing is done.

If the item is greater than `root.data`, the process is symmetric and is left as an exercise (Step 23 and Programming Exercise 1).

Removal from a Red-Black Tree

Removal follows the algorithm for a binary search tree that was described in Chapter 8. Recall that we remove a node only if it is a leaf or if it has only one child. Otherwise, the node that contains the inorder predecessor of the value being removed is the one that is removed. If the node that is removed is red, there is nothing further that must be done, because red nodes do not affect a Red-Black tree's balance. If the node to be removed is black and has a red child, then the red child takes its place, and we color it black. However, if we remove a black leaf, then the black height is now out of balance. There are several cases that must be considered. We will describe them in Programming Project 6 at the end of this chapter.

Performance of a Red-Black Tree

It can be shown that the upper limit in the height for a Red-Black tree is $2 \log_2 n + 2$, which is still $O(\log n)$. As with the AVL tree, the average performance is significantly better than the worst-case performance. Empirical studies (see Robert Sedgewick, *Algorithms in C++*, 3rd edition, [Addison-Wesley, 1998], p. 570) show that the average cost of a search in a Red-Black tree built from random values is $1.002 \log_2 n$. Thus, both the AVL and Red-Black trees give performance that is close to that of a complete binary search tree.

The TreeMap and TreeSet Classes

The Java API has a TreeMap class (part of the package java.util) that implements a Red-Black tree. The TreeMap class implements the SortedMap interface, so it defines methods get, put (a tree insertion), remove, and containsKey, among others. Because a Red-Black tree is used, these are all $O(\log n)$ operations. There is also a TreeSet class (introduced in Section 9.5) that implements the SortedSet interface. This class is implemented as an adapter of the TreeMap class using a technique similar to what was described in Chapter 9 to implement the HashSet as an adapter of the HashMap.

EXERCISES FOR SECTION 11.3

SELF-CHECK

1. Show how the final AVL tree for the "The quick brown fox" changes as you insert "apple", "cat", and "hat" in that order.
2. Insert the numbers 6, 3, and 0 in the Red-Black tree in Figure 11.21.
3. Build the Red-Black tree from the sentence "Now is the time for all good men to come to the aid of the party." Is it the same as the AVL tree?

PROGRAMMING

1. Program the case where the item is greater than root.data.

11.4 2-3 Trees

In this section we begin our discussion of three nonbinary trees. We begin with the *2-3 tree,* named for the number of possible children from each node (either 2 or 3). A 2-3 tree is made up of nodes designated as *2-nodes* and *3-nodes.* A 2-node is the same as a binary search tree node: It consists of a data field and references to two children, one child containing values less than the data field and the other child containing values greater than the data field. A 3-node contains two data fields, ordered so that the first is less than the second, and references to three children: one child containing values less than the first data field, one child containing values between the two data fields, and one child containing values greater than the second data field.

Figure 11.32 shows the general forms of a 2-node (data item is x) and a 3-node (data items are x and y). The children are represented as subtrees. Figure 11.33 shows an example of a 2-3 tree. There are only two 3-nodes in this tree (the right and right-right nodes); the rest are 2-nodes.

A 2-3 tree has the additional property that all of the leaves are at the lowest level. This is how the 2-3 tree maintains balance. This will be further explained when we study the insertion and removal algorithms.

Searching a 2-3 Tree

Searching a 2-3 tree is very similar to searching a binary search tree.

1. **if** the local root is **null**
2.   Return **null**; the item is not in the tree.
3. **else if** this is a 2-node
4.   **if** the item is equal to the data1 field
5.   Return the data1 field.
6.   **else if** the item is less than the data1 field
7.   Recursively search the left subtree.

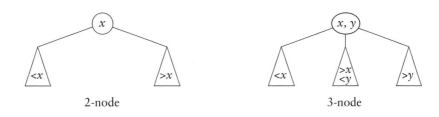

2-node   3-node

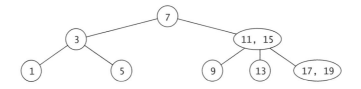

8.   **else**
9.   Recursively search the right subtree.
10.   **else** // *This is a 3-node*
11.   **if** the item is equal to the data1 field
12.   Return the data1 field.
13.   **else if** the item is equal to the data2 field
14.   Return the data2 field.
15.   **else if** the item is less than the data1 field
16.   Recursively search the left subtree.
17.   **else if** the item is less than the data2 field
18.   Recursively search the middle subtree.
19.   **else**
20.   Recursively search the right subtree.

EXAMPLE 11.3   To search for 13 in Figure 11.33, we would compare 13 with 7 and see that it is greater than 7, so we would search the node that contains 11 and 15. Because 13 is greater than 11 but less than 15, we would next search the middle child, which contains 13: success! The search path is shown in color in Figure 11.34.

FIGURE 11.34
Searching a 2-3 Tree

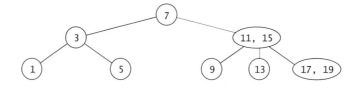

Inserting an Item into a 2-3 Tree

A 2-3 tree maintains balance by being built from the bottom up, not the top down. Instead of hanging a new node onto a leaf, we insert the new node into a leaf, as discussed in the following paragraphs. We search for the insertion node using the normal process for a 2-3 tree.

Inserting into a 2-Node Leaf

Figure 11.35 (left) shows a 2-3 tree with three 2-nodes. We want to insert 15. Because the leaf we are inserting into is a 2-node, then we can insert 15 directly, creating a new 3-node (Figure 11.35 right).

FIGURE 11.35
Inserting into a Tree
with All 2-Nodes

Inserting into a 3-Node Leaf with a 2-Node Parent

If we want to insert a number larger than 7 (say 17), that number will be virtually inserted into the 3-node at the bottom right of the tree, giving the virtual node in gray in Figure 11.36. Because a node can't store three values, the middle value will propagate up to the 2-node parent, and the virtual node will be split into two new 2-nodes containing the smallest and largest values. Because the parent is a 2-node, it will be changed to a 3-node, and it will reference the three 2-nodes, as shown in Figure 11.37.

FIGURE 11.36
A Virtual Insertion

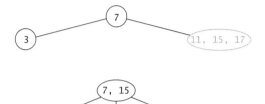

FIGURE 11.37
Result of Propagating
15 to 2-Node Parent

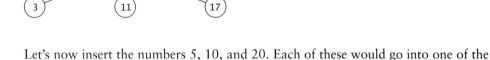

Let's now insert the numbers 5, 10, and 20. Each of these would go into one of the leaf nodes (all 2-nodes), changing them to 3-nodes, as shown in Figure 11.38.

FIGURE 11.38
Inserting 5, 10, and 20

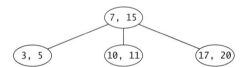

Inserting into a 3-Node Leaf with a 3-Node Parent

In the tree in Figure 11.39 all the leaf nodes are full, so if we insert any other number, one of the leaf nodes will need to be virtually split, and its middle value will propagate to the parent. Because the parent is already a 3-node, it will also need to be split.

For example, if we were to insert 13, it would be virtually inserted into the leaf node with values 10 and 11 (see Figure 11.39). This would result in two new 2-nodes with values 10 and 13, and 11 would propagate up to be virtually inserted in the 3-node at the root (see Figure 11.40). Because the root is full, it would split into two new 2-nodes with values 7 and 15, and 11 would propagate up to be inserted in a new root node. The net effect is an increase in the overall height of the tree, as shown in Figure 11.41.

FIGURE 11.39
Virtually Inserting 13

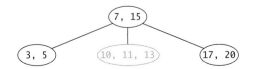

FIGURE 11.40
Virtually Inserting 11

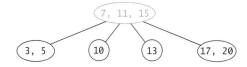

FIGURE 11.41
Result of Making 11
the New Root

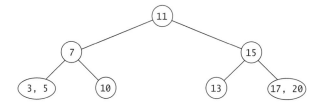

We summarize these observations in the following insertion algorithm.

Algorithm for Insertion

1. **if** the root is **null**
2.   Create a new 2-node that contains the new item.
3. **else if** the item is in the local root
4.   Return **false**.
5. **else if** the local root is a leaf
6.   **if** the local root is a 2-node
7.   Expand the 2-node to a 3-node and insert the item.
8.   **else**
9.   Split the 3-node (creating two 2-nodes) and pass the new parent and right child back up the recursion chain.
10. **else**
11.   **if** the item is less than the smaller item in the local root
12.   Recursively insert into the left child.
13.   **else if** the local root is a 2-node
14.   Recursively insert into the right child.
15.   **else if** the item is less than the larger item in the local root
16.   Recursively insert into the middle child.
17.   **else**
18.   Recursively insert into the right child.
19.   **if** a new parent was passed up from the previous level of recursion
20.   **if** the new parent will be the tree root
21.   Create a 2-node whose data item is the passed-up parent, left child is the old root, and right child is the passed-up child. This 2-node becomes the new root.
22.   **else**
23.   Recursively insert the new parent at the local root.
24. Return **true**.

EXAMPLE 11.4   We will create a 2-3 tree using "The quick brown fox jumps over the lazy dog." The initial root contains *The, quick*. If we insert *brown*, we will split the root. Because *brown* is between *The* and *quick*, it gets passed up and will become the new root.

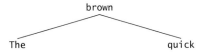

We now insert *fox* as the left neighbor of *quick*, creating a new 3-node.

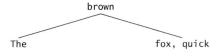

Next *jumps* is inserted between *fox* and *quick*, thus splitting this 3-node, and *jumps* gets passed up and inserted next to *brown*.

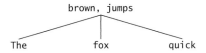

Then *over* is inserted next to *quick*.

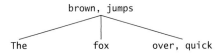

Now we insert *the*. It will be inserted to the right of *over, quick*, splitting that node, and *quick* will be passed up. It will be inserted to the right of *brown, jumps*, splitting that node as well, causing *jumps* to be passed up to the new root.

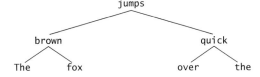

Finally, *lazy* and *dog* are inserted next to *over* and *fox*, respectively.

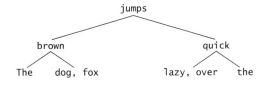

Analysis of 2-3 Trees and Comparison with Balanced Binary Trees

The 2-3 tree resulting from the preceding example is a balanced tree of height 3 that requires fewer complicated manipulations. There were no rotations, as were needed to build the AVL and Red-Black trees, which were both height 4. The number of items that a 2-3 tree of height h can hold is between $2^h - 1$ (all 2-nodes) and $3^h - 1$ (all 3-nodes). Therefore, the height of a 2-3 tree is between $\log_3 n$ and $\log_2 n$. Thus the search time is $O(\log n)$, since logarithms are all related by a constant factor, and constant factors are ignored in big-**O** notation.

Removal from a 2-3 Tree

Removing an item from a 2-3 tree is somewhat the reverse of the insertion process. To remove an item, we must first search for it. If the item to be removed is in a leaf, we simply delete it. However, if the item to be removed is not in a leaf, we remove it by swapping it with its inorder predecessor in a leaf node and deleting it from the leaf node. If removing a node from a leaf causes the leaf to become empty, items from the sibling and parent can be redistributed into that leaf, or the leaf may be merged with its parent and sibling nodes. In the latter case, the height of the tree may decrease. We illustrate these cases next.

If we remove the item 13 from the tree shown in Figure 11.42, its node would become empty, and item 15 in the parent node would have no left child. We can merge 15 and its right child to form the virtual leaf node {15, 17, 19}. Item 17 moves up to the parent node; item 15 is the new left child of 17 (see Figure 11.43).

We next remove 11 from the 2-3 tree. Because this is not a leaf, we replace it with its predecessor, 9, as shown in Figure 11.44. We now have the case where the left

FIGURE 11.42
Removing 13 from a
2-3 Tree

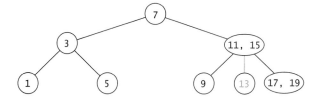

FIGURE 11.43
2-3 Tree After Redistri-
bution of Nodes
Resulting from
Removal

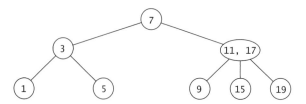

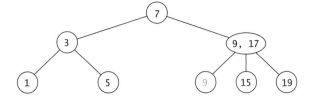

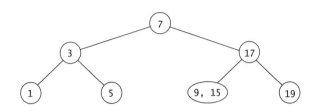

leaf node of 9 has become empty. So we merge 9 into its right leaf node as shown in Figure 11.45.

Finally, let's consider the case in which we remove the value 1 from Figure 11.45. First, 1's parent (3) and its right sibling (5) are merged to form a 3-node, as shown in Figure 11.46. This has the effect of deleting 3 from the next higher level. Therefore, the process repeats, and 3's parent (7) and 7's right child (17) are merged as shown in Figure 11.47. The merged node becomes the root.

The 2-3 tree served as an inspiration for the more general 2-3-4 tree and B-tree. Rather than show an implementation of the 2-3 tree, which has some rather messy complications, we will describe and implement the more general 2-3-4 tree in the next section.

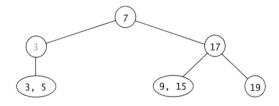

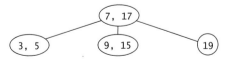

_____

EXERCISES FOR SECTION 11.4

SELF-CHECK

1. Show the following tree after inserting each of the following values one at a time: 1, 4, 9.

2. Show the following tree after inserting each of the following one at a time: 9, 13.

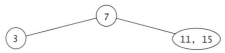

3. Show the 2-3 tree that would be built for the sentence "Now is the time for all good men to come to the aid of their party."

11.5 2-3-4 and B-Trees

The 2-3 tree was the inspiration for the more-general B-tree, which allows up to n children per node, where n may be a very large number. The B-tree was designed for building indexes to very large databases stored on a hard disk.

The 2-3-4 tree is a specialization of the B-tree. It is called a specialization because it is basically a B-tree with n equal to 4. The 2-3-4 tree is also interesting because the Red-Black tree can be considered a 2-3-4 tree in a binary-tree format.

2-3-4 Trees

2-3-4 trees expand on the idea of 2-3 trees by adding the 4-node (see Figure 11.48). This is a node with three data items and four children. Figure 11.49 shows an example of a 2-3-4 tree.

The addition of this third data item simplifies the insertion logic. We can search for the leaf in the same way as for a 2-3 tree. If a 4-node is encountered at any point, we will split it, as discussed subsequently. Therefore, when we reach a leaf, we are guaranteed that there will be room to insert the item.

FIGURE 11.48
2-, 3-, and 4-Nodes

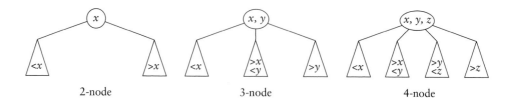

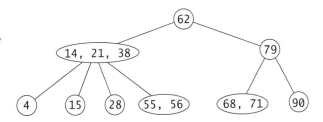

FIGURE 11.49
Example of a 2-3-4 Tree

For the 2-3-4 tree shown in Figure 11.49, a number larger than 62 would be inserted in a leaf node in the right subtree. A number between 63 and 78, inclusive, would be inserted in the 3-node (68, 71), making it a 4-node. A number larger than 79 would be inserted in the 2-node (90), making it a 3-node.

When inserting a number smaller than 62 (say, 25), we would encounter the 4-node (14, 21, 38). We would immediately split it into two 2-nodes and insert the middle value (21) into the parent (62) as shown in Figure 11.50. Doing this guarantees that there will be room to insert the new item. We perform the split from the parent level and immediately insert the middle item from the split child in the parent node. Because we are guaranteed that the parent is not a 4-node, we will always have room to do this. We do not need to propagate a child or its parent back up the recursion chain. Consequently the recursion becomes tail recursion.

In this example, splitting the 4-node was not necessary. We could have merely inserted 25 as the left neighbor of 28. However, if the leaf being inserted into was a 4-node, we would have had to split it and propagate the middle item back up the recursion chain, just as we did for the 2-3 tree. The choice always to split a 4-node when it is encountered while searching for an insertion spot results in prematurely splitting some nodes, but it simplifies the algorithm and has minimal impact on the overall performance.

Now we can insert 25 as the left neighbor of 28 as shown in Figure 11.51.

FIGURE 11.50
Result of Splitting a
4-Node

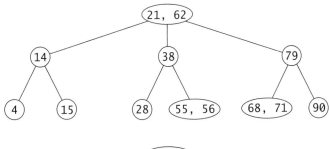

FIGURE 11.51
2-3-4 Tree After
Inserting 25

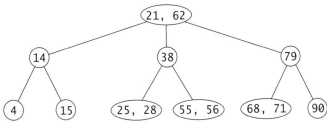

EXAMPLE 11.5   We will again use the sentence "The quick brown fox jumps over the lazy dog." After the first three words are inserted, the root contains *The*, *brown*, and *quick*.

The, brown, quick

This is a 4-node. Prior to inserting *fox*, this node is split.

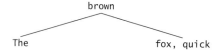

Because *fox* is larger than *brown*, we recursively apply the insert to *quick*. Because *fox* is smaller than *quick*, we obtain the following tree.

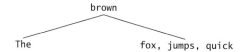

Because *jumps* is larger than *brown* and between *fox* and *quick*, we insert it as follows.

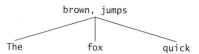

Next, we consider *over*. This is larger than *brown*. The right child of *brown*, however, is a 4-node, so we split it and insert its middle value, *jumps*, next to *brown*.

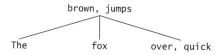

Because *over* is larger than *jumps*, we insert it next to *quick*.

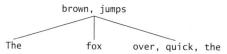

The next word, *the*, gets inserted to the right of *quick*.

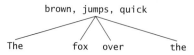

The next word, *lazy*, is larger than *jumps*, and we find that the right child of the node containing *jumps* is a 4-node, so it gets split.

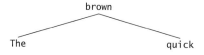

Now we need to insert *lazy*. However, before we insert *lazy*, we observe that the root is a 4-node. So we immediately split it.

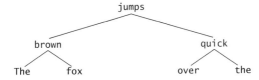

Now we can insert *lazy* next to *over*.

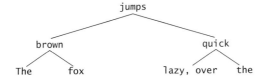

Last, we insert *dog*.

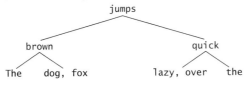

Implementation of TwoThreeFourTree Class

Instead of defining specialized nodes for a 2-3-4 tree, we can define a general node that holds up to three data items and four children. The information will be stored in the array data of size 3, and the references to the children will be stored in the array child of size 4. The information values will be sorted so that data[0] < data[1] < data[2]. The data field size will indicate how many data values are in the node. The children will be associated with the data values such that child[0] references the subtree with items smaller than data[0], child[size] references the sub-tree with items larger than data[size - 1], and for 0 < i < size, child[i] references items greater than data[i - 1] and smaller than data[i].

We show the class Node for a 2-3-4 tree next. Listing 11.5 shows the data field root and inner class Node. The algorithm follows.

LISTING 11.5
The Data Fields of Class TwoThreeFourTree and the Class Node

```
/** Class to represent a 2-3-4 Tree. */
public class TwoThreeFourTree implements SearchTree {

    // Data Fields
    /** The reference to the root. */
    private Node root = null;
```

```java
// Inner Class
/** A Node represents a node in a 2-3-4 tree. This class
    has no methods; it is merely a container of private data.
*/
private static class Node {
    // Data Fields
    /** The size of a node */
    private static final int CAP = 3;
    /** The number of data items in this node */
    private int size = 0;
    /** The information */
    private Comparable[] data = new Comparable[CAP];
    /** The links to the children. child[i] refers to
        the subtree of children < data[i] for i < size
        and to the subtree of children > data[size - 1]
        for i == size. */
    private Node[] child = new Node[CAP + 1];
}
...
}
```

Algorithm for Insertion into a 2-3-4 Tree

1.   **if** the root is **null**
2.   Create a new 2-node with the item.
3.   Return **true**.
4.   **if** the root is a 4-node
5.   Split it into two 2-nodes, making the middle value the new root.
6.   Set index to 0.
7.   **while** the item is less than data[index]
8.   Increment index.
9.   **if** the item is equal to data[index]
10.   Return **false**.
        else
11.   **if** child[index] is **null**
12.   Insert the item into the local root at index, moving the existing data and child values to the right.
        else if child[index] does not reference a 4-node
13.   Recursively continue the search with child[index] as the local root.
        else
14.   Split the node referenced by child[index].
15.   Insert the parent into the local root at index.
16.   **if** the new parent is equal to the item, return **false**.
17.   **if** the item is less than the new parent
18.   Recursively continue the search with child[index] as the local root.
        else
19.   Recursively continue the search with child[index + 1] as the local root.

The **add** Starter Method

If the root is **null**, then a new 2-node is created and becomes the root.

```
/** Insert an Object into the tree.
    pre: item to insert must implement the Comparable interface.
    @param obj The object to be inserted
    @return true if the item was inserted
    @throws ClassCastException if item is not Comparable
*/
public boolean add(Object obj) throws ClassCastException {
    if (root == null) {
        root = new Node();
        root.data[0] = (Comparable) obj;
        root.size = 1;
        return true;
    }
    ...
```

Otherwise, we see whether the root is a 4-node. If it is, then it is split, and the new parent becomes the new root (Step 5).

```
    if (root.size == CAP) {
        root = splitNode(root);
    }
```

Then we recursively insert starting at the root.

```
    return add(root, (Comparable) obj);
}
```

Recursive **add**

We begin by finding index such that the value to be inserted is less than or equal to data[index] or index is equal to the number of data items in the node (Steps 6–8) .

```
/** Recursive method to insert an Object into the tree.
    @param root The local root
    @param obj The item to be inserted
    @return true if the item was inserted, false
            if the item is already in the tree
*/
private boolean add(Node root, Comparable obj) {
    int index = 0;
    while (index < root.size
            && obj.compareTo(root.data[index]) > 0) {
        index++;
    }
    // index == root.size or obj <= root.data[index]
```

Next we see whether the item is equal to data[index]. If so, we return **false** (Steps 9, 10).

```
    if (index != root.size
        && obj.compareTo(root.data[index]) == 0) {
        // Item is already in the tree.
        return false;
    }
```

If child[index] is **null**, insert the item into the local root (Step 12).

```
if (root.child[index] == null) {
    insertIntoNode(root, index, obj, null);
    return true;
}
```

If child[index] does not reference a 4-node, then we recursively continue the insert at this child (Step 13).

```
else if (root.child[index].size < CAP) {
    return add(root.child[index], obj);
}
```

Otherwise we need to split the child and insert the middle value from this child into the current root at index (Steps 14–15).

```
else {
    Node newParent = splitNode(root.child[index]);
    insertIntoNode(root, index,
                    newParent.data[0],
                    newParent.child[1]);
    . . .
```

The newly inserted parent could be equal to the item to be inserted. If it is, then we return **false**. Otherwise we continue to insert recursively either at child[index] or at child[index + 1], depending on whether the inserted item is less than or greater than the newly inserted parent (Steps 16–19).

```
if (obj.compareTo(root.data[index]) == 0) {
    return false;
} else if (obj.compareTo(root.data[index]) < 0) {
    return add(root.child[index], obj);
} else {
    return add(root.child[index + 1], obj);
}
}
```

The **splitNode** Method

The splitNode method takes a 4-node as its parameter (see figure at left). The method changes this node into a 2-node that contains the left data item and the left two children (a), creates a new 2-node with the right data item and the right two children (b), and creates a 2-node to be the parent of these with the middle item as the data item (c).

```
private Node splitNode(Node node) {
    Node newParent = new Node();
    Node newChild = new Node();
    newParent.size = 1;
    newParent.data[0] = node.data[1];
    newParent.child[0] = node;
    newParent.child[1] = newChild;
    newChild.size = 1;
    newChild.data[0] = node.data[2];
    newChild.child[0] = node.child[2];
    newChild.child[1] = node.child[3];
    node.size = 1;
    return newParent;
}
```

The `insertIntoNode` Method

The `insertIntoNode` method shifts the data and child values to the right and inserts the new value and child at the indicated index.

```java
private void insertIntoNode(Node node, int index,
                            Comparable obj, Node child) {
    for (int i = node.size; i > index; i--) {
        node.data[i] = node.data[i - 1];
        node.child[i + 1] = node.child[i];
    }
    node.data[index] = obj;
    node.child[index + 1] = child;
    node.size++;
}
```

We will not discuss deletion, but it is similar to deletion from a 2-3 tree.

Relating 2-3-4 Trees to Red-Black Trees

A Red-Black tree is a binary-tree equivalent of a 2-3-4 tree. A 2-node is a black node (see Figure 11.52). A 4-node is a black node with two red children (see Figure 11.53). A 3-node can be represented as either a black node with a left red child or a black node with a right red child (see Figure 11.54).

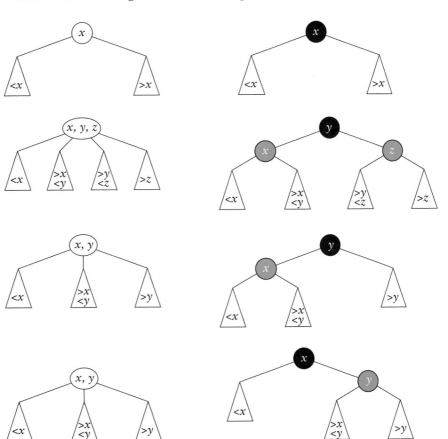

FIGURE 11.52
A 2-Node as a Black Node in a Red-Black Tree

FIGURE 11.53
A 4-Node as a Black Node with Two Red Children in a Red-Black Tree

FIGURE 11.54
A 3-Node as a Black Node with One Red Child in a Red-Black Tree

Suppose we want to insert a value z that is greater than y into the 3-node shown at the top of Figure 11.54 (tree with black root y). Node z would become the red right child of black node y, and the subtree with label $>y$ would be split into two parts, giving the 4-node shown in Figure 11.53.

Suppose, on the other hand, we want to insert a value z that is between x and y into the 3-node shown at the bottom of Figure 11.54 (tree with black root x). Node z would become the red left child of red node y (see the left diagram in Figure 11.55), and a double rotation would be required. First rotate right around y (the middle diagram) and then rotate left around x (the right diagram). This corresponds to the situation shown in Figure 11.56 (a 4-node with x, z, y).

B-Trees

A B-tree extends the idea behind the 2-3 and 2-3-4 trees by allowing a maximum of CAP data items in each node. Other than the root, each node contains between CAP/2 and CAP data items. Figure 11.57 shows an example of a B-tree with CAP equal to 4. The *order of a B-tree* is defined as the maximum number of children for a node, so this is a B-tree of order 5. Except for the root, each node is a leaf node.

B-trees were developed to store indexes to databases on disk storage. Disk storage is broken into blocks, and the time to access a block is significant compared to the time required to manipulate data in once it is in internal memory. The nodes of a B-tree are sized to fit in a block, so each disk access to the index retrieves exactly one B-tree node. The time to retrieve a block is large compared to the time required to process it in memory, so by making the tree nodes as large as possible, we reduce the number of disk accesses required to find an item in the index. Assuming a block can store a node for a B-tree of order 200, each node would store at least 100 items. This would enable 100^4 or 100 million items to be accessed in a B-tree of height 4.

FIGURE 11.55
Inserting into the Middle of a 3-Node (Red-Black Tree Equivalent)

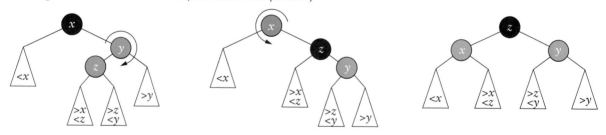

FIGURE 11.56
Inserting into the Middle of a 3-Node (2-3-4 Tree)

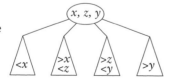

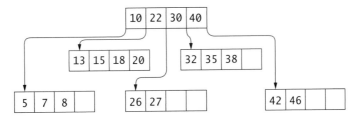

FIGURE 11.57
Example of a B-Tree

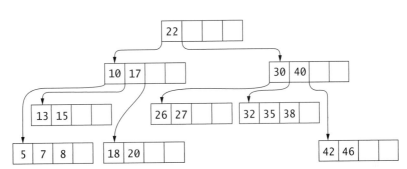

FIGURE 11.58
Inserting into a B-Tree

The insertion process for a B-tree is similar to that of a 2-3 or 2-3-4 tree and each insertion is into a leaf. For example, a number less than 10 would be inserted into the left-most leaf; a number greater than 40 would be inserted into the right-most leaf; and numbers between 11 and 39 would be inserted into one of the interior leaves. If the leaf being inserted into is full, it is split into two nodes, each containing approximately half the items, and the middle item is passed up to the split node's parent. If the parent is full, it is split and its middle item is passed up to its parent, and so on. If a node being split is the root of the B-tree, a new root node is created, thereby increasing the height of the B-tree. The children of the new root will be the two nodes that resulted from splitting the old root. Figure 11.58 shows the B-tree after inserting 17. The node {13, 15, 18, 20} was split, and 17 was passed up. Then the old root node was split, and 22 was passed up to the new root.

Programming the B-tree is left as a project.

<hr>

EXERCISES FOR SECTION 11.5

SELF-CHECK

1. Show the following tree after inserting each of the following values one at a time: 1, 5, 9, and 13.

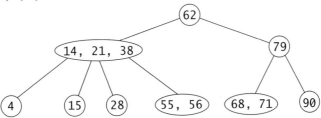

2. Build a 2-3-4 tree to store the words in the sentence "Now is the time for all good men to come to the aid of their party."

3. Draw the Red-Black tree equivalent of the 2-3-4 tree shown in Exercise 1.

4. Draw the 2-3-4 tree equivalent to the following Red-Black tree.

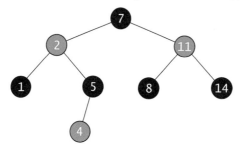

5. Draw a B-tree with CAP = 4 that stores the sequence of integers: 20, 30, 8, 10, 15, 18, 44, 26, 28, 23, 25, 43, 55, 36, 44, 39.

PROGRAMMING

1. Code the find method for the 2-3-4 tree.

2. Code the splitNode method for the B-tree. Leave the values from 0 to CAP / 2 in the original node. Make the value at CAP / 2 the new parent, and move the values from CAP / 2 + 1 up to CAP into a new node. Make child[0] of the new parent the original node, and make child[1] the newly created node.

Chapter Review

♦ Tree balancing is necessary to ensure that a search tree has $O(\log n)$ behavior. Tree balancing is done as part of an insertion or removal.

♦ An AVL tree is a balanced binary tree in which each node has a balance value that is equal to the difference between the heights of its right and left subtrees ($h_R - h_L$). A node is balanced if it has a balance value of 0; a node is left-(right-)heavy if it has a balance of −1 (+1). Tree balancing is done when a node along the insertion (or removal) path becomes critically out of balance; that is, the absolute value of the difference of the height of its two subtrees is 2. The rebalancing is done after returning from a recursive call in the insert or remove method.

♦ For an AVL tree, there are four kinds of imbalance and a different remedy for each.

—Left-Left (parent balance is −2, left child balance is −1): Rotate right around parent.

—Left-Right (parent balance is −2, left child balance is +1): Rotate left around child, then rotate right around parent.

—Right-Right (parent balance is +2, right child balance is +1): Rotate left around parent.

—Right-Left (parent balance is +2, right child balance is −1): Rotate right around child, then rotate left around parent.

◆ A Red-Black tree is a balanced tree with red and black nodes. After an insertion or removal, the following invariants must be maintained for a Red-Black tree.

—A node is either red or black.

—The root is always black.

—A red node always has black children. (A **null** reference is considered to refer to a black node.)

—The number of black nodes in any path from the root to a leaf is the same.

◆ To maintain tree balance in a Red-Black tree, it may be necessary to recolor a node and also to rotate around a node. The rebalancing is done inside the add or delete method, right after returning from a recursive call.

◆ Trees whose nodes have more than two children are an alternative to balanced binary search trees. These include 2-3 and 2-3-4 trees. A 2-node has two children, a 3-node has three children, and a 4-node has four children. The advantage to these trees is that keeping the trees balanced is a simpler process. Also, the tree may be less deep because a 3-node can have three children and a 4-node can have four children, but they still have O(log n) behavior.

◆ A 2-3-4 tree can be balanced on the way down the insertion path by splitting a 4-node into two 2-nodes before inserting a new item. This is easier than splitting nodes and rebalancing after returning from an insertion.

◆ A B-tree is a tree whose nodes can store up to CAP items and is a generalization of a 2-3-4 tree. B-trees are used as indexes to large databases stored on disk. The value of CAP is chosen so that each node is as large as it can be and still fit in a disk block. The time to retrieve a block is large compared to the time required to process it in memory, so by making the tree nodes as large as possible, we reduce the number of disk accesses required to find an item in the index.

Java Classes Introduced in This Chapter

java.util.TreeMap

User-Defined Interfaces and Classes in This Chapter

BinarySearchTreeWithRotate
AVLTree
AVLTree.AVLNode
RedBlackTree

RedBlackTree.RedBlackNode
TwoThreeFourTree
TwoThreeFourTree.Node

Quick-Check Exercises

1. Show the following AVL tree after inserting mouse. What kind of imbalance occurs, and what is the remedy?

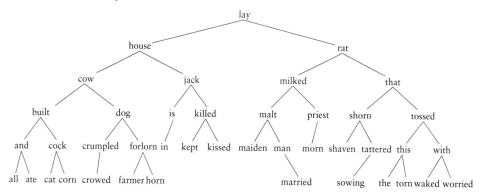

2. Show the following Red-Black tree after inserting 12 and then 13. What kind of rotation, if any, is performed?

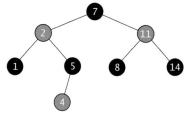

3. Show the following 2-3 tree after inserting 45 and then 20.

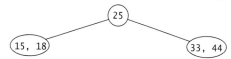

4. Show the following 2-3-4 tree after inserting 40 and then 50.

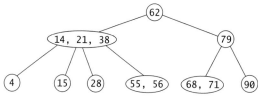

5. Draw the Red-Black tree equivalent to the following 2-3-4 tree.

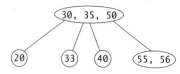

6. Draw the 2-3-4 tree equivalent to the following Red-Black tree.

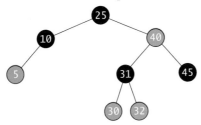

7. Show the following B-tree after inserting 45 and 21.

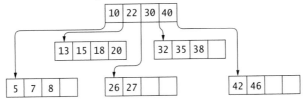

Answers to Quick-Check Exercises

1. When *mouse* is inserted (to the right of *morn*), node *morn* has a balance of +1, and node *priest* has a balance of −2. This is a case of Left-Right imbalance. Rotate left around *morn* and right around *priest*. Node *mouse* will have *morn* (*priest*) as its left (right) subtree.

2. When we insert 12 as a red node, it has a black parent, so we are done. When we insert 13, we have the situation shown in the first of the following figures. This is the mirror image of case 3 in Figure 11.25. We correct it by first rotating left around 12, giving the second of the following figures. Then we change 14 to red and 13 to black and rotate right around 13, giving the tree in the third figure.

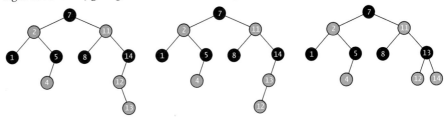

3. The 2-3 tree after inserting 45 is as follows.

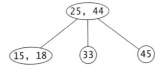

The 2-3 tree after inserting 20 is as follows.

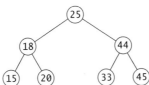

4. When 40 is inserted, the 4-node 14, 21, 38 is split and 21 is inserted into the root, 62. The node 14 has the children 4 and 15, and the node 38 has the children 28 and the 3-node 55, 56. We then insert 40 into the 3-node, making it a 4-node. The result follows.

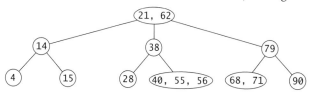

When we insert 50, the 4-node 40, 55, 56 is split and the 55 is inserted into the 2-node 38. Then 50 is inserted into the resulting 2-node, 40, making it a 3-node, as follows.

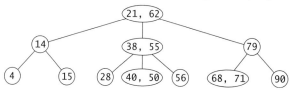

5. The equivalent Red-Black tree follows.

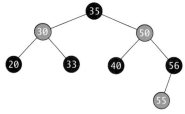

6. The equivalent 2-3-4 tree follows.

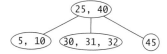

7. Insert 45 in a leaf.

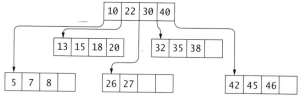

To insert 21, we need to split node {13, 15, 18, 20} and pass 18 up. Then we split the root and pass 22 up to the new root.

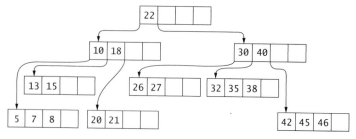

Review Questions

1. Draw the mirror images of the three cases for insertion into a Red-Black tree and explain how each situation is resolved.
2. Show the AVL tree that would be formed by inserting the month names (12 strings) into a tree in their normal calendar sequence.
3. Show the Red-Black tree that would be formed by inserting the month names into a tree in their normal calendar sequence.
4. Show the 2-3 tree that would be formed by inserting the month names into a tree in their normal calendar sequence.
5. Show the 2-3-4 tree that would be formed by inserting the month names into a tree in their normal calendar sequence.
6. Show a B-tree of capacity 5 that would be formed by inserting the month names into a tree in their normal calendar sequence.

Programming Projects

1. Complete the AVLTree class by coding the missing methods for insertion only. Use it to insert a collection of randomly generated numbers. Insert the same numbers in a binary search tree that is not balanced. Verify that each tree is correct by performing an inorder traversal. Also, display the format of each tree that was built and compare their heights.
2. Code the RedBlackTree class by coding the missing methods for insertion. Redo Project 1 using this class instead of the AVLTree class.
3. Code the TwoThreeFourTree class by coding the missing methods. Redo Project 1 using this class instead of the AVLTree class.
4. Code the TwoThreeTree class. Redo Project 1 using this class instead of the AVLTree class.
5. Complete the AVLTree class by providing the missing methods for removal. Demonstrate that these methods work.
   Review the changes required for methods decrementBalance, incrementBalance, rebalanceLeft, and rebalanceRight discussed at the end of Section 11.2. Also, modify rebalanceLeft (and rebalanceRight) to consider the cases where the left (right) subtree is balanced. This case can result when there is a removal from the right (left) subtree that causes the critical imbalance to occur. This is still a Left-Left (Right-Right) case, but after the rotation the overall balances are not zero. This is illustrated in Figures 11.59 and 11.60 where an item is removed from subtree c.

FIGURE 11.59
Left-Left Imbalance with Left Subtree Balanced

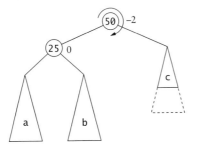

FIGURE 11.60
All Trees Unbalanced After Rotation

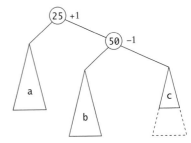

In addition, the Left-Right (or Right-Left) case can have a case in which the Left-Right (Right-Left) subtree is balanced. In this case, after the double rotation is performed, all balances are zero. This is illustrated in the following Figures 11.61 through 11.63.

FIGURE 11.61
Left-Right Case with Left-Right Subtree Balanced

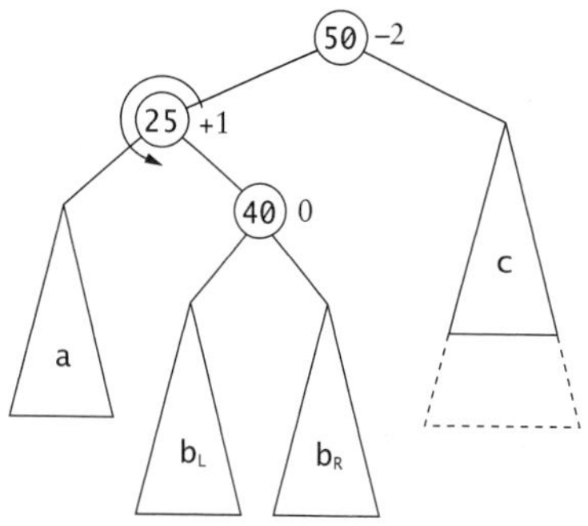

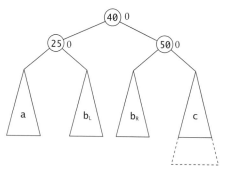

FIGURE 11.62
Imbalance After Single Rotation

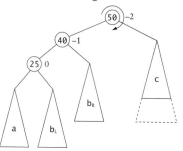

FIGURE 11.63
Complete Balance After
Double Rotation

6. Complete the RedBlackTree class by coding the missing methods for removal. The methods delete and findLargestChild are adapted from the corresponding methods of the BinarySearchTree class. These adaptations are similar to those done for the AVL tree. A data field fixupRequired performs a role analogous to the decrease data field in the AVL tree. It is set when a black node is removed. Upon return from a method that can remove a node, this variable is tested. If the removal is from the right, then a new method fixupRight is called. If the removal is from the left, then a new method fixupLeft is called.

The fixupRight method must consider five cases, as follows:

- **Case 1:** Parent is red and sibling has a red right child. Figure 11.64(a) shows a red node P that is the root of a subtree that has lost a black node X from its right subtree. The root of the left subtree is S, and it must be a black node. If this subtree has a red right child, as shown in the figure, we can restore the black balance. First we rotate the left subtree left and change the color of the parent to black (see Figure 11.64(b)). Then we rotate right about the parent as shown in Figure 11.64(c). This restores the black balance. As shown in the figure, the node S may also have a left child. This does not affect the results.

FIGURE 11.64
Red-Black Removal Case 1

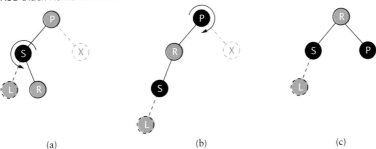

(a)   (b)   (c)

- **Case 2:** Parent is red, and sibling has only a left red child. Figure 11.65(a) shows the case where the red parent P has a left child S that has a red left child L. In this case we change the color of S to red and the color of P to black. Then we rotate right as shown in Figure 11.65(b).

FIGURE 11.65
Red-Black Removal Case 2

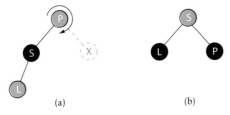

(a)   (b)

- **Case 3:** Parent is red, and the left child has no red children. Figure 11.66(a) shows the case where the red parent P has a left child S that has no children. As in the next two cases, this fixup-process is started at the bottom of the tree but can move up the tree. In this case S may have black children, and X may represent the root of a subtree whose black height is one less than the black height of S. The correction is quite easy. We change P to black and S to red (see Figure 11.66(b)). Now the balance is restored, and the black height at P remains the same as it was before the black height at X was reduced.

FIGURE 11.66
Red-Black Removal Case 3

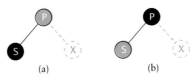

(a)   (b)

- **Case 4:** Parent is black and left child is red. Figure 11.67(a) shows the case where the parent P is black and the left child S is red. Since the black heights of S and X were equal before removing X, S must have two black children. We rotate the child S left and change the color of *P* to red as shown in Figure 11.67(b). Then we rotate right twice, so that *S* is now where *P* was, thus restoring the black balance. However, the black height of *P* has been reduced. Thus we repeat the process at the next level (*P*'s parent).

FIGURE 11.67
Red-Black Removal Case 4

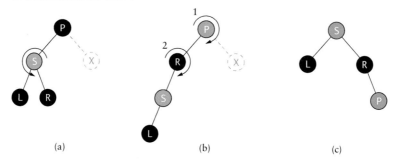

(a)   (b)   (c)

- **Case 5:** Parent is black and left child is black. Figure 11.68(a) shows the case where *P* is back and *S* is black. We then change the color of the parent to red. The black height of *P* has been reduced. Thus we repeat the process at the next level (*P*'s parent).

FIGURE 11.68
Red-Black Removal Case 5

(a)   (b)

12

Graphs

One of the limitations of trees is that they cannot represent information structures in which a data item has more than one parent. In this chapter we introduce a data structure known as a *graph* that will allow us to overcome this limitation.

Graphs and graph algorithms were being studied long before computers were invented. The advent of the computer made the application of graph algorithms to real-world problems possible. Graphs are especially useful in analyzing networks. Thus it is not surprising that much of modern graph theory and application was developed at Bell Laboratories, which needed to analyze the very large communications network that is the telephone system. Graph algorithms are also incorporated into the software that makes the Internet function. You can also use graphs to describe a road map, airline routes, or course prerequisites. Computer chip designers use graph algorithms to determine the optimal placement of components on a silicon chip.

You will learn how to represent a graph, find the shortest path through a graph, and find the minimum subset of a graph.

12.1 Graph Terminology

A graph is a data structure that consists of a set of *vertices* (or nodes) and a set of *edges* (relations) between the pairs of vertices. The edges represent paths or connections between the vertices. Both the set of vertices and the set of edges must be finite, and either set may be empty. If the set of vertices is empty, naturally the set of edges must also be empty. We restrict our discussion to simple graphs in which there is at most one edge from a given vertex to another vertex.

EXAMPLE 12.1   The following set of vertices, V, and set of edges, E, define a graph that has five vertices, with labels A through E, and four edges.

$V = \{A, B, C, D, E\}$

$E = \{\{A, B\}, \{A, D\}, \{C, E\}, \{D, E\}\}$

Each edge is set of two vertices. There is an edge between A and B (the edge {A, B}), between A and D, between C and E, and between D and E. If there is an edge between any pair of vertices x, y, this means there is a path from vertex x to vertex y and vice versa. We discuss the significance of this shortly.

Visual Representation of Graphs

Visually we represent vertices as points or labeled circles and the edges as lines joining the vertices. Figure 12.1 shows the graph from Example 12.1.

There are many ways to draw any given graph. The physical layout of the vertices, and even their labeling, are not relevant. Figure 12.2 shows two ways to draw the same graph.

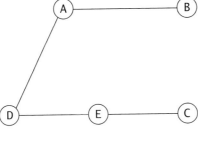

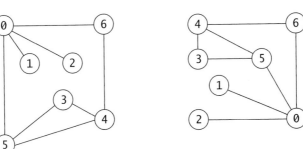

Directed and Undirected Graphs

The edges of a graph are *directed* if the existence of an edge from A to B does not necessarily guarantee that there is a path in both directions. A graph that contains directed edges is known as a *directed graph* or *digraph,* and a graph that contains undirected edges is known as an *undirected graph,* or simply a graph. A directed edge is like a one-way street; you can travel on it only in one direction. Directed edges are represented as lines with an arrow on one end, whereas undirected edges are represented as single lines. The graph in Figure 12.1 is undirected; Figure 12.3 shows a directed graph. The set of edges for the directed graph follows:

$$E = \{(A, B), (B,A), (B, E), (D, A), (E, A), (E, C), (E, D)\}$$

Each edge above is an ordered pair of vertices, instead of a set as in an undirected graph. The edge (A, B) means there is a path from A to B. Observe that there is a path from both A to B and from B to A, but these are the only two vertices in which there is an edge in both directions. Our convention will be to denote an edge for a directed graph as an ordered pair (u, v) where this notation means that v (the destination) is adjacent to u (the source). We denote an edge in an undirected graph as the set $\{u, v\}$ which means that u is adjacent to v and v is adjacent to u. Therefore, you can create a directed graph that is equivalent to an undirected graph by substituting for each edge $\{u, v\}$ the ordered pairs (u, v) and (v, u). In general, when we describe graph algorithms in this chapter, we will use the ordered pair notation (u, v) for an edge.

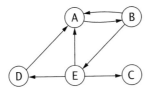

FIGURE 12.4
Example of a
Weighted Graph

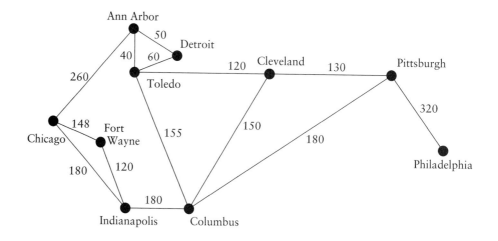

The edges in a graph may have values associated with them known as their *weights*. A graph with weighted edges is known as a *weighted graph*. In an illustration of a weighted graph the weights are shown next to the edges. Figure 12.4 shows an example of a weighted graph. Each weight is the distance between the two cities (vertices) connected by the edge. Generally the weights are nonnegative, but there are graph problems and graph algorithms that deal with negative weighted edges.

Paths and Cycles

One reason we study graphs is to find pathways between vertices. We use the following definitions to describe pathways between vertices.

- A vertex is *adjacent* to another vertex if there is an edge to it from that other vertex. In Figure 12.4, Philadelphia is adjacent to Pittsburgh. In Figure 12.3 A is adjacent to D, but since this is a directed graph, D is not adjacent to A.
- A *path* is a sequence of vertices in which each successive vertex is adjacent to its predecessor. In Figure 12.5, the following sequence of vertices is a path: Philadelphia → Pittsburgh → Columbus → Indianapolis → Chicago.

FIGURE 12.5
A Simple Path

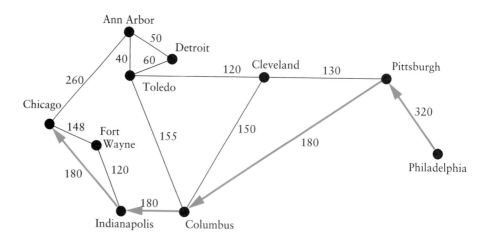

- In a *simple path* the vertices and edges are distinct, except that the first and last vertex may be the same. In Figure 12.5 the path Philadelphia → Pittsburgh → Columbus → Indianapolis → Chicago is a simple path. The path Philadelphia → Pittsburgh → Columbus → Indianapolis → Chicago → Fort Wayne → Indianapolis is a path, but not a simple path. (See Figure 12.6)

FIGURE 12.6
Not a Simple Path

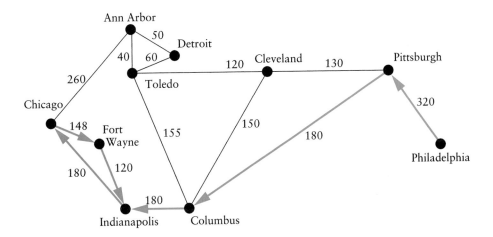

- A *cycle* is a simple path in which only the first and final vertices are the same. In Figure 12.7, the path Pittsburgh → Columbus → Toledo → Cleveland → Pittsburgh is a cycle. For an undirected graph, a cycle must contain at least three distinct vertices. Thus Pittsburgh → Columbus → Pittsburgh is not considered a cycle.

FIGURE 12.7
A Cycle

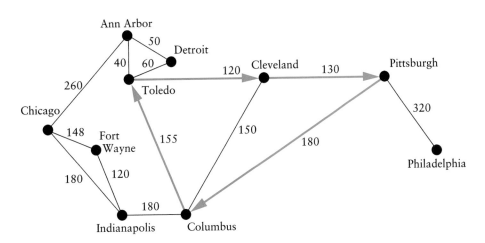

- An undirected graph is called a *connected graph* if there is a path from every vertex to every other vertex. Figure 12.7 is a connected graph, whereas Figure 12.8 is not.

FIGURE 12.8
Example of an
Unconnected Graph

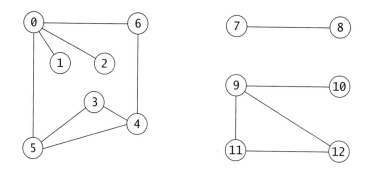

- If a graph is not connected, it is considered *unconnected,* but it will still consist of *connected components.* A connected component is a subset of the vertices and the edges connected to those vertices in which there is a path between every pair of vertices in the component. A single vertex with no edges is also considered a connected component. Figure 12.8 consists of the connected components {0, 1, 2, 3, 4, 5, 6}, {7, 8}, and {9, 10, 11, 12}.

Relationship Between Graphs and Trees

The graph is the most general of the data structures we have studied. It allows for any conceivable relationship among the data elements (the vertices). A tree is actually a special case of a graph. Any graph that is connected and contains no cycles can be viewed as a tree by picking one of its vertices (nodes) as the root. For example, the graph shown in Figure 12.1 can be viewed as a tree if we consider the node labeled *D* to be the root. (See Figure 12.9.)

Graph Applications

We can use graphs to help in solving a number of different kinds of problems. For example, we might want to know whether there is a connection from one node in a network to all others. If we can show that the graph is connected, then a path must exist from one node to every other node.

In college you must take some courses before you take others. These are called prerequisites. Some courses have multiple prerequisites, and some prerequisites have prerequisites of their own. It can be quite confusing. You may even feel that there is

FIGURE 12.9
A Graph Viewed as a
Tree

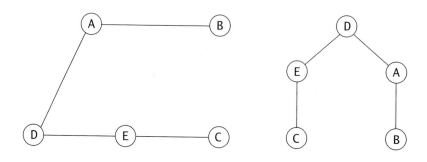

a loop in the maze of prerequisites and that it is impossible to schedule your classes to meet the prerequisites. We can represent the set of prerequisites by a directed graph. If the graph has no cycles, then we can find a solution. We can also find the cycles.

Another application would be finding the least-cost path or shortest path from each vertex to all other vertices in a weighted graph. For example, in Figure 12.4 we might want to find the shortest path from Philadelphia to Chicago. Or we might want to create a table showing the distance (miles in the shortest route) between each pair of cities.

EXERCISES FOR SECTION 12.1

SELF-CHECK

1. In the graph shown in Figure 12.1, what vertices are adjacent to D? In Figure 12.3?
2. In Figure 12.3, is it possible to get from A to all other vertices? How about from C?
3. In Figure 12.4, what is the shortest path from Philadelphia to Chicago?

12.2 The Graph ADT and Edge Class

Java does not provide a Graph ADT so we have the freedom to design our own. To write programs for the applications mentioned at the end of the previous section, we need to be able to navigate through a graph or traverse it (visit all its vertices). To accomplish this, we need to be able to advance from one vertex in a graph to all its adjacent vertices. Therefore, we need to be able to do the following:

1. Create a graph with the specified number of vertices.
2. Iterate through all of the vertices in the graph.
3. Iterate through the vertices that are adjacent to a specified vertex.
4. Determine whether an edge exists between two vertices.
5. Determine the weight of an edge between two vertices.
6. Insert an edge into the graph.

With the exception of item 1, we can specify these requirements in a Java interface. Since a Java interface cannot include a constructor, the requirements for item 1 can only be specified in the comment at the beginning of the interface.

Listing 12.1 gives the declaration of the Graph interface. It includes a nested interface EdgeIterator with methods next and hasNext.

```java
import java.util.*;

/** Interface to specify a Graph ADT. A graph is a set
    of vertices and a set of edges. Vertices are
    represented by integers from 0 to n - 1. Edges
    are ordered pairs of vertices. Each implementation
    of the Graph interface should provide a constructor
    that specifies the number of vertices and whether
    or not the graph is directed.
*/
public interface Graph {

    // Accessor Methods
    /** Return the number of vertices.
        @return The number of vertices
    */
    int getNumV();

    /** Determine whether this is a directed graph.
        @return true if this is a directed graph
    */
    boolean isDirected();

    /** Insert a new edge into the graph.
        @param edge The new edge
    */
    void insert(Edge edge);

    /** Determine whether an edge exists.
        @param source The source vertex
        @param dest The destination vertex
        @return true if there is an edge from source to dest
    */
    boolean isEdge(int source, int dest);

    /** Get the edge between two vertices.
        @param source The source vertex
        @param dest The destination vertex
        @return The Edge between these two vertices
                or an Edge with a weight of
                Double.POSITIVE_INFINITY if there is no edge
    */
    Edge getEdge(int source, int dest);

    /** Return an iterator to the edges connected
        to a given vertex.
        @param source The source vertex
        @return An EdgeIterator to the vertices
                connected to source
    */
    EdgeIterator edgeIterator(int source);

    // Nested interface
    /** Interface for classes that iterate over the edges that are
        connected to a given vertex via an edge.
```

```
        */
        interface EdgeIterator {
            /** Determine whether there are more edges.
                @return true if there are more edges
            */
            boolean hasNext();

            /** Return the next edge in the iteration.
                @return The next edge in the iteration
            */
            Edge next();
        }
    }
```

Representing Vertices and Edges

Before we can implement this interface, we must decide how to represent the vertices and edges of a graph. We can represent the vertices by integers from 0 up to, but not including, |V| (|V| means the *cardinality of V*, or the number of vertices in set *V*). For edges we will define the class Edge that will contain the source vertex, the destination vertex, and the weight. For unweighted edges we will use the default value of 1.0. Table 12.1 shows the Edge class. Observe that an Edge is directed. For undirected graphs we will always have two Edge objects: one in each direction for each pair of vertices that has an edge between them. A vertex is represented by a type **int** variable.

TABLE 12.1
The Edge Class

Data Field	Attribute
private int dest	The destination vertex for an edge.
private int source	The source vertex for an edge.
private double weight	The weight.

Constructor	Purpose
public Edge(int source, int dest)	Constructs an Edge from source to dest. Sets the weight to 1.0.
public Edge(int source, int dest, double w)	Constructs an Edge from source to dest. Sets the weight to w.

Method	Behavior
public boolean equals(Object o)	Compares two edges for equality. Edges are equal if their source and destination vertices are the same. The weight is not considered.
public int getDest()	Returns the destination vertex.
public int getSource()	Returns the source vertex.
public double getWeight()	Returns the weight.
public int hashCode()	Returns the hash code for an edge. The hash code depends only on the source and destination.
public String toString()	Returns a string representation of the edge.

EXERCISES FOR SECTION 12.2

SELF-CHECK

1. Use the constructors in Table 12.1 to create the `Edge` objects connecting vertices 9 through 12 for the graph in Figure 12.8.

PROGRAMMING

1. Implement the `Edge` class.

12.3 Implementing the Graph ADT

Because graph algorithms have been studied and implemented throughout the history of computer science, many of the original publications of graph algorithms and their implementations did not use an object-oriented approach and did not even use abstract data types. The implementation of the graph was done in terms of fundamental data structures that were used directly in the algorithm. Different algorithms would use different representations.

Two representations of graphs are most common:

- Edges are represented by an array of lists called *adjacency lists,* where each list stores the vertices adjacent to a particular vertex.
- Edges are represented by a two dimensional array, called an *adjacency matrix,* with |V| rows and |V| columns.

Adjacency List

An adjacency list representation of a graph uses an array of lists. There is one list for each vertex. Figure 12.10 shows an adjacency list representation of a directed graph. The list referenced by array element 0 shows the vertices (1 and 3) that are adjacent to vertex 0. The vertices are in no particular order. For simplicity, we are showing just the destination vertex as the value field in each node of the adjacency list, but in the actual implementation the entire `Edge` will be stored. Instead of storing `value = 1` (the destination vertex) in the first vertex adjacent to 0, we will store a reference to the `Edge` `(0, 1, 1.0)` where 0 is the source, 1 is the destination, and 1.0 is the weight. The `Edge` must be stored (not just the destination) because weighted graphs can have different values for weights.

For an undirected graph (or simply a "graph"), symmetric entries are required. Thus, if {*u, v*} is an edge, then *v* will appear on the adjacency list for *u* and *u* will appear on the adjacency list for *v*. Figure 12.11 shows the adjacency list representation for an undirected graph. The actual lists will store references to `Edges`.

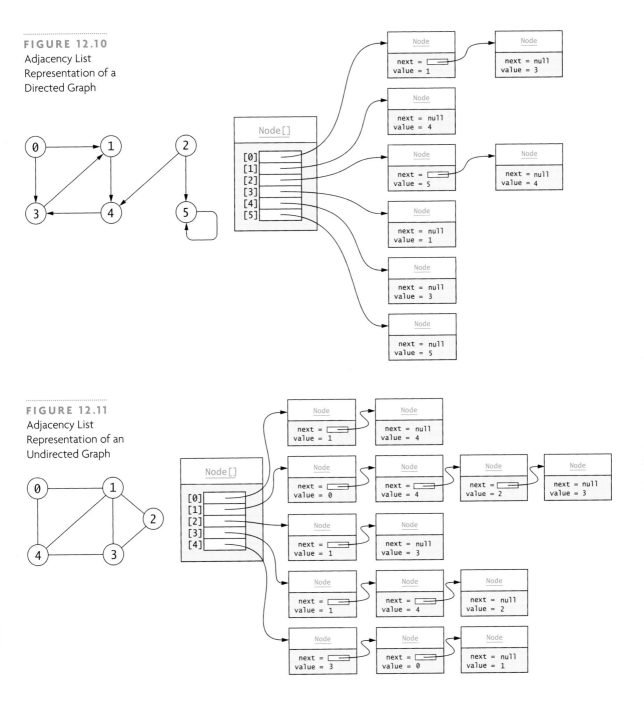

FIGURE 12.10
Adjacency List
Representation of a
Directed Graph

FIGURE 12.11
Adjacency List
Representation of an
Undirected Graph

Adjacency Matrix

The adjacency matrix uses a two-dimensional array to represent the graph. For an unweighted graph the entries in this matrix can be **boolean** values, where **true** represents the presence of an edge and **false** its absence. Another popular method is to use the value 1 for an edge and 0 for no edge. The integer coding has benefits over the **boolean** approach for some graph algorithms that use matrix multiplication.

For a weighted graph the matrix would contain the weights. Since 0 is a valid weight, we will use `Double.POSITIVE_INFINITY` (a special **double** value in Java that approximates the mathematical behavior of infinity) to indicate the absence of an edge, and in an unweighted graph we will use a weight of 1.0 to indicate the presence of an edge.

Figure 12.12 shows a directed graph and the corresponding adjacency matrix. Instead of using `Edge` objects, an edge is indicated by the value 1.0, and the lack of an edge is indicated by a blank space.

If the graph is undirected, then the matrix is symmetric, and only the lower diagonal of the matrix need be saved (the colored squares in Figure 12.13).

Overview of the Hierarchy

We will describe Java classes that use each representation. Each class will extend a common abstract superclass. The interfaces `Graph` and `Graph.EdgeIterator` were introduced in Section 12.2. The class `Edge` was also described in that section.

We will define the class `AbstractGraph` to represent a graph in general. The classes `ListGraph` and `MatrixGraph` will provide concrete representations of graphs using an adjacency list and adjacency matrix, respectively (see Figure 12.14). Both the `ListGraph` and `MatrixGraph` class contain an inner class (indicated by the ⊕ symbol) that we call `Iter`, which implements the `EdgeIterator` interface. The methods provided by these inner classes are the same, but the implementations are different because of the different internal representations of the graph.

FIGURE 12.12
A Directed Graph and the Corresponding Adjacency Matrix

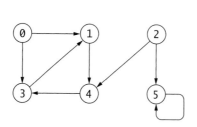

Column

	[0]	[1]	[2]	[3]	[4]	[5]
[0]		1.0		1.0		
[1]					1.0	
[2]					1.0	1.0
[3]		1.0				
[4]				1.0		
[5]						1.0

(Row labels on left side)

FIGURE 12.13
Undirected Graph and Adjacency Matrix Representation

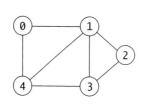

Column

	[0]	[1]	[2]	[3]	[4]
[0]		1.0			1.0
[1]	1.0		1.0	1.0	1.0
[2]		1.0		1.0	
[3]		1.0	1.0		1.0
[4]	1.0	1.0		1.0	

(Row labels on left side)

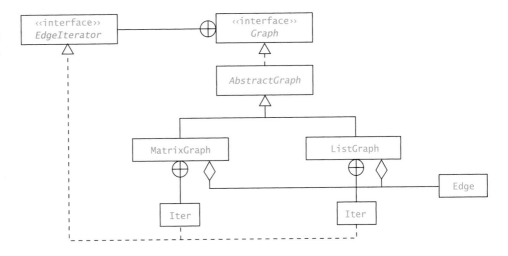

FIGURE 12.14
UML Class Diagram of
Graph Class Hierarchy

Class AbstractGraph

We will use an abstract class, AbstractGraph, as the common superclass for graph implementations. This will enable us to implement some of the methods for the Graph interface in the abstract superclass and leave other methods that are implementation specific to its subclasses. Graph algorithms will be designed to work on objects that meet the requirements defined by this abstract class. This class is summarized in Table 12.2. Note that the methods edgeIterator, getEdge, insert, and isEdge, which are required by the Graph interface (see Listing 12.1), are implicitly declared abstract and must be declared in the subclasses.

TABLE 12.2
The Abstract Class AbstractGraph

Data Field	Attribute
private boolean directed	**true** if this is a directed graph.
private int numV	The number of vertices.
Constructor	**Purpose**
public AbstractGraph(int numV, boolean directed)	Constructs an empty graph with the specified number of vertices and with the specified directed flag. If directed is **true**, this is a directed graph.
Method	**Behavior**
public int getNumV()	Gets the number of vertices.
public boolean isDirected()	Returns **true** if the graph is a directed graph.
public void loadEdgesFromFile(BufferedReader bR)	Loads edges from a data file.

Implementation

The implementation is shown in Listing 12.2. Method `loadEdgesFromFile` reads edges from individual lines of a data file (see Programming Exercise 1).

LISTING 12.2

AbstractGraph.java

```java
/** Abstract base class for graphs. A graph is a set
    of vertices and a set of edges. Vertices are
    represented by integers from 0 to n - 1. Edges
    are ordered pairs of vertices.
*/
public abstract class AbstractGraph implements Graph {

    // Data Fields
    /** The number of vertices */
    private int numV;
    /** Flag to indicate whether this is a directed graph */
    private boolean directed;

    // Constructor
    /** Construct a graph with the specified number of vertices
        and the directed flag. If the directed flag is true,
        this is a directed graph.
        @param numV The number of vertices
        @param directed The directed flag
    */
    public AbstractGraph(int numV, boolean directed) {
        this.numV = numV;
        this.directed = directed;
    }

    // Accessor Methods
    /** Return the number of vertices.
        @return The number of vertices
    */
    public int getNumV() {
        return numV;
    }

    /** Return whether this is a directed graph.
        @return true if this is a directed graph
    */
    public boolean isDirected() {
        return directed;
    }

    // Other Methods
    /** Load the edges of a graph from the data in an input file.
        The file should contain a series of lines, each line
        with two or three data values. The first is the source,
        the second is the destination, and the optional third
        is the weight.
        @param bR The buffered reader containing the data
        @throws IOException if an I/O error occurs
```

```
    */
    public void loadEdgesFromFile(BufferedReader bR)
        throws IOException {
        // Programming Exercise 1
    }
}
```

The ListGraph Class

The ListGraph class extends the AbstractGraph class by providing an internal representation using an array of lists. It overrides the abstract methods edgeIterator, getEdge, isEdge, and insert. It also includes the inner class Iter, which implements the Graph.EdgeIterator interface. Table 12.3 describes the ListGraph class, and Table 12.4 describes the ListGraph.Iter class.

TABLE 12.3
The ListGraph Class

Data Field	Attribute
private List[] edges	An array of Lists to contain the edges that originate with each vertex.
Constructor	**Purpose**
public ListGraph(int numV, boolean directed)	Constructs a graph with the specified number of vertices and directionality.
Method	**Behavior**
public EdgeIterator edgeIterator(int source)	Returns an iterator to the edges that originate from a given vertex.
public Edge getEdge(int source, int dest)	Gets the edge between two vertices.
public void insert(Edge e)	Inserts a new edge into the graph.
public boolean isEdge(int source, int dest)	Determines whether an edge exists from vertex source to dest.

TABLE 12.4
The ListGraph.Iter Class

Data Field	Attribute
private Iterator itr	An Iterator to the list containing the edges.
Constructor	**Purpose**
public Iter(int source)	Constructs an EdgeIterator for a given vertex.
Method	**Behavior**
public boolean hasNext()	Returns **true** if there are more edges.
public Edge next()	Returns the next edge, if there is one.

The Data Fields

The class begins as follows:

```
import java.util.*;

/** A ListGraph is an extension of the AbstractGraph abstract class
    that uses an array of lists to represent the edges.
*/
public class ListGraph extends AbstractGraph {

    // Data Field
    /** An array of Lists to contain the edges that
        originate with each vertex. */
    private List[] edges;
...
```

The Constructor

The constructor allocates an array of LinkedLists, one for each vertex.

```
/** Construct a graph with the specified number of
    vertices and directionality.
    @param numV The number of vertices
    @param directed The directionality flag
*/
public ListGraph(int numV, boolean directed) {
    super(numV, directed);
    edges = new List[numV];
    for (int i = 0; i < numV; i++) {
        edges[i] = new LinkedList();
    }
}
```

The isEdge Method

Method isEdge determines whether an edge exists by searching the list associated with the source vertex for an entry. This is done by calling the contains method for the List.

```
/** Determine whether an edge exists.
    @param source The source vertex
    @param dest The destination vertex
    @return true if there is an edge from source to dest
*/
public boolean isEdge(int source, int dest) {
    return edges[source].contains(new Edge(source, dest));
}
```

Observe that we had to create a dummy Edge object for the contains method to search for. The Edge.equals method does not check the edge weights.

The insert Method

The insert method inserts a new edge (source, destination, weight) into the graph by adding that edge's data to the list of adjacent vertices for that edge's source. If the graph is not directed, it adds a new edge in the opposite direction (destination, source, weight) to the list of adjacent vertices for that edge's destination.

```
/** Insert a new edge into the graph.
    @param edge The new edge
*/
public void insert(Edge edge) {
    edges[edge.getSource()].add(edge);
    if (!isDirected()) {
        edges[edge.getDest()].add(new Edge(edge.getDest(),
                                     edge.getSource(),
                                     edge.getWeight()));
    }
}
```

The getEdge Method

Similar to the isEdge method, the getEdge method also requires a search. However, we need to program the search directly. We create and use an EdgeIterator object itr to access all edges in the list for vertex source. We compare each edge to a target object with source and destination set to the method arguments. The equals method does not compare edge weights, only the vertices.

```
/** Get the edge between two vertices. If an
    edge does not exist, an Edge with a weight
    of Double.POSITIVE_INFINITY is returned.
    @param source The source
    @param dest The destination
    @return the edge between these two vertices
*/
public Edge getEdge(int source, int dest) {
    Edge target =
        new Edge(source, dest, Double.POSITIVE_INFINITY);
    Graph.EdgeIterator itr = new Iter(source);
    while (itr.hasNext()) {
        Edge edge = itr.next();
        if (edge.equals(target)) {
            return edge;   // Desired edge found, return it.
        }
    }
    // Assert: All edges for source checked.
    return target;   // Desired edge not found.
}
```

The ListGraph.Iter Class

Next we turn our attention to the inner class Iter. It has a single Iterator data field itr. The constructor initializes itr to an Iterator returned by method List.iterator. Recall from Chapter 4 that the List.iterator method returns an Iterator object that will iterate through the List object that returns it. The methods of class Iter delegate their work to this Iterator object.

```
/** An iterator to the edges. An EdgeIterator is
    similar to an Iterator except that its
    next method will always return an edge.
*/
private class Iter implements Graph.EdgeIterator {
    // Data Field
    /** An Iterator to the list containing the edges */
    private Iterator itr;
```

```
// Constructor
/** Construct an EdgeIterator for a given vertex.
    @param source The source vertex
*/
public Iter(int source) {
    itr = edges[source].iterator();
}
```

The hasNext method of class ListGraph.Iter merely calls the hasNext method of class List.Iterator.

```
public boolean hasNext() {
    return itr.hasNext();
}
```

The next method casts the result returned by the Iterator.next method to an Edge.

```
public Edge next() {
    return (Edge) itr.next();
}
```

The MatrixGraph Class

The MatrixGraph class extends the AbstractGraph class by providing an internal representation using a two-dimensional array for storing the edge weights

```
double[][] edges;
```

When a new MatrixGraph object is created, the constructor sets the number of rows (vertices) in this array. It implements the same methods as class ListGraph and also has an inner iterator class Iter. The implementation is left as a project (Programming Project 1).

Comparing Implementations

Time Efficiency

The two implementations present a tradeoff. Which is best depends upon the algorithm and the density of the graph. The density of a graph is the ratio of $|E|$ to $|V|^2$. A *dense graph* is one in which $|E|$ is close to but less than $|V|^2$, and a *sparse graph* is one in which $|E|$ is much less than $|V|^2$. Therefore, for a dense graph we can assume that $|E|$ is $O(|V|^2)$, and for a sparse graph we can assume that $|E|$ is $O(|V|)$.

Many graph algorithms are of the form:

1.   **for** each vertex u in the graph
2.   **for** each vertex v adjacent to u
3.   Do something with edge (u, v).

For an adjacency list representation, Step 1 is $O(|V|)$ and Step 2 is $O(|E_u|)$, where $|E_u|$ is the number of edges that originate at vertex u. Thus the combination of Steps 1 and 2 will represent examining each edge in the graph, giving $O(|E|)$. On the other hand, for an adjacency matrix representation, Step 2 is also $O(|V|)$, and thus the overall algorithm is $O(|V|^2)$. Thus, for a sparse graph the adjacency list gives better performance for this type of algorithm, whereas for a dense graph the performance is the same for either representation.

Some graph algorithms are of the form

1.   **for** each vertex u in some subset of the vertices
2.   **for** each vertex v in some subset of the vertices
3.   **if** (u, v) is an edge
4.   Do something with edge (u, v).

For an adjacency matrix representation, Step 3 tests a matrix value and is $O(1)$, so the overall algorithm is $O(|V|^2)$. However for an adjacency list representation, Step 3 searches a list and is $O(|E_u|)$, so the combination of Steps 2 and 3 is $O(|E|)$ and the overall algorithm is $O(|V||E|)$. For a dense graph the adjacency matrix gives the best performance for this type of algorithm, and for a sparse graph the performance is the same for both representations.

Thus, if a graph is dense, the adjacency matrix representation is best, and if a graph is sparse, the adjacency list representation is best. Intuitively, this makes sense, because a sparse graph will lead to a sparse matrix, or one in which most entries are POSITIVE_INFINITY. These entries are not included in a list representation, so they will have no effect on processing time. However, they are included in a matrix representation and will have an undesirable impact on processing time.

Storage Efficiency

Notice that storage is allocated for all vertex combinations (or at least half of them) in an adjacency matrix. So the storage required is proportional to $|V|^2$. If the graph is sparse (not many edges), there will be a lot of wasted space in the adjacency matrix. In an adjacency list, only the adjacent edges are stored.

On the other hand, in an adjacency list, each edge is represented by a reference to an Edge object containing data about the source, destination, and weight. There is also a reference to the next edge in the list. In a matrix representation, only the weight associated with an edge is stored. So each element in an adjacency list requires approximately four times the storage of an element in an adjacency matrix.

Based on this we can conclude that the break-even point in terms of storage efficiency occurs when approximately 25 percent of the adjacency matrix is filled with meaningful data. That is, the adjacency list uses less (more) storage when less than (more than) 25 percent of the adjacency matrix would be filled.

EXERCISES FOR SECTION 12.3

SELF-CHECK

1. Represent the following graphs using adjacency lists.

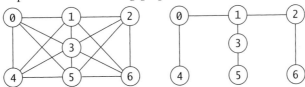

2. Represent the graphs in Exercise 1 using an adjacency matrix.

3. For each graph in Exercise 1, what are the |V|, the |E|, and the density? Which representation is best for each graph? Explain your answers.

PROGRAMMING

1. Implement the `loadEdgesFromFile` method for class `AbstractGraph`. If there are two values on a line, an edge with the default weight of 1.0 is inserted, if there are three values, the third value is the weight.

12.4 Traversals of Graphs

Most graph algorithms involve visiting each vertex in a systematic order. Just as with trees, there are different ways to do this. The two most common traversal algorithms are breadth first and depth first. Although these are graph traversals, they are more commonly called *breadth-first* and *depth-first search*.

Breadth-First Search

In a breadth-first search, we visit the start node first, then all nodes that are adjacent to it next, then all nodes that can be reached by a path from the start node containing two edges, three edges, and so on. The requirement for a breadth-first search is that we must visit all nodes for which the shortest path from the start node is length k before we visit any node for which the shortest path from the start node is length $k + 1$. You can visualize a breadth-first traversal by "picking up" the graph at the vertex that is the start node, so the start node will be the highest node and the rest of the nodes will be suspended underneath it, connected by their edges. In a breadth first search, the nodes that are higher up in the picked-up graph are visited before nodes that are lower in the graph.

Breadth-first search starts at some vertex. Unlike the case of a tree, there is no special start vertex, so we will arbitrarily pick the vertex with label 0. We then visit it by identifying all vertices that are adjacent to the start vertex. Then we visit each of these vertices, identifying all of the vertices adjacent to them. This process continues until all vertices are visited. If the graph is not a connected graph, then the process is repeated with one of the unidentified vertices. In the discussion that follows, we use color to distinguish among three states for a node: identified (light blue), visited (dark blue), and not identified (white). Initially, all nodes are not identified. If a node is in the identified state, that node was encountered while visiting another, but it has not yet been visited.

Example of Breadth-First Search

Consider the graph shown in Figure 12.15. We start at vertex 0 and color it light blue (see Figure 12.16(a)). We visit 0 and see that 1 and 3 are adjacent, so we color them light blue (to show that they have been identified). We are finished visiting 0 and now color it dark blue (see Figure 12.16(b)). So far we have visited node 0.

FIGURE 12.15
FIGURE 12.15
Graph to Be Traversed
Breadth First

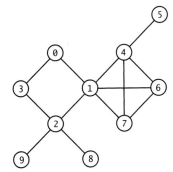

FIGURE 12.16
Example of a Breadth-First Search

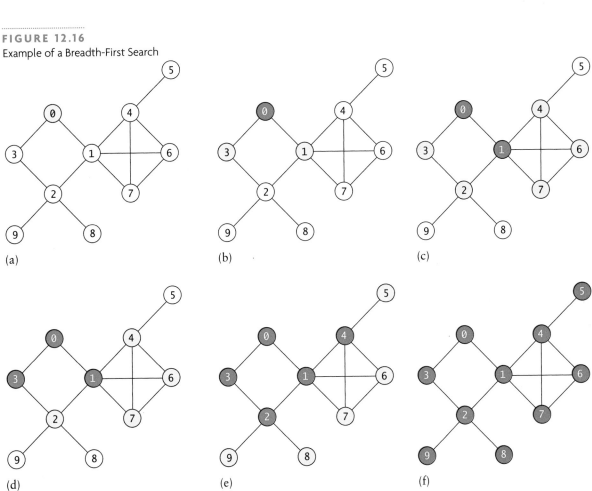

(a)

(b)

(c)

(d)

(e)

(f)

We always select the first node that was identified (light blue) but not yet visited and visit it next. Therefore, we visit 1 and look at its adjacent vertices: 0, 2, 4, 6, and 7. We skip 0, because it is not colored white, and color the others light blue. Then we color 1 dark blue (see Figure 12.16(c)). Now we have visited nodes 0 and 1.

Then we look at 3 (the first of the light blue vertices in Figure 12.16(c) to have been identified) and see that its adjacent vertex, 2, has already been identified and 0 has been visited, so we are finished with 3 (see Figure 12.16(d)). Now we have visited nodes 0, 1, and 3, which are the starting vertex and all vertices adjacent to it.

Now we visit 2 and see that 8 and 9 are adjacent. Then we visit 4 and see that 5 is the only adjacent vertex not identified or visited (Figure 12.16(e)). Finally, we visit 6 and 7 (the last vertices that are two edges away from the starting vertex), then 8, 9, and 5, and see that there are no unidentified vertices (Figure 12.16(f)). The vertices have been visited in the sequence 0, 1, 3, 2, 4, 6, 7, 8, 9, 5.

Algorithm for Breadth-First Search

To implement breadth-first search, we need to be able to determine the first identified vertex that has not been visited, so that we can visit it. To ensure that the identified vertices are visited in the correct sequence, we will store them in a queue (first-in, first-out). When we need a new node to visit, we remove it from the queue. We summarize the process in the following algorithm.

Algorithm for Breadth-First Search

1. Take an arbitrary start vertex, mark it identified (color it light blue), and place it in a queue.
2. `while` the queue is not empty
3.   Take a vertex, u, out of the queue and visit u.
4.   `for` all vertices, v, adjacent to this vertex, u
5.   `if` v has not been identified or visited
6.   Mark it identified (color it light blue).
7.   Insert vertex v into the queue.
8.   We are now finished visiting u (color it dark blue).

Table 12.5 traces this algorithm on the graph shown earlier in Figure 12.15. The initial queue contents is the start node, 0. The first line shows that after we finish visiting vertex 0, the queue contains nodes 1 and 3, which are adjacent to node 0 and are colored light blue in Figure 12.16(b). The second line shows that after removing 1 from the queue and visiting 1, we insert its neighbors that have not yet been identified or visited: nodes 2, 4, 6, and 7.

Table 12.5 shows that the nodes were visited in the sequence 0, 1, 3, 2, 4, 6, 7, 8, 9, 5. There are other sequences that would also be valid breadth-first traversals.

We can also build a tree that represents the order in which vertices would be visited in a breadth-first traversal, by attaching the vertices as they are identified to the vertex from which they are identified. Such a tree is shown in Figure 12.17. Observe that this tree contains all of the vertices and some of the edges of the original graph. A path starting at the root to any vertex in the tree is the shortest path in the original graph from the start vertex to that vertex, where we consider all edges to have the same weight. Therefore, the *shortest path* is the one that goes through the smallest number of vertices. We can save the information we need to represent this tree by storing the parent of each vertex when we identify it (Step 7 of the breadth-first algorithm).

TABLE 12.5
Trace of Breadth-First Search of Figure 12.15

Vertex Being Visited	Queue Contents After Visit	Visit Sequence
0	1 3	0
1	3 2 4 6 7	0 1
3	2 4 6 7	0 1 3
2	4 6 7 8 9	0 1 3 2
4	6 7 8 9 5	0 1 3 2 4
6	7 8 9 5	0 1 3 2 4 6
7	8 9 5	0 1 3 2 4 6 7
8	9 5	0 1 3 2 4 6 7 8
9	5	0 1 3 2 4 6 7 8 9
5	empty	0 1 3 2 4 6 7 8 9 5

FIGURE 12.17
Breadth First Search
Tree of Graph in
Figure 12.15

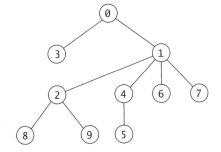

Refinement of Step 7 of Breadth-First Search Algorithm

7.1   Insert vertex v into the queue.

7.2   Set the parent of v to u.

Performance Analysis of Breadth-First Search

The loop at Step 2 will be performed for each vertex. The inner loop at Step 4 is performed for $|E_v|$ (the number of edges that originate at that vertex). The total number of steps is the sum of the edges that originate at each vertex, which is the total number of edges. Thus the algorithm is O(|E|).

Implementing Breadth-First Search

Listing 12.3 shows method breadthFirstSearch. Notice that nothing is done when we have finished visiting a vertex (algorithm Step 8).

This method declares three data structures: int[] parent, boolean[] identified, and Queue theQueue. The array identified is used to keep track of the nodes that have been previously encountered, and theQueue is used to store nodes that are waiting to be visited.

The method returns array parent, which could be used to construct the breadth-first search tree. The element parent[v] contains the parent of vertex v in the tree. The statement

```
parent[neighbor] = current;
```

is used to "insert an edge into the breadth-first search tree". It does this by setting the parent of a newly identified node (neighbor) as the node being visited (current). If we run the breadthFirstSearch method on the graph shown in Figure 12.15, then the array parent will be defined as follows:

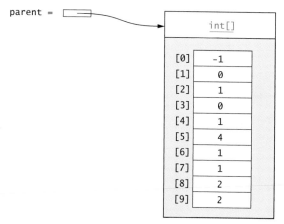

If you compare array parent to Figure 12.17, you can see that parent[i] is the parent of vertex i. For example, the parent of vertex 4 is vertex 1. The entry parent[0] is –1 because node 0 is the start vertex.

Although array parent could be used to construct the breadth-first search tree, we are generally not interested in the complete tree but rather in the path from the root to a given vertex. Using array parent to trace the path from that vertex back to the root would give you the reverse of the desired path. For example, the path derived from parent for vertex 4 to the root would be 4 to 1 to 0. If you place these vertices in a stack and then pop the stack until it is empty, you will get the path from the root: 0 to 1 to 4.

....
LISTING 12.3
Class BreadthFirstSearch.java

```
/** Class to implement the breadth-first search algorithm. */
public class BreadthFirstSearch {

    /** Perform a breadth-first search of a graph.
        post: The array parent will contain the predecessor
              of each vertex in the breadth-first
              search tree.
        @param graph The graph to be searched
        @param start The start vertex
        @return The array of parents
```

```
*/
public static int[] breadthFirstSearch(Graph graph, int start) {
    Queue theQueue = new ArrayQueue();
    // Declare array parent and initialize its elements to -1.
    int[] parent = new int[graph.getNumV()];
    for (int i = 0; i < graph.getNumV(); i++) {
        parent[i] = -1;
    }
    // Declare array identified and
    // initialize its elements to false.
    boolean[] identified = new boolean[graph.getNumV()];
    /* Mark the start vertex as identified and insert it
       into the queue */
    identified[start] = true;
    theQueue.insert(new Integer(start));
    /* While the queue is not empty */
    while (!theQueue.isEmpty()) {
        /* Take a vertex, current, out of the queue.
           (Begin visiting current). */
        int current = ((Integer) theQueue.remove()).intValue();
        /* Examine each vertex, neighbor, adjacent to current. */
        Graph.EdgeIterator itr = graph.edgeIterator(current);
        while (itr.hasNext()) {
            Edge edge = itr.next();
            int neighbor = edge.getDest();
            /* If neighbor has not been identified */
            if (!identified[neighbor]) {
                /* Mark it identified. */
                identified[neighbor] = true;
                /* Place it into the queue. */
                theQueue.insert(new Integer(neighbor));
                /* Insert the edge (current, neighbor)
                   into the tree. */
                parent[neighbor] = current;
            }
        }
        /* Finished visiting current. */
    }
    return parent;
}
}
```

Depth-First Search

Another way to traverse a graph is depth-first search. In depth-first search you start at a vertex, visit it, and choose one adjacent vertex to visit. Then choose a vertex adjacent to that vertex to visit, and so on until you go no further. Then back up and see whether a new vertex (one not previously visited) can be found. In the discussion that follows, we use color to distinguish among three states for a node: being visited (light blue), finished visiting (dark blue), and not yet visited (white). Initially, of course, all nodes are not yet visited. Note that the color light blue is used in depth-first search to indicate that a vertex is in the process of being visited, whereas it was used in our discussion of breadth-first search to indicate that the vertex was identified.

Example of Depth-First Search

Consider the graph shown in Figure 12.18. We can start at any vertex, but for simplicity we will start at 0. The vertices adjacent to 0 are 1, 2, 3, and 4. We mark 0 as being visited (color it light blue; see Figure 12.19(a)). Next we consider 1. We mark 1 as being visited (see Figure 12.19(b)). The vertices adjacent to 1 are 0, 3, and 4. But 0 is being visited, so we recursively apply the algorithm with 3 as the start vertex. We mark 3 as being visited (see Figure 12.19(c)). The vertices adjacent to 3 are 0, 1, and 4. Because 0 and 1 are already being visited, we recursively apply the algorithm with 4 as the start vertex. We mark 4 as being visited (see Figure 12.19(d)). The vertices adjacent to 4 are 0, 1, and 3. All of these are being visited, so we mark 4 as finished (see Figure 12.19(e)) and return from the recursion. Now all of the vertices adjacent to 3 have been visited, so we mark 3 as finished and return from the recursion. Now all of the vertices adjacent to 1 have been visited, so we mark 1 as finished and return from the recursion to the original start vertex, 0. The order in which we started to visit vertices is 0, 1, 3, 4; the order in which vertices have become finished so far is 4, 3, 1.

We now consider vertex 2, which is adjacent to 0 but has not been visited. We mark 2 as being visited (see Figure 12.19(f)) and consider the vertices adjacent to it: 5 and 6. We mark 5 as being visited (see Figure 12.19(g)) and consider the vertices adjacent to it: 2 and 6. Because 2 is already being visited, we next visit 6. We mark 6 as being visited (see Figure 12.19(h)). The vertices adjacent to 6 (2 and 5) are already being visited. Thus we mark 6 as finished and recursively return. The vertices adjacent to 5 have all been visited, so we mark 5 as finished and return from the recursion. All of the vertices adjacent to 2 have been visited, so we mark 2 as finished and return from the recursion.

Finally, we come back to 0. Because all of the vertices adjacent to it have also been visited, we mark 0 as finished and we are done (see Figure 12.19(i)). The order in which we started to visit all vertices is 0, 1, 3, 4, 2, 5, 6; the order in which we finished visiting all vertices is 4, 3, 1, 6, 5, 2, 0. The *discovery order* is the order in which the vertices are discovered. The *finish order* is the order in which the vertices are finished. We consider a vertex to be finished when we return to it after finishing all its successors.

Figure 12.20 shows the depth-first search tree for the graph in Figure 12.18. A preorder traversal of this tree yields the sequence in which the vertices were visited: 0, 1, 3, 4, 2, 5, 6. The dashed lines are the other edges in the graph that are not part of the depth-first search tree. These edges are called *back edges* because they connect a vertex with its ancestors in the depth-first search tree. Observe that vertex 4 has two ancestors in addition to its parent, 3: 1 and 0. Vertex 1 is a grandparent, and vertex 0 is a great-grandparent.

FIGURE 12.18
Graph to Be Traversed
Depth First

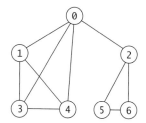

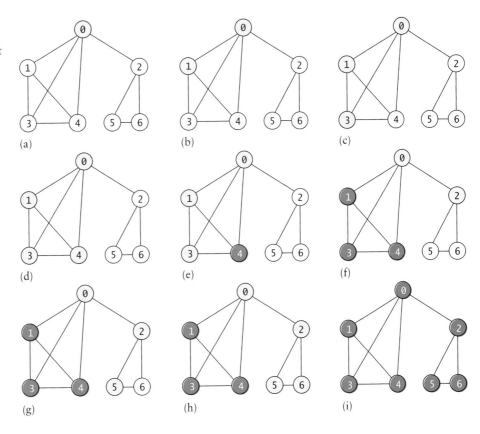

FIGURE 12.19
Example of Depth-First
Search

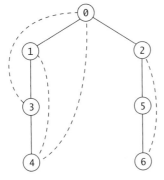

FIGURE 12.20
Depth-First Search
Tree of Figure 12.18

Algorithm for Depth-First Search

Depth-first search is used as the basis of other graph algorithms. However, rather than embedding the depth-first search algorithm into these other algorithms, we will implement the depth-first search algorithm to collect information about the vertices, which we can then use in these other algorithms. The information we will collect is the discovery order (or the visit order) and the finish order.

The depth-first search algorithm follows. Step 5 recursively applies this algorithm to each vertex as it is discovered.

Algorithm for Depth-First Search

1. Mark the current vertex, u, visited (color it light blue), and enter it in the discovery order list
2. **for** each vertex, v, adjacent to the current vertex, u
3.   **if** v has not been visited
4.   Set parent of v to u.
5.   Recursively apply this algorithm starting at v.
6. Mark u finished (color it dark blue) and enter u into the finish order list.

Observe that Step 6 is executed after the loop in Step 2 has examined all vertices adjacent to vertex u. Also, the loop at Step 2 does not select the vertices in any particular order.

Table 12.6 shows a trace of the algorithm as applied to the graph shown in Figure 12.19. We list each visit or finish Step in column 1. Column 2 lists the vertices adjacent to each vertex when it begins to be visited. The discovery order (the order in which the vertices are visited) is 0, 1, 3, 4, 2, 5, 6. The finish order is 4, 3, 1, 6, 5, 2, and 0.

Performance Analysis of Depth-First Search

The loop at Step 2 is executed $|E_v|$ (the number of edges that originate at that vertex) times. The recursive call results in this loop being applied to each vertex. The total number of steps is the sum of the edges that originate at each vertex, which is the total number of edges $|E|$. Thus the algorithm is $O(|E|)$.

TABLE 12.6
Trace of Depth-First Search of Figure 12.19

Operation	Adjacent Vertices	Discovery (Visit) Order	Finish Order
Visit 0	1, 2, 3, 4	0	
Visit 1	0, 3, 4	0, 1	
Visit 3	0, 1, 4	0, 1, 3	
Visit 4	0, 1, 3	0, 1, 3, 4	
Finish 4			4
Finish 3			4, 3
Finish 1			4, 3, 1
Visit 2	0, 5, 6	0, 1, 3, 4, 2	
Visit 5	2, 6	0, 1, 3, 4, 2, 5	
Visit 6	2, 5	0, 1, 3, 4, 2, 5, 6	
Finish 6			4, 3, 1, 6
Finish 5			4, 3, 1, 6, 5
Finish 2			4, 3, 1, 6, 5, 2
Finish 0			4, 3, 1, 6, 5, 2, 0

There is an implicit Step 0 to the algorithm that colors all of the vertices white. This is $O(|V|)$, thus the total running time of the algorithm is $O(|V|+|E|)$.

Implementing Depth-First Search

The class `DepthFirstSearch` is designed to be used as a building block for other algorithms. When constructed, this class performs a depth-first search on a graph and records the start time, finish time, start order, and finish order. For an unconnected graph, or for a directed graph (whether connected or not), a depth-first search may not visit each vertex in the graph. Thus, once the recursive method returns, the vertices need to be examined to see whether they all have been visited; if not, the recursive process repeats, starting with the next unvisited vertex. Thus, the depth-first search can generate more than one tree. We will call this collection of trees a *forest*. Also, it may be important that we control the order in which the vertices are examined to form the forest. Thus, one of the constructors for the `DepthFirstSearch` class enables its caller to specify the order in which vertices are examined to select a new start vertex. The default is normal ascending order. The class is described in Table 12.7, and part of the code is shown in Listing 12.4.

TABLE 12.7
Class `DepthFirstSearch`

Data Field	Attribute
`private int discoverIndex`	The index that indicates the discovery order.
`private int[] discoveryOrder`	The array that contains the vertices in discovery order.
`private int finishIndex`	The index that indicates the finish order.
`private int[] finishOrder`	The array that contains the vertices in finish order.
`private Graph graph`	A reference to the graph being searched.
`private int[] parent`	The array of predecessors in the depth-first search tree.
`private boolean[] visited`	An array of **boolean** values to indicate whether or not a vertex has been visited.
Constructor	**Purpose**
`public DepthFirstSearch(Graph graph)`	Constructs the depth-first search of the specified graph selecting the start vertices in ascending vertex order.
`public DepthFirstSearch(Graph graph, int[] order)`	Constructs the depth-first search of the specified graph selecting the start vertices in the specified order. The first vertex visited is `order[0]`.
Method	**Behavior**
`public void depthFirstSearch(int s)`	Recursively searches the graph starting at vertex s.
`public int[] getDiscoveryOrder()`	Gets the discovery order.
`public int[] getFinishOrder()`	Gets the finish order.
`public int[] getParent()`	Gets the parents in the depth-first search tree.

Each constructor allocates storage for the arrays `parent`, `visited`, `discoveryOrder`, and `finishOrder` and initializes all elements of `parent` to -1 (no parent). In the constructor in Listing 12.4, the **for** statement

```
for (int i = 0; i < n; i++) {
    if (!visited[i])
        depthFirstSearch(i);
}
```

calls the recursive depth-first search method. Method `depthFirstSearch` follows the algorithm shown earlier. If the graph is connected, all vertices will be visited after the return from the initial call to `depthFirstSearch`. If the graph is not connected, additional calls will be made using a start vertex that has not been visited.

In the constructor (not shown) that allows the client to control the order of selection for start vertices, the parameter `int[]` `order` specifies this sequence. To code this constructor, change the **if** statement just shown to

```
if (!visited[order[i]])
    depthFirstSearch(order[i]);
```

The rest of the code is the same.

··

LISTING 12.4
DepthFirstSearch.java

```java
/** Class to implement the depth-first search algorithm. */
public class DepthFirstSearch {

    // Data Fields
    /** A reference to the graph being searched. */
    private Graph graph;
    /** Array of parents in the depth-first search tree. */
    private int[] parent;
    /** Flag to indicate whether this vertex has been visited. */
    private boolean[] visited;
    /** The array that contains each vertex in discovery order. */
    private int[] discoveryOrder;
    /** The array that contains each vertex in finish order. */
    private int[] finishOrder;
    /** The index that indicates the discovery order. */
    private int discoverIndex = 0;
    /** The index that indicates the finish order. */
    private int finishIndex = 0;

    // Constructors
    /** Construct the depth-first search of a Graph
        starting at vertex 0 and visiting the start vertices in
        ascending order.
        @param graph The graph
```

```java
*/
public DepthFirstSearch(Graph graph) {
    this.graph = graph;
    int n = graph.getNumV();
    parent = new int[n];
    visited = new boolean[n];
    discoveryOrder = new int[n];
    finishOrder = new int[n];
    for (int i = 0; i < n; i++) {
        parent[i] = -1;
    }
    for (int i = 0; i < n; i++) {
        if (!visited[i])
            depthFirstSearch(i);
    }
}

/** Construct the depth-first search of a Graph
    selecting the start vertices in the specified order.
    The first vertex visited is order[0].
    @param graph The graph
    @param order The array giving the order
                 in which the start vertices should be selected
*/
public DepthFirstSearch(Graph graph, int[] order) {
    // Same as constructor above except for the if statement.
}

/** Recursively depth-first search the graph
    starting at vertex current.
    @param current The start vertex
*/
public void depthFirstSearch(int current) {
    /* Mark the current vertex visited. */
    visited[current] = true;
    discoveryOrder[discoverIndex++] = current;
    /* Examine each vertex adjacent to the current vertex */
    Graph.EdgeIterator itr = graph.edgeIterator(current);
    while (itr.hasNext()) {
        int neighbor = itr.next().getDest();
        /* Process a neighbor that has not been visited */
        if (!visited[neighbor]) {
            /* Insert (current, neighbor) into the depth-
                first search tree. */
            parent[neighbor] = current;
            /* Recursively apply the algorithm
                starting at neighbor. */
            depthFirstSearch(neighbor);
        }
    }
    /* Mark current finished. */
    finishOrder[finishIndex++] = current;
}
}
```

Testing Method depthFirstSearch

Next, we show a main method that tests the class. It is a simple driver program that can be used to read a graph and then initiate a depth-first traversal. After the traversal, the driver program displays the arrays that represent the search results.

```java
/** Main method to test depth-first search method
    pre: args[0] is the name of the input file.
    @param args The command line arguments
*/
public static void main(String[] args) {
    try {
        BufferedReader bR =
            new BufferedReader(new FileReader(args[0]));
        String nString = bR.readLine();
        int n = Integer.parseInt(nString);
        ListGraph g = new ListGraph(n, true);
        g.loadEdgesFromFile(bR);
    } catch (IOException ex) {
        ex.printStackTrace();
        System.exit(1);     // Error
    }

    // Perform depth-first search.
    DepthFirstSearch dfs = new DepthFirstSearch(g);
    int[] dOrder = dfs.getDiscoveryOrder();
    int[] fOrder = dfs.getFinishOrder();
    System.out.println("Discovery and finish order");
    for (int i = 0; i < n; i++) {
        System.out.println(dOrder[i] + "   " + fOrder[i]);
    }
}
```

EXERCISES FOR SECTION 12.4

SELF-CHECK

1. Show the breadth-first search trees for the following graphs.

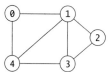 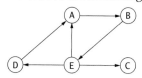

2. Show the depth-first search trees for the graphs in Exercise 1.

PROGRAMMING

1. Provide all accessor methods for class DepthFirstSearch and the constructor that specifies the order of start vertices.
2. Implement method depthFirstSearch without using recursion. *Hint:* Use a stack to save the parent of the current vertex when you start to search one of its adjacent vertices.

12.5 Applications of Graph Traversals

CASE STUDY   Shortest Path Through a Maze

Problem   We want to design a program that will find the shortest path through a maze. In Chapter 7 we showed how to write a recursive program that found a solution to a maze. This program used a backtracking algorithm that visited alternate paths. When it found a dead end, it backed up and tried another path, and eventually it found a solution.

Figure 12.21 shows a maze solution generated by this recursive program. The light gray cells are barriers in the maze. The white squares show the solution path, the black squares show the squares that were visited but rejected, and the dark gray squares were not visited. As you can see, the program did not find an optimal solution. (This is a consequence of the program advancing the solution path to the South before attempting to advance it to the East.) We want to find the shortest path, defined as the one with the fewest decision points in it.

FIGURE 12.21
Recursive Solution to a Maze

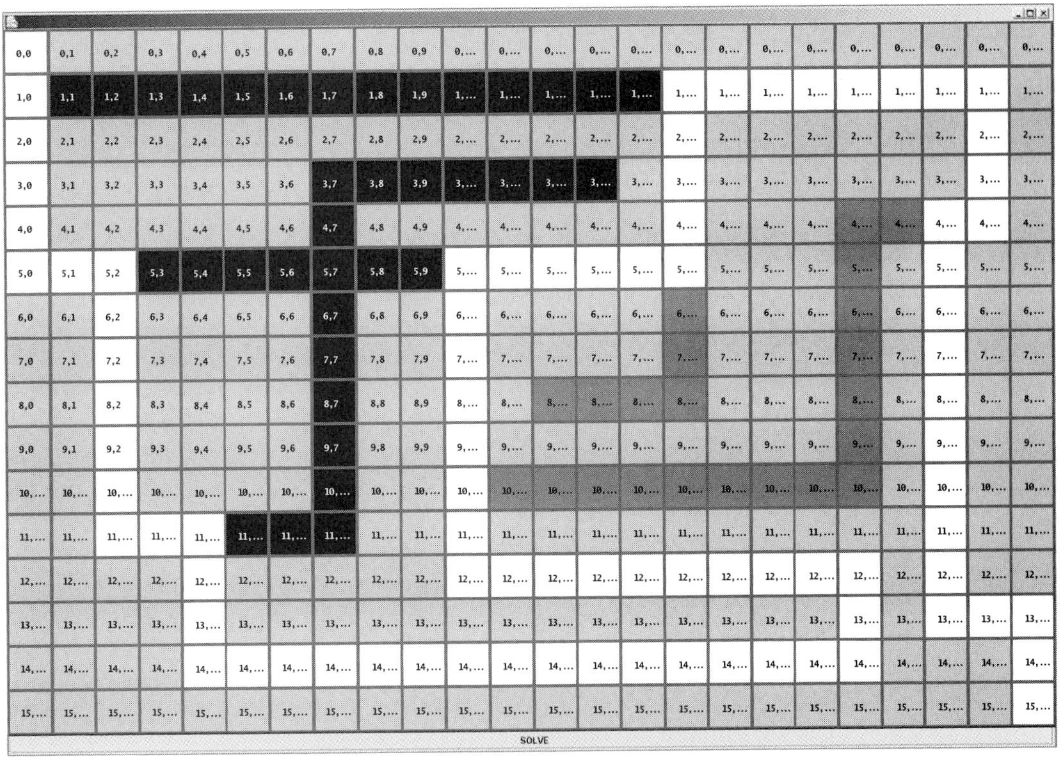

Analysis   We can represent the maze shown in Figure 12.21 by a graph, where we place a node at each decision point and at each dead end, as shown in Figure 12.22.

Now that we have the maze represented as a graph, we need to find the shortest path from the start point (vertex 0) to the end point (vertex 12). The breadth-first search method will return the shortest path from each vertex to its parent (the array of parent vertices), and we can use this array to find the shortest path to the end point. Recall that our shortest path will contain the smallest number of vertices, but not necessarily the smallest number of cells, in the path.

FIGURE 12.22
Graph Representation of the Maze in Figure 12.21

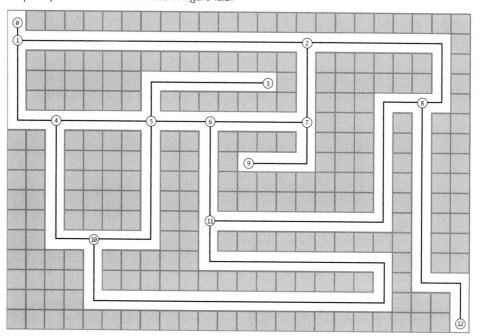

Design   Your program will need the following data structures:

- An external representation of the maze, consisting of the number of vertices and the edges
- An object of a class that implements the Graph interface
- An array to hold the predecessors returned from the breadthFirstSearch method
- A stack to reverse the path

The algorithm is as follows:

1. Read in the number of vertices and create the graph object.
2. Read in the edges and insert the edges into the graph.
3. Call the breadthFirstSearch method with this graph and the starting vertex as its argument. The method returns the array parent.
4. Start at v, the end vertex.
5. **while** v is not −1
6.   Push v onto the stack.
7.   Set v to parent[v].
8. **while** the stack is not empty
9.   Pop a vertex off the stack and output it.

Implementation   Listing 12.5 shows the program. We assume that the graph that represents the maze is stored in a text file. The first line of this file contains the number of vertices. The edges are on subsequent lines. The method loadEdgesFromFile reads the source and destination vertices and inserts the edge into the graph. The rest of the code follows the algorithm.

LISTING 12.5
Program to Solve a Maze Using a Breadth-First Search

```java
import java.io.*;
import java.util.*;

/** Program to solve a maze represented as a graph.
    This program performs a breadth-first search of the graph
    to find the "shortest" path from the start vertex to the
    end. It is assumed that the start vertex is 0, and the
    end vertex is numV-1.
*/
public class Maze {

    /** Main method to solve the maze.
        pre: args[0] contains the name of the input file.
        @param args Command line argument
    */
    public static void main(String[] args) {
        int numV = 0;    // The number of vertices.
        AbstractGraph theMaze = null;
        // Load the graph data from a file.
        try {
            BufferedReader bR =
                new BufferedReader(new FileReader(args[0]));
            String line = bR.readLine();
            numV = Integer.parseInt(line);
            theMaze = new ListGraph(numV, false);
            theMaze.loadEdgesFromFile(bR);
```

```
            } catch (IOException ex) {
                System.err.println("IO Error while reading graph");
                System.err.println(ex.toString());
                System.exit(1);
            }
            // Perform breadth-first search.
            int parent[] =
                BreadthFirstSearch.breadthFirstSearch(theMaze, 0);
            // Construct the path.
            Stack thePath = new Stack();
            int v = numV - 1;
            while (parent[v] != -1) {
                thePath.push(new Integer(v));
                v = parent[v];
            }
            // Output the path.
            System.out.println("The Shortest path is:");
            while (!thePath.empty()) {
                System.out.println(thePath.pop());
            }
        }
    }
}
```

Testing   Test this program with a variety of mazes. Use mazes for which the original program finds the shortest path and mazes for which it does not. For the graph shown in Figure 12.23, the shortest path from 0 to 12 is $0 \rightarrow 1 \rightarrow 2 \rightarrow 8 \rightarrow 12$.

FIGURE 12.23

Solution to Maze in Figure 12.21

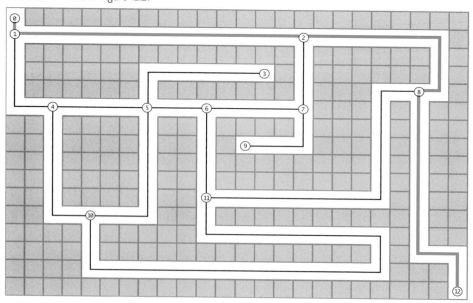

CASE STUDY   Topological Sort of a Graph

Problem   There are many problems in which one activity cannot be started before another one has been completed. One that you may have already encountered is determining the order in which you can take courses. Some courses have prerequisites. Some have more than one prerequisite. Furthermore, the prerequisites may have prerequisites. Figure 12.24 shows the courses and prerequisites of a Computer Science program at the authors' university.

FIGURE 12.24
Prerequisites for a
Computer Science
Program

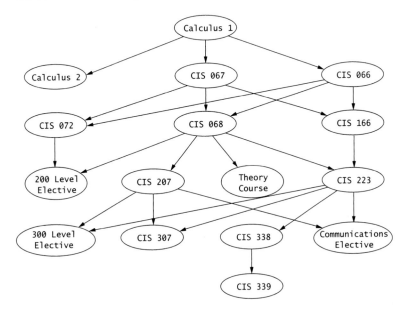

Graphs such as the one shown in Figure 12.24 are known as *directed acyclic graphs (DAGs)*. They are directed graphs that contain no cycles; that is, there are no loops, so once you pass through a vertex, there is no path back to that vertex. Figure 12.25 shows another example of a DAG.

FIGURE 12.25
Example of a
Directed Acyclic
Graph

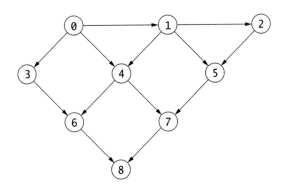

A *topological sort* of the vertices of a DAG is an ordering of the vertices such that if (u, v) is an edge, then u appears before v. This must be true for all edges. For example, 0, 1, 2, 3, 4, 5, 6, 7, 8 is a valid topological sort of the graph in Figure 12.25, but 0, 1, 5, 3, 4, 2, 6, 7, 8 is not, because $2 \rightarrow 5$ is an edge, but 5 appears before 2. There are many valid paths through the prerequisite graph and many valid topological sorts. Another valid topological sort is 0, 3, 1, 4, 6, 2, 5, 7, 8.

Analysis

If there is an edge from u to v in a DAG, then if we perform a depth-first search of this graph, the finish time of u must be after the finish time of v. When we return to u, either v has not been visited or it has finished. It is not possible that v would be visited but not finished, because if it were possible, we would discover u on a path that had passed through v. That would mean that there is a loop or cycle in the graph.

For example, in Figure 12.25 we could start the depth-first search at 0, then visit 4, followed by 6, followed by 8. Then, returning to 4, we would have to visit 7 before returning to 0. Then we would visit 1, and from 1 we would see that 4 has finished. Alternatively, we could start at 0 and then go to 1, and we would see that 4 has not been visited. What we cannot have happen is that we start at 0, then visit 4, and eventually get to 1 before finishing 4.

Design

If we perform a depth-first search of a graph and then order the vertices by the inverse of their finish order, we will have one topological sort of a directed acyclic graph. The topological sort produced by listing the vertices in the inverse of their finish order after a depth-first search of the graph in Figure 12.25 is 0, 3, 1, 4, 6, 2, 5, 7, 8.

Algorithm for Topological Sort

1. Read the graph from a data file.
2. Perform a depth-first search of the graph.
3. List the vertices in reverse of their finish order.

Implementation

We can use our `DepthFirstSearch` class to implement this algorithm. Listing 12.6 shows a program that does this. It begins by reading the graph from an input file. It then creates a `DepthFirstSearch` object `dfs`. The constructor of the `DepthFirstSearch` class performs the depth-first search and saves information about the graph. We then call the `getFinishOrder` method to get the vertices in the order in which they finished. If we output this array starting at `numVertices - 1`, we will obtain the topological sort of the graph.

LISTING 12.6

TopologicalSort.java

```java
import java.io.*;

/** This program outputs the topological sort of a directed graph
    that contains no cycles.
*/
public class TopologicalSort {

    /** The main method that performs the topological sort.
        pre: arg[0] contains the name of the file
             that contains the graph.
        @param args The command line arguments
    */
    public static void main(String[] args) {
        AbstractGraph theGraph = null;
        int numVertices = 0;
        try {
            // Construct BufferedReader for input file.
            BufferedReader bR =
                new BufferedReader(new FileReader(args[0]));
            // Read the number of vertices.
            String line = bR.readLine();
            numVertices = Integer.parseInt(line);
            // Construct the graph.
            theGraph = new ListGraph(numVertices, true);
            // Load the edges from the file.
            theGraph.loadEdgesFromFile(bR);
        } catch (Exception ex) {
            ex.printStackTrace();
            System.exit(1); // Error exit.
        }
        // Perform the depth-first search.
        DepthFirstSearch dfs = new DepthFirstSearch(theGraph);
        // Obtain the finish order.
        int[] finishOrder = dfs.getFinishOrder();
        // Print the vertices in reverse finish order.
        System.out.println("The Topological Sort is");
        for (int i = numVertices - 1; i >= 0; i--) {
            System.out.println(finishOrder[i]);
        }
    }
}
```

Testing   Test this program using several different graphs. Use sparse graphs and dense graphs. Make sure that each graph that you try has no loops or cycles. If it does, the algorithm may display an invalid output.

EXERCISES FOR SECTION 12.5

SELF-CHECK

1. Draw the depth-first search tree of the graph in Figure 12.24 and then list the vertices in reverse finish order.
2. List some alternative topological sorts for the graph in Figure 12.24.

12.6 Algorithms Using Weighted Graphs

Finding the Shortest Path from a Vertex to All Other Vertices

The breadth-first search discussed in Section 12.4 found the shortest path from the start vertex to all other vertices, assuming that the length of each edge was the same. We now consider the problem of finding the shortest path where the length of each edge may be different—that is, in a weighted directed graph such as that shown in Figure 12.26. The computer scientist Edsger W. Dijkstra developed an algorithm, now called Dijkstra's algorithm (E. W. Dijkstra, "A Note on Two Problems in Connection with Graphs," *Numerische Mathematik*, Vol. 1 [1959], pp. 269–271), to solve this problem. This algorithm makes the assumption that all of the edge values are positive.

For Dijkstra's algorithm we need two sets, S and $V–S$, and two arrays, d and p. S will contain the vertices for which we have computed the shortest distance, and $V–S$ will contain the vertices that we still need to process. The entry d[v] will contain the shortest distance from s to v, and p[v] will contain the predecessor of v in the path from s to v.

We initialize S by placing the start vertex, s, into it. We initialize $V–S$ by placing the remaining vertices into it. For each v in $V–S$, we initialize d by setting d[v] equal to the weight of the edge $w(s, v)$ for each vertex, v, adjacent to s and to ∞ for each vertex that is not adjacent to s. We initialize p[v] to s for each v in $V–S$.

FIGURE 12.26
Weighted Directed
Graph

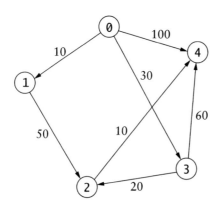

For example, given the graph shown in Figure 12.26, the set S would initially be {0}, V–S would be {1, 2, 3, 4}. The arrays d and p would be defined as follows.

v	d[v]	p[v]
1	10	0
2	∞	0
3	30	0
4	100	0

The first row shows that the distance from vertex 0 to vertex 1 is 10 and that vertex 0 is the predecessor of vertex 1. The second row shows that vertex 2 is not adjacent to vertex 0.

We now find the vertex u in V–S that has the smallest value of d[u]. Using our example, this is 1. We now consider the vertices v that are adjacent to u. If the distance from s to u (d[u]) plus the distance from u to v (that is, $w(u, v)$) is smaller than the known distance from s to v, d[v], then we update d[v] to be d[u] + $w(u, v)$, and we set p[v] to u. In our example the value of d[1] is 10, and $w(1, 2)$ is 50. Since 10 + 50 = 60 is less than ∞, we set d[2] to 60 and p[2] to 1. We remove 1 from V–S and place it into S. We repeat this until V–S is empty.

After the first pass through this loop, S is {0, 1}, V–S is {2, 3, 4} and d and p are as follows:

v	d[v]	p[v]
1	10	0
2	60	1
3	30	0
4	100	0

We again select u from V–S with the smallest d[u]. This is now 3. The adjacent vertices to 3 are 2 and 4. The distance from 0 to 3, d[3], is 30. The distance from 3 to 2 is 20. Because 30 + 20 = 50 is less than the current value of d[2], 60, we update d[2] to 50 and change p[2] to 3. Also, because 30 + 60 = 90 is less than 100, we update d[4] to 90 and set p[4] to 3.

Now S is {0, 1, 3}, and V–S is {2, 4}. The arrays d and p are as follows:

v	d[v]	p[v]
1	10	0
2	50	3
3	30	0
4	90	3

Next we select vertex 2 from *V–S*. The only vertex adjacent to 2 is 4. Since d[2] + $w(2, 4)$ = 50 + 10 = 60 is less than d[4], 90, we update d[4] to 60 and p[4] to 2. Now *S* is {0, 1, 2, 3}, *V–S* is {4}, and d and p are as follows:

v	d[v]	p[v]
1	10	0
2	50	3
3	30	0
4	60	2

Finally we remove 4 from *V–S* and find that it has no adjacent vertices. We are now done. The array d shows the shortest distances from the start vertex to all other vertices, and the array p can be used to determine the corresponding paths. For example, the path from vertex 0 to vertex 4 has a length of 60, and it is the reverse of 4, 2, 3, 0; therefore, the shortest path is 0 → 3 → 2 → 4.

Dijkstra's Algorithm

1. Initialize *S* with the start vertex, *s*, and *V–S* with the remaining vertices.
2. **for** all *v* in *V–S*
3.   Set p[*v*] to *s*.
4.   **if** there is an edge (*s*, *v*)
5.   Set d[*v*] to $w(s, v)$.
    else
6.   Set d[*v*] to ∞.
7. **while** *V–S* is not empty
8.   **for** all *u* in *V–S*, find the smallest d[*u*].
9.   Remove *u* from *V–S* and add *u* to *S*.
10.   **for** all *v* adjacent to *u* in *V–S*
11.   **if** d[*u*] + $w(u, v)$ is less than d[*v*].
12.   Set d[*v*] to d[*u*] + $w(u, v)$.
13.   Set p[*v*] to *u*.

Analysis of Dijkstra's Algorithm

Step 1 requires |*V*| steps.

The loop at Step 2 will be executed |*V* – 1| times.

The loop at Step 7 will also be executed |*V* – 1| times.

Within the loop at Step 7 we have to consider Steps 8 and 9. For these steps we will have to search each value in *V–S*. This decreases each time through the loop at Step 7, so we will have |*V*| – 1 + |*V*| – 2 + · · · 1. This is $O(|V|^2)$. Therefore, Dijkstra's algorithm as stated is $O(|V|^2)$. We will look at possible improvements to this for sparse graphs when we discuss a similar algorithm in the next subsection.

Implementation

Listing 12.7 provides a straightforward implementation of Dijkstra's algorithm using HashSet vMinusS to represent set *V–S*. We chose to implement the algorithm as a **static** method with the inputs (the graph and starting point) and outputs (predecessor and distance array) passed through parameters. An alternative approach would be to make them data fields in a class that contained this method.

We use iterators to traverse vMinusS.

If we used an adjacency list representation for the graph (i.e., class ListGraph, described earlier), then we would code Step 10 (update the distances) to iterate through the edges adjacent to vertex u, and then update the distance if the destination vertex was in vMinusS. The modified code follows:

```
// Update the distances.
Graph.EdgeIterator edgeIter = graph.edgeIterator(u);
while (edgeIter.hasNext()) {
    Edge edge = edgeIter.next();
    int v = edge.getDest();
    if (vMinusS.contains(new Integer(v));
        double weight = edge.getWeight();
        if (dist[u] + weight < dist[v]) {
            dist[v] = dist[u] + weight;
            pred[v] = u;
        }
    }
}
```

....

LISTING 12.7
Dijkstra's Shortest-Path Algorithm

```
/** Dijkstra's Shortest-Path algorithm.
    @param graph The weighted graph to be searched
    @param start The start vertex
    @param pred Output array to contain the predecessors
                in the shortest path
    @param dist Output array to contain the distance
                in the shortest path
*/
public static void dijkstrasAlgorithm(Graph graph,
                                      int start,
                                      int[] pred,
                                      double[] dist) {
    int numV = graph.getNumV();
    HashSet vMinusS = new HashSet(numV);
    // Initialize V-S.
    for (int i = 0; i < numV; i++) {
        if (i != start) {
            vMinusS.add(new Integer(i));
        }
    }
    // Initialize pred and dist.
    Iterator iter = vMinusS.iterator();
    while (iter.hasNext()) {
        int v = ((Integer) iter.next()).intValue();
        pred[v] = start;
        dist[v] = graph.getEdge(start, v).getWeight();
    }
```

```
// Main loop
while (vMinusS.size() != 0) {
    // Find the value u in V-S with the smallest dist[u].
    double minDist = Double.POSITIVE_INFINITY;
    int u = -1;
    iter = vMinusS.iterator();
    while (iter.hasNext()) {
        int v = ((Integer) iter.next()).intValue();
        if (dist[v] < minDist) {
            minDist = dist[v];
            u = v;
        }
    }
    // Remove u from vMinusS.
    vMinusS.remove(new Integer(u));
    // Update the distances.
    iter = vMinusS.iterator();
    while (iter.hasNext()) {
        int v = ((Integer) iter.next()).intValue();
        if (graph.isEdge(u, v)) {
            double weight = graph.getEdge(u, v).getWeight();
            if (dist[u] + weight < dist[v]) {
                dist[v] = dist[u] + weight;
                pred[v] = u;
            }
        }
    }
}
```

Minimum Spanning Trees

A *spanning tree* is a subset of the edges of a graph such that there is only one edge between each vertex, and all of the vertices are connected. If we have a spanning tree for a graph, then we can access all the vertices of the graph from the start node. The *cost of a spanning tree* is the sum of the weights of the edges. We want to find the *minimum spanning tree* or the spanning tree with the smallest cost. For example, if we want to start up our own long-distance phone company and need to connect the cities shown in Figure 12.4, finding the minimum spanning tree would allow us to build the cheapest network.

We will discuss the algorithm published by R. C. Prim (R. C. Prim, "Shortest Connection Networks and Some Generalizations," *Bell System Technical Journal*, Vol. 36 [1957], pp. 1389–1401) for finding the minimum spanning tree of a graph. It is very similar to Dijkstra's algorithm, but Prim published his algorithm in 1957, two years before Dijkstra's paper that contains an algorithm for finding the minimum spanning tree that is essentially the same as Prim's as well as the previously discussed algorithm for finding the shortest paths.

Overview of Prim's Algorithm

The vertices are divided into two sets: *S*, the set of vertices in the spanning tree, and *V–S*, the remaining vertices. As in Dijkstra's algorithm, we maintain two arrays: d[*v*] will contain the length of the shortest edge from a vertex in *S* to the vertex *v* that is in *V–S*, and p[*v*] will contain the source vertex for that edge. The only difference between the algorithm to find the shortest path and the algorithm to find the minimum spanning tree is the contents of d[*v*]. In the algorithm to find the shortest path, d[*v*] contains the total length of the path from the starting vertex. In the algorithm to find the minimum spanning tree, d[*v*] contains only the length of the final edge. We show the essentials of Prim's algorithm next.

Prim's Algorithm for Finding the Minimum Spanning Tree

1.   Initialize *S* with the start vertex, *s*, and *V–S* with the remaining vertices.
2.   **for** all *v* in *V–S*
3.   Set p[*v*] to *s*.
4.   **if** there is an edge (*s*, *v*)
5.   Set d[*v*] to *w*(*s*, *v*).
               else
6.   Set d[*v*] to ∞.
7.   **while** *V–S* is not empty
8.   **for** all *u* in *V–S*, find the smallest d[*u*].
9.   Remove *u* from *V–S* and add it to *S*.
10.   Insert the edge (*u*, p[*u*]) into the spanning tree.
11.   **for** all *v* in *V–S*
12.   **if** *w*(*u*, *v*) < d[*v*]
13.   Set d[*v*] to w(*u*, *v*).
14.   Set p[*v*] to *u*.

In the array d, d[*v*] contains the length of the shortest known (previously examined) edge from a vertex in *S* to the vertex *v*, while *v* is a member of *V–S*. In the array p, the value p[*v*] is the source vertex of this shortest edge. When *v* is removed from *V–S*, we no longer update these entries in d and p.

EXAMPLE 12.2   Consider the graph shown in Figure 12.27. We initialize *S* to {0} and *V–S* to {1, 2, 3, 4, 5}. The smallest edge from *u* to *v*, where *u* is in *S* and *v* is in *V–S*, is the edge (0, 2). We add this edge to the spanning tree, and add 2 to *S* (see Figure 12.28(a)). The set *S* is now {0, 2} and *V–S* is {1, 3, 4, 5}. We now have to consider all of the edges (*u*, *v*), where *u* is either 0 or 2, and *v* is 1, 3, 4, or 5 (there are eight possible edges). The smallest one is (2, 5). We add this to the spanning tree, and *S* now is {0,

FIGURE 12.27
Graph for Example 12.2

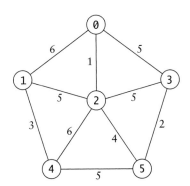

2, 5} and *V–S* is {1, 3, 4} (see Figure 12.28(b)). The next smallest edge is (5, 3). We insert that into the tree and add 3 to *S* (see Figure 12.28(c)). Now *V–S* is {1, 4}. The smallest edge is (2, 1). After adding this edge (see Figure 12.28(d)), we are left with *V–S* being {4}. The smallest edge to 4 is (1, 4). This is added to the tree, and the spanning tree is complete (see Figure 12.28(e)).

FIGURE 12.28

Building a Minimum Spanning Tree Using Prim's Algorithm

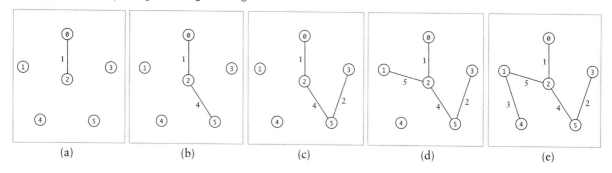

(a)   (b)   (c)   (d)   (e)

Analysis of Prim's Algorithm

Step 8 is $O(|V|)$. Because this is within the loop at Step 7, it will be executed $O(|V|)$ times for a total time of $O(|V|^2)$. Step 11 is $O(|E_u|)$, the number of edges that originate at *u*. Because Step 11 is inside the loop of Step 7, it will be executed for all vertices; thus, the total is $O(|E|)$. Because $|V|^2$ is greater than $|E|$, the overall cost of the algorithm is $O(|V|^2)$.

By using a priority queue to hold the edges from *S* to *V–S*, we can improve on this algorithm. Then Step 8 is $O(\log n)$, where *n* is the size of the priority queue. In the worst case, all of the edges are inserted into the priority queue, the overall cost of the algorithm is then $O(|E| \log |V|)$. We say that the algorithm is $O(|E| \log |V|)$ instead of saying that it is $O(|E| \log |E|)$, even though the maximum size of the priority queue is $|E|$, because $|E|$ is bounded by $|V|^2$ and $\log |V|^2$ is $2 \times \log |V|$.

For a dense graph, where $|E|$ is approximately $|V|^2$, this is not an improvement; however, for a sparse graph, where $|E|$ is significantly less than $|V|^2$, it is. Furthermore, computer science researchers have developed improved priority queue implementations that give $O(|E| + |V| \log |V|)$ or better performance.

Implementation

Listing 12.8 shows an implementation of Prim's algorithm using a priority queue to hold the edges from *S* to *V–S*. The arrays p and d given in the algorithm description above are not needed, because the priority queue contains complete edges. For a given vertex d, if a shorter edge is discovered, we do not remove the entry containing the longer edge from the priority queue. We merely insert new edges as they are discovered. Therefore, when the next shortest edge is removed from the priority queue, it may have a destination that is no longer in *V–S*. In that case, we continue to remove edges from the priority queue until we find one with a destination that is still in *V–S*. This is done with the following loop:

```
do {
    edge = (Edge) pQ.remove();
    dest = new Integer(edge.getDest());
} while(!vMinusS.contains(dest));
```

LISTING 12.8
Prim's Minimum Spanning Tree Algorithm

```
/** Prim's Minimum Spanning Tree algorithm.
    @param graph The weighted graph to be searched
    @param start The start vertex
    @return An ArrayList of edges that forms the MST
*/
public static ArrayList primsAlgorithm(Graph graph,
                                       int start) {
    ArrayList result = new ArrayList();
    int numV = graph.getNumV();
    // Use a HashSet to represent V–S.
    Set vMinusS = new HashSet(numV);
    // Declare the priority queue.
    PriorityQueue pQ =
        new HeapPQwithComparator(new CompareEdges());
    // Initialize V–S.
    for (int i = 0; i < numV; i++) {
        if (i != start) {
            vMinusS.add(new Integer(i));
        }
    }
    int current = start;
    // Main loop
    while (vMinusS.size() != 0) {
        // Update priority queue.
        Graph.EdgeIterator iter = graph.edgeIterator(current);
        while (iter.hasNext()) {
            Edge edge = iter.next();
            Integer dest = new Integer(edge.getDest());
            if (vMinusS.contains(dest)) {
                pQ.insert(edge);
            }
        }
        // Find the shortest edge whose source is in S and
        // destination is in V–S.
        Integer dest = null;
        Edge edge = null;
        do {
            edge = (Edge) pQ.remove();
            dest = new Integer(edge.getDest());
        } while(!vMinusS.contains(dest));
        // Take dest out of vMinusS.
        vMinusS.remove(dest);
        // Add edge to result.
        result.add(edge);
```

```
    // Make this the current vertex.
    current = dest.intValue();
  }
  return result;
}
```

EXERCISES FOR SECTION 12.6

SELF-CHECK

1. Trace the execution of Dijkstra's algorithm to find the shortest path from Philadelphia to the other cities shown in the following graph.

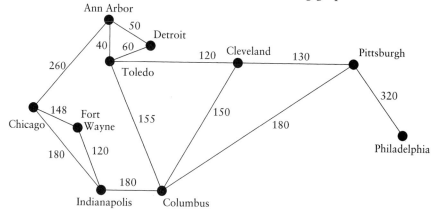

2. Trace the execution of Dijkstra's algorithm to find the shortest paths from vertex 0 to the other vertices in the following graph.

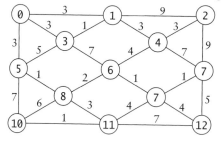

3. Trace the execution of Prim's algorithm to find the minimum spanning tree for the graph shown in Question 2.

4. Trace the execution of Prim's algorithm to find the minimum spanning tree for the graph shown in Question 1.

Chapter Review

◆ A graph consists of a set of vertices and a set of edges. An edge is a pair of vertices. Graphs may be either undirected or directed. Edges may have a value associated with them known as the weight.

◆ In an undirected graph, if $\{u, v\}$ is an edge, then there is a path from vertex u to vertex v, and vice versa.

◆ In a directed graph, if (u, v) is an edge, then (v, u) is not necessarily an edge.

◆ If there is an edge from one vertex to another, then the second vertex is adjacent to the first. A path is a sequence of adjacent vertices. A path is simple if the vertices in the path are distinct except, perhaps, for the first and last vertex, which may be the same. A cycle is a path in which the first and last vertexes are the same.

◆ A graph is considered connected if there is a path from each vertex to every other vertex.

◆ A tree is a special case of a graph. Specifically, a tree is a connected graph that contains no cycles.

◆ Graphs may be represented by an array of adjacency lists. There is one list for each vertex, and the list contains the edges that originate at this vertex.

◆ Graphs may be represented by a two-dimensional square array called an adjacency matrix. The entry $[u][v]$ will contain a value to indicate that an edge from u to v is present or absent.

◆ A breadth-first search of a graph finds all vertices reachable from a given vertex via the shortest path, where the length of the path is based on the number of vertices in the path.

◆ A depth-first search of a graph starts at a given vertex and then follows a path of unvisited vertices until it reaches a point where there are no unvisited vertices that are reachable. It then backtracks until it finds an unvisited vertex, and then continues along the path to that vertex.

◆ A topological sort determines an order for starting activities which are dependent on the completion of other activities (prerequisites). The finish order derived from a depth-first traversal represents a topological sort.

◆ Dijkstra's algorithm finds the shortest path from a start vertex to all other vertices, where the distance from one vertex to another is determined by the weight of the edge between them.

◆ Prim's algorithm finds the minimum spanning tree for a graph. This consists of the subset of the edges of a connected graph whose sum of weights is the minimum and the graph consisting of only the edges in the subset is still connected.

User-Defined Classes and Interfaces in This Chapter

Graph
Graph.EdgeIterator
Edge
AbstractGraph
ListGraph

MatrixGraph
BreadthFirstSearch
DepthFirstSearch
Maze
TopologicalSort

Quick-Check Exercises

1. For the following graph:
   a. List the vertices and edges.
   b. True or false: The path 0, 1, 4, 6, 3 is a simple path.
   c. True or false: The path 0, 3, 1, 4, 6, 3, 2 is a simple path.
   d. True or false: The path 3, 1, 2, 4, 7, 6, 3 is a cycle.

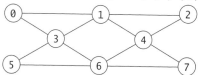

2. Identify the connected components in the following graph.

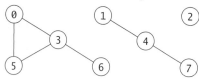

3. For the following graph
   a. List the vertices and edges.
   b. Does this graph contain any cycles?

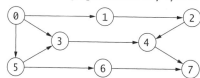

4. Show the adjacency matrices for the graphs shown in Questions 1, 2, and 3.
5. Show the adjacency lists for the graphs shown in Questions 1, 2, and 3.
6. Show the breadth-first search tree for the graph shown in Question 1, starting at vertex 0.
7. Show the depth-first search tree for the graph shown in Question 3, starting at vertex 0.
8. Show a topological sort of the vertices in the graph shown in Question 3.
9. In the following graph, find the shortest path from 0 to all other vertices.

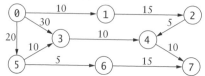

10. In the following graph, find the minimum spanning tree.

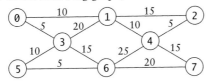

Answers to Quick-Check Exercises

1. a. Vertices: {0, 1, 2, 3, 4, 5, 6, 7}. Edges: {{0, 1}, {0, 3}, {1, 2}, {1, 3}, {1, 4}, {2, 4}, {3, 5}, {3, 6}, {4, 6}, {4, 7}, {5, 6}, {6, 7}}.

   b. True.

   c. False.

   d. True.

2. The connected components are {0, 3, 5, 6}, {1, 4, 7}, and {2}.

3. a. Vertices: {0, 1, 2, 3, 4, 5, 6, 7}. Edges: {(0, 1), (0, 3), (0, 5), (1, 2), (2, 4), (3, 4), (4, 7), (5, 3), (5, 6), (6, 7)}.

   b. The graph contains no cycles.

4. For the graph shown in Question 1:

Column

	[0]	[1]	[2]	[3]	[4]	[5]	[6]	[7]
[0]		1		1				
[1]	1		1	1	1			
[2]		1			1			
[3]	1	1				1	1	
[4]		1	1				1	1
[5]				1			1	
[6]				1	1	1		1
[7]					1		1	

Row

For Question 2:

Column

	[0]	[1]	[2]	[3]	[4]	[5]	[6]	[7]
[0]				1		1		
[1]					1			
[2]								
[3]	1					1	1	
[4]		1						1
[5]	1			1				
[6]				1				
[7]				1				

Row

For Question 3:

Column

	[0]	[1]	[2]	[3]	[4]	[5]	[6]	[7]
[0]		1		1		1		
[1]			1					
[2]				1				
[3]				1				
[4]								1
[5]			1			1		
[6]								1
[7]								

(Row)

5. For Question 1:

```
[0]  →  1 → 3
[1]  →  0 → 2 → 3 → 4
[2]  →  1 → 4
[3]  →  0 → 1 → 5 → 6
[4]  →  1 → 2 → 6 → 7
[5]  →  3 → 6
[6]  →  3 → 4 → 5 → 7
[7]  →  4 → 6
```

For Question 2:

```
[0]  →  3 → 5
[1]  →  4
[2]  →
[3]  →  0 → 5 → 6
[4]  →  1 → 7
[5]  →  0 → 3
[6]  →  3
[7]  →  4
```

For Question 3:

```
[0]  →  1 → 3 → 5
[1]  →  2
[2]  →  4
[3]  →  4
[4]  →  7
[5]  →  3 → 6
[6]  →  7
[7]  →
```

6.

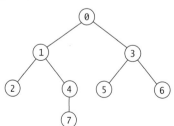

7.

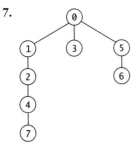

8. 0, 5, 6, 3, 1, 2, 4, 7.

9.

Vertex	Distance	Path
1	10	$0 \rightarrow 1$
2	25	$0 \rightarrow 1 \rightarrow 2$
3	30	$0 \rightarrow 3$ (or $0 \rightarrow 5 \rightarrow 3$)
4	30	$0 \rightarrow 1 \rightarrow 2 \rightarrow 4$
5	20	$0 \rightarrow 5$
6	25	$0 \rightarrow 5 \rightarrow 6$
7	40	$0 \rightarrow 5 \rightarrow 6 \rightarrow 7$ (or $0 \rightarrow 1 \rightarrow 2 \rightarrow 4 \rightarrow 7$)

10.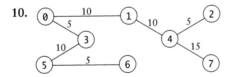

Review Questions

1. What are the different types of graphs?
2. What are the different types of paths?
3. What are two common methods for representing graphs? Can you think of other methods?
4. What is a breadth-first search? What can it be used for?
5. What is a depth-first search? What can it be used for?
6. Under what circumstances are the paths found by Dijkstra's algorithm not unique?
7. Under what circumstances is the minimum spanning tree unique?
8. What is a topological sort?

Programming Projects

1. Design and implement the MatrixGraph class.
2. Rewrite method dijkstrasAlgorithm to use a priority queue as we did for method primsAlgorithm. When inserting edges into the priority queue, the weight is replaced by the total distance from the source vertex to the destination vertex. The source vertex, however, remains unchanged as it is the predecessor in the shortest path.

3. In both Prim's algorithm and Dijkstra's algorithm, edges are retained in the priority queue even though a shorter edge to a given destination vertex has been found. This can be avoided, and thus performance improved, by using a `ModifiablePriorityQueue`. Modify the heap-based priority queue class described in Chapter 8 to implement the `ModifiablePriorityQueue` interface, shown as follows:

```
/** A ModifiablePriorityQueue stores Comparable objects. Items
    may be inserted in any order. They are removed in priority
    order, with the smallest being removed first, based on the
    compareTo method. The insert method will return a value
    known as a locator. The locator may be used to replace a
    value in the priority queue.
*/

public interface ModifiablePriorityQueue {
    /** Insert an item into the priority queue.
        @param obj The item to be inserted
        @return A locator to the item
    */
    int insert(Comparable obj);

    /** Remove the smallest item in the priority queue.
        @return The smallest item in the priority queue
    */
    Comparable remove();

    /** Replace the item at the specified location.

        @param loc The locator value of the current item
        @param newValue The new value
    */
    void replaceItem(int loc, Object newValue);
```

4. Implement Dijkstra's algorithm using the `ModifiablePriorityQueue`.
5. Implement Prim's algorithm using the `ModifiablePriortyQueue`.
6. A maze can be constructed from a series of concentric circles. Between the circles there are walls placed, and around the circles there are doors. The walls divide the areas between the circles into chambers, and the doors permit movement between chambers. The positions of the doors and walls are given in degrees measured counterclockwise from the horizontal. For example, the maze shown in the figure can be described as follows:

Number of circles	4	
Position of doors	Outer circle	85–90
	Next inner circle	26–40, 135–146, 198–215, 305–319
	Next inner circle	67–90, 161–180, 243–256, 342–360
	Innermost circle	251–288
Position of walls:	Outer ring	45, 135, 300
	Middle ring	0, 100, 225, 270
	Inner ring	65, 180

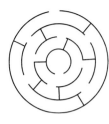

Write a program that inputs a description of a maze in this format and finds the shortest path from the outside to the innermost circle. The shortest path is the one that goes through the fewest number of chambers.

7. In Chapter 7 we discussed the class MazeTest, which reads a rectangular maze as a sequence of lines consisting of 0s and 1s, where a 0 represents an open square and a 1 represents a closed one. For example, the maze shown in Figure 12.21 and reproduced here, has the following input file:

```
0111111111111111111111111
0000000000000000000000001
0111111111111110111111101
0111110000000101011111101
0111111011111110011000001
0000000000000000011011011
1101111011011110110110011
1101111011011110110110011
1101111011010000011011011
1101111011011111111011011
1101111011100000000011011
1100000011011111111111011
1111011111000000000001011
1111011111111111111101000
1111000000000000000001110
1111111111111111111111110
```

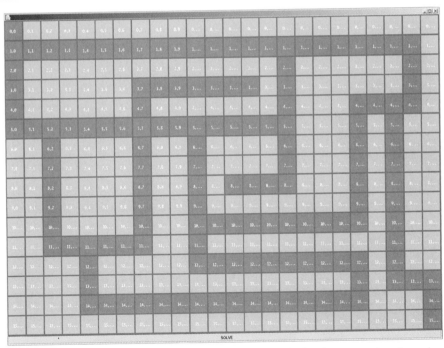

Write a program that reads input in this format and finds the shortest path, where the distance along a path is defined by the number of squares covered.

8. A third possible representation of a graph is to use the TreeSet class to contain the edges. By defining a comparator that first compares on the source vertex and then the destination vertex, we can use the subSet method to create a view that contains only edges originating at a specified vertex and then use the iterator of that view to iterate through edges. Design and implement a class that meets the requirements of the Graph interface and uses a TreeSet to hold the edges.

Introduction to Java

This chapter reviews object-oriented programming in Java. It is oriented to a student who has had a first course in programming in Java or another language and who, therefore, is familiar with control statements for selection and repetition, basic data types, arrays, and methods or functions. If your first course was in Java, you can skim this chapter for review or just use it as a reference as needed. However, you should read it more carefully if your Java course did not emphasize object-oriented design.

If your first course was not in Java, you should read this chapter carefully. If your first course followed an object-oriented approach but was in another language, you should concentrate on the differences between Java syntax and the language that you know. If you have programmed only in a language that was not object-oriented, you will need to concentrate on aspects of object-oriented programming and classes as well as Java syntax.

The chapter begins with an introduction to the Java environment and the Java Virtual Machine (JVM). Next it covers the basic data types of Java, called primitive data types, and provides an introduction to objects and classes. Control structures and methods are then discussed.

The Java Application Programmers Interface (API) provides a rich collection of classes that simplify programming in Java. The first Java classes that we cover are the `String`, `StringBuffer`, and `Math` classes. The `String` class provides several methods and an operator + (concatenation) that process sequences of characters (strings). The `Math` class provides many methods for performing standard mathematical computations.

Next we show you how to design and write your own classes consisting of data fields and methods. We also discuss the Java wrapper classes, which enable a programmer to create and process objects that contain primitive-type values.

We describe a specific format for comments in classes. Using this commenting style enables you to generate HTML pages with clear and complete documentation for classes in the same form as the Java documentation provided on the Sun Web site.

We also review array objects in Java. We cover both one- and two-dimensional arrays.

Finally we discuss input/output. We show how to use the `JOptionPane` class (part of package `javax.swing`) to create dialog windows for data entry and for output. We also show how to use streams and the console for input/output.

Introduction to Java

A.1 The Java Environment and Classes
A.2 Primitive Data Types and Reference Variables
A.3 Java Control Statements
A.4 Methods and Class `Math`
A.5 The `String`, `StringBuffer`, and `StringTokenizer` Classes
A.6 Wrapper Classes for Primitive Types
A.7 Defining Your Own Classes
A.8 Arrays
A.9 Input/Output Using Class `JOptionPane`
A.10 Input/Output Using Streams

A.1 The Java Environment and Classes

Before we talk about the Java language, we will briefly discuss the Java environment and how Java programs are executed. Java, developed by Sun Microsystems Corporation, enjoys its popularity because it is a platform-independent, object-oriented language and because certain kinds of Java programs, called *applets,* can be embedded in Web pages. Being platform independent means that a Java program

FIGURE A.1
Compiling and
Executing a
Java Program

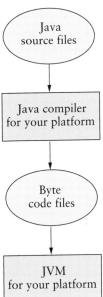

will run on any kind of computer. Although platform independence is a goal for all high-level language programs, it is not always achieved. Java comes closer to achieving this goal than most by providing implementations of the Java Virtual Machine (discussed next) for many platforms.

The Java Virtual Machine

Java is platform independent because the Java designers utilize the concept of a Java Virtual Machine (JVM), which is a software "computer" that runs inside an actual computer. Before you can execute a Java program, the classes in the Java program must first be translated from the Java language in which they were written into an executable form in the traditional way by a compiler program. Instead of a file of platform-dependent machine-language instructions, however, which is the normal output from a compiler, the Java compiler generates a file of platform-independent Java *byte code* instructions. When you execute the program, your computer's JVM *interprets* each byte code instruction and carries it out. The JVM for machines running Microsoft Windows is different from the JVM for UNIX or Apple machines, but they all process byte code instructions in the same way (see Figure A.1).

The Java Compiler

The Java compiler is also platform specific even though it produces the same byte code file for a given Java source program on all platforms. It must be platform specific because it executes machine language instructions for a particular platform, and these instructions are not the same for all platforms.

Classes and Objects

In Java and object-oriented programming in general, the class is the fundamental programming unit. Every program is written as a collection of classes, and all code that you write must be part of a class. In Java, class definitions are stored in separate files with the extension .java; the file name must be the same as the class name defined within.

A *class* is a named description for a group of entities (called *objects* or *instances* of the class) that have the same characteristics. These characteristics are the attributes (*data fields*) for each object and the operations (*methods*) that can be performed on these objects.

If you are new to object-oriented design, you may be confused about the differences between a class and an object. A class is a general description of a group of entities that all have the same characteristics—that is, they can all perform the same kinds of actions, and the same pieces of information are meaningful for all of them. The individual entities are objects. For example, the class House would describe a collection of entities that each have a number of bedrooms, a number of bathrooms, a kind of roof, and so on (but not a horsepower rating or mileage); they can all be built, remodeled, assessed for property tax, and so on (but not have their transmission fluid changed). The house where you live and the house where your best friend lives can be represented by two objects of class House.

Classes extend Java by providing additional data types. For example, the class
String is a predefined class that enables the programmer to process sequences of
characters easily. We will discuss the String class in detail in Section A.5.

The Java API

The Java programming language consists of a relatively small core language aug-
mented by an extensive collection of *packages* (called libraries in other languages),
which constitute the Java application programming interface (API) and give Java
additional capabilities. Each package contains a collection of related Java classes.
We will use several of these packages in this textbook. Among them are the Swing
package, the AWT package, and the util package. You can find out about these
packages by accessing the Java Web site maintained by Sun Microsystems at
http://java.sun.com.

Java documentation is provided as a linked collection of Web pages. In Section A.7,
we will discuss how you can write your own Java documentation that follows this
style.

The import Statement

Next, we show a sample Java source file (HelloWorld.java) that contains an application program (class HelloWorld). Our goal in the rest of this section is to give you
an overview of the process of creating and executing an application program. The
statements in this program will be covered in more detail later in this chapter.

```
import javax.swing.*;

public class HelloWorld {
    public static void main(String[] args) {
        String name = JOptionPane.showInputDialog("Enter your name");
        JOptionPane.showMessageDialog(null, "Hello " + name"
                                      + ", welcome to Java!");
    }
}
```

The Java source file begins with the statement

```
import javax.swing.*;
```

This statement tells the Java compiler to make the names defined in the Swing package accessible to this file. The semicolon at the end of the line is used to terminate
a Java statement.

Class HelloWorld begins with the line

```
public class HelloWorld {
```

which identifies HelloWorld as a public class and makes it visible to other classes (or
the JVM).

Method main

The line

```
public static void main(String[] args) {
```

identifies the start of the definition for method `main`. This is the place where the JVM begins the execution of an application program. The words **public static void** tell the compiler that `main` is accessible outside of the class (**public**), it is a **static** method (explained in Section A.4), and it does not return a value (**void**). The part in parentheses after `main` describes the method's parameters, an array of `Strings`. We always write the heading for method `main` in this way.

Method `main` contains two statements that call methods in class `JOptionPane`, a class in Swing that displays dialog windows (Section A.9). The statement

```
String name = JOptionPane.showInputDialog("Enter your name");
```

displays the following dialog window. The user has typed in the characters `Katherine`.

The characters typed in by the user are stored in a memory cell referenced by the variable `name`. Later, they may be displayed in a message window by the following statement, which is written on two lines. The message window follows the statement.

```
JOptionPane.showMessageDialog(null, "Hello " + name
                                   + ", welcome to Java!");
```

Execution of a Java Program

You can compile and run class `HelloWorld` using an Integrated Development Environment (IDE) or the Java Development Kit (JDK). If you are using an IDE, type this class into the edit window for class `HelloWorld.java` and select **Run**. If you are not using an IDE, you must create this file using an editor program and save it as file `HelloWorld.java`. Then you can use the command

```
javac HelloWorld.java
```

to get the Java compiler to compile it. This will create the Java byte code file called `HelloWorld.class`.

The command

```
java HelloWorld
```

starts the JVM and causes it to execute the byte code instructions in file `Hello World.class`. It begins execution with the byte code instructions for method `main`.

EXERCISES FOR SECTION A.1

SELF-CHECK

1. What is the Java Virtual Machine? Is it hardware or software? How does its role differ from that of the Java compiler?
2. Explain the statement: You can write a Java program once and run it anywhere.
3. Explain the relationship between a class and an object. Which is general and which is specific?

A.2 Primitive Data Types and Reference Variables

Java distinguishes between two kinds of entities: primitive types (numbers, characters) and objects. Values associated with primitive-type data are stored in primitive-type variables. Objects, on the other hand, are associated with reference variables, which store an object's address. We will discuss primitive types and introduce objects in this section; we describe objects in more detail throughout the chapter.

Primitive Data Types

The primitive data types for Java represent numbers, characters, and Boolean values (**true, false**) (see Table A.1). Integers are represented by data types **byte**, **short**, **int**, and **long**; real numbers are represented by **float** and **double**. The range of values for the data types is in increasing order in Table A.1.

Type **char** is used in Java to represent characters. Java uses the Unicode character set (two bytes per character), which provides a much richer set of characters than the ASCII character set (one byte per character) used by many earlier languages. Table A.2 shows the first 128 Unicode characters, which correspond to the ASCII characters. These include the control characters and the Basic Latin alphabet. The

TABLE A.1

Java Primitive Data Types in Increasing Order of Range

Data Type	Range of Values
byte	−128 through 127
short	−32,768 through 32,767
int	−2,147,483,648 through 2,147,483,647
long	−9,223,372,036,854,775,808 through 9,223,372,036,854,775,807
float	Approximately $\pm 10^{-38}$ through $\pm 10^{38}$ and 0 with 6 digits precision
double	Approximately $\pm 10^{-308}$ through $\pm 10^{308}$ and 0 with 15 digits precision
char	The Unicode character set
boolean	true, false

TABLE A.2
The First 128 Unicode Symbols

	000	001	002	003	004	005	006	007
0	Null		Space	0	@	P	`	p
1			!	1	A	Q	a	q
2			"	2	B	R	b	r
3			#	3	C	S	c	s
4			$	4	D	T	d	t
5			%	5	E	U	e	u
6			&	6	F	V	f	v
7	Bell		'	7	G	W	g	w
8	Backspace		(	8	H	X	h	x
9	Tab		)	9	I	Y	I	y
A	Line feed		*	:	J	Z	j	z
B		Escape	+	;	K	[	k	{
C	Form feed		,	<	L	\	l	|
D	Return		-	=	M	]	m	}
E			.	>	N	^	n	~
F			/	?	O	_	o	delete

Unicode for each character, expressed as a hexadecimal number, consists of the three-digit column number (000 through 007) followed by the row number (0 through F). For example, the Unicode for the letter Q is 0051, and the Unicode for the letter q is 0071. The characters in the first two columns of Table A.2 and the Unicode character 007F (delete) are control characters. The hexadecimal digits A through F are equivalent to the decimal values 10 through 15. The hexadecimal number 007F is equivalent to the decimal number $7 \times 16 + 15$.

Java uses type **boolean** to represent logical data. The **boolean** data type has only two values: **true** and **false**. Some languages allow you to represent type **boolean** values using the integers 0 and 1, but Java does not allow you to do this.

Primitive-Type Variables

Java uses declaration statements to declare and initialize primitive-type variables.

```
int countItems;
double sum = 0.0;
char star = '*';
boolean moreData;
```

The second and third of the preceding statements initialize variables sum and star to the values after the operator =. As shown, you can use primitive-type values (such as 0.0 and '*') as *literals* in Java statements. A literal is a constant value that appears directly in a statement.

Identifiers, such as variable names in Java, must consist of some combination of letters, digits, the underscore character, and the $ character, beginning with a letter. Identifiers can't begin with a digit.

PROGRAM STYLE

Java Convention for Identifiers

Many Java programmers use "camel notation" for variable names. All letters are in lowercase except for identifiers that are made up of more than one word. The first letter of each word, starting with the second word, is in uppercase (for example, thisLongIdentifier). Camel notation gets its name from the appearance of the identifier, with the uppercase letters in the interior forming "humps."

Primitive-Type Constants

Java programmers usually use all uppercase letters for constant identifiers, with an underscore symbol between words. The keywords **static final** identify a constant value that is **static** (more on this later) and **final**—that is, can't be changed.

```
static final int MAX_SCORE = 999;
static final double G = 3.82;
```

Operators

Table A.3 shows the Java operators in decreasing precedence. We will not use any of the bitwise operators, shifting operators, or conditional operator. The arithmetic operators (*, /, +, -) can be used with any of the primitive numeric types or type **char**, but not with type **boolean**. This is also the case for the Java remainder operator (%) and the increment (++) and decrement (--) operators.

Postfix and Prefix Increment

In Java you can write statements such as

```
i = i + 1;
```

using the *increment operator:*

```
i++;
```

This form is the *postfix increment.* You can also use the *prefix increment*

```
++i;
```

but the postfix increment (or decrement) is more common.

Operator Precedence

Rank	Operator	Operation	Associativity
1	[]	Array subscript	Left
	()	Method call	
	.	Member access	
2	++	Pre- or postfix increment	Right
	--	Pre- or postfix decrement	
	+ -	Unary plus or minus	
	!	Complement	
	~	Bitwise complement	
	(*type*)	Type cast	
	new	Object creation	
3	*, /, %	Multiply, divide, remainder	Left
4	+	Addition or string concatenation	Left
	-	Subtraction	
5	<<	Signed bit shift left	Left
	>>	Signed bit shift right	
	>>>	Unsigned bit shift right	
6	<, <=	Less than, less than or equal	Left
	>, >=	Greater than, greater than or equal	
	instanceof	Reference test	
7	==	Not equal to	Left
	!=	Equal to	
8	&	Bitwise and	Left
9	^	Bitwise exclusive or	Left
10	|	Bitwise or	Left
11	&&	Logical and	Left
12	||	Logical or	Left
13	?:	Conditional	Left
14	=	Assignment	Right
	*=, /=, %=, +=, -=, <<=, >>=, >>>=, &=, |=	Compound assignment	

When the postfix form is used in an expression (for example, x * i++), the variable i is evaluated and then incremented. When the prefix form is used in an expression (for example, x * ++i), the variable i is incremented before it is evaluated.

EXAMPLE A.1   In the assignment

    z = i++;

i is incremented, but z gets the value i had before it was incremented. So if i is 3 before the assignment statement, z would be 3 and i would be 4 after the assignment. In the assignment statement

    z = ++i;

i is incremented and z gets its new value, so if i is 3 before the assignment, z and i would both be 4 after the assignment statement.

 PITFALL

Using Increment and Decrement in Expressions with Other Operators

In the preceding example, the increment operator is used with the assignment operator in the same statement. Similarly, the expression x * i++ uses the multiplication and postfix increment operators. In this expression, the variable i is evaluated and then incremented. When the prefix form is used in an expression (for example, x * ++i), the variable i is incremented before it is evaluated. However, you should avoid writing expressions like these, which could easily be interpreted incorrectly by the human reader.

Type Compatibility and Conversion

In operations involving mixed-type operands, the numeric type of the smaller range is converted to the numeric type of the larger range. This means that if an operation involves a type **int** and a type **double** operand, the type **int** operand is automatically converted to type **double**. This is called a *widening conversion*.

In an assignment operation, a numeric type of a smaller range can be assigned to a numeric type of a larger range; for example, a type **int** expression can be assigned to a type **float** or **double** variable. Java performs the widening conversion automatically.

```
int item = . . .;
double realItem = item;    // Valid - automatic widening
```

However, the converse is not true.

```
double y = . . . ;
int x = y;   // Invalid assignment
```

This statement is invalid because it attempts to store a real value in an integer variable. It would cause the syntax error possible loss of precision; double, required: int. This means that a type **int** expression is required for the assignment. You can use explicit *type cast* operations to perform a *narrowing conversion* and ensure that the assignment statement will be valid. In the following statement, the expression (int) instructs the compiler to cast the value of y to type **int** before assigning the integer value to x.

```
int x = (int) y;    // Cast to int before assignment
```

Referencing Objects

In Java, you can declare reference variables that can reference objects of specified types. For example, the statement

```
String greeting;
```

declares a reference variable named greeting that can reference a String object. The statement

```
greeting = "hello";
```

specifies the particular String object to be referenced by greeting: the one that contains the characters in the string literal "hello". What is actually stored in the memory cell allocated to greeting is the *address* of the area in memory where this particular object of type String is stored. We illustrate this in Figure A.2 by drawing an arrow from variable greeting to the object that it references (type String, value is "hello"). In contrast, the memory cell allocated to a primitive-type variable stores a value, not an address. Just as with the primitive variable declarations shown earlier, these two statements can be combined into one.

```
String greeting = "hello";
```

String objects are the only ones that can be created by assignment operations such as this one. We describe how to create other kinds of objects in the next section.

Two reference variables can reference the same object. The statement

```
String welcome = greeting;
```

copies the address in greeting to welcome, so String variable welcome also references the object shown in Figure A.2.

Creating Objects

The Java **new** *operator* can be used to create an instance of a class. The expression

```
new String("qwerty")
```

creates a new String instance (object) that stores the character sequence consisting of the first six characters of the top row of letters on the standard keyboard (called a "qwerty" keyboard). The expression new String("qwerty") invokes a special method for the String class called a *constructor*. A constructor executes whenever

FIGURE A.2
Variable greeting
References a String
Object

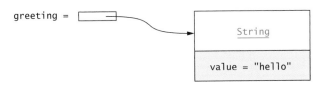

a new object of any type is created; in this case, it initializes the contents of a String object to the character sequence "qwerty".

The object created by the expression new String("qwerty") is an *anonymous* or unnamed object. Normally we want to be able to refer to objects that we create. We can declare a reference variable of type String and assign this object to the reference variable:

```
String keyboard = new String("qwerty");
```

EXERCISES FOR SECTION A.2

SELF-CHECK

1. For the following assignment statement, assume that x, y are type **double** and m, n are type **int**. List the order in which the operations would be performed. Include any widening and narrowing conversions that would occur.
   ```
   m = (int) (x * y + m / n / y * (m + x));
   ```

2. What is the value assigned to m in Exercise 1 when m is 5, n is 3, x is 2.5, and y is 2.0?

3. What is the difference between a reference variable and a primitive-type variable?

4. Draw a diagram similar to Figure A.2 that shows the effect of the following statements.
   ```
   String y = new String("abc");
   String z = "def";
   String w = z;
   ```

A.3 Java Control Statements

The control statements of a programming language determine the flow of execution through a program. They fall into three categories: sequence, selection, and repetition.

Sequence and Compound Statements

A group of statements that is executed in sequence is written as a *compound statement* delimited (enclosed) by braces. The statements execute in the order in which they are listed.

EXAMPLE A.2   The following statements constitute a compound statement:

```
{
    double x = 3.45;
    double y = 2 * x;
    int i = (int) y;
    i++;
}
```

Selection and Repetition Control

Table A.4 shows the Java control statements for selection and repetition. (Java uses the same syntax for control structures as do C and C++.) We assume that you are familiar with basic programming control structures from your first course, so we won't dwell on them here.

In Table A.3, each *condition* is a **boolean** expression in parentheses. Type **boolean** expressions often involve comparisons written using equality (==, !=) and relational operators (<, <=, >, >=). For example, the condition (x + y > x – y) is true if the sum of the two variables shown is larger than their difference. The logical operators ! (not, or complement), && (and), and || (or) are used to combine **boolean** expressions. For example, the condition (n >= 0 && n <= 10) is true if n has a value between zero and 10, inclusive.

Java uses short-circuit evaluation, which means that evaluation of a **boolean** expression terminates when its value can be determined. For example, if in the expression *bool1* || *bool2*, *bool1* is true, the expression must be true, so *bool2* is not evaluated. Similarly, in the expression *bool3* && *bool4*, if *bool3* is false, the expression must be false, so *bool4* is not evaluated.

TABLE A.4
Java Control Statements

Control Structure	Purpose	Syntax

if ... else	Used to write a decision with *conditions* that select the alternative to be executed. Executes the first (second) alternative if the *condition* is true (false).	`if (condition) {`
		`   ...`
		`} else {`
		`   ...`
		`}`

switch	Used to write a decision with scalar values (integers, characters) that select the alternative to be executed. Executes the *statements* following the *label* that is the *selector* value. Execution falls through to the next **case** if there is no **return** or **break**. Executes the statements following **default** if the *selector* value does not match any *label*.	`switch (selector) {`
		`   case label : statements; break;`
		`   case label : statements; break;`
		`   ...`
		`   default : statements;`
		`}`

while	Used to write a loop that specifies the repetition *condition* in the loop header. The *condition* is tested before each iteration of the loop and, if it is true, the loop body executes; otherwise, the loop is exited.	`while (condition) {`
		`   ...`
		`}`

for	Used to write a loop that specifies the *initialization*, repetition *condition*, and *update* steps in the loop header. The *initialization* statements execute before loop repetition begins; the *condition* is tested before each iteration of the loop and, if it is true, the loop body executes; otherwise, the loop is exited. The *update* statements execute after each iteration.	`for (initialization; condition; update) {`
		`   ...`
		`}`

TABLE A.4 (continued)

Control Structure	Purpose	Syntax
do ... while	Used to write a loop that specifies the repetition *condition* after the loop body. The *condition* is tested after each iteration of the loop and, if it is true, the loop body is repeated; otherwise, the loop is exited. The loop body always executes at least one time.	```do { ... { while (condition) ;```

EXAMPLE A.3   In the condition

```
(num != 0 && sum / num)
```

if num is 0, the expression following && is not evaluated. This prevents a division by zero.

EXAMPLE A.4   The operator % in the condition (nextInt % 2 == 0) gives the remainder after an integer division, so the condition is true if nextInt is an even number. If maxVal has been defined, the following loops (**for** loop on the left, **while** loop on the right) store the sum of the even integers from 1 to maxVal in variable sum (initial value 0) and they store the product of the odd integers in variable prod (initial value 1).

```
for (int nextInt = 1;          int nextInt = 1;
        nextInt <= maxVal;      while (nextInt <= maxVal) {
        nextInt++) {                if (nextInt % 2 == 0) {
    if (nextInt % 2 == 0) {             sum += nextInt;
        sum += nextInt;             } else {
    } else {                            prod *= nextInt;
        prod *= nextInt;            }
    }                               nextInt++
}                               }
```

PROGRAM STYLE

Braces and Indentation in Control Statements

Java programmers often place the opening brace { on the same line as the control statement header. The closing brace } aligns with the first word in the control statement header. We will always indent the statements inside a control structure to clarify the meaning of the control statement.

Although we write the symbols } **else** { on one line, another popular style convention is to place the word **else** under the symbol } and aligned with **if**:

```
if (nextInt % 2 == 0) {
    sum += nextInt;
}
```

```
    else {
        prod *= nextInt;
    }
```
Some programmers omit the braces when a true task or false task or a loop body consists of a single statement. Others prefer to include them always, both for clarity and because having the braces will permit them to insert additional statements later if needed.

Nested if Statements

You can write **if** statements that select among more than two alternatives by nesting one **if** statement inside another. Often each inner **if** statement will follow the keyword **else** of its corresponding outer **if** statement.

EXAMPLE A.5   The following nested **if** statement has four alternatives. The conditions are evaluated in sequence until one evaluates to **true**. The compound statement following the first true condition then executes.

```
if (operator == '+') {
    result = x + y;
    addOp++;
}
else
    if (operator == '-') {
        result = x - y;
        subtractOp++;
    }
    else
        if (operator == '*') {
            result = x * y;
            multiplyOp++;
        }
        else
            if (operator == '/') {
                result = x / y;
                divideOp++;
            }
```

 PITFALL

Omitting Braces Around a Compound Statement

The braces in the preceding example delimit compound statements. Each compound statement consists of two statements. If you omit a brace, you will get the syntax error 'else' without 'if'.

PROGRAM STYLE

Writing if Statements with Multiple Alternatives

Java programmers often write nested **if** statements like those in the preceding example without indenting each nested **if**. The following multiple-alternative decision has the same meaning but is easier to write and read.

```java
if (operator == '+') {
    result = x + y;
    addOp++;
} else if (operator == '-') {
    result = x - y;
    subtractOp++;
} else if (operator == '*') {
    result = x * y;
    multiplyOp++;
} else if (operator == '/') {
    result = x / y;
    divideOp++;
}
```

The switch Statement

The **if** statement in Example A.5 could also be written as the following **switch** statement. Each **case** label (for example, '+') indicates a possible value of the selector expression operator. The statements that follow a particular label execute if the selector has that value. The **break** statements cause an exit from the **switch** statement. Without them, execution would continue on to the statements in the next case. The last case, with label default, executes if the selector value doesn't match any case label. (Note that the compound statements for each case are not surrounded by braces.)

```java
switch (operator) {
    case '+':
        result = x + y;
        addOp++;
        break;
    case '-':
        result = x - y;
        subtractOp++;
        break;
    case '*':
        result = x * y;
        multiplyOp++;
        break;
    case '/':
        result = x / y;
        divideOp++;
        break;
    default:
        // Do nothing
}
```

EXERCISES FOR SECTION A.3

SELF-CHECK

1. What is the purpose of the **break** statement in the preceding **switch** statement? List the statements that would execute when operator is '-' with the **break** statements in place and if they were removed.
2. What is the difference between a **while** loop and a **do ... while** loop? What is the minimum number of repetitions of the loop body you can have with each kind of loop?

PROGRAMMING

1. Rewrite the **for** statement in Example A.4 using a **do ... while** loop.

A.4 Methods and Class Math

Java programmers can use methods to define a group of statements that perform a particular operation. Methods are very similar to functions in other programming languages such as C and C++. The Java method minChar that follows returns the character with the smaller Unicode value. The statements beginning with keyword **return** cause an exit from the method; the expression following **return** is the method result.

```
static char minChar(char ch1, char ch2) {
    if (ch1 <= ch2)
        return ch1;
    else
        return ch2;
}
```

The modifier **static** indicates that minChar is a *static method* or *class method*. A static method must be called by listing the name of the class in which it is defined, followed by a dot, followed by the method name and any arguments. This is called *dot notation*. For example, the statement

```
char ch = ClassName.minChar('a', 'A');
```

would store the letter A in ch because uppercase letters have smaller codes than lowercase letters. (If method minChar is called within the class that defines it, the prefix *ClassName.* is not needed.) If the modifier **static** does not appear in a method header, the method is an *instance method*. We describe how to invoke instance methods next and show how to define them afterwards.

The Instance Methods println and print

Methods that are not preceded by the modifier **static** are instance methods. To call or invoke an instance method, you need to apply it to an object using dot notation:

object.method(arguments)

One instance method that is useful for output operations is the method `println` (defined in class `PrintStream`). It can be applied to the `PrintStream` object `System.out` (the console window), which is defined in the `System` class. It has a single argument of any data type. If x is a type **double** variable, the statement

```
System.out.println(x);
```

displays the value of x in the console window. The statement

```
System.out.println("Value of x is " + x);
```

has a `String` expression as its argument (+ means concatenate, or join, strings). The string consists of the character sequence `Value of x is` followed by the characters that represent the value of variable x. If x is 123.45, the output line will be

```
Value of x is 123.45
```

You would get the same effect using the statement pair

```
System.out.print("Value of x is ");
System.out.println(x);
```

The method `print` also displays its argument in the console window. However, it does not follow this information with the *newline* character, so the next execution of `print` or `println` will display information on the same output line.

 PITFALL

Static Methods Can't Call Instance Methods

A static method can call other static methods directly. Also, an instance method can call a static method. However, a static method, including method `main`, can't call an instance method without first creating an object and applying the instance method to that object.

Call-by-Value Arguments

In Java, all method arguments are call-by-value. This means that if the argument is a primitive type, its value (not its address) is passed to the method, so the method can't modify the argument value and have the modification remain after return from the method. Some other programming languages provide a call-by-reference or call-by-address mechanism so that a method can modify a primitive-type argument.

If the argument is of a class type, the value that is passed to the method is the value of the reference variable, not the value of the object itself (see Section A.2). The reference variable value points to the object, allowing the method to access the object itself using the methods of the object's own class. Any modification to the object will remain after the return from the method. This will be discussed in Section A.7.

The Class Math

Class Math is part of the Java language, and it provides a collection of methods that are useful for performing common mathematical operations. These are all **static** methods, so the prefix Math. is required in order to invoke a method of this class.

Table A.5 shows some of these methods. The first column shows the result type for each method followed by its *signature* (the method name and the argument types). For example, for method ceil, the first column shows that the method returns a type **double** result and has a type **double** argument. The data type *numeric* means that any of the numeric types can be used.

TABLE A.5
Class Math Methods

Method	Behavior
static *numeric* abs(*numeric*)	Returns the absolute value of its *numeric* argument (the result type is the same as the argument type).
static double ceil(double)	Returns the smallest whole number that is not less than its argument.
static double cos(double)	Returns the trigonometric cosine of its argument (an angle in radians).
static double exp(double)	Returns the exponential number *e* (i.e., 2.718 ...) raised to the power of its argument.
static double floor(double)	Returns the largest whole number that is not greater than its argument.
static double log(double)	Returns the natural logarithm of its argument.
static *numeric* max(*numeric*, *numeric*)	Returns the larger of its *numeric* arguments (the result type is the same as the argument types).
static *numeric* min(*numeric*, *numeric*)	Returns the smaller of its *numeric* arguments (the result type is the same as the argument type).
static double pow(double, double)	Returns the value of the first argument raised to the power of the second argument.
static double random()	Returns a random number greater than or equal to 0.0 and less than 1.0.
static double rint(double)	Returns the closest whole number to its argument.
static long round(double)	Returns the closest **long** to its argument.
static int round(float)	Returns the closest **int** to its argument.
static double sin(double)	Returns the trigonometric sine of its argument (an angle in radians).
static double sqrt(double)	Returns the square root of its argument.
static double tan(double)	Returns the trigonometric tangent of its argument (an angle in radians).
static double toDegrees(double)	Converts its argument (in radians) to degrees.
static double toRadians(double)	Converts its argument (in degrees) to radians.

Escape Sequences

The `main` method in the following `SquareRoots` class contains a loop that displays the first ten integers and their square roots (see Figure A.3).

```
public class SquareRoots {
    public static void main(String[] args) {
        System.out.println("n \tsquare root");
        for (int n = 1; n <= 10; n++) {
            System.out.println(n + "\t" + Math.sqrt(n));
        }
    }
}
```

The `println` statements use the *escape sequence* \t, the tab character, to align the column label "square root" with the numbers in the second output column (see Figure A.3). An escape sequence is a sequence of two characters beginning with the character \. Some escape sequences are used for special output control characters. Others are used to represent characters or symbols that have a special meaning in Java. For example, a double quote character by itself is a string delimiter, so we need to use the sequence \" to represent the double quote character in a string. Table A.6 lists some common escape sequences and their meaning.

The escape sequence that starts with \u represents a Unicode character. The character code uses four hexadecimal digits, where a hexadecimal digit is formed using four binary bits and ranges from 0 (all bits 0) to F (all four bits 1). The hexadecimal digit A corresponds to a decimal value of 10, and the hexadecimal digit F corresponds to a decimal value of 15.

TABLE A.6
Escape Sequences

Sequence	Meaning
\n	Start a new output line
\t	Tab character
\\	Backslash character
\"	Double quote
\'	Single quote or apostrophe
\udddd	The Unicode character whose code is *dddd* where each digit *d* is a hexadecimal digit in the range 0 to F (0–9, A–F)

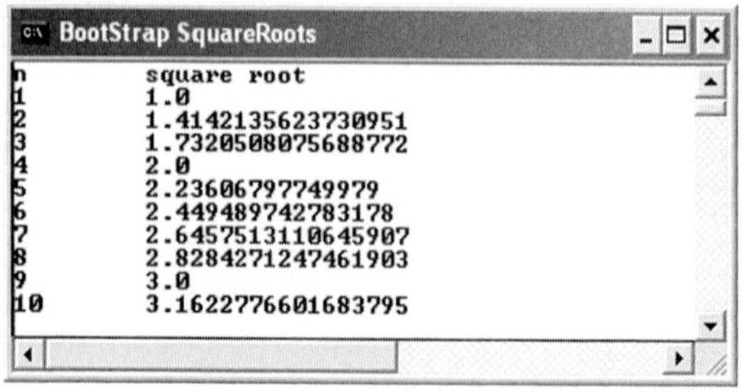

FIGURE A.3
Sample Run of Class
`SquareRoots`

EXERCISES FOR SECTION A.4

SELF-CHECK

1. Identify the escape sequences in the following string. Show how this line would be displayed. Which of the escape sequences could be replaced by the second character of the pair without changing the effect?

```
System.out.println(
    "Jane\'s  motto is \n\"semper fi\"\n, according to Jim");
```

PROGRAMMING

1. Write a Java program that displays all odd powers of 2 between 1 and 29. Display the power that 2 is being raised to, as well as the result, on each line. Use tab characters between numbers.
2. Write a Java program that displays n and the natural log of n for values of n of 1000, 2000, 4000, 8000, and so on. Display the first twenty lines for this sequence. Use tab characters between numbers.

A.5 The String, StringBuffer, and StringTokenizer Classes

In this section we discuss three Java classes that are used to process sequences of characters. We begin with the String class.

The String Class

The String class defines a data type that is used to store a sequence of characters. In this section we describe the Java String class and two related classes: StringBuffer and StringTokenizer.

Table A.7 describes some String class methods. The first column shows the result type for each method followed by its signature. For example, for method charAt, the first column shows that the method returns a type **char** result and has a type **int** argument. The second column describes what the method does. The phrase "this string" means the string to which the method is applied by the dot notation. If type Object is listed as an argument type in column 1, any kind of object can be an argument. (We discuss type Object in Chapter 3.)

Method	Behavior
`char charAt(int pos)`	Returns the character at position `pos`.
`int compareTo(String)`	Returns a negative integer if this string's contents precede the argument string's contents in the dictionary; returns 0 if this string and the argument string have the same contents; returns a positive integer if this string's contents follow those of the argument string. This comparison is case sensitive.
`int compareToIgnoreCase(String)`	Returns a negative, zero, or positive integer according to whether this string's contents precede, match, or follow the argument string's contents in the dictionary, ignoring case.
`boolean equals(Object)`	Returns **true** if this string's contents is the same as its argument string's contents.
`boolean equalsIgnoreCase(String)`	Returns **true** if this string's contents is the same as the argument string's contents, ignoring case.
`int indexOf(char)` `int indexOf(String)`	Returns the index within this string of the first occurrence of its character or string argument, or −1 if the argument is not found.
`int indexOf(char, int index)` `int indexOf(String, int index)`	Returns the index within this string of the first occurrence of its first character or string argument, starting at the specified `index`.
`int lastIndexOf(char)` `int lastIndexOf(String)`	Returns the index within this string of the rightmost occurrence of its character or string argument.
`int lastIndexOf(char, int index)` `int lastIndexOf(String, int index)`	Returns the index within this string of the last occurrence of its first character or string argument, searching backward stopping at the specified `index`.
`int length()`	Returns the length of this string.
`String replace(char oldChar,` `char newChar)`	Returns a new string resulting from replacing all occurrences of `oldChar` in this string with `newChar`.
`String substring(int start)`	Returns a new string that is a substring of this string, starting at position `start` and going to the end of the string.
`String substring(int start,` `int end)`	Returns a new string that is a substring of this string, starting with the character at position `start` and ending with the character at position `end - 1`.
`String toLowerCase()`	Returns a new string in which all of the letters in this string are converted to lowercase.
`String toUpperCase()`	Returns a new string in which all of the letters in this string are converted to uppercase.
`String trim()`	Returns a new string in which all the white space is removed from both ends of this string.

EXAMPLE A.6   Assume that keyboard (type String) contains "qwerty". We evaluate several expressions:

- keyboard.charAt(0) is 'q'.
- keyboard.length() is 6.
- keyboard.indexOf('o') is −1.
- keyboard.indexOf('y') is 5.

The statement

```
String upper = keyboard.toUpperCase();
```

creates a new String object, referenced by the variable upper, that stores the character sequence "QWERTY", but the String object referenced by keyboard is unchanged, as shown here.

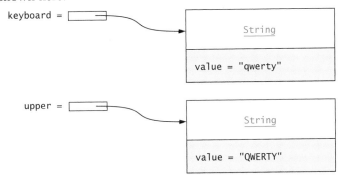

Finally, the expression

```
keyboard.charAt(keyboard.length() - 1)
```

applies two instance methods to keyboard. The inner call, to method length, returns the value 6; the outer call, to method charAt, returns y, the last character in the string (at position 5).

The method substring returns a new string containing a portion of the String object to which it is applied. If it is called with just one argument, the contents of the string returned will be all characters from its argument position to the end of the string. If it is called with two arguments, the contents of the string returned will be all characters from its first argument position up to, but excluding, the character at its second argument position. However, the string to which method substring is applied is not changed.

EXAMPLE A.7   The expression

```
keyboard.substring(0, keyboard.length() - 1)
```

returns a new string "qwert" consisting of all characters except for the last character in the string referenced by keyboard. The contents of keyboard are unchanged.

Strings Are Immutable

Strings are different from most other Java objects in that they are *immutable*. What this means is that you cannot modify a String object. If you attempt to do so, Java will create a new object that contains the modified character sequence. The following statements create a new String object storing the character sequence "Koffman, Elliot" that is referenced by myName (indicated by the blue arrow in Figure A.4). The original String object still exists (at least temporarily) and contains the character sequence "Elliot Koffman", but it is no longer referenced by myName (indicated by the gray arrow in Figure A.4).

```
String myName = "Elliot Koffman";
myName = myName.substring(7) + ", " + myName.substring(0, 6);
```

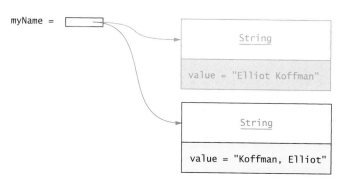

FIGURE A.4
Old and New Strings
Referenced by **myName**

 PITFALL

Attempting to Change a Character in a String

You might try to change the first character in myName using either of the following statements:

```
myName.charAt(0) = 'X';   // Invalid attempt to change character at
                          //    position 0
myName[0] = 'X';          // Invalid attempt to treat string as array
```

Both statements cause syntax errors. The first statement will not work because method charAt returns a value, but a variable must precede the assignment operator. The second statement attempts to change the first character in a string by treating it as an array of characters. You can do this in some programming languages, but not in Java.

The Garbage Collector

Storage space for objects that are no longer referenced is automatically reclaimed by the Java *garbage collector* so that the storage space can be reallocated and reused. The storage space occupied by the first String object in Figure A.4 will be reclaimed by the garbage collector. In other programming languages, the programmer is responsible for reclaiming any storage space that is no longer needed.

Comparing Objects

You can't use the relational (<, <=, >, >=) or equality operators (==, !=) to compare the values stored in strings or other objects. After the assignment

```
String anyName = new String(myName);
```

the condition (anyName == myName) would be **false** even though these variables have the same contents. The reason is that the == operator compares the *addresses* stored in anyName and myName, and the String objects that are referenced by these variables have different addresses (see Figure A.5).

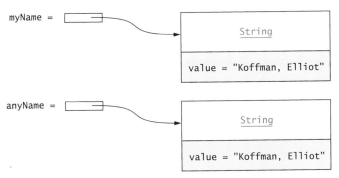

FIGURE A.5
Two **String** Objects at Different Addresses with the Same Contents

After String anyName = new String(myName);

To compare the character sequences stored in two String objects, you need to use one of the Java String comparison methods: equals, equalsIgnoreCase, compareTo, or compareToIgnoreCase. In general, if you want to compare instances of classes that you write, you will need to write at least an equals and a compareTo method for that class.

EXAMPLE A.8   If you execute the statement

```
String otherName = anyName;
```

the variables anyName and otherName reference the same String object:

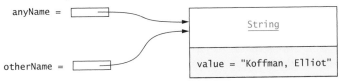

All of the following conditions are then **true**.

```
(anyName == otherName)
(anyName.equals(otherName))
(anyName.compareTo(otherName) == 0)
(anyName.equalsIgnoreCase(otherName))
```

If they had referenced different strings with the same contents, only the first condition would be **false** because of the address comparison. If they referenced different strings that contained the same words but one's contents were in uppercase and the other's contents were in lowercase, only the last condition would be **true**.

The `compareTo` and `compareToIgnoreCase` operators return negative or positive values according to whether the argument, in dictionary order, follows or precedes the string to which the method is applied. If `keyboard` contains the string "qwerty", the expression

```
keyboard.compareTo("rest")
```

is negative because "r" follows "q". For the same reason, the expression

```
"rest".compareTo(keyboard)
```

is positive.

The `compareTo` method performs a case-sensitive comparison, in which all of the uppercase letters precede all of the lowercase letters. If `keyboard` (containing "qwerty") is compared with "Rest", the results are the opposite of what we have just shown for comparing `keyboard` with "rest": `keyboard.compareTo("Rest")` is positive because "R" precedes "q", and `"Rest".compareTo(keyboard)` is negative.

To compare the contents of two strings in alphabetical order regardless of case, use the `compareToIgnoreCase` method: The expressions

```
keyboard.compareToIgnoreCase("rest")
```

```
keyboard.compareToIgnoreCase("Rest")
```

are both negative because "r" follows "q".

The `StringBuffer` Class

Java provides a class called `StringBuffer` that, like `String`, also stores character sequences. However, unlike a `String` object, the contents of a `StringBuffer` object can be changed. Use a `StringBuffer` object to store a string that you plan to change; otherwise, use a `String` object to store that string. Table A.8 describes the methods of class `StringBuffer`. In Table A.8, "this `StringBuffer`" means the `StringBuffer` object to which the method is applied through the dot notation. Methods `append`, `delete`, `insert`, and `replace` modify this `StringBuffer` object.

EXAMPLE A.9 The following statements declare three `StringBuffer` objects using three different constructors. The default capacity of an empty `StringBuffer` object is 16 characters. The capacity of a `StringBuffer` object is automatically expanded to accommodate the character sequence that is stored.

```
StringBuffer sB1 = new StringBuffer();        // Capacity is 16
StringBuffer sB2 = new StringBuffer(30);      // Capacity is 30
StringBuffer sB3 = new StringBuffer("happy"); // Stores "happy"
                                              // Capacity is 21 (16+5)
```

The following statements result in the character sequence "happy birthday to you" being stored in sB3.

```
sB3.append("day me");      // "happyday me"
sB3.insert(9, "to ");      // "happyday to me"
sB3.insert(5, " birth");   // "happy birthday to me"
sB3.replace(18, 20, "you"); // "happy birthday to you"
```

TABLE A.8
StringBuffer Methods in java.lang.StringBuffer

Method	Behavior
void StringBuffer append(*anyType*)	Appends the string representation of the argument to this StringBuffer. The argument can be of any data type.
int capacity()	Returns the current capacity of this StringBuffer.
void StringBuffer delete(int start, int end)	Removes the characters in a substring of this StringBuffer, starting at position start and ending with the character at position end - 1.
void StringBuffer insert(int offset, *anyType* data)	Inserts the argument data (any data type) into this StringBuffer at position offset, shifting the characters that started at offset to the right.
int length()	Returns the length (character count) of this StringBuffer.
StringBuffer replace(int start, int end, String str)	Replaces the characters in a substring of this StringBuffer (from position start through position end - 1) with characters in the argument str. Returns this StringBuffer.
String substring(int start)	Returns a new string containing the substring that begins at the specified index start and extends to the end of this StringBuffer.
String substring(int start, int end)	Return a new string containing the substring in this StringBuffer from position start through position end - 1.
String toString()	Returns a new string that contains the same characters as this StringBuffer object.

 PITFALL

String Index out of Bounds

If an index supplied to any String or StringBuffer method is outside the valid range of character positions for the string object (that is, if the index is less than 0 or greater than or equal to the string length), a StringIndexOutOfBoundsException will occur. This is a run-time error and will terminate program execution. We will discuss exceptions in more detail in Section A.9 and in Chapter 2.

The StringTokenizer Class

Often we want to process individual pieces, or *tokens*, in a string. For example, in the string "Doe, John 5/15/65", we are likely to be interested in one or more of the particular pieces "Doe", "John", "5", "15", and "65". These pieces would have to be extracted from the string as tokens. You can retrieve tokens from a String object using the substring method, but it is easier to use an instance of the class StringTokenizer (part of the Java package java.util).

The statements

```
String personData = "Doe, John 5/15/65";
StringTokenizer sT = new StringTokenizer(personData, " ,/");
```

create a new `StringTokenizer` object, `sT`, for the string `personData` and specify that the space character, the comma (,), and the slash (/) are *delimiter characters* (characters that separate tokens) for this string. The method `sT.nextToken` from class `StringTokenizer` retrieves the next token from string `personData`, using these characters as delimiters. The delimiter characters are not included with the token. The string object is not changed by execution of the `StringTokenizer` methods.

EXAMPLE A.10 The statements

```
String familyName = sT.nextToken();  // stores "Doe"
String givenName = sT.nextToken();   // stores "John"
String month = sT.nextToken();       // stores "5"
String day = sT.nextToken();         // stores "15"
String year = sT.nextToken();        // stores "65"
```

assign to each `String` variable the string shown in the comment on the right. The first time the method `nextToken` is applied to the object `sT`, the first token is extracted. The `StringTokenizer` object keeps track of its place in the string `personData`, so each subsequent call to `nextToken` extracts the next token.

The statements

```
String sentence = "This is a set of seven tokens"
StringTokenizer getWords = new StringTokenizer(sentence);
```

creates a new `StringTokenizer` object `getWords`. Because the constructor does not have a second argument, the default delimiter is implied, which is white space. White space includes the space character, carriage return character, newline character, and tab character.

EXAMPLE A.11 The method `hasMoreTokens` returns **true** if there are more tokens in a string to be extracted. The following loop extracts each token from string `sentence` and displays it in the console window (using `System.out.println`). Loop exit occurs when there are no more tokens.

```
while (getWords.hasMoreTokens())
    System.out.println(getWords.nextToken());
```

Table A.9 summarizes the `StringTokenizer` methods.

TABLE A.9
StringTokenizer Methods in `java.util.StringTokenizer`

Method	Behavior
`StringTokenizer(String str)`	Constructs a new `StringTokenizer` object for the string specified by `str`. The delimiters are "whitespace" characters (space, newline, tab, and so on).
`StringTokenizer(String str, String delim)`	Constructs a new `StringTokenizer` object for the string specified by `str`. The delimiters are the characters specified in `delim`.
`boolean hasMoreTokens()`	Returns **true** if this tokenizer's string has more tokens; otherwise, returns **false**.
`String nextToken()`	Returns the next token of this tokenizer's string if there is one; otherwise, a run-time error will occur.

 PITFALL

Calling nextToken Too Many Times

In the loop in Example A.11, the condition tests whether there are more tokens before invoking method nextToken. If nextToken is called after all the tokens have been extracted, a NoSuchElementException (run-time error) will occur.

EXERCISES FOR SECTION A.5

SELF-CHECK

1. Evaluate each of these expressions.
   ```
   "happy".equals("Happy")
   "happy".compareTo("Happy")
   "happy".equalsIgnoreCase("Happy")
   "happy".equals("happy".charAt(0) + "Happy".substring(1))
   "happy" == "happy".charAt(0) + "Happy".substring(1)
   ```

2. Rewrite the following statements using `StringBuffer` objects:
   ```
   String myName = "Elliot Koffman";
   String myNameFirstLast = myName;
   myName = myName.substring(7) + ", " + myName.substring(0, 6);
   ```

3. You want to extract the words in the string "Nancy* has thirty-three*** fine!! teeth." using a `StringTokenizer` object. What should you use as the delimiter string?

4. What is stored in `result` after the following statements execute?
   ```
   String result = "";
   StringTokenizer sT =
       new StringTokenizer("Let's all learn how to program in Java");
   ```

```
while (sT.hasMoreTokens()) {
    String next = sT.nextToken();
    result = result + next + ", ";
}
```

5. There is an extra ", " at the end of `result`. Write a statement to remove these characters.

6. Rewrite Question 4 using a `StringBuffer` for `result`.

PROGRAMMING

1. Write statements to extract the individual tokens in a string of the form `"Doe, John 5/15/65"`. Use the `indexOf` method to find the string ", " and the symbol / and use the `substring` method to extract the substrings between these delimiters.

2. For Self-Check Exercise 3, write a loop to display all the tokens that are extracted.

A.6 Wrapper Classes for Primitive Types

We have seen that the primitive numeric types are not objects, but sometimes we need to process primitive-type data as objects. For example, we may want to pass a numeric value to a method that requires an object as its argument. Java provides a set of classes called *wrapper classes* whose objects contain primitive-type values: `Float`, `Double`, `Integer`, `Boolean`, `Character`, and so on. These classes provide constructor methods to create new objects that "wrap" a specified value. They also provide methods to "unwrap" or extract an object's value and methods to compare two objects. Table A.10 shows some methods for wrapper class `Integer` (part of `java.lang`). The other numeric wrapper classes also provide these methods, except that method `parseInt` is replaced by a method parse*ClassType*, where *ClassType* is the data type wrapped by that class.

TABLE A.10
Methods for Class `Integer`

Method	Behavior
`int compareTo(Integer anInt)`	Compares two `Integer`s numerically.
`double doubleValue()`	Returns the value of this `Integer` as a **double**.
`boolean equals(Object obj)`	Returns **true** if the value of this `Integer` is equal to its argument's value; returns **false** otherwise.
`int intValue()`	Returns the value of this `Integer` as an **int**.
`static int parseInt(String s)`	Parses the string argument as a signed integer.
`String toString()`	Returns a `String` object representing this `Integer`'s value.

EXAMPLE A.12   The first pair of the following statements creates two Integer objects. The next pair extracts the **int** value contained in each object. The next-to-last statement calls the static method parseInt to parse its string argument to an **int** (not Integer) value. The last statement displays the value (35) wrapped in Integer object i1.

```
Integer i1 = new Integer(35);          // Wraps 35
Integer i2 = new Integer("1234");      // Wraps 1234
int i1Val =  i1.intValue();            // Assigns 35
int i2Val = i2.intValue();             // Assigns 1234
int i3Val = Integer.parseInt("-357");  // Assigns -357
System.out.println(i1.toString());     // Displays 35
```

PROGRAM STYLE

Autoboxing in Java 1.5

In Java 1.5, programmers will not need to be concerned about explicit conversion from primitive numeric types to wrapper types and vice-versa. Java 1.5 will use a facility called *auto-boxing* that will perform this conversion for the programmer. Consequently, if num and sum are type **int**, you will be able to write statements such as

```
Integer numObject = num;
sum = sum + numObject;
```

For the first statement, Java will wrap the **int** value num in a new Integer object. For the second statement, Java will extract the **int** value in numObject and add it to sum.

EXERCISES FOR SECTION A.6

SELF-CHECK

1. Do you think objects of a wrapper type are immutable or not? Explain your answer.
2. For objects i1, i2 in Example A.12, what do the following two statements display?
```
System.out.println(i1.intValue() + i2.intValue());
System.out.println(i1.toString() + i2.toString());
```

PROGRAMMING

1. Write statements that double the value stored in the Integer object referenced by i1. Draw a diagram showing the objects referenced by i1 before and after these statements execute.
2. There is no * (multiply) operator for type Integer objects. Suppose you have Integer objects i1, i2, i3. Write statements to multiply the three type **int** values in these objects and store the product in an Integer object i4.

A.7 Defining Your Own Classes

We mentioned earlier that a Java program is a collection of classes; consequently, when you write a Java program, you will develop one or more classes. We will show you how to write a Java class next.

A class `Person` might describe a group of objects, each of which is a particular human being. For example, instances of class `Person` would be yourself, your mother, and your father. A `Person` object could store the following data:

- Given name
- Family name
- ID number
- Year of birth

The following are a few of the operations that can be performed on a `Person` object:

- Calculate the person's age
- Test whether two `Person` objects refer to the same person
- Determine whether the person is old enough to vote
- Determine whether the person is a senior citizen
- Get one or more of the data fields for the `Person` object
- Set one or more of the data fields for the `Person` object

Figure A.6 shows a diagram of class `Person`. This figure uses the *Unified Modeling Language™ (UML)* to represent the class. UML diagrams are a standard means of documenting class relationships that is widely used in industry. The class is represented by a box. The top compartment of the box contains the class name. The data fields are shown in the middle compartment, and some of the methods are shown in the bottom compartment. Data fields are also called *instance variables* because each class instance (object) has its own storage for them. We discuss UML further in Appendix B.

Figure A.7 shows how two objects or instances of the class `Person` (`author1` and `author2`) are represented in UML. A curved arrow from the reference variable for each object (`author1`, `author2`) points to the object, as we have shown in previous figures. Each object is represented by a box in which the top compartment contains the class name (`Person`), underlined, and the bottom compartment contains the data

FIGURE A.6
Class Diagram for
Person

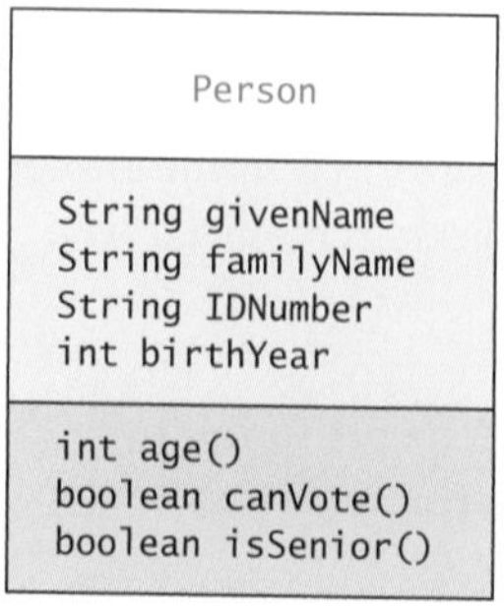

```
         Person

String givenName
String familyName
String IDNumber
int birthYear

int age()
boolean canVote()
boolean isSenior()
```

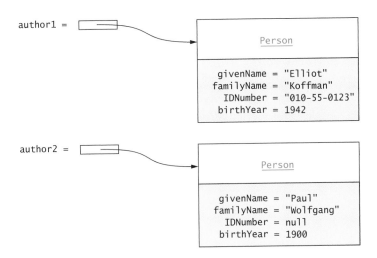

FIGURE A.7
Object Diagrams of
Two Instances of Class
Person

fields and their values. (For simplicity, we show the value of each `String` data field instead of a reference to a `String` object.)

Listing A.1 shows class `Person` and the instance methods for this class. The lines that are delimited by /** and */ are comments. They are program documentation, extremely important for human programmers but ignored by the compiler. We discuss the form of the comments used in class `Person` at the end of this section.

We declare four data fields and two constants (all uppercase letters) before the methods (although many Java programmers prefer to declare methods before data fields). In the constant declarations, the modifier **final** indicates that the constant value may not be changed. The modifier **static** indicates that the constant is being defined for the class and does not have to be replicated in each instance. In other words, storage for the constant VOTE_AGE is allocated once, regardless of how many instances of `Person` are created.

LISTING A.1
Class **Person**

```
/** Person is a class that represents a human being. */
public class Person {
    // Data Fields
    /** The given name */
    private String givenName;
    /** The family name */
    private String familyName;
    /** The ID number */
    private String IDNumber;
    /** The birth year */
    private int birthYear = 1900;

    // Constants
    /** The age at which a person can vote */
    private static final int VOTE_AGE = 18;
```

```java
/** The age at which a person is considered a senior citizen */
private static final int SENIOR_AGE = 65;

// Constructors
/** Construct a person with given values
    @param first The given name
    @param family The family name
    @param ID The ID number
    @param birth The birth year
*/
public Person(String first, String family, String ID, int birth) {
    givenName = first;
    familyName = family;
    IDNumber = ID;
    birthYear = birth;
}

/** Construct a default person. */
public Person() { }

// Modifier Methods
/** Sets the givenName field.
    @param given The given name
*/
public void setGivenName(String given) {
    givenName = given;
}

/** Sets the familyName field.
    @param family The family name
*/
public void setFamilyName(String family) {
    familyName = family;
}

/** Sets the IDNumber field.
    @param ID The ID number
*/
public void setIDNumber(String ID) {
    IDNumber = ID;
}

/** Sets the birthYear field.
    @param birthYear The year of birth
*/
public void setBirthYear(int birthYear) {
    this.birthYear = birthYear;
}

// Accessor Methods
/** Gets the person's given name.
    @return the given name as a String
*/
public String getGivenName() { return givenName; }
```

```java
/** Gets the person's family name.
    @return the family name as a String
*/
public String getFamilyName() { return familyName; }

/** Gets the person's ID number.
    @return the ID number as a String
*/
public String getIDNumber() { return IDNumber; }

/** Gets the person's year of birth.
    @return the year of birth as an int value
*/
public int getBirthYear() { return birthYear; }

// Other Methods
/**  Calculates a person's age at this year's birthday.
    @param year The current year
    @return the year minus the birth year
*/
public int age(int year) {
    return year - birthYear;
}

/** Determines whether a person can vote.
    @param year The current year
    @return true if the person's age is greater than or
            equal to the voting age
*/
public boolean canVote(int year) {
    int theAge = age(year);
    return theAge >= VOTE_AGE;
}

/** Determines whether a person is a senior citizen.
    @param year the current year
    @return true if person's age is greater than or
            equal to the age at which a person is
            considered to be a senior citizen
*/
public boolean isSenior(int year) {
    return age(year) >= SENIOR_AGE;
}

/** Retrieves the information in a Person object.
    @return the object state as a string
*/
public String toString() {
    return "Given name: " + givenName + "\n"
        + "Family name: " + familyName + "\n"
        + "ID number: " + IDNumber + "\n"
        + "Year of birth: " + birthYear + "\n";
}
```

```
/** Compares two Person objects for equality.
    @param per The second Person object
    @return true if the Person objects have same
            ID number; false if they don't
*/
public boolean equals(Person per) {
    if (per == null)
        return false;
    else
        return IDNumber.equals(per.IDNumber);
}
}
```

Private Data Fields, Public Methods

The modifier **private** sets the visibility of each variable or constant to *private visibility*. This means that these data fields can be accessed only within the class definition. Only class members with *public visibility* can be accessed outside of the class.

The reason for having private visibility for data fields is to control access to an object's data and to prevent improper use and processing of an object's data. If a data field is private, it can be processed outside of the class only by invoking one of the public methods that are part of the class. Therefore, the programmer who writes the public methods controls how the data field is processed. Also, the details of how the private data are represented and stored can be changed at a later time by the programmer who implements the class, and the other programs that use the class (called the class's *clients*) will not need to be changed. We explain this concept more thoroughly in Section 1.4.

Constructors

In Listing A.1, the two methods that begin with `public Person` are constructors. One of these methods is invoked when a new class instance is created. The constructor with four parameters is called if the values of all data fields are known before the object is created. For example, the statement

```
Person author1 = new Person("Elliot", "Koffman",
                        "010-055-0123", 1942);
```

creates the first object shown in Figure A.7, initializing its data fields to the values passed as arguments.

The second constructor, the no-parameter constructor, is called when the data field values are not known at the time the object is created.

```
Person author2 = new Person();
```

In this case, the data fields are initialized to the default values for their data type (see Table A.11) unless a different initial value is specified (1900 for `birthYear`). The three `String` data fields are initialized to **null**, which means that no `String` object is referenced. You can use the modifier methods at a later time to set the values of the data fields. The statement

```
author2.setGivenName("Paul");
```

sets the data field `givenName` to reference the `String` object `"Paul"`.

TABLE A.11
Default Values for Data Fields

Data Field Type	Default Value
int (or other integer type)	0
double (or other real type)	0.0
boolean	**false**
char	\u0000 (the smallest Unicode character: the null character)
Any reference type	**null**

The no-parameter constructor is sometimes called the *default constructor* because Java automatically defines this constructor for a class that has no constructor definitions. However, if you define one or more constructors for a class, you must also explicitly define the no-parameter constructor, or it will be undefined for that class.

Modifier and Accessor Methods

Because the data fields have private visibility, we need to provide public methods to access them. Normally, we want to be able to get or retrieve the value of a data field, so each data field in class Person has an accessor method (also called getter) that begins with the word get and ends with the name of the data field (for example, getFamilyName). If we want to allow a class user to update or modify the value of a data field, we provide a modifier method (also called mutator or setter) beginning with the word set and ending with the name of the data field (for example, setGivenName). Currently, there is an accessor and modifer for each data field in this example. However, it would make sense to remove the setIDNumber method so that a person's ID number could not be changed.

The modifier methods are type void because they are executed for their effect (to update a data field), not to return a value. In the method setBirthYear,

```
public void setBirthYear(int birthYear) {
    this.birthYear = birthYear;
}
```

the assignment statement stores the integer value passed as an argument in data field birthYear. (We explain the reason for **this.** in the next subsection.)

The accessor method for data field givenName,

```
public String getGivenName() { return givenName; }
```

is type String because it returns the String object referenced by givenName. If the class designer does not want other users (clients) of the class to be able to access or change the data field values, these methods can be given private visibility.

Use of this. in a Method

Method setBirthYear uses the statement

```
this.birthYear = birthYear;
```

to store a value in data field `birthYear`. We can use **this.***aDataField* in a method to access a data field of the current object. Because we used `birthYear` as a parameter in method `setBirthYear`, the Java compiler will translate `birthYear` without the prefix **this.** as referring to the parameter `birthYear`, not to the data field. The reason is the declaration of `birthYear` as a parameter is local to the method and, therefore, hides the data field declaration.

The Method `toString`

The last two methods, `toString` and `equals`, are found in most Java classes. The method `toString` creates a `String` object that represents the information stored in an object (the *state* of an object). The escape sequence \n is the newline character, and it terminates an output line when the string is displayed. A client of class `Person` could use the statement

```
System.out.println(author1.toString());
```

to display the state of `author1`. In fact, the statement

```
System.out.println(author1);
```

would also display the state of `author1`, because `System.out.println` and `System.out.print` automatically apply method `toString` to an object that appears in their argument list. The following lines would be displayed by this statement.

```
Given name: Elliot
Family name: Koffman
ID number: 010-055-0123
Year of birth: 1942
```

PROGRAM STYLE

Using `toString` Instead of Displaying Data Fields

Java programmers use method `toString` to build a string that represents the object state. This string can then be displayed at the console, written to a file, displayed in a dialog window, or displayed in a Graphical User Interface (GUI). This is more flexible than the approach taken in many programming languages, in which each data field is displayed or written to a file.

The Method `equals`

The method `equals` compares the object to which it is applied (*this* object) to the object that is passed as an argument. It returns **true** if the objects are determined to be the same based on the data they store. It returns **false** if the argument is **null** or if the objects are not the same. We will assume that two `Person`s are the same if they have the same ID number.

```
public boolean equals(Person per) {
    if (per == null)
        return false;
```

```
    else
        return IDNumber.equals(per.IDNumber);
}
```

The second return statement returns the result of the method call

```
IDNumber.equals(per.IDNumber)
```

Notice that we can look at parameter per's private IDNumber because per references an object of this class (type Person). Because IDNumber is type String, the equals method of class String is invoked with the IDNumber of the second object as an argument. If the two IDNumber data fields have the same contents, the String equals method will return **true**; otherwise, it will return **false**. The Person equals method returns the result of the String equals method. In Section 3.5, we discuss the equals method in more detail and will show you a better way to write this method.

PROGRAM STYLE

Returning a Boolean Value

Some programmers unnecessarily write **if** statements to return a **boolean** value. For example, instead of writing

```
    return IDNumber.equals(per.IDNumber);
```

they write

```
    if (IDNumber.equals(per.IDNumber))
        return true;
    else
        return false;
```

Resist this temptation. The **return** statement by itself returns the value of the **if** statement condition, which must be **true** or **false**. It does this in a clear and succinct manner using one line instead of four.

Declaring Local Variables in Class Person

There are three other methods declared in class Person. Methods age, canVote, and isSenior are all passed the current year as an argument. Method canVote calls method age to determine the person's age. The result is stored in local variable theAge. The result of calling method canVote is the value of the Boolean expression following the keyword **return**.

```
    public boolean canVote(int year) {
        int theAge = age(year);      // Local variable
        return theAge >= VOTE_AGE;
    }
```

It really was not necessary to introduce local variable theAge; the call to method age could have been placed directly in the **return** statement (as it is in method isSenior). We wanted, however, to show you how to declare local variables in a Java method. The scope of the local variable theAge and the parameter year is the body of method canVote.

PITFALL

Referencing a Data Field or Parameter Hidden by a Local Declaration

If you happen to declare a local variable (or parameter) with the same name as a data field, the Java compiler will translate the use of that name in a method as meaning the local variable (or parameter), not the data field. So if theAge was also declared as a data field in class Person, the statement

```
theAge++;
```

would increment the local variable, but the data field value would not change. To access the data field instead of the local variable, use the prefix **this.**, just as we did earlier when a parameter had the same name as a data field.

PITFALL

Using Visibility Modifiers with Local Variables

Using a visibility modifier with a local variable would cause a syntax error, because a local variable is visible only within the method that declares it. Therefore, it makes no sense to give it public or private visibility.

An Application That Uses Class Person

To test class Person we need to write a Java application program that contains a main method. The main method should create one or more instances of class Person and display the results of applying the class methods. Listing A.2 shows a class TestPerson that does this. To execute the main method, you must compile and run class TestPerson. As long as Person and TestPerson are in the same folder (directory), the application program will run. Figure A.8 shows a sample run.

LISTING A.2
Class TestPerson

```java
/** TestPerson is an application that tests class Person. */
public class TestPerson {
    public static void main(String[] args) {
        Person p1 = new Person("Sam", "Jones", "1234", 1930);
        Person p2 = new Person("Jane", "Jones", "5678", 1990);
        System.out.println("Age of " + p1.getGivenName() +
                        " is " + p1.age(2004));
        if (p1.isSenior(2004))
            System.out.println(p1.getGivenName() +
                            " can ride the subway for free");
        else
            System.out.println(p1.getGivenName() +
                            " must pay to ride the subway");
```

```
            System.out.println("Age of " + p2.getGivenName() +
                               " is " + p2.age(2004));
            if (p2.canVote(2004))
                System.out.println(p2.getGivenName() + " can vote");
            else
                System.out.println(p2.getGivenName() + " can't vote");
        }
    }
```

FIGURE A.8
Sample Run of Class
TestPerson

Although we will generally write separate application classes such as TestPerson, you could also insert the main method directly in class Person and then compile and run class Person. Program execution will start at the main method, and the result will be the same. If you use separate classes, make sure that you put them in the same folder (directory).

Objects as Arguments

We stated earlier that Java arguments are passed by value. For primitive-type arguments, this protects the value of a method's argument and ensures that its value can't be changed by the method. However, this is not the case for arguments that are objects. If an argument is an object, its address is passed to the method, so the method parameter will reference the same object as the method argument. If the method happens to change a data field of its object parameter, that change will be made to the object argument. We illustrate this next.

EXAMPLE A.13   Suppose method changeGivenName is defined as follows:

```
        public void changeGivenName(Person per) {
            per.givenName = this.givenName;
        }
```

Also suppose a client program declares firstMan and firstWoman as reference variables of type Person. After the method call

```
        firstMan.changeGivenName(firstWoman)
```

parameter per (declared in method changeGivenName) and reference variable firstWoman (declared in the client) will reference the same object. The statement

```
        per.givenName = this.givenName;
```

will set the givenName data field of the object referenced by per (and firstWoman) to reference the same string as the givenName field of this object (the object referenced by firstMan). Figure A.9 shows the givenName data field of the objects referenced by firstMan and firstWoman after the foregoing statement executes.

Reference Variables `firstMan` and `firstWoman`

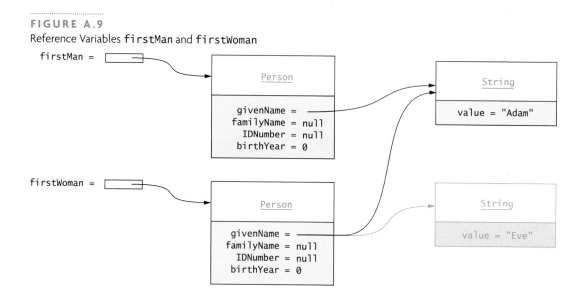

Classes as Components of Other Classes

Class `Person` has three data fields that are type `String`, so `String` objects are *components* of a `Person` object. In Figure A.10 this component relationship is indicated by the solid diamond symbol at the end of the line drawn from the box representing class `String` to the box representing class `Person`. Like the class diagram in Figure A.6 and the object diagrams in Figure A.7, Figure A.10 is a UML diagram, this one showing the relationships between classes. We will follow UML's set of conventions for documenting class relationships in this book.

UML Diagram Showing That `String` Objects Are Components of Class `Person`

Java Documentation Style for Classes and Methods

Java provides a standard form for writing comments and documenting classes, which we will use in this book. If you use this form, you can run a program called *Javadoc* (part of the Java Development Kit) to generate a set of HTML pages describing each class and its data fields and methods. These pages will look just like the ones that document the Java API classes on Sun Microsystems' Java Web site (http://java.sun.com).

The Javadoc program focuses on text that is enclosed within the delimiters /** and */. The introductory comment that describes the class is displayed on the HTML page exactly as it is written, so you should write that carefully. The lines that begin with the symbol @ are Javadoc tags. They are described in Table A.12. We will use the @author tag only in the comment associated with the class, because the class author is also responsible for writing all the methods. We will use one @param tag for each method parameter. We will not use a @return tag for **void** methods. The first line of the comment for each method appears in the method summary part of the HTML page. The information provided in the tags will appear in the method detail part. Figures A.11 through A.13 shows part of the documentation generated by running Javadoc for class Person.

TABLE A.12
Javadoc Tags

Javadoc Tag and Example of Use	Purpose
@author *Koffman and Wolfgang*	Identifies the class author.
@param first *The given name*	Identifies a method parameter.
@return *The person's age*	Identifies a method return value.

FIGURE A.11
Field Summary for Class **Person**

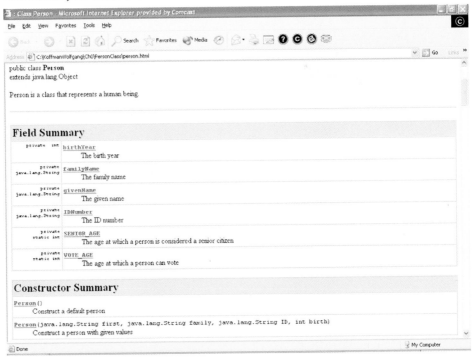

FIGURE A.12
Method Summary for Class `Person`

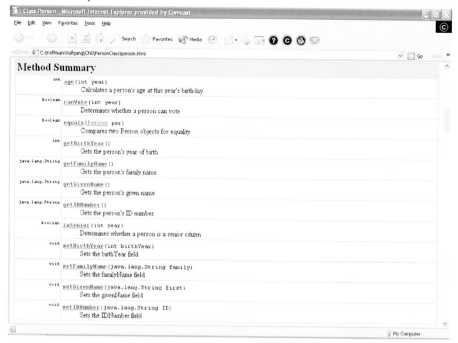

FIGURE A.13
Method Detail for Class `Person`

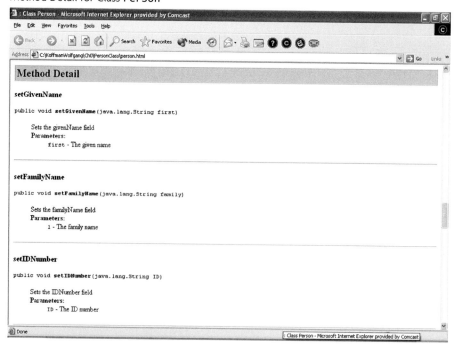

To run the Javadoc program, change to the directory that contains the source files that you would like to process. Then, to create the HTML documentation files, enter the command

> *pathName*\javadoc *className1*.java *className2*.java

where *pathName* is the directory that contains the Javadoc program and the Java source file names (*className1*.java, *className2*.java, and so forth) follow the javadoc command. If you want to show the private data fields and methods, add the command line argument –private. If you want to create documentation files for all the .java files in the directory, use the wildcard * for the class name.

> *pathName*\javadoc –private *.java

Another useful command line argument is –d *destinationFolder*, which allows you to specify a folder or directory other than the source folder for the Javadoc HTML files.

EXERCISES FOR SECTION A.7

SELF-CHECK

1. Explain why methods have public visibility but data fields have private visibility.
2. Download file Person.java from the textbook Web site and run javadoc on it.
3. Trace the execution of the following statements.

```
Person p1 = new Person("Adam", "Jones", "wxyz", 0);
p1.setBirthYear(1990);
Person p2 = new Person();
p2.setGivenName("Eve");
p2.setFamilyName(p1.getFamilyName());
p2.setBirthYear(p1.getBirthYear() + 10);
p2.setIDNumber(p1.getIDNumber().toUpperCase());
if (p1.equals(p2))
    System.out.println(p1 + "\nis same person as\n\n" + p2);
else
    System.out.println(p1 + "\nis not the same person as\n\n" + p2);
```

PROGRAMMING

1. Write a method getInitials that returns a string representing a Person object's initials. There should be a period after each initial. Write Javadoc tags for the method.
2. Add a data field motherMaidenName to Person. Write an accessor and a modifier method for this data field. Modify class toString and class equals to include this data field. Assume two Person objects are equal if they have the same ID number and mother's maiden name. Write Javadoc tags for the method.
3. Write a method compareTo that compares two Person objects and returns an appropriate result based on a comparison of the ID numbers. That is, if the ID number of the object that compareTo is applied to is less than (is greater than) the ID number of the argument object, the result should be negative (positive). The result should be 0 if they have the same ID numbers. Write Javadoc tags for the method.
4. Write a method switchNames that exchanges a Person object's given and family names. Write Javadoc tags for the method.

A.8 Arrays

In Java, an array is also an object. The elements of an array are indexed and are referenced using a subscripted variable of the form:

arrayName[*subscript*]

Next, we show some different ways to declare arrays and allocate storage for arrays.

EXAMPLE A.14   The following statement declares a variable scores that references a new array object that can store five type **int** values (subscripts 0 through 4) as shown. Each element is initialized to 0.

```
int[] scores = new int[5];   // An array with 5 type int values
```

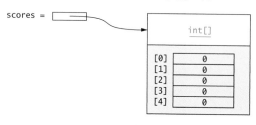

EXAMPLE A.15   The following statement declares a variable names that references a new array object that can store four type String objects. The values stored are specified in the *initializer list*.

```
String[] names = {"Sally", "Jill", "Hal", "Rick"};
```

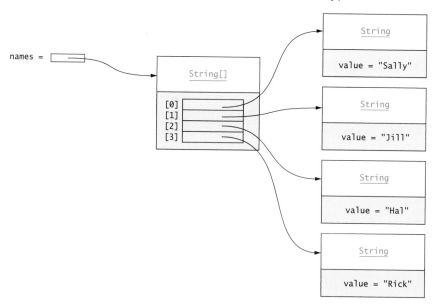

PITFALL

Out-of-Bounds Subscripts

Some programming languages allow you to use an array subscript that is outside of the array bounds. For example, if you attempt to reference scores[5], a C or C++ compiler would access the first memory cell following the array scores. This is considered an error, but it is not detected by the run-time system and will probably lead to another error that will be detected further down the road (before it does too much damage, you hope). Java, however, verifies that the current value of each array subscript is within the array bounds. If it isn't, you will get an ArrayIndexOutOfBoundsException error.

EXAMPLE A.16   The first of the following statements declares a variable people that can reference an array object for storing type Person objects. Storage has not yet been allocated for the array object (or for the Person objects). The second statement assumes that n is defined, possibly through an input operation. The last statement allocates storage for an array object with n elements. Each array element can reference a type Person object, but initially each element has the value **null** (no object referenced).

```
// Declare people as type Person[].
Person[] people;
// Define n in some way.
int n = ...
// Allocate storage for the array.
people = new Person[n];
```

We can create some Person objects and store them in the array. The following statements store two Person objects in array people.

```
people[0] = new Person("Elliot", "Koffman", "010-055-0123", 1942);
people[1] = new Person("Paul", "Wolfgang", "015-023-4567", 1945);
```

PITFALL

Forgetting to Declare Storage for an Array

As just shown, you can separate the declaration of variable people (the array reference variable) from the step that actually allocates storage (people = new ...). However, you can't reference the array elements before you allocate storage for the array. Similarly, if the array elements reference objects, you must separately allocate storage for each object.

Data Field `length`

A Java array has a `length` data field that can be used to determine the array's size. The value of `names.length` is 4; the value of `people.length` is the same as the value of n when storage was allocated for the array. The subscripted variable `people[people.length - 1]` references the last element in array `people`. The following **for** statement can be used to display all the `Person` objects stored in array `people`, regardless of the array size.

```
for (int i = 0; i < people.length; i++ )
    if (people[i] != null)
        System.out.println(people[i] + "\n");
```

 PITFALL

Using `length` Incorrectly

The value of data field `length` is set when storage is allocated for the array, and it is final. Therefore, it can't be changed by the programmer. A statement such as

```
people.length++;    // invalid attempt to increment length
```

would cause a syntax error.

Another common error is using parentheses with `length`. The expression `people.length()` causes a syntax error, because `length` is a data field, not a method, of an array.

Method `System.arraycopy`

Although you can't change the length of a particular array object, you can copy the values stored in one array object to another larger object using method `System.arraycopy`. You can also use `System.arraycopy` to save the data stored in an array object before passing that object as a method argument. That way, if the method changes the data stored in the argument array, you will still have a copy of the original array object.

EXAMPLE A.17 The following statements create a new array tempScores that is twice the size of array scores. Next, we copy the elements in array scores to the first half of array tempScores. Finally, we reset variable scores to reference the same array as tempScores (see Figure A.14). The storage originally allocated to store the elements of array scores can now be reclaimed by the garbage collector.

```
int[] tempScores = new int[2 * scores.length];
System.arraycopy(scores, 0, tempScores, 0, scores.length);
scores = tempScores;
```

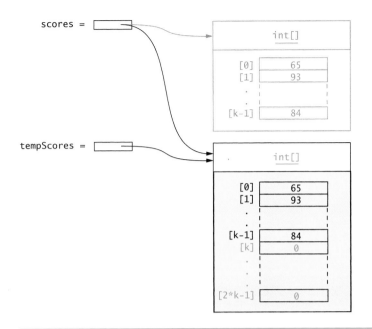

FIGURE A.14
Doubling the Size of
the Array Referenced
by **scores**

A call to method arraycopy has the general form

System.arraycopy(*source*, *sourcePos*, *destination*, *destPos*, *numElements*);

The parameters *sourcePos* and *destPos* specify the starting positions in the *source* and *destination* arrays, respectively. The parameter *numElements* specifies the number of elements to copy. If this number is too large, an ArrayIndexOutOfBounds-Exception error occurs.

Array Data Fields

It is very common in Java to encapsulate an array, together with the methods that process it, within a class. Rather than allocate storage for a fixed-size array, we would like the client to be able to specify the array size when an object is created. Therefore, we should define a constructor with the array size as a parameter and have the constructor allocate storage for the array. Class Company in Listing A.3 has a data field employees that references an array of Person objects. Both constructors allocate storage for a new array when a Company object is created. The client of this class can specify the size of the array by passing a type **int** value to the constructor parameter size. If no argument is passed, the no-parameter constructor sets the array size to DEFAULT_SIZE.

LISTING A.3
Class **Company**

```
/** Company is a class that represents a company.
    The data field employees provides storage for
    an array of Person objects.
*/
```

```java
public class Company {
    // Data Fields
    /** The array of employees */
    private Person[] employees;

    /** The default size of the array */
    private static final int DEFAULT_SIZE = 100;

    // Methods
    /** Creates a new array of Person objects.
        @param size The size of array employees
    */
    public Company(int size) {
        employees = new Person[size];
    }

    public Company() {
        employees = new Person[DEFAULT_SIZE];
    }

    /** Sets field employees.
        @param emp The array of employees
    */
    public void setEmployees(Person[] emp) {
        employees = emp;
    }

    /** Gets field employees.
        @return employees array
    */
    public Person[] getEmployees() {
        return employees;
    }

    /** Sets an element of employees.
        @param index The position of the employee
        @param emp The employee
    */
    public void setEmployee(int index, Person emp) {
        if (index >= 0 && index < employees.length)
            employees[index] = emp;
    }

    /** Gets an employee.
        @param index The position of the employee
        @return the employee object or null if not defined
    */
    public Person getEmployee(int index) {
        if (index >= 0 && index < employees.length)
            return employees[index];
        else
            return null;
    }
}
```

```
/** Builds a string consisting of all employee's
    data, with newline characters between employees.
    @return The object's state
*/
public String toString() {
    StringBuffer result = new StringBuffer();
    for (int i = 0; i < employees.length; i++)
        result.append(employees[i] + "\n");
    return result.toString();
}
}
```

There are modifier and accessor methods that process individual elements of array Company (setEmployee and getEmployee). Method getEmployee returns the type Person object at position index, or **null** if the value of index is out of bounds.

The toString method returns a string representing the contents of array employees. In the **for** loop, the argument in each call to method append is the string returned by applying method Person.toString to the current employee. This string is appended to the string representing the data for all employees with smaller subscripts.

The following main method illustrates the use of class Company and displays the state of object comp.

```
public static void main(String[] args) {
    Company comp = new Company(2);
    comp.setEmployee(0, new Person("Elliot", "K", "123", 1942));
    comp.setEmployee(1, new Person("Paul", "W", "234", 1945));
    System.out.println(comp);
}
```

Array Results and Arguments

Method setEmployees in class Company takes a single argument emp that is type Person[]. The assignment statement

```
employees = emp;
```

resets array employees to reference the array argument. Storage allocated to the array previously referenced by employees can then be reclaimed by the garbage collector.

The return value of method getEmployees is type Person[]. The statement

```
return employees;
```

returns a reference to the array employees.

Arrays of Arrays

A Java array can have other arrays as its elements. If all these arrays are the same size, then the array of arrays is a two-dimensional array.

EXAMPLE A.18 The declaration

```
double[][] matrix = new double[5][10];
```

allocates storage for a two-dimensional array, matrix, that stores 50 real numbers in 5 rows and 10 columns. The variable matrix[i][j] references the number with row subscript i and column subscript j. You can also declare arrays with more than two dimensions.

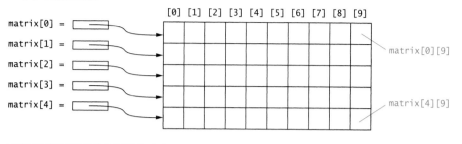

In Java you can have two-dimensional arrays with rows of different sizes. We illustrate this in the next two examples.

EXAMPLE A.19   The declaration

```
char[][] letters = new char[5][];
```

allocates storage for a two-dimensional array of characters with five rows, but the number of columns in each row is not specified. The statements

```
letters[0] = new char[4];
letters[1] = new char[10];
```

define the size of the first two rows and allocate storage for them. The subscripted variable letters[0] references the first row; letters.length is 5, the number of rows in the array; letters[1].length is 10, the number of elements in the row with subscript 1.

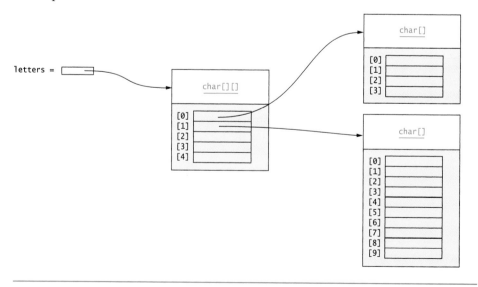

EXAMPLE A.20 The declaration

```
int[][] pascal = {
                    {1},        // row 0
                    {1, 1},     // row 1
                    {1, 2, 1},
                    {1, 3, 3, 1},
                    {1, 4, 6, 4, 1},
};
```

allocates storage for an array of arrays with 5 rows. The initializer list provides the values for each row, starting with row 0. The subscripted variable `pascal[0]` references the one-element array `{1}`, and `pascal[4]` references the array `{1, 4, 6, 4, 1}`. Each row has one more element than the previous one. The values shown above form a well-known mathematical entity called Pascal's triangle. Each element in a row, except for the first and last elements, is the sum of the two elements on either side of it in the previous row. For example, the number 6 in the last row is the sum of the numbers 3, 3 in the previous row. In mathematical notation,

```
pascal[i + 1][j] = pascal[i][j - 1] + pascal[i][j].
```

The first and last elements in each row are 1.

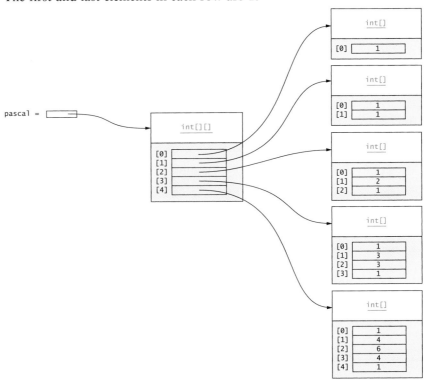

The following nested **for** statements sum all values in the Pascal triangle. In the outer **for** loop header, the expression `pascal.length` is the number of rows in the triangle. In the inner **for** loop header, the expression `pascal[row].length` is the number of columns in the array with subscript `row`.

```
int sum = 0;
for (int row = 0; row < pascal.length; row++)
    for (int col = 0; col < pascal[row].length; col++)
        sum += pascal[row][col];
```

EXERCISES FOR SECTION A.8

SELF-CHECK

1. Show the output that would be displayed by method `main` following Listing A.3.
2. Show that the formula for the interior elements of a Pascal triangle row is correct by evaluating it for each interior element of the last row.
3. What is the output of the following sample code fragment?
```
int[] x;
int[] y;
int[] z;
x = new int[20];
x[10] = 0;
y = x;
x[10] = 5;
System.out.println(x[10] + ", " + y[10]);
x[10] = 15;
z = new int[x.length];
System.arraycopy(x, 0, z, 0, 20);
x[10] = 25;
System.out.println(x[10] + ", " + y[10]+ ", " + z[10]);
```
4. What happens if you make a copy of an array of object references using method `System.arraycopy`? If the objects referenced by the new array are changed, how will this affect the original array?
5. Assume there is no initializer list for the Pascal triangle and you are trying to build up its rows. If row `i` has been defined, write statements to create row `i + 1`.

PROGRAMMING

1. Write code for a method
   `public static boolean sameElements(int[] a, int[] b)`
   that checks whether two arrays have the same elements in some order, with the same multiplicities. For example, two arrays

   | 121 | 144 | 19 | 161 | 19 | 144 | 19 | 11 |

   and

   | 11 | 121 | 144 | 19 | 161 | 19 | 144 | 19 |

   would be considered to have the same elements because 19 appears 3 times in each array, 144 appears twice in each array, and all other elements appear once in each array.
2. Write an `equals` method for class `Company`. The result should be **true** if the employees of one company match element-for-element with the employees of a different company. Assume that the objects referenced by each array `employees` are in order by ID number.

3. For the two-dimensional array letters in Example A.19, assume letters[i] is going to be used to store an array that contains the individual characters in String object next. Allocate storage for letters[i] based on the length of next and write a loop that stores each character of next in the corresponding element of letters[i]. For example, the first character in next should be stored in letters[i][0].

A.9 Input/Output Using Class JOptionPane

Prior to Java 2, it was fairly difficult to perform input/output operations (I/O) in Java. You had to either use the console for I/O, use streams (external files), or build GUIs. Java 2 provided class JOptionPane (part of the Swing package), which facilitates the display of dialog windows for input and message windows for output. We describe two static methods from class JOptionPane in Table A.13. (We discuss more Swing classes in Appendix C.) To use class JOptionPane, you should place the line

```
import javax.swing.JOptionPane;    // Import class JOptionPane
```

or

```
import javax.swing.*;              // Import entire Swing package
```

before the class definition in your source file.

TABLE A.13
Methods from Class JOptionPane

Method	Behavior
static String showInputDialog(String prompt)	Displays a dialog window that displays the argument as a prompt and returns the character sequence typed by the user.
static void showMessageDialog(Object parent, String message)	Displays a window containing a message string (the second argument) inside the specified container (the first argument).

EXAMPLE A.21   The statement

```
String name = JOptionPane.showInputDialog("Enter your name");
```

displays the dialog window shown on the left in Figure A.15. After the OK button is clicked or the Enter key is pressed, variable name references a String object that stores the character sequence "Jane Doe". If Cancel is clicked, variable name stores **null**. The statement

```
JOptionPane.showMessageDialog(null, "Your name is " + name);
```

displays the message window shown on the right in Figure A.15. The first argument specifies the parent container in which this window will be placed. When the argument is **null**, the dialog window is placed in the middle of the screen (the window in which the program is executing).

FIGURE A.15
A Dialog Window (Left)
and Message Window
(Right)

FIGURE A.15
A Dialog Window (Left)
and Message Window
(Right)

Converting Numeric Strings to Numbers

A dialog window always returns a reference to a string. How can we convert numeric strings to numbers? Fortunately, as shown in Table A.14, class Integer provides a static method, parseInt, for converting strings consisting only of digit characters to numbers, and class Double provides a static method, parseDouble, for converting strings consisting of the characters for a real number (or integer) to a type double value.

TABLE A.14
Methods for Converting Strings to Numbers

Method	Behavior
static int parseInt(String)	Returns an **int** value corresponding to its argument string. A NumberFormatException occurs if its argument string contains characters other than digits.
static double parseDouble(String)	Returns a double value corresponding to its argument string. A NumberFormatException occurs if its argument string does not represent a real number.

EXAMPLE A.22   The next pair of statements stores a type **int** value in numStu if answer references a String object that contains digit characters only.

```
String answer =
    JOptionPane.showInputDialog("Enter number of students");
int numStu = Integer.parseInt(answer);
```

 PITFALL

Using Nonnumeric Strings with parseInt, parseDouble

If you pass to parseInt a String that contains characters that are not digit characters, you will get a NumberFormatException error. If you pass to parseDouble a String that contains characters that can't be in a number, you will also get a NumberFormatException error.

GUI Menus Using Method showOptionDialog

Another useful method from class JOptionPane is method showOptionDialog. This method displays a menu of choices with a button for each choice (see Figure A.16). When a button is clicked, the method returns the index of the button pressed (0 for the first button, and so on). The index value can be used in a **switch** statement to select an alternative.

EXAMPLE A.23   The statements

```
String[] choices = {"insert", "delete", "add", "display"};
int selection = JOptionPane.showOptionDialog(null,
                        "Select an operation",
                        "Operation menu",
                        JOptionPane.YES_NO_CANCEL_OPTION,
                        JOptionPane.QUESTION_MESSAGE, null,
                        choices, choices[0]);
```

display the menu shown in Figure A.16. The array choices defines the button labels. After a button is clicked, the value stored in selection will be the index of that button, an integer from 0 to 3.

FIGURE A.16
Displaying a Menu

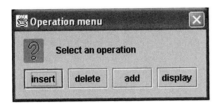

EXERCISES FOR SECTION A.9

SELF-CHECK

1. Show the statements that would be required, using Swing, to read and store the data for a Person object prior to calling the constructor with four parameters.

PROGRAMMING

1. Write a main method that reads the data for two Person objects, creates the objects, and displays the objects and a message indicating whether they represent the same Person.

A.10 Input/Output Using Streams

In this section we will show you the basics of using streams for I/O in Java. An input stream is a sequence of characters representing program data. An output stream is a sequence of characters representing program output. You can store program data in the stream associated with the console, `System.in`. When you type data characters at the console keyboard, they are appended to `System.in`. The console window is associated with `System.out`, the standard output stream. We have used methods `print` and `println` to write information to this stream.

Besides using the console for I/O, you can create and save a text file (using a word processor or editor) and then use it as an input stream for a program. Similarly, a program can write characters to an output stream and save it as a disk file.

Input Streams

To use input streams, a class file must import `java.io`:

```
import java.io.*;
```

You also need to create a `BufferedReader` object:

```
String fileName = args[0];   // The first main parameter
BufferedReader ins =
        new BufferedReader(new FileReader(fileName));
```

Although this looks fairly complicated, you can think of it as "boilerplate" (or a template for creating a `BufferedReader`). The only part of this code that can change is the `String` argument passed to the `FileReader` constructor (`fileName` in this example). Variable `fileName` references the string passed as the first parameter (`args[0]`) to method `main`. This should be the name of a data file that is saved in the same directory as the application class.

The `BufferedReader` constructor needs a parameter that is type `FileReader` (or type `InputStreamReader`). The `BufferedReader` class defines a method `readLine` that can be used to read the next data line in a file (or typed at the console); the method returns a `String` object that contains the characters in that data line.

Console Input

To enable console input, you also must create a `BufferedReader` object:

```
BufferedReader con =
        new BufferedReader(new InputStreamReader(System.in));
```

The `BufferedReader` object con is associated with the standard input stream `System.in`, so you can invoke method `readLine` to read the next data line typed at the keyboard.

Output Streams

To create an output stream, use statements such as:

```
String outFileName = args[1];  // The second main parameter
PrintWriter outs = new PrintWriter(new FileWriter(outFileName));
```

You can apply method `print` or `println` to the `PrintWriter` object `outs`. Variable `outFileName` references the same string as `args[1]`, the string passed as the second parameter to method `main`. This should be the external name of a file. When object `outs` is created, the stream it references is always empty. Any information previously stored in the file whose name is passed to `args[1]` will be lost.

Passing Arguments to Method `main`

Earlier we set the variable `fileName` to reference the same string as `args[0]`, the first parameter for method `main`. You must specify the `main` method parameters before you run an application. When you are using the JDK and therefore running your applications from the console command line (such as an "MS-DOS Prompt" window in Windows), you list the parameters after the name of the class you are executing. For example, if you are running application `FileTest.java` with parameters `indata.txt` and `output.txt`, use the command line

```
java FileTest indata.txt output.txt
```

When you are using an IDE, you can also specify parameters before running an application. (For example, Borland JBuilder provides an option Parameters ... on the Run menu. Selecting this option brings up a window that has a text field with label Parameters. You can type the parameters into this text field. Do not use quotes when typing in parameter names.)

Closing Streams

After processing streams, you must disconnect them from the application. The statement

```
outs.close();
```

does this for stream `outs`. Data to be written to a file is stored in an *output buffer* in memory before it is written to the disk. The `close` statement ensures that any data in the output buffer is written to disk.

 PITFALL

Neglecting to Close an Output Stream

If you do not close a stream, it is not considered an error. However, you may find that not all the information written to the stream is actually stored in the corresponding disk file unless you close it.

Exceptions

Exceptions are program errors that occur during the execution of a program. We will discuss exceptions in great detail in Chapter 2. In this section, we will tell you just enough about them to enable you to use streams for I/O.

When you process streams, there is a reasonable chance that a system error will occur. For example, the system may not be able to locate your file, or an error could occur during a file read operation. For this reason, Java requires you to perform all file-processing operations within the **try** block of a **try-catch** sequence, as follows:

```
try {
    // Statements that perform file-processing operations
}
catch (IOException ex) {
    ex.printStackTrace(System.err);   // Display stack trace
    System.exit(1);     // Exit with an error indication
}
```

If all operations in the **try** block execute without error, the **catch** block is skipped. If an IOException or error occurs, the **try** block is exited and the **catch** block executes. This **catch** block simply displays the sequence of method calls that led to the error (starting with the most recent one and working backwards) in the console window (System.err—the standard error stream) and then exits with an error indication. If we did not exit the **catch** block after catching an error, the program would continue with the first statement following the **catch** block.

A Complete File-Processing Application

We put all these pieces together in this example. In Listing A.4, the main method in class FileTest consists of a **try-catch** sequence. The **try** block creates two BufferedReader objects: ins (associated with a data file) and con (associated with System.in). It also creates a PrintWriter object outs (associated with an output file). The **while** loop invokes method readLine to read data lines from stream ins, storing the information read in the String object first. When the end of the data file is reached, first will contain **null**. If first is not **null** (the normal situation when a data line is read), the user sees a console prompt asking for more data. The data entered by the user is read into the String object second.

```
System.out.print("Type in data to follow " + first + ": ");
String second = con.readLine();     // Read from console
```

Next, the contents of second are appended to first, and the new string is written to the output file.

```
outs.println(first + ", " + second);   // Append and write
```

This process continues until the end of the data file is reached, loop exit occurs, and the files are closed.

LISTING A.4
Class FileTest

```
/** FileTest is an application that illustrates stream operations. */
import java.io.*;
```

```java
public class FileTest {
    /** Reads a line from an input file and a line from the console.
        Concatenates the two lines and writes them to an output file.
        Does this until all input lines have been read.
        @param args[0] The input file name
        @param args[1] The output file name
    */
    public static void main(String[] args) {

        try {
            String inFileName = args[0];    // First main parameter
            String outFileName = args[1];   // Second main parameter
            BufferedReader ins =
                new BufferedReader(new FileReader(inFileName));
            BufferedReader con =
                new BufferedReader(new InputStreamReader(System.in));
            PrintWriter outs =
                new PrintWriter(new FileWriter(outFileName));

            // Reads words and writes them to the output file until done.
            String first = ins.readLine();          // Read from file
            while (first != null) {
                System.out.print("Type in a word to follow "
                                    + first + ": ");
                String second = con.readLine();  // Read from console
                // Append and write
                outs.println(first + ", " + second);
                first = ins.readLine();             // Read from file
            }

            // Close files.
            ins.close();
            outs.close();
        }
        catch (IOException ex) {
            ex.printStackTrace(System.err);    // Display stack trace
            System.exit(1);     // Exit with an error indication
        }
    }
}
```

Figure A.17 shows a sample run. The input file contains the three lines

```
apple
cat
John
```

and the output file contains three lines consisting of a word read from the data file, a comma, and a word typed in at the console.

```
apple, butter
cat, dog
John, Doe
```

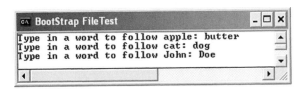

Tokenized Input

Often a data line will consist of a group of data items separated by spaces. You can use a StringTokenizer object to extract the individual items (tokens) from each line in order to process them. The following nested loops add all the numbers read from input stream ins. The outer **while** loop repeats until all the data lines are read. Each data line is read into numberStr and a new StringTokenizer object is created for each line. The inner **while** loop extracts and stores each token in nextNum and then adds it to sum.

```
double sum = 0.0;
String numberStr = ins.readLine();
while (numberStr != null) {
    // Create a new StringTokenizer for the current line.
    StringTokenizer numberStrTokens =
                        new StringTokenizer(numberStr);

    // Add all the numbers on the current line.
    while (numberStrTokens.hasMoreTokens()) {
        double nextNum
                = Double.parseDouble(numberStrTokens.nextToken());
        sum += nextNum;
    }
    numberStr = ins.readLine();  // Read the next line.
}
```

EXERCISES FOR SECTION A.10

SELF-CHECK

1. Show the statements that would be required, using the console for input, to read and store the data for a Person object prior to calling the constructor with four parameters.
2. Answer Exercise 1 using a data file instead of the console.
3. What would happen if the output file name matched the name of a file already saved on disk? What could happen if the user forgets to close an output file?
4. When does the **catch** block in a **try-catch** sequence execute?

PROGRAMMING

1. Write a method for class Person that reads the data for a single employee from a BufferedReader object (the method argument). Assume there is one data item per line.
2. Write a method for class Company that reads the data for the employees array. This method should call the one needed for Programming Exercise 1.

Chapter Review

◆ A Java program is a collection of classes. A programmer can use classes defined in the Java Application Programming Interface (API) to simplify the task of writing new programs, and can define new classes to use as building blocks in future programs. Use

    `import packageName.*;`

or

    `import packageName.ClassName;`

to make the public names defined in a package or a class accessible to the current file.

◆ The Java Virtual Machine (JVM) enables a Java program written for one machine to execute on any other machine that has a JVM. The JVM is able to execute instructions that are written in Java byte code. The byte code instructions are found in the `.class` file that is created when a Java source file is compiled.

◆ Java defines a set of primitive data types that are used to represent numbers (**int**, **double**, **float**, and so on), characters (**char**), and **boolean** data. Characters are represented using Unicode. Primitive type variables are used to store primitive data. The Java programmer can use reference variables to reference objects. Wrapper classes can be used to encapsulate (wrap) a primitive-type value in an object.

◆ The control structures of Java are similar to those found in other languages: sequence (a compound statement), selection (**if** and **switch**), and repetition (**while, for, do ... while**).

◆ There are two kinds of methods: static (or class) methods and instance methods. Static methods are called using

    ClassName.methodName(arguments)

but instance methods must be applied to objects:

    objectReference.methodName(arguments)

◆ The Java `String` and `StringBuffer` classes are used to reference objects that store character strings. `String` objects are immutable, which means they can't be changed, whereas `StringBuffer` objects can be modified. `StringTokenizer` objects can be created for `String` objects. A `StringTokenizer` object is used to extract the individual tokens from a `String` object.

◆ Make sure you use methods such as `equals` and `compareTo` to compare the contents of two `String` objects (or any objects). The operator == compares the addresses of two objects, not their contents.

◆ You can declare your own Java classes and create objects (instances) of these classes using the **new** operator. A constructor call must follow the **new** operator. A constructor has the same name as its class, and a class can define multiple constructors. The no-parameter constructor is defined by default if no constructors are explicitly defined.

◆ A class has data fields (instance variables) and instance methods. The default values for data fields are 0 or 0.0 for numbers, \u0000 for characters, **false** for **boolean**, and **null** for reference variables. A constructor initializes data fields to values specified by its arguments. Generally, data fields have private visibility (accessible only within the class) whereas methods have public visibility (accessible outside the class).

◆ Array variables can reference array objects. You must use the **new** operator to allocate storage for the array object.

```
int[] anArray = new int[mySize];
```

The elements of an array can store primitive-type values or references to other objects. Arrays of arrays (multidimensional arrays) are permitted. The data field length represents the size of an array and is always accessible, but length can't be changed by the programmer. However, an array variable can be reset to reference a different array object with a different size.

◆ Class JOptionPane (part of Swing) can be used to display dialog windows for data entry (method showInputDialog) and message windows for output (method showMessageDialog).

◆ The stream classes in java.io can be used to read strings from the console (System.in) and display strings to the console (System.out). Use statements like

```
BufferedReader con =
            new BufferedReader(new InputStreamReader(System.in));
PrintWriter outs =
            new PrintWriter(new FileWriter(outFileName));
```

to associate the input stream con with the console and the output stream outs with a specified disk file. File operations must be performed within a **try-catch** sequence that catches IOException exceptions. You must close an output file when you have finished writing all information to it.

Java Constructs Introduced in This Chapter

class	**boolean**
main	**public**
int	**private**
double	**new**
char	**static**
final	

Java API Classes Introduced in This Chapter

java.lang.Math	javax.swing.JOptionPane
java.lang.String	java.io.BufferedReader
java.lang.StringBuffer	java.io.FileReader
java.lang.StringTokenizer	java.io.InputStreamReader
java.lang.Object	java.io.PrintWriter
java.lang.Integer	java.lang.FileWriter
java.lang.Double	java.lang.Exception
java.lang.Character	java.lang.NumberFormatException
java.lang.Boolean	java.io.IOException

User-Defined Interfaces and Classes in This Chapter

HelloWorld   TestPerson
SquareRoots   Company
Person   FileTest

Quick-Check Exercises

1. The Java compiler translates Java source code to _____ which are executed by the _____.

2. Java _____ are embedded in _____, whereas Java _____ are stand-alone programs.

3. A Java program is a collection of _____. Execution of a Java application begins at method _____.

4. Java classes declare _____ and _____. Generally, the _____ have public visibility and the _____ have private visibility.

5. An _____ method is invoked by applying it to an _____; a _____ method is not.

6. If you use the operator == with objects, you are comparing their _____, not their _____.

7. To associate an input stream with the console, you must wrap an _____ object in a _____ object.

8. To associate an output stream with the console, you must wrap a _____ object in a _____ object.

9. To associate an input stream with a text file, you must wrap a _____ object in a _____ object.

10. Method _____ of class JOptionPane normally has _____ as its first argument and a _____ as its second argument.

Answers to Quick-Check Exercises

1. The Java compiler translates Java source code to *byte code instructions*, which are executed by the *Java Virtual Machine (JVM)*.

2. Java *applets* are embedded in Web pages, whereas Java *applications* are stand-alone programs.

3. A Java program is a collection of *classes*. Execution of a Java application begins at method *main*.

4. Java classes declare *data fields* and *methods*. Generally, the *methods* have public visibility and the *data fields* have private visibility.

5. An *instance* method is invoked by applying it to an *object*; a *static* (or *class*) method is not.

6. If you use the operator == with objects, you are comparing their *addresses*, not their *contents*.

7. To associate an input stream with the console, you must wrap an *InputStreamReader* object in a *BufferedReader* object.

8. To associate an output stream with the console, you must wrap a *FileWriter* object in a *PrintWriter* object.

9. To associate an input stream with a text file, you must wrap a *FileReader* object in a *BufferedReader* object.

10. Method *showMessageDialog* of class JOptionPane normally has **null** as its first argument and a *prompt string* as its second argument.

Review Questions

1. Discuss how a Java source file is processed prior to execution and why this approach makes Java platform independent.

2. Declare storage for an array of arrays that will store a list of integers in its first row, the squares of all but the last integer in its second row, and the cubes of all but the last two integers in its third row. Assume that the size of the first row and its integer values are entered by the program user. Read this data into the array and store the required squares and cubes in the array.

3. Draw diagrams that illustrate the effect of each of the following statements.

```
String s1 = "woops";
String s2 = new String(s1);
String s3 = s1;
s1 = new String("Oops!");
```

What are the values of s1 == s2, s1 == s3, and s2 == s3? What are the values of s1.equals(s2), s1.equals(s3), s2.equals(s3)? What are the values of s1.compareTo(s2), s1.compareTo(s3), s2.compareTo(s3)?

4. Write a class Fraction with integer numerator and denominator data fields. The default value of denominator should be 1. Define a constructor with two arguments for this class and one with just one argument (the value of the numerator). Define a method multiply that multiplies this Fraction object with the one specified by its argument and returns a new Fraction object as its result. Define a method toDecimal that returns the value of the fraction as a decimal number (be careful about integer division). Define a toString method for this class that represents a Fraction object as a string of the form *numerator / denominator*.

5. Write a main method that reads two Fraction objects using class JOptionPane. Multiply them and display their result as a fraction and as a decimal number using the instance methods defined in Review Question 4. Use class JOptionPane to display the results.

6. Write a main method that reads two Fraction objects from the console. Multiply them and display their result as a fraction and as a decimal number using the instance methods defined in Review Question 4. Use the console to display the results.

Programming Projects

1. Complete the definition of the Fraction class described in Review Question 4. Provide all the methods listed in Review Question 4 and methods to add, subtract, and divide two fractions. Also, provide methods equals and compareTo to compare two Fraction objects.

2. Provide a class MatrixOps that has a two-dimensional array of **double** values as its data field. Provide the following methods:

```
MatrixOps() // Default constructor
MatrixOps(int numNows)  // Sets the number of rows
MatrixOps(int numRows, int numCols)
                // Sets the number of rows and columns
MatrixOps(double[][] mat) // Stores the specified array
void setMatrix(double[][] mat) // Stores the specified array
double[][] getMatrix()  // Gets the array
void setRow(int row, double[] rowVals)
                // Stores the array of rowVals in row
```

```
double[] getRow(int row)  // Returns the specified row
void setElement(int row, int col) // Sets the specified element
double getElement(int row, int col) // Returns the specified element
double sum() // Returns sum of the values in the array
double findMax() // Returns the largest value in the array
double findMin() // Returns the smallest value in the array
double[][] transpose() // Returns the transpose of the matrix
double[] multiply(double[][] mat2)
                  // Returns the product of two matrices
String toString() // Returns a string representing the array
```

3. Modify class `Person` to include a person's hours worked and hourly rate as data fields. Provide modifier and accessor methods for the new data fields and a method `calcSalary` that returns a person's salary. Also, modify method `toString`. Provide a method `calcPayroll` for class `Company` that returns the weekly payroll amount for a company (gross payroll only; don't be concerned about withholding, payroll taxes, and so forth). Write a `main` method that reads the employee data for a `Company` object from a data file. Display the data stored and the calculated payroll in a message window using class `JOptionPane`. Also, write this information to an output file.

4. Write a class that stores a collection of exam scores in an array. Provide methods to find the average score, to assign a letter grade based on a standard scale, to sort the scores so they are in increasing order, and to display the scores. Test the methods of this class.

5. Write a class `Student` that stores a person's name, an array of scores for each person, an average exam score, and a letter grade. Write a class `Gradebook` that stores an instructor's name, a section ID, a course name, and an array of `Student` records. Write the following methods to process this array.

   • Load the array of `Student` records with data read from a text file.
   • Write all information stored to an output file.
   • Calculate and store each student's average exam score in that student's record.
   • Calculate and store the average score for each student in that student's record.
   • Assign a letter grade to each student based on that student's average exam score.
   • Sort the array of student records so that all information is in increasing order by student.
   • Sort the array of student records so that all information is in decreasing order by exam score.

   Write a client program that reads the data for a class and performs all the operations in the list above. Display the information in a `Gradebook` object after all the data is stored and again after all student information been calculated and stored. Also, display the information after sorting it by name and after sorting it by exam score.

Overview of UML

The Unified Modeling Language (UML) represents the unification of earlier object-oriented design modeling techniques. Specifically, notations developed by Grady Booch, Ivar Jacobson, and James Rumbaugh were adapted to form the initial version. This version was submitted to the Object Modeling Group for formal standardization. Since that initial submission, the UML standard has undergone several revisions and continues to be revised.

We call UML a modeling *language* much in the same way we call Java a programming language. There is a formal definition of the syntax and semantics. There are software tools that are used both to draw the diagrams and to capture the underlying design information. These tools can then be used to analyze the resulting model, verify the model's consistency, and generate code.

UML defines twelve types of diagrams. In this text we use only two of them: the class diagram and the sequence diagram. Throughout the text, where we use these diagrams, we provide brief explanations of the diagram and the meaning of the notations used. The purpose of this appendix is to provide a more complete reference to the diagrams as they are used in this text.

In this text, we use a notation that has been adapted from the UML standard to match the syntax of Java more closely. Other books may use slightly different versions of these diagrams that follow the standard syntax, but the principles are the same.

Overview of UML

B.1 The Class Diagram

The *class diagram* shows the classes and their relationships. It is a static diagram that represents the structure of the program. The classes (including interfaces) are represented by rectangles, and lines between the classes represent the relationships. The style of a line, symbols on the ends of the lines, and text placed near the line are used to indicate the kind of relationship being modeled.

A large amount of information about the structure of a program can be represented in a class diagram. If all of the possible information were presented, the diagram would become quite cluttered. Therefore, the practice is to show only the essential information. For example, in a class diagram the complete method declaration can show the method's visibility, return type, name, and parameter types. Sometimes only the method's name is necessary, in which case you would elect to suppress the other information. Also, some methods may not be significant to the discussion, so those methods need not be shown. Sometimes only the class's name is the essential item, and thus the methods and attributes are not shown.

FIGURE B.1
General Representation
of a Class

ClassName
Attributes
Operations

Representing Classes and Interfaces

A class is represented by a rectangle divided into three segments as shown in Figure B.1.

The Class Name

Every class has a name that distinguishes it from other classes. In Java a class may be (and usually is) a member of a package, in which case we may show the complete name including the package name (for example, java.util.Stack). In other cases we just show the class name (for example, Node). Italics indicate abstract classes. The class name is centered in the box representing the class. For example, Figure B.2 shows the abstract class Number and the concrete classes derived from it.

FIGURE B.2
The Abstract Class
Number and Concrete
Subclasses

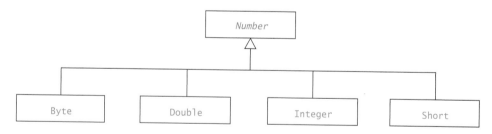

FIGURE B.3
The Interface List

«interface»
List

Interfaces

The word *interface* enclosed in double angle brackets (« and », called guillemets) placed before the class name is used to indicate that this class is an interface. Because interfaces, like abstract classes, cannot be instantiated, the name is shown in italics. See Figure B.3.

FIGURE B.4
Alternative Syntax for
Indicating an Abstract
Class

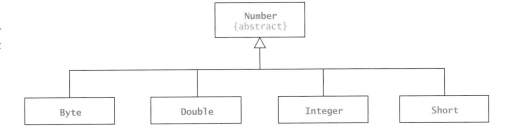

Alternative UML Syntax for Class Names

In other texts you may see the class name in a bold sans-serif font. Also, abstract classes may be indicated by {abstract}, as shown in Figure B.4.

The Attributes

The *attributes* of a class are the data fields. As a minimum we show the name. Optionally we can also show the visibility and type. The visibility is indicated by the symbols shown in Table B.1.

TABLE B.1
Visibility Specifiers

Symbol	Visibility
+	public
-	private
#	protected
~	package

In this text we use the Java language syntax to indicate the type of an attribute by placing the type name before the attribute name. For example the class, Person could have the attributes familyName, givenName, and address, as shown in the following figure.

```
          Person
─────────────────────────
 - String familyName
 - String givenName
 - Address address
```

Where they are not essential to the current discussion, we will omit the visibility indicator, the type, or both, as shown in the following figure.

```
          Person
─────────────────────────
 familyName
 givenName
 address
```

Static attributes are indicated by underlining their name. For example, the class LapTop has the static attribute DEFAULT_LT_MAN.

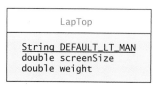

Standard UML Syntax for Attribute Types

In other texts you may see a different syntax for showing the attribute type. The UML standard specifies that the attribute type be specified following the name and separated by a colon.

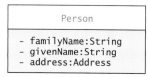

The Operations

The *operations* are the methods of the class. At a minimum, we show the method name followed by a pair of parentheses. An empty set of parentheses does not necessarily indicate that this method takes no parameters. Italics are used to indicate an abstract method, and underlining is used to indicate a static method. For example, Figure B.5 shows the class Passenger with the static method setMaxProcessingTime and the nonstatic methods getArrivalTime and getProcessingTime. The attributes are not shown.

We may also show the visibility, the parameter types, and the return type. The visibility is shown using the same symbols as used for the attributes (see Table B.1). In this text we use the Java method declaration syntax, as shown in Figure B.6 to show the parameter types and return type. A return type of **void**, however, will not be shown.

FIGURE B.5
The Class **Passenger**

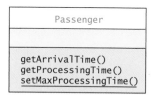

FIGURE B.6
Class **Passenger**
Showing the Return and
Parameter Types of Its
Operations

Standard UML Syntax for Operations

In other texts you may see a different syntax for showing the parameter types and return type. The UML standard specifies that the parameter type be preceded by a colon and shown following the parameter name, and that the return type be shown following the operation name, also preceded by a colon. The class Passenger using this syntax is shown in the following figure.

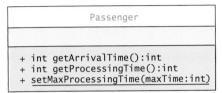

Generalization

UML uses the term *generalization* to describe the relationship between a superclass and its sub-classes. Drawing a solid line with a large open arrowhead pointing to the superclass shows generalization. Figure B.7 shows the class LapTop as a subclass of Computer.

A dashed line with a large open arrowhead is used to show that a class implements an interface. Figure B.8 shows that the abstract class AbstractList implements the List interface and that the classes ArrayList, Vector, and AbstractSequentialList are subclasses of AbstractList. Stack is a subclass of Vector, and LinkedList is a subclass of AbstractSequentialList.

FIGURE B.7

Class LapTop as a Subclass of Computer

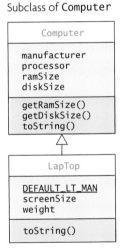

FIGURE B.8

The List Interface and Classes That Implement It

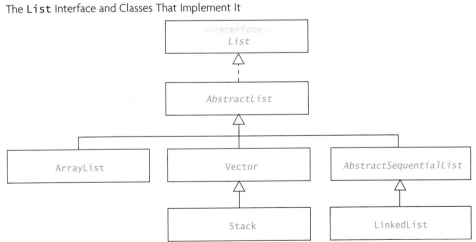

Inner or Nested Classes

A class that is declared within the body of another class is called an inner or nested class. In UML this relationship is indicated by a solid line between the two classes, with what the UML standard calls an *anchor* on the end connected to the enclosing class. The anchor is a cross inside a circle. For example, in Figure B.9 the class Node is declared as an inner class of the class KWLinkedList.

FIGURE B.9
Node as an Inner Class

Association

An *association* between classes represents a relationship between objects of those classes. In object-oriented terminology we say that "object A sends a message to object B." This statement implies two things:

1. There is a method in class B that will receive the message.

2. There must be a reference within class A that references object B.

An association indicates the presence of the reference required by condition 2. Thus, in the analysis process in which we examine a use case and determine the flow of information from one object to another, we identify the requirements for methods and associations. Note that the association may represent a data field or it may represent a parameter.

Figure B.10 shows the UML notation for an association. The *association name*, multiplicities, and roles are all optional. The association name is a name given to the association. The *multiplicity* represents the number of objects of that class that participate in the association. Where the association is implemented as a data field, the *role name* is generally used as the name of the data field. Thus, in ClassA there would be a reference of type ClassB with the name roleB. The role name may have a visibility specifier (see Table B.1). The role and multiplicity may be either above or below the line.

FIGURE B.10
UML Notation for an
Association

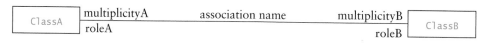

Multiplicity represents the number of objects of the class that are related to the other class. Thus *multiplicityB* represents the number of objects of ClassB that are associated with an object of ClassA, and *multiplicityA* represents the number of objects of ClassA that are associated with an object of ClassB. Multiplicity may be either a single number or a range of numbers. The symbol * is used to indicate an indefinite number. A range of numbers is specified by a low bound followed by a high bound separated by two periods. Examples are shown in the following table:

Multiplicity	Meaning
1	There is only 1.
1..5	There is at least 1, and there may be as many as 5.
3..*	There are at least 3.
*	There could be any number, including 0.

In addition, an arrow can be placed at one or both ends of the line. The presence of an arrow indicates the navigation direction. Thus, if there is an arrow on the ClassB end, then objects of ClassA can send messages to objects of ClassB, but objects of ClassB cannot send messages to objects of ClassA. The absence of arrows generally represents that navigation in both directions is possible, but it may also mean that the navigation is not being shown.

Aggregation and Composition

In those cases where we wish to show that an association definitely is represented by a data field, we place a diamond on the end of the line next to the class that will contain the data field. This represents the *has-a* relationship. If the diamond is open, this is called an *aggregation*, and if the diamond is filled, this is called a *composition*. The difference is that in a composition the component objects are not considered to have an independent existence. For example, an Airplane is composed of two wings, a body, and a tail, none of which would exist unless they were components of an Airplane. This would be modeled as shown in Figure B.11.

On the other hand, a Node in either a linked list or a tree has references to other Nodes, but these other nodes are independent entities, and the value of the reference can be changed. Thus we use the open diamond as shown in Figure B.12. Observe that the references are to the same class (Node).

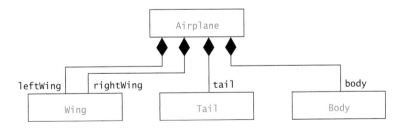

FIGURE B.11
Airplane Composed of Wing, Tail, and Body

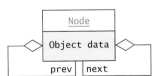

FIGURE B.12
A **Node** in a Double-Linked List

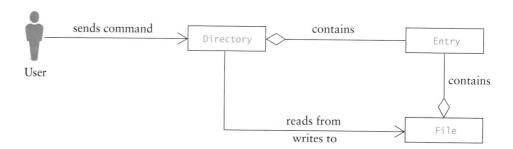

The **Directory** and **File** Classes as Aggregations of **Entrys**

Aggregation is also used to indicate that one class is a collection of objects of another class. For example, the **Directory** and **File** classes are collections of **Entry** objects, as shown in Figure B.13.

B.2 Sequence Diagrams

Sequence diagrams are used to show the flow of information through the program. Sequence diagrams are generally developed on a use case basis and show the message sequence associated with a particular use case. The purpose of developing a sequence diagram is to identify the messages that are passed from one object to another. This then identifies the requirements for the corresponding classes. Recall that if *objectA* sends a message to *objectB*, then

1. *ClassB* must have a method to process that message.

2. *ClassA* must have a reference to an *objectB*.

Thus, when you enter a message on a sequence diagram, you identify a requirement for a method and an association to be entered on the class diagram. Many UML modeling software tools automate the process of keeping the sequence diagrams and class diagram consistent.

Figure B.14 shows an example of a sequence diagram. This is a two-dimensional diagram with time running down the vertical axis and objects listed across the horizontal axis. The ordering across the horizontal axis is insignificant.

Time Axis

Time flows down the vertical axis. Generally the scale is not significant, but for some applications, where timing is critical, a precise timing scale can be used. The sequence along the time axis is significant.

Objects

Objects are listed across the horizontal axis. Their order is insignificant. An object is represented by a rectangle with the name of the object underlined. For anonymous objects, the name of the class is given.

FIGURE B.14
Sequence Diagram Example

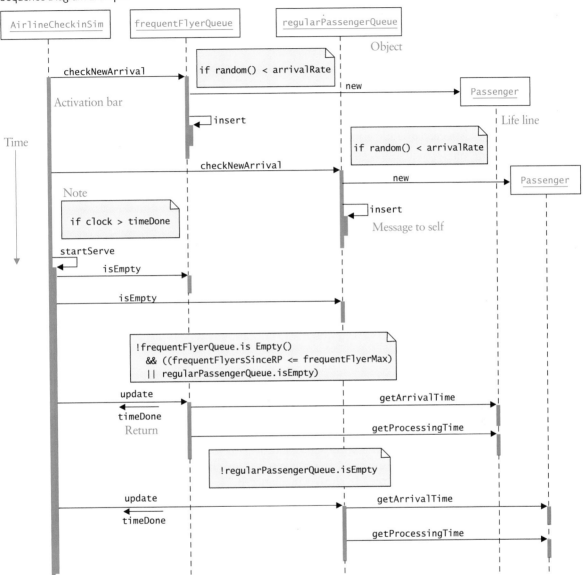

Objects are listed across the top of the sequence diagram unless they are created during the time period represented by the sequence diagram. If an object is created, then it is shown lower in the diagram, at the point at which it is created. As shown in Figure B.14, two Passenger objects are created during the sequence of events depicted.

Life Lines

Flowing down from each object is its *life line*. This is a dashed line that begins when the object is created and ends when the object is destroyed. There is no way to destroy an object explicitly in Java, so the life lines will continue to the bottom of the diagram.

Activation Bars

The thin long rectangles along the life line are *activation bars*. These represent the time that the object is responding to a given message. Note that if a second message is received while a message is being processed, a second activation bar is drawn on top of and to the right of the first activation bar. This can be seen in Figure B.14, where the AirlineCheckinSim object sends itself the startServe message, or where the frequentFlyerQueue and regularPassengerQueue objects send themselves the insert message.

Messages

Messages are indicated by a horizontal arrow from the sending object to the receiving object. The name of the message is shown above the arrow. Optionally, the parameters may be shown in parentheses following the message name. Also, a small reverse direction arrow may be used to indicate a return value with the value shown below it. An example of this is shown in Figure B.14 where timeDone is returned to the AirlineCheckinSim object in response to the update message sent to the frequentFlyerQueue.

Use of Notes

Notes may be used on any UML diagram. They are free-form text enclosed in a rectangle with the upper right corner folded down.

The purpose of the sequence diagram is to identify the sequence of messages that occur during a use case. For a given instance of a use case, not all messages will be sent. For example, as shown in Figure B.14, the checkNewArrival message to the frequentFlyerQueue may or may not result in the creation of a new Passenger object. Notes can be used to document the conditions for sending a message. For example, the checkNewArrival message is sent when the result of the random number generator is less than arrivalRate.

Event-Oriented Programming

Chapter Objectives

◆ To understand how event-driven programming differs from request-response programming

◆ To learn how to design and write event-driven programs using the Java graphics API

◆ To learn about different kinds of events that can occur

◆ To become familiar with the structure of the Java Swing API, including the class hierarchy, user interaction components, and ways to arrange the components

◆ To learn about mouse events and how to draw figures using the mouse

You are accustomed to using an operating system that has a graphical user interface (GUI) for interacting with your computer. The operating system constantly receives inputs from the keyboard, mouse, and communications network. You control the computer's operation by moving the mouse, clicking on icons, or typing information at the keyboard. However, it wasn't always that way. Initially, computers had little direct interaction with human users. Users prepared their programs and data on external media such as magnetic tape, punched paper tape, or punched cards. These were then fed directly to the computer or copied to magnetic tape by another computer whose task was to create batches of programs to be run by the main computer. (We get the term *batch processing* from this practice.) With the development of minicomputers and, later, personal computers, programmers and users were able to interact directly with their programs. With these smaller computers the *request-response* style was developed. The computer prompted the user for input, and the user supplied it.

Batch processing and request-response were not the only ways in which computers were used. Interactive systems, such as airline reservations, bank automated tellers, and military command and control systems provided real-time interaction between many users and a single program, but the request-response model is totally unworkable for these kinds of systems. In the request-response model the logic that requests the data, the logic that processes the data, and the logic that displays the results are all intertwined. Developing logic that can manage numerous different transactions in this model is all but impossible.

Thus the designers of these large, interactive systems separated requesting input, displaying data, and processing data into independent processes that could be considered as executing in parallel. The input process would constantly be ready to receive input. As each individual input was received, a processing process would be activated to process these data. The processing process would then update information that the display process would use to update the display(s).

This model has been adapted to modern personal-computer operating systems through their GUI environments. Each input represents an event. By writing and registering event listeners (methods that listen for and respond to events), we can develop very sophisticated applications that are easier to use. In this chapter we will show how to develop such programs using the Java API's which provide a GUI environment that is operating system independent.

Event-Oriented Programming

C.1 Elements of an Event-Oriented Application

This section will introduce you to event-driven programming. We will write a new interface for the phone directory application from Chapter 1 that processes events that are generated by clicking buttons.

Earlier, we wrote class PDGUI (see Listing 1.4), which used method JOptionPane.show OptionDialog to display a menu of buttons. (See Figure C.1.) When the user clicked a button, a number was returned to the calling program. The calling program then used this number in a **switch** statement to call the appropriate processing routine.

FIGURE C.1

Button Menu displayed
by PDGUI

The code for the main loop is as follows:

```
do {
    choice = JOptionPane.showOptionDialog(
        null,                                   // No parent
        "Select a Command",                     // Prompt message
        "PhoneDirectory",                       // Window title
        JOptionPane.YES_NO_CANCEL_OPTION,       // Option type
        JOptionPane.QUESTION_MESSAGE,           // Message type
        null,                                   // Icon
        commands,                               // List of commands
        commands[commands.length - 1]);         // Default choice
    switch (choice) {
        case 0: doAddChangeEntry(); break;
        case 1: doLookupEntry(); break;
        case 2: doRemoveEntry(); break;
        case 3: doSave(); break;
        case 4: doSaveAndClose(); break;
    }
} while (choice < commands.length - 1);
```

Although this code appears to be fairly straightforward, it presents some potential maintenance issues. The labels for the buttons are given in the array `commands`, which is defined as follows:

```
String[] commands = {"Add/Change Entry",
                     "Look Up Entry",
                     "Remove Entry",
                     "Save Directory",
                     "Exit"};
```

If we were to decide to change the list of options, we would have to change the array `commands` and the **switch** statement. We would have to make sure that `commands[i]` corresponds to **case** i and its associated code after we make the changes.

Instead, it would be more desirable to link the processing routine directly to the button. Thus, when the button is clicked, the processing routine is called with no intervening logic to determine which button was clicked and which routine should process it.

We will next describe how to reimplement the class `PDGUI` so that the processing routines are directly linked to the buttons. This new class, `PDButtonUI`, will have the same functionality as the original `PDGUI`. We can then use this new class as the basis for making the changes just discussed. Making the changes is left as a programming project.

Components and Events

The Java API documentation uses the term *component* to represent the objects that are displayed on the screen and can interact with the user. A button is a type of component. Placing the cursor over the button and clicking the mouse button triggers an *event*.

In the first few sections of the chapter, we will focus on action events (type ActionEvent). We will study action events that are triggered by clicking a mouse button over a GUI component and action events that are triggered by pressing the Enter key on the keyboard after typing in text. Class ActionEvent is a subclass of the abstract class AWTEvent. Both classes are defined in API java.awt.event. Another subclass of AWTEvent is ItemEvent. ItemEvents are triggered by making a selection from a list of items. A third subclass of AWTEvent is MouseEvent. MouseEvents are triggered by pressing and releasing mouse buttons or by dragging the mouse.

Event Listeners

When an event occurs, the button clicked will call each of the *event listeners* that are registered for the event. An action listener is a method that is to be called when an action event occurs. We need to be able to pass the name of this method to the button so that it will know whom to call, just as you need to leave your name and phone number on someone's answering machine if that person is to call you back when available. In the Java programming language, however, we can't treat methods like objects—we can't pass them to other methods as parameters, and other methods can't store them in data fields for later use. Therefore, we enclose the method in a class and pass an object of the class to the button. By defining a common interface for the classes that will enclose action listener methods, we ensure that all button objects have a common way of registering their action listeners and then calling them when the event triggered by clicking that button occurs.

The process by which an event listener is associated with an event is called *registering* the listener for the event. This is done by a method named add*EventType*Listener, where *EventType* is the type of the event. For example, action listeners are registered by calling the method addActionListener. The component object (e.g., a button) maintains lists of the event listeners that are registered for each of its events. When the component determines that an event has occurred, it then calls the event listeners that are registered for that event. This is called *firing an event*. The component does this by calling the fire*EventType* method.

The ActionListener Interface

The ActionListener interface (defined in API java.awt.event) declares just one method, actionPerformed, as follows:

```
interface ActionListener extends EventListener {
    void actionPerformed(ActionEvent e);
}
```

The interface EventListener (defined in java.util) has no methods. Such interfaces are known as *markers*. Marker interfaces are used to give a common name to a family of interfaces and classes. Another example of a marker interface is Cloneable, which you saw in Chapter 3.

EXAMPLE C.1   In the PDGUI class, when the Look Up Entry button is clicked, the loop shown earlier invokes the method doLookupEntry. Since the ActionListener interface requires a method named actionPerformed, we transform method doLookupEntry into method actionPerformed for the class DoLookupEntry, as shown next:

```
/** Class to respond to the Look Up Entry Button. */
private class DoLookupEntry implements ActionListener {
    /** Method to look up an entry.
        pre:  The directory has been loaded with data.
        post: No changes made to the directory.
    */
    public void actionPerformed(ActionEvent e) {
        // Request the name.
        String theName =
            JOptionPane.showInputDialog("Enter name");
        if (theName == null) return; // Dialog was canceled.
        // Look up the name.
        String theNumber = theDirectory.lookupEntry(theName);
        String message = null;
        if (theNumber != null) { // Name was found.
            message =
                "The number for " + theName + " is " + theNumber;
        } else { // Name was not found.
            message =
                theName + " is not listed in the directory";
        }
        // Display the result.
        JOptionPane.showMessageDialog(null, message);
    }
}
```

If you compare this with Listing 1.4, you will see that we changed the method name from doLookupEntry to actionPerformed and then enclosed it in a class named DoLookupEntry. Class DoLookupEntry implements the ActionListener interface. It is an *inner class* because it is wholly contained in class PDButtonUI. All private members of the outer class (for example, theDirectory) are visible in an inner class. Listing C.1, in a later subsection, shows the PDButtonUI class with the DoLookupEntry class as an inner class.

Registering an Event Listener

A button is an object of the class JButton. This class provides the method addActionListener through the superclass AbstractButton (see Figure C.3 for the button class hierarchy; we will discuss other subclasses of AbstractButton later). We use this method to register the action listener as follows:

```
lookupEntryButton.addActionListener(new DoLookupEntry());
```

We can call this method at any time after the object lookupEntryButton is created, but generally we call it right after invoking the constructor to create this JButton object:

```
JButton lookupEntryButton = new JButton("Look Up Entry");
lookupEntryButton.addActionListener(new DoLookupEntry());
```

Creating a User Interface

All user interfaces are displayed within a *window*. The Java GUI API defines three kinds of windows: *frames, dialogs,* and *applets.* Of these, only a frame can stand alone. Frames are implemented by the class Frame and its subclass JFrame. The class Frame is part of the original Java Abstract Window Toolkit (AWT–java.awt), and JFrame is part of the more flexible Swing graphics API (javax.swing). In this text we will use the Swing classes wherever possible.

Therefore we begin our definition of PDButtonUI as follows:

```
/** Class to display and modify a simple phone directory. */
public class PDButtonUI extends JFrame
                        implements PhoneDirectoryUI {
```

This states that our class inherits from JFrame and implements the methods required by the interface PhoneDirectoryUI.

The Constructor

The constructor will then build the contents of the frame. First we place a title on our frame as follows:

```
// Set the title on the top of the frame.
super("Phone Directory");
```

By default, when a frame is closed by clicking on the window close box (✕) or by some other external command, the program that owns it is still running. We can change that default behavior by calling the setDefaultCloseOperation. However, we need to ensure that the phone directory data is written back to the data file. Therefore, we need to respond to the WindowClosing event. We register the event listener for this event as follows:

```
// Define the window close action.
addWindowListener(new WindowClosing());
```

The visible part of the frame is known as the *content pane.* Since we want to display several buttons, these are placed into another *container* that is then placed into the content pane. This container is known as a *panel* and is defined by the class JPanel. We create a panel to hold the buttons as follows:

```
// Create a panel to hold the buttons.
JPanel panel = new JPanel();
```

Now we can create the buttons, register their action listeners, and add them to the the panel. The code to do this for the Look Up Entry button is as follows:

```
// Look Up Entry
JButton lookupEntryButton = new JButton("Look Up Entry");
lookupEntryButton.addActionListener(new DoLookupEntry());
panel.add(lookupEntryButton);
```

These lines are repeated for each button. Finally, the panel is added to the content pane and the frame size set to hold the panel using the statements

```
// Put the panel into the frame.
getContentPane().add(panel);
// Size the frame to hold the panel.
pack();
```

The processCommands Method

As required by the PDUserInterface, we also provide the method processCommands as follows:

```
public void processCommands(PhoneDirectory thePhoneDirectory) {
    theDirectory = thePhoneDirectory;
    show();
}
```

It merely saves the reference to the PhoneDirectory object and shows the frame (see Figure C.2).

FIGURE C.2
Button Based Phone
Directory User Interface

Unlike the JOptionPane-based PDGUI, this method does not contain a loop that waits for input to be entered and then calls the processing routines. Instead, it displays the frame and then releases the processor to perform other tasks. When a button is clicked, the processor executes the instructions in method actionPerformed for that button's listener object.

Listing C.1 shows the classes required for the button-based interface. The constructor creates the GUI window (a frame) as described earlier. Next comes the processCommands method. Then there are five private *inner classes* with methods that respond to different button events. They are similar to class DoLookupEntry shown in Example C.1. We will just show the listener class that responds to the window closing event.

LISTING C.1
PDButtonUI.java

```
import java.util.*;
import java.io.*;
import javax.swing.*;
import java.awt.event.*;

/** Class to display and modify a simple phone directory. */
public class PDButtonUI extends JFrame
                        implements PDUserInterface {

    // Data Field
    private PhoneDirectory theDirectory;

    // Constructor
    public PDButtonUI() {
        // Set the title on the top of the frame.
        super("Phone Directory");
        // Define the window close action.
        addWindowListener(new WindowClosing());
        // Create a panel to hold the buttons.
        JPanel panel = new JPanel();
        // Create buttons and add them to the panel.
```

```
        // Add/Change Entry
        JButton addEntryButton = new JButton("Add/Change Entry");
        addEntryButton.addActionListener(new DoAddChangeEntry());
        panel.add(addEntryButton);
        // Look Up Entry
        JButton lookupEntryButton = new JButton("Look Up Entry");
        lookupEntryButton.addActionListener(new DoLookupEntry());
        panel.add(lookupEntryButton);
        // Remove Entry
        JButton removeEntryButton = new JButton("Remove Entry");
        removeEntryButton.addActionListener(new DoRemoveEntry());
        panel.add(removeEntryButton);
        // Save Directory
        JButton saveDirectoryButton = new JButton("Save Directory");
        saveDirectoryButton.addActionListener(new DoSave());
        panel.add(saveDirectoryButton);
        // Exit
        JButton exitButton = new JButton("Exit");
        exitButton.addActionListener(new DoSaveAndExit());
        panel.add(exitButton);
        // Put the panel into the frame.
        getContentPane().add(panel);
        // Size the frame to hold the panel.
        pack();
    }

    public void processCommands(PhoneDirectory thePhoneDirectory) {
        theDirectory = thePhoneDirectory;
        show();
    }

    // Action Event Listener Classes
    /** Class to respond to the Look Up Entry button. */
    private class DoLookupEntry implements ActionListener {
        ...
    }
    // Insert listener classes for other buttons.

    /** Class to respond to the WindowClosing event. */
    private class WindowClosing extends WindowAdapter {
        /** Method to save the directory to the data file and close
            the data file.
            pre:  The directory has been loaded with data.
            post: The current contents of the directory have been
                  saved to the data file, and the data file is closed.
        */
        public void windowClosing(WindowEvent e) {
            theDirectory.save();
            System.exit(0);
        }
    }
}
```

PITFALL

Not Registering a Listener

If you forget to register an event listener for a GUI component, the component will still be displayed, but clicking on that component will have no effect. This will not cause a syntax error or exception.

EXERCISES FOR SECTION C.1

SELF-CHECK

1. What is an event, and how are events generated? What does it mean to register for an event?
2. What is an action listener? How does Java determine which `actionPerformed` method to execute when an action event is generated?
3. What is a `Container`? A `Panel`? The `contentPane`?
4. What does the `Container` method add do?
5. Explain the effect of executing each of the following statements. What can you say about class `HelloMonitor`?
   ```
   JButton aButton = new JButton("Hello");
   aButton.addActionListener(new HelloMonitor());
   panel.add(aButton);
   // Put the panel into the frame.
   getContentPane().add(panel);
   ```

PROGRAMMING

1. Write statements to create a button with label Submit, and register class `DoSubmit` as an action listener for this button.
2. Write class `DoSubmit` and include an `actionPerformed` method that displays a message window showing the message "Thanks for the submission" when button Submit is clicked.
3. Write class `DoSave` for the phone directory problem.

C.2 Overview of the AWT and Swing Hierarchy

Whole books have been written on the Abstract Window Toolkit (AWT) and Swing. In this section we give a brief overview of the class hierarchy and discuss how the different classes interact. Figure C.3 shows the Swing and AWT class hierarchy. The Swing classes are extensions of the AWT classes.

A `Component` is a graphics object that can be displayed on a screen and can interact with a user. A `Container` is a component that can contain other components. The `JComponent` is the base class for all other Swing components except the top-level containers `JFrame`, `JDialog`, `JApplet`, and `JWindow`. Objects of class `JComponent` and its subclasses must be placed in a containment hierarchy that is rooted in one of the top-level containers. Therefore all applications we develop will begin with a `JFrame` that will contain the other components either directly or indirectly. For more information about the various classes in AWT and Swing, you can consult the online documentation of the Java API provided at the Sun Java Web site (`www.java.sun.com`).

FIGURE C.3
Swing and AWT Class Hierarchy

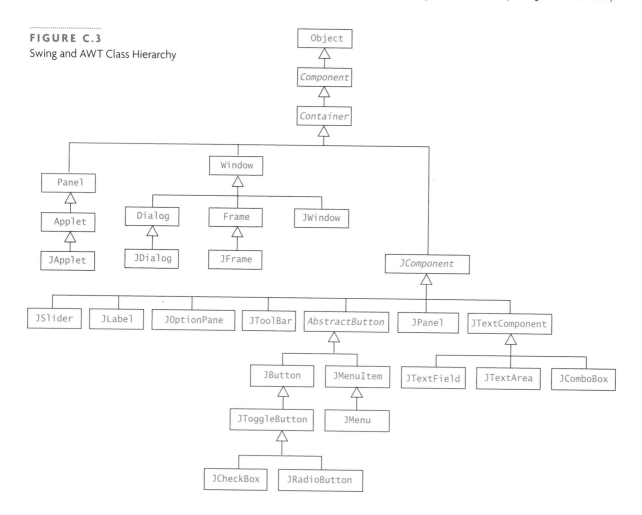

EXAMPLE C.2

Figure C.4 shows an empty `JFrame`. Other components are not directly added to a `JFrame`, but rather are added to the `JFrame`'s content pane, shown in Figure C.4.

FIGURE C.4
Empty Frame Demo

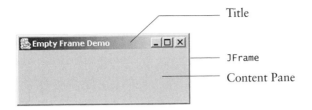

The `JPanel` is a generic container that can be used to contain other components or as a painting surface. We will use `JPanel` as the base class for customized components in our GUI examples, and we will use `JPanel`s as building blocks to lay out the components of our applications.

Example and Overview: Two Circles

Figure C.5 shows a `JFrame` whose content pane contains two `CirclePanel`s, which are extensions of `JPanel`, which is in turn an extension of `JComponent`. Each of these components contains two other components: a `MyCircle` and a `JButton`. The containment hierarchy is shown in Figure C.6. The containment hierarchy is a UML diagram. A filled-in diamond shows containment. The containment hierarchy shows that objects of `MyCircle` and `JButton` are contained in an object of class `CirclePanel` that is, in turn, contained in an object of class `TwoCircles`. The classes are shown in Listings C.2, C.3, and C.4. A `CirclePanel` object is a panel containing a button and a `MyCircle` object. A `MyCircle` object is a panel in which a green rectangle is drawn. A red circle may or may not be drawn over the rectangle. The constructor for class `CirclePanel` creates a `MyCircle` object and registers an instance of `ToggleState` as the listener for events generated by clicking the button in this panel. It also adds the button and `MyCircle` object to the panel.

```
theCircle = new MyCircle();
onOffButton = new JButton("On / Off");
onOffButton.addActionListener(new ToggleState());
add(theCircle, BorderLayout.CENTER);
// Section C.3 discusses Layouts.
add(onOffButton, BorderLayout.SOUTH);
```

FIGURE C.5
`TwoCircles`

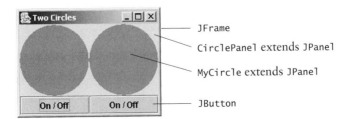

FIGURE C.6
TwoCircles
Containment
Hierarchy

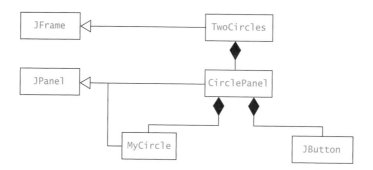

Method main creates a new TwoCircles object (a subclass of JFrame). Its constructor puts two CirclePanel objects in a row in this object using a Grid layout (explained in Section C.3).

```
getContentPane().setLayout(new GridLayout(1,2));
getContentPane().add(new CirclePanel());
getContentPane().add(new CirclePanel());
```

Clicking the button in either of these panels generates an action event that invokes method actionPerformed (a member of inner class ToggleState) for that panel.

```
public void actionPerformed(ActionEvent e) {
    theCircle.toggleState();
}
```

The method actionPerformed invokes toggleState, which complements the **boolean** flag showCircle for that panel and causes the panel to be repainted.

```
public void toggleState() {
    showCircle = !showCircle;
    repaint();
}
```

Invoking method repaint causes the paintComponent method to execute.

```
public void paintComponent(Graphics g) {
    super.paintComponent(g);
    g.setColor(Color.GREEN);
    g.fillRect(0, 0, size, size);
    if (showCircle) {
        g.setColor(Color.RED);
        g.fillOval(0, 0, size, size);
    }
}
```

The Graphics class is an abstract class that provides the interface between the Java API and the physical device on which the image is created. When the paintComponent method is called, a concrete object that is specific for the physical device (such as the graphics display) is passed as this parameter. A summary of the Graphics class is presented later in this section.

The first statement in the body is required. The next two statements draw a green rectangle. The **if** statement draws a red circle over this rectangle if showCircle is true.

 **PITFALL**

You shouldn't call the method paintComponent directly. It should always be invoked indirectly by calling repaint. The actual painting is done in a separate execution thread under the control of what is known as the window manager. A call to repaint tells the window manager to schedule the component for repainting as soon as possible. Also, paintComponent needs a Graphics object, which is obtained by the window manager.

LISTING C.2
TwoCircles.java

```java
import java.awt.*;
import java.awt.event.*;
import javax.swing.*;

/** TwoCircles is a simple event-oriented application that
    displays two circles and two buttons. The buttons are
    placed below the circles. The buttons are labeled on/off.
    When a button is clicked, the state of the circle is toggled.
*/
public class TwoCircles extends JFrame {

    // Constructor
    /** Construct a TwoCircles object. Set the title and
        default close operation. Using a grid layout add
        two CirclePanel objects. Finally, pack the frame
        and set it visible.
    */
    public TwoCircles() {
        super("Two Circles");
        setDefaultCloseOperation(JFrame.EXIT_ON_CLOSE);
        getContentPane().setLayout(new GridLayout(1,2));
        getContentPane().add(new CirclePanel(100));
        getContentPane().add(new CirclePanel(100));
        pack();
        setVisible(true);    // Show the JFrame.
    }

    // Main Method
    /** Instantiate a TwoCircles object.
        @param args Not used. */
    public static void main(String[] args) {
        TwoCircles tc = new TwoCircles();
    }
}
```

```
.........................
LISTING C.3
CirclePanel.java

import java.awt.*;
import java.awt.event.*;
import javax.swing.*;

/** A CirclePanel will contain a circle and a button. */
public class CirclePanel extends JPanel {

    // Data Fields
    /** The button object */
    JButton onOffButton;
    /** The Circle object */
    MyCircle theCircle;

    // Constructor
    /** Construct a CirclePanel object. */
    public CirclePanel(int size) {
        setLayout(new BorderLayout());
        theCircle = new MyCircle(size);
        onOffButton = new JButton("On / Off");
        onOffButton.addActionListener(new ToggleState());
        add(theCircle, BorderLayout.CENTER);
        add(onOffButton, BorderLayout.SOUTH);
    }

    // Inner Class
    /** The action listener for the button. */
    private class ToggleState implements ActionListener {
        public void actionPerformed(ActionEvent e) {
            theCircle.toggleState();
        }
    }
}
```

```
.........................
LISTING C.4
MyCircle.java

import javax.swing.*;
import java.awt.*;
import java.awt.event.*;

/** Class MyCircle is a JPanel that consists of a circle enclosed
    in a square. The square is always displayed, but the circle can
    be turned on and off.
*/
public class MyCircle extends JPanel {

    // Data Fields
    /** The size */
    private int size;
    /** Display state for the circle */
    private boolean showCircle = true;
```

```java
// Constructors
/** Construct a MyCircle object of the specified size.
    @param size The size of the circle in pixels
*/
public MyCircle(int size) {
    this.size = size;
    // Encapsulate the object's dimensions in a Dimension object.
    Dimension dims = new Dimension(size, size);
    // Set the object's dimensions.
    setPreferredSize(dims);
    setMaximumSize(dims);
    setMinimumSize(dims);
}

/** Toggle the state of the circle. */
public void toggleState() {
    showCircle = !showCircle;
    repaint();     // Calls paint to redraw the object.
}

/** Paint the component when it changes. This method is called
    by the Swing API.
    @param g The graphics object used for painting. */
public void paintComponent(Graphics g) {
    super.paintComponent(g);
    g.setColor(Color.GREEN);
    g.fillRect(0, 0, size, size);
    if (showCircle) {
        g.setColor(Color.RED);
        g.fillOval(0, 0, size, size);
    }
}
}
```

JFrame

The class JFrame will be the top-level container for our GUI applications. Generally our application main class will be derived from JFrame, which the main method will instantiate. Table C.1 gives a summary of selected members of the JFrame class and its superclasses.

TABLE C.1
Summary of JFrame

Constant	Usage
EXIT_ON_CLOSE	Argument to setDefaultCloseOperation.
Constructor	**Behavior**
JFrame()	Constructs a new JFrame with no title and initially invisible.
JFrame(String title)	Constructs a new JFrame with the specified title and initially invisible.

TABLE C.1 (continued)

Method	Behavior
Container getContentPane()	Returns the content pane object, which can then be manipulated by adding components and changing its layout manager.
void setDefaultCloseOperation(int operation)	Sets the operation that will happen when the user initiates a close on this frame.
void setContentPane(Container contentPane)	Replaces the current content pane with the specified one. Generally a JPanel is used as the content pane.
void setTitle(String title)	Sets the title.
void setMenuBar(MenuBar bm)	Sets the menu bar for this frame.
void setSize(int width, int height)	Sets the window size to the number of pixels specified by its arguments.
void pack()	Causes the window to be sized to fit the preferred size and layout of its subcomponents.
void show()	Makes the window visible.

JPanel

A JPanel is a general-purpose intermediate component. It is used to organize the other components. It can also be used as the basis for a customized component and as a drawing surface. Table C.2 shows the different constructor options for JPanel. The default is *double buffering* and flow layout. The choice of double buffering allows for flicker-free updates at the cost of additional memory. (Actual drawing is done in one buffer, while the other buffer is being displayed. When the drawing updates are complete, the buffers are swapped very quickly so that the change is not noticeable to the human eye.) The default layout for the panel is flow layout, which results in a left-to-right placement of the components in the order in which they were added. If not all components fit, later components will be inserted below the earlier ones, in left-to-right order. The different layout managers will be discussed in Section C.3.

The methods unique to JPanel are minimal and are used to change the "look and feel," a subject beyond the scope of this text. Instead, you are more likely to use the methods inherited from JComponent, Container, and Component. These methods are summarized in Table C.3.

TABLE C.2
Constructors for JPanel

Constructor	Behavior
JPanel()	Constructs a JPanel with double buffering and flow layout.
JPanel(LayoutManager layout)	Constructs a JPanel with double buffering and the specified layout manager.

TABLE C.3
Summary of JPanel Inherited Methods

Method	Behavior
void add(Component c)	Adds the specified component to the panel at the next position.
void add(Component c, Object pos)	Adds the specified component to the panel and notifies the layout manager to add it to the position indiated by the second argument.
void paintComponent(Graphics g)	Paints the component.
void repaint()	Schedules repainting of this component. This method is called by client programs whenever the content of the component is changed and should be repainted. Client programs should call only this method and never call paintComponent directly.

Graphics

The Graphics class provides the ability to do the actual drawing (called image rendering) in a device-independent manner. The Graphics class is an abstract class. The Java API provides the correct concrete class when the paintComponent method is called. A summary of selected methods of this class is given in Table C.4.

TABLE C.4
Selected Methods of the Graphics Class

Method	Behavior
void drawLine(int x1, int y1, int x2, int y2)	Draws a line, using the current color, from (x1, y1) to (x2, y2).
void drawOval(int x, int y, int width, int height)	Draws the outline of an oval that is tangent to the bounding rectangle specified by x, y, width, and height. (See Figure C.7.)
void drawPolygon(Polygon p)	Draws the outline of a polygon defined by the Polygon object.
void drawRect(int x, int y, int width, int height)	Draws the outline of the specified rectangle.
void fillOval(int x, int y, int width, int height)	Fills an oval bounded by the specified rectangle. (See Figure C.7)
void fillPolygon(Polygon p)	Fills a closed polygon defined by the specified Polygon object.
void fillRect(int x, int y, int width, int height)	Fills the specified rectangle.
Color getColor()	Returns the current color.
void setColor(Color c)	Sets this graphics context current color to the specified color.
void setPaintMode()	Sets the painting mode to overwrite the destination with the current color.
void setXORMode(Color c)	Sets the painting mode such that if the same figure is drawn twice, all pixels are restored to their original values.

FIGURE C.7
Graphics Coordinates
and Bounding Rectangle
of an Oval

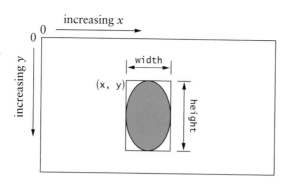

FIGURE C.7
Graphics Coordinates
and Bounding Rectangle
of an Oval

Graphics Coordinates

All graphics coordinates are in units of pixels. The size of a pixel is dependent on the actual output device. The origin is the upper left corner. Increasing x moves to the right. Increasing y moves down. (See Figure C.7.)

EXERCISES FOR SECTION C.2

SELF-CHECK

1. _____ is the top-level container for GUI applications.
2. A _____ is a general-purpose intermediate component used to organize the other components.
3. A JPanel can also be used to _____.

PROGRAMMING

1. Create a modified version of TwoCircles to show just the outline of a circle in green.
2. Create a modified version of TwoCircles to display a dialog that asks "Do you really want to do this?" *Hint:* Use JOptionPane to display the dialog. Try clicking on the button for the other circle when the dialog is displayed. What happens?

C.3 Layout Managers

The Java API provides different *layout managers* to position components within the display area of a container component. This frees the user from having to manipulate the graphics coordinates, although this option is still available. The layout managers we use are listed in Table C.5.

Layout Manager	Description
BorderLayout	Arranges objects in five areas of the container: north, west, center, east, and south.
FlowLayout	Arranges objects in left-to-right order across the container, flowing down to the next row when a row is filled.
BoxLayout	Arranges objects in a single row or column.
GridLayout	Arranges objects in a two-dimensional grid.

The layout manager can be specified as an argument of the JPanel constructor, or it can be set in any Container by calling the method setLayoutManager. In this section we will describe the BorderLayout, FlowLayout, BoxLayout, and GridLayout.

Border Layout

The default layout for the JFrame's content pane is Border Layout. This layout defines five areas: north, south, east, west, and center. These are shown in Figure C.8. Notice that the north and south areas extend across the width of the container.

The following code fragment shows how components are added to each of the areas. It is not necessary to fill each of the layout areas, however.

```
// Add the labels to the content pane.
Container contentPane = getContentPane();
contentPane.add(north, BorderLayout.NORTH);
contentPane.add(south, BorderLayout.SOUTH);
contentPane.add(east, BorderLayout.EAST);
contentPane.add(west, BorderLayout.WEST);
contentPane.add(center, BorderLayout.CENTER);
```

The program to draw Figure C.8 is shown in Listing C.5.

FIGURE C.8
Border Layout

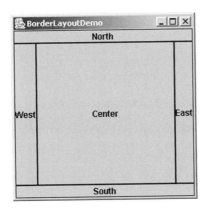

LISTING C.5

BorderLayoutDemo.java

```java
import java.awt.*;
import javax.swing.*;
import javax.swing.border.*;

/** BorderLayoutDemo generates a simple frame that shows the positions
    available in a BorderLayout. */
public class BorderLayoutDemo extends JFrame {

    // Main Method
    public static void main(String args[]) {
        // Construct a BorderLayoutDemo object.
        JFrame frame = new BorderLayoutDemo();
        // Display the frame.
        frame.show();
    }

    // Constructor
    public BorderLayoutDemo() {
        // Set the title.
        setTitle("BorderLayoutDemo");
        // Set the default close operation to exit on close.
        setDefaultCloseOperation(JFrame.EXIT_ON_CLOSE);
        // Create five labels: "North", "South", "East", "West",
        // and "Center".
        JLabel north = new JLabel("North", JLabel.CENTER);
        JLabel south = new JLabel("South", JLabel.CENTER);
        JLabel east = new JLabel("East", JLabel.CENTER);
        JLabel west = new JLabel("West", JLabel.CENTER);
        JLabel center = new JLabel("Center", JLabel.CENTER);
        // Place a black border around each label.
        Border blackBorder =
            BorderFactory.createLineBorder(Color.BLACK);
        north.setBorder(blackBorder);
        south.setBorder(blackBorder);
        east.setBorder(blackBorder);
        west.setBorder(blackBorder);
        center.setBorder(blackBorder);
        center.setPreferredSize(new Dimension(200,200));
        // Add the labels to the content pane.
        Container contentPane = getContentPane();
        contentPane.add(north, BorderLayout.NORTH);
        contentPane.add(south, BorderLayout.SOUTH);
        contentPane.add(east, BorderLayout.EAST);
        contentPane.add(west, BorderLayout.WEST);
        contentPane.add(center, BorderLayout.CENTER);
        // Size the frame to fit.
        pack();
    }
}
```

Flow Layout

The default layout manager for JPanel is Flow Layout. This is the simplest layout; items are placed left to right until the maximum width is filled, then they are placed on successive rows, much as words are placed in a paragraph. Figures C.9 and C.10 show examples of flow layout.

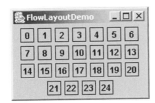

Figure C.9 shows the original output of the program that places 25 labels into a JPanel. Figure C.10 shows the frame after it has been resized using the mouse. Notice that by constraining the width, components are placed on successive lines. Also notice that because the components on the last line do not fill the full width, they are centered. This is the default behavior; the method setAlignment can be used to change it. Listing C.6 shows the program that generated these figures.

LISTING C.6
FlowLayoutDemo.java

```java
import java.awt.*;
import javax.swing.*;
import javax.swing.border.*;

/** FlowLayoutDemo generates a simple frame that shows how components
    are arranged using FlowLayout. */
public class FlowLayoutDemo extends JFrame {

    // Main Method
    public static void main(String args[]) {
        // Construct a FlowLayoutDemo object.
        JFrame frame = new FlowLayoutDemo();
        // Display the frame.
        frame.show();
    }

    // Constructor
    public FlowLayoutDemo() {
        setTitle("FlowLayoutDemo");
        setDefaultCloseOperation(JFrame.EXIT_ON_CLOSE);
```

```
        // Create a JPanel to hold some labels.
        JPanel aPanel = new JPanel();
        // Define the preferred size for the labels.
        Dimension preferredSize = new Dimension(20, 20);
        Border blackBorder =
            BorderFactory.createLineBorder(Color.BLACK);
        // Create some labels and add them to the panel.
        for (int i = 0; i < 25; i++) {
            JLabel aLabel =
                new JLabel(Integer.toString(i), JLabel.CENTER);
            aLabel.setPreferredSize(preferredSize);
            aLabel.setBorder(blackBorder);
            aPanel.add(aLabel);
        }
        setContentPane(aPanel);
        pack();
    }
}
```

Box Layout

Box Layout places components in either a horizontal or vertical arrangement. In contrast to Flow Layout, components do not wrap to the next line.

The BoxLayout constructor requires a reference to the container as one of its arguments. Therefore, to set a vertical layout, the following sequence of code is required:

```
JPanel panel = new JPanel();
panel.setLayout(new BoxLayout(panel, BoxLayout.Y_AXIS));
```

To set a horizontal layout, replace Y_AXIS with X_AXIS. Listing C.7 shows the program that creates the GUI in Figure C.11 for the button-based phone directory user interface.

FIGURE C.11
Box Layout

LISTING C.7
BuildBoxLayout.java

```
import java.awt.*;
import java.awt.event.*;
import javax.swing.*;

/** Demonstration of the Box Layout. */
public class BuildBoxLayout extends JFrame {
    public static void main(String[] args) {
        JFrame frame = new BuildBoxLayout();
    }
```

```java
public BuildBoxLayout () {
    setDefaultCloseOperation(EXIT_ON_CLOSE);
    // Create a panel to hold the buttons.
    JPanel panel = new JPanel();
    panel.setLayout(new BoxLayout(panel, BoxLayout.Y_AXIS));
    // Create buttons and add them to the panel.
    // Add/Change Entry
    JButton addEntryButton = new JButton("Add/Change Entry");
    panel.add(addEntryButton);
    // Look Up Entry
    JButton lookupEntryButton = new JButton("Look Up Entry");
    panel.add(lookupEntryButton);
    // Remove Entry
    JButton removeEntryButton = new JButton("Remove Entry");
    panel.add(removeEntryButton);
    // Save Directory
    JButton saveDirectoryButton =
        new JButton("Save Directory");
    panel.add(saveDirectoryButton);
    // Exit
    JButton exitButton = new JButton("Exit");
    panel.add(exitButton);
    // Put the panel into the frame.
    getContentPane().add(panel);
    // Size the frame to hold the panel.
    pack();
    show();
}
}
```

Grid Layout

Grid Layout places components in a rectangular grid. The container is divided into equal-sized rectangles, and one component is placed in each rectangle. Figure C.12 shows a grid that consists of five rows and 10 columns. Listing C.8 shows the program that generated Figure C.12.

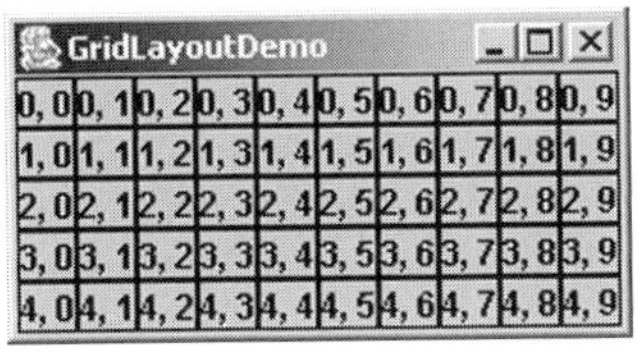

FIGURE C.12
Grid Layout
Demonstration

LISTING C.8
GridLayoutDemo.java

```java
import java.awt.*;
import javax.swing.*;
import javax.swing.border.*;

/** GridLayoutDemo generates a simple frame that shows how components
    are arranged using Grid Layout. */
public class GridLayoutDemo extends JFrame {
```

```
// Main Method
public static void main(String args[]) {
    // Construct a GridLayoutDemo object.
    JFrame frame = new GridLayoutDemo();
    // Display the frame.
    frame.show();
}

// Constructor
public GridLayoutDemo() {
    setTitle("GridLayoutDemo");
    setDefaultCloseOperation(JFrame.EXIT_ON_CLOSE);
    // Create a JPanel to hold a grid.
    JPanel thePanel = new JPanel();
    thePanel.setLayout(new GridLayout(5,10));
    Border blackBorder =
        BorderFactory.createLineBorder(Color.BLACK);
    // Create some labels and add them to the panel.
    for (int i = 0; i < 5; i++) {
        for (int j = 0; j < 10; j++) {
            JLabel aLabel = new JLabel
                (Integer.toString(i) + ", "
                + Integer.toString(j),
                JLabel.CENTER);
            aLabel.setBorder(blackBorder);
            thePanel.add(aLabel);
        }
    }
    setContentPane(thePanel);
    pack();
}
}
```

Combining Layouts

By combining layouts, you can make more complicated arrangements. You can place panels within panels, each with different layout managers. The layout shown in Figure C.13 can be made by placing one panel set to Border Layout into the "center" of the content pane and placing another panel set to Grid Layout into the "south" of the content pane. You could also create the grid layout shown in Figure C.12 by creating a panel with a vertical Box Layout, each component of which is a panel with a horizontal Box Layout containing ten components. The code for each nested layout is left as an exercise.

FIGURE C.13
Combined Layout Demo

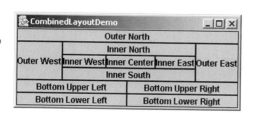

EXERCISES FOR SECTION C.3

SELF-CHECK

1. Describe the characteristics of the following layout managers:
   Border Layout
   Box Layout
   Grid Layout
   Flow Layout
2. What is the default layout for class JFrame? for class JPanel?
3. Why are layout managers useful?

PROGRAMMING

1. Create a frame that has a grid of labels that looks like this:

yellow		white		blue
		green		
	orange		purple	
green		red		blue
yellow			orange	

2. Create a frame that has a grid of labels that looks like Figure C.13.
3. Create a frame that looks like Figure C.12 using nested BoxLayout managers.

C.4 Components for Data Entry

A primary purpose of the Swing API is to enable a programmer to develop a GUI for a Java application. A GUI has several purposes:

1. To enable the user to provide input data to an application
2. To enable the user to control the action of the application
3. To display information or results to the user

We have shown how to control actions using buttons. In this section, we describe Swing components that enable the user to enter data; these include the JCheckBox, JRadioButton, and JComboBox for indicating choices, and the JTextField for entry of text. To display information, Swing uses JLabel, JTextField, and JTextArea. In this section we will describe each of them individually and demonstrate their use in very simple applications. In the next section we will then use some of them to build a more complicated application in which changes to input in one are reflected in the values displayed by the others.

Check Box

FIGURE C.14
Check Box Demo

A *check box* (JCheckBox) is a type of button. It is displayed with a label or icon next to a small square box. When the check box is selected, a check mark appears in the box. Also, when the user selects or deselects the check box (either way, by clicking it), its registered ActionListener is called. Figure C.14 shows a pair of check boxes. Listing C.9 shows the program to generate Figure C.14.

LISTING C.9
CheckBoxDemo.java

```java
import java.awt.*;
import java.awt.event.*;
import javax.swing.*;
import javax.swing.event.*;
import java.io.*;

/** CheckBoxDemo generates a simple demonstration of check boxes. */
public class CheckBoxDemo extends JFrame {

    // Data Fields
    JCheckBox greenEggs;
    JCheckBox ham;

    // Main Method
    public static void main(String args[]) {
        // Create a CheckBoxDemo object.
        JFrame aFrame = new CheckBoxDemo();
        // Show it.
        aFrame.show();
    }

    // Constructor
    public CheckBoxDemo() {
        setTitle("CheckBoxDemo");
        setDefaultCloseOperation(JFrame.EXIT_ON_CLOSE);
        // Create a JPanel to be used as the content pane.
        JPanel aPanel = new JPanel();
        aPanel.setLayout(new BoxLayout(aPanel, BoxLayout.Y_AXIS));
        // Create two check boxes and add them to the panel.
        greenEggs = new JCheckBox("Green Eggs");
        greenEggs.addActionListener(new GreenEggsChanged());
        aPanel.add(greenEggs);
        ham = new JCheckBox("Ham");
        ham.addActionListener(new HamChanged());
        aPanel.add(ham);
        setContentPane(aPanel);
        pack();
    }
```

```
        // Action Listener Classes
        private class GreenEggsChanged implements ActionListener {
            public void actionPerformed(ActionEvent e) {
                if (greenEggs.isSelected()) {
                    System.out.println("Green Eggs is selected");
                }
                else {
                    System.out.println("Green Eggs not selected");
                }
            }
        }

        private class HamChanged implements ActionListener {
            public void actionPerformed(ActionEvent e) {
                if (ham.isSelected()) {
                    System.out.println("Ham is selected");
                }
                else {
                    System.out.println("Ham not selected");
                }
            }
        }
    }
}
```

Radio Button

FIGURE C.15
Radio Button Demo

A *radio button* (JRadioButton) is similar to a check box in that it can be selected or deselected. There are two differences: Selection is indicated by having a small circle appear filled in rather than a square containing a check mark, and, more importantly, only one of a group of radio buttons may be selected at a time. Figure C.15 shows three radio buttons.

To facilitate the mutual exclusion, radio buttons are placed into a ButtonGroup. When one object in a ButtonGroup is selected, the others are automatically deselected. A ButtonGroup is not a Component. It is not displayed, and event listeners cannot be registered to it. The event listeners are registered to the individual buttons. Listing C.10 shows the program that created Figure C.15. Notice that a common ActionListener is registered for each of the buttons. When the buttons are created, the name of the selection is set as the *action command* of the associated ButtonModel using the statement:

```
    radioButtons[i].getModel().setActionCommand(selections[i]);
```

The method getSelection in the class ButtonGroup returns the ButtonModel of the selected button, not the button itself. We can then use the method getActionCommand to retrieve the selected item using the statement:

```
    String choice = buttonGroup.getSelection().getActionCommand();
```

LISTING C.10
RadioButtonDemo.java

```java
import java.awt.*;
import java.awt.event.*;
import javax.swing.*;
import javax.swing.event.*;
import java.io.*;

/** RadioButtonDemo generates a simple demonstration of
    radio buttons. */
public class RadioButtonDemo extends JFrame {

    // Data Fields
    String[] selections = {"Bacon", "Ham", "Sausage"};
    JRadioButton[] radioButtons =
        new JRadioButton[selections.length];
    ButtonGroup buttonGroup;

    // Main Method
    public static void main(String args[]) {
        // Create a RadioButtonDemo object.
        JFrame aFrame = new RadioButtonDemo();
        // Show it.
        aFrame.show();
    }

    // Constructor
    public RadioButtonDemo() {
        setTitle("RadioButtonDemo");
        setDefaultCloseOperation(JFrame.EXIT_ON_CLOSE);
        // Create a JPanel to be used as the content pane.
        JPanel aPanel = new JPanel();
        aPanel.setLayout(new BoxLayout(aPanel, BoxLayout.X_AXIS));
        // Create a button group for the buttons.
        buttonGroup = new ButtonGroup();
        // Create radio buttons and add them to the panel.
        // Also add them to the button group.
        ActionListener newSelection = new SelectionChangeMade();
        for (int i = 0; i < selections.length; i++) {
            radioButtons[i] = new JRadioButton(selections[i]);
            radioButtons[i].getModel().setActionCommand(selections[i]);
            radioButtons[i].addActionListener(newSelection);
            buttonGroup.add(radioButtons[i]);
            aPanel.add(radioButtons[i]);
        }
        setContentPane(aPanel);
        pack();
    }

    // Action Listener Classes
    private class SelectionChangeMade implements ActionListener {
        public void actionPerformed(ActionEvent e) {
            String choice =
                buttonGroup.getSelection().getActionCommand();
            System.out.println(choice + " is selected");
        }
    }
}
```

Combo Box

A *combo box* combines a button or editable field and a drop-down list. Normally the current selection is displayed, as shown in Figure C.16. When the button is clicked, a menu of choices is displayed, as shown in Figure C.17. A combo box is created using the statement:

```
comboBox = new JComboBox(selections);
```

where *selections* is an array of objects that define the set of choices. Items can be added to the list of choices using the method `addItem` and removed using the method `removeItem`. The selected item can be retrieved using `getSelectedItem` (return type is `Object`) and can be reset using `setSelectedItem` (argument type is `Object`). Listing C.11 shows the program that generated Figures C.16 and C.17.

FIGURE C.16
Combo Box Showing
Selected Item

FIGURE C.17
Combo Box Showing
Selections Available

LISTING C.18
ComboBoxDemo.java

```java
import java.awt.*;
import java.awt.event.*;
import javax.swing.*;
import javax.swing.event.*;
import java.io.*;

/** ComboBoxDemo generates a simple demonstration of a combo box. */
public class ComboBoxDemo extends JFrame {

    // Data Fields
    String[] selections = {"Bacon", "Ham", "Sausage"};
    JComboBox comboBox;

    // Main Method
    public static void main(String args[]) {
        // Create a ComboBoxDemo object.
        JFrame aFrame = new ComboBoxDemo();
        // Show it.
        aFrame.show();
    }
```

```
// Constructor
public ComboBoxDemo() {
    setTitle("ComboBoxDemo");
    setDefaultCloseOperation(JFrame.EXIT_ON_CLOSE);
    // Create a JPanel to be used as the content pane.
    JPanel aPanel = new JPanel();
    // Create the combo box.
    comboBox = new JComboBox(selections);
    comboBox.addActionListener(new SelectionChangeMade());
    aPanel.add(comboBox);
    setContentPane(aPanel);
    pack();
}

// Action Listener Classes
private class SelectionChangeMade implements ActionListener {
    public void actionPerformed(ActionEvent e) {
        String choice = (String)comboBox.getSelectedItem();
        System.out.println(choice + " is selected");
    }
}
}
```

Text Field

A *text field* (JTextField) is a component that allows for the display and editing of a single line of text. The Java API also provides components for display and editing of multiple lines. A summary of selected constructors and methods of JTextField and its superclasses is shown in Table C.6.

Figure C.18 shows a simple text field with 10 columns that was generated by the program shown in Listing C.12. Pressing the Enter key generates an action event.

TABLE C.6
Summary of JTextField

Constructor	Behavior
JTextField()	Constructs a new JTextField.
JTextField(int columns)	Constructs a new empty JTextField with the specified number of columns.
JTextField(String text)	Constructs a new JTextField with the specified text.
JTextField(String text, int columns)	Constructs a new JTextField with the specified text and number of columns.
Method	**Behavior**
void addActionListener(ActionListener l)	Adds the specified action listener to receive action events from this text field.
String getText()	Returns the text contained in the text field.
void setText(String t)	Sets the text of the text field.

FIGURE C.18
Text Field Demo

LISTING C.12
TextFieldDemo.java

```java
import java.awt.*;
import java.awt.event.*;
import javax.swing.*;

/** TextFieldDemo provides a simple demonstration of data input
    from a JTextField. */
public class TextFieldDemo extends JFrame {

    // Data Field
    JTextField textField;

    // Main Method
    public static void main(String[] args) {
        JFrame aFrame = new TextFieldDemo();
        aFrame.show();
    }

    // Constructor
    private TextFieldDemo() {
        setTitle("Text Field Demo");
        setDefaultCloseOperation(JFrame.EXIT_ON_CLOSE);
        // Create a panel for the content pane.
        JPanel aPanel = new JPanel();
        // Add a label.
        aPanel.add(new JLabel("Enter a number"));
        // Create a text field.
        textField = new JTextField(10);
        // Register action listener.
        textField.addActionListener(new NumberEntered());
        // Add it to the panel.
        aPanel.add(textField);
        // Set the panel to be the content pane.
        setContentPane(aPanel);
        // Size the frame.
        pack();
    }

    // Inner Action Listener Class
    private class NumberEntered implements ActionListener {
        public void actionPerformed(ActionEvent e) {
            String text = textField.getText();
            int value = 0;
            try {
                value = Integer.parseInt(text);
                System.out.println("Number entered: " + value);
            }
```

```
                    catch (NumberFormatException ex) {
                        System.err.println("Invalid entry " + text);
                    }
                }
            }
        }
    }
```

Label

In Listing C.12 the statement

```
    aPanel.add(new JLabel("Enter a number"));
```

adds a label to the panel. As its name implies, a label is a string of characters. You can specify the string when you create the label, as shown here, or you can specify it later using method setText. You can retrieve the text in a label using method getText (returns a String). If you declare data field result as a label

```
    private JLabel result = new JLabel();
```

and add result to aPanel, you can use the following statement in the **try**-clause (as a replacement for the call to println) to display the result as a label under the text field:

```
    result.setText("Number entered: " + value);
```

Text Area

A text area is another component that can be used to enter data or to display information to the user. The statement

```
    JTextArea textArea = new JTextArea(2, 20);
```

declares a text area with two lines and 20 columns. A text area is like a text field except that it can show more than one line of information. You can use methods setText and getText with a text area just as you use them with a text field (or label). You can use them in combination to append information to what is already in a text area:

```
    textArea.setText(textArea.getText() + newInformation);
```

The user can also edit information that is typed into a text area or a text field prior to pressing the Enter key. The edited text is what is retrieved by the getText method.

EXERCISES FOR SECTION C.4

SELF-CHECK

1. Which of the data entry components (check box, radio button, combo box, or text field) is appropriate for the following situations?
   a. Recording answers in a multiple-choice exam
   b. Entering the state or province in a data entry form that is collecting address information
   c. Entering the city in a data entry form that is collecting address information
   d. Allow the user to select several different breakfast items from a menu

PROGRAMMING

1. A GUI that displays three button groups, containing radio buttons and a text area, is shown in Figure C.19. Whenever one of the radio buttons is changed, the text should be updated. Write the program.

FIGURE C.19
Radio Button Exercise

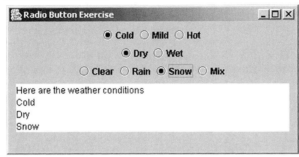

2. Revise the program written in Exercise 1 to use check-boxes rather than radio buttons in the third row. Eliminate the "mix" option, but let the user select both rain and snow. If clear is selected, then deselect rain and snow.

C.5 Using Data Entry Components in a GUI

In this section we will show how to use some of the data entry components to build an application in which changes entered in one component are reflected in the values displayed by the others.

CASE STUDY   Liquid Volume Converter

Problem   In Europe and Canada gasoline is measured in liters, whereas in the United States it is measured in (U.S.) gallons. We want to write an application that will take a value in one unit and display it in the other.

Analysis   Based on the problem statement, we can identify two use cases:
- User enters a value in gallons
- User enters a value in liters

These are further expanded in Table C.7:

TABLE C.7
Use Cases for Liquid Volume Converter

User Action	System Response
User enters a value in gallons.	The system updates the corresponding value in liters. If the value entered is not a valid number, an error message is displayed.
User enters a value in liters.	The system updates the corresponding value in gallons. If the value entered is not a valid number, an error message is displayed.

Design   Class `VolumeConverterGUI`

The main class for this application, `VolumeConverterGUI`, will be a `JFrame`. The content pane will be set to a 2×2 grid layout. The left column will contain the labels "Gallons" and "Liters," and the right column will contain two text boxes corresponding to the adjacent labels (see Figure C.20). `ActionListener` classes will be registered to each of the text fields. When a text field is changed, its contents are converted to a `double` value. This value is then converted to the opposite liquid volume unit, and the result displayed in the other text field. We will also need to develop a class to perform the conversions.

FIGURE C.20
`JFrame VolumeConverterGUI`

Class `VolumeConverter`

This class provides the conversion from gallons to liters. Its design is summarized in Table C.8.

TABLE C.8
`VolumeConverter` Class Design

Data Field	Attribute
`private static final double` `LITERS_PER_GALLON`	The conversion factor.
Method	**Behavior**
`double toGallons(double value)`	Converts input value from liters to gallons.
`double toLiters(double value)`	Converts input value from gallons to liters.

Implementation Class `VolumeConverterGUI`

Listing C.13 shows the code for the main class. The constructor lays out the four components: two `JLabels` and two `JTextFields`. The `JTextField` objects are data fields so that the inner classes can access them.

The two inner classes are very similar. One converts from gallons to liters, and the other converts from liters to gallons. Objects of these inner classes are registered to the corresponding text fields using the statements:

```
gallonsField.addActionListener(new NewGallonsValue());
litersField.addActionListener(new NewLitersValue());
```

In the listener class `NewGallonsValue`, the statements

```
double gallonsValue = Double.parseDouble(gallonsField.getText());
double litersValue = VolumeConverter.toLiters(gallonsValue);
litersField.setText(Double.toString(litersValue));
```

retrieve the value in `gallonsField`, convert it to liters, and then place that value in `litersField`.

LISTING C.13
VolumeConverterGUI.java

```java
import java.awt.*;
import java.awt.event.*;
import javax.swing.*;

/** VolumeConverterGUI is a GUI application that converts
    values in gallons to liters and vice versa.
*/
public class VolumeConverterGUI extends JFrame {

    // Data Fields
    /** Text field to hold gallons value */
    private JTextField gallonsField;
    /** Text field to hold liters value */
    private JTextField litersField;

    // Main Method
    /** Create an instance of the application and show it.
        @param args Command Line Arguments - not used
    */
    public static void main (String[] args) {
        JFrame frame = new VolumeConverterGUI();
        frame.show();
    }

    // Constructor
    /** Construct the components and add them to the frame. */
    public VolumeConverterGUI() {
        super("Liquid Volume Converter");
        setDefaultCloseOperation(EXIT_ON_CLOSE);
        // Get a reference to the content pane.
        Container contentPane = getContentPane();
```

```java
            // Set the layout manager to grid layout.
            contentPane.setLayout(new GridLayout(2, 2));
            contentPane.add(new JLabel("Gallons"));
            gallonsField = new JTextField(15);
            gallonsField.addActionListener(new NewGallonsValue());
            contentPane.add(gallonsField);
            contentPane.add(new JLabel("Liters"));
            litersField = new JTextField(15);
            litersField.addActionListener(new NewLitersValue());
            contentPane.add(litersField);
            // Size the frame to fit.
            pack();
        }

        // Inner Classes
        /** Class to respond to new gallons value. */
        private class NewGallonsValue implements ActionListener {
            /** Convert the gallons value to corresponding liters value.
                @param e ActionEvent object - not used
            */
            public void actionPerformed(ActionEvent e) {
                try {
                    double gallonsValue = Double.parseDouble
                        (gallonsField.getText());
                    double litersValue =
                        VolumeConverter.toLiters(gallonsValue);
                    litersField.setText(Double.toString(litersValue));
                } catch (NumberFormatException ex) {
                    JOptionPane.showMessageDialog(null,
                                                "Invalid Number Format",
                                                "",
                                                JOptionPane.ERROR_MESSAGE);
                }
            }
        }

        /** Class to respond to new liters value. */
        private class NewLitersValue implements ActionListener {
            /** Convert the liters value to corresponding gallons value.
                @param e ActionEvent object - not used
            */
            public void actionPerformed(ActionEvent e) {
                try {
                    double litersValue = Double.parseDouble
                        (litersField.getText());
                    double gallonsValue =
                        VolumeConverter.toGallons(litersValue);
                    gallonsField.setText(Double.toString(gallonsValue));
                } catch (NumberFormatException ex) {
                    JOptionPane.showMessageDialog(null,
                                                "Invalid Number Format",
                                                "",
                                                JOptionPane.ERROR_MESSAGE);
                }
            }
        }
    }
}
```

Class **VolumeConverter**

The implementation of the VolumeConverter class is shown in Listing C.14. The two methods toGallons and toLiters either multiply or divide by the conversion factor as appropriate.

LISTING C.14
VolumeConverter.java

```java
/** VolumeConverter is a class with static methods
    that convert between gallons and liters.
*/
public class VolumeConverter {

    /** The number of liters in a gallon.
    */
    private static final double LITERS_PER_GALLON = 3.785411784;

    /** Convert a value in liters to gallons.
        @param liters The value in liters
        @return The value in gallons
    */
    public static double toGallons(double liters) {
        return liters / LITERS_PER_GALLON;
    }

    /** Convert a value in gallons to liters.
        @param gallons The value in gallons
        @return The value in liters
    */
    public static double toLiters(double gallons) {
        return gallons * LITERS_PER_GALLON;
    }
}
```

Testing   Figure C.21 shows two examples of running the VolumeConverterGUI: one in which the value for gallons is entered and the other in which the value for liters is entered. We know that the conversion factor is 3.785411784. By entering 10 as the number of gallons, we can see that the conversion factor is being multiplied correctly. By entering 37.85 as the number of liters, we can see that the conversion factor is being divided correctly as well. If we enter all 10 digits, the gallons display will be 10 exactly. You should also test this with invalidly formatted numbers to verify that an appropriate error message is displayed.

FIGURE C.21
Test of Liquid Volume Converter

....
TABLE C.9
The NumberFormat Class

Method	Behavior
`String format(double number)`	Formats a **double** value.
`static NumberFormat getCurrencyInstance()`	Returns a NumberFormat object that is configured to convert numbers to the currency format of the default locale.
`static NumberFormat getNumberInstance()`	Returns a NumberFormat object that is configured to convert numbers to ordinary numbers (with a fraction part) in the format of the default locale.
`static NumberFormat getPercentageInstance()`	Returns a NumberFormat object that is configured to convert numbers to percentages (i.e., fractions are multiplied by 100, and a percentage indicator is provided) in the format of the default locale.
`void setMaximumFractionDigits(int newValue)`	Sets the maximum number of digits allowed in the fraction portion.

Limiting the Number of Significant Digits

Some of the numbers in Figure C.21 have many more decimal places than needed. The Java API java.text contains the class NumberFormat, which can be used to format numbers either as pure numbers or as currency values. The formatting depends on the Locale, a class that encapsulates culture and language differences. Your computer is probably configured so that the default locale is appropriate for where you are. For example, if you live in the United States, then the default locale is appropriate for the United States. If you live in the United Kingdom, then the default locale is appropriate for the United Kingdom. To use the NumberFormat class, you must first create an instance. The NumberFormat class itself is an abstract class. It includes factory methods to create appropriate concrete instances. It also has modifiers that allow you to set the number of integer and fraction digits. The methods in this class are summarized in Table C.9.

All of the get*Xxxxx*Instance methods also have a form that takes a Locale object as a parameter. This allows you to create a NumberFormat object for a specific locale. We show how to use the Number instance and the format method in the following example.

EXAMPLE C.3   We can modify the VolumeConverterGUI to display only two fraction digits as follows:

1. We add a declaration for a NumberFormat to the data fields:

    ```
    NumberFormat numberForm;
    ```

2. We initialize this data field in the constructor as follows:

    ```
    numberForm = NumberFormat.getNumberInstance();
    numberForm.setMaximumFractionDigits(2);
    ```

3. In the NewGallonsValue class we change the statement that sets the litersField to

litersField.setText(numberForm.format(litersValue));

4. In the NewLitersValue class we change the statement that sets the gallonsField to

gallonsField.setText(numberForm.format(gallonsValue));

The modified display is shown in Figure C.22. Notice that an input value of 37.85 liters produces a display of "10" gallons instead of "9.998912181755918". Also notice that an input of 1000 gallons gives a value of "3,785.41"

FIGURE C.22
Modified Liquid Volume Converter

Liquid Volume Converter			Liquid Volume Converter	
Gallons	10		Gallons	1000
Liters	37.85		Liters	3,785.41

Formatting Currency for Different Locales

You can obtain NumberFormat instances that are configured to convert numbers to local currency representation using the statement

NumberFormat format = getCurrencyInstance(locale);

where locale is a Locale object. You can consult the Java documentation on how to specify the locale and how to obtain a list of locales that are available on your computer. There are also defined constants in the API java.util that map to some locales. For example, Locale.US is a locale for the United States.

EXAMPLE C.4

Figure C.23 shows the value 12345.67 formatted as currency in different locales. Notice that both Germany and France use the comma to separate the integer portion from the fraction, whereas in both the United States and the United Kingdom the period is used. Also notice that in Germany the period is used to group thousands, in France the space is used to group thousands, and in the United States and the United Kingom the comma is used. Listing C.15 shows the code to generate this figure.

FIGURE C.23
Currency Display Demonstration

Message

The value 12345.67
As US Currency $12,345.67
As UK Currency £12,345.67
As German Currency 12.345,67 €
As French Currency 12 345,67 €

OK

....

LISTING C.15

CurrencyDemo.java

```java
import java.util.*;
import java.text.*;
import javax.swing.*;

/** Program to demonstrate different currency formats. */
public class CurrencyDemo {

    public static void main(String[] args) {
        NumberFormat usa =
            NumberFormat.getCurrencyInstance(Locale.US);
        NumberFormat uk =
            NumberFormat.getCurrencyInstance(Locale.UK);
        NumberFormat de =
            NumberFormat.getCurrencyInstance(Locale.GERMANY);
        NumberFormat fr =
            NumberFormat.getCurrencyInstance(Locale.FRANCE);

        double value = 12345.67;

        String result = "The value " + value
                        + "\nAs US Currency " + usa.format(value)
                        + "\nAs UK Currency " + uk.format(value)
                        + "\nAs German Currency " + de.format(value)
                        + "\nAs French Currency " + fr.format(value);

        JOptionPane.showMessageDialog(null, result);
        System.exit(0);
    }
}
```

EXERCISES FOR SECTION C.5

SELF-CHECK

1. How can you obtain a formatting with three decimal places?
2. How can you obtain currency formatting that is appropriate to the location in which the user is using the program?

PROGRAMMING

1. Write a distance converter that converts from miles to kilometers. There are 1.609344 kilometers in a mile. Display the result with only one fraction digit.

C.6 Menus and Toolbars

Menus and toolbars are another way for a user to indicate choices or initiate actions in a GUI application. Menus may be hierarchical; that is, selecting a menu choice can bring up a submenu. Generally the top level of a menu is placed on a menu bar that sits at the top of the window, just under the frame border. With Java Swing, the menu bar may be positioned like any other component. Menus can also be made to "pop up" in response an event such as a mouse click. In addition to the `JMenuItem`, most Swing components may be used as menu items. Other features of menu items are the following:

- Icons can augment or replace menu items.
- Keyboard accelerators (shortcuts) and mnemonics may be assigned.

A toolbar is a group of buttons, combo boxes, and other components together in a repositionable panel. The toolbar may be dragged into its own child window or anchored along the edge of a frame. In many GUI applications toolbars duplicate the functionality of menus. For example, the toolbar icon showing a folder opening () duplicates the effect of selecting Open from the File menu. This duplication is accomplished by assigning the same `ActionListener` to the menu item and to the button in the toolbar.

The Classes `JMenuItem`, `JMenu`, and `JMenuBar`

Because `JMenuItem` is an extension of `AbstractButton`, a `JMenuItem` object can display text or an icon. It also fires action events when activated. Figure C.24 shows an example menu with five menu items. The first item consists only of an icon that represents the "new" action (the blank, dog-eared page). The second item contains both an "open" icon (the opening folder) and text "Open . . ." The third contains text and an accelerator (or shortcut), "Ctrl+S"; the fourth only text; and the final item a mnemonic, indicated by the underscore under the x. Table C.10 shows a subset of the constructors and methods of the `JMenuItem` class.

Note that an accelerator is a key combination that invokes the menu item's action listeners. A mnemonic is a key that, when pressed while the menu is displayed, will activate the action listeners without the user having to select the menu item with the mouse.

FIGURE C.24
Example of a Menu

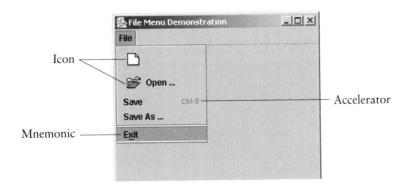

TABLE C.10

Constructors and Methods of `JMenuItem`

Constructor	Behavior
`JMenuItem()`	Creates a `JMenuItem` with no set text or icon.
`JMenuItem(Icon icon)`	Creates a `JMenuItem` with the specified icon.
`JMenuItem(String text)`	Creates a `JMenuItem` with the specified text.
`JMenuItem(String text, Icon icon)`	Creates a `JMenuItem` with the specified text and icon.
`JMenuItem(String text, int mnemonic)`	Creates a `JMenuItem` with the specified text and keyboard mnemonic. The **int** value is the key code, defined by the class `KeyEvent`.
Method	**Behavior**
`void setAccelerator(KeyStroke keystroke)`	Sets the key combination that invokes the menu item's action listeners without the user navigating the menu hierarchy.
Methods Inherited from `AbstractButton`	**Behavior**
`void setIcon(Icon icon)`	Sets the default icon.
`void setText(String text)`	Sets the text.
`setMnemonic(int mnemonic)`	Sets the mnemonic. The **int** value is the key code, defined by the class `KeyEvent`.
`void addActionListener(ActionListener l)`	Adds an `ActionListener` to this menu item.

You create a menu as a new `JMenu` object, passing the menu name as an argument. Then you create each individual menu item (type `JMenuItem`) and add it to the `JMenu` object (using method add). The File menu in Figure C.24 was constructed with the following sequence of Java statements:

```
JMenu fileMenu = new JMenu("File");
JMenuItem newItem = new JMenuItem(newIcon);
JMenuItem openItem = new JMenuItem("Open ...", openIcon);
JMenuItem saveItem = new JMenuItem("Save");
JMenuItem saveAsItem = new JMenuItem("Save As ...");
JMenuItem exitItem = new JMenuItem("Exit", KeyEvent.VK_X);
saveItem.setAccelerator(KeyStroke.getKeyStroke('S',
                                        Event.CTRL_MASK));
fileMenu.add(newItem);
fileMenu.add(openItem);
fileMenu.add(saveItem);
fileMenu.add(saveAsItem);
fileMenu.addSeparator();
fileMenu.add(exitItem);
```

A `JMenuBar` is a class designed to hold top-level menus. The next step would be to create a new `JMenuBar` object, add the `JMenu` object to it, and then place the `JMenuBar` in the container using method `setJMenuBar`.

```
JMenuBar menuBar = new JMenuBar();
menuBar.add(fileMenu);
setJMenuBar(menuBar);
```

Icons

An icon is a small fixed-size picture. It is used to decorate buttons and other components. Icons must implement the Icon interface as defined in Table C.11.

TABLE C.11
The Interface Icon

Method	Behavior
int getIconHeight()	Returns the icon's height.
int getIconWidth()	Returns the icon's width.
void paintIcon(Component c, Graphics g, int x, int y)	Draws the icon at the specified location using the given graphics context.

The class ImageIcon implements the Icon interface. It uses an image file (such as a GIF or JPEG file) to create the icon. The image file must be created by a drawing or paint program. You don't have to create all your own image files, because there are many predefined image files available in libraries. Table C.12 gives a subset of the ImageIcon class constructors.

TABLE C.12
A Subset of the ImageIcon Constructors

Constructor	Behavior
ImageIcon()	Creates an uninitialized image icon.
ImageIcon(String filename)	Creates an image icon from the specified file.
ImageIcon(String filename, String description)	Creates an image icon from the specified file and with the specified description that is meant to be a brief textual description of the object.

Toolbars

The JToolBar class is a container that can be oriented either horizontally or vertically. A toolbar contains icons that can be selected by a mouse click. Often a toolbar is used as an alternative to a menu. The toolbar shown in Figure C.25 has icons for creating a new document, opening a document, and saving a document (the diskette). The mouse can drag the toolbar to any of the four sides of a container or into its own window (see the figure).

FIGURE C.25
Examples of Different
Toolbar Positions

The icons shown in Figure C.25 are created using the following statements:

```
Icon newIcon = new ImageIcon("new.gif",
                             "Create a new document");
Icon openIcon = new ImageIcon("open.gif",
                             "Open an existing document");
Icon saveIcon = new ImageIcon("disk.gif",
                             "Save file to disk");
```

Each GIF file above displays an icon for the specified button (new, open, or save) when painted. JButtons with these icons are then created:

```
JButton newButton = new JButton(newIcon);
JButton openButton = new JButton(openIcon);
JButton saveButton = new JButton(saveIcon);
```

ActionListeners must be registered for the buttons in the normal way. Generally the same action listener object is registered for each button as was registered for the corresponding menu item. Finally, the buttons are added to the toolbar, and the toolbar is added to the content pane.

```
JToolBar toolBar = new JToolBar();
toolBar.add(newButton);
toolBar.add(openButton);
toolBar.add(saveButton);
getContentPane().add(toolBar, BorderLayout.NORTH);
```

This code added the toolbar to the NORTH position of the content pane. The other positions shown in Figure C.25 are the result of using the mouse to drag the toolbar to different positions. You can place the toolbar in any one of the four BorderLayout edge positions.

CASE STUDY   A Drawing Application

Problem   We want to write an application that will let us draw different shapes of different sizes. The shape to be drawn is to be selected either from a menu or from a toolbar. A menu to specify the color of the shape and the color of the border should also be provided. The list of available figures should be variable. The user specifies the names of the classes that draw the figures on the command line when the application is started.

Analysis   In this case study we will be concerned with initializing the application and building the menus and toolbar. The case study in the next section will complete the design of the application by including the drawing of the figures.

When the program is started, the JFrame should include two menus and a toolbar. One menu offers the choice of setting the interior color or setting the border color as shown in Figure C.26. The other should offer the choice of shapes to be drawn, as shown in Figure C.27. The choice of shapes should also be provided by a toolbar.

FIGURE C.26
DrawApp Showing
Color Menu and
Toolbar

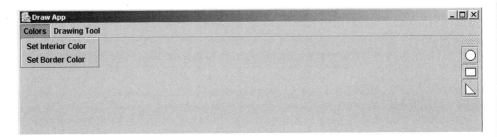

FIGURE C.27
DrawApp Showing
Drawing Tool Menu
and Toolbar

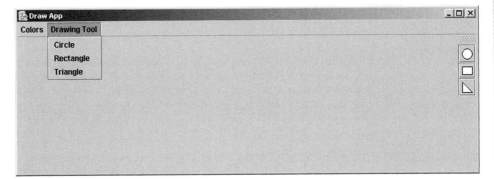

Design   The DrawApp class will be an extension of the JFrame class. The constructor will perform the following steps:

1. Build a list of prototype figures based on the list of class names provided as input.
2. Build a list of icons, one for each figure kind.
3. Build the drawing tool menu that is used to select which figure is to be drawn.

4. Build the drawing tool toolbar.
5. Build the color chooser menu.
6. Create a menu bar and add the drawing tool menu and the color chooser menu to it.
7. Add the menu bar to the frame.
8. Add the toolbar to the frame.
9. Create a panel for the drawing objects and add it to the frame.

In Section 3.6, we described a drawable shape class hierarchy (see Figure C.28) and a simple test application that drew some figures of fixed size and at fixed locations. Also, in Section 3.8 we described the object factory design pattern, in which the set of choices was determined by giving a list of classes in the command line that ran the application. We will use the drawable shape classes and factory design pattern in our solution.

To use the drawable shapes class hierarchy, the `DrawableInt` interface must be modified to add the following abstract methods. Each class that implements `DrawableInt` must also be modified to define these methods.

TABLE C.13
Abstract Methods to Be Added to `DrawableInt`

Method	Behavior
`int getWidth()`	Returns the width.
`int getHeight()`	Returns the height.
`String getName()`	Returns the name to be used in the menu.
`DrawableIcon getIcon(int size)`	Creates an icon for this figure to be used in the toolbar.

Rather than creating images of each figure for the icons, we take advantage of the fact that our figures can draw themselves. Thus, we can create a class `DrawableIcon` (see Table C.14) that implements the `Icon` interface. The only tricky part about this is that the `paintIcon` method is passed the coordinates of the upper left corner, but each of the figures we implemented has a different origin (the rectangle's origin is the upper left corner, the circle's is the center, and the triangle's is the lower left corner). Each `DrawableIcon` class will set the position of the object that will draw the figure in the icon as needed. The `DrawableRectangle` will use an origin of (0, 0), the `DrawableCircle` will position itself to (size/2, size/2), and the `DrawableTriangle` will position itself to (0, size). The parameter `size` is the size of the square in which the icon image is drawn. Setting these origins will result in the figures appearing inside the square as shown in Figure C.27.

FIGURE C.28
Drawable Shapes
Class Hierarchy

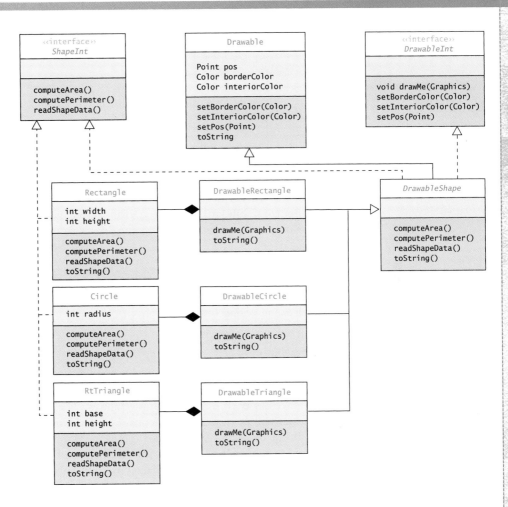

TABLE C.14
The DrawableIcon Class

Data Field	Attribute
DrawableInt theFig	Reference to the figure that is to be drawn in this icon.
int x0	The *x*-coordinate of the origin relative to the upper left corner.
int y0	The *y*-coordinate of the orgin relative to the upper left corner.
Constructor	**Behavior**
DrawableIcon(DrawableInt f)	Creates an icon based on the supplied DrawableInt. The figure will be placed so that the upper left corner is at (0, 0)

TABLE C.14 (continued)

Method	Behavior
void paintIcon(Component c, Graphics g, int x, int y)	Paints the figure for the icon with the upper left corner at the specified coordinates using the specified graphics environment.
int getWidth()	Gets the width of the Icon.
int getHeight()	Gets the height of the Icon.

Three ActionListeners are needed: one to respond to the Drawing Tool menu selections (ToolSelector), one to respond to the Select Fill Color menu selection (ChangeFillColor), and one to respond to the Select Outline Color menu selection (ChangeOutlineColor).

Implementation

Listing C.16 shows the code for the DrawApp class. The main method calls the constructor for class DrawApp, passing on the array of command-line parameters:

```
DrawApp drawApp = new DrawApp(args);
```

In the constructor, the statement

```
loadFigKinds(args);
```

calls method loadFigKinds (not shown) to load array theFigKinds. This method is very similar to method loadShapes in Listing 3.21. The array theFigKinds contains prototype instances of each of the drawable figures. These prototypes are also the figure objects that will be drawn in the icons. The constructor calls on helper methods createDrawingToolMenu, createDrawingToolToolBar, and createColorMenu to create the drawing tool menu, drawing tool toolbar, and color menu, respectively. Then it adds them to a menu, which is placed in the frame along with a panel where the figure will be drawn.

The method createDrawingToolMenu registers action listeners for each menu item (a figure kind) using the statement

```
item.addActionListener(new ToolSelector(theFigKinds[i]));
```

and method createDrawingToolToolBar does the same using the statement

```
aButton.addActionListener(new ToolSelector(theFigKinds[i]));
```

These statements instantiate listener class ToolSelector. The statement

```
this.desiredFig = desiredFig;
```

stores a reference to the appropriate figure kind prototype (theFigKinds[i]) in each listener object.

When the user makes a selection from the toolbar or the drawing tool menu, an event is fired, which is processed by the actionPerformed method for the corresponding listener object. The method ToolSelector.actionPerformed copies the figure prototype referenced by this object into the DrawApp's selectedFigure data field.

```
    selectedFig = desiredFig;
```

For the two choices in the color menu—Set Interior Color and Set Border Color (method not shown)—the `JColorChooser` class is used to present a color chooser dialog. The return value from the `showDialog` method is saved in either the `currentInteriorColor` or the `currentBorderColor` data field. We cycle through array `theFigKind` to set the color values in the figure prototypes. This has two effects: The selected color will then be used in a new figure to be drawn, and the icon colors are updated. Thus the icons always display the user's most recently selected colors.

The actual drawing of the figures is handled by the `DrawingPanel` class, which we will describe in Section C.7.

LISTING C.16
DrawApp.java

```java
import javax.swing.*;
import java.util.*;
import java.awt.*;
import java.awt.event.*;

/** Simple Drawing Application. This program draws selected
    figures. The list of available figures is provided as a command-line
    argument. The figure to be drawn is selected via a menu or a
    toolbar button.  The interior and border colors are selected by
    a menu choice.
*/
public class DrawApp extends JFrame {

    // Data Fields
    /** Currently selected figure kind to be drawn. */
    private DrawableInt selectedFig = null;
    /** Currently selected border color. */
    private Color currentBorderColor = Color.BLACK;
    /** Currently selected interior color. */
    private Color currentInteriorColor = Color.WHITE;
    /** Array of figure prototypes. */
    private DrawableInt[] theFigKinds;

    // Constructor
    /** Construct a DrawApp object.
        @param args An array of strings containing DrawableInt class
        names.
    */
    private DrawApp(String args[]) {
        // Set title.
        super("Draw App");
        // Set frame size.
        setSize(750, 750);
        // Set default close operation.
        setDefaultCloseOperation(JFrame.EXIT_ON_CLOSE);
        // Load the figure kinds.
        loadFigKinds(args);
```

```java
            // Create drawingToolMenu.
            JMenu drawingToolMenu = createDrawingToolMenu();
            // Create drawingToolToolBar.
            JToolBar drawingToolToolBar = createDrawingToolToolBar();
            selectedFig = theFigKinds[0];
            // Create the color choice menu.
            JMenu colorMenu = createColorMenu();
            // Create a menu bar to hold the menu.
            JMenuBar menuBar = new JMenuBar();
            menuBar.add(colorMenu);
            menuBar.add(drawingToolMenu);
            // Set the menu bar in the frame.
            setJMenuBar(menuBar);
            // Add the toolbar to the frame.
            getContentPane().add(drawingToolToolBar, BorderLayout.EAST);
            // Add the DrawPanel to the frame.
            getContentPane().add(new DrawPanel(this),
                            BorderLayout.CENTER);
        }

        /** Load and instantiate the figure prototypes based on the names
            of the DrawableInt classes listed in the command-line argument.
            @param args An array of strings containing DrawableInt class
                        names
        */
        // Insert loadFigKinds here (see loadShapes in Listing 3.21)

        /** Method to create the drawing tool menu. This method loops
            through array theFigKinds and creates a menu item for each
            entry. It then creates an action listener that will select
            this figure when the actionPerformed method is called.
            @return A reference to the JMenu object that is created
        */
        private JMenu createDrawingToolMenu() {
            JMenu drawingToolMenu = new JMenu("Drawing Tool");
            for (int i = 0; i < theFigKinds.length; i++) {
                // Create a menu item for this figure kind.
                JMenuItem item = new JMenuItem(theFigKinds[i].getName());
                // Set the action listener.
                item.addActionListener(new ToolSelector(theFigKinds[i]));
                // Add the item to the menu.
                drawingToolMenu.add(item);
            }
            return drawingToolMenu;
        }

        /** Method to create the toolbar. This method loops through
            array theFigKinds and creates a button for each entry, using that
            figure kind to construct an icon.  It then creates an action
            listener that will select this figure when the actionPerformed
            method is called.
            @return A reference to the JToolBar object that is created
```

```
        */
        JToolBar createDrawingToolToolBar() {
            JToolBar drawingToolToolBar = new JToolBar(JToolBar.VERTICAL);
            for (int i = 0; i < theFigKinds.length; i++) {
                JButton aButton = new JButton(theFigKinds[i].getIcon(16));
                aButton.addActionListener
                        (new ToolSelector(theFigKinds[i]));
                drawingToolToolBar.add(aButton);
            }
            return drawingToolToolBar;
        }

        /** Method to create the color menu. The menu will contain two
            commands: Set Interior Color and SetBorder Color. For each
            command a JColorChooser dialog is displayed, and the user's
            choice is saved in the appropriate attribute for each of the
            figures in array theFigKinds.
            @return A reference to the JMenu object that is created
        */
        private JMenu createColorMenu() {
            JMenu colorMenu = new JMenu("Colors");
            JMenuItem setInteriorColor =
                new JMenuItem("Set Interior Color");
            setInteriorColor.addActionListener(new SetInteriorColor());
            colorMenu.add(setInteriorColor);
            JMenuItem setBorderColor = new JMenuItem("Set Border Color");
            setBorderColor.addActionListener(new SetBorderColor());
            colorMenu.add(setBorderColor);
            return colorMenu;
        }

        /** Access the currently selected figure.
            @return The currently selected figure
        */
        public DrawableInt getSelectedFig() {
            return selectedFig;
        }

        /** Main method. This method instantiates a DrawApp object
            and shows it.
            @param args An array of DrawableInt class names
        */
        public static void main(String args[]) {
            DrawApp drawApp = new DrawApp(args);
            drawApp.show();
        }

        // Inner Classes
        /** Common ActionListener for the figures menu and the
            figures toolbar.
        */
        private class ToolSelector implements ActionListener {
```

```java
        // Data Fields
        /** Figure prototype to be selected when this action
            listener is fired. */
        private DrawableInt desiredFig;

        // Constructor
        /** Construct a ToolSelector object with the specified
            figure prototype.
            @param desiredFig The figure prototype to be selected
        */
        public ToolSelector(DrawableInt desiredFig) {
            this.desiredFig = desiredFig;
        }

        // Methods
        /** Set the selected figure to the desired figure when
            the action is performed.
            @param e Not used
        */
        public void actionPerformed(ActionEvent e) {
            selectedFig = desiredFig;
        }
    }

    /** ActionListener class for the Set Interior Color command. */
    private class SetInteriorColor implements ActionListener {
        /** Method actionPerformed displays the color chooser
            dialog and then sets the interior color of each of the
            figure prototypes. The display is then repainted
            @param e - Not used
        */
        public void actionPerformed(ActionEvent e) {
            currentInteriorColor =
                JColorChooser.showDialog(DrawApp.this,
                                         "Select Interior Color",
                                         currentInteriorColor);
            for (int i = 0; i < theFigKinds.length; i++) {
                theFigKinds[i].setInteriorColor
                    (currentInteriorColor);
            }
            repaint();
        }
    }

    /** ActionListener class for the Set Border Color command */
    // Insert setBorderColor similar to setInteriorColor

}
```

EXERCISES FOR SECTION C.6

SELF-CHECK

1. Why must we extend the DrawableInt interface to include the methods getName, getMnemonic, getShortcut, and getIcon?
2. Why must we extend the DrawableInt interface to include the methods getWidth and getHeight?

PROGRAMMING

1. Code the methods getWidth, getHeight, getName, getMnemonic, getShortCut, and getIcon for the DrawableShape classes defined in Section 3.7.
2. Code method loadFigKinds.
3. Code method setBorderColor.

C.7 Processing Mouse Events

A commonly used input device for GUI applications is the mouse. We have seen how clicking a button on the screen triggers the ActionListener associated with that button. All of these examples have involved mouse-clicked events, but there are other possible mouse events. These are listed in Table C.15. Because Java is designed to be platform independent, there are no specific events for the different buttons on a two- or three-button mouse. The mouse button that caused the event is obtained from the getButton method of the MouseEvent and may have the value BUTTON1, BUTTON2, or BUTTON3. Table C.16 shows the methods defined in the MouseEvent class.

TABLE C.15
Mouse Events

Mouse Event	Cause
MOUSE_CLICKED	A mouse button is pressed and released.
MOUSE_PRESSED	A mouse button is pressed.
MOUSE_RELEASED	A mouse button is released.
MOUSE_MOVED	The mouse position has changed.
MOUSE_DRAGGED	The mouse position has changed while a button is pressed.
MOUSE_ENTERED	The mouse cursor enters the visible part of the component's geometry. If one component is on top of another, then only the top component receives the event.
MOUSE_EXITED	The mouse cursor exits the visible part of the component's geometry.

TABLE C.16
MouseEvent Class (Selected Methods)

Method	Behavior
`Point getPoint()`	Returns the x, y position of the event relative to the component that receives the event.
`int getButton()`	Returns which, if any, of the mouse buttons has changed state. Possible values are `BUTTON1`, `BUTTON2`, `BUTTON3`, or `NOBUTTON`.

Two interfaces are defined for event listeners for these events: `MouseMotionListener` (see Table C.17), which responds to the `MOUSE_MOVED` and `MOUSE_DRAGGED` events, and `MouseListener` (see Table C.18), which responds to all others. There is also the `MouseInputListener` interface, which combines these two (multiple inheritance is allowed for interfaces). All methods take as an argument the `MouseEvent` object that caused the method to be invoked.

TABLE C.17
MouseMotionListener Interface

Method	Behavior
`void mouseDragged(MouseEvent e)`	Invoked when the mouse is moved while a button is pressed.
`void mouseMoved(MouseEvent e)`	Invoked when the mouse is moved while no button is pressed.

TABLE C.18
MouseListener Interface

Method	Behavior
`void mouseClicked(MouseEvent e)`	Invoked when the mouse button has been clicked (pressed and released) on a component.
`void mouseEntered(MouseEvent e)`	Invoked when the mouse enters a component.
`void mouseExited(MouseEvent e)`	Invoked when the mouse exits a component.
`void mousePressed(MouseEvent e)`	Invoked when the mouse button is pressed.
`void mouseReleased(MouseEvent e)`	Invoked when the mouse button is released.

MouseAdapter and MouseMotionAdapter

The `MouseAdapter` and `MouseMotionAdapter` classes are abstract classes that facilitate writing mouse listeners. They implement the `MouseListener` and `MouseMotionListener` interfaces by providing required methods that do nothing. The user can then extend these classes by overriding only those methods for mouse events that are being used by the application, instead of having to implement all of the methods specified in the interfaces.

CASE STUDY   A Drawing Application (Continued)

Problem   In Section C.6 we introduced an application that will let us draw different shapes of different sizes. We specified how the shape to be drawn and its color were determined. However, we did not specify how to draw the figures themselves.

We will specify the origin of the selected figure by pressing the mouse button at the desired point. Then, as the mouse is dragged, the shape outline should expand by following the current mouse position. When the mouse button is released, the shape should be filled with the selected interior color and permanently placed on the drawing canvas.

Analysis   We will need to respond to the MOUSE_PRESSED, MOUSE_DRAGGED, and MOUSE_RELEASED events. We will also need a method to draw the shape outline continuously to represent the current mouse position. This is known as *rubber banding* because the shape seems to stretch like a rubber band. (See Figure C.29.)

FIGURE C.29
Example of Rubber
Banding

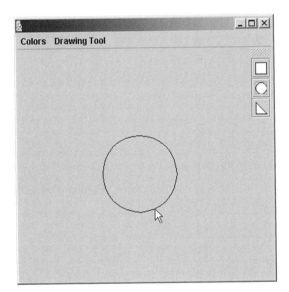

As the mouse is dragged, we need to erase the previously drawn shape outline, calculate the new size, and then draw a new outline. To support this, the Graphics class has a special mode known as *exclusive or* (XOR). When an image is drawn in XOR mode, it is drawn in such a way that if it is drawn again, the old image is erased and the original canvas is restored.

Design   To provide a container for the DrawableFigures and to respond to the mouse events, we create a class DrawPanel as an extension to JPanel. This class has data fields and methods shown in Table C.19.

TABLE C.19
Design of the DrawPanel Class

Data Field	Contents
DrawApp parent	A reference to the parent DrawApp so that the method getSelectedFig can be accessed.
DrawableInt[] figsList	The array of figures that have been drawn.
int numFigs	The number of figures that have been drawn.
DrawableInt currentFig	The figure currently being drawn or **null**.
Constructor	**Behavior**
DrawPanel(DrawApp p)	Registers the MouseListener and MouseMotionListener.
Method	**Behavior**
void paintComponent(Graphics g)	Paints all of the figures in the figsList.

FIGURE C.30
Sequence Diagram for
Adding a New Figure

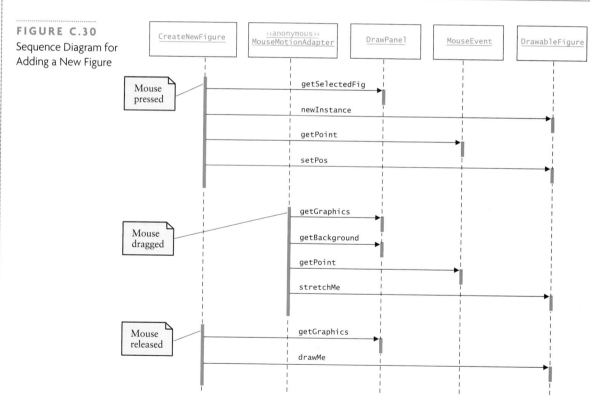

Figure C.30 shows the sequence diagram for the process of adding a new figure. The mouse pressed event is passed to the CreateNewFigure object. The class Create-

NewFigure is an extension of the AbstractMouseListener and is registered as the mouse listener for the DrawPanel. It then obtains the selected figure from the DrawPanel using the getSelectedFig method. Next it gets a new instance of the selected figure by calling the newInstance method. The new figure is positioned at the current mouse position by passing the result of the MouseEvent.getPoint method to the new figure's setPos method.

As the mouse is dragged, the mouseDragged method of an anonymous MouseMotionListener is called. This method gets the current graphics context and current background color from the DrawPanel via the getGraphics and getBackground methods. It then gets the current mouse position using the MouseEvent.getPoint method. These values are then passed to the figure's stretchMe method.

When the mouse is released, the figure is added to the figure list and it is permanently drawn using the drawMe method.

The stretchMe Method

To facilitate rubber banding we add method stretchMe to the DrawableShape class and its subclasses. This method sets the paint mode to XOR and performs the following steps:

Algorithm for stretchMe Method

1. If the outline was previously drawn in XOR mode, draw the current figure's outline in XOR mode. This erases the old figure.
2. Set the size based on the new mouse position.
3. Draw the outline in XOR mode.
4. Set a flag to indicate that the figure's outline has been drawn.

Implementation The code for the stretchMe method of the DrawableCircle class follows. (Refer to Listing 3.18 for the DrawableCircle class.) This method is called by the MouseMotionListener.mouseDragged method whenever the mouse position changes. The code for this method first sets the drawing color to the figure's borderColor and then sets the drawing mode to XOR using the provided background color. If an outline was previously drawn, it is redrawn so that the previous version is erased. Then the new radius is calculated based on the figure's center and current mouse position. Then the figure's outline is drawn in XOR mode.

```
public void stretchMe(Graphics g, Point stretchPoint,
                Color background) {
    g.setColor(drawable.borderColor);
    g.setXORMode(background);
    if (drawable.stretchableOutlineDrawn) {
        g.drawOval(drawable.pos.x - circle.radius,
                drawable.pos.y - circle.radius,
                2 * circle.radius,
                2 * circle.radius);
    }
```

```
            double deltaX = drawable.pos.x - stretchPoint.x;
            double deltaY = drawable.pos.y - stretchPoint.y;
            circle.radius = (int) Math.sqrt(deltaX * deltaX
                                            + deltaY * deltaY);
            g.drawOval(drawable.pos.x - circle.radius,
                       drawable.pos.y - circle.radius,
                       2 * circle.radius,
                       2 * circle.radius);
            drawable.stretchableOutlineDrawn = true;
            g.setPaintMode();
    }
```

The code for the stretchMe methods of other figure kinds is left as an exercise. There is one complication, however. If the mouse is moved to the left of or above its starting position, the resulting width or height is negative. In this case the origin x or y coordinate must be set to the mouse position coordinate and the sign of the width or height reversed.

Listing C.17 shows the code for the DrawPanel class. The mouse event listeners do most of the work. The class CreateNewFigure is an extension of the MouseAdapter. This class overrides the methods mousePressed and mouseReleased.

The current Graphics object and background color for the DrawPanel are obtained by the getGraphics and getBackground methods of JComponent. These are callable from the MouseMotionListener because it is nested within the DrawPanel class.

When the mouse button is pressed (responded to by method CreateNew-Figure.mousePressed), a copy of the selected figure is created by calling the figure's newInstance method, and the figure's origin (position of the mouse click) is saved with the new figure in data field currentFig:

```
    currentFig = parent.getSelectedFig().newInstance();
    currentFig.setPoint(e.getPoint());
```

When the mouse button is released (responded to by method CreateNew-Figure.mouseReleased), the currentFig is added to the figsList, and the drawMe method is invoked to draw it.

```
    figsList[numFigs++] = currentFig;
    currentFig.drawMe(getGraphics());
```

We register the mouse motion listener using the following code:

```
    addMouseMotionListener(new MouseMotionAdapter() {
        public void mouseDragged(MouseEvent e) {
            if (currentFig != null) {
                currentFig.stretchMe(getGraphics(),
                                     e.getPoint(),
                                     getBackground());
            }
        }
    });
```

This is an example of using an anonymous inner class as an event listener. This syntax is discussed below. When the mouse is dragged, the listener object created by this code is invoked and the `currentFig`'s `stretchMe` method is called.

Whenever the window is resized or moved, the `paintComponent` method is called (by Swing). This method first calls its parent `paintComponent` to repaint the background, and then loops through the `figsList` and paints each figure by calling its `drawMe` method.

Testing   Figure C.31 shows an example of the `DrawApp` with several different figures drawn.

 PITFALL

Forgetting to Call `super.paintComponent`
The first statement of paintComponent should always be
    super.paintComponent(g);
This results in the component's background being drawn and, as a side effect, the previously drawn stuff's being erased. If you forget to do it, the results can be quite surprising.

FIGURE C.31
Sample Run of DrawApp

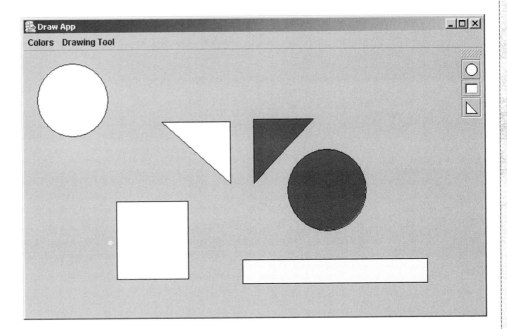

SYNTAX **Anonymous Classes**

FORM

new *Base*() {*class body*}

EXAMPLE

```
new ActionListener() {
    ActionPerformed(ActionEvent e) {
        theCircle.toggleState();
    }
}
```

We can then use this expression in a statement to register an action listener as follows:

```
onOffButton.addActionListener(new ActionListener() {
    public void actionPerformed(ActionEvent e) {
        theCircle.toggleState();
    }
});
```

INTERPRETATION

An anonymous class that is either an implementation of *Base* (if *Base* is an interface) or an extension of *Base* is created with the methods defined in the class body implementing or overriding the corresponding methods in *Base*. Then an instance of this class is created. The class that is created is an inner class of the class in which this expression occurs.

PROGRAM STYLE

Use of Anonymous Classes

The syntax for anonymous classes can be quite confusing, so we have avoided it so far in the text. However, its use is quite common in Java event-oriented programs. Its proponents say that placing the code for an action listener right where it is registered to the component leads to more understandable code. However, if the processing is several lines of code long, the overall logic of creating and laying out the components can be lost. Thus, using anonymous classes is appropriate only for event listeners that require a few lines of code. Also, if you need to use a class in more than one place, it would make more sense to give it a name rather than to define it each time.

LISTING C.17
DrawPanel.java

```java
import java.awt.*;
import java.awt.event.*;
import javax.swing.*;
import java.util.*;

/** The DrawPanel is the canvas on which the figures are drawn. */
public class DrawPanel extends JPanel {

    /** The maximum number of figures */
    private static final int MAX_FIG = 25;
    /** The list of figures */
    private DrawableInt[] figsList = new DrawableInt[MAX_FIG];
    /** The number of figures that have been drawn */
    private int numFigs = 0;
    /** Currently selected figure prototype */
    private DrawableInt currentFig = null;
    /** Reference to parent frame to access selectedFigure */
    private DrawApp parent;

    /** Construct a DrawPanel object. The constructor registers
        the mouse listeners.
        @param p Reference to parent DrawApp
    */
    public DrawPanel(DrawApp p) {
        // Save reference to parent.
        parent = p;
        // Add the mouse listeners.
        addMouseListener(new CreateNewFigure());
        addMouseMotionListener (new MouseMotionAdapter() {
                public void mouseDragged(MouseEvent e) {
                    if (currentFig != null) {
                        currentFig.stretchMe(getGraphics(),
                                             e.getPoint(),
                                             getBackground());
                    }
                }
        });
    }

    /** Method to paint the component. This method is called
        by Swing and should not be called directly.
        @param g The graphics object to do the painting
```

```java
    */
    public void paintComponent(Graphics g) {
        // Always call super.paintComponent first.
        super.paintComponent(g);
        // Draw the figures.
        for (int i = 0; i < numFigs; i++) {
            figsList[i].drawMe(g);
        }
    }

    // Inner Class
    /** Class to create a new figure when the mouse button is pressed
        and released. */
    private class CreateNewFigure extends MouseAdapter {
        /** When the mouse is pressed and the figures array
            is not full, a new figure is created
            with its orgin at the current point.
            @param e MouseEvent
        */
        public void mousePressed(MouseEvent e) {
            if (parent.getSelectedFig() != null && numFigs < MAX_FIG) {
                currentFig =
                    parent.getSelectedFig().newInstance();
                currentFig.setPoint(e.getPoint());
            } else {
                currentFig = null;
            }
        }

        /** When the mouse is released, the current figure is
            redrawn as a final figure by calling its drawMe method.
            @param e MouseEvent
        */
        public void mouseReleased(MouseEvent e) {
            if (currentFig != null) {
                figsList[numFigs++] = currentFig;
                currentFig.drawMe(getGraphics());
                currentFig = null;
            } else {
                JOptionPane.showMessageDialog
                    (null, "Sorry too many figures");
            }
        }
    }
}
```

EXERCISES FOR SECTION C.7

PROGRAMMING

1. Code the stretchMe method for the DrawableShape classes in Section 3.6.
2. Add a new figure, the rhombus (diamond), as shown, to the set of DrawableShapes.

3. Create an anonymous listener class for class ComboBoxDemo shown in Listing C.11.

Chapter Review

- In event-oriented programming the computer responds to the actions of the user or other external events. This is distinguished from the action-response mode of interacting with a program, in which the user responds to requests (prompts) from the computer. Event-oriented programming allows for much more complicated interactions between the computer and user and for simultaneous response to multiple users and other interfacing systems.

- An event is an occurrence that is initiated either by the user or by an external system or program. An event may also be internally initiated by another event. In event-oriented programming, the program responds to events. You write methods to respond to events that are encapsulated into classes that implement a listener interface that is specific to the event type. Objects of these classes are known as event listeners, and event listeners are registered with the component that recognizes the occurrence of the event. For example, a Swing JButton object recognizes that the mouse is clicked while the cursor is inside the JButton's graphic representation. The JButton object will then call the actionPerformed method of any ActionListener objects that have registered with the JButton object.

- Event-oriented programming is used for coding graphical user interfaces (GUIs). Events are triggered by the motion of the mouse, the pressing of mouse buttons, and the pressing of keyboard keys.

- Java has an extensive framework of GUI components in the AWT and Swing packages. The AWT package was part of the original Java release, and Swing represents an extension of this framework. A GUI component is an object that has a graphical representation on the screen and that interacts with the user. Components that can contain other components are called containers.

◆ The JFrame is the Swing top-level container, which is used to build GUI applications. The JPanel is a general-purpose container that can be used to group other components. The Graphics class provides the methods to create the displayed image on the screen or on another graphics device. The Graphics class has both a paint mode, in which image elements (pixels) are set permanently on the display canvas, and an XOR mode, in which image elements are set in such a way that if they are redrawn, the image is erased.

◆ A LayoutManager arranges the components in a container for display on the screen. Java provides several layout managers, including Border Layout, Flow Layout, Box Layout, and Grid Layout.

◆ Java components for interacting with the user include check boxes, radio buttons, and combo boxes for selecting from a set of choices, and text fields and text areas for entry and display of text.

◆ The Locale class encapsulates different language and cultural variations. The NumberFormat class enables formatting of numbers as ordinary numbers, currency, or percentages in accordance with the conventions of the default locale. A Locale for other languages and countries can be created and used to initialize the NumberFormat for that language and culture.

◆ You can also issue commands to a GUI application through menus and toolbars. Menu selections can have a shortcut or accelerator key associated with them, so that the command can be activated without the menu being displayed. Menu selections can also have a mnemonic, a key that will activate the menu selection when the menu is displayed. Both menu selections and toolbar buttons may have icons associated with them. An icon is a small picture that is representative of the action being selected.

◆ Whenever the cursor that is driven by the mouse is displayed in a portion of a component, one or more mouse events are triggered. Mouse events include the mouse entering a component, leaving a component, moving inside a component, the mouse button pressed, released, or clicked (pressed and released quickly).

Java API Classes Introduced in This Chapter

java.awt.event.ActionListener
java.awt.event.ActionEvent
java.util.EventListener
javax.swing.JButton
javax.swing.JFrame
javax.swing.JPanel
java.awt.event.WindowAdapter
java.awt.Graphics
Javax.swing.ButtonGroup
javax.swing.JRadioButton
javax.swing.JTextArea
javax.swing.JTextField
java.text.NumberFormat
java.util.Locale

javax.swing.JMenu
javax.swing.JMenuItem
javax.swing.JMenuBar
java.awt.event.KeyEvent
javax.swing.Icon
javax.swing.ImageIcon
javax.swing.JToolBar
javax.swing.JColorChooser
java.awt.event.MouseEvent
java.awt.event.MouseAdapter
java.awt.event.MouseMotionAdapter
java.awt.event.MouseListener
java.awt.event.MouseMotionListener

User-Defined Interfaces and Classes in This Chapter

DoLookupEntry
PDButtonUI
CirclePanel
TwoCircles
MyCircle
BorderLayoutDemo
FlowLayoutDemo
BuildBoxLayout
GridLayoutDemo
CheckBoxDemo

RadioButtonDemo
ComboBoxDemo
TextFieldDemo
VolumeConverterGUI
VolumeConverter
CurrencyDemo
DrawApp
DrawableIcon
DrawingPanel

Quick-Check Exercises

1. How does the event-oriented model differ from the query-response model?
2. When a GUI button is pressed, an _____ object is fired, which invokes its _____ method, passing the _____ object as an argument.
3. The method _____ is used to register an `ActionListener` for an _____.
4. Can more than one ratio button be selected at a time? If yes, how is this done?
5. What does the grid layout do?
6. What are the names of the areas in the border layout?
7. How do you combine layouts?
8. How is the number ten thousand formatted in the United States? In Germany?
9. How do you specify that you want only two fractional digits in the display of a number?
10. The _____ responds to events generated by the movement of the mouse, and the _____ responds to other mouse events.

Answers to Quick-Check Exercises

1. In the event-oriented model the program responds to external events generated by the user. In the query-response model, the program prompts the user for inputs.
2. `ActionEvent`, `actionPerformed`, `ActionEvent`
3. `addActionListener`, `ActionEvent`
4. Yes; they must be placed within different `ButtonGroups`. Buttons in the same `ButtonGroup` are mutually exclusive.
5. It arranges components in a rectangular grid with a specified number of rows and columns.
6. NORTH, SOUTH, EAST, WEST, and CENTER.
7. You can combine layouts by creating `JPanel` objects and placing them into the frame's content pane using the top-level layout, and setting this layout using the desired layout manager. Each `JPanel` can then have its own layout manager assigned. If necessary this can be repeated by placing `JPanels` within the `JPanels`.
8. In the United States: 10,000. In Germany: 10.000.
9. Create a `NumberFormat` object using the `getNumberInstance` method. Then apply method `setMaximumFractionDigits(2)` to the `NumberFormat` object. Finally, use the `NumberFormat` object's `format` method to format the number.
10. `MouseMotionListener`, `MouseListener`.

Review Questions

1. Write an action listener class that will increment the variables `count1` and `count2` when buttons `button1` and `button2` are clicked, respectively.

2. Assume `button1` and `button2` are variables of type `JButton`. Write statements to register action listeners for them.

3. Assume that you have an array of type `JRadioButton[]`. Write a loop that adds each radio button to a `JPanel` and a `ButtonGroup` and register an action listener for each button.

4. Write code to create a grid of buttons that represents a calculator. Provide the ten digits, the decimal point, and the operations +, −, ×, ÷, C, and CE.

5. Write code to create a `JPanel` that contains a `JTextField` at the top and a set of radio buttons at the bottom.

6. Write code that contains a grid of `JPanel`s, all gray. When the mouse enters a panel, change its color to green, and when it leaves reset the color to gray.

Programming Projects

1. Modify `PDButtonUI` to make the changes discussed at the beginning of this appendix. Specifically:
   - Provide separate buttons for "Add Entry" and "Change Entry"
   - Remove the buttons "Save Directory" and "Exit".
   - The file should be automatically saved whenever the window is closed.

2. Write a program that is a simple calculator that contains a `JTextField` and a grid of buttons. Provide the ten digits, the decimal point, and the operations +, −, ×, ÷, C, and CE. C will completely reset the calculator, and CE will reset the current entry. Clicking one of the arithmetic operators will perform the selected operation, using the currently displayed value as the right-hand operand and the previously displayed value as the left-hand operand, and then display the result. When a number or the decimal point key is pressed after an operator key or C is pressed, the currently displayed value will be saved to become the left-hand operand, and the value associated with this key will be displayed. Additional numbers (and decimal point) will be entered to the right of the display. The decimal point may be entered only once. Pressing CE will clear the display, but the saved value will be retained.

3. Write a GUI program to convert between dollars and euros. The program should allow the amount to be specified either in dollars per euro or euros per dollar using radio buttons. The user enters the amount to be converted in a text field. The converted currency should be displayed in a second text field in the format appropriate for the locale: dollars in the US locale, and euros in a European locale such as Germany.

4. Write a program to convert the price of fuel expressed in dollars per gallon to euros per liter. The currency conversion factory should be expressed either in dollars per euro or euros per dollar. Use a text field to input the price of fuel.

5. Write a program to illustrate the Towers of Hanoi game. The Towers of Hanoi consists of a board with three pegs. At the beginning of the game, a set of rings ranging from the largest on the bottom to the smallest on the top is on one of the pegs, as shown in Figure C.32. As the game is played, rings are moved from peg to peg, but the rings on each peg are always in order of size, with the smallest on top and the largest on the bottom. This program does not have to play the game; it just has to illustrate the board.

Your program should have a menu command that lets the user select the number of rings. The display should fit within the frame, as shown in Figure C.32. Whenever the frame is resized, the board should be resized and redrawn.

FIGURE C.32
Design of the Towers of Hanoi Board

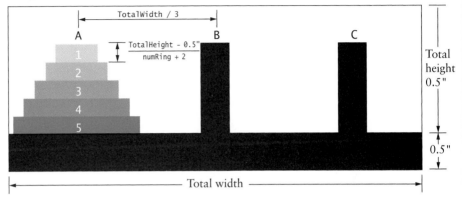

6. Write a GUI that you could use in a hotel room to order breakfast. Each item description and price appears as a label alongside a check box. You will select each item you want to order by setting its check box. When you are done, click the submit button, and the items you selected should be listed in a text area along with the total cost.

7. Write a GUI that could be used by a Web-based company to receive billing information. Use a set of radio buttons to enter the person's title (Mr., Ms., Dr.), a text box for name, a text field for the street address, a text field for city, a text field for ZIP code, a combo box for state, a combo box for the user's credit card type, a text field for the credit card number, a combo box for expiration month, and a combo box for expiration year. After the user clicks a Submit button, if some information is missing, display in a text area the names of any fields that are not set. Otherwise, display a summary of the information that was entered in the text area.

8. Write a GUI that could be used with the `Media` hierarchy project in Chapter 3 (Project 5). Use a combo box to select the operation that the user wishes to perform: add an item, retrieve an item's stored information given its title, display all items for a particular artist, display all items for a particular kind of media. When adding an item, use a set of radio buttons to designate its type and use check boxes and text fields to enter other kinds of information.

9. Redo Project 7 using a menu for the different user choices. Based on the user's choice, display an appropriate GUI in a panel. For example, if the user selects Add an Item from the menu, the GUI should allow the user to enter the desired information using radio buttons, check boxes, text fields, and other such components. If the user selects Retrieve an Item, the GUI displayed should have a text field in which the user can enter the title, and it should have a text area for displaying the information retrieved.

Glossary

2-3 tree A search tree in which each node may have two or three children.

2-3-4 tree A search tree in which each node may have two, three, or four children.

2-node A node in a 2-3 or 2-3-4 tree with two children.

3-node A node in a 2-3 or 2-3-4 tree with three children.

abstract class A class that contains at least one abstract method.

abstract data type An implementation-independent specification of a set of data items and the operations performed on those data items.

abstract method The specification of the signature of a method without its implementation. Abstract methods are declared in interfaces and abstract classes. A concrete class that is a subclass of an abstract class or an implementation of an interface must implement each abstract method declared in the abstract superclass or interface.

abstraction A model of a physical entity or activity.

accelerator A key combination that invokes a menu item's action listeners without requiring the user to navigate the menu hierarchy.

acceptance testing A sequence of tests that demonstrates to the customer that a software product meets all of its requirements. Acceptance testing generally is observed by a customer representative.

action event An event caused by a user's action, such as pressing a key or clicking a GUI button.

action listener An object that contains a method that responds to an action event. An action listener is an event listener for an action event. See also *event listener*.

activation bar The thick line along the life line in a sequence diagram that indicates the time that a method is executing in response to the receipt of a message.

activation frame An area of memory allocated to store the actual parameters and local variables for a particular call to a method. In Java, references to activation frames are stored on the run-time stack. When a method is called, a new activation frame is pushed onto the stack, and when a method exits, the activation frame is popped.

actor An entity that is external to a given software system. In many cases an actor is a human user of the software system, but an actor may be another system.

adapter class A class that provides the same or very similar functionality as another class but with different method signatures. The actual work is performed by delegation to the methods in the other class.

address A number that represents an object's location in memory.

adjacency lists A representation of a graph in which the vertices (the destinations) adjacent to a given vertex (the source) are stored in a list associated with that vertex. The actual edge (source, destination, weight) from the source vertex to the destination may be stored.

adjacency matrix A representation of a graph in which the presence or absence of an edge is indicated by a value in a matrix that is indexed by the two vertices. The value stored is 0 for no edge, 1 for an edge in an unweighted graph, and the weight itself for a weighted graph.

adjacent [vertex] In a directed graph, a vertex, v, is adjacent to another vertex, u, if there is an edge, (u, v), from vertex u to vertex v. In an undirected graph v is adjacent to u if there is an edge $\{u, v\}$ between them.

aggregation An association between two classes in which one class is composed of a collection of objects of the other class.

analysis In the waterfall model, the phase of the software life cycle (workflow in the Unified Model) during which the requirements are clarified and the overall architecture of the solution is determined.

ancestor A node in a tree that is at a higher level than a given node and from which there is a path to that node (the descendant).

ancestor-descendant relationship A generalization of the parent-child relationship. (See *ancestor* and *descendant*).

anchor The symbol, $\oplus$, that is used in a UML class diagram to indicate that a class is an inner class of another class.

anonymous object An object for which there is no named reference. The Java **new** operator returns a reference to an anonymous object.

anonymous reference A reference to an object that itself has no name. Anonymous references are the result of a cast operation.

applet A top-level Java GUI class that is intended to be displayed in a frame that is under the control of a web browser.

assertion A statement about the current value of one or more variables.

association A relationship between two classes.

attributes The set of data values that determine the state of an object. Generally the attributes of a class are represented by data fields within the class.

auto-boxing A new Java feature (in Java 1.5) that performs automatic conversion between the primitive types and their corresponding wrapper classes.

AVL tree A self-balancing binary search tree in which the difference between the heights of the subtrees is stored in each tree node. The insertion and removal algorithms use rotations to maintain this difference within the range –1 to +1.

back edges An edge that is discovered during a depth-first search that leads to an ancestor in the depth-first search tree.

backtracking An approach to implementing a systematic trial-and-error search for a solution. When a dead-end is reached, the algorithm follows a path back to the decision point that lead to the dead-end, then moves forward along a different path.

balanced binary search tree A binary search tree in which the height of each pair of subtrees is approximately the same.

base case The case in a recursive algorithm that can be solved directly.

batch processing A way of using a computer in which a series of jobs (individual programs) are collected together and then executed sequentially.

big-O notation The specification of a set of functions that represent the upper bound of a given function. Formally the function $f(n)$ is said to be $O(g(n))$ if there are constants $c > 0$ and $n_0 > 0$ such that for all $n > n_0$, $cg(n) \geq f(n)$.

binary search The process of searching a sorted sequence that begins by examining the middle element. If the middle element is greater than the target, then the search is applied recursively to the lower half; if it is less than the target, the search is applied recursively to the upper half.

binary search tree A binary tree in which the items in the left subtree of a node are all less than that node, and the items in the right subtree are all greater than that node.

binary tree A tree in which each node has 0, 1, or 2 children. The children are distinguished by the names left and right. If a node has one child, that child is distinguished as being a left child or a right child.

black-box testing A testing approach in which the internal structure of the item being tested is not known or taken into account in the design of the test cases. The test cases are based only on the functional requirements for the item being tested.

block A compound statement that may contain local variables and class declarations.

bottom-up design A design process in which the lower-level methods are designed first. A lowest-level method is one that does not depend on other methods to perform its function.

boundary condition A value of a variable that causes a different path to be taken. For example in the statement if `(x > C) { ... } else { ... }` the value of C is a boundary condition.

branch coverage A measure of testing thoroughness. Each alternative from a decision point (`if`, `switch`, or `while` statement) is considered a branch. If a test exercises a branch, then that branch is considered covered. The ratio of the covered branches to the total number of branches is the branch coverage. See also *path coverage*, and *statement coverage*.

branch In a tree, the link between a parent node and one of its children.

breadth-first search A way of searching through a graph in which the vertices adjacent to a given vertex are all examined and placed into a queue. Once all the adjacent vertices are examined, the next vertex is removed from the queue. Thus vertices are examined in increasing distance (as measured by the number of edges) from the starting vertex.

breadth-first traversal See *breadth-first search*.

breakpoint A point in a program at which the debugger is instructed to suspend execution when it is reached. This allows for examination of the value of variables at a given point before execution is resumed.

B-tree A balanced search tree in which each node is a leaf or may have up to n children and $n-1$ data items. The leaves are all at the bottom level. Each node (except for the root) is kept at least half full. That is, each node has between $(n-1)/2$ and $n-1$ data items. The root is either a single node (leaf) or it has at least one data item and two children.

bubble sort A sort algorithm that makes several passes through the sequence being sorted. During each pass, adjacent items are examined and, if out of order, swapped. If there are no exchanges on a given pass, then the process is complete. The effect of each pass is that the largest item in the unsorted part of the sequence is moved to (bubbles to) the end of the sequence.

bucket hashing See *chaining*.

bucket The list of keys stored in a hash table entry that uses chaining. All the keys in the list map to the index of that table entry.

byte code The platform-independent representation of a Java program that is the output of the Java compiler and is the input to the Java Virtual Machine (JVM). The JVM then interprets this input to execute the program.

casting When applied to a reference to an object, casting re-interprets that reference to refer to an object of a different type. The object must be of the target type (or a subclass of the target type) for the cast to be valid. When applied to a primitive numeric value, a cast represents a conversion to an equivalent value of the target primitive numeric type.

catch block The sequence of statements that will be executed when an exception is caught by a **catch** clause.

catch clause The specification of an exception type and the statements to be executed when an exception of that type is caught. One or more **catch** clauses follow a **try** block, and will catch the exceptions thrown from that **try** block.

chaining An approach to hashing in which all keys that are mapped to a given entry in the hash table are placed into a list. The list is called a bucket.

check box A GUI component which may be either selected or de-selected. The component is generally shown as a small square box, and the selected state is indicated by a check-mark symbol. Several check boxes may be presented to give the user the choice of one or more from a group of possible values See also *radio button* and *combo box*.

checked exception An exception that either must be declared in a throws declaration or caught by a **try-catch** sequence.

child A node in a tree that is the immediate descendant of another node.

class diagram A UML diagram that shows a number of classes and the relationships between them.

class method See *static method*.

class The fundamental programming unit in a Java program. A class consists of a collection of zero or more data fields (instance variables) and zero or more methods that operate on those data fields.

client A class or method that uses a given class.

cloning The process of making a deep copy of an object.

closed-box testing See *black-box testing*.

collection hierarchy The hierarchy of classes in the Java API that consists of classes designed to represent collections of other object.

collision The mapping of two or more keys into the same position in a hash table.

combo box A GUI component which is a combination of a button or editable field and a drop-down list. The drop-down list is a set (or menu) of choices, only one of which may be selected at a time. The current selection is displayed in the button of field, but when selected by a mouse click, the drop-down list is displayed, allowing the selection of one of the other choices. See also *check box and radio button*.

complete binary tree A binary tree in which each node is a leaf or has two children.

component testing The testing of an individual part of a program by itself. In a Java program a component may be a method or a class.

component In a GUI application, an object displayed on the screen that can interact with the user.

component class A class whose objects are part of another object. See *composition*.

composition The association between two classes in which objects of one class are part of another class. The parts generally do not have an independent existence, but are created when the parent object is created. For example an `Airplane` object is composed of a `Body` object, two `Wing` objects, and a `Tail` object.

compound statement Zero or more statements enclosed within braces { ... }.

concrete class (actual class) A class for which objects can be instantiated.

connected components A set of vertices within a graph for which there is a path between every pair of vertices.

connected graph A graph that consists of a single connected component.

construction phase The phase of the Unified Model of the software life cycle during which most of the activity is devoted to writing the software.

constructor A method that initializes an object when it is first created.

container In a GUI application, a component that contains other components.

content pane In a Swing GUI application, the component of a frame in which the application places the components to be displayed.

contract The specification of the pre- and postconditions of a method.

cost of a spanning tree The sum of the weights of the edges.

coverage testing See *branch testing*.

cycle A path in a graph in which the first and final vertices are the same.

data abstraction The specification of the data items of a problem and the operations to be performed on these data items that does not specify how they (the data items) will be represented and stored in memory. See also *abstract data type*.

data field (instance variable) A variable that is part of a class.

debugging The process of finding and removing defects (bugs) from a program.

deep copy A copy of an object in which data field values and references to immutable objects are simply duplicated, but each reference to a mutable object references a copy of that object. If there are mutable references in any object that is copied, these also reference a copy of that object. The effect is that you can change any value in a deep copy of an object without modifiying the original object.

default constructor The no-parameter constructor that is generated by the Java compiler if no constructors are defined.

default visibility The same as *package visibility*.

defensive programming An approach to designing a program that builds in statements to test the values of variables that might result in an exception or run-time error (to be sure that they are valid) before statements that use the variables are executed.

delegation The implementation of a method in one class that merely calls a method in another class.

delimiter characters Characters which are defined to separate a string into tokens.

depth (level) The number of nodes in a path from the root to a node.

depth-first search A method of searching a graph in which adjacent vertices are examined along a path until a dead end is reached. The search then backtracks until an unexamined vertex is found, and the search continues with that vertex.

depth-first traversal See *depth-first search*.

deque A data structure that combines the features of a stack and queue. Items may be inserted in one end, and removed from either.

descendant In a tree, a lower node that can be reached by following a path from a given node.

design The process by which classes and methods are identified and defined to create a program that satisfies a given set of requirements.

detail message An optional string to be displayed when an exception is thrown that provides additional information about the conditions that led to the exception.

dialog In a GUI application, a window that provides information or asks for data entry.

digraph See *directed graph*.

directed edge An edge in a directed graph.

directed acyclic graph A directed graph that contains no cycles.

directed graph A graph in which every edge is considered to have a direction. If u and v are vertices in a graph, then the presence of the edge (u, v) indicates that v is adjacent to u, but u may not be adjacent to v. Contrast with *undirected graph*.

discovery order The order in which vertices are discovered in a depth-first search.

double buffering In a GUI application, updates to the image are made in one area of memory while the image being displayed is based on another area of memory. When all of the updates are complete, the memory areas are swapped and the new image is displayed.

downcast A reinterpretation of a reference from a superclass to a subclass. In Java, downcasts are tested for validity. See also *casting*.

driver A method whose purpose is to call a method being tested and provide it with appropriate argument values. Usually the result of executing the method is displayed immediately to the user.

edges In a graph, the links between pairs of vertices.

elaboration phase The phase in the Unified model of the software life-cycle during which the software architecture is defined.

escape sequence A sequence of characters beginning with the backslash (\) which is used to indicate another character that cannot be directly entered. For example the sequence \n represents the newline character.

Euler tour A path around a tree, starting and ending with the root. The tree is always kept to the left of the path when viewed from the direction of travel along the path.

event listener An object that is registered to respond to an event. The object's class contains a method that is called when the event occurs.

event The occurrence of an external input or an internal state change.

exclusive or (XOR) A graphics drawing mode in which drawing a shape twice has the effect of erasing the original shape from the image.

extending The process of adding functionality by defining a new class that adds data fields and/or adds or overrides methods of an existing class.

external node See *leaf*.

Extreme Programming A software development process in which programmers work in pairs. One programmer writes methods while the other designs tests for those methods. The programmers alternate roles. The programmers also share a workstation so that when one programmer is using the workstation the other is observing.

factory method A method that is responsible for creating objects of a class. Generally a factory method will be associated with an abstract class or interface and will choose an appropriate concrete class that extends the abstract class or implements the interface based upon parameters passed to the factory method and/or system parameters. Returns a reference to a new object of this concrete class.

finally block A block preceded by the key word `finally`. Part of the `try-catch-finally` sequence.

finish order The order in which the vertices are finished in a depth-first search. A vertex is considered finished when all of the paths to adjacent vertices have been finished.

firing an event The process of indicating that an event has occurred.

forest A collection of trees that may result from a depth-first search of a directed graph or an unconnected graph.

frame A top level container in a GUI application. A frame consists of a window with a border around it.

full binary tree A binary tree in which the nodes at all but the deepest level contain two children. At the deepest level, all nodes that have two children are to the left of those that have no children, and there is at most one node with a left child that is between these two groups.

functional testing Testing that concentrates on verifying that software meets its functional requirements.

garbage collector The process of reclaiming memory that no longer has a reference to it. This process generally runs in the background.

generalization The relationship between two classes in which one class is the superclass and the other is a subclass. The superclass is a generalization of the subclass.

generic type A type that is defined in terms of another type where that other type may be specified as a parameter. For example the class List<E> is a List designed to hold objects of type E, where E may be any other class and is specified when the object is created.

glass-box testing Testing that takes the internal structure of the unit being tested into account.

graph A mathematical structure consisting of a set of vertices and edges. The edges represent a relationship between the vertices.

hash code A function that transforms an object into an integer value that may be used as an index into a hash table.

heapsort A sort algorithm in which the items being sorted are inserted into a heap, then removed one at a time.

height of a tree The number of nodes in a path from the root to the deepest leaf.

Huffman code A varying length binary code in which each symbol is assigned a code whose length is inversely proportional to the frequency with which that symbol appears (or is expected to appear) in a message. The resulting coded message is the minimum possible length.

image rendering The process of creating an image in a device-dependent form for display on that device. During this process, the values of individual pixels are determined.

immutable A class that is immutable has no methods to change the value of its data fields. An immutable object can't be changed.

implement (an interface) To provide in a class an implementation of all of the methods specified by an interface.

inception phase In the Unified model of the software life cycle, the initial phase of a project in which the requirements are first identified.

increment operator The operator that has the side effect of adding one to its operand.

index A value that specifies a position within an array.

infix notation Mathematical notation in which the operators are between the operands.

information hiding The design principle that states that the internal data representations of a class cannot be used or directly modified by clients.

inherit To receive from an ancestor. In an object-oriented language, a subclass inherits the visible methods and data fields from its superclass. These inherited methods and data fields appear to clients of the subclass as if they were members of that class.

initializer list A list of values, enclosed in braces, that initializes the values in an array.

inner class A class that is defined within another class. Methods of inner classes have access to the data fields and methods of the outer class in which they are defined and vice versa.

inorder predecessor For a binary search tree, the inorder predecessor of an item is the largest item that is less than this item. The node containing an item's inorder prececessor would be visited just prior to that item in an inorder traversal.

insertion sort A sorting algorithm in which each item is inserted into its proper place in the sorted region.

instance method A method that is associated with an object. Contrast with *static method*.

instance variables A variable of a class that is associated with an object (i.e., a data field of an object). Contrast with *static variable*.

instance See *object*.

instanceof operator The Java operator that returns true if a reference variable references an instance of a specified class or interface.

integration testing Testing in which the interaction of the components or units of a software program are validated.

interface The external view of a class. In Java, an interface is a class that defines nothing more than public abstract methods and constants.

internal node A node in a tree that has one or more children. Contrast with *leaf*.

interpret To translate or understand the meaning of. The Java Virtual Machine interprets the machine-independent byte code in terms of specific machine-language instructions for the computer on which it is executing.

iteration In a loop, a complete execution of the loop body. In the Unified model of the software life cycle, a sequence of activities that results in the release of a set of software artifacts.

iterator An object that accesses the objects contained in a collection one at a time.

Javadoc The commenting convention defined for Java programs. Also the program that generates documentation from the comments that follow this convention in a program.

key A value or reference that is unique to a particular object and thereby identifies that object (e.g., a social security number).

Last In, First Out (LIFO) An organization of data such that the most recently inserted item is the one that is removed first.

last-line recursion A recursive algorithm or method in which the recursive call is the last executable statement.

layout manager An object in a GUI application that manages the visual arrangement of components in a container.

leaf (node) A node in a tree that has no children. Contrast with *internal node*.

left rotation The transformation of a binary search tree in which the right child of the current root becomes the new root, and the old root becomes the left child of the new root.

level of a node The number of nodes in a path from the root to this node.

life line The dotted vertical line in a UML sequence diagram that indicated the life time of an object.

linear probing A collision resolution method in which sequential locations in a hash table are searched to find the item sought or an empty location.

linear search A search algorithm in which items in a sequence are examined sequentially.

link A reference from one node to another.

literal A constant value that appears directly in a statement.

logic error An error in the design of an algorithm or program. Contrast with *syntax error*.

logical view A description of the data stored in an object that does not specify the physical layout of the data in memory.

loop invariant An assertion that is true before each execution of the loop body and is true when the loop exits.

many-to-one mapping An association among items in which more than one item (a key) is associated with a single item (a value).

marker An interface that is defined with no methods or constants. It is used to give a common name to a family of interfaces or classes.

merge The process of combining two sorted sequences into a single sorted sequence.

merge sort A sorting algorithm in which sorted subsequences are merged to form larger sorted sequences.

message to self A message that is passed from an object to itself. It represents a method calling another method within the same class.

message In an object-oriented design, a message represents an occurrence of a method call.

method A sequence of statements that can be invoked (or called) passing a fixed number of values as arguments and optionally returning a value.

method declaration The specification of the name, parameters, and return type of a method. See also *signature*.

method overloading The presence of multiple methods in a class with the same name but different signatures.

method overriding The replacement of an inherited method with a different implementation in a subclass.

minimum spanning tree A subset of the edges of a connected graph such that the graph remains connected and the sum of the weights of the edges is the minimum.

mnemonic A character that can be used to select a menu item from the keyboard when the menu is displayed.

multiple inheritance Inheriting from more than one superclass.

multiplicity An indication of the number of objects in an association.

narrowing conversion A conversion from a type that has a larger range of values to a type that has a smaller one.

nested class See *inner class*.

network A system consisting of interconnected entities.

new operator The Java operator that creates objects (or instances) of a class.

newline The special character that indicates the end of a line of input or output.

node An object to store data in a linked list or tree. This object will also contain references to other nodes.

object An example or instance of a class. Internally, it is an area of memory that is structured as defined by a class. The methods of that class operate on the values defined within this memory area.

object-oriented design A design approach that identifies the entities, or objects, that participate in a problem or system and then designs classes to model these objects within a program.

onto mapping A mapping in which each value in the value set is mapped to by at least one member of the key set.

open-box testing See *glass-box testing*.

operations The methods defined in a class.

operator For classes, operator is another name for *method*. For primitive types, it represents a pre-defined function on one or two values (for example addition).

output buffer A memory area in which information written to an output stream is stored prior to being written to disk.

override Replace a method inherited from a superclass by one defined in a subclass.

package visibility A level of visibility whereby variables and methods are visible to methods defined in classes within the same package.

package A grouping of classes under a common package name.

panel A general purpose GUI component that can be used as a drawing surface or to contain other GUI components.

parent The node that is directly above a node within a tree.

partitioning The process of separating a sequence into two sequences; used in quicksort.

path coverage A measure of testing thoroughness. If a test exercises a path, then that path is considered covered. The ratio of the covered paths to the total number of paths is the path coverage. See also *branch coverage*, and *statement coverage*.

path In a graph, a sequence of vertices in which each vertex is adjacent to its predecessor.

phase In the Unified Model of the software life cycle, the span of time between two major milestones.

physical view A view of an object that considers its actual representation in computer memory.

pivot In the quicksort algorithm, a value in the sequence being sorted that is used to partition the sequence. The sequence is partitioned into values that are less than or equal to the pivot, and values that are greater than the pivot.

polymorphism Many forms or many shapes. In a Java program a method defined in a superclass (or interface) may be called through a reference to that superclass (or interface). The actual method executed is the one that overrides that method and is defined in the concrete subclass object that is referenced by the superclass (or interface) variable.

pop Remove the top element of a stack.

postcondition An assertion that will be true after a method is executed assuming that the preconditions were true before the method is executed.

postfix increment The increment operator (e.g., i++) that has the side effect of incrementing the variable to which it is applied, but its current value is the value of the variable before the increment takes place (e.g., i).

postfix notation A mathematical notation in which the operators appear after their operands.

precedence The degree of binding of infix operators. Operators of higher precedence are evaluated before operators of lower precedence.

precondition An assertion that must be true before a method is executed for the method to perform as specified.

prefix increment The increment operator (e.g., ++i) that has the side effect of incrementing the variable to which it is applied, and its current value is the value of the variable after the increment takes place (e.g., i + 1).

private visibility A level of visibility whereby variables and methods are visible only to methods defined in the same class.

procedural abstraction The philosophy that procedure (method) development should separate the concern of *what* is to be achieved by a procedure (or method) from the details of *how* it is to be achieved.

protected visibility A level of visibility whereby variables and methods are visible to methods defined in the same class, subclasses of that class, or the same package.

proof by induction A proof method which demonstrates that a proposition is true for a base case (usually 0) and then demonstrates that if the proposition is true for an arbitrary value (k) is it then true for the successor of that value ($k + 1$).

pseudocode A description of an algorithm that is structured similar to a programming language implementation, but lacks the formal syntax and notation of a programming language. Generally pseudocode will use common programming language decision and looping constructs.

pseudorandom A computer-generated sequence of values that appear to be random because they pass various statistical tests that are consistent with those that would be produced by a truly random sequence.

public visibility A level of visibility whereby variables and methods are visible to all methods regardless of which class or package they are defined in.

quadratic probing In a hash table, a collision resolution technique in which the sequence of locations that are examined increases as the square of the number of probes made.

queuing theory The branch of mathematics developed to solve problems associated with queues by developing mathematical models for these problems.

quicksort A sorting algorithm in which a sequence is partitioned into two sub-sequences, one that is less than or equal to a pivot value and the other that is greater than the pivot value. The process is then recursively applied to the sub-sequences until a sub-sequence with one item is reached.

radio button A GUI component which may be either selected or de-selected. The component is generally shown as a small open circle, and the selected state is indicated by a filled-in circle. Radio buttons are grouped into a button group so that only one item in the group may be selected at a time. See also *check box* and *combo box*.

random access The ability to access any object in a collection by means of an index.

recursive case A case in a recursive algorithm that is solved by applying the algorithm to a transformed version of its parameter.

recursive data structure A data structure that is defined in terms of itself.

recursive method A method that calls itself.

Red-Black tree A self balancing binary search tree that maintains balance by distinguishing the nodes by one of two states: "red" or "black". Algorithms for insertion and deletion maintain the balance by ensuring that the number of black nodes in any path from the root to a leaf is the same.

reference variable A variable that references an object.

registering (listener for event) The process by which a listener object is associated with an event. This is done by calling a method defined by the component that recognizes the event and passing a reference to the listener object.

regression testing Testing that ensures that changes to the item being tested do not invalidate previously verified functions.

rehashing The process of moving the items in one hash table to a larger hash table using hashing to find each item's new location.

request-response A program that issues a request to the user and then waits for input.

requirements specification A document that specifies what a program or system is to do without specifying how it is done.

reusable code Code written for one program that can be used in another.

right rotation The transformation of a binary search tree in which the left child of the current root becomes the new root, and the old root becomes the right child of the new root.

root The node in a tree that has no parent and is at the top level.

rubber banding Continuously erasing and redrawing a shape so that it follows the mouse position.

run-time error An error that is detected when the program executes. In Java, run-time errors are detected by the Java Virtual Machine.

starter method See *wrapper method*.

seed The initial value in a pseudorandom number sequence. Changing the seed causes a different sequence to be generated by the pseudorandom number generator.

selection sort A sort algorithm in which the smallest item is selected from the unsorted portion of the sequence and placed into the next position in the sorted portion.

self-balancing search tree A search tree with insertion and removal algorithms that maintain the tree in balance. See *balanced binary search tree, AVL tree, Red-Black tree, 2-3 tree,* and *2-3-4 tree.*

sequence diagram A UML diagram that shows the sequence of messages between objects that are required to perform a given function or realize a use case.

set difference For sets A and B, A–B is the subset of a set, A, that does not contain elements of some other set, B.

set intersection A set of the elements that are common to two sets.

set union A set of the elements that are in one set or the other.

shallow copy A copy of an object that only copies the values of the data fields. If a data field is a reference, the original and the copy reference the same target object.

Shell sort A variation on insertion sort in which elements separated by a value known as the gap are sorted using the insertion sort algorithm. This process repeats using a decreasing sequence of values for the gap.

sibling One of two or more nodes in a tree that have a common parent.

signature A method's name and the types of its parameters. The return type is not part of the signature because it is illegal to have two methods with the same signature and different return types.

simple path A path that contains no cycles.

simulation The process of modeling a physical system using a computer program.

single-step execution In debugging, the process of executing one statement at a time so that the user may examine the values of variables after each statement is executed.

software life cycle The sequence of phases that a software product goes through as it is developed.

spanning tree A minimum subset of the vertices of a connected graph which still results in a connected graph.

stack trace A listing of the sequence of method calls that starts where an error is detected and ends at the program invocation.

state The current value of all of the data fields in an object.

statement coverage A measure of testing thoroughness. If a test exercises a statement, then the statement is considered covered. The ratio of the covered statements to the total number of statements is the statement coverage. See also *branch coverage*, and *path coverage.*

static method A method defined within a class, but not associated with any particular object of that class.

static variable A variable defined in a class that is not a member of any particular object, but shared by all objects of the class.

step into When debugging in single-step mode, setting the next statement to be executed to be the first statement of the method. Each individual statement in the method is executed in sequence.

step over When debugging in single-step mode, setting the method call to be treated as a single statement.

stepwise refinement The process of breaking a complicated problem into simpler problems. This process is repeated with the smaller problems until a problem of solvable size is reached.

strongly typed language A programming language in which the type of objects is verified when arguments are bound to parameters and when values are assigned to variables. A syntax error occurs if the types are not compatible.

structure chart A diagram that represents the relationship between problems and their subproblems.

structured walkthrough A design or code review following a defined process in which the author of a program leads the review team through the design and implementation, and the reviewers follow a check-list of common defects to verify that these defects are not present.

stub A dummy method that is used to test another method. A stub takes the place of a method that the method being tested calls. A stub will typically return a known result.

subclass A class that is an extension of another class. A subclass inherits the members of its superclass.

subset A set that contains only elements that are in some other set. A subset may contain any or all of the elements of the other set or it may be the empty set.

subtree of a node The tree that consists of this node as its root.

superclass A class that has a subclass. See *subclass*.

syntax error An error that violates the syntax rules of the language. Syntax errors are generally the result of a mistake in entering the program into the computer (typographical error) or a misunderstanding of the language syntax. Syntax errors are detected by the compiler.

system analyst A person who analyses a problem to determine the requirements for a software program.

system testing Testing of a complete program or solution to a problem.

tail recursion See *last line recursion*.

test case An individual test.

test framework A set of classes and procedures used to design and conduct tests.

test harness A method that executes the individual test cases of a test suite and records the results.

test suite A collection of test cases.

throw an exception Indicate that the situation that causes an exception has been detected.

token A character or string extracted from a larger string. Tokens are separated by *delimiters*.

top-down design A design process which represents the solution to a higher module in terms of the solution to one or more lower level modules.

topological sort An ordering of a sequence of items for which a partial order is defined that does not violate the partial order. For example if *a* is defined to be before *b* (*a* is a prerequisite of *b*) by the partial order, then *a* will not appear later in the sequence than *b*. A partial order is defined by a directed acylic graph.

transition phase In the Unified Model of the software life cycle, the phase in which the software product is turned over to the end users.

tree traversal The process of systematically visiting each node in a tree.

try-catch-finally sequence A sequence consisting of a **try** block followed by one or more **catch** clauses and optionally followed by a **finally** block. Or a **try** block followed by a **finally** block. Exceptions that are thrown by the **try** block are handled by the **catch** clauses that follow it. Statements in the **finally** block

are executed either after the **try** block exits normally, or when a **catch** block that handles an exception exits.

try block A block preceded by the reserved word, **try**. Part of the **try-catch-finally** sequence.

type cast The process of converting from one type to another.

unchecked exception An exception which does not have to be declared in a **throws** statement or have the statements which might throw it enclosed within a **try** block.

undirected edge An edge in an undirected graph.

undirected graph A graph in which no edge has a direction. If *u* and *v* are vertices in a graph then the presence of the edge {*u*, *v*} indicates that *v* is adjacent to *u*, and *u* is adjacent to *v*. Contrast with *directed graph*.

Unified Model A software development life cycle model that is defined in terms of a sequence of phases and workflows. The workflows are exercised during each iteration of each phase, but the distribution of the amount of effort for each workflow varies from iteration to iteration.

Unified Modeling Language (UML) A language to describe the modeling of an object-oriented design that is the unification of several previous modeling systems. Specifically, the modeling techniques developed by Booch, Jacobson, and Rumbaugh were combined to form the initial version. UML has since evolved and is defined by a standard issued by the Object Modeling Group.

unit testing Testing of an individual unit of a software program. In Java, a unit is generally a method or class.

unnamed reference See *anonymous reference*.

unwinding the recursion The process of returning from a sequence of method calls and forming the result.

upcast Casting a reference to a superclass or interface type.

use case The documentation of the sequences of interactions between a computer system and its user needed to accomplish a given process.

user interface (UI) The way in which the user and a program interact, or the class that provides this interaction.

version control The process of keeping track of the various changes that are made to a program as it is developed or maintained.

vertices The set of items that are part of a graph. The vertices are related to one another by edges.

waterfall model A software development model in which all of the activities of one workflow are completed before the next one is started.

weight A value associated with an edge in a weighted graph.

weighted graph A graph in which each edge is assigned a value.

widening conversion A conversion from a type that has a smaller set of values to one that has a larger set of values.

window A top level container in a GUI application. Generally a window is a rectangular area on the display surface. See also *frame*.

workflow In the Unified Model of the software life cycle, a sequence of activities performed by participating workers and the artifacts they produce.

wrapper class A class that encapsulates a primitive data type.

wrapper method A method whose only purpose is to call a recursive method, perhaps providing initial values for some parameters, and returning the result. Also called a starter method.

Index

Page references followed by italic *t* indicate material in tables.

A

AbstractButton class, 751, 756
abstract classes, 138–142
  features comparison, 142*t*
  and interfaces, 141
AbstractCollection class, 242
abstract data types, 1–2
  described, 13–19
AbstractGraph class, 624–627
abstraction, 1–2
  to manage complexity, 11–13
AbstractList class, 195, 242, 741
AbstractMap class, 490
abstract methods, 15, 138–142
  omitting definition in subclass, 140
AbstractMouseListener class, 803
AbstractSequentialList class, 195, 241, 741
AbstractSet class, 490
Abstract Windows Toolkit (AWT), 756
acceptance testing, 87
  software life cycle, 6*t*
accessor methods, 705
action command, of radio button, 773
ActionEvent class, 750
ActionListener interface, 750–751
  processing mouse events, 799
activation bars, 746
activation frame, 343–345
activities, in software life cycle, 6, 6*t*
actors, 10
actual classes, 138, 141
  features comparison, 142*t*
actual objects, 141
adapter class, 264
addActionListener method, 750
add method
  ArrayBasedPD class, 41
  ArrayList class, 198
  BinarySearchTree class, 413–414
  Collection interface, 240
  KWArrayList class, 202–203
  KWListIter class, 230–233
  LinkedListRec class, 364
addOrChangeEntry method, 79, 199–200
  ArrayBasedPD class, 32–33, 38

address, object reference in memory, 679
add starter method
  AVL trees, 568
  Red-Black trees, 583–584
  2-3-4 trees, 599
adjacency list, 622–623, 630
adjacency matrix, 622, 623–624, 630
adjacent vertex, 616
Agent class, 318
aggregation, 743–744
AirlineCheckinSim class, 318, 319, 321, 323–326, 745, 746
airline passenger service simulation (case study), 317–329
airline reservation systems, 747
algorithm efficiency, 108–117
analysis phase, in software life cycle, 4*t*, 6, 7–8
ancestor-descendant relationship, 389
anchor, 742
anonymous classes, 806
anonymous object, 680
anonymous reference, 146
Applet class, 756
applets, 670, 752
architectural design, 6*t*
areas, of geometric shapes (case study), 183–184
argument list, 130
arguments
  arrays, 719
  call-by-value, 686
  objects as, 709–710
  passing to method main, 727
ArithmeticException class, 62*t*, 69, 126
arithmetic operators, 676, 677*t*
ArrayBasedPD class, 28, 30–53
ArrayIndexOutOfBoundsException class, 62*t*, 63–64, 68, 69
  falling off either end of array in sorting, 544
  out-of-bounds subscripts, 715
ArrayList class, 195–197, 741
  applications, 198–200
  forgetting to cast item retrieved from, 199
  implementation, 201–205
  for implementing heaps, 426–429
  implementing Queue interface using, 307, 308
  implementing stacks with, 263, 265–267

limitations, 206
methods, 197*t*
using subscripts with, 197
ArrayQueue class, 301, 311–315
  in airline passenger simulation, 318
arrays, 714–716. *See also* recursive array search; sorting
  of arrays, 719–722
  data field length, 716
  data fields, 717–719
  disadvantages, 194
  forgetting to declare storage for, 715
  hash table performance compared, 473
  for implementing heaps, 426–429
  implementing Queue interface using circular, 309–315
  implementing stacks using, 265–267
  out-of-bounds subscripts, 715
  recursive algorithm to search, 339–340
  recursive array search, 353–360
Arrays class, 506–509, 507*t*
ArraySearch class, 91–92
artificial intelligence, 337
AssertionError class, 67, 69
assertions, 105, 107
assert statement, 107
assignment, 38, 141
association, 742–743
attributes, 739–740
attribute types, 739–740
  standard UML syntax, 740
@author Javadoc tag, 711*t*
auto-boxing, 699
automated tellers, 747–748
AVLNode class, 565–567
AVLTree class, 565–566
AVL trees
  critically unbalanced trees, 563–565
  implementing, 565–567
  inserting into, 567–572
  left-left tree balancing, 561
  left-right tree balancing, 562–563
  performance, 573
  removal from, 573
AWTEvent class, 750
AWT package, 672

B

backtracking, 377–382
balanced parentheses, checking for (case study), 256–261

Q

quadratic growth rate, 115*t*, 115–116
quadratic probing, 470–471
quadratic sort, 511
  comparison of, 520*t*
quality assurance (QA) organization, testing by, 93
queue abstract data type, 296–299
Queue interface, 298–299
  implementing using circular array, 309–315
  implementing using Java's LinkedList, 307–309
  implementing using single-linked list, 305–307
queue of customers, 297–299
  case study, 300–304
  maintaining, 300–304
queues
  simulating waiting lines using, 316–331
  stack contrasted, 295
queuing theory, 316
quicksort, 536–544
  Dutch National Flag problem, 547–550
  performance comparison, 551*t*
QuickSort class, 538
qwerty keyboard, 679–680

R

radio button, 773–774
RadioButtonDemo class, 774
radix sort, 553
random access, 193
Random class, 329
random method, 327, 329
random numbers, 329
readData method, 78
readInt method, 71–72
reallocate method
  ArrayBasedPD class, 41
  KWArrayList class, 204–205
rebalanceLeft method, 569–572, 573
rebalanceRight method, 569, 572, 573
Rectangle class, 163, 164–166, 171–172
recursion, 337–338
  backtracking, 377–382
  efficiency, 350
  infinite, and stack overflow, 347
  iteration compared, 349
  last-line, 349–350
  problem solving using, 367–376
  in quicksort method, 538
  recursive definitions of mathematical formulas, 346–352
  run-time stack, 343–345
  tail, 349–350
  unwinding, 343
recursive add method
  AVL trees, 568–569
  Red-Black trees, 584–585
  2-3-4 trees, 599–600

recursive algorithms, 337–338
  design steps, 340–342
recursive array search
  binary, 355–360
  linear, 353–355
recursive case, of recursive algorithm, 340
recursive data structures, 361–366
  trees, 388
recursive methods, 337–338, 341
  proving correctness of, 342–343
  tracing, 343
RecursiveMethods class, 340–342
recursive thinking, 338–345
RedBlackNode class, 580–581
RedBlackTree class, 580–581
Red-Black trees, 454, 574
  insertion into, 575–585
  performance, 586
  relating 2-3-4 trees to, 601–602
  removal from, 585–586
registering, listener for event, 750, 751
regression testing, 97
rehash method, 482
remainder operator, 676, 677*t*
removal
  from AVL trees, 573
  from binary search trees, 415–420
  form Red-Black trees, 585–586
  from heaps, 425–426
  from heaps implemented as ArrayList, 427–429
  of list node, 365–366
  node from double-linked lists, 214–215
  nodes from linked lists, 208, 211
  from 2-3 trees, 592–593
remove method
  Collection interface, 240
  HashtableChain class, 486
  HashtableOpen class, 482
  HeapPriorityQueue class, 433–434
  Iterator and List compared, 221
  KWArrayList class, 204
repaint, 758, 759
repetition condition, 681–683
  do ... while statement, 682*t*
  for statement, 681*t*
replace method, 363–364
request-response style, 747
requirements specification, 3, 4*t*, 5, 6*t*, 7
  phone directory program case study, 21–22
@return Javadoc tag, 711*t*
reusable code, 13
reuse, 157
right-left tree, 563
right-right tree, 563
right rotation, 557–558
right subtree, 557
role name, 742
root, 389
rotation, self-balancing search trees, 556–560

RtTriangle class, 163, 165
rubber banding, 801
run-time errors, 61–65
RunTimeException class, 67, 68, 126, 127
  subclasses, 62*t*, 69
run-time stack, 343–345

S

save method, 33, 39
SearchTree interface, 409
  target is not Comparable, 411
selection, Java control statements, 681–683
selection sort, 510–512
  other quadratic sort methods compared, 520*t*
  performance comparison, 551*t*
SelectionSort class, 511–512
selector, **switch** statement, 681*t*, 684
self-balancing search trees, 555–556
  AVL trees, 561–573
  balance and rotation, 556–560
  B-trees, 602–603
  Red-Black trees, 574–586
  2-3 trees, 587–593
  2-3-4 trees, 594–601
sequence of statements, 680
Serializable interface, 405
serialized object, 405
  modifying class file of, 406
setAlignment method, 767
set difference, 455
setElementOfX method, 63, 64
Set interface, 241, 454–458
  implementing, 490
set intersection, 455
SetIterator class, 491–492
setLayoutManager method, 765
set method, 198
sets, 454–458
  creating set view of maps, 491
  lists compared, 458
set union, 455
shaker sort, 552
shallow copy, 150–151
ShapeInt interface, 164, 165, 167–168
Shell sort, 521–525
  performance comparison, 551*t*
ShellSort class, 524–525
shifting operators, 676, 677*t*
Short class, 141
short data type, 674*t*, 674–676
shortest path, 634
  finding shortest path from one vertex to all other vertices, 651–656
  through maze (case study), 645–648
showOptionDialog method, 725
siblings, 389
Sierpinski fractal, 386
signature, 130, 687
significant digits, 784
simple path, graphs, 617